Evolution
of
Educational Doctrine:
Major Educational Theorists
of the
Western World

Edward J. Power

BOSTON COLLEGE

Evolution
of
Educational Doctrine:
Major Educational Theorists
of the
Western World

 APPLETON-CENTURY-CROFTS
EDUCATIONAL DIVISION
New York MEREDITH CORPORATION

678–1

Library of Congress Card Number: 69–14530

PRINTED IN THE UNITED STATES OF AMERICA
390–71500–X

ACKNOWLEDGMENTS

The quotations from Cassiodorus are reprinted from L. W. Jones' translation, *Cassiodorus, An Introduction to Divine and Human Readings,* New York, Columbia University Press, 1946, by permission of the Columbia University Press.

The quotations from Hugh of St. Victor are reprinted from Jerome Taylor's translation of *The Didascalicon of Hugh of St. Victor,* New York, Columbia University Press, 1961, by permission of the Columbia University Press.

The quotations from Jean Jacques Rousseau are reprinted from Barbara Foxley's translation of *Emile; Or, Education,* Everyman's Library Edition, New York, E. P. Dutton & Company, Inc., 1938, by permission of E. P. Dutton & Company, Inc. and J. M. Dent & Sons, Ltd.

The quotations from John Dewey are reprinted from his *Democracy and Education,* New York, The Macmillan Company, 1916, Copyright 1916 by The Macmillan Company.

To Helen

⋟ Preface ⋞

With multiple issues facing them, contemporary educators understandably spend little time applying historical tests to current objectives and practices or studying the pedagogical wisdom of their predecessors. The contexts of modern education are activity, experiment, and novelty of design; its great moments are counted by doing that which, hopefully, has not previously been done. Ordinary schoolmasters are called ordinary because they stay within familiar boundaries; their teaching follows accepted, even traditional, canons of educational technique. So doing, they may really be extraordinary teachers, but go unrecognized because they are ignored in publicity releases; their work has few, if any, newsworthy features, and seldom elicits praise or subvention, either from foundations or government agencies. Research proposals or novel teaching techniques are given the center of the educational stage, rather than theories concerning teaching and learning, which have changed only slightly in centuries of educational practice. Perhaps we should expect this, for in education's long history, school administrators and teachers thought infrequently about fundamental educational issues. Yet need persists for reexamining basic educational assumptions, or sometimes simply returning to them.

Too often, it may be argued, the general function of schools—of all education—is misread; and however this general function is divided into various special functions in everyday teaching and learning, it should be apodictically clear that schools must not be the toys of ardent researchers, testing places for avant-garde pedagogic technique, or laboratories for educationist and statistical technicians. Schools should surely want up-to-date methods and curricula, and unquestionably research has its proper role for keeping schools abreast of the broad front of rapidly expanding knowledge. Yet schools must concentrate on educating students; other phases of school life must be subordinate to this primary objective.

This book is not concerned directly with the manifold issues of contemporary education; that in it any schoolmaster shall find solutions to his pressing classroom difficulties is extremely unlikely. It does, however, present many important educational issues—even now current—in the theories and practices of great educators.

The title, *Evolution of Educational Doctrine: Major Educational Theorists of the Western World,* needs some explanation. The term evolution is intended to imply a forward thrust of educational judgments, from one theorist to

vii

another, and from one society to another. For example, Isocrates' literary human-ism was accepted, first by Quintilian and then by Cassiodorus and Erasmus, although literary humanism in Erasmus' teaching code was altered greatly from its use in the school of Athens' most illustrious teacher. Such are the metamor-phoses I want to identify and elaborate, and following them in the history of educational thought is, for our purposes here, called evolution. Educational theory could not have been born, or have survived, without social, political, and economic life, and the totality of educational doctrine cannot be under-stood and evaluated apart from steadying insights derived from broad social histories. However, except in Chapter 1, where the birth of an independent philosophy of education is traced, the history of educational theories of societies is not chronicled. We grant, for example, the persistent Roman drive to have an intellectual culture not unlike the Greeks in content and quality, yet we have not tried to show the historical unfolding of this determination from Rome's archaic years to, say, the time of Cicero and Quintilian. But the princi-pal features of Greek education, defended by Greek theorists, are reviewed as they were accepted and sometimes altered by the Romans, the Christians, and, indeed, most modern educators. This book consciously skirts an emphasis on social processes which may have influenced both the indigenous and bor-rowed features of education in any state or nation. What I want to demonstrate, along with the principal theoretical positions and amendments to them, is a continuity in educational theory; and while I should not like to state that nothing is ever new in it, I am always impressed by that which is perennial in educational theory.

In thirteen chapters fourteen famous educational theorists are presented. What justification can be given for my selections? The book itself answers this question better than any prefatory remarks, but the reader has a right to know the general theme dominating its early planning. Wanting to give reasonably broad coverage within the Western world, and also to show the tenacity of certain aspects of theory, I decided to select theorists from each of the major periods in educational history. Isocrates, Plato, and Quintilian speak for the ancients and, in a sense, they spoke to all teachers who followed them. Isocrates was included because of his preoccupation with literature and the perfection of oral and written composition. While Isocrates did not write a constitution for formal education, he commissioned the schools of his time to concentrate on words and made schooling predominantly a literary exercise; this commis-sion was perpetuated in schools throughout the Western world from his time forward.

In opposition to the literary humanism of Isocrates, we have Plato's de-termination to search for truth and to use the instruments of literature and rhetoric to move from the level of opinion to dependable and scientifically verifiable knowledge. Plato was never content to listen only to speeches; he wanted to examine evidence and he counseled his students and pedagogical fol-lowers to do the same. Words were necessary, but Plato asked for more: mathe-matics and science were for him the best vehicles in the pursuit of certitude. Plato was the leading spokesman for scientific humanism. Despite their leader-ship along competing educational paths, both Isocrates and Plato eschewed the day-to-day involvements in translating educational theory into practice. Quintilian took the educational doctrine of Isocrates and fitted it to the classroom: he elaborated the literary humanism of Isocrates by writing the *Education of an Orator,* an educational handbook which dominated educational thought and practice for the next thousand years.

Cassiodorus' importance, and his right to be included in a book on the history of educational theory, rests on his ability to adapt the code of Quintilian so as to enable Christians to pursue a relative kind of literary scholarship while permitting their anti-classical, pro-Christian sentiments to remain intact. His educational theory quieted the most urgent anxieties his Christian confreres had about the dangers inherent in classical literature, by teaching them how to use the seven liberal arts without at the same time learning to love them. He made literary education respectable in a Christian environment.

Yet, even while Cassiodorus was writing his famous *Introduction to Divine and Human Readings,* the Christian world was losing its contacts with the classical past. And as Christians ranged farther away from Italy—the European center for classical study in the fifth and sixth centuries A.D.—this literary loss was greater. Latin was a literary language, but it was a language of ritual as well, and became absolutely essential to the ecclesiastical future of the Roman Catholic Church. Thus, Alcuin, as an educator, was faced with a twofold task: to rescue Latin from linguistic misuse and abuse; and to reassure the Christian community that this classical language, along with its literary corpus, could be studied, not perhaps with impunity, but with certain safeguards.

Hugh of St. Victor and John of Salisbury took Christian learning over its last great hurdle by providing a theoretically sound method for studying any type of literature from any source; thereafter, in theory at least, Christians were allowed the freedom of inserting the whole of classical literature in their school syllabus. Neither was content with the age-old device advanced by St. Augustine of selecting materials from decontaminated classical sources and then providing the student with a handbook of rhetoric and grammar from which he could learn the rules. They wanted to study all classical literature, and their theories allowed them to add a revised technique for textual exposition: allegorical interpretation. The importance of Hugh and John, then, is to be found in a theory of education allowing the entire body of the classics to enter the Christian school. Since both belonged to the twelfth century, both were responsible for kindling the spirit of inquiry which dominated, and contributed to the greatness of, medieval universities.

Erasmus belongs in any account of the world's great educational theorists, because he produced the most reasoned justification for using literary means to educate "good" men. This may not have been important in itself, but when we see how education became preoccupied with moral formation from the time of the Renaissance throughout the entire modern period, we should be willing to listen to the principal architect of the theory detailing the organization of literary materials toward the objective of moral perfection.

Comenius proved to be the apostle of progress for modern education: he counseled greater attention to the training of the senses and the acquisition of sensory knowledge; he advocated more generous educational opportunity for all classes of men and women; and he took the first steps toward creating pedagogical techniques based on a natural psychology of learning. Such credentials almost certainly qualify him for a place among the world's great educators.

Despite the unquestioned worth of Comenius' educational labor, the bases for his stance were often little more than humanistic sentiments and unerring intuition. The generous educational doctrine he preached needed theoretical strength that could be found only in updated philosophical and psychological wisdom: both were the contribution of John Locke, and Locke stands as a groundbreaker for educational practices that could deal with the realities of life by first replacing the literary commitment schools' curricula had made to the past. Locke, moreover, prepared the way for Rousseau and the theory of natural education, a theory that in the long run initiated a revolution in modern education.

Rousseau's prominence in the history of educational theory is seldom a subject for debate, but Pestalozzi, standing somewhat in Rousseau's shadow, needs to be seen as more than a mere methodologist, who took Rousseau's best ideas and geared them for classroom use. Pestalozzi's intense humanism—translated best as his love for man—coupled with a conviction that education can improve the quality of life in society led him to revitalize pedagogy by capitalizing on natural learning processes and pragmatic educational goals. Pestalozzi provided the theoretical basis and the practical means for popular education.

Education's great forward thrust was made with some uncertainty, with some confusion of purpose and means. From Herbart's point of view its greatest deficiency was its lack of scientific justification, so he endeavored to construct a science of education based on ethics and psychology. In the long run he succeeded, not perhaps by articulating a definitive science of pedagogy or a formalized and rigid approach to teaching, but by setting in motion the idea that a human occupation as important as education requires verifiable objectives and procedures. Pedagogy as a science owes much to Herbart, and because so much of his work anticipated the modern science of education, he merits consideration in this book.

Finally, John Dewey, whose stature as an educational theorist is unquestioned, is invited to join this company of illustrious men because of his determination to reshape educational goals and practices and make them relevant and meaningful for contemporary life. Dewey should not be characterized as an enemy of the past—to do so would be unfair—but as a friend of the present. Meaningful education for contemporary life was his pedagogic motto.

These men are imposing witnesses to the forward movement of educational theory, and their testimony is always worth hearing. Yet, it may be argued that some important names are missing. Why? To defend our exclusions would require extensive digressions, and any defense, especially if it runs counter to a confirmed, private opinion, is bound to be weak. As we read the record of educational theory's history, the theorists included in this book are outstanding, and we leave it to the text itself to provide further documentation.

The reader may note some unevenness in biographical comments: in every case, only those data important for illuminating a theoretical posture were developed because it seemed outside this book's ambit to give a comprehensive account of a man's life. Besides, since the theories of some famous educators were generated partly in the ferment of their own scholastic endeavor either as students or teachers, some advantage was seen in relating the growth and grafting of pedagogical creeds to their academic and personal lives.

A book of this kind necessarily owes a great deal to the work of others, and I have done my best in the notes to indicate the sources—books, articles, monographs, and, of course, the writings of the great educators themselves—to which I am indebted. Permission generously given by various publishers to quote from their publications is gladly acknowledged.

In addition, I am grateful to Prof. William W. Brickman, of the University of Pennsylvania, for his many perceptive suggestions while the book was still in manuscript, and to my colleague, Prof. Pierre D. Lambert, for his critical reading of the galleys.

Demonstrating educational theory at work as it advanced through history, removing it from theoretical discussion, and indicating how it makes a difference when students and teachers enter classrooms are this book's broad purposes. Whether for the general reader, interested in critical educational questions, or for students in graduate or undergraduate classes, we hope the book may contribute to a revitalization of contemporary educational theory and thus to all formal education.

E. J. P.

❧ Contents ❧

Evolution

of

Educational Doctrine:

Major Educational Theorists
of the
Western World

ᔐ 1 ᔒ

Educational Theory: Origins and Prospects

I

POLITICAL THEORY AND EDUCATION

Although theories of education have formed part of every society's intellectual resources, they have not always been distinguished clearly from simple attitudes toward life and living; nor have they always been accorded, even in somewhat advanced cultures, an independent intellectual or academic status. Primitive men, concerned about training their sons, formed certain opinions about the nature of education—about what skills should be emphasized and what goals should be achieved. Yet they never bothered to codify these opinions in special categories of thought, although they were preserved in general social traditions. From our point of view this was an oversight, but no matter. Even in eras where certain cultures advanced far beyond primitive associations, education was so ingrained in a way of life that any theory regarding either its ends or means was superfluous. Despite being taken for granted, and without having any special code, education was, nevertheless, both imperative and highly regarded; its relevance to life was not gainsaid.[1]

In archaic Greece, connections between politics and education become more obvious, and we begin to find the origins of educational theory, for men now began to think of alternatives in the purposes and means of education. Theories about appropriate learning and effective teaching were first handmaidens of political theory, then of philosophy; finally, during the Hellenistic period, the alternatives available in educa-

[1] In a remarkable book, *Life and Education in Early Societies* (New York, The Macmillan Company, 1949), Thomas Woody traces both the rise of educational consciousness and the evolution of pedagogical practice among primitive and ancient people.

1

tional content and purpose came to be taken more seriously, and educational theory was able to claim and obtain an independent academic and intellectual status.[2]

In the early Greek city states a citizen was a knight dedicated to state service, and, while his dedication went unquestioned, he performed civic duties in a highly independent way. In a word, being a good citizen meant being an effective soldier, with skills distinct from those proper for the ordinary mass of mankind. Wholly military, these skills involved mainly horsemanship and weaponry; basic to them were physical strength, stamina, and the virtue of courage. The young citizen's education and training were directed toward military efficiency and personal valor; before every citizen was the goal, and the hope, of some day performing a heroic deed.[3] Educational policy was unencumbered by alternatives; what was clear on the level of policy could easily be converted into precise practices: the curriculum, if we may so dignify it, faithfully served ends acknowledged as proper for education. The wisdom of traditional policies went unchallenged; besides, debate in the face of clear social necessity was inevitably unproductive of change. Educational theory needed neither honoring nor special notice; its principal message was clear, uncomplicated, and supported by tradition's incontestable authority. Education's aim was to prepare citizens for essentially military duties and services.[4]

Had Greek aristocrats been able to stop the calendar, they might have enjoyed their traditions untroubled by change, and the pleasant knightly culture extant in ancient Greece could stand as their principal heritage. But the calendar would not be frozen; life moved, and by the seventh century B.C. the old knightly culture was out of step. In the first

[2] Despite the undocumented tradition that educational theory originated with Plato, H. I. Marrou, *A History of Education in Antiquity* (New York, Sheed and Ward, 1956), p. 100, proposed an obviously more tenable alternative interpretation. While not denying Plato's interest in educational issues, and his ability to handle them with depth and perception, Marrou asserted that, as an independent study, educational philosophy began with Hellenistic scholars and philosophers.

[3] See C. H. Whitman, *Homer and the Heroic Tradition* (Cambridge, Mass., Harvard University Press, 1958); and J. Drever, *Greek Education: Its Practices and Principles* (London, Cambridge University Press, 1912).

[4] Frederick A. G. Beck, *Greek Education: 450–350* B.C. (New York, Barnes & Noble, Inc., 1964), p. 129, in understatement confirms this position: "The old Homeric training—an education designed and developed for a leisure class of knightly warriors—laid more emphasis on sport than on music. This sport was, of course, in earlier times partly, if not mainly, a means of preparing oneself, and keeping fit, for the business of war." Aristophanes, *Clouds*, 961–1023, not only expressed a conservative attitude, but was something of a historian, when he dramatized the values of physical training with military-civic purposes. It is hard to explain the prominence of the Greek paidotribe in education unless one recognizes the homage paid to physical formation. If it was too early for sport for sport's sake, the military ideal must have been taken into account, or almost taken for granted. Plato (*Gorgias*, 504a; *Protagoras*, 313a) as a near-contemporary observer, should be consulted too.

place, tactical innovations in military science reduced a person's importance; a citizen was no longer an army. Instead of the mounted horseman carrying out personal expeditions, or the cavalry moving forward in concerted military maneuver, the new military science specified an infantry unit and directed it to the field to fight as a unit. Personal courage and skill still counted, but now as contributions to the infantry company, and the versatility common among tactically archaic military men was neither especially evident nor necessary.

Training the infantry soldier, while still important and regularly given top priority, held no monopoly. But a people who had lived long with honored traditions were not likely to jettison them arbitrarily, if at all; they tried to salvage something. What was no longer deemed essential to the citizen's military education could be retained in a sporting tradition, and a vast system of sporting education came into existence. Now education has two goals: one is utility centered—constructed from everything necessary for the soldier-citizen; the other is leisure or sport. Even when these two goals were not hostile, questions of balance needed answering. When should military training begin? Should it intermingle with pure sport? How could sporting education serve military objectives? Could sport be relegated to a preparatory role? Who should teach? How much time should be devoted to various kinds of education or training? These simple questions, which we perhaps should think unworthy of educational theory, set men to the difficult task of making judgments about the education of human beings.[5]

Plato questioned the teaching of wrestling in the gymnasium and counseled reform: he prized wrestling but opposed professionalism, and he refused to allow schools to produce gladiators.[6] He was especially sensitive to the vast problem of character education. He argued that wrestling, in serving only military objectives, would lack human goals, and in becoming a crude professional sport it would surely subvert the making of honorable men. His doctrine of music for the mind and gymnastics for the body contained important distinctions relevant to educational purposes and means, but these distinctions were not self-applying

---

[5] A number of authors have handled the evolution of Athenian education from its archaic origins to the point where choices had to be made between sport and leisure-time education, on the one hand, and cultural and intellectual formation, on the other. Beck, *op. cit.*, pp. 72–146, gives the details of traditional practice—the conventional education acceptable both to Plato and Isocrates—and is well worth reading, but Marrou, *op. cit.*, pp. 3–14 and 36–46, bores more deeply into the causes of educational ferment, and his work should be preferred. K. J. Freeman, *Schools of Hellas, An Essay on the Practice and Theory of Ancient Greek Education from 600 to 300 B.C.*, 3d ed. (New York, The Macmillan Company, 1922) contains a wealth of information and is always good, as is LaRue Van Hook, *Greek Life and Thought* (New York, Columbia University Press, 1937). W. Barclay, *Educational Ideals in the Ancient World* (London, Collins, 1959), contains valuable insights and is worth careful study; along with E. B. Castle, *Ancient Education and Today* (Baltimore, Penguin, 1961).

[6] Plato, *Laws* VII, 795d–796a; VIII, 814cd.

and needed, as Plato understood so well, considerable thought and elaboration. Isocrates could scoff at time spent in the gymnasium; his school's curriculum never had any place for sport, but he tempered his public statements, for his audience wanted to be true to its past, and Isocrates preferred to avoid acquiring a reputation as a revolutionary educator.[7] Xenophon preferred less time for music—the soul, he thought, should care for itself—and more attention to training men for the hazards of military life. He wrote of Persia and commended to his fellow citizens as a worthy model the educational program supposedly followed by Cyrus. However, most of the things he wrote about he learned in Sparta.[8]

With alternatives—first, those arising from a separation of education for military purpose and sporting value, and then those arising through contact with other systems—concerning what education might be, theory became important. But the problems inaugurating educational theory were, in the light of future events, relatively minor. Educational theory was forced to grow up.

Besides military changes and a sporting tradition, economic and political adjustments further complicated the educational issue. Greek aristocrats—mainly in Athens—were determined to maintain a position of social exclusiveness. Economically, the noncitizen middle class became more powerful and prosperous; politically, the power of the old families was waning. Tradition could bar the door to a noncitizen intent on entering the military establishment, but tradition was unable to keep the prosperous middle class from the playing fields. Aristocrats could exclude all but citizens from the old gymnasia—where admission depended on credentials of birth, especially admission to the Academy and Lyceum— but they had no control over the construction of private gymnasia free from obstacles to admission where hoi polloi could play their games. The Athenian aristocrat wanted to be exclusive, as we have said, and to preserve his position he turned to the intellectual arena, where he was confident noncitizens would not follow.[9]

---

7 Isocrates, *Antidosis* 241.

8 In Xenophon's plan there is nothing to remind us of cultural formation—no reading, writing, literature or mathematics. Although he cannot obliterate the historical fact of Socrates' interest in broad culture in the *Memorabilia* IV, vii, 3, he interprets this interest to suit himself and make it entirely practical. In *Cyropaedia* I, 2, 15, he rejects cultural education altogether and concentrates on the acquisition of certain basic skills necessary for the defense of the city.

9 It is easy to overlook the import of the sporting tradition in the development of Greek educational theory and practice, because modern education lacks any counterpart for the sporting tradition. Good accounts of the growth and application of this tradition may be found in E. Norman Gardiner, *Athletics of the Ancient World* (New York, Oxford University Press, 1930) ; his *Greek Athletic Sports and Festivals* (New York, The Macmillan Company, 1910) ; and C. A. Forbes, *Greek Physical Education* (New York, Appleton-Century-Crofts, Inc., 1929) . Longer views regarding the germination of this tradition are tested with ingenuity by William R. Ridington, *The Minoan-Mycenaean Background of Greek Athletics* (Philadelphia, Westbrook Publishing Co.,

With this move—about 590 B.C.—we have the origin of liberal education, and now educational theory takes another step forward.[10] The step, halting and immature, was that of an infant discipline in need of mothering by an older and more certain body of knowledge. Because of the connections maintained between education, training, and citizenship, and because preparation for the duties and responsibilities of citizenship were still important, a natural and happy affinity was continued between education and practical politics. The legendary Law of Lycurgus laid the foundations for the Spartan way of life; despite the obvious fact that this way was neither literary nor intellectual, education, or better, training, was absolutely essential. Thus, although certainly subordinate to political thought, and often obscured by it, Sparta had an educational theory. For Spartans no aspect of life was more important than education; for centuries they used it to perpetuate their hard and inflexible social system.[11] In Athens, even the Laws of Solon and the Constitutions of Cleisthenes, while having in view primarily the regulation of society, paid scant heed to education; the fragmentary evidence suggests that these codes were both regulatory and hortatory. In order to ordain and sustain a political system with preconceived objectives, Greek politicians regularly depended on the agencies of education: they understood education to be a social instrument.[12] Certainly their traditions supported this

1935). Perhaps Lorenz Grasberger's first two volumes of a three-volume work, *Erziehung und Unterricht im klassischen Alterthum mit besonderer Rücksicht auf die Bedürfnisse der Gegenwart, nach den Quellen dargestellt* (Würzburg, Stahel'sche Buchhandlung, 1864–1881), is still the definitive treatment of the Greek athletic tradition. Yet, A. L. Bondurant, *Ancient Athletics, Their Use and Abuse* (Emory University, Banner Press, n.d.); A. J. Butler, *Sport in Classic Times* (London, Benn, 1930); F. A. Wright, *Greek Athletics* (London, Cape, 1925); and H. A. Harris, *Greek Athletes and Athletics* (Bloomington, Indiana University Press, 1966), might be consulted too. For further analyses of economic and social ferment in Greece, see G. Glotz, *Ancient Greece at Work* (London, Routledge & Kegan Paul, Ltd., 1926); and, though its principal focus is on a somewhat later period, M. Rostovtzeff's, *The Social and Economic History of the Hellenistic World* (New York, Oxford University Press, 1941), contains impressive and perceptive interpretations.

10 This broad issue is treated by many authors; as a matter of fact, it is the rare book on Greek educational history that neglects it. Attention is directed particularly to John F. Dobson, *Ancient Education and Its Meaning to Us* (New York, Longmans, Green and Company, 1932); E. C. Moore, *The Story of Instruction: The Beginnings* (New York, The Macmillan Company, 1936); and A. S. Wilkins, *National Education in Greece in the Fourth Century Before Christ* (New York, G. E. Stechert and Co., 1911).

11 Scholars have shown very little interest in Spartan education, probably because once the basic story was told few amendments were needed. Although Xenophon, *The Constitution of Sparta;* Plutarch, *Lycurgus;* and Plato, *Laws* I, describe a Sparta of about the fourth century B.C., and show no connection to earlier periods, we may accept their reports with considerable confidence, because Sparta was not only conservative, she was reactionary, and lived out a determination to resist any natural development of custom or tradition.

12 See Freeman, *op. cit.*, p. 57; Marrou, *op. cit.*, p. 382; Robert J. Bonner, *Aspects of Athenian Democracy* (Berkeley, Calif., University of California Press, 1933); and T. A. Sinclair, *A History of Greek Political Thought* (London, Routledge & Kegan

belief. How could it be used, and sometimes be redesigned, to serve changing goals and changing political systems?

No one seriously doubts Plato's capacity for writing a book on educational theory, a theory able to stand independently of politics and economics.[13] His not having done so allows few inferences about the possibilities of educational theory, although it indicates Plato's principal intellectual preoccupations. He thought of education as a process preparing citizens to take a responsible place in civic society; goals and content should be ordered to serve this severely practical ideal. Beginning with the unassailable assumption that a theory of education unrelated to social theory as a whole is meaningless, he sketched an ideal society in the *Republic* and made practical recommendations to support it in the. *Laws.*[14] In both works the function of education was to perpetuate the state's best traditions; but in a larger sense the state's institutions were devised to make the state itself one huge educational instrument.

Plato was not alone in making this assumption: the best traditions of education and statecraft, and some of the best Greek minds too, were on his side. Even before Plato's time Athens was a kind of big school. The theater, the public assembly, the festivals, to name only the most visible Greek institutions, had clear, although often unnamed, educational objectives. In the broad sense, education in Athens was provided by mere membership in the community; in a somewhat narrower sense, formal education deliberately aimed at the development of civic virtue. Plato's political theory made room for this point of view, for it conceived of the state as a means of providing broad opportunities for the individual's welfare and of molding individuals to enjoy the benefits the state could offer.[15] With such convictions, it was hardly possible for Plato to elaborate an independent theory of education, although he could have discussed many theoretical points about education, which were treated in

Paul, Ltd., 1959) ; F. M. Cornford, *Before and After Socrates* (London, Cambridge University Press, 1962) ; and J. P. Mahaffy, *Old Greek Education* (London, Kegan Paul, Trench, Trubner & Co., 1881) .

13 Testimony to Plato's ability to have formulated an independent philosophy of education is given by John E. Adamson, *The Theory of Education in Plato's Republic* (London, Swan Sonnenschein and Co., 1903) ; Bernard Bosanquet, *The Education of the Young in the Republic of Plato* (Cambridge, Mass., Harvard University Press, 1901) ; Warner Fite, *The Platonic Legend* (New York, Charles Scribner's Sons, 1934) ; and, of course, Werner Jaeger's incomparable *Paideia: The Ideals of Greek Culture* (Oxford, Basil Blackwell, 1939) .

14 On the question of Plato's goals for the educational process and for the production of citizens able to play their part in the life of the civic community, see A. E. Taylor, *Plato: The Man and His Work*, 6th ed. (London, Methuen, 1949) , pp. 125 ff. In this connection, see also G. C. Field, *Plato and His Contemporaries: A Study of Fourth-Century Life and Thought* (London, Methuen, 1948) ; Richard Livingstone, *Plato and Modern Education* (London, Cambridge University Press, 1944) ; and R. C. Lodge, *Plato's Theory of Education* (London, Routledge & Kegan Paul, Ltd., 1947) .

15 Plato, *Republic*, 590e.

relation to politics, apart from any particular political system. That he did not indicates a clear allegiance to the objectives of his political theory; but possibilities for an independent theory of education are nowhere denied.

A few examples may help make the point: Can virtue be taught? The answer meant much to Plato's political theory. It stands, moreover, as a cardinal and perennial question in education; but no answer, not even Plato's partial one, is irrevocably bound to political philosophy. In or out of the *Republic,* the teacher must know how to handle the problem of virtue. In the *Republic,* where Plato speaks to the issue, we find virtuous citizens produced by certain kinds of learning. Plato does not identify knowledge and virtue, but in the *Republic,*[16] the *Meno,* and the *Theaetetus,*[17] the acquisition of knowledge requires effort on the learner's part, and this effort has educational significance. He almost says the discipline of learning either produces or leads to virtue, and, while he may not have meant to initiate a doctrine of mental discipline, he set the first boundaries for its classic codification.

What shall be taught? This is too large a question even for Plato. Yet with supreme confidence he advanced a doctrine of differentiation: some citizens can profit from one kind of education; others from another; and all education depends on the student's capacity. Plato was certainly not first in promoting class or elite education, but his divisions and distinctions relative to educational opportunity became conventional wisdom in educational theory. Besides educating citizens for their proper place in society, and in addition to considering where girls should fit into education, Plato had something to say about elementary schools. In the music school, Plato wanted more mathematics and science,[18] and had his recommendations been followed it would have been a nine-year school with three-year periods each for music, literature, and mathematics. Next he cast a critical eye at Greek gymnasia and recommended an upgrading: the purely physical part of secondary education was proscribed from competing with intellectual formation.[19] Although sport was not expunged from the school's studies, it was subordinated to mathematics and science. A page was borrowed from the Sophist's book on educational organization, for Plato, too, wanted to take the boys from playing fields and put them in classrooms. And as part of the reformed syllabus for secondary education, Plato devised a new discipline and a new method for teaching and learning. Without becoming a day-to-day literary master, Plato could deal with techniques of teaching and learning.

The military features of higher learning were suppressed and re-

16 *Ibid.,* 401e.
17 Plato, *Theaetetus,* 193c and 197c.
18 Plato, *Republic,* 524b.
19 *Ibid.* VII, 537b.

placed with scientific instruction. Whether or not Plato had the Academy in mind in elaborating a theory of higher learning is a moot point. Indeed, remarkable parallels exist between Plato's Academy and his advice in the *Republic* about who should enter institutions of higher learning and what should be studied there.[20] The similarities between an actual and an ideal school should not preoccupy us. In the final analysis Plato was simply reserving a scientific and dialectical higher education for the very best students, for those who some day would be political leaders.

Our purpose here, without going into detail on Plato's thought, is to show how he handled specifically educational questions, questions properly theoretical, because they cannot be answered by collecting information, by conducting experiments, or by testing. Plato knew what it meant to be an educational philosopher, and he knew a theory of education was possible, but he saw no compelling reason for severing educational theory from political doctrine. Given the intellectual context of the time, he would have deplored taking such a step.

Isocrates can make a better claim than Plato to being an educational theorist, yet even Isocrates was preoccupied with politics. While not liking to admit it publicly, he often agreed with Plato's political doctrines and believed, with Plato, that education should be an instrument for making a public man. In the long run, because Isocrates' views were more limited than Plato's, he did not have to contend with the impressive interacting forces between educational practice and political philosophy. His thought was less recondite, less philosophical, and, according to his own definition, more practical. But at this point we are not interested to explain Isocratic educational thought; instead, we want to see how he contributed to an authentic and independent theory of education.

Here Isocrates performed a service Plato either never thought about or refused to recognize. Isocrates opened his school with a public announcement of its objectives in *Against the Sophists:* he wrote that it was founded to produce responsible public men and effective orators.[21] Students from his school would some day, if Isocrates had his way, be ruling Athens and other states. *Against the Sophists* is neither a political diatribe nor a discourse; and although by no means a complete theory of education, it forms part of such a theory, and is used by Isocrates to show how education can be philosophized about without hauling in politics and economics, although unquestionably at the outset some clearheaded assumptions are made about both. Nearly a half-century later (353 B.C.) Isocrates again turns to theory and essays to defend his educational plan

---

[20] For a fuller discussion of this point, see my article, "Plato's Academy: A Halting Step Toward Higher Education," *History of Education Quarterly*, IV, 3 (September, 1964), pp. 155–166.

[21] Isocrates, *Against the Sophists*, 3–6.

and school program before his fellow citizens. Here, too, we find a faint relationship between education and Isocrates' political philosophy, but he was able to write about, and propose, a theory of education without making it part of a book on politics. This later work was *Antidosis*.

We can follow Isocrates' development of educational theory, and we sense how far he could go in the face of a general unwillingness to separate anything—drama, music, or educational theory—from a politically dominated vision of the world. Still, it would probably be wrong, even with *Against the Sophists* and *Antidosis* before us, to argue that Isocrates was a professional educational theorist. He was a teacher committed to teaching a political philosophy and practice, and he was ready to discuss educational problems only when they appeared on the political avenues he was traveling. Isocrates' books mark him more a political theorist and journalist than an educational thinker, and he himself wanted to be known, not as a teacher or educational philosopher, but as a political scientist.[22]

Despite Isocrates' tendency to subordinate education to political theory, he sometimes philosophized about distinct pedagogical issues, and some of them, interestingly enough, are with us still. Yet, Isocrates remains a friend of educational theory, and a quick example may clinch the point: Both Plato and the Sophists debated the possibilities of teaching virtue. The Sophists believed virtue was produced by direct teaching; at least their advertisements and public utterances contained this implication. Plato, on the other hand, wavering on the verge of making knowledge and virtue equivalent, was saved by sober judgment from such an extremity, and finally settled on saying that discipline of learning may lead to virtue. Isocrates, opposing both the Sophists and Plato, confidently established virtue as a natural endowment. Persons are either virtuous or not, and no pedagogic technique can alter this indelible fact. Instruction, however, may enable virtuous men to apply their "good" plans more effectively, and, in addition, teaching can test a boy's virtue. In other words, teachers of rhetoric, by finding good boys in their schools and expelling bad ones, can serve effectively as guardians of public policy.[23]

Thus disposing of virtue, Isocrates turned totally to his educational aim: civic efficiency through rhetoric. Although not equating virtue and rhetoric, as one author says,[24] his innocence of that fault does not make him the champion of a pedagogy centered first on finding, and then on teaching, truth. Isocrates called himself a philosopher and maintained steadfastly that his educational program had sound philosophical roots; yet he denied the relevance of Plato's educational theory, centered as it

---

[22] For a summary of Isocrates' writings, see pp. 31–32.
[23] See *Against the Sophists*, 3–10, 14–15, 18; *To Nicocles*, 12; and *Antidosis*, 190–192.
[24] Beck, *op. cit.*, p. 256.

was on science, and chose instead to place total confidence in literary knowledge. Expression meant more than thought, and, while not ignoring thought, he nevertheless geared his teaching program to produce flawless writers and speakers.[25]

In company with Plato and the Sophists, Isocrates hoped to educate leaders by teaching young aristocrats.[26] Plato's aristocracy was one of intelligence; the Sophists founded their elite largely on financial ability, and Isocrates wanted students able to demonstrate their genius with words. An educational program with such clear rhetorical objectives was hard to find, so Isocrates was something of a pioneer. Imitation of superior models, he decided, should be the principal technique in teaching rhetoric and oratory. Where were these models? Some came from the best Athenian orators; some were found in extant poetry; but Isocrates prepared many himself. His decisions relative to specific models are less important than the doctrine of imitation itself; originating with Isocrates it was eventually accepted by every teacher placing value on classical education's objectives.[27] A number of improvements and additions to its technique followed, but, whenever and wherever it dominated teaching, Isocrates' counsel and example lurked in the background, giving the technique classical authenticity and tone. Although Isocrates was not a philosopher or "friend of wisdom" like Plato, and no modern philosopher wants him as a mentor, we owe him much, for he created a choice between an education with dialectical tensions and one dominantly literary. Herein lies his real greatness, and it is pointless to debate his limitations and weaknesses.

Staying with educational thought as a handmaiden of politics, we come next to the Sophists. This is hardly the place for a recapitulation of Sophistic doctrine—assuming a common one for them, which is doubtful —or for a description of their school practices, yet something of both is necessary in order to appreciate their educational context, at once hemmed in by political idealism and the compulsions of tradition.[28]

We should begin by recognizing the political conditions around the beginning of the fifth century B.C. that were responsible for introducing

---

25 Isocrates, *Antidosis,* 275.

26 Isocrates, *Areopagiticus,* 44–46.

27 R. Johnson, "Isocrates' Methods of Teaching," *American Journal of Philology,* LXXX, I, 317 (January, 1959), pp. 297–300; and my article, "Class Size and Pedagogy in Isocrates' School," *History of Education Quarterly,* IV, 4 (Winter, 1966), pp. 22–33.

28 Despite the inevitable difficulties in making valid judgments about the Sophists and their theoretical stance, the literature on them is brief but good: M. Untersteiner, *The Sophists,* tr. by K. Freeman (Oxford, Blackwell, 1954); E. A. Havelock, *The Liberal Temper in Greek Politics* (London, Jonathan Cape, Ltd., 1957); H. Gomperz, *Sophistik und Rhetorik,* (Leipzig, B. G. Teubner, Verlagsgesellschaft, mbH, 1912); F. J. Copleston, *A History of Philosophy: Greece and Rome,* I (New York, Image Books, 1962); and E. Duprell, *Les Sophistes: Protagoras, Gorgias, Prodicus, Hippias* (Neuchâtel, Editions du Griffon, 1948).

the Sophists to Athens. Athens had plenty of teachers, as we have seen, so it was not a vacuum the Sophists came to fill. The fortunes of war compelled Athens to create a navy, but sailors were scarce among free citizens because their skills were said to be illiberal. Urgent military need dictated a reluctant surrender of tradition to reason: sailors were induced to bear arms for Athens and were thus invited to fulfill duties heretofore reserved to citizens. The navy's military performance incurred a social debt recognized by both sides, and the aristocracy, to pay this debt, lowered standards for citizenship and, with a surprising display of generosity, enfranchised the sailors. But solving this problem according to a code of simple equity created other problems. Most significantly for education, the political act of enfranchising hundreds made citizens of men unprepared for Athenian citizenship according to established custom and law. Neither the sailors nor members of their families had ever danced in the music school or played in the gymnasium. In no sense were they public men, and in hardly any sense were they ready even for minimal civic responsibilities. Should they return to school to work their way up the ladder of political culture? Or were shortcuts available? To sit as schoolboys at the feet of primary masters was out of the question, so a shortcut was chosen. The need was real and urgent for a quick and effective education to put students in contact with culture. And teachers were needed to perform the monumental task of closing the gap between culture and educational opportunity. The run-of-the-mill Athenian schoolmaster was not qualified to offer such instruction; the better professors in schools where this function might have been performed refused to participate: they opposed on principle the liberalization of traditional qualifications for citizenship. A new class of teachers was needed, and necessity again became the mother of invention: many teachers from outside Athens paid heed to the call, and, flying the banner of wise men or sophists, they offered their teaching to anyone who wanted it.

Beginning with older students first, because adults refused to spend much time in school, the Sophists devised an abbreviated program of studies. Though it was much shorter than the traditional elementary curriculum, the Sophists maintained that this course could meet the test; it could achieve the end of political effectiveness, or what the Sophists liked to call political virtue.[29]

The connection between Sophistic teaching and politics should not be dismissed, nor should the Sophists be charged with ignorance of, or indifference to, political theory. But in their work as teachers, their private political faith was inconsequential; as teachers they could allow political philosophy to make holiday, for their aim was to teach social and political success and not make converts to their politics. Assuming

[29] If Protagoras can be accepted as their spokesman, and if Plato is a fair reporter, we have the fundamentals of their teaching practice outlined in *Protagoras*, 325–335b.

that knowledge can improve human character, they discarded a traditional belief making virtue an innate gift and replaced it by establishing nature as a foundation for education. Refusing to follow dogmas limiting the efficacy of education to liberations of natural endowment, the Sophists created a new theory wherein education was assigned a principal responsibility for making men, and introduced a liberal influence to educational theory by emphasizing nurture over nature. In addition, they reformed the entire structure of classical education by infusing it with intellectual objectives, and removed sport from the gymnasium to replace it with literature and other intellectual subjects. In time—when adult education was less desperately needed—Athenian schoolboys abandoned the playgrounds to populate classrooms. Thus, in practices reflected both in the content and level of teaching, the Sophists, by the middle of the fifth century B.C., had founded literary secondary education.

It is always hazardous to generalize about sophistic teaching; first, because the Sophists, not being a corporation of masters, may not have followed a common teaching plan; second, with the exception of a few fragments, we know little first hand about them. Plato and Aristotle tell us a lot about the Sophists, but we know that neither was friendly to them. We shall, nevertheless, try to summarize their teaching theories. While we are not certain of their inability to create an independent theory of education, such a theory, it must be admitted, remains unrevealed in the arcana of the past. Perhaps their best contributions were toward a theory of education. Also, they belong in the history of evolution because they put man inside the evolutionary process. In addition to man, they put morality, law, and justice into an evolutionary scheme and asserted that the values ascribed to them were derived from custom and convention and not from absolute principle or divine authority. They were confident, moreover, of man's progress and accepted neither cyclical nor regressive doctrines of history. Their social views were democratic, despite their apparent willingness to forget them for profit; they stood ready to teach anyone, and their theory countenanced no class or social boundaries to knowledge. Finally, they were relativists: practice was knowledge's ultimate test.

If the Sophists failed to create a theory of education, they nevertheless added a number of new dimensions and hastened the day when educational theory could stand alone. We should not want to leave them without at least mentioning the most prominent of these new dimensions. First, being responsible for a new higher education—literary secondary education—they were the custodians of the most advanced instruction in fifth-century Athens. They sponsored new curricula and new fields of study; language and logic were upgraded, and studies in grammar and rhetoric assumed a greater seriousness of purpose. Literature and mathematics aimed at dual goals of knowledge and discipline. Thus the Sophists promoted the disciplinary values of education and kept them alive to influence later ancient and medieval teachers. All their innovations were aimed at practical results, and here the Sophists' reputation for effective teaching seems most secure. Their theory was largely anticipatory; yet, although severely fragmented, it was forced throughout history to contend with the determined opposition of Plato's scientific humanism, on the one hand, and Isocrates' literary humanism—a refined type of sophistic teaching—on the other.

II

PHILOSOPHY AND EDUCATION

Only twice in its long history has educational theory been wedded to academic-historic philosophy: first, when Aristotle, after leaving the friendly atmosphere of Plato's Academy to make his own way, made it part of ethics and metaphysics; and, second, when John Dewey expanded educational theory and invited it to replace philosophy in the university's curriculum. We need elaborate only the first of these intellectual movements. We study Aristotle here and neglect Dewey, although both were engaged in welding educational theory to philosophy, because Aristotle participated in and made important contributions to the origin of educational theory.[30] Dewey sought to re-engage philosophy and educational theory when the latter was already securely established; its independent status was assured. Apparently even the elaborate exertions of Dewey were insufficient to make serious inroads on this independence.

In saying that philosophy was the custodian of educational theory only twice in the latter's long history, we do not argue that educational theory is an objectively constituted discipline without any need to consult with other disciplines, such as philosophy or sociology, or even to accept their conclusions. We intend only this: educational theory, as Aristotle handled it, was an adjunct to philosophy, merely one of the problems to be dealt with in constructing a total world view.[31] This does not mean that philosophy is foreclosed from making positive contributions to educational theory; such a conclusion is unworthy of debate, and impossible to defend. As part of philosophy, educational theory enjoyed the status of a speculative discipline; standing independently it became a practical discipline. In this latter role it was invited to supply principles

[30] The road he chose to take is partly mapped by H. F. Cherniss, *Aristotle's Criticism of Plato and the Academy,* I (Baltimore, The Johns Hopkins Press, 1944).

[31] See Werner Jaeger, *Aristotle: Fundamentals in the History of His Development,* tr. by Richard Robinson, 2d ed. (Oxford, Oxford University Press, 1962).

and policies on which to base educational procedures. Thus educational theory rejected the limits of speculative philosophy, where it was allowed to promote education as an important human occupation but enjoined from superintending pedagogy in action.

Aristotle left undisturbed the universal assumption that education is a business for human beings, but this was no curtailment to speculation. In philosophizing about the education of men, whether in the *Politics,* the *Ethics,* or the *Metaphysics,* he distinguished theoretical from practical reason. Theoretical reason aims at a virtue which is intellectual; practical reason's goal is political and moral virtue. Aristotle recognizes both as relevant to, perhaps outcomes of, an educational process, yet he avoided direct involvement in educational theory because he preferred to express his attitudes within the boundaries of theoretical reason. And theoretical reason, it should be stressed, functions purely on its own account, with no end beyond itself: the products of theoretical reason are purely speculative.

Aristotle's emphasis on speculative knowledge—knowledge for its own sake, later a fundamental plank in the doctrine of liberal education —directed philosophers and educators to think about "right education," or how education ought to be judged on a purely abstract, antiseptic level. In selecting the road of abstraction Aristotle used terms somewhat foreign to the more practical political orientations of Plato and Isocrates.

In company with his illustrious predecessors, Aristotle was concerned with virtue, and this was inevitable, for virtue dominated the educational discussions of the Greeks. Plato and Isocrates, we know, prized nature first, and doubted that education could implant virtue in an ignoble soul. The Sophistic departure from this doctrine, however much welcomed by the ordinary man, was deplored by Athens' stationary schoolmasters and upset them. In addition to eroding tradition, it threatened the entire structure of a class society. Aristotle, while not siding with the Sophists, was somewhat more precise and philosophical in his theory of virtue than either Isocrates or Plato. He refused to equate knowledge and virtue; nor would he endorse unequivocally the unguarded assumption that virtue begins and ends with a naturally noble soul. "There are three things," he said, "which make men good and virtuous; these are nature, habit, and reason." [32]

Aristotle, we have said, would not argue about nonhuman virtue, so, by nature, he meant man's nature, or soul, and distinguished three types of activity for it. He made activity a fundamental quality of the soul.

[32] *Politics* VII, 13. For a comprehensive interpretation of Aristotle's educational position, see John Burnet, *Aristotle on Education,* 5th ed. (Cambridge, Mass., Harvard University Press, 1928) ; and Thomas Davidson, *Aristotle and Ancient Educational Ideals* (New York, Charles Scribner's Sons, 1892) . A more recent study, of which Aristotle forms a part, is William K. Frankena, *Three Historical Philosophies of Education: Aristotle, Kant, and Dewey* (Chicago, Scott, Foresman and Co., 1965) .

Beginning at the lowest level, activity was vegetative and manifested itself in growth, reproduction, and decay. The next level, animal activity, had principal features of sensation, appetite, and locomotion. The soul's vegetative and animal activities are found in all life. On the third level, man is clearly distinguished from other forms of life: the soul's activity here is reason.

In Aristotle's analysis habit was more than an unfolding of a natural endowment, although an enviable natural endowment was the best foundation for goodness and virtue. And habit, though learned behavior, was not always conscious; it was, Aristotle said, learning to do right by doing it. On a level where appetite and reason were not combined, virtue appeared to Aristotle to be an acquired habit, and he put it in the category of "the things we have to learn before we can do them, we learn by doing them."

The distinction between practical and theoretical reason led to the conclusion that the former directs the soul's appetitive activities, while the latter, functioning on the level of speculation, makes universal truth its goal.

Education, a social and political process, belonging to practical reason, was something to be managed for men's good, and Aristotle allowed education, as a day-to-day business, to remain subservient to politics. As a theorist, however, anxious for insight into "right education," he preferred to constrain it to the boundaries of theoretical reason and thus forged a relationship to philosophy never since completely severed. This relationship between philosophy and educational theory is fully justified so long as educational theory is allowed the status of an independent study, but Aristotle's liberalism did not extend far enough even to permit a partial or temporary secession of education from philosophy.

It is quite regularly thought, though perhaps mistakenly, that Aristotle's definition of educational theory and its subordination to philosophy were accorded special reverence in the early Christian and Medieval worlds. Christians began, the assumption runs, by embracing all of Aristotle, and their Medieval successors followed suit. In the first place, Aristotle was paid scant heed even by his contemporaries, and, as we shall see, a variety of factors combined to redirect educational thought during the Hellenistic years. Aristotle's codifications and crabbed involutions, buried away in speculative philosophy, were largely ignored except in schools of philosophy dedicated to him, where his books were studied as philosophical classics. Still, philosophy was a minority culture—further subdivided by contending schools of thought—during these long years; and despite the often important things some philosophers said about education and other issues besetting mankind, their words fell on deaf ears.

In the second place, the idea that Aristotle's philosophy of education guided schools throughout the early and late Christian Middle Ages, down through the Renaissance of the fourteenth century, while containing some elements of truth, ignores the historical importance of Jerome, Augustine, Cassiodorus, and Alcuin in the formative centuries of the Christian West, and it slights the highly significant place of Hugh of St. Victor and John of Salisbury in Medieval educational theory, and of Erasmus in Renaissance educational thought and practice.[33]

Because Aquinas used Aristotle, Aristotle's theory of education, the argument goes, must have played a prominent role in Medieval education. But Aristotle, we must remember, did not write a complete theory of education and, therefore, could not have bequeathed one to Aquinas. Nor did Aquinas write a theory of education. What he said about it stayed in Aristotle's categories of thought, and he left to others the task of shaping and articulating a total educational plan.[34] Medieval educational theory, moreover, was largely a settled issue by Aquinas' time, and we have no evidence for believing he took exception to its principal positions. And these positions bore no clear debt to Aristotle. After Aristotle, educational theory took an entirely new direction; one not altered materially until the time of John Dewey. With this new direction we must now concern ourselves.

III

TOWARD AN INDEPENDENT THEORY OF EDUCATION

Conditions in the Hellenistic world making possible a disengagement of educational theory from politics, on the one hand, and from philosophy, on the other, were generated partly within education itself and partly in a society education was expected to serve.[35] In the most advanced of the city-states of Greece—Athens—to whom the majority of Hellenistic municipalities looked for guidance on cultural issues, education was an accredited member of the cultural family. The various threads forming the fabric of classical culture were hard to identify; education was one

---

33 R. R. Bolgar, *The Classical Heritage and Its Beneficiaries* (London, Cambridge University Press, 1954), pp. 149–162, lays to rest the old myths surrounding the continuity of an Aristotelian philosophical tradition from classical times to the early scholastic period. Bolgar's book is a brilliant contribution to our understanding of perennial features of classical education.

34 Especially Hugh of St. Victor and John of Salisbury. For their places in Medieval educational theory, see pp. 161–184.

35 Attention is again called Rostovtzeff, *op. cit.*, especially pp. 1059–1095; and George Grote's monumental twelve-volume work, *A History of Greece from the Earliest Period to the Close of the Generation Contemporary with Alexander the Great* (London, John Murray (Publishers) Ltd., 1869–1870). See also, W. W. Tarn, *Hellenistic Civilization*, 2d ed. (London, Edward Arnold (Publishers) Ltd., 1934).

thread, but being almost part of the fabric itself no Athenian argued about principals and subordinates. Education was simply part of Greek life; neither of the terms "servant" or "master" would have had much meaning. Yet, the Hellenistic world, despite its ardent wish to be true to an authentic Greek heritage, was new and different; classical traditions were too distant to flow naturally and effortlessly into society's life. When culture was not imbibed by living, new means were needed, so schools were designed to communicate the classical inheritance. This was a new assignment for formal education, and from now on our knowledge of the classical tradition comes from the sole, and often unsatisfactory, medium of school learning. Retaining its essentially moral features, education, nevertheless, became more dependent on books and developed an unmistakably scholastic image.

Although the institutionalization of schooling for continuing the classical heritage was one important factor allowing, or forcing, educational theory to grow up, it was not alone, and may not have been most important. When we think of the person in the city-state, we think first of a man who has subordinated his individuality to a higher collective good. While it is true that some erosion of the collective spirit is observable as early as the fifth century B.C., along with definite individualistic tendencies, the old theory remained in force: a citizen paid his first allegiance to the city-state; other allegiances then fell in line. Further liberalization was held in check by the internal political structure of society, and classical men could cultivate the collective attitude and live according to its prescripts because their city was real and touched almost every segment of their lives. Hellenistic man, however, no longer lived in a city-state, although he lived in a city, and he considered himself a citizen, not of the city, but of the world. Without any clear political duties much beyond political housekeeping, he could easily believe his first duty was to himself. Thus, when men rejected political idealism, it followed that education should sever bonds with politics too. With education no longer a humble reflection of corporate life, the ground was ready to plant seeds for an educational theory directed toward the perfection of personalities rather than public men. If perfecting oneself became the one task worthy of a lifetime's devotion, it is not surprising that men began to think more profoundly about education.

The record supports the conclusion: ideas about education became a common currency of intellectual exchange. Earlier in authentic classical times we heard prominent thinkers theorizing about education and its relationship to state ends; now others are debating the pros and cons of educational opportunity befitting a citizen of the world. A formidable array of educational theorists begin to publish their formulas on teaching and learning, on pedagogy and its services to culture, for an anxiously waiting Hellenistic audience.

Among the first, standing on the early fringe of Hellenism, was Aristippus of Cyrene (435–350 B.C.). He with others—all called Lesser Socratics to distinguish them from Plato's disciples—established schools where they essayed to teach wisdom, or embraced wisdom rather than practical efficiency as their ideal. This lone, though important, feature expressed their independence of the Sophists, and some such expression may have been necessary, because they used the usual sophistic techniques, such as public displays to attract students, teaching by contract, and organizing courses of study lasting two or three years. Aristippus' theory reminds us more of Isocrates and the Sophists than of Plato or Socrates: emphasizing the moral side of education, and seeking the development of personality and the elaboration of inner life, he set a course for moving teaching away from the political ideal long inherently identified with the environment of the ancient city. Individual development and personal self-realization were the goals for all human endeavor: to help persons reach these goals was the business of education.

In his educational program outlined in *On Education* (in all he seems to have written six books, none now extant),[36] Aristippus departed from Socrates' and Plato's affirmations respecting the role of science and truth in teaching, and accepted instead the dialectical techniques made famous by Socrates,[37] and nailed them to his educational mast. The conceptual dogmatism of Plato was rejected in favor of argumentation. Aristippus and his colleagues, not especially interested in the elaboration of specific doctrinal truths, wanted mental exercise. Using an approach centering on argumentation—and one bound to have an abundance of negative content—Aristippus tolerated the mathematical and scientific courses in Plato's plan as preparatory disciplines, and argued for a school syllabus whose dominant tone was literary. Following Aristippus, whose work anticipated Hellenistic theory, the curriculum should involve students in the study of poetry and language. Not forgetting moral formation, Aristippus recommended literature for the moral lessons it contained; yet he wanted the classics taught for their own sake, and when his students attended the theater he wanted them prepared to criticize what they found there.

In educational theory Aristippus occupies middle ground between Plato and the Sophists; his theory laid the foundation for a transition from classical to Hellenistic educational theory and practice. Other more authentic Hellenists followed his model.

Chrysippus (c. 300 B.C.), the great Stoic and champion of Hellenism, accepted the new political order with its goals of personal fulfillment. His theory of education recognized the person as a potential citizen of the world, and he tried to offer an educational code commensurate with this

---

36 Diogenes Laertius, *Lives of Eminent Philosophers* II, 85.
37 *Ibid.*, 91–93.

high goal. Unavoidably Chrysippus neglected many things necessary to a complete theory, yet he felt, no doubt, that working within a general ideological structure he was absolved from saying everything. In any case, his views on education had enough permanence to last until Quintilian could notice and approve them. Chrysippus began with the assumption, made also by Aristippus, that education should have a dominant literary tone: the school henceforth was defined as a literary agency. With this commitment to the written word and language, his recommending great care in selecting a nursemaid for the child elicits no surprise. No doubt he wanted her to be moral; ideally she should be a philosopher; what he really meant to say was that her speech should be pure.[38] In addition, he was anxious to change the beginning school age. Plato thought six might be a good time to start, and Aristotle talked about five; Chrysippus recommended three.[39] He was not alone in making such an advanced recommendation—many of his contemporaries shared this view—but his audience was too conservative for such innovations: they listened politely and continued to accept seven as the beginning school age.

Ancient schoolmasters observed only two motives for learning: fear and use. Since schoolboys had some difficulty in seeing the utility of their studies in Hellenistic schools, the former rather than the latter motive usually took precedence. Chrysippus could think of nothing much better than corporal punishment to keep the boys in line, so his objections are stilled,[40] but he did recognize excessive brutality in the schools as a possible impediment to learning. Quintilian, we shall see, seconding Chrysippus' concern, decisively opposed brutal school practices, but Quintilian reasoned from the advantage of a more enlightened educational environment, and even then he was not successful in modifying school practices much.

On more essential elements of school practice Chrysippus is clearer: he enthusiastically endorsed the study of Homer, and thus associated himself with authentic classical traditions. The whole Greek heritage should be absorbed by Hellenistic culture, and, he thought, this could be done by teaching all of Homer: nothing should be expurgated or brought up to date. Whatever Homer wrote was assumed to have real meaning for Greek culture, so learning Homer, Chrysippus said, should be a continuous effort to understand him, even when it meant using all the resources of dialectic. Nothing was left out, not even the "law of gesture," [41] and everything was analyzed. If this put a great burden on schools, it was no less a clear commission for them: their job was to extract meaning from the literature of the classical past. As a corollary to this commission,

[38] Quintilian, *Education of an Orator* I, i, 4.
[39] *Ibid.* I, i, 16.
[40] *Ibid.* I, iii, 14.
[41] *Ibid.* I, xi, 12.

Chrysippus recommended the study of grammar. Despite the dedicated efforts of Protagoras, Plato, and Chrysippus himself to produce a creative rather than a critical grammar, the codification of grammar was a slow and uneven endeavor. In a somewhat fragmented form grammar was difficult to study; yet, in following Chrysippus' advice, the schools made a brave beginning in giving grammar an unassailable place in the school's program. Besides grammar, Quintilian tells us, Chrysippus wanted rhetoric taught too, with all its embellishments, calling it the "science of speaking correctly." [42]

Theophrastus (c. 370–286 B.C.), standing somewhat in the shadow of Aristotle, assumed the directorship of the Lyceum in 323 B.C.[43] But before this he had a reputation in his own right, perhaps because of his willingness on occasion to differ forthrightly from his teacher Aristotle. He was a popular teacher, for even if Diogenes Laertius is plainly wrong in saying that two thousand students regularly attended his lectures,[44] a reduction of this estimate fifty times gives him more students than most stationary masters wanted, and more students, too, than ordinary Sophists attracted. Besides teaching, Theophrastus was a prolific writer, expressing views on subjects ranging from astronomy to rhetoric. In keeping with the temper of the times, his educational philosophy was solitary: he refused to wed it either to politics or philosophy. The author of four books on educational theory (none now extant) —*Of the Education of Kings, Of the Education of Children* (two books with the same title) , and *Of Education*—he wrote, in addition, a dozen books on rhetoric containing curricular materials along with theoretical justifications for teaching oratory.

Perhaps more than his Hellenistic colleagues, he made rhetoric the heart of education; through its good offices the religion of culture was served best. And he was listened to, for Quintilian acknowledged that "after him we may note that the philosophers, more especially the leaders of the Stoic and Peripatetic schools, surpassed even the rhetoricians in the zeal which they devoted to the subject." [45] Yet, with all his zealous effort, Theophrastus could not revive the old oratory full of political significance. The Hellenistic world, although it wanted classical models, downgraded deliberative oratory because the imperial state refused to countenance political debate over its policies. When Hellenistic men wanted to speak they chose safe topics and purged their orations of political meaning. Theophrastus found the solution: display oratory.[46] Delivering orations, speakers exercised their skill on highly artificial subjects and tried to keep the traditions and techniques of classical oratory inviolate.

42 *Ibid.* II, xv, 34.
43 Diogenes Laertius, *op. cit.* V, 36.
44 *Ibid.* V, 37.
45 Quintilian, *op. cit.* III, i, 15.
46 *Ibid.* III, vii, 1.

The code of Hellenistic rhetoric demanded an employment of classical vocabulary, an additional burden on the already heavily loaded student, in order to keep tradition and language pure. A man was identified by his speech, and Theophrastus was sensitive to this because he was once accused of being a foreigner by an old Athenian woman who noticed the archaisms of his language. His critic was both right and wrong: Theophrastus, a native of Eresus, and an adopted son of Athens, wanted to demonstrate his allegiance to the classical past.

Theophrastus gave rhetoric pride of place in the curriculum, but he left some room for literature. Good speaking, though essential, he agreed, is inelegant and empty without the content, range, and charm supplied by the genius of classical poets. Reading the poets, he said, "is of great service to the orator." [47]

Clearchus of Soli, an educator of the third century B.C., in his *On Education* (no longer extant), and Cleomenes, of the second century B.C., in *The Schoolmaster* (not extant), added little to educational theory. Education, they acknowledged, needed careful study, and both believed in perpetuating classical traditions by promoting primarily literary objectives for the school. They engaged in rhetorical and grammatical discourse, emphasized ephebic training without being too serious about it, and gave full attention to artistic and literary education. No doubt Clearchus and Cleomenes commanded an audience, and their views were important, yet, compared to other theorists of the period, they were paid scant heed. The keen observer, Quintilian, chose to follow other Hellenists whose views were expressed with greater generality and who were, therefore, better witnesses in the trial determining education's objectives.

One better witness was Aristoxenus (third century B.C.). In his *Rules of Pedagogy* (not now extant) he shared the advanced views of his colleagues, especially with respect to the enormously inflated role rhetoric was assigned for perpetuating Greek culture. He, as they, was absorbed in the idea that educational institutions should aim directly at cultural transmission. Literature could support this purpose, but the superior sign of culture was a man's ability to express himself using all the refinements of rhetorical art. Chrysippus only advocated the law of gesture—or chironomy—but Aristoxenus went beyond this to extract principles from rhythm and melody for application to gesture, word arrangement, and vocal inflection. His rhetorical doctrine made a euphonious combination of sounds as necessary in speaking as in singing or reciting poetry, and variations in arrangement and sound were determined by an oration's nature. Not many generations before, Plato had accused rhetoric of being theoretically barren; but the picture was changing, and Aristoxenus took the vanguard helping fill rhetoric's scientific and theoretic arsenal.

For all the energy spent by Hellenistic theorists to project rhetorical

[47] *Ibid.* X, i, 27.

education to the pinnacle, the incisive criticisms of Plato did not die easily.[48] Before rhetoric could take an unchallenged position at the top of the educational ladder, it was essential to deflate the significance of Plato's assertion that rhetoric was a mere knack, akin to cooking, something learned by experience. Almost every Hellenist tried to discount Plato's reasoned arguments in *Gorgias,* but in the end Cleanthes became their spokesman. Cleanthes (c. 331–232 B.C.) is credited with *Of Education, Of Usages, Of Dialectic, Of Moods or Tropes,* and *Of Predicates* (none extant). A native of Assos, he was, according to Diogenes Laertius, a boxer converted to Stoicism; upon Zeno's death he became president of the Poecile, the Stoic school in Athens, which should cast some doubt on the story depicting him as a man of modest ability. His profound dedication to education as the principal avenue to Greek culture led him to write five books on education wherein his special interest in rhetoric and the doubt Plato had raised about its being a true art were displayed. While these doubts remained current, to assault them was essential for rhetoric to retain its position as the kingpin of Hellenistic education. So Cleanthes undertook to idealize oratory as the true goal of education. Rhetoric, he said, is the art of speaking well, and the orator knows how to speak well. If he is asked for evidence to support his assertion, Cleanthes answers that even philosophers are unable to answer such questions about their doctrines. Proof that rhetoric is an art, he avers, can be supplied quickly: "Art is a power reaching its ends by a definite path, that is, by ordered methods," [49] and no one doubts the significance to good speaking of method and order. The definition that art consists in perceptions agreeing and cooperating to the achievement of some useful end sustained rhetoric. This weak argument silenced Plato's imposing objections because Cleanthes' colleagues were too anxious to extol rhetoric to demand more proof or stronger reasoning. Cleanthes thus abetted a grammatical-rhetorical monopoly and added stability to the already formidable shape of Hellenistic techniques and theories. His reputation as a spokesman may be measured by the willingness of Quintilian to quote Cleanthes' proofs; although Quintilian cannot be a disinterested observer where oratory is concerned, his partiality is really beside the point: Quintilian's *Education of an Orator* is as much a description of Hellenistic pedagogy as a plan for the future of education.

The last prominent Hellenist, Zeno (333–261 B.C.), was, in a sense, the most effective of all. As the founder and principal teacher of the Stoic school of philosophy, he was in an excellent position to express his doctrines in terms giving them philosophical respectability. His two books on education (neither extant)—*The Usual Greek Education* and a *Handbook of Rhetoric*—handle the conventional preoccupations of Hellenistic

48 See pp. 69–74.
49 Quintilian, *op. cit.* II, xvii, 41.

theorists: education's importance as a transmitter of culture and rhetoric's singular role as a means to effect it. Lavish in his praise of rhetoric and speaking in favor of purple passages, with their grace, charm, and force, he remembered to insist on oratory steeped in meaning; without profound meaning, embellishments and flourishes meant nothing. He distinguished two types of speech: one, continuous, was called rhetoric; the other, concise, was labeled dialectic. The distinction, however, did not matter because according to Zeno the two are intimate: one is like a closed fist; the other like an open hand.

The details of speech distract us from Zeno's best work, where his broader insights are most revealing. Although Zeno would hardly qualify as an original thinker, he collated diverse attitudes about teaching, learning, and curricula and summarized them for Hellenistic schoolmasters and for everyone interested in following the educational model of Hellenism. An expression of Hellenistic educational theory approached its final form with Zeno. His theory commended the mature, educated man as the standard for educational practice. Obviously teachers begin with children, but they must not teach them as children, or even give special attention to their interests and needs. Their objective is to start the child down the cultural road, and with this rigid aim it was entirely unnecessary to think of the child as a child at all or to introduce any techniques of pedagogy appropriate to the education of children. Hellenistic education, moreover, had an intense interest in the education of the whole man. Schoolmasters were not concerned only with the intellect, the will, or the body: their approach to culture was total. Yet, we must realize, this was theory; and in practice they failed to educate the whole man almost as miserably as future generations of schoolmasters were to fail.

When the theory of whole-man education was not followed, and this was often, we should judge, moral education did not suffer. Moral education was the objective the ancients had sought with so much vigor, and the ideal of classical living, expressed most concretely in the literature of the classical period, was the ideal Hellenists tried to embrace. They were remarkably successful in reviving the past, making it live in their students' minds, and thus they believed they were successful in achieving the moral objective of teaching by forming citizens of the world.

Zeno read the signs of the times, and of classical culture too, so he declared technical education anathema. Not that technical education was unavailable in the Hellenistic world, and no one questioned its utility. It represented nothing of the classical inheritance, so its case was closed. This inheritance was promoted in the only possible way, by a literary type of education, and every effort was made to keep traditions pure. Constant watch was kept over the literary syllabus to assure its authenticity and purity.

So we reach the end of the road: educational theory is able to stand alone as a subject worthy of study, able to attract the attention of good minds. Hellenistic educational philosophers did this for their discipline, but they did even more: instruction was now a matter for the schools, and the schools were directed to transmit an inheritance from the past; by accepting a preoccupation with grammar and rhetoric the commission could be fulfilled.

In tracing the evolution of educational theory from its subordinate supporting role in politics and philosophy to a position of undeniable significance as a separate discipline worthy of thought and effort, we have moved over terrain somewhat unfamiliar to many readers. Unavoidably we sometimes get ahead of the story, and refer to points treated more completely later. In this chapter we wanted to show how educational theory reached a mature academic level. Now in succeeding chapters we can turn to theories of education as they were formulated, sometimes fully, often partially, sometimes subordinate to politics, often independent, against the background of a discipline that has come of age, and by men whose work has a coveted position in the history of educational thought.

❧ 2 ❧

Isocrates: A Theory of Literary Humanism

I

THE MAN AND HIS WORK

Late in the fifth century B.C. Athens was overrun with Sophists offering to sell their teaching for almost any price. Not content to wait until the end of the course, or to trust their students, they demanded escrow deposits to assure payment of tuition fees. Doubtless a business arrangement of this kind gives us little evidence about the quality of their teaching; yet we are on fairly safe ground in assuming that many Sophists in Athens during this half-century of ferment were excellent teachers.

The Sophists are highly interesting and important to the history of learning; without them neither Isocrates nor Plato could have reached his full stature, and the conflict between literary and scientific humanism would not have been joined on the same level of significance. Yet despite the Sophists' importance both to education and philosophy—they were the first secondary-school teachers and the first pragmatists—our interest in them is tangential to a study of Isocrates' role in the evolution of educational doctrine.[1]

The importance of the Sophists here, however, is not their role as effective and unquestionably popular teachers,[2] but their place as Isoc-

[1] See E. A. Havelock, *op. cit.*, chapters eleven and twelve. We should understand from the first that the Sophists were recognized as seekers after wisdom; they were often called philosophers. In the fifth and fourth centuries B.C., the term Sophist was employed without invidiousness. Beck, *op. cit.*, pp. 147–187, has an excellent chapter on the Sophists, as does Marrou, *op. cit.*, pp. 46–60.

[2] Among the most popular Sophists who occupied this role were Prodicus, Protagoras, and Theramenes. Isocrates' contact with Gorgias was probably not in the ordinary role of a student. He is said to have associated with Gorgias only after he had opened his school (R. C. Jebb, *Attic Orators*, New York, The Macmillan Company, 1893, II, 5), and, while this may be true, he had undoubtedly developed an earlier sympathy

25

rates' principal mentors. Among them apparently was Socrates, who, though never a Sophist in the later meaning of the term, had a reputation as a friend of wisdom and a dialectician. No one spent many hours with the venerable Socrates without learning something. Isocrates' favorable financial and social standing makes it appear more likely that he had close contact with Socrates and Plato. Isocrates was nine years older than Plato; Socrates was several years the senior of both. Tradition supports the belief that Isocrates was exposed to the leading teachers of Athens.

His father invested in a small factory employing thirty or forty men to manufacture musical instruments; the investment repaid him in influence and wealth and he gave Isocrates the best educational advantages. What the Isocratic future might have been—he may even have fulfilled the prophecy of Socrates reported by Plato in the *Phaedrus*, viz., "a certain philosophy is inborn in him," had his father's fortune remained intact—can only be speculated about.[3] Fate raised its ugly hand and the family's assets deteriorated; its members were faced with the unhappy prospect of mere subsistence living. Rather than accept this, Isocrates decided to earn his way, but he had no reputation as a teacher; writing was his only saleable skill, so he became a legal journalist for litigants in Athenian courts.[4]

Isocrates, in later years, took no pride in this work, although we are unconvinced about his misgivings during this quasilegalistic interlude. He expended honest effort, prepared effective defenses for his clients—if the few extant forensic speeches are authentically Isocratic—and was well paid. He later shuns any involvement with the law courts,[5] as does his adopted son, Aphareus, and some admirers, yet the experience was too

for Gorgias' rhetorical theories, probably from Theramenes. (S. Wilcox, "The Scope of Early Rhetorical Instruction," *Harvard Studies in Classical Philology*, LIII (1942), 121–155.) Otherwise we are at a loss to explain his reaction to Plato's *Gorgias*, already extant when his school's prospectus, *Against the Sophists*, was composed. For the teaching enterprises of the Sophists and some of the intellectual interplay among them, see M. Untersteiner, *op. cit.*

[3] Many commentators speak of Isocrates' association with Socrates. Jebb, *op. cit.*, p. 4, for one, is quite confident of its intimate qualities. My own view is that Plato is merely having a little fun at Isocrates' expense. The latter was then only about twenty-six years old and was engaged in what Plato regarded as an unbecoming vocation: writing of legal speeches. The chronology seems to me to be unimportant; the dramatic date in Plato's *Phaedrus* is really what counts. Plato was simply saying that Isocrates had not lived up to his potential either as a writer or teacher. For other views, see R. L. Howland, "The Attack on Isocrates in the Phaedrus," *Classical Quarterly*, 31 (July, 1937), pp. 151–159; and G. J. De Vries, "Isocrates' reaction to the Phaedrus," *Mnemosyne*, 4a, Ser. VI (1953), pp. 39–45.

[4] We need not dwell on legal customs here, but we should point out that at this time in Athens each litigant served as his own attorney. Litigants, therefore, regularly employed others to prepare their speeches for them. See Robert J. Bonner, *Lawyers and Litigants in Ancient Athens* (Chicago, University of Chicago Press, 1927).

[5] See Isocrates, *Antidosis*, 37. If this is not a denial, it is, at least, an assertion that his literary sights were always higher.

real to be wished away. Outright denials are supplemented with explanations that Isocrates did not write these speeches for the courtroom but simply as models for his school.[6]

We are tempted to shelve the whole question as picayunish, although if we do we should be misreading the real reason for the Isocratic denials. Isocrates understood, when his disciples did not, why these legalistic orations had to be reinterpreted, and what appears to be a pettifogging disclaimer is really a fundamental point. Yet even Isocrates has no license to rewrite history. This is why he tried: when he established a school with oratory, rhetoric, and eloquence as its principal objects, he retreated from an earlier position, viz., that speech is intended to serve legal and political expediency. Thus Plato's oblique charge against Gorgias and rhetoric contained an allegation that rhetoric was unable to contradict, despite Isocrates' diligent efforts. Isocrates became committed to a responsible oratory recognizing truth and justice. His oratory, raised to a philosophic level, was intended as a handmaiden both to truth and justice, i.e., it was expected to honor and advance both in the day-to-day contacts of men in society. Isocratic philosophy was not destined for the dungeons of unreality and irrelevance; it could achieve viability only by permeating the lives of men and renewing its relevance and effectiveness. In such a doctrine the instruments of oratory must assume broader dimensions if they are to proceed with assurance toward creating a more responsible and virtuous public life. Plato and Isocrates differed on many things, but nowhere were their differences more marked than here: for Plato truth and justice were apprehended only after a long, patient, and exhausting intellectual search; Isocrates believed in the self evidence of most, if not all, virtues. Such elusive things as the good, the true, and the just were for Isocrates almost totally bereft of anagogical character. He was impatient with most Sophists and Platonists who were consciously or unconsciously distracting students from the virtues of good life. He refused to expend the effort formulating special meanings or methods for philosophy. Must men spend a lifetime learning the bare elements of justice? Such conditions or demands make effective statesmanship impossible; and in practice men must assume the mantle of statesmen without the benefits of extended years of exposure to political-philosophical seminars. Isocrates could cite examples from his own experience, and from the common traditions of Greek political life, where they had done so. Were these men different politically? Were they more effective? Did they

---

[6] This hypothesis, although not original with Jebb, is repeated by him, *op. cit.,* p. 28. He credits Westermann, *History of Greek Oratory,* with its formulation (I have been unable to obtain a copy of this old book, published around 1839). George Kennedy, *The Art of Persuasion in Greece* (Princeton, N.J., Princeton University Press, 1963), pp. 71–74, discusses Isocrates' speeches and their use. See also, J. W. H. Atkins, *Literary Criticism in Antiquity* (Cambridge, Cambridge University Press, 1934), pp. 129 ff.

have any greater—or less—devotion to the political weal? No public man, according to Isocrates, had conducted the agonizing and unrewarding pursuit outlined by Plato. Successful public men ignored the traps of dialectic, depended on common sense interpretations of virtue, and welded these interpretations into responsible oratory. Isocrates' writings regularly reflect an undisguised and dogmatic assumption that Platonic sophistry is sham. There was no place for Platonic-like philosophizing in his theory of education, and he tried to expurgate it from pedagogy when he opened his own school. Yet his position was vulnerable, because of his career as a writer of law-court speeches, and he tried to cover his oratorical tracks. He did not relish being charged with shallowness, nor did he want to place his educational venture in jeopardy, so he made room for philosophy in the curriculum. This was not simply a concession to the popular movement upgrading philosophical study, for Isocrates acknowledged the worth of general ideas. Yet he assigned philosophy to a low rung on the scholastic ladder; it was a study for boys, not a conversion and a way of life for men.[7]

His bond with Socrates was not intimate, although he admired the old philosopher enough to strike a parallel between his own misfortunes, described in the *Antidosis,* and those of Socrates, described by Plato in the *Apology*. Emotional kinships may have been present: Socrates never became a statesman, although his exploits as a citizen-soldier are legendary. Socrates is strikingly a creation of Plato, and Plato preferred to keep him out of the political arena. Plato makes Socrates reflect his own inability, bred of political connections and miscalculations, to be active in politics. Plato preferred a real political world to one of speculation and utopia.[8] Socrates, we assume, remained aloof by choice. Isocrates' weak voice and retiring nature kept him from public life; this is a personal admission.[9] Yet possibly neither physical deficiencies nor temperamental shortcomings were compelling; Isocrates may have preferred the tranquility of a position enabling him to comment on public affairs and affording him the luxury of political involvement without the liability of political responsibility. History records another parallel. Both Socrates and Isocrates achieved their greatest political fame through their students or disciples. For Socrates this was sheer accident; Isocrates may have planned to perpetuate his name and philosophy in his students.

Our knowledge of Isocrates' personal affairs—except for his father's

[7] In fairness to Isocrates, one should be at pains to indicate that the meaning of philosophy was unsettled in this age. Anyone who was interested in things of the mind would lay claim to the title of philosopher. After separate schools of philosophy were distilled, allegiances became more definite and the term philosopher assumed a more professional and particular significance. For some further insight into the origins and constituents of the philosophic life, see H. I. Marrou, *op. cit.*, pp. 206–210.

[8] Plato himself is the witness here (*Epistolae* VII, 324c).

[9] In *Panathenaicus*, 10, Isocrates says: "For I was born more lacking in the two things which have the greatest power in Athens—a strong voice and ready assurance—than, I dare say, any of my fellow citizens."

enterprise, some fragmentary information about his brothers and a sister, his marriage late in life, and some scandal about affairs either with men or women—is scanty. We should like to know the physical details of his school, its name, its curriculum and methods, where the students came from and how many there were. Tradition says the school was small,[10] but some writers confidently contradict that tradition. All agree that Isocrates conducted the best known school of antiquity.[11]

Isocrates removes part of the veil covering his personal affairs in the *Antidosis*. As a literary vehicle he used it to expound his educational doctrine, but prior to this it was a real litigation involving him as one of the principals.[12] For this reason and also because of some misunderstanding concerning Isocrates' wealth, we might look at the case. The chief source of revenue for Athens during most of the fifth century was the tribute paid by allies and subjects. Eventually these sources were exhausted and the state, to maintain a certain stability of income, obtained the proceeds from mines at Laurium and Thrace, rents from state property, and court fees and fines. Resident aliens were required to pay a poll tax. Although citizens paid no direct tax, a system of liturgies was in vogue whereby public services were sponsored by wealthier citizens and metics, provided they had sufficient wealth to qualify. During one period, when Isocrates was conducting his school, the burdens of government expense exceeded the income from voluntary support, so a unique method was employed to raise money. The 1200 wealthiest citizens were divided into twenty companies of sixty persons. These companies were further divided, so that a varying number of persons—probably from two to twelve—supported one trireme.[13] The financial responsibility of each individual trierarch was decided after some method of property evaluation was instituted. Evidently these evaluations of wealth were made, not by outside agencies or committees of citizens, but by the elected chairman of each small group. This method had weaknesses which led to its eventual demise, to be followed by another, surer method of approaching equity. It was this newer adaptation of tax collection, one involving Isocrates directly and unhappily, that laid the historical foundation for his *Antidosis*.

Citizens were taxed as individuals in each group, but payments were

10 See pp. 44–45.

11 Johnson surveys some of the opinion on this point (R. S. Johnson, "Isocratic Methods of Teaching," *American Journal of Philology*, LXXX (January, 1959), pp. 25–36.

12 See Robert J. Bonner, "The Legal Setting of Isocrates' Antidosis," *Classical Philology*, 15 (April, 1920), pp. 193–197.

13 A trireme was a ship. The state supplied only the hull and some of the rigging; the duty and expense of fitting the galley and training the oarsmen were laid upon the wealthiest citizens, each in his turn. This public burden was called the trierarchy, and the trierarch, who sailed with the ship, was responsible for the good repair of the trireme at the end of his period of office, usually one year. (J. B. Bury, *A History of Greece*, New York, Modern Library, 1922, p. 318.)

made by the group. Whenever some members of the group were unable or unwilling to forward their share of the levy, the government-revenue council compiled a list of the wealthiest men in the group and exacted the entire amount from them. Following traditional terminology, although benevolence was absent, this payment was called a liturgy. Those who performed it were left to recover whatever they could from other members of their tax group.

So Isocrates, despite the tradition of his being one of the 1200 wealthiest citizens of Athens, may simply have been a victim of circumstances, i.e., the wealthiest man in a group, when he was called upon to perform the liturgy. We are unable to confirm the tradition that he was a fully qualified member of the financial elite; he may or may not have been able to bear the tax burden. In any case, the state-revenue council saddled him with the responsibility, made him liable for the tax payment, and left him to his own devices for gaining relief from his colleagues. Isocrates paid the tax bill and began litigation to recover. If his own account is accurate, the trial court's verdict was inequitable: misjudging his financial ability, the court refused to use the force of law to help him recover money paid to fulfill obligations not solely his.

His fellow citizens treated him unfairly, and we have labeled him a tax dodger who, despite great wealth, refused to bear his just share. Critics are amused with his use of the *Antidosis* to introduce, in Socratic fashion, a tragic episode in his life; and we are unsympathetic with his loss and his unfair treatment in court. His fellow citizens knew him as an extraordinarily successful professor of oratory. The glory of the Sophists was fading and Plato's fame was largely in the realm of promise. His countrymen, moreover, believing they knew his financial abilities as well as his bookkeeper, drew unfair conclusions on the basis of prejudicial or inaccurate evidence. And Isocrates was a man who depended on justice and enthusiastically counted on a quality of fair play to sustain a responsible moral balance! Little wonder, then, that Isocrates ventured again into the public domain to inform his fellow citizens; not, to be sure, to plead poverty, but to reveal the theory basic to his oratorical teaching. Misjudging him on a profane level of wealth, made a misunderstanding of the bases for his reputation as a responsible, thorough, and efficient teacher all the more likely.[14] If a quality of comic-tragedy appears in an old man using taxation and its frequently regressive means as a springboard for discussing rhetorical theory, we may forgive him, for he had real anxieties concerning the stability of his reputation as a teacher, and its influence on his students. When Plato castigated and ridiculed the Sophists, most of the objects of his scorn were already dead, but he was not really arguing with dead men; nor was Isocrates when he sought vindication through the *Antidosis*.

---

[14] Arete still had its traditional meaning, and, on this point, Isocrates was especially sensitive. See *Antidosis*, 275.

Later we shall discuss Isocrates' educational ideas and his methods of teaching, but now, in connection with the man's life and work, we offer a quick summary of his writings. Evidence showing the importance of this man to the history of learning is too often camouflaged: the conventional wisdom takes Isocrates' influence for granted, thus conferring on him an historical anonymity. One need only count pages in standard histories of education to confirm this point. He is either paid scant heed or ignored completely. Plato takes the leading role, supported, after a long historical step, by Quintilian. But Quintilian was not a true disciple of Plato; he taught, thought, and wrote in the tradition of Ciceronian and Isocratic eloquence. Without Isocrates what would Quintilian have been? History frees us from wondering how the systems of secondary education conducted by the Jesuits and the followers of Johann Sturm would have fared without Isocrates. Isocrates was the theorist to whom both these systems and the entire tradition of literary humanism are indebted.

Neither excellence nor influence is so evident in Isocrates' educational writings as in his school: Cicero's praise is unrestrained when he compares the Isocratic school and the Trojan horse and avers that only heroes came from both.[15]

Many ancient and modern writers were more productive than Isocrates; Plato's and Aristotle's bibliographies are bulkier. In all, Isocrates produced about sixty works, although only twenty-one discourses and nine letters survived. Some of his writings are either uneven or weak, for as Isocrates grew older he leaned more heavily on the past and, as in the *Antidosis*, often included generous extracts from earlier discourses. And we must not believe that all his writings touched humanity deeply—that quality distinguishing living from ephemeral literature. Yet, what he wrote kept scholars with him for centuries; even in the past half-century, critical works on Isocrates, in a half-dozen languages, number more than 500.[16]

---

15 *De Oratore*, II, 94.

16 Isocratic writing may be given a three-fold classification: forensic speeches, political discourses, and educational discourses. The latter interest us here, although the political discourses contain scholastic implications warranting close attention. Six forensic speeches were written early in his career; he and his disciples tried to forget them. They were *Against Lochites* (c. 394), *Span of Horses* (c. 397), *Aergineticus* (c. 394), *Against Euthynus* (c. 403), *Trapeziticus* (c. 394), and *Callimachus* (c. 402). Three were hortatory—*To Demonicus* (c. 372), *To Nicocles* (c. 374), and *Nicocles* (c. 372)—in which he exhorted the Greeks on ethics and tried to lay a foundation for practical morality. These discourses, though less artistic than Plato's dialogues, form at once an intellectual fellowship with and separate him from Plato. Isocrates was determined to deal with ethical questions—an issue common to Greek thinkers in the era of Socrates —but not on a theoretical level. Where Plato sought the foundations of morality or virtue, Isocrates tried to make virtue operative. He was willing to assume the ultimate meaning of virtue, Plato was not. Three—*Busiris* (c. 391), *Helen*, and *Evagorus*—belong to a category of display oratory in which Isocrates tries in a half-frivolous way to use a mythological theme to communicate a useful lesson. Two are clearly educational: *Against the Sophists* (c. 391)—a prospectus for his school, unfortunately not complete —and the *Antidosis* (c. 353), a long treatise on his educational hopes, theories, and

Isocrates did not want to be immunized from politics; he was too devoted a patriot to cut himself off from the political world. And he would not have had good credentials for tutoring statesmen if he had withdrawn from the realities of life to a mental refuge; yet he did not want to expose himself to the distractions and tensions of active political life either. To satisfy a desire for political involvement, he became a political commentator; and he became a teacher of oratory because he wanted to exert an effective influence on politics.

II

THE ISOCRATIC BASES OF CULTURE

No one can speak with confidence on the personal relationship between Plato and Isocrates. A close acquaintance may be assumed: both, long-time residents of Athens, were engaged in the profession of higher education, and both were under the intellectual wing of Socrates. Because of basic differences on fundamental philosophical and rhetorical questions, it is easy to believe that genuine cordiality was lacking in their relationship: [17] instead, it may have been one of admiration or pitying good will. We have no way of knowing.[18] In the *Gorgias* Plato shows his doubts about teaching political virtue; yet such teaching was the principal object and the primary commitment of Isocrates' school.[19] In other words, Plato was not simply opposing Isocratic methods, but the very heart of Isocrates' theory of teaching. And we have yet to learn how the *Gorgias*,

accomplishments. *Panathenaicus* (c. 342) in theme and tone is partly educational and partly political and thus belongs both to this and the next category. Six—*Panegyricus* (c. 381) , *Philip* (c. 346) , *Plataicus* (c. 373) , *Peace* (c. 355) , *Archidamus* (c. 366) , and *Areopagiticus* (c. 355) —are distinctly political, treating of government and political policies. Focus is on Athens, but the lessons of political philosophy extend beyond the city-state. The nine letters, because of their emphasis, are classified among the political discourses.

17 A dialogue is extant portraying Plato and Isocrates in conversation at Plato's country estate (Diogenes Laertius, *op. cit.*, III, 9) but this is inconclusive, possibly fictional. Though the harmony of friendship was unlikely, there were keenly aware of each other.

18 Platonic references to Isocrates: *Phaedrus, Gorgias, Euthydemus*. Isocratic references to Plato: *Against the Sophists, Helenae, Encomium, Panathenaicus, Antidosis*.

19 In this chapter and in the ones that follow, we shall have occasion to make many allusions to rhetoric as a part of schooling and as a political way of life. Since rhetorical instruction is somewhat foreign to contemporary educational practice, the following commentaries on it, especially on its standing in the ancient world, are recommended: S. Wilcox, "The Scope of Early Rhetorical Instruction," *Harvard Studies in Classical Philology*, LIII (1942) , pp. 121–155; H. Ll. Hudson-Williams, "Thucydides, Isocrates, and the Rhetorical Method of Composition," *Classical Quarterly*, 42 (July, 1948) , pp. 76–81; Gomperz, *op. cit.*; Jaeger, *op. cit.*, pp. 294 ff.; Marrou, *op. cit.*, pp. 194–205; and Charles S. Baldwin, *Ancient Rhetoric and Poetic* (New York, The Macmillan Company, 1924) .

with all its artistry, wit, and condemnation, affected the foremost teacher of antiquity. On the other hand, Isocrates plants doubt in the minds of Athenians about the authenticity of sophistic teaching—where he classifies Plato—when, in *Against the Sophists,* he deplores the unrealism of their teaching, the airy nothingness of their curriculum, and their irresponsibility for not accepting a clear commission to educate effective citizens.[20] In the eyes of one, the other was either engaged in fraudulent art or could not comprehend the realities of educational theory and practice. Although too early for pamphlet warfare, it was not too early for intellectual differences and personal animosities: Isocrates' observations are biting too, although his rhetoric eschews paradox, a tool employed with superb skill by the philosophers, when he focuses on Plato's *Gorgias* in *Against the Sophists.*

The timing of Isocrates' adoption of education and his assignment of it to an ancillary role to politics is imprecise. He opened a school in Athens when he was about forty-four, in 392 B.C., after having conducted one briefly at Chios, 404–403 B.C.[21] His first published academic theories, recorded in *Against the Sophists,* while incomplete, are nevertheless interesting and worth study. The essay's title makes a good beginning, for, although Isocrates admits being a Sophist—a man involved in intellectual and literary pursuits—he wants to distinguish his ideals of culture from other Sophists whose ideals are different or hostile. Poetry was the cultural pillar of archaic Greece, but this respected inheritance was somewhat illusory and did not satisfy the new ethical mindedness of Athenians.[22] It did not satisfy Isocrates either, although he hesitated to reject it outright because of his deep patriotism and profound reverence for everything Greek. New cultural axes were rhetoric and philosophy—to use the latter term in the Pythagorian sense of a search for ultimates—and neither was acceptable to Isocrates. Rhetorical culture, embraced by the vulgar Sophists, according to Isocrates, made teaching and exposure synonymous. But these were not the Sophists with whom Isocrates had studied; less responsible, more flamboyant Sophists now in Athens purveyed in caricature the teaching tradition of this old and respected cadre of teachers. Philosophic culture aimed at scientific humanism essaying to give statesmen a firm intellectual foundation from which the virtues of truth and justice could be given a political application. When Isocrates wrote *Against the Sophists,* Plato was not yet famous—a point leading

20 *Against the Sophists,* 21. For a discussion of Isocrates' cultural and educational ideals, and a source to which I am indebted, see Jaeger, *op. cit.,* III, pp. 46–155.

21 Jebb, *op. cit.,* p. 6, does not doubt the authenticity of the Chios school. He is impressed especially by Aristotle's comments, quoted by Cicero (*Brutus,* 48). It appears to be an insignificant point, and the evidence offered does not seem to me to be highly convincing.

22 The relationship between myth, poetry, and education in the period of early Greek education is treated by Beck, *op. cit.,* pp. 17–71.

some commentators to conclude that Isocrates did not have Plato in mind—but he was widely known in Athens and, moreover, was already advocating acquiring scientific, positive knowledge about virtue.

Against the Sophists, abundantly negative, gives us a fairly clear idea of the things Isocrates opposed. He wanted to assure prospective students of the uniqueness of his school and of the importance he attached to political responsibility, and moreover, he wanted to warn his fellow citizens of the dangers inherent in the teachings of other schools. Not all Sophists were condemned, but those he opposed were opposed with vehemence.

The Sophists were already vulnerable because of their superficial teaching, lack of solid technique, extravagant promises, and insistence on payment in advance; but, Isocrates wrote, these were only the outward signs of their decadence. If Athenian teachers were to be criticized, it was important to make the criticisms specific and thus absolve teachers to whom the indictment did not apply. He recommends that Sophists openly disclose the structure of their art: "If all who are engaged in the profession of education were willing to state the facts instead of making greater promises than they can possibly fulfill, they would not be in such bad repute with the lay public." [23]

What facts are they to state? First, he wants the common teachers of oratory to renounce their promise to teach a prose or oral composition capable of passing muster for any occasion. Both Isocrates and these Sophists wanted political commentators and analysts to make neat, pointed, comprehensive addresses extemporaneously. But here the similarity ended. Such oratory, Isocrates said, required the prerequisites of solid intellectual foundations and keen moral sensitivities; without them oratory would be either perceptive and immoral or superficial and amoral. Neither fulfilled the Isocratic standard of responsible oratory.

Isocrates objected to the attenuated goals of vulgar sophistic oratory, and charged it with shoddy technique. The ordinary Sophist lacked a thorough teaching method, being content to have pupils commit to memory either famous orations or pet Sophistic compositions. When this part of instruction was finished, they began memorizing dialogues renowned for their qualities of sublety and artistry. This was all the students had when they terminated their quick but crude course of study, and though enabling them to win arguments, its long-term results were barren and dangerous. Sophistic teaching reminded Aristotle of a shoemaker who, instead of teaching apprentices how to make shoes, simply showed them several pairs.[24] Granted, all Sophists did not resort to such flagrantly shallow techniques, yet Isocrates is still stressing devotion to study and practice prior to writing technical expositions, although no-

23 *Against the Sophists* 1.
24 Aristotle, *Against the Sophists* XXXIV, 7.

where does he intimate that examples or models be expunged from the rhetorician's pedagogy. We must try to grasp Isocrates' vision in order to understand his school practices. His school was closed to hoi polloi; and his adherence to democratic processes in education was remarkably low. He began with an aristocracy of ability, and never saw any possibility of educating anyone who was without talent, but he always valued nonintellectual aristocratic qualities. Next came diligent and intensive study to lay a foundation for later composition and oratory. For study—his syllabus of teaching was fairly broad, as we shall see—models were used. One must, therefore, be careful about taking at face value his chastisement of the Sophists for depending solely on models, for this technique in teaching rhetoric knows no greater champion than Isocrates; from him to Cicero, Quintilian, and the Humanists of the fourteenth century it was given pride of place in educational methodology. But we must guard against modifying the tone of *Against the Sophists* by inserting Isocratic doctrines here that belong to later discourses; at best, it is possible only by inferences drawn from this essay to know how he would correct the mistakes of his colleagues.

Responsible oratory is the central theme of *Against the Sophists:* its realization depends partly on a curriculum formed on the fundamentals of a good education—Plato and Isocrates disagreed on these fundamentals—and partly on the morals and intellectual integrity of teachers. Isocrates' charge is serious: "They pretend to search for truth, but straightaway at the beginning of their professions attempt to deceive us with lies." [25] What were teachers doing to elicit such a response from a man known for his moderate and discreet language? Who were they, and how did Isocrates know so much about their intellectual and moral standards?

Isocrates is not talking about Plato here, although he does not exonerate Plato's disciples. His target is the ordinary Sophist. The question of how Isocrates knew what other teachers were doing is easy to handle: the city-state was small; sophistic teachers made almost daily advertisements of their wares. Anyone who wanted to know what they promised had only to listen as they carried on public tub-thumping activities. Isocrates was sure of the facts. Apparently he was sure, too, that it is impossible to teach students what to do and how to become happy and prosperous. Besides, Sophists sold this precious knowledge for a trifling fraction of its worth. This bothers Isocrates, for, he argues, if they have knowledge to lead their students to inevitable prosperity, why are they themselves in such dire need—Sophists were usually poor—and why, if they know so much about the future, are they unable to say anything meaningful about the present? Reasonable, thinking men, Isocrates concludes, are certain to

---

25 Isocrates, *Against the Sophists*, 2.

reject these pretensions and condemn sophistic studies for not being true disciplines of the soul.[26]

Isocrates finds both the Sophists and the teachers of political discourse (not further identified) guilty of fraudulent educational practices and of corrupting Athenian youth. The former are guilty because they promised to teach truth, but did not possess it; the latter were condemned because they professed to teach clever oratory while at the same time acknowledging their complete indifference to truth. Isocrates' teaching practices were not immunized from these indictments either by the excellence of his school's reputation or by his own stature as an educator; because this was so, he devotes more than passing notice to these charges of fraudulence in the *Antidosis*.[27] But we should not now try to follow the academic reminiscences of the old master, for in doing so we run the risk of being distracted from his negative approach to the fundamentals of a good education. These fundamentals, it is true, are not reported as precise revelations in *Against the Sophists;* nevertheless, they are worth our attention.

Without referring to the pedagogic techniques involved in securing it, Isocrates gives pride of place to information. We must see information within the context of his educational goal, one of educating a public man, an orator, capable of holding his own in political disputes and determined to dominate political dialogue with preconceptions about what was best for Athens. What public man could do this without a mind enriched with knowledge? So Isocrates projected a broad curriculum; when he opened his school the course of study contained at least a dozen subjects for the boys to master. Teachers can endorse with enthusiasm pedagogic practices centered on information, but they can also approve those parts of an educational program whose object is to whet ingenuity and imagination. We may assume Isocrates' concurrence with a program for developing a discipline of curiosity and awe of learning; if he had been guiding the educational ship a millennium after the classical period he would surely have stressed discipline. Yet, for his time, preoccupation with informational aspects of education was warranted: when libraries existed they were not readily available, nor did they contain the appurtenances of reference books, encyclopedias, anthologies, or dictionaries of information. Skill was subordinated to information. Isocrates wanted graduates of his school to employ information with facility in forging oral and written orations; the information he transmitted in his classroom was reaped from the literature available to him in Athens.

The third ingredient for forming a public man was character. Isocrates reports his doubts about the ability of the Sophists or the stationary teachers to teach students how to be good, honest, true men. He knew the

26 *Ibid.*, 3–7.
27 *Antidosis*, 30.

hazards in translating the heart of these virtues from the order of wisdom to prudence; he doubted, moreover, the possibility of attaining ultimate knowledge of virtue, yet he wanted oratory to be grounded on a bedrock more stable than whim or convention. On a priori grounds he attested to man's innate knowledge of the good and the true; differences between justice and inequity, truth and error did not have to be taught. The burden of character education was refining intuitions of virtue: Isocratic pedagogy not only affirmed the worth of this undertaking, but made it imperative. Positive affirmations in Isocratic educational theory can be stated quickly under the general thesis of responsible oratory.

We turn now from his teaching prospectus, to which he was constant for a half-century, to a product of his advanced maturity where he reflected on an illustrious career and reaffirmed his pedagogic convictions, the *Antidosis*.

The *Antidosis*, a broadly-gauged document modeled after Plato's *Apology*, is literature's first autobiography. A political discourse, it supplemented *On Peace* and *Areopagiticus* and further contributed to Isocrates' unpopularity in Athenian political circles; a book on education, it embodied the essential structure of literary humanism. We may dismiss its literary and political dimensions and implications to summarize Isocrates' educational views.

1. To see the *Antidosis* in its historical context, we should know Isocrates was involved in a lawsuit over taxes, but the oration does not contain a transcript of the actual trial.[28] The charge Isocrates answers was commonly made against the Sophists: youth were corrupted by their training, which gave them an unfair advantage in the courts. The image of his school and its teaching practices had been tarnished by a shadow of Platonic doubt cast over teachers of rhetoric. First and foremost, Isocrates wanted to be freed from guilt by association: he wanted to secure his reputation as an extraordinary teacher. The preliminary verbal skirmishes recorded in *Against the Sophists* are reconstructed to form an intellectual battleground.

2. The power of a teaching based on his theory to affect not just a few moralists but the body politic is dogmatically assumed, and this unassailable assumption permeates the entire discourse. This assumption, however, should not be misunderstood, for Isocrates is not advocating popular education; he asserts that teachers who follow in Plato's footsteps have little practical influence because they deal in producing either recluses or antiseptic philosophers, whereas his teaching aims at finishing a practical politician who will affect all the people of the state. In his own school he tried to secure this aim by accepting students whose family backgrounds tended to guarantee leadership roles for them. He never retreated very far from the view that the education of potentially pow-

28 See R. J. Bonner, *op. cit.*, pp. 193–197.

erful men—usually members of the nobility—is of first importance and that the teacher's work, because he is molding the minds of prospective leaders, is more important than the legislator's.[29]

3. On the level of method, the influence of Isocrates is most obvious, for the techniques of models and imitation became permanent features of what later ages called classical education. Yet, in his adherence to models Isocrates was not concerned solely with technique; his political philosophy was shaped by tradition and he believed a reverence for the best from the past could be inculcated most effectively by exposing students regularly to the "oldest speeches and the oldest laws."[30] He was disturbed by a new philosophy of education which embraced the thesis that "men [should] love the oldest laws and the newest speeches," because this thesis contained a political contradiction. To follow old laws and new speeches meant political paralysis at a halfway house between conservativism and reform.

4. If Athenians looked for evidence of the efficacy of Isocrates' pedagogy, they found it in his students, who usually became remarkably influential and effective in their own cities. But early in his career Isocrates demurred from accepting responsibility for his students' futures because he wanted to disassociate himself from the arrogant claims of the Sophists. This question of responsibility, however, was a good one: To what extent is a school responsible for the success or failure of its students? Isocrates began by minimizing the school's responsibility; but later when he could point with pride to illustrious products from his school, as he does in *Antidosis,* for whom he can take credit, he is anxious to accept responsibility;[31] but he must do so cautiously, almost equivocally. His most eminent Athenian student was the deposed and exiled Timotheus, who twice raised Athens to the pinnacle of political success. The old master was put in a dilemma: Timotheus' discipleship was clear, but Isocrates could hardly claim Timotheus unless he was also prepared to accept scorn and recrimination from Athenians who now doubted the stature of Timotheus and thus, by direct association, the effectiveness of Isocrates' political teaching.

5. Isocrates was preoccupied with money and reckoned it a sign of success rather than a mark of intellectual decadence. But again we must make allowances in our judgments, for it is unlikely that he was a vulgar materialist. He wanted mainly to clear the air and set aright a prevailing Athenian attitude assuming it improper for teachers to be well-paid or wealthy. The preoccupation with money arose from his determination to have teachers accepted as professional persons and allowed to seek with impunity the financial, political, and social positions approved for mem-

29 *Antidosis,* 79–80.
30 *Ibid.,* 82.
31 *Ibid.,* 95–96.

bers of other professions.[32] That Isocrates was not altogether successful is imprinted indelibly on the historical record, yet all teachers who followed him somehow stand in his debt for his affirmations relative to teachers' professional status.

6. Isocrates was intent on making an unassailable case for rhetorical education—education aimed principally at political efficiency—while at the same time deflating the educational dogmas of the philosophers. At best, his efforts achieved only partial success, for although the arguments in support of rhetoric are convincing, the attack on philosophy runs aground because of his inability to assess the public's attitude toward philosophy and from this attitude to form a basis for an indictment of philosophy. In the end he admits this deficiency and admits, too, that his position is neither convincing nor clear.[33]

7. Uncertainty over the origin of ideas is common in the history of culture, so the Isocratic credo, affirming the critical significance of education, need not be tested for originality. He put it this way: whoever is able to influence the minds of the young can control the destiny of the state. This influence, of course, was directed at basic civic education aimed at the building of political virtue. But education did not stop here; it could offer opportunities for training political leaders. This second level was higher education and, according to Isocrates, it bore responsibility for developing men's ability to understand one another. More precisely, higher education meant education in the use of speech full of meaning about the essential affairs of politics and life.[34]

8. Isocrates believed that he had the credentials of a philosopher and that his school course contained the elements of a philosophical education. But his definition of philosophy was his own. In this narrow context he talks about true philosophic teaching and parallels it with gymnastic pedagogy. Again he turns back the clock, fully content to stand by his earlier statement in *Against the Sophists.*[35] Isocrates' mind had not changed in nearly a half-century: nature, practice, and training were still the items demanding the educator's attention.

9. There was a combativeness to Isocrates' nature that even old age did not erode; it was difficult for him to be positive about his teaching theories despite their half-century of usefulness. He could not resist criticizing his colleagues; and his special criticism was reserved for teachers who discounted the value of paideia, or who despised paideia as an educational objective. These teachers, he says, are of two types: those who say that education in speech and action is impossible (meaning that efforts to

---

[32] *Ibid.*, 157.

[33] *Ibid.*, 168.

[34] *Ibid.*, 180–181; See also LaRue Van Hook, "Alcidamas Versus Isocrates; the Spoken Versus the Written Word," *Classical Weekly*, XII (1929), pp. 89–94.

[35] *Against the Sophists*, 16–19.

train expression and reason on the intellectual level, and right judgment and prudent living on the moral level are futile) ; and those who, while admitting the possibility of such training or education, insist that deterioration is the only certain outcome. In other words, education makes men morally worse, not because education is inherently evil, but because teachers are deliberately deceitful. Isocrates responds to the first allegation by making this basic point: education takes time; teachers are involved in the process of molding souls, a goal that cannot be achieved quickly.[36] The Sophists, promising to teach more quickly than before, had disillusioned the educated community of Athens, and when the Sophists could not educate a good citizen in two years, a natural, though perhaps invalid, belief arose that teaching could not produce a good citizen at all. The second attitude put all teachers in jeopardy; if all were guilty of deceit, none could maintain a good reputation. How could teachers be respectable professional men when as a group they were tarnished with an indictment that they deliberately perverted their pupils? A refutation of this charge can hardly be expected, for it is incapable of being answered evidentially or empirically. Despite this, there is no weakness in Isocrates' response when he states simply that a teacher of quality could not be induced, whatever the rewards, to damage his students, who are always his best recommendation.[37]

10. Isocrates is painfully aware of competition; he fears Plato most because Plato's theory obviously abhors a rhetorical emphasis in education. Isocrates feels compelled to criticize Plato's theory and its subordination of rhetoric to philosophy, for not engaging in debate would have been tantamount to surrender. Isocrates would not have been disturbed if the Academy's curriculum had simply excluded rhetoric, for such an exclusion could be interpreted merely as a selection of curricular emphasis in the education of public men. But Plato did not ignore rhetoric; he called it a study without roots, detached from ultimate knowledge of virtue, and unacceptable as an adequate education for a political scientist. There is a story that Aristotle parodied a line from Euripides: " 'Twere shame to hold our peace, and let Isocrates speak." The implication is clear: Platonists were not going to allow teachers of rhetoric to have a monopoly. With Plato's obvious concurrence, Aristotle proposed a theory of rhetoric for precise application to political teaching; thus, the Platonic challenge to Isocrates' system of teaching was not merely academic. Unavoidably it hurt Isocrates' school and provoked his resentment against both Plato and Aristotle.[38]

---

[36] *Antidosis*, 209–214; for some interpretations of this hope, see P. G. Neserius, "Isocrates' Political and Social Ideas," *International Journal of Ethics*, XLIII (1932–33) , pp. 307–328.

[37] *Antidosis*, 217 and 220.

[38] Jaeger, *op. cit.*, III, 147. Isocrates' resentment is unveiled throughout *Antidosis*.

11. Isocrates found himself in the uncomfortable position of questioning the value attributed to certain subjects in the Academy, while offering the same subjects in his own school. Dialectic, astronomy, and mathematical science were accorded nominal curricular standing,[39] yet he wanted to clarify his doubt that these subjects had the value that their professors said they had. He began by assuming their practical uselessness and compromised this attitude only when it was clear that neither the temper of the times nor the popular views of intellectuals would accept such an unequivocal evaluation. He regarded the Academy's curriculum as preparatory to the study of philosophy, but he demurs from saying so explicitly. For him, we must remember, philosophy's object was to refine and articulate the implications of common sense. Isocrates needed to define Greek paideia, although it was hard for him to be positive because Plato had already brought the main problems to light, and there was relatively little left to say. He was at pains to be different from Plato or, when this was impossible, at least to reflect a negative attitude toward the theory Plato had already established as being educationally true.

12. We have already referred to the strange intellectual fellowship between Isocrates and the Sophists. For example, Isocrates says men cannot achieve true science; they are capable only of arriving at opinion.[40] Taking a line from the Sophists' book, he defines the philosopher as one who has practical wisdom. This skirted the current central issue in education: knowledge of good and evil. Time and again Plato defined the issue; but Isocrates, for whom the problem and the central issue were the same, tried to find the solution in practical interpretations stripped of abstract and theoretical meaning. So Isocrates falls into the philosophically untenable trap of maintaining that right opinion is a product of genius: it cannot be produced by teaching.[41] With some lack of clarity Isocrates charged Plato and Socrates with a consistent overemphasis on the value of paideia. Can we be certain that Isocrates' criticism was invalid?

13. Despite Isocrates' dogmatic assumption relative to an excessive emphasis on the power of education, he avoided a doctrine that would have put schools in jeopardy by giving people a platform from which they could ignore teaching with impunity. Anyone who showed his interest in wealth and success, and who assumed that rhetorical training was an instrument for achieving both, was emotionally incapable of formulating such a doctrine regardless of the intellectual temptations in evidence. Isocrates wanted to give teachers a theory protecting teaching from any indictment that instruction was unnecessary and, at the same time, establishing the primacy of a rhetorically committed pedagogy. He

[39] For the content of these studies, see pp. 46–47.
[40] *Antidosis*, 271.
[41] *Ibid.*, 274.

did this by affirming the power of rhetorical education to perfect human nature, although he refused to accept the philosopher's creed that positive knowledge is possible and that it can guarantee virtue. In the Platonic philosophical tradition the ultimate convergence of knowledge and virtue is a moot point; in the Isocratic teaching tradition the final identity of knowledge and virtue is categorically rejected.

14. Despite Isocrates' fame as a teacher, the *Antidosis* itself admits that Isocrates' theories of teaching were neither fully understood nor approved in Athens. Our first reaction is surprise, for Athenians were enamoured of education and were constantly searching for and testing new teaching devices and doctrines, and they were anxious to learn from any teacher who wanted to teach. In these receptive attitudes toward education, the Sophists read their invitation to come to Athens. Yet Isocrates, offering a course far superior to the program of even the best Sophists, was unable to communicate his educational ideals or garner allegiance to his pedagogical practices from his fellow citizens. One reason for his unpopularity in Athens was that his teaching created a new elite (only students who promised to be a credit were admitted to his school) to replace the old, now discredited aristocracy of birth. Since the time of Solon the masses had nurtured democratic tendencies and they refused to acknowledge or approve a system of education ignoring them.[42]

We are ready at last to state quickly and simply the cultural objective of Isocratic teaching and to identify the principal means for securing this objective. The aim of Isocrates' school and the hope expressed for his theory of education was to produce "those who manage well the circumstances which they encounter day by day, and who possess a judgment which is accurate in meeting occasions as they arise and rarely misses the expedient course of action; next, those who are decent and honorable in their intercourse with all with whom they associate, tolerating easily and good-naturedly what is unpleasant or offensive in others and being themselves as agreeable and reasonable to their associates as it is possible to be; furthermore, those who hold their pleasures always under control and are not unduly overcome by their misfortunes, bearing up under them bravely and in a manner worthy of our common nature; finally, and most important of all, those who are not spoiled by successes and do not desert their true selves and become arrogant, but hold their ground steadfastly as intelligent men, not rejoicing in the good things which have come to them through chance rather than in those which through their own nature and intelligence are theirs from birth." [43]

How was such a man to be educated? In the next part we shall try to elaborate the means, but here it is enough to say that literature, con-

[42] See Bury, *op. cit.*, pp. 368–373.
[43] *Panathenaicus*, 32–33.

taining the finest thoughts and expressions of mankind, was the principal vehicle: this was literary humanism. Men were made better by sharing fully in the twin inheritances of thought and expression; thus, the common meeting place for good minds in all education was literature. From its careful study attitudes of humanness and tolerance could be shaped; and from it, too, would come refinement of taste, demeanor, and expression. The surest sign of good thinking was evidenced by the right word: the literary humanism of Isocrates was preoccupied with expression and assumed that refined and precise speech was supported by clear and incisive thought.[44]

III

ISOCRATES THE EDUCATOR

Historians of ancient education have been speculating about the enrollment in Isocrates' school.[45] While enrollment can hardly be taken as a critical historical datum—and evidence supporting even the best opinions on the subject is not too good—these speculations may bring to light some little known dimensions of Isocrates' basic teaching method. If Isocrates was teaching as many as 100 students a year, his pedagogy would not have been the same as if he had taught only 100 students during his entire career. Freeman believes that Isocrates had a huge school attracting an annual clientele of 100 students; [46] Isocrates himself speaks of having had more pupils than all the other schools combined.[47] Marrou, on the other hand, describes the Isocratic school as an elite institution supplying an academic adventure of rare quality to carefully selected and highly motivated persons. Is there any way of illuminating these divergent views, for apparently they cannot be reconciled?

Taking Isocrates at his word is not always satisfactory, not because he tries to mislead us, but because what he says is often ambiguous. When he said he had more students than all the other schools, he may not have meant in a single school year but for the half-century of the school's existence. When we read that Isocrates was rich and assigned a trierarchy, it is perhaps natural to envision large numbers of students in his class-

[44] H. Ll. Hudson-Williams, "A Greek Humanist," *Greece and Rome*, 9 (1940), pp. 166–172; and Moses Hadas, *Humanism: The Greek Ideal and Its Survival* (New York, Harper & Brothers, 1960).

[45] Most recently by Marrou, *op. cit.*, p. 82; and R. S. Johnson, "A Note on the Number of Isocrates' Pupils," *American Journal of Philology*, LXXVIII (July, 1957), pp. 297–300. Parts of this section of the chapter were published in my article "Class Size and Pedagogy in Isocrates' School," *History of Education Quarterly*, VI (Winter, 1966), pp. 22–32.

[46] Freeman, *op. cit.*, p. 191.

[47] *Antidosis*, 41.

rooms, for if he did not charge Athenians tuition, as pseudo-Plutarch asserts in the *Life of Isocrates,* he must have had a non-Athenian enrollment large enough to make his enterprise profitable and him a rich man. Demosthenes, however, states that Athenians were charged. Perhaps the misunderstanding arises from Isocrates' own comments: he says he received payments from foreigners and that his wealth came chiefly from foreign gifts.[48] He implies, but he does not assert, that this was his only source of income; nor does he unequivocally deny charging fees to Athenians. If we are correct in assuming that all students were charged tuition, fewer students paying the rate of 1000 drachmae for the full course were needed to put Isocrates in the enviable financial position tradition attributes to him.

We need not doubt his wealth or his ability to share in the support of public services, an assessment amounting to about 2000 drachmae. But if he had 100 students a year, would it have made sense for him to try to reduce or remove the trierarchy? Johnson, using leads from income analysis, maintains that if Isocrates had 100 pupils annually his financial opulence would have made him a fable of antiquity.[49] History contains no such fable. If, however, he had 100 pupils during his school's existence, his income would have been about three times greater than that of a lower-middle-class family—540 drachmae per year [50]—or quite enough to make him comfortable and enough, also, to lead to the assignment of the trierarchy. Adding the gifts Isocrates received from Nicocles—twenty talents, or about 120,000 drachmae—and a payment of one talent from Timotheus, we have our man of wealth.

Guided by income analysis, Johnson concluded by concurring with Marrou that Isocrates' school was small, never enrolling more than six or eight students at a time. Building on this analysis, Johnson hypothesizes a smaller number of students for the Sophists than popular legend assigns. Although current thought usually credits Sophists with a large number of students, advanced opinion favors a reassessment of old myths and a more modest estimate of the popularity of Sophistic schools. The ordinary Sophist's school was likely no larger than the one Isocrates conducted.

Apart from method, the enrollment debate is interesting; besides, it is relevant to technique. What is gleaned from Isocratic writings and commentaries on pedagogic practice must be set in the context of the small class. At this point we should turn to technique and try to reconstruct the Isocratic plan of teaching.

We begin by assuming that Isocrates had good credentials as an

48 *Ibid.,* 39, 146, 164.

49 Johnson, *op. cit.,* pp. 297–300.

50 G. Glotz, *Ancient Greece at Work,* (London, Routledge & Kegan Paul, Ltd., 1926), p. 236.

educator in the ancient world; any other assumption makes it impossible to take Isocrates seriously. He was neither an ignored nor rejected prophet in his own land, but a teacher and political commentator who altered the course of political and educational history. Laistner says of him: "In a half-century devoted to teaching and writing Isocrates more than any other man prepared men's minds for the new era brought to birth by the genius of Alexander." [51] Despite his undoubted genius for influencing the thinking of his contemporaries, he was not altogether successful in obtaining support for his political programs because they were arrogantly aristocratic; and his educational theory and practice were certainly misunderstood, otherwise *Antidosis* would not have been written. Perhaps we shall never know fully the pride of place Isocrates' pen managed to secure for him in the affairs of Athens; and perhaps we shall never see clearly all the relationships between Isocratic educational theory and modern humanism in literature and learning, yet it is becoming apodictically clear, regardless of the extent and depth of his direct influence on learning, how his theory rode through much of educational history as a subculture, effective but unnoticed. Today, Isocrates is too often unrecognized—while Plato is honored as a pioneer in educational philosophy—and his name is never found over the portals of schools of education. His existence as an educator of unassailable stature is a fact of which many professors of education are completely unaware.[52]

Whether or not Isocrates is known and appreciated today is really irrelevant to the central point of his influence on most Western education. Perhaps knowledge of Isocrates is needed less because the shadows of influence cast by Cicero and Quintilian are so long. This is the point: Had it not been for Isocrates, neither Cicero nor Quintilian, both of whom acknowledge indebtedness to him, might have plowed the furrow of humanistic culture so deeply or so impressively.[53] Isocrates is not as well known or appreciated as he should be, yet this can be deplored too much, and too much time can be wasted by indicting the past for its indifference to him. The record of history is his unimpeachable witness.

The place to begin a consideration of Isocratic methods and any analysis of technique is with objectives. What were his teaching goals? How did he try to shape student minds? Now we are dealing with questions which admit of little or no debate: Isocrates founded a school and

[51] M. L. W. Laistner, "The Influence of Isocrates' Political Doctrine on some Fourth-Century Men of Affairs," *Classical Weekly*, XXIII (1930), p. 131; and P. Merlin, "Isocrates, Aristotle, and Alexander the Great," *Historia*, III (1954), pp. 60–81. Isocrates was unsuccessful in influencing the political attitudes of his fellow citizens because he defended aristocratic political principles, whereas they had already embraced democratic attitudes.

[52] See LaRue Van Hook, "Some Aspects of Isocrates' Writings," *Classical Weekly*, XLI (1947–48), pp. 98–103.

[53] S. E. Smithurst, "Cicero and Isocrates," *Transactions and Proceedings of the American Philological Association*, 84 (1953), pp. 262–320.

conducted it for about a half-century with the principal purpose of preparing statesmen. Isocrates was a remarkably successful teacher precisely because he was single-minded and unwavering in his goals. He refused to waste time testing the validity of the assumption that it was possible to educate statesmen; he did not indulge in agonizing analyses relative to truth, justice, and virtue; he based his teaching program on commonsense, which for him was philosophy, and aimed for his goal. It is worthwhile to inquire below the level of goals, and to ask of Isocrates how he would make not a mind, not a man, but a statesman. We need not think of contemporary curricular theories at this point, for a comparison of today's curricula and Isocrates' syllabus would hardly be a meaningful exercise. Yet it is reasonable to ask what subjects were taught. Goals can be reached only by using certain means, and education has not changed so much in twenty or more centuries to make the application of this principle obsolete. Bodies of knowledge were organized into subjects, although they were not isolated or departmentalized. If we work our way through the writings of Isocrates we shall probably be able to reconstruct, somewhat tentatively, the curriculum of the school: grammar, composition, essay writing, elocution, history, archeology, jurisprudence, citizenship, religion, ethics, philosophy, geography, political science, and strategy.[54] The outstanding omission here is mathematics, indeed a surprising one in view of the willingness of Isocrates to accept mathematics as part of an intellectual foundation necessary to a public man. Possibly Isocrates meant only the keeping of household accounts, a lower-level accomplishment without standing in the studies of the school.

Grammar may have been a very elemental study of the structure of language, for Isocrates antedated by three centuries Dionysius Thrax's codification of grammar, although the Sophists had done preliminary and cursory work on codes of correct speech. In any case, grammar in its infancy did not include the Hellenistic appurtenances, except possibly for the reading of the poets. Composition, essay writing, and elocution belonged to rhetoric, or were later wedded to it, and are mentioned here only to give a more precise notion of what the students did. Isocrates wanted statesmen who could write and speak; apparently the distinction to be made between composition and essay writing was one of degree. Graduates of the school undertook careers as political pundits or journalistic commentators on the vital questions of the day; it is barely possible that essay writing was a highly professionalized study, while composition was general and applied to the foundations and the skill of good writing. Elocution's importance is elevated when we recognize, despite the possibility of having something published in written form, that the

---

[54] See A. Burk, *Die Pädagogik des Isokrates,* (Würzburg, Becker, 1923) , pp. 118–119; and R. S. Johnson, "Isocratic Methods of Teaching," *American Journal of Philology,* LXXX (January, 1959) , pp. 25–36.

most convenient way to publish was to read what was written to an audience. It was not imperative for the author to recite his essay—he could have a reader—but publication was more impressive when the author himself did the reading. For the day-to-day involvements of the public man the relevance of elocution cannot be gainsaid.[55]

Religion was simply a knowledge of the gods who occupied, even in this day, a prominent place in Greek life. Few Athenians had any real faith in the gods and most were convinced only of their reality in myth; they were all atheists, but for purposes of display they wanted an intimate knowledge of the gods. References to characters in Greek mythology served to embellish a speech; the orator who did not know his gods could not expect the people's support or respect.

What methods did Isocrates employ in teaching these subjects? We may be certain of his effectiveness as a teacher; the remarkable success of his students is the best testimony we have for knowing we are not dealing with an opportunistic pedagogue who parlayed a good reputation out of the fragments of self-serving publicity. The *Antidosis* gives us some insight into the foundation of his method. He was dedicated to teaching the art of discourse and began, he says, at the beginning: Our ancestors invented and bequeathed to us two principal arts—physical training for the body and philosophy for the mind. While a distinction may be made between the two, they need not be separated sharply, for similar methods of instruction, exercise, and discipline are common to both. This is a clue to his technique:

> For when they take their pupils in hand, the physical trainers instruct their followers in the postures which have been devised for bodily contest, while the teachers of philosophy impart all the forms of discourse in which the mind expresses itself. Then, when they have made them familiar and thoroughly conversant with these lessons, they set them at exercises, habituate them to work, and require them to combine in practice the particular things which they have learned, in order that they may grasp them more firmly and bring their theories into closer touch with the occasions for applying them —I say "theories," for no system of knowledge can possibly cover these occasions, since in all cases they elude our science. Yet those who apply their minds to them and are able to discern the consequences which for the most part grow out of them, will often meet these occasions in the right way.[56]

Prophetic anticipations taking into account a physiology of learning are shadowy and imprecise in the thought of Isocrates, but they are there. He detected the correspondence of mind-body relationships and believed,

---

[55] H. Ll. Hudson-Williams, "Isocrates and Recitations," *Classical Quarterly,* 43 (1949), pp. 65–69.

[56] *Antidosis,* 183–185.

obviously, that the teacher of letters could imitate the paidotribe. But we can make too much of this, as it is possible to make too much of direct Isocratic influences on the methodology of modern education. There is no evidence whatever, and we have no hope of uncovering any, to lead us to suppose that the methodological revolution instigated by Rousseau, haltingly applied by Pestalozzi, and codified by Dewey and his progressive followers had its origin with Isocrates. History and educational theory often make strange bedfellows. Isocrates would have pushed aside the general thesis of modern pragmatists—though he was often pragmatic—because of the support they could give to the lesser Sophists against whom he employed his artistry in pedagogic polemic. He was not merely opposing Plato, who was, he thought, swamped in the world of ideas, when he made mental and physical training analogous. Paidotribes, who were themselves educated men, had perfected a technique which, he believed, could be applied to academic training. Because of the nature of their teaching, or coaching, paidotribes needed a technique for teaching students the skills of the palaestra; besides, they understood the futility of trying to teach skills by lecturing or of improving the speed and endurance of a stadium runner by telling him how to run. Yet they did not reject theory, for they recognized the importance of general rules relative to running—pace, position, conditioning, etc.—none of which come from practice alone.

Taking a page from the paidotribe's book, Isocrates recognized the need for basing instruction on a realistic physiology of learning; from his own experience he discerned the place of a psychology of learning. Even with these discoveries in his possession, he came perilously close to jeopardizing his reputation as an educator. He lived the double life of a publicist and a teacher. Rarely do we find him publicizing the vital ingredients of art and skill in teaching, save when he wanted to start a school and attract students, and again when he felt that his educational program had been unjustly criticized by his fellow citizens. Had his sense of mission been somewhat more profound and his dedication to a more generous distribution of learning more exacting, he would have spent less time trying to reform the Greek polity according to his own political views and would have let teachers know more about the results of his experiments with teaching.

In some respects he reminds us of Wolfgang Ratke (1571–1635) who, believing he had found the key to success in teaching and learning, proudly boasted of his ability to teach twice as much in only half the time and steadfastly refused to disclose his secrets to an anxiously waiting educational fraternity. Ratke wanted to profit from his "discovery" by patenting it; Isocrates, deeply engaged in acrid pedagogical competition in Athens, did not choose to put his ideas in the public domain. Philanthropy, whether with money or ideas, was not an Isocratic virtue. This striking quality of egoism, which somehow ill-befits the man, makes us struggle through the underbrush of his thought, almost at times to invade his subconscious, to reconstruct the main lines of congruence between his educational theory and his practice.

Undoubtedly the dimensions of his system were limited, admitting for proper and careful tutelage only a small number of students; but it is reasonable to suspect—though he was not engaged in preparing teachers, which he might have done had he really wanted to disseminate his treasury of educational ideals—that he sensed a certain danger in sending from his school too many emissaries of his thought and thus increasing the dangers of having his secrets spread unevenly throughout the Greek world. If he was inflexibly protective about his techniques of teaching, this rigidity must be regarded as a minor fault in Isocratic educational thought. We should not like to describe Isocrates as a pedagogic miser whose best thoughts were discounted on the scales of pettiness and avarice.

Lest our interpolations relative to the character of the man plow too deep a furrow of imperfection, or of humanness, let us return once more to the major elements of his technique and bare them as best we can. He admitted, we have said, only a few students to his classes because of his extraordinary concern for care. Quintilian noticed this point and made much of it—that care in education was the primary current deficiency—in the famous *Education of an Orator*. Care had nothing whatever to do with discipline: it meant simply that only a few students at a time could be taught effectively. Books were not readily available, and few schoolmasters could afford them. Thus, there was usually only one copy of any instructional material. In addition to this, so far as instructional practices were concerned, each student was dealt with individually. Because of deficiencies in the quantity of teaching materials, to say nothing whatever about their quality and how the master would embellish them to suit his own instructional purpose, large classes were out of the question. Still, the method of class instruction was neither unknown to nor unused by Isocrates. The Sophists thrived on it when they had large classes, which may not have been often. Isocrates used group methods only for stamping in the details of learning. Here we begin to sense some of the methodological differences between Isocrates and Plato; their disputes were not always hinged on the sharp edge of theory: instruction in Plato's school was largely informal, taking place in what might be regarded as casual, at least unconventional, educational settings. The informalities in the Platonic system of teaching admitted several students and it was not in the wine or olive shop but in the dining room that the finest instruction took place. Exercise, practice, stamping in, were all accomplished through the art of discourse and the friction of mind on mind. Yet even at this point Plato and Isocrates should not have prolonged their dispute:

Plato's students were being schooled on the level of higher education, roughly equivalent to the American college, while the students of Isocrates were probably only secondary-school boys.[57]

Regardless of the number of subjects which found a place with Isocrates, the main purpose of the school was to teach rhetoric and to prepare young men for positions where they could become statesmen of first rank. With this goal uppermost in his mind Isocrates employed techniques that have since become regarded in Western education generally as techniques par excellence of rhetoric: rules and models.

Isocrates was not original in his use of either, for the history of Greek pedagogy to his time is filled with examples of the employment of both. The Sophists devised rules for rhetoric, and as the centuries wore on the arsenal of rules became greater and greater until only rules remained. Students pored over these rules, unwittingly and perhaps unwillingly paralyzing rhetoric. While not entirely original, Isocrates did make a distinctive contribution to rhetoric by adding rules, and these rules remained so long as rhetoric occupied a place of prominence in the schools. Isocrates more than any other teacher of rhetoric enhanced its position, and he, almost alone among ancient masters, may be absolved from having led it to separate life from learning. Isocrates' precise contributions to the rhetorical code belong to another side of the story, one told well by other authors.

The models employed by teachers who preceded Isocrates were either their own orations or excerpts from Homer or lesser known Greek poets. Some were only barely acceptable as rhetorical models, being barren of the techniques oratory needed to keep pace with a world in transition. Isocrates replaced them with his own works. In the preparation of these orations he again exemplifies the depth of his pedagogic insight by calling on his students for help, and they, under his guidance, shared in the work of composition, learning by demonstration and by doing. These polished orations were used as models for years.

Isocratic rhetorical teaching stood on the broad foundation of rules and models, and to both he made, as we have said, some important contributions. But the uniqueness of his teaching, found principally in minor techniques and methodological devices, has yet to be fully explored.

It may be hazardous to begin by believing in the distinctiveness of Isocrates' day-to-day teaching techniques, for he gives us few insights into them, and his contemporaries, his students, and later commentators, all

---

[57] Evidence on this is not impressive, I grant, yet the entire temper of Isocratic teaching would certainly suggest secondary education. Moreover, according to Bury, *op. cit.*, p. 818, Aristotle completed the Isocratic school course and then enrolled in Plato's Academy. If we are willing to admit the Academy to the arena of higher education, we may conclude that Aristotle was preparing for higher learning by attending Isocrates' school.

leave us too much in the dark on the matter. Perhaps they overlooked technique because, in company with Plato, they thought it unimportant in the education of highly intelligent students, or possibly they were so engrossed with the main lines of Isocratic methodological thinking they would not stoop to deal with what seemed to be mere detail. Or they may have regarded Isocrates as a competitor of Plato in the arena of general educational ideas and ideals and have been unwilling, by mentioning the everyday techniques of their champion, to make him appear with feet of clay. But if we are to assume this, we must at the same time be prepared to admit that the disciples of Isocrates did not really understand him at all, or at best only partially, because Isocrates preached a doctrine of culture that while not illuminating the formative process of shaping the whole man—an idea, almost a compulsion, shared by most Greek teachers —was able to describe the elements and separate stages of the educational act. Because of his insights into the fundamentals of teaching, he should have been more acceptable to the common man. Common men are uncomfortable with mystery, and Plato's long course with its extraordinary demands on time and intelligence had more than its share. Yet it would be manifestly unfair to Isocrates to say that he took a simple road to culture because it would be more popular: after all, Isocrates deplored as much as Plato the sham and fraud among the Sophists. Still, it was Plato and his followers, not the Sophists—despite their specialty and their weakness, described by Isocrates in *Against the Sophists*—whom Isocrates feared professionally. Plato was his competition.

There is little reason to doubt Isocrates' sincerity when he makes everything in education depend on the proper cooperation of art and nature. This central principle should make him at once an exponent and surely a firm friend of educational methodology. And he was. First, we should say he was an empiricist. That is, he based his entire system of teaching on the principle of imitation—a principle neither invented by him nor one that ceased with his retirement. Imitation became an indelible feature in the technique of teaching literature and rhetoric from the time of Isocrates forward.

Imitation of models was the hub around which methodology turned; the spokes were shaped by the following techniques, not always used in concert, but all available for use depending on the turn of the instructional wheel. The small enrollment in Isocrates' school allowed him the luxury of instructing a few students at a time. The initial phase of the instructional process was really an exercise in tutoring, where Isocrates could take one or, at the most, two students and instruct them carefully in the basic principles of a subject. This required a well-educated and versatile master, for instructional tools were primitive; he worked with few of the appurtenances of contemporary education. Books for student use were usually unavailable; the library was probably small and unsuitably stocked; materials for writing and composition were crude when judged by the standards of modern times. Despite these handicaps, shared by all classical teachers, Isocrates, drawing on the resources of his personal library, could be a textbook, a library, and a literary and writing master all wrapped into one. When he completed the first phase of teaching he moved to the second, drill. Under the direct supervision of the teacher students were called upon, now not as individuals but in groups, to drill and fix the material they had learned. This technique was justified on the grounds that it gave students an opportunity to master fundamental knowledge. Despite Isocrates' unwillingness to accept the dogmatic assumptions of Plato with respect to basic truth and fundamental philosophical principles, he did demand that students master the content of his teaching syllabus. Nothing on the level of necessary knowledge was thought too insignificant for unrelenting, repeated attention. And at this point we begin to see faint signs of a teaching technique made famous in later centuries by the Jesuits: use of competition among students for excellence in learning. Even today this technique occupies a place in methodology, although now it has fewer dedicated adherents than it did in the fifteen centuries following Isocrates.

Unfortunately we know almost nothing of the day-to-day application of the technique of competition in the Isocratic classroom, but it is fair to assume that it offered generous opportunities for students not only in learning the matter of their study but in fixing and elaborating it by the friction of mind on mind. One pupil was pitted against another, making mastery of knowledge and skill a highly personal challenge. In addition, we must remember Isocrates was preparing future orators, and he wanted them from the first to have the experience of intellectual analysis in debate. Isocrates knew ability had no substitute; but he knew too that unrefined ability could make no impression in public life or political affairs.

The instructional process is dominated by the teacher. There is never any hint that Isocrates sat quietly in the back of the room watching the students go through their learning exercises, marveling at their progress, and resisting all temptations to intervene to clarify points, make important distinctions, and correct errors in form or content. Fairness to the method, to the whole teaching art of Isocrates, requires the assertion that he was never content with mere facility in speech, although we know how he prized speech and established it as a distinctive human ability. It is important to understand speech in its Greek context, including both reason and expression and not merely an aptitude for empty, albeit effective, oratory. On this point principally, Isocrates has been frequently and unfairly maligned; too many commentators have dismissed him as only another Sophist, more sophisticated perhaps and more widely respected, who wanted nothing more than eristic competence—an ability to win an argument whatever the intellectual costs. To state Isocrates' objective more exactly and with complete fairness is to indicate his unwavering allegiance to man as a thinking and speaking animal: thought and expression were for him the distinctive human abilities. Thus, it is easy to envision Isocrates suspending the classroom debates and personally intervening to sharpen the students' understanding of what they were saying and the implications of their thought. The criticism implied in the statement that Isocrates' philosophy was praiseworthy if not profound is more damaging to his theory of teaching than has generally been supposed: it carries with it an almost unavoidable conclusion that though the old master was a seeker of the good he was incapable of understanding it. The indictment is not altogether without substance, for Isocrates did dispute the Platonic assertion that knowledge of the good, on an ultimate, highly philosophical level, was possible. He was content to accept the virtues of both goodness and truth on the uncomplicated level of common sense. An undeniable element of relativism taints his thought, but it was not a crass or irresponsible relativism: he believed men could come to a fuller understanding of their intuitions of goodness and truth. In his teaching he pried and pushed his students constantly and unrelentingly toward this understanding; it was the bedrock for responsible oratory.

After students had been drilled in content and its more profound implications Isocrates led them to rhetoric. Rhetoric as then conceived, deprived of its arsenal of rules and models added by Hellenistic rhetors, included oral and written composition. Avoiding detail on the study of rhetoric seems imperative here, but we are able to say that Isocrates paralleled his instruction with medical teaching, stressed diagnostic techniques relevant in debate, allowed for practice and application, and aimed at fluency.

The foregoing contains the main body of method; added to it are other instruments of teaching which may be touched quickly in the interest of completeness. Isocrates wanted his students to have a good foundation in knowledge, not because he thought of knowledge as having any independent value but because it was necessary to effective oratory. Yet knowledge alone was insufficient; even fluency was not enough: style was the indispensable key to effective oratory. Here, of course, Isocrates and Plato did not agree. In *Gorgias* Plato downgrades the preeminence of style and treats Gorgias to what must have been a unique experience. Gorgias' reputation as a teacher of rhetoric was unequalled and Plato turns him into a skeleton of pretensions and unfounded assumptions. The Platonic attack on rhetoric's central position in education was an obstacle to a friendly reception for Isocratic educational theory. The famous Isocratic apology for this theory reads as if it were written with a copy of the *Gorgias* on the desk. Yet Isocrates listened to what Plato had to say about rhetoric and may often have agreed, for he made analysis and stylistic criticism important tools in method.

In some of his teaching Isocrates may have used the lecture, and his technique compares favorably with that of the Medieval university professor who conducted an exercise in dictation enabling students to record the contents of manuscripts often possessed only by himself. In addition to lecturing, which must have been used sparingly, for it had no currency among Greek teachers, Isocrates often assigned several books for critical and analytical study. The aftermath of this study was a general discussion participated in by all students: study in isolation was not common practice in this famous school. Even from this technique there were frequent departures, for some such books were not intended to be studied and discussed but only read for the information they contained. After all, many important books do not contain bases for discussion; in Isocratic pedagogy geography and history were in this category, but it would be foolhardy to suppose an orator could be educated without some knowledge of these two important areas. Isocrates did not ignore them, but he did not give them a place in his syllabus of learning equal to grammar, composition, and essay writing.

Finally, Isocrates took his stand alongside those who sought integration of knowledge, not only in its presentation and mastery but in its application. Isocrates hoped to produce an orator—a learned man—with an integrated personality and a balanced, informed, and disciplined mind as well; these attitudes toward education made his brand of literary humanism entirely acceptable to Cato, Cicero, and Quintilian.

⫸ 3 ⫷

Plato: A Theory of Scientific Humanism

I

LIFE AND WORK

Biographical data on Plato are probably fuller than on any other great figure of antiquity.[1] Yet, even accepting this as a fair statement, many details of his career are obscure because tradition is often uncertain and incomplete. Time has not eroded his reputation as a writer and philosopher; his stature in the history of culture must have generated envy in the heart of every academician who followed in his wake. Almost from the beginning of his literary life, his pen guaranteed distinction, and even in history he never enjoyed the equivocal luxury of obscurity or anonymity.

Autobiographical comments in Plato's writings suggest that his parents imposed a pedagogical regimen consistent with the conventional patterns of Athenian education. And the conventional education in Athens during Plato's youth is fairly well known: it consisted of a few years of primary schooling, where boys learned to read, write, and count; a few more years of physical training in the palaestra; and a final stage in the music school, where they learned instrumental music, dancing, and singing, and where they were exposed to Greek literature preserved mainly in an oral tradition. Our knowledge of Plato's early life confirms our belief in the aristocratic orientation of his elemental schooling. His tuition could hardly have taken a nonaristocratic direction, for his family belonged to this class, and its members were expected to be social and

[1] See, for example, R. S. Bluck, *Plato's Life and Thought* (London, Routledge & Kegan Paul, Ltd., 1949) ; A. E. Taylor, *Plato: the Man and His Work* (New York, The Dial Press, Inc., 1927) ; Warner Fite, *The Platonic Legend* (New York, Charles Scribner's Sons, 1934) ; and Paul Shorey, *What Plato Said* (Chicago, University of Chicago Press, 1933) .

political leaders. His family's claim to an aristocratic status was based on the usual pedigree of the times—birth and wealth.

When Plato was ready to pursue a career in active politics, Athenian politics were contaminated by ferment and recrimination: Athens had achieved a level of singular significance in the greater Greek world; then rather quickly and dramatically she slipped from this pinnacle. Briefly she was restored to her place in the political sun by the active support and guidance of Athenian aristocrats who temporarily assumed the reins of active government. But during this interlude of aristocratic restoration to power, little of lasting value was accomplished, and democratic elements in society became more certain than ever before that the aristocratic party was the natural enemy of good and equitable government. A discredited aristocracy was deprived of power in state affairs. Because Plato was a member of the aristocracy, it was difficult for him to claim any immunity from the contempt Athenians heaped on his party. But his association with aristocratic statesmanship and his attraction to practical politics were dictated by something deeper than class allegiance: members of his immediate family held positions of leadership in the aristocratic party; most of his relatives and almost all his friends were members of that party. He had been reared in an aristocratic political tradition; naturally, he followed the political footsteps of his ancestors.

The trail blazed by his ancestors was uncertain and hazardous and ultimately turned him away from rather than toward a life of active politics. We sense a certain nostalgia in his political writings, especially in the *Republic* and the *Laws,* for a political life he could not embrace. There is no reason to debate the point: he surely would have preferred a life of active politics to a political utopia, and a literary utopia at that; but this road was blocked by ideological barricades, and he was realistic enough to see that if he were to make an impact on political life he would have to concentrate on doing what was possible.[2] Besides recognizing the realities of a dangerous political situation, Plato doubted the competence of statesmen who tried to be political leaders without having a foundation in political philosophy. Isocrates believed that being a good man, or perhaps a well-intentioned man, was the essential qualification for a statesman; and he consistently and cogently opposed Plato's doctrine that political action must be grounded in theory.[3] Plato knew the doubts other political scientists had about the worth of political philosophy and its relationship to effective and dedicated statesmanship; but neither doubt nor counsel of caution deterred him; instead they confirmed his resolution to articulate a political theory and to establish it as the bedrock of political action. He settled for utopia because this was the only avenue open to him; yet, even in a utopia—or possibly especially because

2 See Marrou, *op. cit.,* pp. 63–64.
3 Taylor, *op. cit.,* p. 125.

it was a utopia—he could lay out the principal tenets of political thought.

No special obstacles stood in Plato's way when he chose a literary career. Members of the democratic party would almost certainly have been apprehensive had he entered active politics, and after the death of Socrates, when Plato was often accused of sedition, it would have been impossible for him to follow such a career. Partly by temperament and partly by talent Plato was qualified for a literary career; and one seemed to flow rather naturally from his close contacts with Greek literati. So for public consumption, and to satisfy his political enemies, Plato became a poet.

Plato was no ordinary poet. Before becoming a poet he studied philosophy and sensed its importance. His fellowship with Socrates confirmed his interest in philosophy, but even before Socrates entered his life he had read or studied under most of the important philosophers of the day. Despite these philosophic interests of his youth, it would be impossible to ignore the Socratic influence in forming attitudes that committed Plato to a scholarly career dominated by speculation and contemplation. After the Socratic interlude Plato began a serious study of most of the extant philosophical systems. His study took him beyond Socrates to the earlier philosophers and the principal Sophists. But too much can easily be made of this stage of scholarship, for philosophy even in the hands of its best agents was unsystematic, and so it remained until the Hellenistic Age was well advanced.

The most important single event in Plato's life was a tragic one: the death of Socrates at the hands of political persecutors. Even if Plato and Socrates had been nothing more than good friends, this tragedy would have shocked the younger man severely. After Socrates' death two things became clear to Plato. First, he saw a need for perpetuating the memory of his martyred friend. The Socratic message, he was convinced, was important for all men to know, and the Socratic crusade to upgrade intelligence and understanding should not be allowed to wither and die. Second, it was expedient that he should leave Athens. His relationship with Socrates was common knowledge, and persecutors of Socrates stood ready to indict Plato as a ringleader of insurrection. Plato's security would have been in constant jeopardy if he had remained in this suspicion-laden climate. Besides having compelling reasons for leaving Athens, Plato was attracted by the wide world; he felt the need to know it, and Athens, especially in its state of unrest, offered little to satisfy his intellectual appetite. So Plato went first to Megara and while there, so our sources tell us, studied under Euclid. How long he remained with Euclid, who became his close friend, and the precise nature of their academic relationship remains a mystery. After his stay in Megara and his studentship with Euclid, he traveled to Egypt, Cyrene, Magna Graecia (now southern Italy), and Sicily. This part of Plato's life is veiled in obscurity. We are uncertain, for example, whether or not he returned to Athens after having studied with Euclid in Megara. If he interrupted his self-imposed exile and returned to Athens, he may have opened a school. This was not the Academy. In Sicily he entered upon a quasi-active political career, as a counselor or advisor to the tyrant.[4]

The sojourn in Egypt had the following consequences relative to the further maturation of Plato's thought: an increased emphasis on mathematics as a tool for philosophy and a more profound knowledge of the Pythagorean school.

His immersion in practical politics came to an unhappy conclusion. He fell out with the tyrant, lost his advisory commission, and was arrested and released in the custody of the Spartan ambassador, who sold him as a slave. He was ransomed from servitude by a certain Anniceris, a Cyrenian, and returned to Athens. Plato's durability was remarkable. Despite the unrewarding, even dangerous, outcome of his first tour of duty, he accepted a second invitation to act as a political advisor in Sicily. Maybe Plato should have known better, for history repeated itself, and now almost seventy years old, Plato again returned to Athens.

Scandal treads regularly on the periphery of the lives of most illustrious men; Plato was no exception. The precise nature of the alleged indiscretions is unclear, and friendly commentators disbelieve the story and testify to its total lack of factual foundation. Besides scandalous activity, Plato was often accused of flagrant breaches of courtesy. In addition to arrogance and unfriendliness he is accused of hostility toward his disciples, censoriousness, self-love, and sedition. His detractors say, moreover, that he had neither the temperament, skill, nor perseverance to be the author of works credited to him. Plagiarism is the most serious charge leveled against him. But we should not take this charge seriously, for it has no evidence to support it. It is easy to see why some of his critics should have doubted his originality: Plato was one of the first philosophers to exploit the philosophic tradition; he knew the philosophical literature and used it in his own writings. But Plato could use his predecessors without copying them; their ideas inspired him and led him more deeply into his discipline.

Plato's style of writing was novel. Some commentators maintain that Plato first used the dialogue for teaching in the Academy and found it too effective to abandon when the dimensions of his teaching were broadened. But they are only guessing. No evidence supports the belief that Plato used dialogues in the classroom; in fact, we know relatively little about either his teaching technique or the instructional materials

4 J. Burnet, *Greek Philosophy* (New York, The Macmillan Company, 1950), p. 213; Taylor, *op. cit.*, p. 6; and Field, *op. cit.*, p. 18. Illegitimate monarchs—that is, monarchs who were not hereditary kings—were called tyrants. The word was in itself morally neutral and did not imply that the monarch was bad or cruel.

he used. It is entirely possible that Plato used neither the techniques of dialogue nor the content of his poetic dialogues in the classrooms of the Academy.[5] He may have reserved the dialogue as a writing technique; in more than fifty authentic Platonic written works no other method is used. Doubtless he was capable of other literary techniques, for his fifty-year literary career dispels any question about his versatility as a composer or his mastery of style. Material on which to base a judgment is abundant: no Platonic work intended for public view has been lost.

A word might be added on the nature of ancient philosophical teaching. Four principal schools were current in antiquity; all had mother houses in Athens and daughter houses throughout the ancient world. One school represented Plato's idealism, another Aristotle's realism, another Epicurus' hedonism, and the fourth Zeno's stoicism. Teaching methods were similar in all schools.[6] Because philosophy was a minority culture pursued only by talented and dedicated students, enrollment was limited. A commitment to philosophy was essential if a student aspired to the title of philosopher, but it was always possible for young men to satisfy their curiosity by making preliminary studies of various philosophical doctrines without becoming a convert to any. So most schools of philosophy offered an introductory course and admitted anyone who was interested. In this course students studied what we would call a history of philosophy. The syllabus was abbreviated, according to present standards, beginning with the pre-Socratics—as it does today—and proceeding so far as philosophy's history had gone. Interestingly enough, the record of philosophy's beginnings has been little changed by time: we know neither more nor less about the pre-Socratics than did philosophy students in these early schools. The next step after the introductory course, and one presuming a commitment to philosophy, was to study the classical doctrines to which a particular school subscribed: in schools following Plato, the writings of Plato were studied, while in schools following Aristotle, Epicurus, or Zeno their respective philosophical classics were the textbooks. So in addition to preserving philosophical thought in a living tradition, the philosophical fraternity actually used the written doctrines of its masters as textbooks in the schools and thus bestowed on them a quality of permanence.

In this chapter we shall try to illustrate the basic points in Plato's educational thought by studying *Protagoras, Gorgias,* and *Phaedrus.* In the first dialogue Plato exposes the dichotomous structure of Socratic and Sophistic educational goals and methods; in the second he tries to establish the foundations of rhetoric, and in the third he explores the relationships and counterclaims of rhetoric and philosophy.

Only the very brave would attempt to offer a brief summary of

---

5 See my article, "Plato's Academy: A Halting Step Toward Higher Education," *History of Education Quarterly,* IV (September, 1964), pp. 155–166.

6 Marrou, *op. cit.,* pp. 207–210.

Plato's philosophy. At one time it was thought possible to summarize Plato by going through his dialogues and selecting the central ideas in them.[7] While in the thicket of his thought, one could categorize the major ideas and conclude that he had grasped Platonic philosophy by the roots. We have come to learn, however, the complexity of Plato and to understand the fruitlessness of simply isolating major ideas. Their meaning is really disclosed in a context. But this is not the place either for a summary of Plato's philosophy or an explanation of means for understanding it. Plato's thought is an extension of Socratic emphasis, and he, like Socrates, was preoccupied with moral philosophy; his concern for moral questions—a common concern among Plato's contemporaries—and his attraction to scientifically based ethics are fairly obvious. Socrates stopped with moral philosophy, but Plato plowed the mysteries of the universe and of man's mind to sow the seeds of intellectual philosophy as well. Plato, we have said, knew his philosophic predecessors and used them effectively; and these predecessors, because they were highly naturalistic in their outlook, had devised a method that Plato adopted and used successfully: the scientific method. In his hands it gave philosophy a scientific foundation and thus provided a framework for scientific humanism.

With this brief introduction to Plato's life and work we can turn to the three dialogues mentioned above. A general summary of Plato's educational thought follows in Part V of this chapter. Such a summary has been made by other authors,[8] so here we shall look for cornerstones of his theory and see, if we can, how Plato used them to reject the pedagogic creed of Isocrates.

II

PRETENSIONS OF SOPHISTRY

We have seen how Isocrates used *Against the Sophists* for denouncing Sophistic educational practice as being inadequate to man's and society's needs.[9] The Sophists, he wrote, had missed the point: their teaching was superficial and succeeded only in communicating a few rhetorical tricks enabling a debater to win. Isocrates gained many Athenian converts to his view, but the Sophists nevertheless had a cadre of fairly solid support.

---

[7] This technique and its consequences are discussed by Jaeger, *op. cit.*, I, pp. 77–86.

[8] For entirely adequate reviews of Plato's educational thought, see John E. Adamson, *The Theory of Education in Plato's Republic* (New York, The Macmillan Company, 1903) ; R. C. Lodge, *Plato's Theory of Education* (London, Routledge & Kegan Paul, Ltd., 1947) ; and Walter Moberly, *Plato's Conception of Education and Its Meaning Today* (New York, Oxford University Press, 1944) .

[9] *Against the Sophists*, 2.

Plato was even more critical and went beyond Isocrates to formulate an educational doctrine prescribing a foundation of knowledge and a grounding in philosophy as antecedents to rhetoric.

In his earlier dialogues [10] Plato had opened the debate on the relationship between knowledge and virtue; his starting point was the Socratic assertion that some relationship exists between knowledge and virtue, and, though no guarantee can be given, virtue might be produced by learning. Despite Plato's meaningful introduction to the problem in earlier dialogues, his solution was tentative and imprecise until he came to *Protagoras*. *Protagoras* may be taken as complementary to Isocrates' *Against the Sophists,* although the common elements flow mainly from an abhorrence that both share for sophistic culture. In *Protagoras* Plato grappled with the fundamental sophistic educational premises; he begins by opposing them with his own theory of education.

Not only does Plato deal with educational problems in great depth, but by setting the scene properly he shows how they are both broad and significant. The important Sophists, along with their students, appear in the dialogue, and, in addition, many interested Athenian citizens are there. The dialogue begins when Hippocrates, apparently a pupil or friend, awakens Socrates early one morning. He tells Socrates of Protagoras' recent arrival in Athens and exudes enthusiasm over the prospect of studying with him.[11] Socrates is excited too and shows his interest, for he is dedicated to learning—a true sign of his humility; if Protagoras has intellectual gifts to distribute, he wants his share. In an ensuing conversation Socrates tries to elicit from Hippocrates the precise nature of Protagoras' teaching specialty: he wants to know what his young friend expects to learn from this famous Sophist. In pursuing the question further, Socrates asks Hippocrates to consider the wisdom of studying under a physician if he wants to enter the medical profession, or to choose a sculptor for his instructor if he is looking forward to a career as a creative artist. Protagoras is a Sophist, is Socrates' point, and thus the right teacher for a young man who wants to become a Sophist. Unless Hippocrates wants to be a Sophist, he should seek another mentor.[12] The dialectical thrust is effective, especially for the reader whose sympathies lie with logical analysis, but Hippocrates is not convinced, and we should not expect him to be. He doubts that Protagoras' teaching syllabus is narrowly technical or that it is incapable of opening broad vistas in liberal learning. He eschews the specialties, he says, and aspires to the profession of a public man.

[10] According to W. R. M. Lamb, Introduction to *Plato*, vol. 5 (New York, G. P. Putnam's Sons, 1925), p. xii, the *Apology, Crito, Euthyphro, Charmides, Laches,* and *Lysis.*

[11] See Jaeger, *op. cit.,* I, pp. 107–125, for an excellent analysis of *Protagoras. Protagoras,* 310 af.

[12] *Ibid.,* 312 a.

Protagoras has a good reputation as a teacher and man of letters; apparently Plato acknowledged his credentials, for no other Sophist is accorded the same respect or spared the artistic scorn Plato reserved especially for Sophists. From our vantage point in history, we know how the Sophists were maligned by their pedagogical colleagues, and how they were condemned all together, although in fact they were disparate teachers. We note the significance in Plato's willingness to take Protagoras' educational doctrine seriously and give it a fair hearing. Because Protagoras' teaching was dangerous, Plato wanted to submit it to a searching philosophical diagnosis. Protagoras was a real historical figure who came to Athens to teach; along with teaching he helped develop the Greek language and worked to build a foundation on which it could grow.[13]

We come to the first question. Is Protagoras, in company with other Sophists, engaging in a specialty by preparing young men to be Sophists, or does his teaching aim at liberal culture? It could be argued that Sophists were preparing orators who, in the Athenian cultural complex, were men well versed in all the arts of mind and expression. But this is not a good answer. The general question Socrates asks is about balance in the structure of liberal and special education. Put another way, it inquires into the relationship between liberal culture and technical training.[14] During their walk in the garden Socrates tries to show Hippocrates the complexities of and apparent conflict between liberal and technical knowledge; and here Plato demonstrates an important pedagogic device: men begin to learn only when they are able to make a confession of ignorance.

In essaying to sharpen Hippocrates' critical attitudes, Socrates makes a penetrating and meaningful analogy: Protagoras has come to teach in Athens and he has advertised to teach all knowledge for a fee. Socrates believes this is analogous to the salesman who sells goods for money. But there is a difference and it is not in the Sophist's favor. What one buys from a salesman can be taken home to be tested and used. But young men who pay for Protagoras' teaching are buying a mystery: they know neither its substance nor effects.[15] Socrates can speak for himself: "You are going to commit your soul to the care of a man whom you call a Sophist. And yet I hardly think that you know what a Sophist is; and if not, then you do not even know whether you are committing your soul to good or to evil." [16]

These are preliminaries, but they are important. The two friends agree to seek out Protagoras and elicit from him a statement covering the

13 Taylor, *op. cit.*, p. 141.
14 *Protagoras*, 312 b.
15 *Ibid.*, 313 a–314 b.
16 *Ibid.*

aim and scope of his teaching. They go to Callias' house where Protagoras is a guest, and they find a crowd has preceded them, for Protagoras' arrival in Athens is known and a chorus of admirers is waiting anxiously to greet him. Protagoras is strolling in the garden with an entourage of students; he is talking constantly and they are listening to every word. But Protagoras is not the only Sophist at Callias' house. Hippias of Elis is presiding from an armchair; a number of people are sitting on benches listening to him. He is expounding problems in astronomy. Prodicus of Ceos is there too, but he is still in bed. Admirers are gathered in the chamber sitting on the floor or on chairs or sofas waiting for him to speak.

Socrates introduces Hippocrates to Protagoras and mentions that Hippocrates hopes to become his student. Hippocrates, he avers, aspires to politics and wants Protagoras' help in preparing for this profession. Socrates carefully appends a sly recommendation: Hippocrates is the son of a rich and noble family and, moreover, is ambitious and capable. Then, in a most solicitous manner, Socrates asks Protagoras to explain his educational theory and practice. Rather than being apprehensive about explaining his theory, Protagoras seems pleased, even honored, to have Socrates show an interest in his work. He readily accedes to the request, inquiring whether the discourse is to be public or private.[17] Either is acceptable, although we detect Socrates' preference—it may only be a dramatic device—for meeting Protagoras in open dialectical combat.

From the familiarity of their greeting and the easy confidence evident in their conversation, we may assume some previous contact between the principal adversaries in this dialogue. This, at least, is the tone Plato sets, although it may be a technique for showing the civility of men of culture, or an attempt to identify Socrates as a thinker whose credentials no Sophist could have misread.

Protagoras begins, somewhat hesitatingly, with a long speech to give the yin and the yang of his teaching. He intends to handle the question with a long and generous answer. It becomes apparent, however, how often a long and ponderous speech can miss the point. Protagoras does not represent his pedagogy as something new and up-to-date, but as old and well-established.[18] He is aware of the mistrust certain people had for Sophists and their innovations in education; he wants everyone to know he is not engaging in something novel but in something time-honored. In other words, he wants to build upon, and be recommended by, the educational prestige of the great poets, from Homer to Simonides, and to use their reputations to support his own practices. Protagoras does not fear publicity; he thinks the more people know about his teaching the better they will like it. He is a publicist as well as a professional teacher of high

17 *Ibid.*, 317 cd.
18 *Ibid.*, 316 d.

culture who is interested in educating men, but he wants to show a profit from his work. He indicates with an air of genuine sincerity how much he welcomes this opportunity to explain the nature of his profession; his demeanor is that of a man who believes profoundly in what he is doing— he thinks, too, a new admirer is won—and he shows confidence. He shows no reluctance whatever to a public display and extends an invitation to Prodicus, Hippias, and their followers to come and listen too. The stage is set for debate. It begins with Socrates speaking: "I will begin again at the same point, Protagoras, and tell you once more the purport of my visit: this is my friend, Hippocrates, who is desirous of making your acquaintance; he wants to know what will happen to him if he associates with you. That is all I have to say." [19] Protagoras' answer is likewise brief: "Young man, if you associate with me, on the very first day you will return home a better man than you came, and better on the second day than on the first, and better every day than you were the day before." [20]

In this way the unresolved problem of earlier dialogues is resumed: how can education make men better? More specifically, how can sophistic education do it? Socrates says that if a young man wanted to be an artist and apprenticed himself to a great painter everyone would know how he wanted to be better; or if he wanted to be a flute player, he would study under a master player, and everyone would understand the young man's goal. Socrates' question implies: what particular art or special knowledge do Sophists have? [21] Protagoras senses these implications and hedges by saying he is unable to speak for all Sophists.

Protagoras willingly identifies his particular art as political, and professes to teach men how to be good citizens. This was not the first, nor yet the last, time such a grandiose claim was made for the power of teaching; and it is based on the clearly stated conviction that political virtue can be taught. This statement interests Socrates immensely and it opens the gate to the heart of the debate. Socrates responds by admitting that if he were responsible for drawing up the laws of nature, political virtue would indeed be a product of teaching; but taking reality as it is and not as he should like it to be, Socrates wants to register his doubt about the validity of Protagoras' categorical claim. He thinks that in the assembly and in public life questions dealing with technical or special professions are answered by men who know most about them. If a layman offered his opinion on architecture and shipbuilding, for example, he would be jeered from the platform.[22] But on political matters, Socrates continues, there are no specialists, because there is no special art concerning them; every person, whether he is a carpenter, a blacksmith, a cobbler, a sailor, a

19 *Ibid.*, 318.
20 *Ibid.*, 318 b.
21 *Ibid.*, 312 e–318 c.
22 *Ibid.*, 319 bc.

merchant, a rich man, a poor man, a noble, or a slave, gives advice, and no one silences him because everyone believes politics is a matter of opinion and that political prudence cannot be taught.[23] Socrates refers to the low correlation between the political abilities of fathers and sons; his own observations, plus the common experience of mankind, compel him to assert that virtue cannot be taught.[24]

The Socratic assertion challenges one of the principal justifications of the unbridled optimism of sophistic teaching that the bounds of educational achievement are limitless.[25] This open-ended quality assigned to teaching contributed greatly to the Sophists' popularity, for the education they offered could raise people to new stations and be a substitute for heritage, prestige, and wealth. Socrates acknowledges the Sophists' success in forming men's minds, but he refuses to recognize an essential relationship between forming minds and reforming souls or restructuring men's moral stature. After tasting the sweetness of approval and popularity in one dimension of teaching—the communication of the arts of mind—the Sophists boldly assumed competence in communicating the virtues of the soul as well. In questioning the power of moral education, Socrates is challenging Protagoras, the real leader of the school of thought that holds the issue of ethical and political education to be central, to disclose the pedagogic secret for teaching political virtue. Protagoras is not yet aware of the fundamental purpose of Socrates' probing, so he responds rather easily and expresses his confidence that social science can achieve appropriate goals in ethical and political teaching. He is himself, he says, a social-science teacher.[26]

Protagoras takes a long time to explore Socrates' assertion: "I never thought that human ingenuity could make men good." [27] We should be prepared for a generous speech on such a fundamental point, and a man of considerable stature is needed to make it, for, obviously, they are now boring beneath the surface of pedagogic technique. Few Sophists were prepared to handle Socrates' summons, and Plato wanted no straw man for Socrates to dispose of; Protagoras was a good choice.

Protagoras begins his speech with a myth and hopes in this way to demonstrate his educational views. He alludes to sociological theories and seems to update his interpretation of education's sociological bases;

23 *Ibid.*, 319 d.

24 *Ibid.*, 320 b.

25 Marrou, *op. cit.*, pp. 48–49, comments on this point. He also admits that evidence on the real nature of sophistic theory and methods is too scant for an objective analysis. Havelock, *op. cit.*, p. 209; and J. Anderson, *Socrates as an Educator* (Sydney, Angus and Robertson, 1962), pp. 203–213, both concerned about sophistic method, are somewhat critical of Socrates' teaching techniques. See also, E. A. Havelock, "The Evidence for the Teaching of Socrates," *Transactions of the American Philological Association*, 65 (1934), pp. 282–295.

26 *Protagoras*, 319.

27 *Ibid.*, 319 b and 328 e.

moreover, he returns to an earlier criterion: although the Sophists found their teaching foundations in the past they were decidedly progressive teachers. In this long, profound speech we note a mastery of style and a brilliant illustration of a variety of types of eloquence. Socrates, a humble man, admits his defeat, at last overwhelmed by the power of Protagoras' argument; he even joins in applause. But what passes for uncritical admiration is really an ironical way of refusing to compete with Protagoras on the level of oratory, where Protagoras holds undisputed supremacy. He wants to lead Protagoras into a dialectical discussion, and he is successful in coaxing his adversary onto his own terrain where he overpowers him. His dialectical art is effectively displayed in the debate that follows.

Socrates begins by asking what appears to be an antiseptic question: Is virtue a unity, and are justice, prudence, and piety parts of it, or are they different names for the same thing? [28] The question seems superficial to Protagoras, so he boldly follows Socrates. He has not fully appreciated the point of the question; moreover, he does not know Socrates' thesis that virtue is knowledge, and he fails to understand Socrates' steady progress towards it.[29] Throughout the conversation Socrates tries to keep Protagoras confused about his real aim, although if we are familiar with the earlier dialogues we are aware of it. Pursuing the point of the unity or diversity of virtue, Socrates asks this question: If we possess virtue, must we have all its parts? Socrates asks first whether justice must be the same as piety; then he puts the same question pertaining to prudence and wisdom; finally he raises it again with respect to prudence and justice.[30] Socrates tries to wrest from Protagoras an acknowledgement of the essential identity of justice and piety or, failing in this, an admission that they are similar and related. Protagoras unwillingly concedes the point. Then Socrates moves to other pairs of virtues in order to elicit another concession. All this strikes Protagoras as very strange, and somewhat hesitatingly he admits their similarity. Like most people who approach the problem of virtue from a common-sense level he is inclined to emphasize differences among the virtues rather than similarities. Protagoras tries without much success to illuminate this point.

By now Protagoras begins to see the depth of the water; he senses the currents are getting too strong—he is in greater trouble than he supposed —and he searches for something to buoy him up. To escape the dialectical trap Socrates has laid he uses the device of petulance and ill humor. The discussion is in jeopardy; Protagoras shows signs of refusing to con-

28 *Ibid.*, 329 c.

29 Socrates' and Plato's views are not easily separated on ethical questions; see M. A. Adam, *Plato: Moral and Political Ideals* (Cambridge, Mass., Harvard University Press, 1913) ; and R. C. Lodge, *Plato's Theory of Ethics: The Moral Criterion and the Highest Good* (New York, Harcourt, Brace and Company, 1928) .

30 *Protagoras,* 329 d.

tinue. The debate is resumed only when Protagoras is permitted to re-direct it. He thinks he can find a topic more to his liking and one where he can appear to better advantage.

They turn to a critical examination of poetry and perhaps indirectly to a test of its relevance in sophistic education. But here again Protagoras meets his match when Socrates skillfully turns the discussion back to a question of true virtue. By masking his true purpose, and cleverly per-verting the meaning of an illustrative poem, Socrates demonstrates a method for proving anything; and he adds another principle: no one errs willingly.[31]

Then Socrates asks Protagoras what he thinks about reason and knowledge. Protagoras thinks they are the highest human powers. The ultimate question, as Socrates poses it, is whether or not knowledge can help man to act rightly; if a man knows what is good, is he insulated from any influence motivating him toward evil? Protagoras now doubts the effectiveness of knowledge; and his doubt is dictated partly by authori-tative cultural snobbery. His position is indeed surprising, for the Sophists as zealous upholders of intellectual culture should have had a high estimate of the power of knowledge. Again Protagoras threatens to with-draw from the discussion to find a more comfortable and less embarrass-ing place in the audience. But Socrates is too clever to allow his carefully baited hook to be reeled in without a prize. He tantalizes Protagoras with the attractive prospect of examining imperative considerations of stan-dards for human living; once more Protagoras is plunged into the swirl-ing and deadly waters of Socratic dialectic.

Throughout the discourse Socrates has maintained, though only for the purpose of argument, that what is pleasant is good: such is the stan-dard for human purpose in behavior. The Sophists assembled in the audience agree to this proposition and indicate their assent. Protagoras, apparently reassured by evidence of general agreement, makes no objec-tion to Socrates' thesis, although he began by distrusting it. This shift in attitude depicts the Sophists, and their most illustrious spokesman, Pro-tagoras, as being uncertain of their art. So these great Sophistic teachers find themselves reduced to the level of hoi polloi, whose opinion Socrates had originally adopted. He has succeeded in putting the Sophists in a seri-ous intellectual predicament: in the final analysis they were no more astute, and held no more basic positions on education, morality, virtue, and knowledge, than the ordinary mass of mankind. In a word, they were hedonists. But Socrates does not press this point; as a matter of fact, he makes no special reference to it, for apparently he prefers not to destroy the Sophists as teachers. Without delay he proceeds to capitalize on the

---

[31] *Ibid.*, 345 e. These are by no means new issues to Greek thinkers, which may explain why Plato is able to be so complete. See Theodor Gomperz, *Greek Thinkers*, vols. II and III (New York, Charles Scribner's Sons, 1905) .

implications in this hedonist principle for which he has elicited their agreement. If pleasure is the standard, if it dominates men's actions, then no one voluntarily chooses anything less than the best; and what is commonly thought to be immorality among men who respond only to the goal of pleasure is nothing more than faulty knowledge or reasoning. Socrates' principle can be repeated: a man never aims to do what is evil. By this argument Socrates leads the Sophists to accept his clever paradox: no one falls into error consciously; and Socrates is not especially concerned about the meaning of error.[32]

Scholars have criticized this dialogue for its slow and meandering progress and for its indecisive conclusion. To some extent Socrates anticipates this objection. He says: "The only reason I ask all these questions is to find out about virtue, and learn what it really is. If that could be discovered, I know it would clear up the question you and I have been talking about for so long, you asserting, and I denying, that virtue could be taught." [33] The question about the nature of virtue must be answered before anyone can talk about the possibility of its being taught. Socrates' conclusion—that virtue is knowledge—is more than a preliminary point; it quite clearly makes the teaching of virtue possible. At the end of the debate we find Socrates and Protagoras changing places. Socrates, who began by believing virtue could not be taught, is now using the dialectical apparatus to wed virtue and knowledge; while Protagoras, who explained virtue could be taught, is desperately denying what he had dogmatically assumed: if virtue is not knowledge it obviously cannot be taught.[34] The dialogue ends with Socrates marveling at the incompatibility between Protagoras' earlier and now subsequent assertion with respect to knowledge and virtue; and the reader leaves *Protagoras* understanding the Socratic theory: virtue grounded on a foundation of true value is the bedrock of education.

Plato succeeds in demonstrating the foundation in knowledge education must have if it is to form men responsibly, and he also succeeds in illustrating Socratic pedagogy at its best. Plato remained faithful to the Socratic principle of rejecting all dogmatic instruction; moreover, he was careful not to allow his intellectual idol to engage in dogmatic teaching either.[35]

On a practical level, seeing the dialogue in its temporal context and in opposition to sophistic culture, it is evident that despite their contributions to teaching methods and pedagogic style, and despite, too, their

32 Jaeger, *op. cit.*, II, 121, and *Protagoras,* 358 b and 358 d.
33 *Ibid.,* 360 e.
34 *Ibid.,* 316 a.
35 For a more elaborate analysis of Plato's philosophy of knowledge, see Francis M. Cornford, *Plato's Theory of Knowledge* (London, Paul, Trench, Trubner & Co., Ltd., 1949) ; and Norman Gully, *Plato's Theory of Knowledge* (London, Methuen and Co., Ltd., 1962) . On the point of dogmatic teaching, see Jaeger, *op. cit.*, p. 122.

success in broadening the curriculum by introducing new subjects, the Sophists misunderstood the fundamental bases of education. This was the most damaging of all demonstrations. Socrates never claimed to be a teacher; Protagoras did; yet we are constantly treated to evidences of Socrates' superior caliber as a teacher, one whose teaching method is always useful. And this Socratic superiority stands on something more solid than mere technique or an especially attractive personality; it was grounded on his ability to make moral and intellectual education complement one another. His fundamental assumption was that morality and knowledge are related, but this was an assumption the Sophists regularly refused to accept.[36]

III

SUBORDINATION OF RHETORIC

Protagoras and *Gorgias* are important planks in the platform of Plato's educational thought. In *Protagoras* Socrates tests the pretensions of sophistry and gives Plato a framework for elaborating his views on knowledge vis-à-vis virtue. The *Gorgias* is less discursive than the *Protagoras;* one discipline—rhetoric—is subjected to rigorous dialectical scrutiny.

Because a plan of teaching based on rhetoric enjoyed pride of place in Athens,[37] Plato's critical analysis had to be made cautiously and the stage had to be set carefully. To have introduced an advocate for rhetoric whose stature was doubtful would have been undramatic and ineffective; Plato was too good an artist to miss this. He chose the greatest rhetorician of antiquity, or at least of the fifth century B.C., Gorgias of Leontini. Gorgias is credited with bestowing on rhetoric its educational and political orientation; he was the authentic spokesman for rhetoric as an educational and political way of life.[38] Not only were his own credentials

[36] *Ibid.,* p. 123. Although it is hazardous to try to make Plato speak to us, the implications of Socratic and Platonic educational thought are nicely presented by Richard Livingstone, *Plato and Modern Education* (Cambridge, Cambridge University Press, 1944).

[37] Rhetoric's place in early education, frequently referred to in these pages, is not easily appreciated today, because oratory—or the spoken word—is much less a universal tool of the educated man than it was in ancient times. We learn to write our thoughts while ancient men learned to speak theirs. Rhetoric's pride of place in ancient formal teaching is explained somewhat in the following: C. S. Baldwin, *Ancient Rhetoric and Poetic* (New York, The Macmillan Company, 1924); M. M. Odgers, "Quintilian's Rhetorical Predecessors," *Transactions of the American Philological Association,* 65 (1935), pp. 25–36; D. L. Clark, *Rhetoric in Greco-Roman Education* (New York, Columbia University Press, 1957); and M. L. Clarke, *Rhetoric at Rome* (London, Cohen and West, 1953).

[38] Marrou, *op. cit.,* pp. 52–54; H. Gomperz, *Sophistik und Rhetorik* (Leipzig, Teubner, 1912); and Beck, *op. cit.,* pp. 173–179.

good and universally attested, his pupils—especially Isocrates [39]—had carried on the rhetorical tradition in education with more than modest success. Gorgias was the embodiment of the art of rhetoric, as Protagoras, in the earlier dialogue, was the embodiment of the art of sophistry.

It is not easy today to appreciate the significance of ancient rhetoric; first it was a study, and second a way of life. In classical times, "rhetor" was the correct name for the statesman; [40] and in the ancient democracy of Athens the foremost tool for effective statesmanship was oratory. Gorgias proposed to educate political scientists by making rhetoric the core of his teaching, and Isocrates, who adopted this program, never thought of his teaching in any context other than that of preparing men to govern the state. Quite appropriately the dialogue involves us as spectators in a discussion of rhetoric's nature; we are brought face to face with a subject whose purposes are broad and powerful, a discipline by no means concerned only with mere words, but one going beyond words to the influence they can exert.

Rhetoric was a complex art with extraordinary appeal; otherwise Plato should not have noticed it, and misinterpretations regarding its force and purpose as well as its friends and foes were always possible. A quick but superficial reaction is to label Plato an enemy of rhetoric. Such a judgment is unfair and unsupported, for Plato was interested not in destroying rhetoric but in finding its appropriate place in an educational hierarchy. He never doubted rhetoric's instrumental value—he was himself a skillful practitioner of the art—but he wanted rhetoric used responsibly and this was possible only when it was subordinated to a knowledge of fundamental values.

Gorgias refuses to accept Socrates' characterization of rhetoric as an instrument; [41] he assigns it a more prominent role and illustrates his meaning by telling us of cases where eloquence has persuaded sick people to follow prescribed medical therapy. His advocacy for rhetoric is at once broad, arrogant, and naïve: all specialists and professional men must master rhetoric and to it they must subordinate their professional knowledge.[42]

Socrates finds it hard to take Gorgias' assertion seriously, but he is unwilling to quibble about such a superficial article in Sophistic faith. He wants to move to more essential items in Gorgias' conception of rhetoric, and he does so by getting Gorgias to say that teachers of rhetoric are able to impart this art to students and along with it the prudence to employ it justly and responsibly. Underlying this proposition is the dogmatic assumption that Gorgias and all teachers of rhetoric know what is

39 Untersteiner, *op. cit.,* pp. 93–94.
40 Jaeger, *op. cit.,* II, 127.
41 *Gorgias,* 450 c.
42 *Ibid.,* 456 b–457 c.

good and just and that their pupils either begin with an intuitive understanding of goodness and justice or they learn it from their teachers. Knowledge is at a discount; technique is now the Sophists' educational goal. Yet, if intuitive knowledge is lacking, the Sophist must teach virtue, although Protagoras had concluded his debate with Socrates by doubting the teacher's ability to do so; and Socrates has already demonstrated for us how neither a Sophist nor anyone else can teach what he does not know.[43]

Plainly Gorgias has gone too far in his unsupported assumptions and Socrates applies enough dialectical pressure to force his distinguished opponent into an untenable intellectual position. Gorgias is not happy about his defeat—a defeat shared in by all Sophists, who are now humiliated by having the glaring weakness of their system exposed—and with ill-concealed bad humor he withdraws from the discussion apparently leaving Socrates the victor. But the Sophists are not beaten so easily; if Gorgias withdraws he has not conceded. His place is taken by his pupil, Polus, who thinks he can resolve the dilemma Socrates has set and thus deliver Gorgias and sophistic pedagogy from a serious predicament.

Polus represents the younger generation or, perhaps more exactly, students of rhetoric who are insensitive to questions of morality and are impressed with the power rhetoric gives them. Rhetoric, Polus quite frankly admits, is absolutely indifferent to questions of morality; it is not concerned with moral questions on any fundamental level but accepts convention, or what society calls its moral code, in a routine fashion. This is an important point; it dramatically and forcefully demonstrates that if anyone was tampering with the morals of Athenian youth, it was not Socrates but the Sophists themselves. Perhaps this tampering with moral values was unintentional, for Gorgias eschews moral nihilism; yet Polus shows us where sophistic teaching can lead. Neither Polus nor Callicles, a practicing orator who appears in the dialogue as a substitute for Polus, is interested in the moral law. Both are amoral and candidly make the right of the stronger as the highest moral law. Finally we have, if not a definition of rhetoric, at least its main attraction—the power it generates in the person, who then wields it in the political arena. As the debate proceeds Socrates' position earns our allegiance, and we prepare for the Sophists' capitulation. Gorgias' arguments have been demolished; Polus has succeeded only in undermining the image of rhetoric; but we have been listening to academic rhetoricians who, having exhausted their ammunition, are now forced to fall back to their last line of defense. They call upon Callicles, a man of the world who uses rhetoric every day; Athenians were always ready to admire his type. He represents the best in academic rhetoric, but he also represents rhetoric at work in real life.

43 *Ibid.,* 459 c.

Plato is reluctant to stop with the defeat of the schoolmasters, for rhetoric is deeply ingrained in Athenian life and the Athenian people must be given an elementary demonstration of its weaknesses before they will relegate it to its proper instrumental role. Plato was not trying to destroy rhetoric—he saw its value and used it himself—and he did not criticize it only because it lacked a theoretical basis, although this reason would have been sufficient.[44] By now rhetoric and philosophy had established their independent positions and stood as hostile cultures; the former was draining off prospective philosophy students with attractive promises for a quicker and more practical education. Plato's school and the relevance of his teaching were threatened by the increasing popularity of rhetorical teaching. Thus an element of self-justification invades Plato's argument.

We cannot be certain that Plato was thinking of Isocrates when he wrote this dialogue, nor do we have good evidence for supposing that Isocrates had a copy of *Gorgias* on his writing table when he prepared *Against the Sophists,* but Plato was aware of and focused on indictments drawn relative to the worth of philosophical teaching. Put quickly, Isocrates said philosophy was good if not studied too long; he added that its principal function was to correlate general ideas. Where Isocrates was preoccupied with misgivings about his reputation as a teacher, Plato saw the dangers in the contemporary trend to downgrade philosophy and praise rhetoric; moreover, he fully understood the charges against philosophy and was able to express them more effectively and forcefully than any of philosophy's enemies.

With Callicles speaking for rhetoric, the direction of the debate is altered somewhat. Socrates knows that rhetoric's defenses so far have been built around its utility, for both Gorgias and Polus have been at pains to prove that for optimum effectiveness all special knowledge must be subordinated to eloquence. But this emphasis on eloquence leaves the entire field of theory untouched, and Socrates is anxious to learn more about the theoretical foundation supporting oratory. When Socrates asked Polus to explain the meaning of rhetoric, he wanted to know its theory as well as the art involved in its implementation. He is aware of the techniques forming its practical dimensions, and he knows that these techniques can be improved by practice. When he hears no satisfactory statement of theory, he wonders whether or not rhetoric is supported by theory. If it is not, he argues, or if teachers of rhetoric are unable to explain the theory, then they must retract their assumptions about theory and allow rhetoric to stand nakedly as a knack obtained by practice or experience. Now Socrates delivers his major blow: if experience alone counts, can teachers of rhetoric justify their profession? What do they

---

44 See E. Black, "Plato's View of Rhetoric," *Quarterly Journal of Speech,* XLIV (December, 1958) , pp. 361–374.

have to teach? An authentic science contains knowledge related to its nature and purpose; moreover, it explains its procedures and regulates them to serve its principal purpose. Since Sophistic rhetoric neglects all these points, Socrates concludes that it is not an authentic science.[45]

Socrates puts rhetoric in an unenviable position; his paradox dethrones it and reduces it to a level where its reputation and stature are no better than cookery. His conclusion provokes an emotional outburst from Polus and Callicles, but this should not surprise us. They try to parry Socrates' rapier-like thrust by saying that rhetoric is clearly an important instrument because it exercises tremendous influence in politics. Their reaction—almost a common-sense point of view—is fairly simple and is based on the assumption that because an instrument can be used to exert force and power it therefore becomes highly significant. Socrates does not deny the considerable influence rhetoric can have over political decisions and he acknowledges the refinements and elaborations that have been made in techniques for educating and influencing people, but these accomplishments, he contends, are founded on unsophisticated ideas and faulty knowledge. The exchange touches philosophies of power and culture and gives Plato an opportunity to explain his meaning of paideia.[46] Paideia, by which the Greeks meant something broader than education, is translated best as culture. In Plato's view culture was not just a state in human development, where men became skillful in employing their faculties; it connoted perfection of character in accordance with nature. Rhetoric's importance, he reasons, is not that it is an instrument for men to exert force over others, but that it can be a tool for fathoming the depths of human nature and thus can help men perfect themselves culturally.

Plato does not want us to miss the object lesson in this dialogue: the dialectic of Socrates cannot be matched by the rhetorical devices either of Polus or Gorgias. Both are well trained, but both are ignorant of Socratic dialectic; they are skilled in methodical tactics but lack logical precision in argument and, worst of all, are devoid of objective knowledge. They demonstrate an empty and imprecise rhetoric that stands as an ominous obstacle to a valid philosophy of life. If Socrates' criticisms are right, rhetoric cannot help being empty and imprecise, for without ethical principles for guidance, it is blind to everything save personal ambitions and appetites for power.[47]

Callicles does not follow the younger Polus in his naïve assumption that everyone naturally tries to gain power. Along lines that remind us of Isocrates, he establishes a standard for human conduct on convention and

[45] *Gorgias,* 456 ab.
[46] *Ibid.,* 470–487.
[47] *Ibid.,* 471 de, and Jaeger, *op. cit.,* p. 135.

common sense. He denounces Socrates for assuming that men must learn the difference between right and wrong, and takes the position, apparently still alongside Isocrates, that men have intuitive knowledge of right and wrong. They naturally pursue the course of right action.

When the argument touches the nature of official law and conventional morality, Callicles' doctrine becomes repugnant, for he holds that laws are made by weak people to suit their own ends. The strong, he claims, have been hobbled by the weak; his social theory is based on a struggle for existence, and education plays only a minor role. It is but a formalized means for deceiving and misleading strong men to support a law protecting the weak. He tries to relate his thesis to a philosophy, about which, he says, Socrates is always talking, which ultimately dominates man and turns him on himself—socially and politically man becomes a recluse. According to Callicles, this is philosophy's inevitable tendency and its greatest deficiency.[48]

Callicles ends his performance with an appeal to Socrates to abandon philosophy—he is wasting his great intellectual talent with it—and to embrace rhetoric or political oratory where the prospects for success are greater.[49]

Without reviewing details, we see the inevitability of defeat for the last of rhetoric's defenders. Callicles fought to preserve the sophistic system of education and he defended it somewhat more effectively than either Gorgias or Polus, but his greater effectiveness was also a signal of greater danger, so it is important that his arguments be controverted convincingly. This is all clear to Plato. To deliver the final blow to rhetoric and its advocates, Socrates reuses an argument he had made in *Protagoras*. Here he develops it this way. The Sophists' educational system aimed at preparing people for civic life. Instruction was given in the practices of statecraft, and tangentially it dealt with educational sociology or the relationship of education to the state. Beneath the obvious aim of sophistic education was an emphasis on training public leaders who could be successful in turning existing conditions to their own advantage. They conceived the relationship between education and the state as a one-sided affair, and they were totally indifferent to political reform; despite the possibility of its being degenerate the state was accepted as a model and a standard for education. In a word, rhetoric had no objective standard.

In the *Gorgias* Plato's principal purpose is to show that education must find, define, and understand a standard for its own regulation. To find, define, and understand this standard, education needs the help of philosophy; a groundless, aimless discipline of rhetoric is of no help.

---

[48] *Gorgias*, 484–487.
[49] *Ibid.*, 486 d.

IV

INTEGRATION OF RHETORIC AND PHILOSOPHY

In *Protagoras* and *Gorgias* Plato illustrates how empty rhetoric can be, and he records a number of exaggerated claims made for it; yet he never meant to annihilate it. Rhetoric was useful to philosophy—we know how a philosophical rhetoric was developed later—and Plato wanted to use its best qualities in the service of philosophy. He never apologized for expressing his own thought in an attractive and balanced way, and, though he refused to extol the virtues of rhetoric, he had both a theory of rhetoric and a not inconsequential rhetorical power.

We should say at once that Plato's purpose in the *Phaedrus* is often misunderstood and that the obvious topic—love—is simply a point of departure, a way of returning to rhetoric to give him a chance to re-examine the relationship between philosophy and rhetoric. The *Phaedrus* illuminates Plato's theory of rhetoric and shows that a validly conceived rhetoric does belong in a system of education. After studying this dialogue Aristotle began a campaign to include rhetoric in the curriculum of Plato's Academy.[50] This must have both surprised and concerned the Sophists, for their involvement in education was principally as teachers of rhetoric; and teaching rhetoric was left mainly to them and Isocrates. If philosophers were going to teach rhetoric, and especially if Plato was to offer it in his school, it would mean, in addition to losing good students, a deterioration in the Sophists' prestige as specialists in a branch of knowledge.

Plato was anxious to return to the subject of rhetoric because he wanted to make a positive contribution to the discussion of its place in education, and he was determined to disprove the sophistic dogma that philosophy was useless. In addition, this could be another opportunity to show rhetoric's dependence on dialectic. The dialogue opens with a discussion of two sides of rhetoric: one side is clearly pretechnical with a dedication to superior oratory, and superior oratory demands, on the one hand, a profound knowledge of subject matter and, on the other, a valid philosophical framework to impose order on knowledge; the other side, obviously technical, is concerned with the mechanics of rhetoric, which are described in the handbooks of the rhetors.[51]

The date of *Phaedrus'* composition is disputed, but we need not be

---

[50] See Harold F. Cherniss, *Aristotle's Criticism of Plato and the Academy* (Baltimore, The Johns Hopkins Press, 1944).

[51] See O. L. Brownstein, "Plato's Phaedrus: Dialectic as the Genuine Art of Speaking," *Quarterly Journal of Speech*, LI (December, 1965), pp. 392–398.

delayed by it here, except to note that Plato wrote the *Phaedrus* after Isocrates' pedagogic theory and practice were well known in Athens. In Isocrates' exegetic treatment of rhetoric he had placed natural talent, practice, and knowledge in a hierarchy. For Isocrates, natural talent was most important; practice and knowledge were given comparatively modest places in the structure. The unavoidable question, and one not neglected by Plato was: If natural talent is the critical item in the formation of an orator, why should teaching be given so much attention? And neither Isocrates nor any Sophist ever doubted the efficacy of teaching. Although Plato can praise Isocrates and for dramatic purposes envision an illustrious career for him,[52] he is at pains to correct the misleading doctrine allegedly found in Isocrates' *Against the Sophists*. In other words, Plato is anxious to attach considerably greater weight to knowledge and practice in the education of the orator than Isocrates had assigned. Isocrates had emphasized intuition and seemed to belittle learning. But the learning at which he cast aspersions was not the philosophy of Plato but the formal teaching of the old-fashioned Sophists whose adherence to rules made rhetoric barren and almost unbearable. Plato thinks pride of place should be given to knowledge, and in his system development of knowledge would begin with logical training as a prerequisite to philosophy. All this was a matter of teaching. Besides, logical training was construed as being absolutely indispensable to learning anything else. Plato's aim, made evident in *Gorgias,* is to reform rhetoric by rebuilding it as a true science, to make it a discipline with a positive foundation in knowledge first and then a set of rules or skills to be mastered. When Socrates said rhetoric failed to meet the test of true Greek science, he did not mean that rhetoric could not achieve this status, but only that it had not done so with its improper orientation. Plato uses his artistic tools to restructure rhetoric in the *Phaedrus.* The combinations which he expects to lead toward a satisfactory reformation of academic rhetoric are: integration of rhetoric and philosophy, enabling the latter to provide illumination and substance for the former; use of a pleasing and incisive form to make intellectual content more effective; and a combination of truth and expression to make the orator a full and true political man. Plato's technique for reviving a responsible and relevant rhetoric was accepted and followed by all classical schools of philosophy until the end of the Hellenistic period.[53] During this same period teachers of rhetoric became familiar with Plato's oratorical theories, but they absorbed them slowly and allowed them to dominate their system of teaching only when it was too late. But their reluctance to accept Plato's doctrine is understandable: rhetoric and philosophy, as we

[52] *Phaedrus*, 279 b.
[53] The impact of Plato's school is worth considering; see F. W. Russell, *The School of Plato* (London, Methuen and Co., Ltd., 1896) .

have said, were hostile cultures and we should hardly expect a rhetorician to accept from a philosopher edicts on the organization or teaching of his discipline. Despite the inability of Plato's creed to fully penetrate rhetorical teaching, by the time Cicero appeared on the oratorical scene Plato's synthesis was somewhat more acceptable and teachers of rhetoric were using it; the Platonic influence was undoubtedly felt by Quintilian when he composed the famous *Education of an Orator.*

We are familiar with the length of the school course as it is defined by Plato in the *Republic.*[54] For the uninitiated, or for those who definitely oppose philosophical education, the detours and the standards in the course would seem to be too long or too difficult. Surely such an educational program appears disproportionately long and difficult to anyone who expects to be educated quickly by absorbing a few tricks. Plato wants to make sure his position is clear, for the Sophists had gained a great deal of mileage out of teaching on a superficial level. Plato can defend the long course only by stating a fundamental tenet of his educational philosophy: learning must always aim at the highest goal; no one should be led to believe there is an easy or clear path to oratorical excellence.[55] In Plato's conception, the orator is more than a skillful speaker; he is also a fully moral man. To achieve this full moral development the long and arduous philosophical road was inevitable. Plato was impatient with teachers of rhetoric who followed the principle that good teaching was based on probabilities or plausible evidence. He demanded the certain foundation of truth, and to truth he appended eloquence. The marriage of truth and eloquence, or philosophy and rhetoric, is consummated in the *Phaedrus.*

V

PLATO'S ACADEMY

Plato's fame in the history of education rests on his utopian plan for education and not on his work as a teacher in the Academy. This may be one reason why so little is known of the pedagogic details of this famous school.[56]

When Plato opened the Academy in 387 B.C., what were his academic goals? Was the school a front for political subversion; or was it an intel-

---

[54] For what must be the most succinct and precise description of this course, see Marrou, *op. cit.,* pp. 76–77. See also, Bernard Bosanquet, *The Education of the Young in the Republic of Plato* (Cambridge, Mass., Harvard University Press, 1917).

[55] *Phaedrus,* 273 e–274.

[56] Some parts of this chapter appeared in my article, "Plato's Academy: A Halting Step Toward Higher Education," *History of Education Quarterly,* IV (September, 1964), pp. 155–166.

lectual monastery where scholars of similar taste could find an escape
from the real political world? Did he expect to test educational plans for
the *Republic* and the *Laws?* Did he essay to educate a class of political
scientists to positions of leadership in the ancient world and at the same
time impress them with the supreme value of justice and truth? Was
Plato's Academy a utopia in action? Most likely it was less than this. Was
he only embarking on a commercial venture, where profitable employment corresponded to taste and personality? We must not forget that
most stationary schoolmasters were engaged in a commercial venture.[57]

The Academy, we know, was dedicated to the muses and, with a
shrine in the garden, was legally incorporated as a religious fraternity.
Doubtless this was done to impress a suspicious Athenian population, who,
despite its own agnosticism, wanted to preserve a veneer of orthodoxy.
Socrates was brought to trial because he was suspected of harboring athe-
istic tendencies and because he was thought to be corrupting youth;
Protagoras acknowledged his uncertainty about the gods, was declared
anathema as a result, and all his books were burned.[58] Plato could ill
afford further legal lapses; he had already experienced too many brushes
with the law. The magistrates watched him, for they understood his
attachment to Socrates and his dedication to the Socratic doctrine. Yet
while students in the Academy were going through the motions of
belonging to a religious fraternity, they were caricatured as studying bot-
any and zoology in the comedy of Epicrates. The students are on a field
trip and with their teachers are trying to classify vegetables, grass, and
shrubs. A good deal of action and a commendable degree of glee are
expressed in this scene: if it is a good witness, the Academy was a happy
school. It is quite possible that Plato or other teachers sent the boys—and
the two girls who are said to have matriculated—out to experience and
classify specimens and natural phenomena, but it is hard to see how any
legitimate inference can be drawn from this about the studies that dominated the curriculum, the contributions this technique made to the
study of natural science, or the general methodology of the school. In fact
one may be well advised to take this parody as nothing more than an
amusing incident, for Plato is very clear when he has Socrates say that the
trees and fields could teach him nothing.

What appears to be a safe assumption can be used as a starting point
to establish a correspondence between Plato's written and oral teaching.

---

57 It would be unhistorical and unfair to attribute only commercial motives to
Aristotle and Isocrates, but it is impossible, especially in the case of Isocrates, to ignore
the commercial dimension. This was criticism Isocrates himself had to contend with.
See *Antidosis,* 3–5. For further insight into Plato's motives, see H. F. Cherniss, *The
Riddle of the Early Academy* (Los Angeles, University of California Press, 1945) ; and
Eduard Zeller, *Plato and the Other Academy* (New York, Longmans, Green & Com-
pany, 1876) .

58 Freeman, *op. cit.,* p. 230.

We have no incontrovertible evidence for asserting that Plato taught as he wrote, although it would be strange, indeed, to discover that he preferred the dialectical tone and method for written discourse but shunned them in the schoolroom; and we would find it stranger still if the content of Platonic teaching were inconsistent with the content of his writing. Still resting on the weight of the original, but untested, assumption we move to the cautious conclusion that Plato was a master not unlike Socrates and that students studied what Plato thought would lead them to truth, the same general themes that formed his writing. Yet surely the rejoinder could be offered that Plato's writings are philosophical discourses appropriate only for the higher rungs of the educational ladder; boys do not begin their studies with philosophy. Plato knew what every other philosopher must know: philosophy without a foundation of knowledge is a cold, barren, almost useless thing.

Where did the Academy course begin? Is it not possible that Plato accepted his students only when they were mature, when they had completed their preliminary education and were ready to embark on the extremely demanding but highly rewarding study of philosophy? This is a reasonable position but it is not supported by fact. Plato had severe misgivings about the quality of lower education in Athens: he, we are quite certain, wanted a lesser emphasis on sport, a greater emphasis on mathematics, and a careful expurgation of literature.[59] These were not merely superficial criticisms that could be passed off lightly; they were sincere and incisive and they shook the foundations of Athenian school practice. Even if Plato had found contemporary education impeccable, he could not have admitted students to the philosophical or dialectical syllabus without propaedeutics, and none were available in the conventional Greek school: intellectual education terminated with the elementary school.

We should pause to refresh our memories relative to Plato's major criticisms of classical education, and to see more clearly why Plato could not conduct the Academy according to the standard practice of the day. The principal source of our knowledge about Plato's utopian educational and political system is the *Republic* and the *Laws,* and for the best view both should be consulted. Plato is interested in building souls, a practical consideration that whets his interest in education. As an aside to those who deny to educational theory a place in teacher-education curricula, Plato reminds us that theory or philosophy is at once an important and practical undertaking. Who can contribute to the building of souls if he understands neither the soul itself, the material out of which it is to be perfected, or the integration of the two into an enlarged image of the soul and its structure? The highest virtue is education and its rationale is

---

[59] See *Republic,* VII, 298, 536; II, 377; X, 595; *Laws,* VII, 810.

philosophically set forth as an essential and permanent presupposition of Greek culture.

We have drifted away from the principal issue and must return to Plato's reaction to the prevailing system of education in Athens during the hundred years before the Persian Wars. He is concerned exclusively with the content of education and tries to set fundamental lines for it. The natural way to educate men, he concludes, is to follow the traditional system, divided into gymnastics and music; so he takes these as his basis. Despite his radical criticism of certain aspects of traditional education, he has a conservative's wish to cling to things that have demonstrated their worth. Before we listen to him we must know that his philosophy of education stands on the foundations of traditional Greek education, or better, traditional Greek culture. He tried to avoid any sharp break with tradition, and when this attitude was coupled with an admiration of old Greek paideia and the living heritage of the Greek people, his philosophy achieved an historic character. His criticisms of old Greek education are not merely digressions, they are essential parts of his philosophy of education.[60]

Plato begins with musical education and treats it comprehensively by including not only sound and rhythm but speech as well. The section on music is long and complicated; pursuing details here might become dangerously arid, but it revolves about the philosopher's interest in speech and in knowing whether a given sentence is true or false. The informational and educational value of words depends on their truth. And now the myths which formed the Greek classics were called up for intensive diagnosis.[61] Plato knew no other way to begin teaching, and he was unable to find any other content for music schools. Still he recognized the danger of young minds being exposed to a carelessly formed curriculum, and he proposed a perceptive expurgation of the tales and legends that filled the teaching of the poets. He had something to say about athletics too, and close attention should be paid to the order assigned to this discussion. Musical education came first, because in the nature of things it belongs first: a well-developed body cannot make the soul good, but a fine soul can help the body attain perfection. His plan boils down to this: give the young a good intellectual education and let them look after the details of physical education themselves.[62] He endorsed a rigorous physical training program aimed not at amusement and recreation but at preparing young men for anything.

Finally, in this sketch of Plato's major criticisms of traditional edu-

[60] Plato, *Republic*, II, 367 e; VII, 521 de. See R. L. Nettleship, *The Theory of Education in Plato's Republic* (London, Oxford University Press, 1935); and F. H. Lane, *Elementary Greek Education* (Syracuse, Bardeen, 1895).

[61] Plato, *Republic*, II, 377 a; III, 392 b; X, 595 a; *Laws*, VII, 810 c and 811 b.

[62] Plato, *Republic*, III, 410 c–412 a. See also, W. L. and C. L. Bryan, *Plato the Teacher* (New York, Charles Scribner's Sons, 1897).

cation, we come to the ancient doctrine that crudely kept women from formal learning, a doctrine that seems to have been based on insecurity and misunderstanding, or one that simply followed an ominous voice from the *Book of History:* "the hen who does the crowing at dawn brings ruin upon the family." Plato's interest in female education is not in their role as wives or mothers but as guards of the state. He believes women are capable of making a creative contribution to the community, but he does not expect them to do it through family life. Women are physically weaker than men but this should not keep them out of what traditionally was a man's world. If they do the same work as men, they should have the same training and education; [63] they should follow a curriculum of gymnastics and music. Plato could be even more incisive: he believed that social limitations in Athens made it impossible for women to develop their natural gifts. If we take the broad view of Plato's recommendations for the education of women, and subtract everything aimed at producing Amazons, what remains is essentially the modern educational program for women.[64]

We have remained away from school long enough and should be ready to return to the Academy. We suppose that if Plato's recommendations were followed in the lower schools, viz., that music, literature, and mathematics were given deserved attention, and that if the students in the Academy were taught anything, they would certainly have been taught arithmetic, geometry, stereometry, mathematical astronomy, and mathematical harmonics. In none of these studies would we find any specialization or technical or utilitarian emphasis. Their purpose was to train minds and prepare them for the supreme study—dialectics—around which Plato places severe restrictions and for which he assigns imposing prerequisites. Yet we may be somewhat ahead of the story—or ahead of the development of these mathematical studies. According to Plato's own testimony neither mathematical astronomy nor harmonics was discovered by this time, and even stereometrics may have developed too late to find a place in the Academy's curriculum.[65] Some commentators have excluded arithmetic too, giving the reason that boys already knew it. But this is a hasty conclusion. Greek schools did not teach arithmetic as we know it today because a suitable notation for calculation was lacking. Arithmetic was much too difficult for elementary school children. They learned to count—on their fingers—but they did not calculate. Arithmetic was a theory of number, clearly out of place on the elementary level.[66] So if we restore arithmetic, as a theory of number, and by a

63 Plato, *Laws,* VII, 794 c; 802 e; 813 b.
64 Plato, *Republic,* V, 451 d–457 b; *Laws,* VII, 804 d–805 b; 813 b.
65 Plato, *Republic,* II, 528 b–530 c.
66 From Plato's description of arithmetic, we know how it was studied in traditional Greek education. See *Republic,* VII, 522 c; and *Laws,* VII, 819 c.

process of elimination exclude astronomy, harmonics, and stereometrics, plane and solid geometry are left.

Testimony to the effect that the higher mathematics was studied, even developed, in the Academy needs judicious handling. We have Aristotle as a silent witness, a student in Plato's school for twenty years, who gives no indication of having studied advanced mathematics while he was there. Yet we are fairly certain that outstanding mathematicians were associated with the school and that distinct mathematical advances originated in it.[67] We know, too, of Plato's interest in the higher mathematics.[68] Yet we must conclude that advanced courses were not taught in mathematics or dialectics; students were not ready for them. It is most unlikely that Plato lectured in the Academy on the doctrine of Ideas; and it is improbable that Eudoxes or Helicon led students pell-mell into the deeper mysteries of mathematics. Plato had high hopes for his students but he could not teach them what they were not ready to learn, and for this reason neither the highest philosophy nor the highest mathematics could find a formal place in the school. Still, it is not inconceivable that both found their way into the Academy in an informal way. Students read Plato's dialogues and they knew of the mathematical achievements of the men attached to the Academy. We can readily see how they might raise occasional questions on what they had heard or read. This was probably the standing assigned to these higher studies, but even this place is not too secure when we recall Aristotle's difficulties in interpreting some of Plato's works.[69] In his long association with Plato he must never have asked what Plato meant, or if he did, Plato did not answer. When this personal and advanced side of teaching could ignore the genius of Aristotle, we may fairly doubt the accessibility of the great masters to Academy students. It is doubtful, moreover, that as a regular procedure Plato discussed his recondite philosophical doctrines with his students; he may never have done so. We are left with the tentative conclusion, supported by reasonable but not conclusive testimony, that the curriculum of the Academy was much narrower than Plato would have liked and that it bore remarkably little resemblance to the course of higher studies he devised for the intellectual elite in utopia. Still, the curricular question remains up in the air; our best information leads us to believe that the Academy course was really a course in mathematics.

If we accept the hypothesis that the Academy curriculum was mainly mathematical, we can go on to explore some other features of this famous school. All the marks of an elite boarding school are there; it may even have been the first fraternity house. When students sought postelementary

[67] The most prominent was Eudoxes of Cnidus; see Diogenes Laertius, *Lives of Eminent Philosophers*, VIII, 87.

[68] Plato, *Republic*, 514 a.

[69] Aristotle, *Physics*, I, 191 b.

education they formed independent associations or agreements with important masters. Higher education in classical Greece was unsystematic, yet this did not rule out an intimate relationship between teachers and students: fraternities of teachers and students were everywhere recognized and approved. Breaking these intimate bonds, through which moral training might flow, was grounds for rebuke. Whatever hostility Athens showed the Sophists (it must have been insignificant judging from their general popularity) stemmed from two sources: one was a fraternal integration in the teacher's art—Sophists often taught so many students that intimacy was out of the question—the other was that Sophists promised to teach virtue but collected all fees for such instruction in advance. This anomaly often goes unnoticed, yet it is evident that the Sophist did not trust his teaching or the efficacy of the virtue he purveyed, or he would have been willing to wait for his money.

Young men who came to Plato's school were prepared to spend their days and nights in study, learning, and training. The Academy was a school, home, church, and moral society all in one. But this was no problem. The student body was small—possibly never more than a dozen —and the teaching staff probably never exceeded four or five. Few servants were needed to man the establishment. So standing at the threshold of the Academy the student could sense that the portals opened on an intellectual experience of rare quality.[70]

When we think of methodology in lower or higher education, we are disposed to think of teaching the average student along with several others. But to ascribe methods of large, conventional classes to the Academy's teaching procedure is no more accurate than to accept descriptions of teaching and learning in the *Republic* as reports on Academy practices. The Academy was the first progressive school. Its educational program was informal; students were expected to plan their studies and to take full responsibility for their future. They turned to their teachers for assistance as a last resort. And then the teachers did not tell them what to do or think, but only guided them toward understanding and ultimately— perhaps many years later—to truth. Plato was teaching young men, and he did not expect too much. Instruction was partly tutorial and partly generalized discussion; the latter was intended to stimulate thought and to reveal the possibilities of dialectical techniques. Plato prized dialectic and showed preferences for its techniques in his dialogues. No methodologist would approve Plato's imprecise arrangements on the level of technique, and supervising teachers are horrified by the lack of lesson plans and proximate objectives. It was not that Plato rejected system or precision or

[70] J. P. Maguire, "Individual and the Class in Plato's Republic," *Classical Journal*, 60 (January, 1965), pp. 145–150. Maguire is concerned here, not with the student or the class in pedagogy, but with the person as an actual unit in Plato's theory of the state. Yet, inferences may be drawn that are applicable to Plato's theory of education.

that he did not understand their significance. He believed that system was unnecessary where advanced students with exceptional intellectual acumen were concerned. Intuitively he knew what we have since learned: the best education for the exceptional man is the worst possible education for the rank and file.

The level of instruction in the Academy and the length of its course offer plenty of room for speculation. Aristotle spent twenty years in the Academy, or in study with Plato, and left apparently well satisfied with his academic experience. A short course of intermediate quality could not have retained Aristotle for so long, but for most students the course was much shorter. Still, the course must have been more extensive than the Sophists' and longer, too, than Isocrates'.[71]

A word should be added on materials of instruction; little more than a word can be said. Real models were probably used for classification, if we accept the amusing story told by the comic poet Epicrates, and when they were not available the furnishings of the school were pressed into service. But this was the lighter side of the instructional program. What was the context in which geometry and arithmetic were taught? Geometry was the mathematical study par excellence, and arithmetic, lifted above the commercial level of keeping accounts, followed at a respectable distance. Geometric reasoning is centered on intellectual figures and proceeds with an extreme distrust of anything bearing on sense experience. This geometric approach was popularized by Euclid (330–275 B.C.) and was applied in the Academy. The geometry studied by Plato's students was comprised of theorems, with their attendant proofs based on a number of original definitions, axioms, and postulates. The logic of the proofs and their purely rational character were emphasized. The problems were purely speculative and did not touch practical applications involving numbers or calculations of surfaces or volumes. Such practical application may have been appropriate for future surveyors, contractors, engineers, or masons, but it was judged to be outside the boundaries of liberal education and foreign to the realm of mathematics proper. The same attitude applied to arithmetic. It was a theory of whole numbers disdaining the problems of real life; properties of whole numbers, odds and evens, were studied. Distinctions were made between prime numbers and the product of these numbers, between equal and unequal numbers, multiples and submultiples, superpartials and sub-superpartials. To these were added ratios and means, and finally what can be called arithmology—mysticism of number or, in a Christian setting, a theology of numbers. Perhaps the Academy course was fuller than

---

[71] W. B. Ready, "Plato and the Essential Education," *Education*, 68 (September, 1947), pp. 11–15; and George Kennedy, *The Art of Persuasion in Greece* (Princeton, N.J., Princeton University Press, 1963), pp. 18–22.

we at first supposed. It may have been demanding enough to keep young men at their desks for nine years.

Students lived a good life in Plato's school, where few opportunities were lost to cultivate their aristocratic tendencies. They were encouraged to share actively in the social-intellectual life of the school; to have done otherwise would have ill-befitted bright young men. The Academy had no disciplinary problems; the only regulations were those relative to the use of wine at dinners, and these dinners were both culinary and intellectual marvels. Plato's Academy was a place for learning; it was also a place for living.

❧ 4 ❧

Quintilian: The Rebirth of Literary Humanism

I

LIFE AND WORK

If we begin by looking for something unique in Quintilian's life and work, we are struck by the fact of his rise in Rome to a position of pedagogical supremacy without being a Roman at all. He was born in the picturesque town of Callagurris in northern Spain about A.D. 35. Like the early lives of other great men, about which we should like to know more, Quintilian's childhood and early adolescent years were spent in relative obscurity. Almost nothing is recorded about his primary or secondary schooling [1] or the environment for learning in this Spanish setting. The economic circumstances of his family are also in doubt, although his father, it is said, was an important teacher of rhetoric whose reputation was recognized from Spain to Rome.[2] But nothing very definite can be inferred from this claim, for rhetoricians of good repute were often poor men, though some were rich and powerful.

The historical record of Quintilian's early years becomes clearer after his first journey to Rome. By then he was about fifteen or sixteen years old and was perhaps drawn to Rome by attractions that influence so many young men to leave the vicinity of their birth: opportunity and adventure. Spain then was a Roman province, so there was nothing ex-

[1] Quintilian's *grammaticus,* or secondary-school teacher, is alleged to have been Remmius Palaemon, a man of unusual reputation in Rome (Suetonius, *Of Grammarians and Rhetors,* 23, 2; 3, 4.) In *Suetonius,* translated by J. C. Rolfe, Loeb Classical Library (Cambridge, Mass., Harvard University Press, 1920), vol. II, *Lives of Illustrious Men*). But even if this item is factual, it does not illuminate the record of his early education, although we might be justified in assuming that his secondary schooling followed conventional patterns. See W. M. Smail, *Quintilian on Education* (Oxford, Clarendon Press, 1938), p. vi.; and Tom B. Jones, *The Silver-Plated Age* (Sandoval, New Mexico, Coronado Press, 1962), pp. 41–42.

[2] See H. E. Butler, *Quintilian* (Cambridge, Mass., Loeb Classical Library, Harvard University Press, 1922), Introduction, I, p. vii.

traordinary about Quintilian's seeking political or academic preferment in the vast potentialities of the Eternal City. In any case, shortly after his arrival in Rome he became associated with Domitius Afer.[3]

The nature of Quintilian's attachment to Domitius Afer is imprecisely known: he may have been a *famulus*—a tutor or high-grade servant; or the relationship may have been a pederastic one, common in Greek societies but rare in Rome. We are nearer the truth when we recognize the association as one of pupil to teacher and an authentic continuation of an old and respected Roman teaching tradition. Cicero explains this tradition and relates something of the nature of his early education: he tells how he was assigned to an old and trusted friend of the family to be trained for public life.[4] The Roman system of education made the family, principally the father and mother, responsible for elemental education. Mothers were concerned with moral formation in its earliest stages and, thus, because the first years of education were critical for moral development, may have been the most important teachers. When the child's maturity made it less likely that the mother's influence would be felt so keenly, the superintendence of a boy's formation was assumed by his father. He lived, worked, listened to, and traveled with his father, and following this informal regimen it was hoped that few opportunities for training, adventure, or simply exposure to public life would be missed. No law required fathers to supplement their educational resources, but a solid tradition recommended that other teachers take their turn at training before the boy was deposited on the threshold of public life. Old and trusted friends, or perhaps relatives, were recruited to help prepare young men for life in political society. No term was set for this apprenticeship. A young man could remain with his older mentor as long as he wanted, or as long as the mentor would have him, or until the death of one or the other. Cicero's apprenticeship lasted eight years and was interrupted only by the death of his teacher. It should be noted that the man who assumed the responsibility of preparing a boy for public life was not a teacher in the conventional sense. He may have been a lawyer, a physician, an engineer, or a merchant. Whatever his profession, the boy attached to him lived with and learned from him and accompanied him along the various avenues opening on public life. Whether or not any syllabus of law or public philosophy was available to which a serious mentor might expose his younger charge is a moot question. In our more literate age we have come to accept the written word as commonplace, and it is hard to imagine a course of study preliminary to

---

3 Domitius was a distinguished Roman rhetorician and lawyer, and from all accounts was admirably equipped to guide a young man toward public life. See Smail, *op. cit.*, p. vi; but the best witness is Quintilian himself: *Institutio Oratoria*, IV, ii, 86; VII, ii, 5; ii, 24; IX, ii, 73.

4 Cicero, *de Am.*, 1; *Brut.*, 306; and Aubrey Gwynn, *Roman Education from Cicero to Quintilian* (London, Oxford University Press, 1926), pp. 64–66.

public life being totally devoid of literary content. But if we understand the prescriptive role of Roman tradition we know, despite the undeniable claims of literary education, why literary training could have been ignored. In any case, whatever the content of the course, and whatever the length of time needed to master it, we are quite certain that Domitius Afer was to Quintilian what any other Roman citizen was to a boy he had taken as a protégé. No other interpretation is necessary, nor would any other seem appropriate.

Cicero's apprenticeship to public life was interrupted by the death of his teacher, and here there is a striking parallel between the lives of Cicero and Quintilian; Quintilian remained with his teacher—the guide, philosopher, and friend—until Afer's death in A.D. 58. Quintilian's course under this famous man could have extended to eight years; in any case, it went beyond the two years recommended by conventional practice. When Quintilian lost his teacher he returned to Spain, where he remained for about eight years. The Chronicle of Jerome confidently puts Quintilian back in Rome in A.D. 68.[5] We need not be preoccupied with the chronology of these events, for they are not especially important. Quintilian is in Rome again, and now, at age thirty-three, he appears to be fully prepared to assume the mantle of a teacher of rhetoric.

Details are lacking relative to Quintilian's preparation for teaching, at a time when teachers were too often indifferent to the skill and learning they brought to their profession. Rome followed the code of Classical and Hellenistic education in believing an elementary teacher was qualified if he could read. The preparation for secondary-school teachers was not much better, nor were the announced qualifications much higher, although some knowledge of grammar was usually indispensable. But even here the handbook was a crutch available to the least worthy; students could be put to work memorizing rules and literature, and both protected the ignorant schoolmaster. All teachers—good or bad—had to work in the context of this teaching tradition. Excellence too often went unrewarded and unrecognized.[6]

The motivation driving a young man forward toward the teaching profession, when the profession seemed to have so little to offer and so little to recommend it, is obscure. In Quintilian's case we suspect he was motivated by tradition and the opportunity to follow in the footsteps of his father; besides he had been in touch with good teachers and illustrious men who had a rhetorical background. Even if the Spanish town of his birth could not offer the kind of study he needed to prepare himself for a career in rhetoric, he had the tuition of his father, whose ministrations must have compensated for any lack of general opportunity for

[5] Gwynn, *op. cit.*, p. 181.

[6] See F. G. Kenyon, *Books and Readers in Ancient Greece and Rome* (New York, Oxford University Press, 1932).

study. When he arrived in Rome in A.D. 68 he was prepared to teach; almost at once he must either have opened a school or tutored students, because in the relatively short space of four years—and only thirty-seven years old—he had achieved enough distinction to be considered for the state chair of Latin rhetoric, to which Vespasian appointed him in A.D. 72.

The temptation to delve into the qualities of Roman rhetoric (which was not really Roman, but Greek rhetoric all over again) is one we shall have to resist. It is doubtful that such a discussion would illuminate Quintilian's theories of education.[7] But we should say that Quintilian assumed, following Cicero, the impossibility of a discrete non-Greek rhetoric. When Cicero and Quintilian shaped rhetoric for Latin's use, they did nothing more than translate Greek rhetoric for application to Latin. Quintilian even distrusted translation, believing no doubt something would be lost; he was content to use Greek words themselves.[8]

The search for imposing Roman educational figures brings the historian quickly to Quintilian; because of his great influence on later education he must be given an unchallenged place in the vanguard of Latin educational theorists and practitioners. It is doubtful that anyone—even Cicero—could match him. By holding the state chair of rhetoric for more than twenty years, he demonstrated dramatically his great stature as a teacher. And we marvel not only at his longevity in a position for which competition was keen and hazardous, but at his income from teaching as well. While the multiple difficulties in interpreting the real value of Quintilian's income must be recognized, tradition, nevertheless, gives him first place among the world's teachers. His annual salary, in today's terms, some say, surpassed $40,000, but this is extravagant; his actual annual income from teaching was probably one-tenth of that.[9]

After twenty years of teaching, and not yet an old man, Quintilian was ready to retire; perhaps his good income over the years plus the

[7] The evolution of Latin rhetoric and its bondage to Greek rhetoric are treated in a delightful book by Jones, *op. cit.*, pp. 37–59; see also, D. L. Clark, *op. cit.*; M. L. Clarke, *op. cit.*; and Moses Hadas, *History of Latin Literature* (New York, Columbia University Press, 1952).

[8] This imitation of Greek rhetoric often gave Latin rhetoric an unrealistic character. Rules that were meaningful and useful in Greek rhetoric were transferred to Latin rhetoric even when they had no application to Latin. See H. Nettleship, *The Study of Latin Grammar among the Romans in the First Century A.D.*, Lectures and Essays, Second Series (London, Oxford University Press, 1895), pp. 144–171; Marrou, *op. cit.*, p. 281; and Edward J. Power, *Main Currents in the History of Education* (New York, McGraw-Hill Book Company, Inc., 1962), pp. 140–141.

[9] Smail refers to a salary of 900 pounds supplemented by gifts from grateful students (*op. cit.*, p. vi). We know from Quintilian (*op. cit.*, IV, i, 19) that he was also engaged in pleading before the courts. This is further attested to in the commentaries of Juvenal and Martial. Quintilian must have tried to avoid the ivory tower and the ·dangers inherent in it. For a broader view of Roman teachers' salaries see R. P. Robinson, "The Roman Schoolteacher and His Reward," *Classical Weekly*, XV (1921), pp. 57–61.

pressures of high-level teaching made retirement all the more attractive. At any rate, he withdrew from active teaching, apparently to live a life of leisure and contemplation. But his leisure was short lived. Friends importuned him to write an educational guide or textbook containing advice for them to follow in the education of their own children. This was not the first appeal, nor yet the last, for a pedagogical handbook, and Quintilian's format for explaining educational theory was the format adopted by most, if not all, humanist educational writers from the fourteenth to the sixteenth centuries.[10]

He performed his commission with consideration and care, not unmindful that his two sons could benefit from his prescriptions, but he could not follow his own advice to writers. He had said that a manuscript when finished should be laid aside for ten years. If, after ten years, its merits were evident, it should be published. If, however, the aging process kindled doubt about its quality, it should then be banished to the caskets of oblivion. After more than two years of preparation and revision (he could not afford the ten-year wait), Quintilian was ready to show the work to his friends. They must have been overwhelmed at the breadth of this magnum opus; it was much more than a simple guide to the education of a friend's child; it purported to be a discussion of the multiple issues surrounding teaching and learning from a child's birth to his final formation as an accomplished orator.[11] The masterpiece was entitled *Institutio Oratoria,* or *Education of an Orator.*

II

THE ENVIRONMENT FOR TEACHING

Quintilian begins at the beginning with preliminary studies or those most appropriately followed at home. References to the first years of education and training are found throughout Book I of the *Education of an Orator.* Conventional practices in Rome, having by now reformed the archaic tradition that assigned to mothers the role of infant teaching, allowed parents the luxury of delegating infant education and training

10 E. R. Curtius, *European Literature and the Latin Middle Ages* (New York, Harper and Row, Publishers, 1963), pp. 436 ff., indicates the merits of Quintilian's plan of literary instruction and shows how his method of teaching literature influenced the writers of the Middle Ages. Bolgar, *op. cit.,* pp. 31–37, while agreeing that Quintilian's influence should not be ignored, argues that important departures were made from Quintilian's literary code.

11 Quintilian, *op. cit.,* preface, 4–9. In addition to responding favorably to his friends' request, Quintilian wanted to put his thoughts on education before the public in an authentic treatise. Two works attributed to him were in circulation, and, although based on his lectures, were actually published by some of his students. These works did not meet with his approval.

to nurses. Thus, the nurse was a teacher during a most critical time of formation; it is but natural that Quintilian should have concerned himself with her qualifications. And he could argue, because the nurse was the child's first teacher, for greater care in her selection than in the selection of any other teacher. Nurses, of course, were not responsible for literary education—the principal avenue to intellectual culture—but they had an immensely important position in laying foundations for it: in Quintilian's theory moral virtue came before and was the bedrock of intellectual development.

Although parents had relinquished to nurses their day-to-day function as moral teachers—and even if they were not conscious of having done so the fact that nurses were almost constantly with the children made it clear that their influences would prevail—Quintilian was not prepared to write an educational constitution justifying or acknowledging parental abdication from the sphere of moral teaching. He is at pains to emphasize the role of the nurse, but he is also vitally concerned with parental qualifications and responsibilities for shaping a man's moral life. We approach Quintilian's statements on parental qualifications with some misgivings, for with attitudes generated out of our own experiences, we are unable to see how these qualifications could, first, be set and, second, complied with. Within the context of his time he must have seen some possibility of regulating marriage choices to the end where only those couples capable of educating children properly would be authorized to procreate them. None of the machinery for accomplishing such a herculean feat is revealed however, and we are left helplessly to wonder whether Quintilian was expressing only a pious hope. However, Quintilian was a realist and we would be surprised to learn that he was only toying with our minds. Because Quintilian's remarks on this point are sketchy, we are left with the precise knowledge only that he wanted to emphasize parental responsibility; even if the parents did not themselves become pedagogues, they were always to be superintendents of the educational process.

If it is too much to expect parents to be with their children always, and if nurses, too, must release them for free play, then there are times when boys are left to themselves. But these free hours reserved supposedly for leisure and recreation are often as formative as the hours spent in learning the intellectual lessons of the schoolmaster or the moral lessons of the pedagogue. They must not be left unguarded; for the first time in the theory of education place is given to the guidance of informal learning where the principal textbooks are a boy's companions. We note that Quintilian says nothing about the care of girls and in ignoring them he confirms a precedent and sets a course that is honored for the next thousand years. But he does have a great deal to say about the education of boys—the whole of the treatise is devoted to them—and at this point he wants parents and nurses to weigh the qualifications of a boy's companions. Just what guardians of youth were to look for in playmates is unclear, but the admonition is definite: the informal contacts of a boy are to be subject to a detailed and constant scrutiny. To neglect this is to run the risk of having the good instruction of the home undermined on the playground; to attend to it carefully is to guarantee that moral values inculcated at home will be strengthened by life's daily contacts. Perhaps many educators before Quintilian realized the significance of informal education, but none before him had set the theoretical foundation for the environment for moral education so precisely.

The role of parents and nurses in directing the education of the young belongs naturally enough under the general heading of early home training, and early home training is two-sided. One side is moral, the foundation for which Quintilian is interested in laying carefully; inculcation of knowledge is the other. We understand Quintilian's determination to integrate these two sides when we recall his educational aim—the perfect orator. Quintilian says "the first essential for such an one is that he should be a good man, and consequently we demand of him not merely the possession of exceptional gifts of speech, but of all the excellences of character as well." [12]

In Chapters two and three we listened to spokesmen for moral education, and by now we are sensitive both to the order and meaning of this formation. Men, Isocrates argued, are good after they assimilate their intuitive knowledge of virtue; but Plato was unconvinced by this. He maintained that knowledge of virtue was the product of long, arduous, and profound study. For his part, Quintilian puts moral philosophy at a discount. He does not believe education can produce a good man, and he tends to discredit philosophy: "For I will not admit that the principles of upright and honorable living should, as some have held, be regarded as the peculiar concern of philosophy." [13] Because of Isocrates' great influence on Quintilian, which Quintilian himself acknowledges,[14] we find the latter echoing the counsel of the most famous schoolmaster of antiquity when he asserts that the ideal orator is the only person who can make a genuine claim to the title of philosopher. Before formal training in oratory begins, Quintilian maintains, young men should be habituated to the arts of right living; and this habituation comes more from practice than from learning. Again the importance of home education is emphasized and the dual roles of parents and nurses are accentuated.

Quintilian has been accused of aiming too high by establishing the development of a perfect orator as the goal for the educational program. Certainly his aim is high but its height is mitigated somewhat when we

12 *Ibid.,* I, i, 9.
13 *Ibid.,* I, i, 10.
14 *Ibid.,* II, xv, 4.

understand that, while perfect eloquence is a goal not beyond the reach of
the human intellect, this goal is seldom attained. He justified setting such
a goal as follows: "those whose aspirations are highest, will attain to
greater heights than those who abandon themselves to premature despair
of ever reaching the goal and halt at the very foot of the ascent." [15]

Level of aspiration is supremely important to Quintilian, but it must
not be allowed to remain a point of pure theory. The ideal of excellence
must be communicated to boys from the start, and nurses and parents, if
they are good educators, will never permit a boy to forget it. In his
discussion of early home training Quintilian admonishes fathers to conceive the highest hopes for their sons from the moment of their birth.
These high hopes will inspire fathers to exert extraordinary care in planning and directing the son's education. In Quintilian's code boys do not
lack ability to master the various arts involved in oratory; they lack care.
Thus Plato's preoccupation with an aristocracy of talent is shelved, and
Quintilian asserts his lack of confidence in the assumption that only a few
men have the capacity to profit from advanced education, or that the
majority of men are so retarded as to render higher education for them a
waste of time and effort. Quintilian preaches the doctrine of optimism
and contends that teachers will find most boys quick to reason and ready
to learn. Curiosity and willingness to learn are instinctive attributes of
youth, and boys always show promise of many accomplishments until
faulty pedagogy causes natural talent to atrophy and innate curiosity to
disappear. These deplorable demonstrations of wasted youth are not
dictated by depravity of natural gifts but by a lack of care.

Care is exercised principally by nurses and parents. The conventions
of Roman society may have made the nurse's position more important
than the parents'. At any rate, Quintilian is on sure footing when he
identifies the nurse as the first person the child hears, and because children are both imitative and impressionable they will retain best what
they learn first. While good impressions appear to have a certain
permanence, poor or bad impressions are even more durable. Quintilian
strengthens his stand by affirming that although what is good readily
deteriorates, no one can convert vice into virtue.[16] And what can be said
of vice and virtue on the level of moral formation can also be said about
correctness and incorrectness in style of speech. Quintilian would never
allow a boy to become accustomed, even in his most infant years, to a
style of incorrect speech that subsequently would have to be unlearned.
The assumption is evident: relearning is more difficult than learning.
Although he does not go into detail on the quality or breadth of a nurse's
education, we know that she is supposed to be a well-educated person. He
is likewise somewhat imprecise about the qualities of parental education,

[15] *Ibid.,* I, i, 20.
[16] *Ibid.,* I, i, 5.

although he admits a desire to see parents as highly educated as possible, and he is not thinking only of fathers. To go beyond fathers is strange and somewhat novel in this educational age, and the point is not pressed by Quintilian. He would have been uneasy as a champion for the education of women, and he was not. Yet, it may be argued, he was fully aware of the role mothers played in the formation of their children and he wanted some development of their intelligence, although this development may have fallen short of the best formal education.[17]

Even parents who themselves did not have a good education should not for that reason neglect their son's education; they should recognize their weakness and devote their best energies in those areas where good example is crucial. The thought here is good, though realization may have been difficult. It is hard to explain how an uneducated parent, although he may appreciate the importance of education, can involve himself intimately in the educational process. It is a monumental task for even the best-educated parents.[18]

Quintilian, as we have noted, set as his object the education of the perfect orator; without involving ourselves in detail we can perhaps delineate the general approaches selected to achieve that end.[19] The first book of the *Education of an Orator* dealt with preliminary education, preliminary to the school of rhetoric, and treated of infant education in the home, moral teaching under the supervision of parents and nurses, and the teaching responsibilities of the grammar master. With the latter the boy began his first schooling. In his discussion of preliminary education, Quintilian calls our attention to the duties and qualifications of parents and nurses—these are points that bear repetition because of the importance attached to them—and moved forward in his analysis to the duties and qualifications of the grammar master, the introduction of lessons in Greek, the teaching of the alphabet and handwriting, and the preparation of lessons for strengthening memory.

The only one of these items that needs brief annotation here—the

---

[17] It is plainly impossible to give all the background here, but it is important to know that Quintilian was reflecting deep respect for Rome's past by trying to perpetuate some of its most honored educational traditions. For pictures of education in Roman society, see Woody, *op. cit.*, pp. 503–509; M. Rostovtzeff, *The Social and Economic History of the Roman Empire* (London, Oxford University Press, 1926), pp. 33 ff.; J. Carcopino, *Daily Life in Ancient Rome* (New Haven, Yale University Press, 1941); Ludwig Friedlander, *Roman Life and Manners under the Early Empire*, 4 vols. (London, George Routledge and Sons, Ltd., 1908–1913); and we should not neglect E. Jullien, *Les Professeurs de Littérature dans l'Ancienne Rome* (Paris, Ernest Leroux, 1885), whose book on Roman education is as comprehensive and definitive as Gwynn's *Roman Education from Cicero to Quintilian*. Gwynn's title is somewhat misleading because he devotes almost one third of his book to Quintilian.

[18] See G. Kennedy, "An Estimate of Quintilian," *American Journal of Philology,* XXXXII (1962), pp. 130–146.

[19] E. Brandenburg, "Quintilian and the Good Orator," *Quarterly Journal of Speech*, XXXIV (February, 1948), pp. 23–29.

others may be taken care of in a subsequent general treatment—is the introduction of Greek. Doubtless the modern reader is surprised at finding Greek a curricular entry so early in the educational program, and when the surprise wears away he is reminded that contemporary foreign language programs in the elementary school are not authentic evidences of curricular revolution. The pattern for teaching Greek in the elemental program recommended by Quintilian was not in every detail a prophetic anticipation of contemporary foreign language teaching in elementary schools. In the first place—perhaps the significant difference is found here—Greek was not sharing a place with Latin, the vernacular, but it completely preempted Latin teaching. In the first four or five years of schooling Greek was the only language taught, and Latin, because it was the language of the street had to wait its turn.[20] In the second place, Romans, largely because of their feelings of cultural inferiority, were preoccupied with Greek; it opened avenues to Greek literature and thus to the recognized core of Greek culture. Their preoccupation dictated preferential treatment for Greek. No such rationale supports contemporary programs; although when the cultural justification is advanced for them, it is mere broadening that is sought, and desires for this greater breadth are not generated by inferiority complexes. Given the reasons why Greek was important to Romans, it was easy for Quintilian to justify a Greek-first practice: it was simply easier for teachers to teach Greek, and for boys to learn it, if they did not at the same time have to contend with the grammatical mysteries of their native tongue.[21]

Book two proceeds to schools of rhetoric and, in addition to an explanation of the rudiments of rhetoric, handles teaching issues broadly related to the teaching of rhetoric.[22] The book is fairly general, and

---

[20] Quintilian, *Inst. Ora.,* I, i, 12–14.

[21] The language question—bilingualism and all its aspects—is not only large but extremely important in Roman education. Quintilian, again, is not a frontiersman but is perpetuating a tested tradition. Because of the centrality of this issue, the following authors who treat it are recommended: A. S. Wilkins, *Roman Education* (Cambridge, Cambridge University Press, 1905); Gwynn, *op. cit.,* pp. 34–58; William Barclay, *Educational Ideals in the Ancient World* (London, William Collins Sons & Co., Ltd., 1959); Marrou, *op. cit.,* pp. 255–273; J. W. Mackail, *Latin Literature* (New York, Charles Scribner's Sons, 1923), pp. 197–204; and William A. Smith, *Ancient Education* (New York, Philosophical Library, Inc., 1955), pp. 150–196. All this attention in formal teaching was given to a Roman elite. In spite of a general lack of sensitivity to the needs of non-aristocrats, F. F. Abbott, *The Common People of Ancient Rome* (New York, Charles Scribner's Sons, 1911), p. 176, believes the average citizen was probably literate. For another side, see S. L. Mohler, "Slave Education in the Roman Empire," *Transactions of the American Philological Association,* 71 (1940), pp. 262–280.

[22] *Inst. Ora.,* II, ii–iv. Our general willingness to believe that Quintilian was a broad educational thinker is contested by F. H. Colson, *Quintiliani Institutionis Oratoriae,* Liber I (Cambridge, Cambridge University Press, 1924), p. xxv, when he writes that Quintilian's book is not a whole treatise on education, or even a book on how to teach rhetoric, but a treatise on rhetoric. Although not stressing the narrowness of Quintilian's approach to education, Hermann Weimer, *Concise History of Education*

because it avoids the technical problems connected with rhetorical teaching and centers on general questions of teaching and learning may be read with profit by the contemporary student of education. Books three through eleven almost swamp us in the rhetorical apparatus and are so encumbered with technicalities that to explore them carefully would require the motivation of an antiquarian. The discussion centers on necessary qualifications for the professional rhetorician: invention, arrangement, eloquence, memory, and delivery. Rule and rationale are offered in great detail, for Quintilian is certain that the syllabus of rhetoric so far developed, one mainly Greek in origin, could be communicated but could not be improved. Moreover, he honored the ancient dictum of Hellenistic pedagogy, to make haste slowly and to leave nothing out. In the twelfth book he treats of oratorical rules, the ways of preparing and pleading cases in the courts or the assembly, styles of eloquence most appropriate on various occasions, the time for the orator to withdraw from public life, and the studies and occupations best suited to the solitude of retirement.[23]

In his review of the ancient literature on pedagogy, from which he admits learning a great deal, he finds that writers too often refuse to talk about methods of teaching.[24] Apparently they consider technique too pedestrian a subject to command their attention. They could not have thought it inconsequential, although we know that Plato was convinced of the capacity of a good mind to rise above particular techniques. Quintilian does not eschew method, nor does he regard a discussion of its application beside the point in his classic analysis of teaching and learning. Thus in the twelve books, and usually as a corollary to the content under examination, methods of teaching are recommended, explained, and evaluated. He is intent on revealing methods of teaching which will enable students to acquire a knowledge of the art of oratory, an understanding of the laws of rhetoric, and a general facility that will nourish their powers of speech and eloquence. It is only fair to say that he tries to avoid the usual results of textbook study, especially of textbooks on rhetoric, which led to, or aimed at, excessive detail in learning and thus

from Solon to Pestalozzi (New York, Philosophical Library, Inc., 1962), chap. two, argues that Quintilian's theory of education lacks high purpose. He believes that Quintilian stayed on the safe level of considering an individual's education and technical problems of instruction and that he avoided the basic issues in education vis-à-vis the state because the Roman emperors would have been displeased with any theory of education aimed at state reform. Not pushing the point quite as far, but making it nonetheless, is K. Price, *Education and Philosophical Thought*, second edition (Boston, Allyn and Bacon, Inc., 1967), pp. 82–83.

23 *Inst. Ora.*, XII, iii, viii, ix, x, xi, 21–24; see E. P. Parks, *The Roman Rhetorical Schools as a Preparation for the Courts Under the Early Empire* (Baltimore, The Johns Hopkins Press, 1945).

24 *Inst. Ora.*, II, v. See also, Merle M. Odgers, "Quintilian's Use of Earlier Literature," *Classical Philology*, 28 (July, 1933), pp. 182–188.

impaired or crippled all the nobler elements of style. It is a question of balance, emphasis, and goal, for we are quite certain that Quintilian was not leading a crusade to expurgate the rhetorical syllabus. Detail was important to him, but it was not an obsession. According to Quintilian, the dry bones of learning offered in pedantic instruction only exhausted the life blood of imagination and made formal study barren and almost unbearable. Quintilian hopes his recommended methods will have flesh on them for kindling the imagination; his methodological theory seeks to rescind the precedents followed by most teachers of rhetoric.[25] His goal is high and his conception of rhetoric is broad; and as this conception is translated into a volume of twelve books, we come face to face with a brief but effective demonstration of everything potentially useful in the formation of an orator.

Before looking at the precise elements of his teaching techniques and their application to curricula, we should present his views on two issues that always had a relationship to a general theory of education. One pertains to the age for beginning formal schooling, the other weighs the relative merits of public or private instruction. Classical Greek education had not questioned the conventional wisdom that made age seven the beginning school age, nor had its most illustrious representatives ever felt compelled to formulate a theoretical basis for the determination of a schooling age. This could hardly have been an oversight, for the best Greek minds converged on pedagogy to handle even less important details in their own way. What they did not include, we may conclude, was rejected. Even Plato assumed that seven was the age for introducing the child to formal education, and he showed greater willingness than any of his colleagues to question or depart from standard practices. Yet in Plato's utopian plan for education there were provisions for infant, or what we call kindergarten, education, although this plan, it should be noted, was never put to a pragmatic test. The Romans tried to be true to their educational past and to preserve worthy and respected traditions, but when a beginning-school age was in question they were willing to follow their Greek models. Despite Quintilian's determination to preserve national traditions, and to graft Greek practices to them, he was not adamant in his allegiances to either. In his best moments he could remonstrate with the educational inheritance and be tantalized by the possibility of beginning formal education for some students before age seven, and he could question the dogmatic assumption that before seven youth can neither endure the strain of learning nor profit from instruction.

The practice of allowing a child's mind to lie fallow until a certain magic age is mildly resisted; children, Quintilian says, who are capable of

25 Merle M. Odgers, "Quintilian's Rhetorical Predecessors," *Transactions of the American Philological Association*, 65 (1935), pp. 25–36.

profiting from moral training in the conventional preschool years should also be capable of mastering the elements of literary education. During these infant years instruction may be absorbed slowly and imperfectly—and note is taken of opinions doubting the efficacy of results obtained from such early efforts and expenditures of energy—but a clear warning is inserted against despising or despairing of even limited progress and partial mastery. Quintilian's admonition is expressed this way: "Though the knowledge absorbed in the previous years may mean but little, yet the boy will be learning something more advanced during that year, in which he would otherwise have been occupied with something more elementary." [26] Wasting the earliest years of youth cannot be justified, and excuses for withholding instruction because of age are hard to find and harder to defend, especially when we follow Quintilian's rationale: elemental literary education is almost exclusively mnemonic, and the memory faculty of the young is exceptionally retentive.[27]

Next we come to the place for teaching. "This therefore is the place to discuss the question as to whether it is better to have the boy educated privately at home or hand him over to some large school and to those whom I may call public instructors." [28] Eminent authorities, beginning with Aristotle,[29] had defended the superiority of public instruction; they detected a social dimension to learning and thought it could be pursued best in a school where boys had direct social and intellectual contacts with their fellows. A political consideration was involved also: young men learning in concert would become more profoundly attuned to their patriotic duties and the nature of the national state.

Many good witnesses could be summoned from the history of education to testify against Quintilian and thus put private (tutorial) instruction in a more favorable light. Quintilian does not ignore these authorities. He notes the special virtue his predecessors attached to private education and permits them to talk about the two most serious faults of public teaching. First, they opposed public education because it contained potential threats to morality, and these threats, they said, were most critical in the early years of schooling, when boys often were at the mercy of immoral public teachers. Athenian legislators had enacted laws to protect the morals of youth in their relationships with primary schoolmasters. We know that one of the principal reasons for the existence of Greek pedagogues—moral, not intellectual, masters—was to supervise young men as they traveled to and from school and to wait within shouting distance of the primary school ready to respond to a summons for help

26 Quintilian, *Inst. Ora.*, I, i, 18.
27 *Ibid.*, I, i, 19.
28 *Ibid.*, I, ii, 1.
29 Thomas Davidson, *Aristotle and Ancient Educational Ideals* (New York, Charles Scribner's Sons, 1892) , pp. 214–224.

in resisting temptations posed by or advances of the primary masters. If the public teacher was not a good man, it would be difficult to see how he could be an instrument for forming virtuous character. History hardly supports Quintilian in doubting the greater security of students' morals when in the custody of private masters, and he was forced to acknowledge public teaching's flagrant violations of the people's trust. The second objection is somewhat less serious and can be posed more easily. It arises out of the contention that a teacher who must devote attention to several pupils will not teach them as well as if he were responsible for only one.

Quintilian can answer the first objection himself:

> It is held that schools corrupt the morals. It is true that this is sometimes the case. But morals may be corrupted at home as well. There are numerous instances of both, as there are also of the preservation of a good reputation under either circumstance. The nature of the individual boy and the care devoted to his education makes all the difference. Given a natural bent toward evil or negligence in developing and watching over modest behavior in early years, private tutelage will provide equal opportunity for wrong doing. The teacher employed at home may be of bad character, and there is just as much danger in associating with bad slaves as there is with immodest companions of good birth. On the other hand, if the bent is toward virtue, and parents are not afflicted with a blind and torpid indifference, it is possible to choose a teacher of the highest character (and those who are wise will make this their first object), to adopt a method of education of the strictest kind and at the same time to attach some respectful man or faithful freed man to their son as his friend and guardian, that his unfailing companionship may improve the character even of those who gave rise to apprehension.[30]

With this statement Quintilian believes he has stilled the fears of advocates of private education who saw morality undermined in public teaching, and he focuses attention next on the issue of instructional efficiency. There may be prophetic anticipations in his remarks, although the method of simultaneous instruction is still well over the educational horizon, for in Quintilian's discourse we think we see the germ of an idea that later brought this method into full bloom. Quite clearly this great Roman master prefers the broad daylight of a respectable school to the solitude and obscurity of private tutoring.[31] With views formed largely by his Roman experience, he argues that the best teachers are always anxious to have large classes; they judge their skill and learning worthy of huge audiences. Inferior teachers, however, suspecting their own de-

[30] Quintilian, *Inst. Ora.*, I, ii, 4–5.
[31] *Ibid.*, I, ii, 10.

fects, reconcile themselves to teaching a single pupil and become, on the level of practice, not masters but pedagogues. In addition, Quintilian wants us to realize that a good teacher must be a superior technician if purpose and direction in learning are to be given to large numbers of pupils. He does not believe a teacher's time is used wisely in directing one pupil; moreover, he believes a good teacher with only one pupil is wasting his talent.[32] Besides, the variations among subjects are taught more effectively to a class. Both stimulation for the teacher and opportunity for students to learn are greater in group learning; Quintilian does not want teachers to overlook the learning outcomes from the friction of mind on mind possible only in public teaching. Finally, Quintilian expresses confidence that a good teacher will not overburden himself with pupils and that he will not try to teach more pupils than he can manage effectively.[33]

Further justifications for education in common are possible, and Quintilian advances his personal views in order to clinch the debate. When we recall his commitment to educating an orator, one who regularly will be exposed to public view, we understand why he should demand educational experiences accustoming the student to conduct himself with talent and confidence in public exercise. Neither talent in debate nor confidence for performing public duties is generated in the environment of a recluse. Again we can let Quintilian speak for himself. The future orator, he begins, must expose his mind to

> constant stimulus. Whereas retirement such as has just been mentioned induces languor and the mind becomes mildewed like things that are left in the dark, or else flies to the opposite extreme and becomes puffed up with empty conceit; for he who has no standard of comparison by which to judge his own powers will necessarily rate them too high. Again, when the fruits of his study have been displayed to the public gaze, our recluse is blinded to the sun's glare, and finds everything new and unfamiliar, for though he has learned what is required to be done in public, his learning is but the theory of a hermit. I say nothing of friendships which endure unbroken to old age having acquired the binding force of a sacred duty.[34]

The values of incidental or accidental learning are not neglected. In a school with many students boys learn not only what they are taught, but acquire things taught others as well; they hear merits praised and faults corrected and can profit when the indolence of a comrade is rebuked or his industry is commended.

---

32 *Ibid.,* I, ii, 12.
33 *Ibid.,* I, ii, 16.
34 *Ibid.,* I, ii, 18–20.

III

THE ENVIRONMENT FOR LEARNING

Consistent with the general thesis in his great handbook, Quintilian never tired of arguing that education's great object is to create or foster mental activity. Throughout the *Education of an Orator* we find him speaking of sharpening intelligence, native powers, and capacities.[35] This was a basic plank in his platform, and in later educational ages it was used to build a total teaching program. It was used, for example, in the Jesuit code of education, the *Ratio Studiorum*,[36] where an identical emphasis was put on stimulating, exciting, and sharpening mental activity, and we find contemporary educational theorists defending a similar proposition when they describe the mind as an instrument to be sharpened rather than a box to be filled.

An integral principle in his theory—one adopted by many modern ʳactices [37]—is contained in the admonition to accommodate the teach-.ʌg syllabus to a student's intellectual ability and level of interest; in other words, students' individual characteristics must be considered, for they are relevant both to methods and to objectives of teaching. The fairly modern psychological principle of apperception is here too. Without using the term itself Quintilian disclosed his keen psychological intuitions by explaining that new experiences are assimilated against a background of previous experience; and he proceeded from this valid psychological assumption to advise teachers to begin their instruction at a point which coincides with the student's achievement level. Quintilian also endorses the principle of learning readiness, but when he speaks of readiness he in no sense antedates connectionistic psychology; he is thinking, rather, of a fund of experience, which in the terminology of modern education is called "orientation" or "introduction." Quintilian is never out-of-date; he even alludes to opinions concerning the priority to be assigned to nature and nurture. And he appears to recommend teaching techniques based on the hypothesis that nurture can correct nature.[38] If Quintilian was right, and if modern educators who accept nurture as having a dominant role are also right, we should be pleased, for nurture offers some hope that the work of moral and intellectual

[35] *Ibid.*, I, ix, 26–27; i, 1–3; iii, 1–3, 10–15; II, xix, 1–3; iv, 6–8; viii, 1–5; iv, 6–8; III, ii, 1; XII, i, 19.

[36] There is considerable literature on this educational process, but the best is Allan P. Farrell, *Jesuit Code of Liberal Education* (Milwaukee, Bruce Publishing Co., 1938).

[37] M. L. Geany, "Quintilian and Modern Education," *Catholic School Journal*, XLVII (November, 1947), pp. 305–306.

[38] Quintilian, *Inst. Ora.*, II, xix, 1–3; XII, i, 19.

masters will be efficacious; if the citadel of nature is impregnable, little hope is justified. Apparently Quintilian followed Isocrates, who constructed his rhetorical theory on the foundation of natural ability; but Quintilian went beyond Isocrates to predict that training and education could correct weaknesses of nature: he believed the faculties of memory, imagination, and sense perception could be improved by study even when in original nature they were weak or poor.[39]

We have referred to Quintilian's edict about the care to be exercised in learning and how he enjoined teachers to take each item in the syllabus step by step. He honored the watchword, "make haste slowly." Neither he nor his classical predecessors ever swallowed the myth that learning is easy; they understood it as a slow, cumbersome, sometimes difficult, and arduous ordeal. And to complicate it further, part of the learning process must almost certainly involve learning how to learn. Learning how to learn is a popular concept in contemporary education and its promise has yet to be fully tested, but we should demur from acknowledging this as an entirely novel idea, for the code of discipline in learning promulgated by Quintilian, and before him by Plato and Aristotle, made learning how to learn its principal object. Perhaps we should not be satisfied with the fairly simple directions Quintilian gives. He says that a theory of learning containing a commitment to fostering mental activity has two practical dimensions: formation and information. Both are supported by the good foundation provided during the earliest stages of education. But during the more advanced stages his theory affirms the necessity of appropriate techniques for securing these two dimensions: drill, repetition, and stimulation. Drill reinforces information, as a stamping-in process, and it leads to formation because of the inevitable involvement of discipline. Stimulation comes in part from the teacher's good scholarly example and, in part, from the student's joy in learning what he does not know.

Quintilian is both eloquent and picturesque when he explains why teaching must be accommodated to the maturity of pupils. He can give his own testimony:

> If [a teacher] is engaged on the task of training unformed minds and prefers practical utility to a more ambitious program, [he must] not . . . burden his pupils at once with tasks to which their strength is unequal, but . . . curb his energies and refrain from talking over the heads of his audience. Vessels with narrow mouths will not receive liquids if too much be poured into them at a time, but are easily filled if the liquid is admitted in a gentle stream, or, it may be drop by drop; similarly you must consider how much a child's mind is capable of receiving: the things that are beyond their grasp will not enter their minds which have not opened out sufficiently to take

[39] *Ibid.*, I, x, 34–49.

them in. It is a good thing therefore that a boy should have companions whom he will desire first to imitate then to surpass: thus he will
be led to aspire to higher achievement. I would add that the instructors themselves cannot develop the same intelligence and energy
before a single listener as they can when inspired by the presence of
a numerous audience.[40]

Some commentators on Quintilian's *Education of an Orator* have
detected in it a theoretical justification for cocurricular activities.[41] They
are impressed by his attitude toward relaxation and amusement as
important devices in the education of young people. Games, he wrote,
provide a ready mirror for the character of participants. But we look in
vain if we try to find an endorsement of heavy contact sports or any
assurance that games are certain roads to character formation. They are
only one way of identifying strengths and weaknesses in character. In
countenancing the worth of sport Quintilian was not blazing a new trail;
Plato, in the *Statesman,* was able to make a similar statement: "The
natures of individuals must be tested in play . . . the teacher should
endeavor to direct the pupils' inclinations, desires and preferences, by the
help of amusements, to their final aim in life." [42] Plato reaffirms this
position in the *Laws.* The weight of Quintilian's assertion relative to the
importance of relaxation and play would not be impressive if his argument stopped here and if Plato alone could be called upon for support.
Quintilian is sensitive to the stresses and strains of serious learning and
he recognizes that recreation gives students an opportunity to regain
vigor and zeal either through intervals of rest or by a redirection or
distraction of energy. Learning activities likely to be most productive are
based on a student's good will toward his studies, and the generation of
good will remains pretty much a mystery; recreation which offers some
balance between study and play may help to engender good will. So
holidays enabling students to leave their books for extended periods are
counted to be beneficial: when they return they have greater enthusiasm
for learning. In addition to extended holidays, Quintilian recommends
brief periods of respite from work. The prescription for work and play,
however, must be administered with care: if teachers refuse to give boys a
holiday, dislike for study may result; on the other hand, if teachers are
excessively indulgent, students may become accustomed to idleness.
These points are made incisively and they are convincing. But Quintilian
has more to say; he does not want to be incomplete. Games that capitalize

40 *Ibid.,* I, ii, 27–29.
41 E. Bennett, "Ancient Schoolmaster's Message to Present-day Teachers," *Classical
Journal,* IV (February, 1909) , pp. 149–164; and C. S. Brembeck, "Talk With Quintilian,"
Journal of Teacher Education, VII (September, 1956) , pp. 195–200.
42 For amplification of this point, see R. Rusk, *Doctrines of the Greater Educators*
(New York, The Macmillan Company, 1962) , pp. 6–7; and R. C. Lodge, *Plato's Theory
of Education* (London, Routledge & Kegan Paul, Ltd., 1947) .

on the tactic of competition are given special notice; although the rules for playing these games are lacking, their object is clear. They were not contests of physical dexterity or strength but mental contests where boys quizzed one another; an informed mind and a quick and ready wit were qualities that made for excellence. But excellence was only one thing the teacher looked for, and it was not the most important thing at that. Remembering that character revealed itself in contests, the teacher observed the boys carefully to detect any bad habits. When a bad habit disclosed itself, the teacher took action at once, and his therapy was grounded on the principle that a bad habit breaks easier than it bends. Boys should be taught to act unselfishly and honestly, and self-control must be instilled; in Quintilian's school, games were laboratories for assessing and inculcating virtue. He borrows a phrase from Virgil—"so strong is custom formed in early years" [43]—to caution us against laxity in supervision of the future orator.

Quintilian couples relaxation and play with an attitude toward corporal punishment, and he thereby reveals the general temperament of his school. Schoolmasters were expected to be stern and severe; the schoolmaster who had a reputation for moderate discipline had also a reputation for mediocrity. In an age when good reputations were hard to get and easy to lose, the schoolmaster applied his almost unlimited authority to chastise with zeal and devotion. He had to be careful not to punish a free child by an undignified method, but he could live with this proscription and allow it to influence only the anatomy not the ardor of a beating. Any boy could be beaten with limitless intensity, but a free child was not to be struck in the face.

Quintilian tries to avoid all corporal punishment. His view is inspired in part by a feeling that flogging—a regular custom of the day—is fit only for slaves, and to punish a free person in this way is a form of degradation. If, moreover, a student is insensitive to instruction and ignores reproof, flogging only hardens his nature and makes him less receptive to training and education. Although these warnings are valid and are offered with genuine force, they are, nevertheless, somewhat beside the point: Quintilian is convinced that the imposition of force of any kind is really unnecessary if teachers are thorough disciplinarians and competent instructors. Beating, pain, and fear breed shame, and shame unnerves and depresses the mind and motivates the child to avoid or loathe education. Scholarly and skillful teachers understand the genuine motives of education and know that competition, commendation, attraction to the teacher's person, and interest in learning are more effective motives than any kind of corporal punishment. Discipline, that is, good order in the classroom, was understood as an instrument, not an end, of education; in Quintilian's code perverting discipline was doubly damned. Knowing

43 Quintilian, *Inst. Ora.*, I, iii, 13.

that children under the control of masters were almost helpless and easily victimized, he refused to endorse any school practice that allowed masters an unrestricted disciplinary authority over them.[44]

Quintilian opened new frontiers for educational methodology, and despite the fact that his recommendations were not at once translated to practice, these radical views on teaching and learning processes became the foundation stones for modern pedagogic techniques. Little that is now an approved part of teaching practice escaped his notice. For the first time teachers were told to study the psychological structure of pupils and to learn and then apply fundamental principles of teaching and learning. They are told, too, to probe the phenomenon of motivation and to approach it as something more than simply telling a child to learn. While a simple recommendation concerning the importance of learning may certainly stimulate students, it lacks both permanence and force. Quintilian counted most on motives generated out of the froth and foam of learning itself, and of all such motives competition caught his fancy.[45] Although we should hesitate in assigning primacy here—competition had unquestionably been used before—we can attribute to him a cohesive attitude that regarded competition as a technique for learning, and we can recognize that he was among the first educational philosophers to establish it as an educational technique of unassailable worth.

Regardless of Quintilian's attachment to the technique of competition, he knew he had not discovered the philosopher's stone of education. And his faith in this technique was not blind: students of unequal ability or educational background could not profit from competition, although students matched for maturity and ability could. Even better, a student could be enjoined to compete against his own record of achievement. Yet, there were still problems of management, for improperly used competitive techniques could distort personalities, kindle animosities among students, or breed indifference to learning. Doubtlessly Quintilian began his disquisition on competition with the assumption that potential orators would be boys with superior intellectual aptitudes, and he tended to neglect students who would not be spurred by praise, delighted with success, or ready to weep over failure.[46] If we are interested most in the education of boys of average ability, we may find Quintilian's advice incomplete, though by no means useless.

Students should be commended for their achievement, and Quintilian did not reserve commendation for the superior performance of bright children. The teacher who praises the bright boy should commend the slower learner as well, for the latter has perhaps met the limit of his

44 *Ibid.*, I, iii, 18.
45 For the context, see O. E. Nybakken, "Progressive Education in the Roman Empire," *Classical Journal,* 34 (1938–1939) , pp. 38–42.
46 Quintilian, *Inst. Ora.*, I, ii, 21–22; iii, 6–7.

ability, while the bright child frequently has not. Quintilian accepted the positive effect of praise on motive almost without question. He did not take into account what we have since learned, that praise may not always live up to its promise: it may support one successful student and distract another. Yet this was only a slight blemish on his record, and rather than focus on recommendations that are now judged incomplete, we should point to the depth of his pedagogic intuitions. He knew, for example, that praise was good even for the student who failed, and contemporary studies have confirmed his judgment on this point.

A student's attraction to the teacher as a motivational element requires some interpretation. When Quintilian introduced this point he was thinking of elementary education—the grammar school—where the relationship between teachers and pupils would have to be close. On this educational level the importance of the teacher would be magnified, for he is the principal creator of the child's learning environment and his personal qualities unquestionably affect a student's feeling for him. If we take Quintilian's remarks to mean that the best teachers should be assigned to the earliest levels of education, we understand his determination to construct teaching and learning as a progressive enterprise wherein the critical worth of teachers to students declines as students ascend the educational ladder.[47] If formal education is geared to the development of intellectual and moral autonomy, it becomes clear why freedom should be progressive, making a teacher's role less vital as the higher rungs of the educational ladder are reached. So one should be careful about taking Quintilian as an authority for the proposition that the person of the teacher is the critical force in the learning process.[48] While it may be pleasant for students to learn from someone for whom they have genuine affection, they often learn exceptionally well under the direction of capable teachers for whom they have no special liking. Attraction of the subject itself would appear to be the overriding factor generating motivation; but we have yet to learn the complete answer to the question Quintilian asked: "How is interest in a subject generated? He did not try to persuade us to downgrade scholarship or skill as imperative qualifications for the good teacher, nor does he divert us from concluding that these are the qualities most attractive to students, qualities that in the long run may have a decisive effect on motivation. If, in addition, Quintilian was affirming the delight students feel in maintaining a fraternal association with a dynamic and provocative teacher, we should be anxious to sustain him, for we know that his argument was neither ill-conceived nor narrow.

The *Education of an Orator* is permeated by the doctrine that the average child is both intelligent and eager to learn.[49] This is a valid, if

47 *Ibid.*, I, iv, 6–18.
48 *Ibid.*, I, i, 10–12.
49 *Ibid.*, I, i, 1.

optimistic, assumption—at least, there is little good evidence to contradict it—and Quintilian used it almost uncritically to substantiate his contention that whenever a boy failed in attaining his educational goals the teaching or training processes were at fault. Somewhere along the line either schools or teachers, or both, had failed to capitalize on native talent by draining or misdirecting the natural intellectual aptitudes of the student. Correlative with this assumption is the conviction that good will toward learning is necessarily an original factor. Good will may be supported and sustained by exceptional teaching but it is always present in the beginning. The best teaching takes this good will—or natural curiosity—and makes the content of the school's syllabus its object. Whether or not Quintilian was right—that students are intrinsically motivated to learn and do not learn only when bad teaching stops them —need not be debated here. But recognizing Quintilian's position is enough to lead us to the next plank in his pedagogical platform: teachers should beware of overteaching or of intervening needlessly between students and their studies. If we had a full view of present teaching practices, we would think they are not following Quintilian's code closely. But his warnings were not directed at us; he had the narrow grammarian or rhetorician in mind, the man who refused to liberate the student from either him or his handbook.[50]

Quintilian recommends a strategic withdrawal, and he cautions teachers against doing so much for their pupils that they are deprived of real opportunities for learning. Following the same tack, he asks teachers to be prudent with the technique of repetition. Earlier he had affirmed the importance of repetition as a principle of learning and advocated its constant employment, but needless repetition is deadening; it not only saps energy and curiosity, it also leads students to doubt the significance of an educational process that places a premium on teaching students things they have already mastered. Quintilian was among the first educators to recognize genuine differences among students, and he was one of the first theorists to recognize the need for a meaningful teaching response to these differences. A distinct irritant in educational practice seemed to Quintilian to be a childish treatment of mature students. This practice was demeaning, for it put a mature student in an unfavorable light with his fellows; besides, it made the educational setting less attractive and therefore undermined basic motivation.

We come next to the qualities Quintilian looked for in good teachers. He is explicit only where he directs his attention to the teacher of rhetoric, but it is fair for us to say that in dealing with qualities for teachers of rhetoric he meant to extend his terms to all teachers. Consistent with his earlier views on the importance of forming a student's character, Quintilian demands an unimpeachable character as the first requirement for the teacher. In book two, where the topic is the teacher

[50] *Ibid.*, II, i, 1–18.

of rhetoric, character has first claim on his attention, and this special emphasis is justified: "The reason which leads me to deal with this subject in this portion of my work is not that I regard character as a matter of indifference where other teachers are concerned (I have already shown how important I think it in the preceding book), but that the age to which the pupil has now attained makes the mention of this point especially necessary." [51] Boys were first exposed to the teacher of rhetoric in early adolescence and they continued with him until they were young men: in consequence, it was particularly important for the teacher's character to be above reproach and, in addition, for him to have a special talent for shaping character in young men of bold spirit. It was not sufficient, Quintilian argued, for the teacher merely to set an example of the highest personal self-control; he must also govern the behavior of his pupils by strict discipline. But we suspect from what we already know of his attitudes on discipline that Quintilian's disciplinary prescription included equal parts of moderation and strictness. His argument here gave special force to the creed that schoolmasters act *in loco parentis;* with this authentic commission teachers were raised above the level of intellectual masters and became educators in the richest meaning of the term. Quintilian's interpretation of *in loco parentis* was generous. He encouraged teachers to adopt parental attitudes and to regard themselves as agents for persons who committed children to their care. When he takes up some details of caring for young men, we should let him speak for himself:

> Let him, the teacher, be free from vice himself and refuse to tolerate it in others. Let him be strict but not austere, genial but not too familiar: for austerity will make him unpopular, while familiarity breeds contempt. Let his discourse continually turn on what is good and honorable; the more he admonishes, the less he will have to punish. He must control his temper without however shutting his eyes to faults requiring correction: his instruction must be free from affectation, his demands on his class continuous, but not extravagant. He must be ready to answer questions and put them unasked to those who sit silent. In praising the recitations of his pupils he must be neither grudging nor over-generous: the former quality will give them distaste for work, while the latter will produce a complacent self-satisfaction. In correcting faults he must avoid sarcasm and above all abuse: for teachers whose rebukes seem to imply positive dislike discourage industry. He should declaim daily himself, and what is more, without stint, that his class may take his utterances home with them.[52]

Then he returns to the subject of discipline with some practical advice about its administration. Boys in ancient schools were apparently

[51] *Ibid.,* II, ii, 2.
[52] *Ibid.,* II, ii, 5–8.

as active and restless as boys in schools today. At any rate, Quintilian found it necessary to register his disapproval of the prevailing practice of allowing boys to stand up or leap from their seats in an expression of approval or delight at what they saw or heard.[53] He wanted young men to be temperate even when manifesting profound feelings and concluded that a school discipline permitting students to render spontaneously their reactions to lectures or recitations usurped a teacher's authority and should not be countenanced. Students will learn more if they depend on the master's judgment and wait for his evaluation of an oration's effectiveness. Although the practice was common enough in Roman schools, Quintilian refused to approve student applause that was mutual and indiscriminate; he considered such actions impolite, unseemly, theatrical, and unworthy of a decently disciplined school. Such actions, moreover, were powerful foes to genuine study.

A good teacher will demand a serious atmosphere and good decorum when he calls upon students to declaim; he must insist on receiving an attentive and quiet hearing from the class when he himself takes the rostrum. To reverse the standards of acceptability would be educationally unsound: a teacher should never try to adapt his oration to the pupils' standard; their speeches must suit the standards he sets.[54]

Quintilian believed it necessary to restate cautious reminders already given parents relative to a school's ability to form morals. Besides, he has a word of advice to teachers to avoid putting boys and young men in the same class; if they are mixed the moral education of the boys may suffer. Quintilian knew how often boys were led astray by older companions and he believed in an ounce of prevention; moreover, he wanted to be sure that neither corruption nor any suspicion of it infected schools patterned after his model.[55]

When he had handled issues of teachers' qualifications and the administration of discipline, Quintilian was ready to tackle other disputed questions in education. One such question, somewhat related to a master's qualifications, seemed to plague parents when they faced the responsibility for choosing a teacher for their boy. Should they attach a boy just beginning his study of rhetoric to an eminent teacher, or should they choose an acceptable but inferior master instead? It was not unusual for parents to take the latter, assuming, no doubt, that an inferior or mediocre master was easier to understand and imitate and far more willing to involve himself in the tiresome and unglamorous duty of dwelling on rudiments than was the superior teacher. Parents were right in asking why boys should be enrolled with the best masters who charged high fees when what appeared to be the same instruction could be had

[53] *Ibid.,* II, ii, 9.
[54] *Ibid.,* II, ii, 13.
[55] *Ibid.,* II, ii, 15.

from less renowned masters at lower rates. Quintilian had an answer ready; he always recommended the most eminent teacher. He based this recommendation on the proposition that a bad start is hard to overcome; he maintained, moreover, that the responsibility for ridding students of pedagogical fault and error is exceptionally burdensome to later teachers. In a word, reteaching is harder than teaching; and he cites examples of famous teachers who demanded double fees from students who had studied under other masters. Quintilian is specific and his advice is good:

> The mistake to which I am referring is, however, twofold. First they regard these inferior teachers as adequate for the time being and are content with their instruction because they have a stomach that will swallow anything: this indifference, though blameworthy in itself, would yet be tolerable, if the teaching provided by these persons were merely less in quantity and not inferior in quality as well. Secondly, this is still a commoner delusion, they think that those who are blessed with the greatest gifts of speaking will not condescend to the more elementary details, and that consequently they sometimes disdain to give attention to such inferior subjects of study and sometimes are incapable of doing so. For my part I regard the teacher who is unwilling to attend to such details as being unworthy of the name of teacher: and as for the question of capacity, I maintain that it is the most capable man, who, given the will, is able to do this with most efficiency.[56]

The eloquent man who becomes a teacher attains excellence in the profession only when he adds prudence and judgment and a broad knowledge of teaching techniques to his oratorical ability; and even then he must be ready to descend to the pupils' level if he is to be most effective: a rapid walker walking with a small child will give the child his hand and reduce his speed to avoid moving at a pace beyond the strength or endurance of his little companion.[57] Quintilian employs this analogy to illustrate how teachers must reach for students if they are to be effective.

It is a common human experience that attainment is almost always below the goals set, yet Quintilian recommended establishing the highest goals for teaching and learning. We would not want to misinterpret him here. He did not advocate unrealistic or impossible goals, but reasonable ones set high enough to stretch the best minds. He refused to underestimate the ability or drive of young people. This doctrine, with its almost universal appeal, must always be applied prudently, but especially so when teachers are dealing with students of varying abilities. Quintilian's own teaching experiences must have been atypical, for despite his recognition of individual differences, it is unlikely that he ever taught

56 *Ibid.*, II, iii, 3–5.
57 *Ibid.*, II, iii, 7–8.

many students on the lower quartiles of capacity; yet we know he approved of teaching techniques which guaranteed to every student some degree of success.[58] He understood the importance of success and its relationship to motivation as well as we do.

Every teacher consciously or unconsciously assesses a pupil's ability as a corollary to teaching. In Quintilian's day teachers had few tools at their disposal to help them form judgments of a pupil's ability, and the tools they had, which consisted largely of mnemotechniques, lacked sophistication. Quintilian had high hopes for the boy with a good memory; in his code this was the first and surest sign of ability. And neither Quintilian nor anyone else could gainsay its standing, for in an age when neither aids to memory nor general compilations of knowledge which could have replaced a well-stocked memory were available, a highly retentive memory was exceedingly important. Orators and scholars carried their bibliographies in their minds. These conditions went a long way toward justifying Quintilian's view.

Facility in imitation was assigned second place as an index of capacity. The implication is fairly obvious: based on good mental capacity the general memory function may be improved by practice and discipline. Quintilian's position antedated any searching inquiry of general memory functions and their improvement, so he could argue with passion, and without psychological evidence opposing him, for the development of a pupil's memory. A well-stocked memory, in addition to being a catalogue of knowledge, gave students a sense of power and a feeling of self-reliance. On this memory foundation rested the entire cultural structure; and associated with it were bases for imagination and keenness of intellect. When the orator spoke or wrote, a full memory gave him factual materials, a rich vocabulary, a sense of rhythm, and style. While Quintilian was ready to believe that the capacity to remember was an endowment of nature, he never doubted the role nurture might play. And when nurture vis-à-vis memory comes into the picture the conditions which enable it to function most profitably are motivation, understanding, and concentration. First, the student must be interested in what is to be memorized; this is the motivational level. Without interest the student would not make the initial effort to memorize. Subsumed to interest, but hardly secondary in importance, the student must understand what he is asked to memorize. This emphasis on memorizing, an emphasis which must strike us as strange, was given in the context of an ancient methodology for teaching reading. Quintilian was heir to this tradition and he sought to perpetuate it. Reading meant memorizing, but as a preliminary it meant preparing the lesson by separating words, punctuating sen-

[58] Gwynn, *op. cit.*, p. 189, is very clear on this point: "True to his promise, Quintilian begins his theory of education with the child's first lessons; and it is plain from the outset that he is writing for the children of the rich."

tences, learning the meaning of archaic words and phrases, and understanding the story. Teachers helped students prepare the reading lesson; memorizing was a student's own responsibility.

We do not need details here, but we should note that what teachers did then was later called prelection. The burden of this technique, in addition to teaching reading itself, was to sharpen students' understanding of classical literary models. Finally, concentration was necessary. Motivation and understanding were essential preliminaries to concentration; in its simplest form concentration meant mustering all the powers of attention for application to the memory task.

Most ancient educators—Quintilian among them—and many modern educators thought imitation was the methodological sine qua non of classical teaching, and they were determined to be true to the past. Despite the qualifications we should add to bestow an authentic character on this teaching tradition, it was undoubtedly true that in good hands imitation was a decidedly useful technique for achieving the goals of teaching and learning that Quintilian and his ancient colleagues prized most. In bad hands it resulted in little more than a narrow and pedantic approach to learning. The method of imitation, or teaching with models, was given clear and vigorous theoretical support by Isocrates. But once setting his compass by imitation, Isocrates was faced with the unenviable task of finding usable models for justifying his theory. When he was unable to find appropriate models in extant literature—which was often —he prepared his own. Quintilian, however, was in a far happier situation; he could stand confidently by the theory of imitation and depend for his models on a literary world that by now was wearing a new face: Greek and Latin literature was extensive and available. But even with so much literary excellence at his disposal, Quintilian did not believe it necessary to go much beyond Cicero for his models. Cicero had assimilated what was best from the corpus of oratory, and Quintilian could find no better author in his bibliography; time and again he sends his students and readers to consult Cicero.

Neither Isocrates nor Quintilian regarded imitation as superficial copying or mere rote. Ancient writers, noted for their excellence, were used as guides, and a student's mind was formed on the models selected. Properly used imitation was a technique enabling students to apprehend and assimilate grand ideas, effective methods, and meaningful sentiments. The difference between sentiment and idea is nice, but Quintilian was not bothered too much by it. He linked sentiments and ideas and related them also to drive and motivation. In his teaching imitation meant, first, reading literary models to absorb the grand ideas they contained and, second, rereading them to note how these ideas were presented with force, appeal, logic, and eloquence.[59]

---

[59] Gwynn, *ibid.*, p. 220, phrases Quintilian's preoccupation with imitation eloquently. Imitation is such a favorite device with Quintilian that it is impossible to be

The *Education of an Orator* contains directions to writers of compositions, term papers, and essays. The work was intended to be useful; in a sense it was a handbook for teachers and students. It, of course, had been prepared in response to an appeal from Quintilian's friends for a document to guide them in directing education. In this genre Quintilian never tired of reminding his readers that writing was a slow, cumbersome, and difficult enterprise. He told them to begin with a draft, and to regard the draft as a structure which needs to be filled out, finished, and polished. He told them, too, to be tentative not only in their draft, but in every stage of writing, and to use an eraser freely. It can be as important to good writing as a pen. Every aspiring writer, if he follows Quintilian, will be dominated by the dictum that good writing is only achieved by rewriting.[60]

When students do not see the need for careful revision of everything they write—and it may be too much to expect them to begin with this attitude—it is the teacher's responsibility to instill attitudes of self-criticism. And Quintilian did not believe it was easy for teachers to habituate students to subject everything they wrote to correction, refinement, and revision. At first the teacher must show the student where his writing needs improvement and how he can improve it; but as he works with students he must seek also to sharpen their powers of criticism and help them construct objective attitudes about, and standards for, their own compositions. If they are never fully satisfied with the quality of their writing they will respond better to outside criticism of it, and these critiques should center on aspects of writing often ignored by authors: use of words, clearness in expression, and mechanics of style. The point Quintilian was anxious to drive home was simply this: good writing is an outcome of learning. If the objective of good writing is to be reached, the student must be humble and docile, otherwise he will neither listen to nor profit from criticism of his writing. But writing is more than skill or mechanical technique; it presumes clear and correct thinking. And nowhere in Quintilian's book do we find the dogma that thinking cannot be improved by practice. Such a proposition would stand in sharp contrast to Quintilian's theory of learning, which consistently defended this principle: we learn to think better by thinking, the same way we improve any of our abilities.[61]

Admonitions offered relative to teaching and learning are garnished by an additional word of advice to the student who may despair of ever reaching the pinnacle of success. Despair is needless Quintilian says, for if a student has talent, which includes health, capacity, and ambition, and if he has interested teachers, a fine record is possible even though his rank

complete here, but for striking examples, see *Inst. Ora.,* I, iii, 1; IX, i, 30; IX, ii, 35 and 58; X, i, 3, 21, 27; X, ii, 1.

[60] He says the sum of the whole matter is this: "Write quickly and you will never write well, write well and you will soon write quickly" (*ibid.,* X, iii, 10) ; and X, iv, 1.

[61] Almost the whole of Book X could be quoted to support this view.

in class may not be first, but only second or third. Awareness of a relationship between achievement and capacity is important; students should find satisfaction in whatever degree of success they obtain if their efforts have fully exploited their capacities. The vital objective here is not accumulation of knowledge but a development of mental faculties; and now we see that Quintilian's educational goal is lower than Plato's—forming the soul and contemplating the good. But Quintilian took no pride in being like Plato, and it is fair to say that the greater realism of his pedagogy gave it an effectiveness and an influence that Plato's theories never matched. Comparisons of the educational attitudes of Isocrates and Quintilian lead us to believe that the latter owed a great debt to the former.[62]

IV

THE CONTENT OF EDUCATION

Curriculum, in the theory of Quintilian, had the status of an instrument; its proper function was to provide intellectual roads for students to follow toward the destination of superior oratory. When we examine Quintilian's recommendations on the content of education, we are struck by his preoccupation with grammar and rhetoric and by the fact that he was not an innovator at all but a conservative educator whose principal purpose was to clarify and transmit the best traditions of teaching and learning. If he were interested merely in transmitting and codifying Hellenistic educational practices, he would have been content to assign to grammar and rhetoric exclusive positions in the school's curriculum. But the commission he accepted was broader than this, and he sensed that Hellenistic educators, despite their determination to be Greek-like, had lost important parts of classical pedagogy. When he clarified traditional education, he brought to light some parts of the classical syllabus that had been allowed to die over a period of 400 years. So when Quintilian talks about curricula and assigns pride of place to grammar and rhetoric, he is at pains to leave room for other studies as well.

If grammar and rhetoric were the only subjects in the curriculum, one could ask questions about their order and continuity, but since they were not alone such questions have a more imperative character. Besides, in the many-sided curriculum, the teacher is required to decide whether to teach one subject at a time or to teach several subjects at once.[63]

---

[62] Quintilian is willing to acknowledge his indebtedness to Isocrates. He says his views on rhetoric are "derived from Isocrates, if indeed the treatise on rhetoric which circulates under his name is really from his hand" (*Ibid.,* II, xv, 4) .

[63] This practice has sometimes been understood as a kind of electivism. See H. E. Burton, "The Elective System in the Roman Schools," *Classical Journal,* 16 (1920–

Roman education recognized two answers to questions relative to the order and number of studies, and each answer had its zealous adherents. Quintilian could hardly avoid taking sides, for these were practical questions which demanded some answer. On the one hand there were teachers who said that no more than one subject should be taught at a time. They supported their contention, moreover, by maintaining that if students were required to study a number of subjects at once they would end up in confusion. To demand so much would make it almost impossible to learn anything at all. On the other hand, there were apparently successful teachers who rejected the one-subject doctrine to support pluralistic teaching. They argued that integration, understanding, and a true unification of knowledge were possible only when the student studied a number of subjects simultaneously. They were remarkably unimpressed with the widely circulated assumption that students had neither the time nor the energy to undertake serious study of more than one subject. And they eschewed a compromise which would have allowed multiple studies in higher learning while proscribing them in elementary education. They showed no sympathy whatever for the boy who was said to be over-burdened by scholarly toil.

Quintilian quite readily aligned himself with the latter position; he asserted that the strength and agility of the human mind enable students to study a number of subjects at once.[64] Examples are drawn both from education and husbandry to illustrate the weakness of the proposition that crippling fatigue is an unavoidable outcome when a student undertakes to study several subjects at once. No age, he avers, is less susceptible to fatigue than youth, and, though this assertion may be surprising, he says that experiments can prove how the mind, hardened by experiences with learning, becomes more receptive.[65] The example he used for proof is interesting: he directs our attention to children, who with only about two years of undirected learning, are able to form words correctly. What they have accomplished as infants forms the basis for their entire language system and remains with them throughout life. Yet slaves who try to learn Latin when they are well into their maturity find mastery of it extremely difficult and must apply themselves to its study for several years.[66]

Youth is the time for learning. By nature children are better fitted to endure the toil required for learning. In addition, they follow their teachers unquestioningly, and because critical judgments do not impede them they are able to learn more at a faster rate than if they were

1921) , pp. 532–535; S. L. Mohler, "The Iuvenes and Roman Education," *Transactions of the American Philological Association,* 68 (1937) , pp. 442–479; and Quintilian, *Inst. Ora.,* II, iv, 5–7; III, ii, 64; XII, xi, 31.

64 *Ibid.,* I, x, 1–5; I, xii, 1–2.
65 *Ibid.,* I, xii, 8.
66 *Ibid.,* I, xii, 10.

mature. Thus Quintilian reserved to youth the time for education, confident in his judgment that at no other time in life would a child have greater freedom to lay the foundation so essential to superior oratory. Yet Quintilian is anxious, as we have noted, to make adequate provisions for recreation and distraction from study. Despite the importance of learning, and the special aptitude children have for it, they must not be overtaxed by academic labor, for this will either make them lazy or breed in them a persistent dislike for study. With these preliminaries out of the way, we can turn to Quintilian's school syllabus.

Primary education—where boys learned to read and write—is taken for granted. The grammarian is assigned two responsibilities: teaching the art of speaking correctly and instructing the student in the interpretation of the poets. But neither correct speech nor poetic study can be approached mechanically; so the grammarian's teaching must involve, in addition to mechanics, the theory of writing and the art of reading. Then there was criticism which had to be learned and applied to both. But this was not all; grammar would be empty and meaningless deprived of a background in knowledge; for completeness grammar was complemented by music and geometry. But this was not enough for Quintilian, so he added philosophy, claiming that it was essential to grammar because most great Latin poets dealt with philosophic subjects in their verse.[67]

When Quintilian opened the curricular door to philosophy, he, at the same time, provided critics and followers with a means of misinterpreting him. Philosophy is admitted to the curriculum, so Quintilian must be a true disciple of Plato. But this is a shortsighted argument. Philosophy is allowed to enter the grammar school, but it enters only as an instrument for understanding literature, and its place is clearly inferior to rhetoric, which had first claim on higher learning. All this reminds us of Isocrates, not Plato, for it was Isocrates who said that philosophy could be studied by boys for the general ideas it contained, on the condition that only a limited amount of time be devoted to it. Quintilian echoes the sentiments of Isocrates and rejects Plato's enthronement of philosophy as the kingpin of higher learning; scientific humanism is neither endorsed nor befriended by Quintilian.

The two sides of grammatical study are clearly stated: one is the structure of language, which on occasion can be trivial and dry; the other is the acquisition of knowledge by reading, and reading was guided by the needs of superior oratory. In teaching reading, in addition to making the selections meet the test of relevance, such things as rhythm in breathing, proper sense of timing, rate, animation, modulation, and sense of sentence completion were attended to. In most instances their perfection depended on an application of the principle of learning by doing. Both

---

67 *Ibid.*, X, i, 35; XII, ii, 10–23.

sides of the grammatical study were essential; the elimination or de-emphasis of either would surely spell grammar's failure. Although grammar was a preliminary study, Quintilian had no intention of treating it as an inferior subject. He saw it as a branch of knowledge necessary in youth—as a foundation for rhetoric—and pleasant in old age, and he regarded it as a sweet companion in retirement. The admonition is moving: "The elementary stages of the teaching of literature must not therefore be despised as trivial. It is of course an easy task to point out the difference between vowels and consonants, and to subdivide the latter into semivowels and mutes. But as the pupil gradually approaches the inner shrine of the sacred place, he will come to realize the intricacy of the subject, an intricacy calculated not merely to sharpen the wits of a boy, but to exercise even the most profound knowledge and erudition." [68]

It was always difficult to know where the instructional responsibilities of the grammarian ended and where those of the rhetorician began; strained relations had existed between teachers on these two levels for centuries. The grammarian was miffed when schools of rhetoric built curricula that included studies traditionally assigned to schools of grammar. Their action not only cast a shadow of doubt over the quality of his teaching, but deprived him of a livelihood as well. And when grammarians reacted to threats on their reputation as teachers and their professional security by broadening their curricula to include subjects normally found in schools of rhetoric, teachers of rhetoric became uneasy and critical. Compromise was always possible, because it required only mutual assent to an arbitrary curricular line of demarcation. But what could so easily be obtained in theory, was apparently impossible in practice. In the end grammarians and rhetoricians tried to maintain that their differences were based on fundamental issues and by perpetuating their acerbic controversy, and this myth, the quality of education suffered. Quintilian read the record perceptively and set out to make peace between the two disciplines that were trying their best to be hostile. He did what lesser educators were unwilling to do: prescribe the curriculum for grammar teachers by assigning to them the study of the structure of language, literature, music, and geometry. The grammarian's syllabus stopped with these subjects.

Before we close the book on grammar schools and the obligations of their teachers, a word should be added on the study of music and geometry. Quintilian began by doubting the need to justify music's place in the curriculum of the grammar school, and then went to great lengths to do what he said did not need doing. He calls upon the wisdom of ancient educators, formulas of philosophers, and common beliefs of

[68] *Ibid.,* I, iv, 6–7.

mankind to confirm the value of music for forming the body and the soul. In this view, music was expected to exert a disciplinary influence, and discipline, of course, was prized, but it did not satisfy Quintilian. He saw another dimension to music, one clearly utility-centered, although its object was not to produce a performer for the stage. Both instrumental and vocal music could benefit the future orator by shaping his mode of expression, developing vocal utterance, and lending rhythm to gesture and bearing—in a word, it could add grace and harmony in speech and movement—but there was still another side to music that meant even more. When Quintilian looked back to classical education, he found a model in the Athenian music school, and he tried to follow it.[69] Athenian music schools had put more emphasis on literature than on instrumental or vocal music, and by adapting his curriculum to this ancient model Quintilian was able to stress the literary side of musical instruction to provide a broad foundation of general information for his prospective orator. In the curriculum proposed by Quintilian, music had a prominent role—he continued a well-authenticated tradition that music was good for the soul—but it was the music of poetry not of rhythm and harmony that dominated the course.

Classical schools tended to avoid mathematical studies, especially on the lower levels of schooling, for what seemed then to be compelling reasons: the mathematical apparatus lacked a notation which could be easily manipulated in computation, so arithmetic became, or had to become, a theory of number and was too difficult for elementary or secondary school boys. Geometry, despite its fundamentally rational character and its ability to proceed without arithmetic notations, was caught in a net of application. It was a tool for the surveyor, the engineer, and the navigator. The classical teacher had little time for either branch and was content to ignore mathematics until Plato came to its rescue. But even the genius of Plato appeared too late to influence the curriculum of classical schools, although his message relative to the importance of mathematical studies in any syllabus of liberal education did not die with him. It was read by Hellenistic teachers who, perhaps thinking it authentically classical, enthusiastically inserted mathematics in the curricula of their scientific secondary schools. Thus harbored, mathematics stayed alive, although neither the scientific schools nor their mathematical courses ever achieved any degree of popularity. Here, in the record of these schools, Quintilian found geometry and raised it to the level of a liberal study.[70] The question is moot whether he was guided by Plato or only accepted geometry as a study whose distinctive rational character intrigued him. In any case, the confident assumption was made that geometry opened avenues to intellectual discipline, while

[69] *Ibid.,* I, x, 9–12.
[70] *Ibid.,* I, x, 33–37.

incidentally putting the future orator in intimate touch with symbols and numbers. The orator had use for both, and we are left to revise our portrait of Quintilian somewhat: a common belief among scholars that disinterested curiosity was the main force behind every element of his theory contains a measure of truth, but it is not altogether innocent of wishful thinking. Geometry was approved as a curricular entry in the grammar school not only for its liberalizing or disciplinary values, but because it was useful in developing powers of logic and knowledge of numbers and symbols. Unquestionably Quintilian was a scholar, and the orators ushering forth from his school were to have been scholars too. But he was a scholar who could value good tools.

The content of secondary education is fixed, and the responsibilities of grammar teachers are clear; what follows is higher education, the academic province of teachers of rhetoric. But before Quintilian would elaborate his curricular theory for this level of education, he reaffirmed an earlier conclusion that the boundary between grammar and rhetoric must be rigorously respected.[71] At first we are awed by his preoccupation with what appears to be a picayune point, but as we study the history of education from his time forward, and notice how often different levels of education were unable to agree on precise articulation, our attitude changes. His intuitive grasp of fundamental and perennial educational issues is amazing. His preoccupation with fixing and respecting boundaries between grammar and rhetoric grew out of apprehensions that grammarians would try to retain students too long on an elementary level, and thus retard intellectual progress, or that teachers of rhetoric would prematurely undertake instruction in eloquence. He was right more often than he was wrong in suspecting that teachers of higher schools would abandon their proper functions to descend to lower levels of teaching, while teachers in grammar schools would exceed theirs. Quintilian's advice was good, but it stands mainly as an ignored guideline in the history of learning.

Teachers of rhetoric are to begin where teachers of grammar stop; their educational goal is to teach young men the theory of eloquence and how to be eloquent in practice.

The objectives of higher education are stated simply and directly, but beneath the surface, and partially concealed by simplicity and directness, is a vast corpus of rhetorical theory and skills waiting to be mastered. And before a young man can become an accomplished orator it must be mastered.[72] We can only skim the surface of Quintilian's direc-

---

[71] *Ibid.,* II, i, 4–8.

[72] A number of good works center on this point; see especially, F. W. Householder, *Literary Quotation and Allusion in Lucian* (New York, Columbia University Press, 1941) ; S. F. Bonner, *Roman Declamation* (Berkeley, University of California Press, 1950) ; Clyde Pharr, "Roman Legal Education," *Classical Journal,* 34 (February, 1939) ,

tions to teachers of rhetoric, for in the *Education of an Orator* he reserves books two through eleven to amplify them. It is doubtful that Quintilian adds much of substance to Greek or Latin rhetoric; his purpose was to take both as he found them and erect a pedagogic structure around them, a structure to guide all teachers of higher education. To follow Quintilian through these books so full of rhetorical rule and regulation would swamp us in detail and would add little or nothing to his stature as an educator of unassailable worth: it is enough to say that Quintilian wrote a handbook for rhetoric which, if followed, would teach students to write and speak effectively and eloquently.

In addition to rules and regulations for rhetoric, and techniques for applying these rules in oral and written composition, we have Quintilian's recommendations on the orators and historians students should read.[73] These are made in the context of earlier recommendations directed at teachers of grammar about building a foundation of general knowledge. We may conclude this annotation of Quintilian's curricular theory by referring to the criteria he used for choosing authors to be read in schools of rhetoric. He does not think it difficult to establish these criteria. Only the best writers should occupy the student's time, and among the best authors Quintilian preferred to stay with the ones renowned for transparency of style and lucidity of expression. He recommended Livy over Sallust, although in general he thought Cicero was superior to all others and directed teachers to use literary models in the order of their resemblance to Cicero.[74]

Quintilian ends his disquisition on the curriculum with a word of advice to students: he admonishes them to love their teachers no less than their studies, and to regard their teachers as parents, not indeed of their bodies, but of their minds.[75]

---

pp. 257–270; and J. W. H. Atkins, *Literary Criticism in Antiquity* (New York, Peter Smith Publisher, 1952).

[73] Quintilian, *Inst. Ora.*, X, i, 72–81.

[74] *Ibid.*, X, i, 105.

[75] *Ibid.*, II, ix, 1.

⋟ 5 ⋞

Cassiodorus: A Christian Formulation
of Literary Humanism

I

INTRODUCTION

The historical step from Quintilian to Cassiodorus is long, and the educational chronology of this interval, despite its inevitable and unfortunate lacunae, is unquestionably full of peaks and valleys. In taking this step we should not forget that educational interest did not cease with Quintilian, or lie dormant, and then revive with Cassiodorus; schools carried on the tested traditions of the past—the schools of the Empire—and there were innovating schools, if we may call them schools, trying to inculcate Christian virtue while at the same time inoculating Christian students against pagan conventions and values.[1] Thus, without going into great detail, it is important for us, before we try to determine the stature of Cassiodorus and the extent of his educational and pedagogic innovations, to trace the evolution of classical learning to his time. In this way we shall have a view of what he was trying to alter and, at the same time, understand what some of his Christian predecessors thought education should be and how they believed the classical tradition could be adjusted to accommodate the objectives of a Christian life. With this background clear in our minds—the evolution of classical education through the Roman system, and Christian education with its implicit

[1] I have argued elsewhere [*Main Currents in the History of Education* (New York, McGraw-Hill Book Company, 1962), pp. 183–191] that Christian schools were only infrequently scholastic in their methods and goals. G. Hodgson, *Primitive Christian Education* (Edinburgh, T. & T. Clark, 1906); and A. T. Drane, *Christian Schools and Scholars,* new ed. (New York, Benziger Bros. Inc., 1924), describe the evolution and contributions of catechumenal, catechetical, and cathedral schools.

dilemmas—we shall then be ready to describe the accomplishments of Cassiodorus and interpret their influences on teaching and learning processes.

At the outset, it is possible to state in an uncomplicated and general way the real achievement of Cassiodorus, although to do him and the innovations he recommended complete justice a more extensive discussion will be needed later. Cassiodorus found the inherited classical educational apparatus impractical; his whole educational purpose was to convert what may be called the tradition of Quintilian to useful rather than ornamental ends. And if we think we are dealing with a practical educator rather than a theoretician, we may be right, but this does not remove the principal actor in this chapter from the arena of educational doctrine. Cassiodorus, somewhere along the line, became painfully aware of the unreality and the meaninglessness of classical education as it operated in his own day, and he tried to reconstruct it. But, as we have said, to understand his proposed reconstructions we shall have to look more closely at the educational program with which he had to deal.

II

THE BACKGROUND OF CLASSICAL EDUCATION

Although ancient education came eventually to be dominated by grammar and rhetoric, prior to the fifth century B.C. Greeks were quite content to offer their youths training that would prepare them to be good fighting men, well versed in religious practices and social traditions. The training program was commissioned to form citizens—a citizen's most important civic duty being bearing arms to defend the city-state—and it was considered too important a mission to be left to parents. Schools were organized for the purpose of teaching, or for developing certain physical-military skills; and, in addition, probably with equivalent value, there were studies in music and in the works of Homer.[2] The two sides of the curriculum—physical and musical—were aimed at a common objective, civic virtue. In other words, the educational program in force near the later boundary of the Greek archaic period was primarily moral rather than intellectual; special value was attached to the good man skilled in fighting; scant heed was paid to intellectual achievement. With this unique orientation the program was bound to respect and perpetuate a sporting tradition.[3]

Had Greek society of the fifth century B.C. remained unchanged

2 Beck, *op. cit.,* pp. 72–85.

3 See E. N. Gardiner, *Athletics of the Ancient World* (New York, Oxford University Press, 1930) .

socially and politically, these pleasant educational activities undoubtedly would have represented the high point in Greek educational achievement. Change, however, did occur. Democracy emerged, although never without intransigent opposition, and the comfortable and uncomplicated syllabus for civic education was obliged to embrace novel skills involved with composing, recording, and interpreting speech. A premium was placed on these skills, for rhetoric, or oratory, now took its place alongside civic virtue as necessary equipment for the responsible and interested citizen. This is surely the positive side of the picture: the utility of grammar, and more especially rhetoric, as implements for conducting political affairs democratically. But there was another side, one represented by the hard-core aristocrats, who refused to respond affirmatively to democratic anticipations. They too needed tools to attack the predatory threat of hoi polloi; so for purposes of defense they turned to the literary tools of grammar and rhetoric, and they regularly, as in the works of Plato, employed rhetorical artistry to impede or halt the progress of democracy.

After a brief period for adjustment, Greek, especially Athenian, education turned its attention to communicating literary skills, and for the first time in Greek educational history the writing and reading master took precedence over the paidotribe. And to achieve ends now set for it, this type of education needed a new class of teachers more thorough in their grammar (reading) and more sophisticated in their rhetoric (composition) than any of the old reading and writing masters had been. There was continuous disapproval of this turn of events; we see that Plato, Isocrates, and even Aristophanes,[4] could make the new education the topic for critical essays and dramas. Yet, despite the cogency of their arguments and the artistry in which they were clothed, the loyal opposition could not turn back the clock of history or redirect the course of social and political events. A new genre was born, and it had qualities of permanence; the new education elevated the tools of literary learning and made them equivalent to the broader objectives of civic virtue that were still embraced in the educational process.

Without going very deeply into the purposes of the new education, one sees almost immediately their quality of relevance. Reading and oratory occupied important positions in the syllabus of the new schools because they had real meaning for life. And this meaning was consolidated in the everyday work of teachers who came to conduct the schools —the grammarians and the rhetors.

The teacher of grammar was a teacher of reading, and this meant more than just recognizing words and signs; it meant being able to render a written passage correctly and intelligently in spoken form. So the teacher of grammar taught voice control and expression, but, more

---

4 Plato's *Gorgias,* Isocrates' *Against the Sophists,* and Aristophanes' *The Clouds.*

importantly, he had to be sure that his students understood what they were reading. They were expected to be able to explain the origins of words, the senses in which they were used in a passage, the way they had been used by some of Greece's heroes, and, above all, they were expected to be able to deliver a meaningful commentary on the subject matter. Besides all this, or prior to it, they had to separate words, punctuate sentences, and generally prepare the material for reading in the first place. Memorizing was the last step in the reading exercise. When the reading lesson was finished the reader was supposed to know just about everything about the passage, and he should have it committed to memory. In teaching grammar, reading played a dominant role, but it was not to displace music, poetry, and simple arithmetic (counting). Moreover, reading interests were supposed to be comprehensive rather than inclusive. Thus, grammar-school education assumed a rather general form; grammarians were expected to lecture on all topics treated by the authors they used, and in a fairly comprehensive course of reading they hoped to cover everything that a reasonably well educated man might need to know.[5]

Although the boundary line between grammar schools and schools of rhetoric was never established with precision—leading to controversies among the teachers in these schools—it is fair to say that instruction in the school of rhetoric began where the grammarian stopped.[6] The purpose of rhetorical teaching, if inflated, was nevertheless clear: to cover everything a man should know in order to compose and deliver a good speech. The breadth of this objective implied two teaching dimensions: theoretical and technical; the former dealt with the content of an oration, the latter with the rules for composition and delivery. Proper training in rhetoric would finish a man's education, and, together with accomplishments gained in the grammar schools, should furnish him with the most complete education he could desire. This was, of course, the ideal, and, safe to say, it was not often realized in practice. The best teachers of rhetoric offered as much solid education as time permitted and spent what time remained drilling students in the art of speaking effectively. Eventually a large body of rules came to be prescriptive for oratory, so the worst teachers of rhetoric could occupy themselves with teaching and drilling on these rules. In the last analysis, it was the level of oratorical accomplishment that students wanted that decided how

---

[5] See Freeman, *op. cit.*, pp. 88–89; Marrou, *op. cit.*, 151–157; Plato, *Politicus*, 277e–278a, and 285c; Plato, *Protagoras*, 326d; Xenophon, *Memorabilia*, IV, iv, 7; Plato, *Laws*, 811. The evolution of arithmetic teaching is really another story and needs no emphasis here. Yet, part of the story begins here. See, for example, D. V. Schrader, "The Arithmetic of the Medieval Universities," *The Mathematics Teacher*, LX (March, 1967), pp. 264–278; and Nicomachus of Gerasa, *Introduction to Arithmetic*, translated by M. L. D'Ooge (New York, Robbins and Karpinski, 1926).

[6] This is essentially Quintilian's account of teaching hostilities (*Inst. Ora.* II, i, 1–13).

ideal or how practical the rhetorical course would be. After all, teachers had to earn a living; they were dependent on their students. Yet whether or not one wanted to approve either the goals or the content of the rhetorical course, clearly this course stood on the threshold of life. The preparation offered students, quite irrespective of its fundamental quality, what was in the long run useful. Rhetoric had meaning for the citizen in his everyday world; even when it was irresponsible it was not irrelevant.[7]

While grammar and rhetoric dominated Athenian and most Greek education and came to be almost synonymous with classical education, neither had a monopoly. Educators arose who disputed the worth of rhetoric and challenged the position of supremacy it occupied. Perhaps what they really meant was not that the purposes of rhetoric were bad when properly circumscribed and substantially integrated with responsibility and truth, but that rhetoric was far too pretentious. Despite the varied and often intensive attacks on schools of rhetoric, no other plan for education arose to seriously challenge these schools; thus, whatever setbacks rhetoric suffered were only temporary and generally inconsequential. From the time of Isocrates to that of Quintilian, rhetoric held undisputed control over the field of education.

Yet rhetoric did change or, better, the society that championed it changed. The Alexandrian world had little room for democracy; the old city-state with its citizen-soldiers became obsolete; the tools important to a citizen in classical Athens had almost no meaning as civic tools to inhabitants of the Empire of Alexander. But the Greeks in the Empire, or those thousands of people who had succumbed to the inspirations of Greek life and genius, wanted to live in the glorious past; at least, they wanted to live in the literary past. In real life, whatever their ambitions, the natural links between literature and everyday interests and needs were disassociated. With the Alexandrians the connection between literature and life, and between oratory and real political life, came to an end. Literature stopped being an instrument for the artistic expression of contemporary culture and came instead to be a means of education.

This was a development of the greatest importance, for from this time forward contacts with the classical inheritance were always made through the schools.

Roman literature, moreover, began at the point reached by Greek

---

[7] See Ennodius of Pavia, *Letters*, I, 5, 10; Marrou, *op. cit.*, pp. 194–206, and pp. 284–292; E. J. Parks, *The Roman Rhetorical Schools as a Preparation for the Courts Under the Early Empire* (Baltimore, The Johns Hopkins Press, 1945); and C. S. Baldwin, *Ancient Rhetoric and Poetic* (New York, The Macmillan Company, 1926). Despite the undeniable worth of these accounts, the direction of rhetoric and its content may be mined from the pages of Quintilian. See also, W. G. Rutherford, *A Chapter in the History of Annotation* (London, Macmillan & Co., Ltd., 1905), pp. 97–179.

literature in the Hellenistic age; the latter had lost its touch with life and contemporary culture; the former never had any of these contacts to lose. The language of Roman literature was always artistic and scholarly and remote from ordinary speech; it tried to remain true to its own national traditions, but it regularly imitated Greek literary techniques. Both literary traditions, the Greek and the Roman, were firmly linked to the past; perhaps the only way to come in close contact with these traditions was by means of a systematic approach, and when this approach was devised or refined from the old grammatical and rhetorical traditions, it became the fixed content for the schools.

The Greeks in the Hellenistic world never stopped to test the validity of the assumption that the best traditions of their heritage rested on the foundations of their classics; they could and did make literature the center of their lives. Even when professional men became renowned in their specialties, neither they nor their contemporaries were satisfied unless they added to their professional skill the embellishments of literary culture. All this was perhaps natural enough; the allegiance of Hellenistic men to classical Greece is not impossible to understand and approve. But the Romans followed the same path, even though it was more difficult for them, and they were not content with one literature or one language; they had to have two, both Latin and Greek.[8]

The Roman plan for classical education had hardly been adopted when the great Quintilian discovered that its curriculum was too narrow and that it somehow missed the point in preserving the moral tradition of Latin teaching. He could approve bilingualism as necessary for mining the treasures of Greek and Latin literature, and he could endorse the broad sweep of grammar and rhetorical schools, but he could not continue to advocate an educational program with oratory as its goal that did not have greater scope. He wanted a more comprehensive curriculum —one that contained advanced studies—aimed at producing a new kind of orator; moreover, he wanted an order of studies beginning with the cradle that would presumably guarantee the forming of a moral man. "A good man skilled in speaking" may not now be a high sounding objective for the educational enterprise, but in preparing for this objective Quintilian meant that educational experiences should be broad, refined, and profound; he was not satisfied with the fashionable oratory of his day.

Despite Quintilian's strong sense of reform, neither he nor his pedagogic contemporaries caught the real nature of a political world in ferment. The old order may have needed orators of the classical model; at any rate, the educational program tried to prepare them. And the reforms Quintilian suggested may have broadened this older model, but they did not go beyond the courtroom or the assembly—the centers of government in which specialists in oratory might have been needed—to

8 Gwynn, *op. cit.*, pp. 34–45; and Wilkins, *op. cit.*, pp. 25 ff.

the offices and the bureaus of government, which now needed only competently trained civil servants.

Quintilian was listened to, and even when his famous work was lost, or available only in fragments, its principal precepts, retained in an oral and a teaching tradition, were followed. From the time of Quintilian to that of Cassiodorus, the schools were dominated by a code of liberal learning that had been defined by Quintilian. Apart from its progressive approach to technique, which did an immense amount of good for pedagogy after the fourteenth century, this was a code that in its content was out-of-date the very day it was proposed. Thus, education during the greater part of the first five centuries of the Christian era was laboring under two tremendous handicaps: the archaic prescriptions of Quintilian and the decay of the Roman political structure upon which the schools rested for support.

Cassiodorus himself had been educated in the tradition of Quintilian, and there is no evidence that he disbelieved the worth of his own schooling. Yet, he saw that all men would not live the literary-political life he had lived and that governmental processes—or even the broader social complex—had no great need for men with such training. To put it quite bluntly, Quintilian's plan perpetuated another kind of irrelevance and for that reason must be judged defective. Moreover, Cassiodorus came to see that learning has use; obviously its use could not be found in studied oratory. Not only did society not require such erudition or eloquence, it actively distrusted such rhetorical weapons. If Cassiodorus was right in thinking learning should be an instrument, he had first to set the learning apparatus in a Christian light and then to convert this involved classical apparatus to practical ends. All this could be done without altering one word of Quintilian's methodology; but it could not be done unless the content of the classical curriculum was brought down to the level of day-to-day application.

There was another course open to Cassiodorus, but he chose not to take it because he recognized the "great longing for secular letters (a great part of mankind believed that through these schools it attained worldly wisdom)." [9] He could have jettisoned the content of classical schooling, keeping only the structure, and followed the admonitions of some of his Christian predecessors, who had counseled Christians to stay completely away from everything the Pagans had taught.[10] That he did not do so is a sign of the depth of his educational insights; a pure

[9] Cassiodorus, *An Introduction to Divine and Human Readings,* translated by L. W. Jones (New York, Columbia University Press, 1946), p. 67.

[10] Tertullian, *On the Argument of Proscription,* 7, could say "what is there in common between Athens and Jerusalem, the Academy and the Church?" But Tertullian was only the most outspoken, for even the most educated of the early Fathers could sometimes share his view. See E. K. Rand, *Founders of the Middle Ages* (Cambridge, Mass., Harvard University Press, 1929), p. 41.

Christian curriculum would not have been any more meaningful in the broad social and political complex than the nostalgically oratorical educational plan had been. He selected the road of compromise, one that had been sketchily marked out for him by some earlier Christian educational thinkers. It is not entirely fair to Cassiodorus to say that he selected the course because it had a Christian endorsement; the matter cannot be settled so easily, for other courses not so favorable to a redefined educational syllabus with the classical categories as its inspiration had been endorsed by Christian thinkers too.[11] Cassiodorus embraced the liberal arts for two reasons: first, he wanted to provide a strong foundation for divine studies, for he was certain that knowledge of the scriptures and theological advancement could not be obtained without a thorough command of the skills of language and literature; second, he believed that the comprehensiveness of the traditional program, which he was never content merely to describe, with its grounding in grammar and rhetoric, was most suited to effecting the active use of official Latin, a language that seemingly had to be used by government officers, local administrators, and businessmen, to say nothing of that vast body of clergymen who would use Latin in the conduct of divine service and in ecclesiastical administration.[12]

The outcomes of most classical educational programs were highly visible: in a phrase, they were pointed toward eloquence in public. It is not hard to believe that Quintilian still treasured the image of the public man, and there is no need here to retrace the pride of place given to public-man education in the history of the Roman system. Cassiodorus and his followers aimed at changing this: the outcomes of education now were not to be so visible; correct thinking in private, whether in the scholar's study or in the administrator's office, or even in the clergyman's chambers, was accorded first order of importance. This attention to private accomplishment, more than anything else, proved that the educational stage was being refurbished. Indeed, the world in which oratory had flourished, and for which there was sometimes a real need, was dying; the new order that replaced the old had no need for, and little knowledge of, popular assemblies or political debates. For several centuries to come, educated Christians would be living and working in an ecclesiastical-feudal society, and the educational traditions of the past, with their oratorical goals, could not be expected to help them much. Because Cassiodorus became interested in education, and because he reset the stage for relevance in learning, students who followed him were not often faced with such a learning dilemma.

11 Both in the Eastern and Western churches canonical edicts said bluntly, "Have nothing to do with pagan books" (*Apostolic Constitutions,* Funk edition, I, 6, 1–6) .
12 E. K. Rand, "The New Cassiodorus," *Speculum,* XIII (October, 1938) , pp. 433–447.

III

THE DILEMMA OF CHRISTIAN EDUCATION

When stated now the accomplishment of Cassiodorus may appear unimpressive, and although his contemporaries may not have heeded his words or based their educational programs on his theories, the medieval world did. But he forged his theory of education, not in the medieval world, but in the early Christian world, when Christians were not yet sure what direction their learning should take. One side of the picture is now clear: Cassiodorus was championing a kind of education that was in fact a compromise between two extreme positions. One would have excised the classics from the educational syllabus; the other would have continued the classics as the best, if not the only, means to solid learning. As we have said, he could have followed either extreme and have found illustrious company. That he did not is a credit to him, but we must try to see how he plowed his way through the field of educational controversy and how he emerged from the controversy unscathed. His reputation as a Christian was apparently so strong that his assertion of the worth of the liberal arts, and his making them an unavoidable ingredient in his educational program, did not put his reputation for orthodoxy in jeopardy.[13]

The fact that classical education survived the ages that gave it birth and offered it early nurture is due in no small measure to Christianity. Had there been no Cassiodorus to weld together a Christian-classical education and supply a theory to sustain it through predominantly Christian periods, the course of classical education might have been different. We have no evidence for saying that classical education would have dropped out of sight, for one cannot read a history that was never acted out, but we can guess that classical education would have existed as a minority culture on the fringe of learning and scholarship rather than as a principal component in the mainstream of intellectual life. But when one stood at the threshold of the sixth century, the place of the classics in Christian learning and life was by no means clear. Was the classical heritage to be studied by Christians? If the answer to this question was in the affirmative, there followed inevitably the question: how was it to be studied? Throughout the five centuries preceding Cassiodorus there was no unequivocal or unanimous answer.[14]

While these uncertainties may have been supported by good excuses,

---

13 E. K. Rand, *Founders of the Middle Ages*, pp. 242–244.
14 See Werner Jaeger's excellent analysis, *Early Christianity and Greek Paideia* (Cambridge, Mass., The Belknap Press of Harvard University, 1961), pp. 86–102.

it must also be clear that the decisions about the place or meaning of the classical inheritance were never, or hardly ever, made on the level of principle. They were made on the level of tradition: what had the Fathers said about the place, or the role, classical, or pagan, education should occupy in the formation of the Christian intellect? [15]

Some of the Fathers were aware of the common element in classical and Christian traditions: responsibility of the person. In the former, responsibility stopped with the temporal and with the individual's search for happiness within the world. In the latter, although the temporal features might not be eschewed or rejected out of hand, all things were ultimately measured by an otherworldly yardstick. Sometimes the Christian temperament was so intractable, or the Christian single-mindedness so extreme, that the division was easily made between the road to salvation and the road to evil: whatever the former may have been in the language of the educator, the latter was almost always sure to cite the classics as insidious and invidious. Undoubtedly many Christians found a great deal of comfort in being so positive about the things they accepted and the things they condemned. They looked for their references among the Fathers, and when they looked hard enough they found them. But while they looked they were usually exposed to the views of some Fathers, for example, Jerome, who caused them some concern. Jerome was not on the side of the extremists: he could and did see some use to the classics, and he could never bring himself to counsel complete indifference to them. He was the product of an age that grew up with a classical education—one that was Christian and that hated the immorality of the pagan way of life, and that way of life was sometimes reflected in the best of the classical literature—but one that wanted to retain the familiar appurtenances of classical civilization. In a word, these were people who wanted to be good Christians, but they wanted the culture of the classical world without the pagan principles it subserved.[16] During these tempestuous years Christian children were sent to classical schools, because usually there were no other schools for them to attend, and Christians taught in these schools. Moreover, these Christian teachers taught the classics, even when they did not believe in everything the classics contained, and this sometimes caused them real difficulties, especially in the face of Julian's edict.[17] It is easy to believe that Christian teachers in the classical schools shared a heritage of belief in the worth of classical education; moreover, the chroniclers of this age certainly suggest that Christian

15 R. P. C. Hanson, *Tradition in the Early Church* (London, SCM Press, Ltd., 1962) ; and R. R. Bolgar, *The Classical Heritage and Its Beneficiaries* (Cambridge, Cambridge University Press, 1954) , pp. 45–46.

16 Rand's chapter on "St. Jerome the Humanist," *Founders of the Middle Ages*, pp. 102–134, is especially significant for seeing Jerome's position of compromise.

17 R. R. Bolgar, *op. cit.,* p. 47; and Marrou, *op. cit.,* p. 324, discuss the import of the edict pronounced in A.D. 362 and rescinded in 364.

teachers were respected in their profession and that they did not place a different value on the subject matter of classical schools than the one accorded it by their pagan colleagues.[18]

Neither teachers nor students—nor learned men generally—irrespective of their religious beliefs, wanted to cut themselves off from civilization. Many Christians doubted that the dangers to their faith were so great as some anticlassical debaters claimed. These latter were for the most part religious zealots; they saw the world around them as evil; they were convinced that the classics represented human reason, always a danger to their faith; and they demanded an uncompromising severance from everything that the classical world and its literary spokesmen had to offer. Yet, this was a minority view, despite its broad currency provided by dedicated and articulate keepers of the Christian conscience. The majority view, and one that could obtain the guarded endorsement of most Fathers, assumed that in the new Christian society much of the content and style of pagan education could be preserved, although paganism itself would have to be purged from it. Fundamentally their attitude was one of compromise, and this was the attitude that Cassiodorus eventually adopted.[19]

The progress of the opinions held by the Fathers, which, as we have said, came in time to be supported by most Christians, was uneven. And this unevenness put many a Christian mind in a dilemma.

Perhaps the first of the Fathers to see, and express with some clarity, the worth of the classics in education was Clement of Alexandria.[20] Clement, however, died in the early third century, so there was plenty of time for Christians of those early centuries to cultivate their doubts, first embracing pagan education and then fleeing from it. If Clement's was the first voice to still some of the hesitations and offer the more balanced views of compromise, it is clear that Christians had to live a long time without relief from anxiety over what they and their children studied. Clement was perhaps not the best guide. He was often obscure, and sometimes he was charged with heterodoxy by his more rigid Christian companions. His view, moreover, was bound to be somewhat misleading: it was based on the proposition that the value of pagan studies is to be found principally in the mental and moral discipline they cultivated. In other words, Clement was almost indifferent to the content of the classics, or, better, he took this content for granted. He had been schooled with it

---

[18] Bolgar, *op. cit.*, p. 47; and M. L. W. Laistner, *Christianity and Pagan Culture, In the Later Roman Empire* (Ithaca, New York, Cornell University Press, 1951), pp. 59 ff.

[19] See E. G. Sihler, *From Augustus to Augustine, Essays and Studies Dealing With the Contact and Conflict of Classic Paganism and Christianity* (Cambridge, University Press, 1923). Cassiodorus' position is revealed in the conclusion to Book II; see Cassiodorus, *op. cit.*, pp. 204–209.

[20] R. E. Witt, "The Hellenism of Clement of Alexandria," *The Classical Quarterly*, XXV (1931), pp. 195–204.

and was convinced that it was harmless; moreover, he advanced the theory that classical literature had its source in the corpus of Jewish writings and thus shared many traditions in common with Christianity.[21] No one could make him apologize for his steady reading of the classics, and, apparently, even in his famous catechetical school in Alexandria, he offered the students, Christians and non-Christians alike, a steady diet of classical learning.[22] This was all fine for the scholar, who could look past the information and the tales contained in classical literature to the disciplines it could inculcate, but it was hardly convincing to the Christian who did not probe quite so deeply. He could not find the disciplines because he was distracted by the anti-Christian sentiments he thought classical literature contained; and compared to Clement, the Christian of the West was faced with a somewhat more difficult problem. He read and tried to study Latin literature, whereas Clement had been preoccupied with Greek literature. The former was less philosophical in tone and turned more often on themes that were wanton, lewd, and lustful. Clement's argument came in time to be accepted, but not until its source was almost completely forgotten, and too late to have any definitive effects on Christian educational thinking.[23]

A pupil, colleague, and successor to Clement in the Alexandrian school, Origen, accepted the classics for the same reason his master had, but he consistently refused to admit that they made any impression on him. In a similar vein, Origen never admitted or acknowledged any indebtedness to his teacher, Clement. Origen must have had more than his share of arrogance, for he could borrow from his predecessors and at the same time publicly scorn them.[24]

So if we turn to the Alexandrian school for guidance on this question of the value or the danger of classical education, we shall almost at once be put in a dilemma by the arguments of its most famous spokesmen. Clement advocated the use of the classics; [25] Origen used the classics, but refused to admit their worth and took special cheer in advocating a wholehearted policy of flight from them.[26]

Fortunately the cautious policy framed by Clement, against aban-

21 J. E. Sandys, *A History of Classical Scholarship*, vol. I (New York, Hafner Publishing Co., 1958) , p. 325.

22 Charles Kingsley, *Alexandria and Her Schools* (Cambridge, The Macmillan Company, 1854) , p. 131.

23 Frank P. Cassidy, *Molders of the Medieval Mind* (St. Louis, Mo., B. Herder Book Co., 1944) , p. 51.

24 R. B. Tollington, *Clement of Alexandria, A Study in Christian Liberalism*, vol. I (London, Williams and Norgate, Ltd., 1914) , p. 20; and Bolgar, *op. cit.*, p. 49.

25 Clement put it this way: "But he who calls what is useful for the advantage of the Catechumens, and especially when they are Greeks . . . must not abstain from erudition, like irrational animals; but he must collect as many aids as possible for his hearers" (*Stromata*, VI, xi, *The Ante-Nicene Fathers*, p. 500) .

26 Tollington, *op. cit.*, pp. 20 ff; William Fairweather, *Origen and Greek Patristic Theology* (New York, Charles Scribner's Sons, 1901) , pp. 10 ff.

donment of the classics, was not completely lost; a century and a half after his death it reappeared and was dignified in the pronouncements of four Christian scholars all of whom were thorough students of the classics and completely orthodox Christians: St. Basil of Caesarea, St. Gregory Nazianzen, Theodore of Mopsuestia, and St. John Chrysostom.[27] They found merit in the style of classical literature and were impressed with the methods of classical scholarship. They could and did recommend the study of the classics on these bases, but they were even more impressed with the possibilities classical studies contained for elevating the minds of those who were systematically exposed to them. These Christian scholars, true exponents of Christian Humanism, amplified and enlarged the disciplinary argument of Clement; where Clement had found the classics good for dispelling prejudice, they found them good for teaching faultless style and impressing high ideals on the minds of their Christian readers.[28] In theory all this was a great step forward, but when these scholars passed from the educational scene, the influence of their defense of classical studies began to wane. The West began to lose touch with Greek literature, to which these ideas could be most efficaciously applied. However, as a reasoned defense of classical studies they were retained in the Eastern Church, and despite the unquestioned orthodoxy of the protagonists for this view the voices of cultural suspicion and condemnation were again heard in the West.[29]

The loudest voice was Tertullian's, and it was the most uncompromising of all. Yet, even in his studied objections to the bulk of classical education, he had to admit that Christian children should learn to read and write and that they should have some of the general knowledge that only the conventional grammar schools could supply. There seemed to be no way out: pagan education was essential. But in almost the same breath Tertullian proscribed all classical schools.

Tertullian was admittedly hard to follow; he preached a bold doctrine, but in the last analysis it was a doctrine of despair. It is not surprising that his advice was not followed by the majority of Christian thinkers; but it was accepted by significant portions of the Christian community and served for centuries as a serious impediment to a doctrine of balanced compromise making the structure of classical education, with its unchristian elements purged away, the basic framework for Christian teaching and learning. The advice of Tertullian did little more than retard the resolution of the Christian's dilemma; it was not Tertul-

---

27 Bolgar, *op. cit.,* p. 49; Rand, *Founders of the Middle Ages,* pp. 109, 227, and 234; Marrou, *op. cit.,* pp. 314–326.

28 Edgar J. Goodspeed, *A History of Early Christian Literature* (Chicago, University of Chicago Press, 1942) ; Alvin Lamson, *The Church of the First Three Centuries* (Boston, Walker, Wise, and Company, 1860) , p. 75; and Bolgar, *op. cit.,* p. 50.

29 A good example of this suspicion—although not a condemnation of classical studies—is St. Basil's *On the Reading of the Profane Authors* (Sermons, XXII) .

lian but Jerome and Augustine who found the key for resolving the dilemma. To these men, then, credit must be given for pointing the direction Christian education was to take.[30]

Jerome's credentials as a Christian scholar need not be recounted here, and to seriously question them is to cast doubt about his right to speak as a Christian Humanist or to appear as a leading policy maker for Christian education. Even Jerome was not immune to uncertainties or fluctuations in mood about the right of classical studies to appear in a Christian educational setting. He did not always trust his own intuitions about the values of scholarship, and, on occasion, as after his famous dream, he could resolve to abjure all pagan studies.[31] But his resolution was not inflexible, and he returned to his books to pursue his studious ways as before. At the outset the reader may wonder about the point of being reminded of Jerome's career, about his becoming the victim of urgent anxiety and his absolute rejection of learning, and then his return to his old scholarly habits and his great books. In the end it is the career of Jerome more than his documented advice that really makes the point. He created a legend of Christian scholarship, and despite what he said or did not say about classical studies, his scholarship spoke for itself and was there for Christian scholars to admire and emulate. If they found his example in need of some support from precept, they could point to his willingness to ignore the content of classical literature and concentrate on style. Literary study had for him an attenuated meaning; it was purely formal, for its end was not to fathom the meaning of a classic but to abstract from it lessons that could be learned about grace and elegance of expression and the beauty of the written word. This is a lesson that a more literate age finds difficult to learn, but it was easy for Jerome, and it inaugurated a method which went a long way toward consolidating the place of classical literature in Christian curricula: formal study of the classics.[32]

Jerome's example, and to some extent his advice, allowed Christians to escape the dilemma without really resolving it. The point may be academic, for in the end, and for whatever reasons, Christian students could enjoy the luxuries of classical studies. But, at best, this was a mixed blessing: whenever they took a classic in hand they had to be sure that their preoccupation with form could immunize them from the contagions of content. Christian teachers and students were understandably uneasy about following the generous prescriptions of Jerome. Something more

---

30 Bolgar, *op. cit.*, p. 50.

31 See E. K. Rand, *Founders of the Middle Ages*, pp. 103–134. For the report of Jerome's famous dream, see *Selected Letters of St. Jerome*, translated by F. A. Wright (Cambridge, Mass., Loeb Classical Library, Harvard University Press, 1923), XVI, pp. 125–127.

32 This, Jerome's position, was attested to by Cassiodorus, *op. cit.*, pp. 119–120; and by Erasmus, *Letters*, I, edited by P. S. Allen, Oxford, 1906, p. 332. See also, Bolgar, *op. cit.*, pp. 51–52.

needed to be added. The additions, the classifications, or the formulas were left to Augustine to supply.

Many an inarticulate Christian wanted to derive benefits he thought were reserved for students of the classics, and, it is true, most Christians had the feeling that the example of Jerome was sound from the standpoints of both scholarship and faith. But Jerome had offered no solution to the problem a Christian scholar would inevitably face in keeping form separate from content. Jerome's enthusiasm for style was so great that he could easily be unaffected by content; the usual Christian student was never certain that his own dedication to literary form would disinfect the immorality and impiety in the pagan legacy. A formula was most desperately needed, and it had to be one simple enough to be understood and comprehensive enough to be effective.

Augustine had a plan that fulfilled these specifications. It was so simple that it is indeed surprising that no one had seriously advanced it before. He told Christians to cull from the pagan literary inheritance all those elements that ran counter to Christian convictions and thus to preserve civilization without preserving paganism itself. He advanced a formula that all Christian Humanists found useful: selection.[33] While it is true that selection could be employed with greater facility when there was more of the classical legacy to choose from, as in the High Renaissance, it could nevertheless serve a highly valuable purpose when the corpus of classical learning in the hands of the Christian community was restricted.

This general formula led naturally to other specific recommendations. Selection could hardly be trusted to the uninitiated; the student himself could not be expected to go through the classics sifting the good from the bad. Someone would perform this service for him; the products of this service were compendia of various sorts representing broad ranges in quality. These compendia were intended to be summaries of essential information. In this way the most serious defect of Jerome's practice was set aright, for now students would be absolved from ignoring the content of classical works. But in providing a solution to one problem, another was raised: what about the teaching of style, on the one hand, and inculcating an appreciation of artistic expression, on the other? Augustine did not have to look far for the answer. He said that technical works on style could supply what was needed. What he must have had in mind were classical grammars setting forth the rules of style supplemented by handbooks containing examples of style. These examples may have been excerpted from classical works, although Augustine is on record as saying that the Bible itself could be used to furnish all the examples a student might need.[34]

---

[33] *Ibid.*, p. 53. St. Augustine himself informs us about his appraisal of the arts. See *Retractions*, I, 6 (Knöll edition, C.S.E.L., XXXVI, 16, 44).

[34] *Ibid.*, IV, 2 and 20.

While the prescriptions of Augustine fulfilled a temporary need and succeeded in preserving Christian contacts with classical culture, they inevitably promoted a separation between Christian thought, on the one hand, and authentic classical learning, on the other. Each succeeding generation of students, depending as it did upon the work of ardent excerpters, moved further and further away from the genius of a classical work that could never be caught in expurgations and excerptions.

Thus, the precepts of Augustine, despite their temporary worth, had a value that tended to evaporate as they moved up the road of educational history. Although Augustine's formula was never completely forgotten and has always been invested with a quality of permanence in the Christian intellectual community, it by no means meant that Christian educational theory was finalized or that Christian educators could lay aside their work, content in the knowledge that nothing more needed to be done toward bringing about a satisfactory accommodation of classical and Christian education.[35]

Even if this had been so, and Christian educational theory made to stand still, the social world could not be made to heed demands for immobility. Jerome and Augustine spoke to a world that would listen, but the world changed, and by the end of the fifth century their advice did not have the full ring of relevance. They, after all, were treading the same path Quintilian had marked out and they had not taken into account the fact that the public oration, the object of classical education, would be superseded by private study, away from the arena, and that educational programs henceforth would need to prepare public men for the offices and the market place and not just for the forum. Work remained to be done within the broad framework of Christian education; Cassiodorus was again the right man at the right time. It was left to him to try to install the classics with a new perspective, narrower than before, it is true, but vastly more practical in their application.

IV

THE EDUCATIONAL WORK OF CASSIODORUS

Before we look at the ways in which Cassidorus reshaped Christian education along lines that would not obliterate its relationships to reservoirs of classical learning, note should be taken of the man himself. There is no need to recite his biography, for the details of his life are not our

---

35 See G. L. Ellspermann, *The Attitude of the Early Christian Latin Writers Toward Pagan Learning and Literature* (Washington, D.C., Catholic University of America Press, 1949) ; and Rand's excellent chapter in *Founders of the Middle Ages,* pp. 251–284.

principal interest here, but we will probably understand the man better if we know something about him.[36]

Cassiodorus—whose complete name was Flavius Magnus Aurelius Cassiodorus Senator—was born about 480 in southern Italy into a distinguished and prominent family. For generations members of his family had served a variety of political leaders, almost always successfully, and this tradition of political service was continued by Cassiodorus himself. He entered public life in 503 as an assessor—an assistant magistrate, the most specialized of the learned professions—held various government positions for the next thirty years, and in 533 was appointed Praetorian Prefect, the highest post of his career. The office of Prefect was important and its incumbent was invested with a good deal of power: he promulgated imperial laws and edicts, nominated and supervised provincial governors, removed and punished erring political servants, and served as a judge on certain public issues. Cassiodorus held this office for four years, and, after completing his tour of duty, retired from public life.

When Cassiodorus approached the age where he might have anticipated the pleasures of quiet retirement, we find him casting about for a new career. During his political life, and during interludes of unemployment, he had tried his hand at writing. The principal products of this labor were *Variae, Chronicon,* and *Gothic History.* So perhaps it was not unnatural for him at the twilight of life to try to make a mark on intellectual history. It is hardly certain that Cassiodorus had a change of heart with respect to religion—for his private spiritual feelings are not clearly recorded—but it is safe to say that in turning his attention to another career, evidences of religious sensitivity became more apparent. Both in literary and nonliterary activities he began to attract attention: he wrote *De Anima,* based on St. Augustine, Cicero, and Claudianus Mamertus, and shortly followed that with a *Commentary on the Psalms;* moreover, he appealed to Christians to resist the new Gothic invasion that seized Rome between the years 546 and 548. Cassiodorus, in the capacity of an emissary, traveled to Constantinople to implore the Emperor to reconquer Italy. While in Constantinople he was exposed on a fairly profound level to the theory of Jewish theological teaching, and, in addition, he had an opportunity to meet scholars who had dedicated most of their adult lives to the preservation and editing of manuscripts. We may guess that these experiences, plus his own interest in the study of the Scriptures, were important factors contributing to his decision to play

---

[36] No one has written a biography of Cassiodorus. The principal source for details on his life and career is his own *Variae,* prepared and edited during the final years of his public life. See A. Van de Vyver, "Cassiodorus et son oeuvre," *Speculum,* VI (1931), pp. 245–247. Jones, *op. cit.,* pp. 7–32, gives a good summary of the important events of Cassiodorus' life; and R. W. Church, *Miscellaneous Essays* (London, The Macmillan Company, 1891), pp. 155–204, is excellent, not only for Cassiodorus' public career, but for a detailed study of his character as well.

a more vital role in the extension of the Christian ministry. Cassiodorus was too old to be a cleric, even if his station in life had permitted,[37] and the work of the ordinary schools seemed fitted to neither his personality nor his interest, so he turned to the establishment of a monastery. Thus, upon his return to Italy, Cassiodorus founded a double monastery on his ancestral estates at Scylaccium. One section of the monastery was reserved for hermits; the other was organized for those who wished to live a less austere life as well as a more communal one. The latter was called Vivarium. At this second monastery Cassiodorus spent the remaining years of his life and made his historic contributions to education.

These contributions took various forms; some were highly practical, others were mainly theoretical, but all belong in the broad category of educational doctrine. In a way all his work is related to *An Introduction to Divine and Human Readings,* and we can look at it from the perspective of this codification of Christian education. In other words, when we ask what was Cassiodorus' influence on education, we are at the same time asking what message did *An Introduction to Divine and Human Readings* have for the Christian educational world.

We can begin by saying that the *Introduction* served as a guide and an inspiration to librarians to search out copies of works recommended by Cassiodorus. In addition, the manuscripts collected and preserved by Cassiodorus provided a steady source for knowledge of the Fathers and the important Latin authors.[38] Both patristic and classical literature might have survived without Cassiodorus' labor, but, as it is, credit should go to him for having kept them in a reasonably accessible form.

If we look more closely at these points, we recognize Cassiodorus as one of the first Christian educators to make the monastery a place of study as well as a place of seclusion where members of the monastic community would have ample opportunity to cultivate the spiritual life.[39] He wanted his monks to be spiritual, there is no question of that, but he wanted them to be something more as well. They were to be studious and to some extent learned. But neither was possible without proper implements. At this point Cassiodorus began to collect as many manuscripts as possible and then to duplicate them; in this way several

[37] Jean Leclerq, *The Love of Learning and the Desire for God* (New York, New American Library of World Literature, 1962) , p. 28, is positive that Cassiodorus was not a cleric: "Cassiodorus was simply not a monk. Therefore, one can easily see that the director of the Vivarium, although he shares the life of the monks, organizes and even directs it, is not a monk and does not think as a monk. He never received the vocation, and lacks that experience." Few scholars interested in Cassiodorus are so certain of this, although I am inclined to agree with Leclerq, for I think whatever evidence there is supports his conclusion.

[38] F. Holmes Dudden, *Gregory the Great,* vol. II (London, Longmans, Green & Company, Ltd., 1905) , p. 170.

[39] Dudden, *ibid.,* p. 172, says that Cassiodorus "was the first man in Italy to recognize the possibilities of the convent as a school for liberal culture."

monks might use them to further their scholarly purposes.[40] We need not be interested here in the development of the monastic ideal, but we cannot help noting that, for perhaps the first time in monastic history, manual labor is interpreted more broadly than as merely toiling in the fields or the shops. For, as part of his literary monasticism, Cassiodorus told the monks that instead of working in the fields they could fulfill their religious requirement of labor by copying manuscripts. Moreover, the founder of literary monasticism seems to reserve special praise for the monks who worked in the monastic publishing plant: "Among those of your tasks which require physical effort the scribe, if he writes correctly, appeals most to me . . . for by reading Divine Scripture he wholesomely instructs his own mind and by copying the precepts of the Lord, he spreads them far and wide. Happy his design, praiseworthy his zeal; to preach to men with the hand alone, to unleash tongues with the fingers, to give salvation silently to mortals to fight against the illicit temptations of the devil with pen and ink. Every word of the Lord, written by a scribe is a wound inflicted on Satan." [41]

The collection and multiplication of manuscripts was an important part of the work undertaken by Cassiodorus and his monks, but he did not want to stop with this. From the first Cassiodorus attracted to the monastery a small but capable group of grammarians and translators who worked on the texts as they became available, translating, correcting, and editing them. The scholarly tasks successfully completed by these monks included assembling the complete body of scripture from the text of St. Jerome, translating many of the Fathers, translating and assembling the works of early Church historians, preparing Biblical commentaries, translating the *Antiquities* of Josephus, and dividing the Bible into chapters and adding appropriate titles and summaries.[42]

In fulfilling the role of a librarian, Cassiodorus was interested in every phase of the preservation and duplication of manuscripts. And he did not wait for manuscripts to come to him or to be discovered by accident, but he actively sought them out and was prepared, evidently, to pay well for them whenever their contents seemed to merit the expenditure. Cassiodorus' stance may not have been that of the disinterested scholar; although the motive for scholarship is evident, it is always subsumed to religion. When the monks were dealing with manuscripts, he admonished them to regard their work with the greatest care because he believed they were involved in a sacred enterprise. The corrector's work was especially critical—and this is easily understood—but it was not only accuracy that was sought but some beauty of expression as well. He asked

40 G. L. Hurst, *An Outline of the History of Christian Literature* (New York, The Macmillan Company, 1926) , p. 151.

41 Cassiodorus, *op. cit.*, p. 133.

42 *Ibid.*, pp. 28–29.

his correctors to correct with care and to form corrected letters to correspond to the original text and thus to convey the impression that everything in the manuscript was the work of the scribe. He believed it entirely inappropriate for anything unsightly to appear in the glorious works the monks were preparing and he would have been greatly disappointed if anything remained in the manuscripts to offend the eyes of students who subsequently used them. The correctors were asked to consider the nature of their task, how they were serving not only themselves but all Christians as well, and how they were guarding the Church's principal treasures and lighting the souls of men. He told them to "take pains lest there be any residue of faultiness in its truth, of alteration in its purity, of erroneous letters in its correctness." [43]

No detail in the process of copying was overlooked. Punctuation and spelling were matters for special attention, although they would not seem to us today to be worth all the attention Cassiodorus gave them. But if we insist on such a judgment we shall miss an important part of the copying process that engaged these monks. They were not, of course, using duplicating machines, but were sitting at desks in a large room, and with their pens in hand were taking dictation from a reader who occupied a prominent place in the front of the room. As the reader read from the manuscript, it was expected that copying monks would catch his words and record them faultlessly without the reader having to punctuate the text or spell the words. Surely this was asking a great deal for an age which was somewhat illiterate, or at least less literate than our own, and in this setting Cassiodorus' admonitions to his scribes seem more realistic and to the point. He is simply saying that copyists must be prepared adequately in punctuation and spelling if their writing is to be accurate and fast. Experience proved that these matters could not be ignored, and there must have been recurring difficulties both with spelling and punctuation, for Cassiodorus, at age ninety, was still concerned with correct spelling and produced a fairly useful work on the subject.[44]

The internal composition of the copied manuscripts was of course intended to be accurate; the texts copied were to be handled carefully, and their editing was to be done with great pains. This was all natural enough, for neither Cassiodorus nor anyone else could justify the spurious reproduction of texts. But Cassiodorus did not stop here: the binding process was of concern to him too. He recommended that blank pages be

---

[43] *Ibid.*, p. 111. This admonition was for the most part observed and it, along with the generally favorable light Cassiodorus cast on learning, has led to some extravagant recitations of his place in scholarly history. G. L. Hurst, *op. cit.*, p. 151, says, for example, "in [him] the West had the greatest individual contributor to the preservation of learning prior to the Middle Ages."

[44] This work was *De Orthographia*. It along with his other writings led Dudden, *op. cit.*, p. 173, to refer to "complementary elements of Italian monasticism: Benedict, the saint, and Cassiodorus, the savant."

added to the manuscript to allow for additions whenever they were made necessary by the discovery of new sources of information. As with their content, the binding of manuscripts was undertaken from a religious perspective; "in addition to these things we have provided workers skilled in bookbinding, in order that a handsome external form may clothe the beauty of sacred letters; in some measure, perhaps, we imitate the example of the parable of the Lord, who amid the glory of the heavenly banquet, has clothed in wedding garments those whom he judges worthy to be invited to the table." [45]

One must stand in awe of a man capable of undertaking the establishment of an innovating monastery when he himself had attained an age somewhere between sixty and seventy. Whatever one may think of the educational influences of monasticism in general, it is certainly true that this monastery was unusual, and that it differed from anything preceding it. The place was not a university in either the medieval or the modern sense, but in its own day it performed a remarkably useful service to scholarship and learning, for it developed and handed on a level of scholarly accomplishment unequaled in the West for another 400 years.[46]

Besides being a fairly gifted librarian who could collect, arrange, edit, and reproduce manuscripts, Cassiodorus was an author whose influence—although it cannot be traced by direct routes to European centers of learning—was unquestionably considerable. His most important book was an *Introduction to Divine and Human Readings,* and taken as a whole it prescribed a cultural program for Christian use. Book II of the *Introduction* took its place alongside the works of Capella, Boethius, Priscian, and Donatus as one of the important schoolbooks of the Middle Ages.[47]

The *Introduction* was written around 550 as a handbook for the house; a contemporary printed edition would run about 140 pages. It was intended as a syllabus and bibliographical guide for the monks at Vivarium, but the intentions its author had for it were underestimated. In some places it seems to have served as the only textbook a student used throughout his entire educational program, and even in the early medieval university it was still in use as a book for the arts course. Its wide and persistent use for almost 500 years implies, first, that its content was judged acceptable and that its fusing of classical learning to Christian education could be tolerated, and, second, that good schoolbooks

45 Cassiodorus, *op. cit.,* p. 134.

46 A great deal of testimony supports this conclusion. See, for example, E. K. Rand, "Cassiodorus," *Speculum,* XIII (October, 1938) , pp. 433–447; L. W. Jones, "Notes on the Style and Vocabulary of Cassiodorus' *Institutiones,*" *Classical Philology,* XL (January, 1945) , pp. 24–31; and L. W. Jones, "The Influence of Cassiodorus on Medieval Culture," *Speculum,* XX (October, 1945) , pp. 433–442.

47 *Ibid.,* p. 441.

were not easy to procure. The *Introduction,* especially Book II, was all too often the best the masters could offer their students. Considering Cassiodorus' purpose in writing the *Introduction to Divine and Human Readings,* we should be willing to acknowledge that its textbook qualities were limited. Certainly Book II was a discourse on the seven liberal arts, a discourse justified in Book I along these lines: by cultivating secular learning Christians will have at their disposal a means for knowing the Scriptures more fully and more accurately. But it was an attenuated discourse, little more than a digest or an annotation of what previous scholars had said about grammar, rhetoric, logic, astronomy, music, geometry, and arithmetic. And each of these studies was put in a context where its liberal nature was suppressed or ignored while practical outcomes were emphasized.

Had Cassiodorus' advice been taken at full value—assuming that sources were available for students to consult—we would be left with a document that sounded the balanced doctrine of compromise between divine and liberal learning and that pointed the way for students to effect this compromise by using the tools of liberal learning that are touched on in Book II. We know now that only the doctrine was heeded, and the bibliographical handbook was used as a text. And here Cassiodorus set a precedent too, for this type of book remained in constant favor for another 1000 years; Cassiodorus' example—techniques of literary digestion—was eagerly followed by Isidore of Seville and hundreds of other authors who employed compilation and excerption in the same way. Perhaps Cassiodorus may be forgiven, for all unknowingly he inaugurated the age of the anthology, and many of the anthologies that came into use, many based on Cassiodorus' *Introduction,* were far inferior to the one he had produced.

What has been said about Cassiodorus' famous book, while not illuminating its content, has been sufficient to indicate its general nature. And what counts is not so much what Cassiodorus wrote about the arts but the pedagogical message that his *Introduction* contained, first, the authenticity of classical education's claim for a place in Christian schools and, second, the way this classical knowledge might be used to serve the fundamental objectives of Christian education.

Quintilian had not been completely forgotten by Christian educators, although his advice was no longer part of the living educational tradition; it had to be mined from literary sources. At best these sources were none too good: sometimes they were incomplete or just plain wrong; on rare occasions the *Education of an Orator* was available, but only in fragments. Even when a good portion of Quintilian's work was available, it was too theoretical for most Christian appetites. So the end result was that neither Quintilian's *Education of an Orator* nor the teaching tradition it had set in motion served as a practical guide to schoolmasters.

When we add these facts to the imprecision surrounding the Christian teaching tradition itself—one body of opinion denying the worth of classical learning altogether and another body of opinion acknowledging, in guarded terms, the utility of classical educational apparatuses—we have a chaotic situation. Cassiodorus counseled compromise but in doing so he avoided the stigma of innovation: he simply admitted the worth of classical authors for forming Christian intellects. This was a first and a necessary step, for unless this admission was made and its implications followed the old impasse would have reappeared. Before Cassiodorus could say anything meaningful about grafting the methods of classical scholarship to Christian education, it had to be established that this could be done with relative impunity and that it was worth doing at all.

In following the legacy of classical education up to Cassiodorus, one must be sensitive to a number of implicit contradictions. Some of these were not revised out of the legacy when it was used to shape new educational patterns, and, it must be admitted, Cassiodorus allowed some of them to remain. Perhaps the most persistent of these contradictions was to be found in the fact that the educational apparatus, protected by dogmatic assumptions, was Roman in style and technique and was integrally related to the Roman political system. When this system was fragmented a vacuum was created on the level of educational purpose; in setting different goals for education, although employing many of the same means, Cassiodorus performed a useful service. What he did was to undertake the mission of a transmogrifier; he moved educational theory from the library to the schoolroom; he gave the contents of the trivium and the quadrivium a practical orientation. In the tradition of Quintilian both had remained faithful to liberal learning; Cassiodorus reoriented both and called upon the arts to perform useful services.

On such points as imitation and selection Cassiodorus could make the adaptation from the level of theory to that of practice with relative ease, and he could then hope that schoolmasters were willing to listen to him and follow his advice. But so long as imitation meant writing like the ancients had written and not separating form from content, or so long as selection meant taking the whole of a given classic and studying it with thoroughness and completeness, Christian leaders and Christian teachers were understandably anxious and usually balked at following these school practices. On a more comprehensive level Cassiodorus took grammar and rhetoric out of their oratorical contexts and related them, as tools, to the broader aspects of Christian learning. In all, as we look back on these accomplishments of transmogrification, we are tempted to conclude that Cassiodorus did not do anything very great; we are almost inclined to think that what was done was almost inevitably done, that Cassiodorus was more a victim of circumstances than a leader of education. These temptations should be resisted, for we have really no right to look at Cassiodorus' work through glasses tinted for the sun of our own times; whether or not an event has historical significance is a judgment to be made in an appropriate context: to make our context correlative with Cassiodorus' is both unhistorical and unfair. Yet, what Cassiodorus needs is not defense but illumination, and with this in mind the following general points seem worth making:

1. As the founder of literary monasticism, he was responsible for a greater, although admittedly uneven, dissemination of learning throughout the West. In the first place, as we have said, his principal book, *Introduction to Divine and Human Readings,* was used as a textbook and a bibliographical reference for centuries. In some schools, and in some genres, it was used more extensively than in others, but whenever it was used, and with whatever care, it always conveyed the message that classical learning could help Christians understand their faith better; in addition, classical learning could make life in temporal society more fruitful and satisfying. Despite the importance of the *Introduction,* we should not allow another side of Cassiodorus' influence, which was not cultivated by this book, to be slighted. By making a commitment to literary monasticism Cassiodorus preserved and perpetuated the classical tradition: he collected manuscripts on the classics as well as on the Fathers and put his monks to work reproducing them. How much or how little a few copying monks could do is not the point at issue here, for no one believes that one monastery could supply the legitimate literary requirements of all Europe. What is important is the precedent of literary monasticism: from Cassiodorus' time forward it was a respectable commission for monks to accept.

2. Wide erudition is accepted by Cassiodorus and he means to include secular learning. The balance he maintained between the two books of the *Introduction* is evidence of this. Had he despaired of learning, either divine or secular, he would not have entered the field of education at all; had he doubted the need or the utility of secular learning, he would not have written Book II of the *Introduction.* Moreover, if he had thought the secular had only a propaedeutic role for divine study, he would have made this point in Book I and left it at that. But he saw clearly that the claims secular learning could make were not limited to a preparatory role, so he spoke out for them in a way that was somewhat unusual for an age accustomed to looking heavenward.

3. Although Cassiodorus could argue that secular learning was both wanted and needed, he did not, as we have said, follow the avenues that had been marked out by Quintilian. His shift in emphasis meant that Quintilian's oratorical tradition was summarily abandoned; when the arts were studied they were not to be pursued with the expectation that they would serve as foundations for the eloquent speech. Their new role was to provide students with a basic literary education, one that led to competence in conducting the everyday affairs of church and state and

commerce. It is probably true that even before Cassiodorus abandoned the oratorical tradition in education the drift among educators was in that direction, for Christians had never been able to see too clearly the relevance of such studies to their educational objectives. Despite this tendency, it should be noted that Cassiodorus was not merely endorsing the trend, nor was he content to describe the current educational practices; his purpose was to improve them. This meant, first of all, that the linguistic discipline was to be set within the framework of the time. Neither the language structure of Cicero nor the vocabulary used in classical periods had much meaning for the sixth century; the tempers of learning and of the times were too different to continue the rigorous classical approach.[48] So Cassiodorus could be something less than a classical purist and still recommend a relevant education in the linguistic discipline. In fact, language became tremendously important in Cassiodorus' syllabus, even though the old classical models were enjoined. This was a sign that the contacts with the classical past had pretty well disappeared and that the only way an accurate Latin could be perpetuated was in the schools. More clearly than perhaps ever before the schools now became the principal agents for preserving and passing on the cultural inheritance. With this new responsibility, it is understandable that they should be given greater attention and their methods subjected to more searching scrutiny.

4. The question might well be asked: Why was Cassiodorus listened to, when others who had made somewhat the same plea for secular learning had so little influence in reforming the schools? This is not an easy question to answer, and any answer must suffer from being somewhat incomplete. No doubt the security of Cassiodorus' reputation as an orthodox Christian added considerable weight to the *Introduction*. It was considered to be entirely safe advice. But could not the same thing be said about St. Jerome and St. Augustine? The difference is not in their reputation or in the clear orthodoxy of their counsel, but in the fact that where St. Jerome stopped largely on the level of example, and St. Augustine mainly on the level of theory, Cassiodorus descended to the day-to-day problems of the classroom. He dealt with instruments; his predecessors stayed largely with example and precept.

5. Candor demands the admission that Cassiodorus did not stay with the best authors when he justified an encyclopedic view of learning, and this must always be something of a thorn in the side of those who admire Cassiodorus' accomplishments most. Yet, it is something that can be explained. If Cassiodorus had limited his literary recommendations to only the very best of the classical writers, he might have made his con-

---

[48] See Mary Gratin Ennis, *The Vocabulary of the Institutiones of Cassiodorus, With Special Advertence to the Technical Terminology and Its Sources* (Washington, D.C., Catholic University of America Press, 1939) ; and Bolgar, *op. cit.*, pp. 35–37.

temporaries recoil from learning altogether, for they were not ready to deal with the best. He thought it was possible to obtain broad learning by going to the easier writers, although he did not do so exclusively, and not to make his students dig for treasures in mines that were more difficult to excavate. The announced purpose of the *Introduction,* and this purpose was applied indiscriminately, was to provide an easy and safe equivalent to traditional education for the monks in the monastery. Traditional education was to be conducted into the new age on the vehicles of grammar and logic. The former was accorded an unassailable position. Cassiodorus wrote that "Grammar is skill in the art of cultivated speech—skill acquired from famous writers of poetry and prose; its function is the creation of faultless prose and verse; its end is to please through skill in finished speech and blameless writing." [49] It might be argued that this justification was not so different from anything Quintilian might have said, and the argument would have merit, but where Quintilian thought of the orator using speech in public, Cassiodorus thought of speech—both oral and written—as a private accomplishment, as important in one's study or in the teacher's classroom as on the public rostrum.

Finally, logic was raised to a more respectable level in the school's program of studies. In the development of logic, and in the eventual subordination of rhetoric to it (this ran counter to the Roman tradition, which had put rhetoric first) , the Middle Ages—especially tenth and eleventh century logicians—were indebted to Cassiodorus, Isidore, and Capella.[50] They had also part of Aristotle, it is true, either in translation or through commentaries, but they may have had to depend as much on the general surveys of Cassiodorus, Isidore, and Capella, which were encyclopedic yet brief, superficial, obscure, and sometimes plainly wrong. In any event, both the rise of logic to a position of greater importance in school learning and the continuation of classical bodies of knowledge about logic were outcomes for which Cassiodorus was partly responsible.[51]

[49] Cassiodorus, *op. cit.,* p. 146.
[50] See C. S. Baldwin, *Medieval Rhetoric and Poetic* (New York, The Macmillan Company, 1928) .
[51] See Paul Abelson, *The Seven Liberal Arts* (New York, Teachers College, Columbia University, 1906) .

✠ 6 ✠

Three Medieval Educators:
Alcuin, Hugh of St. Victor, John of Salisbury

I

MEDIEVAL EDUCATION

The three centuries separating Cassiodorus from Alcuin are of slight interest to the chronicler of progress in educational theory. In general these were conservative centuries without visionary spokesmen willing to reconstruct or even to build on the past; they were filled instead with schoolmasters who listened to the voice of caution and undertook, with fragile instruments, to perpetuate traditions about which they were ambivalent and unsure. When a progressive appeared—and Gregory the Great may be called a progressive—it was to turn back the calendar from classical education, or a classically oriented education, to a thoroughly Christian syllabus.[1] This had been tried before, briefly and without success, after Julian's famous edict had removed Christian teachers from the schools; lack of success was due in part to the attenuated test the syllabus was given because the edict was rescinded, but in a broader sense it is difficult to see how an educational program built only on Christian readings could have supplied even a minimum of what the limited learned world thought it wanted. Gregory could eschew grammar and rhetoric, and all the usual instruments of classical education, because of his exalted position and partly because he already had these tools; and

---

1 Some may reject the idea that Gregory was progressive; yet, he was asking what the Church and Christian education had to do with an outworn culture. For Gregory's attitude, expressed in his own words, see *Epistle,* XI, 54, in Migne, *Patrologia Latina,* LXXVII, 1171C and LXXV, 516B. Rand, *Founders of the Middle Ages,* pp. 28–32, regards Gregory as a progressive.

he could disbelieve the worth of Latin teaching because he lived in a society that knew and spoke Latin effortlessly, if not always faultlessly. But what was to be done on the outskirts of the Christian world, where Latin was not the vernacular and where, because it was thought to be a divine language, it was absolutely essential to the conduct of divine services and ecclesiastical business? [2] So the ringing declamations and disciplinary epistles of Gregory counted for little, and his counsel for a special kind of progressivism went unheeded. Teachers did their best with the earlier admonitions of Cassiodorus; they tried to convert the classical educational program, clearly no longer useful in pure form, to the demands of practical necessity. When they had his work, Cassiodorus was their best guide; without him they turned to the elaborate exertions of Isidore of Seville, who in his *Etymologies* [3] had copied large portions of Cassiodorus' annotations on the seven liberal arts. What they had to follow, either for theory or for day-to-day teaching materials, was none too good. These were truly dark days for learning, and we should recognize them for what they were; but we should not want to punish the poor schoolmasters who labored in monasteries and municipal schools to bring a little light to the few disorderly schoolrooms that survived.

The long chronological step from Cassiodorus to Alcuin may be made quickly. While it may be extravagant to claim that nothing of consequence took place during these bleak centuries, it is surely not too much to say that history records almost nothing requiring more from us than a passing glance. Yet there was always need for some learning: the Christian Church had long since become a bookish religion, and ecclesiastical business expanded, with a preoccupation for religious administration; civic affairs, too, came to demand the superintendence of literate men as the economic world began to break the chains of feudalism. The Cassiodoran idea that learning might serve a man both in his study and in the market place was never completely realized,[4] but at least learning objectives were moved permanently away from their early connections with the classical public forum. Education approached the threshold of professionalism or vocationalism. But this approach was only on the vague level of hope; the need was clear, almost desperate, but tools were unavailable to accomplish what needed doing. The Church stood ready to encourage educational endeavors; on many occasions priests were directed to spend part of their day teaching the children in their parishes; and this teaching was to be offered to all, without respect to social

---

[2] According to Bede, Latin, Greek, and Hebrew were divine languages (*De Orthographia,* Keil edition, *Gramm. Lat.,* VII, 261). See also, W. Levison, *England and the Continent in the Eighth Century* (Oxford, Oxford University Press, 1946), p. 70.

[3] *Etymologiae sive Origines Libri XX,* rec. W. M. Lindsay, *Scriptorum Classicorum bibliotheca Oxoniensis,* Oxford, 1911.

[4] Cassiodorus, *op. cit.,* pp. 67–68.

standing or ability to pay.[5] Unfortunately, too few priests were available to work on this elementary level, and the results of such teaching were unexceptional; but there were some good results.

In Ireland and England, where the effects of the Roman collapse were not so disastrous, learning stood on solider ground. One of the strangest paradoxes in the history of learning is found in the fact that the greater the distance classical learning ranged from the centers of classical culture the better the chance it had for being perpetuated in the three tumultuous centuries following the sixth century. The centers of classical culture in the West, and their immediate environs, depended for the continuation of their contacts with their classical past more on the informal teachings from the structure of their society than on the schools or on the written classics themselves. But in countries where these informal instruments of instruction were never a clear part of the way of life, knowledge of the classical past had always been made to depend on its written record. In these lands, it is true, contacts with classical times and with classical ways of thinking and acting were always somewhat artificial, and in the beginning, at least, were regarded as something like abrasive intruders; but once the inroads were made they did not depend so heavily on a political or social system. They may have had less relevance to life, but in this fact they gained their strength: the practical necessities of life neither justified nor constituted an argument against their right to a place in formal learning. However, in the centers of classical culture in the West, the schools were less depended upon; yet, even when the schools played a part, they themselves were intimately bound up with, and dependent upon, the political system. When this whole system suffered a premature demise, the avenues through which classical ideas passed were cut; and the corpus of the classical tradition, sustained only orally and informally, was left without any dependable means for perpetuating itself. Thus we find the principal reason for the modest flourishing of classical learning at the outskirts of the Roman Empire during the very years that learning was undergoing its sharpest decline nearer its place of birth.[6]

If these were happier circumstances, and indeed they so appear, they were not entirely devoid of serious and persistent obstacles to an understanding and appreciation of the classics. Even when the Irish monks were enthusiastic about the possibilities for classical knowledge being a secure beam in the structure of divine study, it was usual for them to

---

[5] In 529 the Second Council of Vaison enjoined all parish priests to teach boys and thus prepare fitting successors to themselves. See Marrou, *op. cit.*, p. 336.

[6] For an elaboration of these important evolutions, see M. L. W. Laistner, *Thought and Letters in Western Europe, A.D. 500–900* (New York, The Dial Press, Inc., 1957) ; R. L. Poole, *Illustrations of the History of Medieval Thought and Learning* (New York, The Macmillan Company, 1920) , pp. 8–14; and Bolgar, *op. cit.*, pp. 91–93.

approach classical learning with a disinterested style; they did in fact become exponents of an artistic and contemplative monasticism. In addition, they may be counted as the first scholars who studied the classics as they were to be studied from that time on, against a cultural background without any other contacts with ancient civilization. Yet, in this pioneer venture all the obstacles were found: to use the classics they had to know Latin, at least, and whatever their progress in Latin, and often it was barely passable, there is no hard evidence that they accomplished much in the study of Greek.[7] But Latin was not an easy language to learn and too few aids were at their disposal. They used the traditional instruments of secular learning, but these instruments were too often crude and fragmented. Parts of classical grammars, which they regularly copied and used, were written for students who spoke Latin, so from a variety of sources they culled lists of vocabularies and tried to teach this unfamiliar language to their students. Progress was always slow and uneven; their best efforts led them to reconstruct a Latin with a poverty of vocabulary, overlaid with idiomatic inconsistencies. The result was surely poor quality scholarship, but this counted for less than the heroic efforts they made to do what had not been done before. They constructed the crude machinery for approaching the classical heritage along lines that all future generations were to follow—dictionaries, word lists, and extrapolations from the ancient texts themselves. In a word, the Irish monks made classical learning entirely bookish; this approach was followed wherever Irish teaching models were accepted.[8]

The brave beginnings of the Irish were continued with somewhat greater success among the Anglo-Saxons; and now we meet the monks and scholars who broke ground for Alcuin. It would be incorrect to suppose that the glories of Irish learning and scholarship became the small change of history, for their accomplishments even from this point on were significant, but after the middle of the seventh century they produced little of consequence for pedagogic technique. Now the centers for the new learning, especially for the pedagogy associated with it, became Canterbury and York, and the future of pedagogic theory and practice was in their hands.[9]

These places were Church establishments, and in the efforts of the Church to advance the fundamentals of learning we begin to see more

---

[7] James J. Walsh, *High Points of Medieval Culture* (Milwaukee, The Bruce Publishing Company, 1937), pp. 19–35, is far too generous in his praise of Irish scholarship. More balanced views are offered by: J. J. Auchmuty, *Irish Education* (London, George C. Harrap & Co., Ltd., 1937); and John Healy, *Ireland's Ancient Schools and Scholars* (Dublin, Sealy, Bryers, and Walker, 1893).

[8] Bolgar, *op. cit.*, p. 94.

[9] See E. M. Wilmot-Buxton, *Alcuin* (New York, P. J. Kenedy & Sons, 1922), pp. 64–84; and Bolgar, *op. cit.*, p. 95.

clearly the kind of commitment the Church was required to make to secular learning, not because the Church had finally decided that it needed the ornaments of the seven liberal arts, but because the Church needed a clergy literate in Latin to carry out the essential mission of its divine character. Few historians of Church-related education overlook the sharp rebuke Pope Gregory delivered to Bishop Desiderius, and too often they take this disciplinary epistle as a statement of firm and inflexible policy guiding the Church and her bishops on secular education.[10] Gregory's letter is a classic instance of a man looking at the world but seeing and understanding only a small part of it. Gregory assumed incorrectly that Desiderius was doing work better left to others when he taught boys Latin grammar; and he based this assumption on evidence from Italy, where Latin was still a vernacular. It apparently never occurred to him that this was not true in Gaul. Poor Desiderius was only doing what any conscientious bishop should have done: teaching classes of boys the language they needed for their religious vocation; no one else was prepared to fulfill this elemental function. Perhaps the Saxon schools were in even worse shape than those of Gaul; the social traditions of the Anglo-Saxons, moreover, contained poorer foundations for elementary classical learning. In the long run, these disadvantages probably proved to be blessings in disguise.

The Anglo-Saxons did not begin with a bold plan to recover the methods of the secular schools for use in teaching Latin under the general superintendence of the Church. What was later hailed as a bold plan began almost by accident and proceeded slowly and in short steps. Clerics educated in the secular schools of the Mediterranean world came to England to find the English Church needing the kind of linguistic training course they themselves had; and, doubting that their faith had suffered from secular methods, they naturally showed greater sympathy for secular learning than their English counterparts, who had heard lurid tales about the dangers in the classics. All this was in the nature of a good omen, but structures for educating an entire nation are not built in a day, a decade, or even a lifetime. Teaching Latin to students who had no social affinity for it required special techniques that the emissaries from the lower part of the continent did not have. Too frequently, moreover, they lacked pedagogic knowledge, and the techniques they brought, or the ones they remembered from their own school days, were not especially helpful. After all the problem was new and they were unprepared to master it. Yet they did not come completely empty handed, and the

---

10 Because of the distance from Rome, Ireland was less affected by Gregory's progressive policies. For the letter, see *Epistle, op. cit.* For the character of the ancient Irish Church, see the introduction to J. H. Todd, *St. Patrick the Apostle of Ireland* (Dublin, Hodges, Smith & Co., 1864).

classical techniques they remembered were adopted, imitated, and modified until eventually techniques were hammered out for teaching Latin and parts of the classics to an entirely new clientele.[11]

We need not examine the first steps of this methodology now, for they appear with many refinements in the pedagogy of Alcuin. Yet, a few beacons along the road of progress should be identified.

Ancient grammarians took a great deal for granted; they wrote for students who spoke Latin, or a vernacular akin to Latin, and offered no hints on teaching the language to boys for whom it was a complete mystery. These Latin grammars were often available in the great English monastic and cathedral libraries, and they, along with fragments of classical literature, were the bases on which a new class of English teachers could build.[12] The strong tendency of ancient grammarians to philosophize about language, and the models of literature contained in the classics themselves, needed reworking in order to distill something for day-to-day use. Bede, Boniface, and Tatwine, among the first teachers in England to recognize the pedagogical problem, began by admitting that the presently available materials were pedagogically useless; and from this admission they proceeded to construct pragmatically sound techniques for teaching Latin. They compiled their own grammars, although none was original save in methodology.[13] The books of Bede and Boniface, more successful than those of Tatwine, were used regularly in York and Jarrow, the two best-known schools of the time. The latter school was directed by Bede; the former by Egbert.[14] On the pedagogic foundations laid at York and Jarrow Alcuin built his theory and practice of education, one stimulating the renaissance of the ninth century.

Here, at the Carolingian doorstep, we should interrupt natural historical development to say something about the basic assumptions in medieval educational theory and to add a word of justification for the personality emphases of this chapter. Alcuin's right to appear is based on his contributions to elementary education and to the teaching of an accurate Latin. It may be asked why Hugh of St. Victor is chosen instead of, say, Vincent of Beauvais, and John of Salisbury rather than Theodore of Chartres. And, moreover, why the name of Abelard, the most famous of all medieval teachers, does not figure larger; and why Albert the Great, Thomas Aquinas, and Peter the Lombard are neglected. Any

---

11 See J. W. Thompson, *The Medieval Library* (Chicago, University of Chicago Press, 1939), p. 31; L. J. Paetow, *The Arts Course at Medieval Universities* (Urbana, Illinois, University of Illinois Press, 1910); and Bolgar, *op. cit.*, pp. 99–100.

12 *Ibid.*, p. 104.

13 See Levison, *op. cit.*, p. 70; and M. Roger, *L'Enseignement des lettres classiques d'Ausone à Alcuin* (Paris, A. Silvaire, 1905), p. 332. Tatwine's grammar—*De Octo Partibus Orationis*—was never published.

14 A. F. West, *Alcuin and the Rise of the Christian Schools* (New York, Charles Scribner's Sons, 1892), p. 37.

principle of selection can be debated, but the fundamental assumption here is that these three men—Alcuin, Hugh, and John—were most influential in charting the course of medieval studies. The scholastics, including Thomas Aquinas and his disciples, were not educational theorists except either by accident or indirection; when they treated of pedagogical questions it was always as an aside to broader philosophical or intellectual issues. Even Thomas' disquisition on the teacher, *De Magistro,* for all its superior qualities of reasoned argument, treats teaching philosophically and not pedagogically. It may be doubted that many teachers, taking for granted the possibilities of teaching and the teacher's agent-role in learning, listened to Thomas or altered their practices if they read *De Magistro.* Similarly, we see Scholasticism, not as educational theory, but as an instrument of theory, with its most pronounced application in the universities and in learned circles generally, rather than in schoolrooms where teachers and students were laying the necessary foundation. Within the broad limits of medieval educational theory, we assume, Alcuin, Hugh, and John dealt with the most persistent and basic issues.

In this interpolation, something should be said about medieval educational theory, where Alcuin, Hugh, and John worked, and the assumptions of which they regularly accepted: education aims mainly at the civilization of intellect and must concentrate on the schooling of clerics for otherworldly goals.[15] In part, medieval education agreed with the classical program preceding it and the humanistic teaching succeeding it; but where both classical and humanistic educational systems put moral formation first, medieval education centered on intellectual development. It is strange, but true, that an age so concerned with ecclesiastical business and the erection of structures and formulas for the salvation of souls missed an opportunity to convert education to moral purposes. Perhaps, having so much confidence in the Church's moral influence, it was possible to believe that formal avenues of education could be freed for the noble work of mental development, or that the surest way to morality and eventual salvation was dependable knowledge. It is plainly wrong to think that preoccupations with things of the mind meant that the relevance of divine revelation could be gainsaid; one road to virtue, the one guarded by the school, must have been knowledge.

The twelfth century was the golden age of medieval educational speculation.[16] But prior to this, representative works on educational theory were composed by Cassiodorus, Isidore of Seville, Rabanus Maurus, and Alcuin. The position of Alcuin among pre-twelfth-century educators appears to give him an enviable precedence and therefore

15 D. D. McGarry, "Renaissance Educational Theory," *Historical Bulletin,* 32 (May, 1954), pp. 195–209.

16 See C. H. Haskins, *The Renaissance of the Twelfth Century* (Cambridge, Mass., Harvard University Press, 1927), pp. 1–29.

justifies his place in this chapter. Among the twelfth-century theorists themselves—one Frenchman, two Germans, and one Englishman—pride of place goes to Hugh of St. Victor, principally for the *Didascalicon,* or the *Study of Reading,* and John of *Salisbury,* for his *Metalogicon.* Theodore of Chartres—*Heptateuchon,* or a *Library of the Seven Liberal Arts*—and Conrad of Hirschau—*Didascalion,* or *Dialogue on Authors*— merit notice, although neither wrote with the same breadth of vision as Hugh or John, nor did they have the same influence on the content or method of teaching in medieval schools.

II

ALCUIN

When Alcuin was only a small boy he entered the famous York monastic school, and before leaving he was its master, having succeeded Egbert, the school's founder. The details of Alcuin's early education are little known,[17] and, although some of these details can be found in his writings, they are not especially important, except for showing Alcuin's reactions to conventional elementary education. Bede and Egbert, in company with other Anglo-Saxon scholars, were trying to forge an elementary curriculum guaranteeing an accurate Latin.[18] They made a good start, but it was Alcuin who grafted to it the sound techniques of pedagogy. Undoubtedly Alcuin had some reputation as a skillful teacher before Charlemagne invited him to Frankland, but because Alcuin's work achieved full maturity in the Palace School, we should try to see it there.[19] Before Charlemagne invited Alcuin from York to his capital, he tried to upgrade learning in his dominions in another way. He engaged the services of the famous scholar, Peter of Pisa, undoubtedly a greater ornament to broad scholarship than Alcuin, but Peter's services were ineffective in rejuvenating learning. So Peter was dismissed and Alcuin was summoned to take his place.[20]

If, as the record suggests, Peter was interested in writing polished verses, and reading classical authors, when an integration of the classics to Christian thought and an application of learning to practical needs

---

[17] The best biographies are: C. J. Gaskoin, *Alcuin, His Life and His Works* (New York, G. P. Putnam's Sons, 1904) ; and G. F. Browne, *Alcuin of York* (London, J. Murray, 1908) .

[18] The Venerable Bede, *The Ecclesiastical History of the English Nation,* (London, J. M. Dent & Sons, Ltd., 1954) .

[19] See J. B. Pitra, *Histoire de St. Léger* (Paris, Bossard, 1846) , pp. 24–34.

[20] Einhard, *Life of Charlemagne* (Cincinnati, Ohio, American Book Company, 1883) , pp. 44 ff., implies that Peter taught Charles grammar; and Wilmot-Buxton, *op. cit.,* pp. 80–82, places Peter at the court and makes a reference to his dismissal. See also, Bolgar, *op. cit.,* pp. 106–109.

was required, it is easy to understand Charles' allowing him to return to his native land. This was not the way to inaugurate a large-scale educational reform. Charles thought the Palace School could be a hub around which educational reform could turn, but reform was impossible if teachers and students in the School set their sights on ornamentation rather than on practical knowledge. As a principal educational institution, the Palace School was expected to be an intellectual oasis on which other schools could draw. So much is clear from the commission tendered to Alcuin and in the capitularies Charles issued.[21]

The first palace schools, intended to prepare young men for the clergy, and usually part-time ventures, were conducted by a priest or bishop who instructed the boys when his other court duties permitted. By the eighth century the palace school had broadened its perspectives somewhat and allowed boys not aspiring to the priesthood to benefit from the instruction it offered. But these schools influenced only students who attended, and in even the best palace schools instructional opportunities were uneven and frequently chaotic.[22]

Alcuin's plan and hope was to take the program of teaching developed at York, with its emphasis on teaching a practical and correct Latin grammar, and apply it to centers of learning in Frankland; in turn these centers could disseminate the "new learning" to surrounding areas and thus popularize elementary education. Once the teaching of Latin was solidly established, allowing both civil and ecclesiastical governments to conduct their business with skill and literacy, the program could be broadened to include fresh subjects for which the European world had an obvious need. All this was Alcuin's mission, and Charles, himself only partly literate, merits praise for having concurred in Alcuin's aspirations to bring new life to the world of learning.[23] Alcuin's twofold service to learning can be stated now: he transplanted to the continent pedagogic techniques invented at York, and he improved the discipline of teaching and applied it to subjects besides Latin. Thus he accelerated popular learning.[24]

A visit to Alcuin's Palace School would be illuminating, for Alcuin's teaching methods were being severely tested: Charles himself was a pupil, along with his queen and other members of his family and royal household. If Alcuin's teaching should prove no more satisfactory to Charles than had Peter's, Alcuin's hopes of spreading practical education

21 L. Wallach, "Charlemagne and Alcuin: Studies in Carolingian Epistolography," *Traditio,* 9 (1953), pp. 127–154; and L. Wallach, *Alcuin and Charlemagne: Studies in Carolingian History and Literature* (Ithaca, N.Y., Cornell University Press, 1959).

22 See J. B. Mullinger, *The Schools of Charles the Great* (New York, G. E. Stechert & Company, 1911).

23 West, *op. cit.,* pp. 48–49.

24 B. W. Wells, "Alcuin the Teacher," *The Constructive Quarterly,* VII (1919), pp. 531–538; and Bolgar, *op. cit.,* p. 109.

throughout the continent would have ended quickly. His pupils wanted knowledge fast and without cultural accompaniments and embellishments. To accommodate these appetites, Alcuin employed the question-and-answer method. Allowing for his pupils' untutored minds this method was probably the right one, and we hear Alcuin reading a question and then supplying the answer. Since few of his pupils could read or write, we suppose he repeated the questions and answers until both were fixed in their minds. At the end of a school session students knew they had learned something.[25]

Alcuin started with grammar because, according to current definition, grammar teaching contained everything for a basic education. But Alcuin could not stop with grammar, for neither his students nor his theory countenanced such narrow limits for learning. So using catechetical methods, he introduced his students to arithmetic, astronomy, rhetoric, and dialectics. In so doing he confirmed tradition: the seven liberal arts are foundations for knowledge. While the arts were treated unevenly, and some hardly at all, enough was done so Alcuin could square his teaching practices and curricular preferences with traditions tested and retested from the time of Cassiodorus. Actually Alcuin gave the seven liberal arts a near monopoly in learning; he went beyond Cassiodorus' assertion that the arts were merely useful for divine learning and made them indispensable foundations for divine study. Despite the arts' importance, they should not be loved, for they were merely stepping-stones to loftier learning objectives.[26]

Because of its basic position in the curriculum, along with its impractical and archaic techniques, grammar teaching needed reorganization more than any other subject in the Palace School. And since grammar figured so prominently in his hopes for popular learning in the Empire, Alcuin spent much time on a pedagogy related to it. Using textbooks he had brought from York, Alcuin read their dialogues to his class and thus helped his students associate words and find literary meaning. This was almost painless effort, but vocabulary needed more attention than his simple texts gave. Available word lists were too often barren and unbearable; and they gave students no hints about using words in active speech or writing. So in order to handle the elementary but important matter of word-learning, Alcuin took Bede's grammar and rewrote it along conversational lines.[27] Now his students had an interesting story to follow, and in reading it, or in hearing it read, they were

25 A. L. Maycock, "Bede and Alcuin," *Hibbert Journal*, XXXIII (1934–1935), pp. 402–410; and C. H. Beeson, *A Primer of Medieval Latin* (Chicago, University of Chicago Press, 1925), pp. 155–159.

26 E. M. Sanford, "Alcuin and the Classics," *Classical Journal*, XX (1925), pp. 526–533.

27 Bolgar, *op. cit.*, p. 112. See Joseph Freudgen, *Alkuins pädagogische Schriften* (Berlin, Walther Vogel, 1889).

introduced to vocabulary, elementary syntax, and some general knowledge. The planned reading book, then, stands as Alcuin's principal pedagogical achievement, and while it appears inconsequential alongside the involved theories of, say Plato, it occupies a permanent position in language teaching. In any case, depending on memory, it supplied students with a working vocabulary, along with grammatical form, and filled what up to then was largely a linguistic vacuum.[28]

In addition to linguistic studies, undoubtedly having first place in Alcuin's curriculum, because they opened gateways to accurate scriptural reading, some time was spent on versification. Besides, if the *Propositions of Alcuin* was actually a textbook, elementary mathematical studies were there too. Of fifty-three propositions, only a few needed geometric or algebraic applications for solution; the rest were exercises in ingenuity.[29] Astronomy was limited mainly to calculating seasons of the year; the date for Easter was still debated, and Alcuin and Charles wanted to be correct.[30]

The value of this education is not difficult to assess: it was a limited but competent elementary education.[31] And on this the historical stature of Alcuin must rest.

Alcuin's educational efforts were not restricted to the classroom. He prepared instructional materials for other teachers, and he advanced an educational theory to support his interpretations of the seven arts of popular elementary education.[32]

In one sense, Alcuin's basic premise relative to the seven liberal arts differs only slightly from Augustine's or Cassiodorus', or from the conventional wisdom of Christian education, but in another Alcuin's approach is more progressive than anything so far stated. He agreed with his Christian predecessors that the arts were important to all learning; he said they were indispensable. But where Augustine found the arts to be outside divine learning and gave them only qualified entrance to schools, and where Cassiodorus, admitting their practical worth found their excellence attested in divine writing, Alcuin claimed to find the arts imbedded in Christian culture. Although inferior, there is no question of decontamination, for they belong naturally to Christian learning.[33] Had he been more of a scholar Alcuin would have seen the error of his ways, for later, even Erasmus, unheralded for his sensitivities to dangers in the

---

28 West, *op. cit.*, pp. 92–93.

29 Alcuin, *Propositiones ad acuendos juvenes,* in Migne, *Patrologia Latina* (Paris, J. P. Minge, 1863), 1145–1160.

30 Paul Abelson, *The Seven Liberal Arts* (New York, Teachers College, Columbia University, 1906), pp. 98–102.

31 L. Wallach, "Education and Culture in the Tenth Century," *Medievalia et Humanistica,* 9 (1955), pp. 18–22.

32 See W. Schmitz, *Alcuins Ars Grammatica* (Berlin, Duncker & Humblot, 1908).

33 West, *op. cit.*, p. 97.

classics, erected safeguards before students were allowed to make determined assaults on classical treasures. Alcuin's theory was faulty, and his open-armed embrace of the arts was technically incorrect; yet he was listened to, and part of the Christian's dilemma relative to pagan learning was abandoned. Christian schools welcomed the arts, and students studied them with impunity. Still, even now there were safeguards—possibly recognized by Alcuin: his students were mere beginners who seldom probed the classics deeply enough to meet any danger to their faith.[34]

Without a separate book on educational theory, Alcuin's views on the subject must come from his general educational writings, but this has the advantage of demonstrating Alcuin's respect for the integrity of a theory grounded in practice. His textbook *On Grammar*—where he states the bulk of his theory—has two parts: the first, a dialogue between a fourteen-year-old and a fifteen-year-old pupil and Alcuin, treats of philosophy and liberal studies in general; the second—also a dialogue—takes up the subject of grammar.[35] In the first dialogue Alcuin tries to convince his readers of the relevance of the seven liberal arts to Christian learning, and he implies that they are integral parts of Christian wisdom. There were some unguarded assumptions here, we should think, but from now on the burden of proof rested with anyone wanting to restrict or proscribe liberal learning. We no longer hear expressions of cautious compromise, nor do we observe debates on the number of the arts or on their identity. Alcuin's simple pronouncement is definitive. His pupils ask: "Open to us, as you have often promised, the seven ascents of theoretical discipline." And Alcuin replies: "Here, then, are the ascents of which you are in search, and O that you may ever be as eager to ascend them as you now are to see them. They are grammar, rhetoric, dialectics, arithmetic, geometry, music, and astrology. On these the philosophers bestowed their leisure and their study." [36]

The second dialogue takes students into the study of grammar proper. And here Alcuin borrows from authorities and writers preceding him, so there is little original content in his book. But he handled it wisely, and his book has some good scholarship and pedagogy. The initial assumptions are hard to follow, but the book gets better. He assumes that correct Latin grammar is determined by nature, reason, authority, and usage.[37] These terms were used by ancient grammarians and their meaning was clear, but Alcuin's is not. This article of grammatical faith, however, did not bother the beginning student; in any case, neither

---

[34] O. F. Long, "The Attitude of Alcuin Toward Virgil," *Studies in Honor of Basil L. Gildersleeve* (Baltimore, The Johns Hopkins Press, 1902) , pp. 377–386.

[35] Alcuin, *Ars grammatica*, in Migne, *Patrologia Latina*, CI, 101.849–902.

[36] Quoted in West, *op. cit.*, p. 97.

[37] Bolgar, *op. cit.*, p. 110; and Alcuin, *Ars grammatica*, CI, 858.

Alcuin nor his students dwelt on it. They started with the meaning of a letter, in Alcuin's definition "the least part of an articulate sound." [38] Alcuin divided grammar twenty-six ways and defined them all, but for the subject as a whole he said: "Grammar is the science of written sounds, the guardian of correct speaking and writing." [39] Burrowing into Alcuin's grammar now is an arid exercise, so we shall resist a weak temptation, but it must be said that Alcuin shrinks grammar almost beyond recognition. Standing on classical traditions, grammar included the arts of writing and speaking, a study of great poets and orators, and was a kind of general education. Now technical, and almost barren, it dwells on etymology, with syntax, orthography, and prosody almost completely neglected. Despite Alcuin's heavy debt to Donatus, and sometimes to Isidore, the long-term reaction to his work was one of slavish praise, and *On Grammar* was preferred to other grammar texts. But again the right man has appeared at the right time in educational history; this elementary, often crude treatise on grammar was just what students needed. It was important to creep first through the mysteries of Latin before they made a headlong assault on the classics.

Some parts of Alcuin's *On Grammar* may have been lost—especially the end of the book—yet it is hard to believe its ambitions were any greater than we have indicated. In keeping the book within rather severely circumscribed boundaries, Alcuin sensed accurately the danger of offering untutored students too much. Had he saddled them with the full weight of classical grammar, they would surely have abandoned its study, and, after all, what they needed was simple and accurate learning, not erudition.

Next came *Orthography*,[40] intended as a guide to correct spelling, although remarks concerning pronunciations, meaning, and accurate usage of words are appended. It is hard to know, either from fragmentary testimony about the book or about its contents, whether it was intended for schoolboys or scribes. It had some value for both, we should think.

Despite Alcuin's attention to elementary education, that he had some interest in higher studies is evidenced in his *On Rhetoric and the Virtues*.[41] Here, again using dialogues, Charles and Alcuin first discuss the elements of rhetoric with special application to civil affairs and then give a brief description of the four cardinal virtues—prudence, justice, fortitude, and temperance. The book, not strictly rhetorical, deals rather with rhetoric's applications. Its sources are Cicero and Isidore, the latter quite frequently simply copied and the former used always with some loss

38 *Ibid.*
39 *Ibid.*
40 Alcuin, *De Orthographia*, Aldo Marsili, ed., (Pisa, Vallerini, 1952) .
41 Alcuin, *De rhetorica et de virtutibus*, Carl Halm, ed., (Leipzig, B. G. Teubner, 1863) , pp. 525–550.

and injury.[42] Next came *Dialectics,* but the book does not go deeply into the subject; [43] Alcuin's source is plainly Isidore, which probably explains its superficiality. Alcuin wanted to avoid overburdening his students, for medieval logic, still in its infancy, was distrusted, and there was some wisdom in skirting the subtleties and difficulties introduced in the books of Boethius and Aristotle.

The list of Alcuin's pedagogic writings is closed with *On the Seven Arts* and the *Propositions of Alcuin.* In the former Alcuin wants to say something more about the arts, but he succeeds only in being redundant; Cassiodorus is his authority on grammar and rhetoric, and he is unable even to equal Cassiodorus' abridgement.[44] *Propositions* was a compilation of puzzles, intended no doubt to give students practice with words and to stimulate imagination and ingenuity.[45] It had plenty of company in medieval schools.

The tendency to regard Alcuin's work as a collection of failures and unrealized ambitions is supported by the fact that his books on education were superficial, disorganized, and often plainly wrong; nevertheless, they had enough solid value, especially in technique, to renew medieval elementary education and commit it to accuracy.[46] Besides, Alcuin's example as a teacher adds a new dimension and makes us think that Alcuin's books and methods should not be judged apart from their time, nor apart from his unselfish, gentle, and sensible approach to teaching. The educational and spiritual welfare of students was uppermost in his mind, and he elaborated a pattern for educators to follow. We see his work most clearly, not as a reviver of fragmented school learning—although even here he is due some credit—but as an inspirer of Christian educational ideals.[47]

We have noticed the details of Alcuin's teaching and its relationship to educational theory. The evidence on all his work, subjected to the obliterating forces of time, is fragmentary; yet even the fragments suggest the general pattern of his achievements. These achievements, however, should make us cautious about wanting to link him with the great Renaissance, where such figures as Petrarch and Erasmus played leading roles; if he did, indeed, lead a renaissance it was minor, though important, and had nothing in common with a cult of antiquity so visible in the four-

---

[42] See W. S. Howell, *The Rhetoric of Alcuin and Charlemagne* (Princeton, N.J., Princeton University Press, 1941).

[43] Alcuin, *De dialectica,* in *Patrologia Latina,* CI 101.951–976.

[44] West, *op. cit.,* p. 108, raised some doubt that Alcuin was the author.

[45] Alcuin, *Propositiones ad acuendos juvenes,* CI 1145–1160. See Bolgar, *op. cit.,* p. 113.

[46] See L. Wallach, "Alcuin on Sophistry," *Classical Philology,* 50 (1955), pp. 259–261.

[47] See Gerald Ellard, *Master Alcuin, Liturgist; A Partner of Our Piety,* (Chicago, Loyola University Press, 1956); and E. S. Duckett, *Alcuin, Friend of Charlemagne* (New York, The Macmillan Company, 1951).

teenth century. His work, always Christian and guided by a thoroughly Christian mentality, aimed to supply textbooks and techniques for the education of priests for the Church and laymen for civil government. Always elementary in character, it freed him, his followers, and students from much classical study, although his pedagogy, because of its emphasis on elementary teaching, affected the future of learning. His commitment to the seven liberal arts was clear but limited, and he left to others the job of finding the true genius of a classical education.[48] Thus terminating our study of Alcuin, we complain not of his inadequacies, but marvel at his ability to accomplish so much.

III

HUGH OF ST. VICTOR

The long interval between the death of Alcuin and the advent of the twelfth century is a period distinguished by its conservative character. Scholars and churchmen were content to review and rely on Christian doctrine as it filtered down through the ages from the Fathers. Their principal tool for keeping abreast of tradition was grammar, since the time of Alcuin a staple in the school; but grammar was an indispensable vehicle for communication and not a discipline or a technical acquirement. Fluency was the object sought; depth was not required, and elegant scholarship was virtually unknown. The schoolmaster's task was relatively simple: he drilled boys in books of rules and abstracts; the most popular textbooks were the grammars of Donatus, Priscian, and Alcuin.[49] Classical authors were used sparingly, if at all, and in the ordinary school the only contact a student had with the classics was in the brief lectures of his master. This, on the whole, was an efficient system, and it performed reasonably well in teaching an accurate Latin; but it became too narrow to satisfy the aspirations of twelfth-century scholars attuned to innovation. While not wanting to alter established Church doctrines, they hoped to range beyond the dimly outlined traditions that were maintaining these doctrines to find intellectual supports for faith; in other words, they wanted Christian doctrine to have a cultural basis.[50]

This upgrading of learning began with protests not unlike those made by Bernard of Chartres, who believed that hurrying through grammar was a mistake. Bernard could argue, and men like John of

---

48 See Bolgar, *op. cit.*, pp. 116–117.

49 See L. J. Paetow, *The Battle of the Seven Liberal Arts* (Berkeley, Calif., University of California Press, 1914).

50 See H. O. Taylor, *The Medieval Mind*, 4th ed., 2 vols., (London, The Macmillan Company, 1930).

Salisbury could take up his argument and extend it, that grammar was the basis of all culture. As part of his plea for grammar, he could say, moreover, that it should be learned slowly and thoroughly; it should be learned, not from schoolmasters' simple manuals, but from the classics themselves; and when he sent students to the classics they were not to treat all classical authors alike.[51] They should concentrate on the best authors. We have John of Salisbury's word for the method of teaching grammar Bernard endorsed, but it is hard to know whether Bernard invented this system or simply inherited it from his astute predecessors. The latter is probably correct, for this method must have been the product of evolution; it did not appear suddenly in the twelfth century.[52] In any case, when recognized and accepted, it both broadened and improved grammar, and with this the age was virtually ready for a transformation from a simple knowing of the Christian tradition to a dialectical approach for mastering, organizing, interpreting, and applying it. Now the overarching question facing twelfth-century scholars was: What does this knowledge mean? With only a little knowledge, Christian scholars forgot about order. They tried to learn everything and left it to individual ingenuity to distill meaning. But with so much more to choose from, they faced a central issue in the philosophy of education: what should be studied, and why? Twelfth-century theorists recognized this valid problem in education and tried to solve it. Of the twelfth-century theorists tackling it, Conrad of Hirschau, Theodore of Chartres, and Hugh of St. Victor were most successful in producing guides for their contemporaries to follow. The aim was set by Hugh in the preface to his *Didascalicon:* "The things by which every man advances in knowledge are principally two—namely, reading and meditation. Of these, reading holds first place in instruction, and it is of reading that this book treats, setting forth rules for it. For there are three things particularly necessary to learning for reading: first, each man should know what he ought to read; second, in what order he ought to read, that is, what first and what afterwards; and third, in what manner he ought to read." [53]

The opinion, later expressed so succinctly by John of Salisbury, that little is concealed from the man who reads much,[54] was taken seriously by many twelfth-century educators. By reading, they did not mean, as we might suppose, a cursory exploration of some parts of classical or divine literature; they meant to convey the identity of reading and education. In other words, when they wrote of reading, they were writing about the

[51] Bernard's method of teaching grammar, and his supreme confidence in the subject, is reported by John of Salisbury. See Daniel D. McGarry, *The Metalogicon of John of Salisbury* (Berkeley, Calif., University of California Press, 1955), pp. 62–70.

[52] See R. P. McKeon, "Rhetoric in the Middle Ages," *Speculum,* XVII (1942), 1–32.

[53] Jerome Taylor, *The Didascalicon of Hugh of St. Victor* (New York, Columbia University Press, 1961), p. 44.

[54] McGarry, *Metalogicon,* pp. 64–65.

curriculum to be followed by anyone who hoped to be decently educated. And when they had finished with their speculation about reading, they had constructed a theory of curriculum. But they were not content to merely collect and classify the mass of unspecialized knowlege then available; they were intent on imposing order or structure on knowledge and to subordinate everything to a few general ideas.

Techniques contributing to order and arranging subordination took some time to develop. First, they had to find suitable classifications, and here logical philosophy was of considerable help; but even at its best philosophy was sometimes overburdened with parts of knowledge that refused to fit into any scheme. Much of the content of the classics still wore a pagan garb, and with all their skill medieval logicians were unable to "trim its hair or pare its nails." Yet the pioneers in this herculean task of imposing order on knowledge could begin by arranging the things that would fit, and they could, for the time being, ignore loose ends. At this point we meet Theodore of Chartres who, in *Heptateuchon*, compiled in a massive volume the accepted subject matter for each of the seven arts. One may question the originality of Theodore's work, for he only combined in one manuscript the contents of standard textbooks on the arts, but content was not the issue at stake; intention and structure counted, and he tried to reveal them in his famous work. In the preface he talks about his intention: human knowledge is one, its unity and single purpose being related to man's final end. Within the context of Theodore's thought, wisdom, the goal of life, is cultivated by philosophy, and the seven liberal arts provide the foundation for philosophy. The quadrivium, Theodore says, contains material for thought; the trivium aims at the development of necessary means of expression. Thus Theodore can begin with grammar and provide a structure of knowledge leading all the way to wisdom. Containing more hope than realization, Theodore's work is, nevertheless, a bold beginning; it expresses an educational doctrine, aimed at the cultivation of thought and expression, that occupies a permanent place in educational philosophy.[55] Erasmus, four centuries later, used almost the same language to substantiate his preoccupation with classical education; and even in the twentieth century books on educational philosophy written by Christian humanists have similar emphases.

A contemporary of Theodore's, Conrad of Hirschau, wrote his *Dialogue on the Authors* about 1150, and he accepts Theodore's fundamental assumption: knowledge is one, and teachers must keep this in mind when organizing knowledge for classroom use.[56]

[55] Daniel D. McGarry, "Renaissance Educational Theory," *Historical Bulletin,* 32 (May, 1954), pp. 195–209, discusses Theodore's *Heptateuchon* at some length as a preliminary to the educational theory of the Humanists; see also, Bolgar, *op. cit.,* p. 231.

[56] Conrad of Hirschau, *Dialogus super auctores sive Didascalion,* edited by Schepss (Würzburg, Beck, 1889).

The common practice among ancient grammarians had been to preface the reading of a classic with a few introductory remarks. Thus students learned something about their reading lesson before they started; they learned about the text itself—a kind of elementary textual criticism—and they had the main details on the author and the story. Later grammarians used prelectic somewhat more broadly and not always successfully from a purely pedagogical point of view. They burdened their students with their own erudition. Much of what they said was of no help to the students in reading and hardly qualified as literary criticism. Yet it was an interpretation of the material. This practice spread north, and by the twelfth century it was well known to medieval masters. But they hesitated to use this elaborate technique of prelection until they discovered that it could serve as a means of gathering together the loose ends of classical literature—the things that were offensive to a tender Christian conscience. But this was not just a matter of reducing the thresholds of timidity; it was a way to bring all knowledge into the fold. Allegorical interpretation, thus, became an instrument for unification of knowledge. With Conrad we have an opportunity to see how the old style of interpretation was used for a new purpose. He advised teachers to jettison the old illustrative lecture and replace it with one based on philosophical judgment.[57] Now teachers could take the classics as a whole, or whatever classics they had in the school's syllabus, and interpret everything in them. Conrad proposed to define all classical knowledge in a hierarchy of Christian learning. The key to this technique, unrecognized but described by Conrad, is to distinguish between the intention of the classic's author and the work's final cause, which is a reflection of God's mind. This distinction allowed any book to find its proper place in the totality of experience. Coupled with the dogmatic assumption that the whole of human experience is dominated by religious faith, this new technique overcame the last obstacles to opening the gateways to classical literature and allowing this literature to permeate all Christian education. Christian educational thinking had come a long way since the time of Cassiodorus, who willingly admitted the arts to Christian schools, but only because they were useful intruders.

The task facing Hugh, then, was to go beyond the somewhat modest beginnings of Theodore and Conrad. When he did he kept before him the fundamental problem they had discussed, the problem of interpreting all knowledge by approved means so that everything might, as Vives was to say later, "be put into its proper nest." [58] Because Hugh was a more theoretical thinker than either Theodore or Conrad, and because

---

57 *Ibid.*, p. 46; and Bolgar, *op. cit.*, pp. 216–217.

58 J. L. Vives, *Introductio ad Sapientiam*, quoted by F. Watson in *Vivès on Education* (Cambridge, The University Press, 1913), p. XXXIX.

he meant to give his views general application, we should look closely at his comments about this important part of educational theory.

Didascalicon, On the Study of Reading, was composed in Paris sometime between 1120 and 1130 by a native of Halberstadt who in the years of early youth had entered the Augustinian house at Hamersleben to learn his letters and had stayed on to become a monk. Born in 1097 to a noble family, there was apparently some parental objection to Hugh's becoming a cleric, but this objection was either overcome or ignored, so we have brief, incomplete glimpses of Hugh, first in Germany and then at the Abbey of St. Victor, in Paris. Hugh arrived in Paris about 1115, continued his studies, took his vows, became a teacher in the Abbey school, and finally became its master. He continued as the school's master until his death in 1140 or 1141. The details of his life are little known, but fortunately they seem to be of slight consequence in interpreting his services to learning.[59]

The theoretical problem posed for Hugh was one of subordinating the search for knowledge in the separate sciences to the search for wisdom consonant with the religious ends of man. While it is true that this was not a critical issue in his time—for there was little knowledge that urgently needed reorganization—it later became a critical issue, and Hugh's theory, while in the long run hardly definitive, was unquestionably beneficial. At the same time, we should remember, Hugh's theoretical subordination of parts of knowledge to a whole was to a great extent an elaboration of a hierarchical system started by Aristotle and perpetuated by Boethius.[60] Hugh's genius, then, must be found, not in his originality, but in his ability to take neglected ideas and graft them to a new educational code.

Hugh begins with the assumption that philosophy is a handmaiden to wisdom; he calls it "the art of arts and the discipline of disciplines—that, namely toward which all arts and disciplines are oriented." [61] The magnificence of philosophy has never shone brighter than in the constructions of Hugh, for he asserts at the outset that philosophy contains the totality of man's intelligent response to his environment. But it would not do to talk about philosophy only in grandiose terms, because this would not help to organize knowledge into meaningful parts, each of which could be directed toward the ultimate purpose of philosophy. So Hugh, sensitive to this problem of communication, wants to "distinguish the individual arts from one another by dividing philosophy into its

---

[59] See Jerome Taylor, *The Origin and Early Life of Hugh of St. Victor; an Evaluation of the Tradition* (Notre Dame, Ind., University of Notre Dame Press, 1957).

[60] Taylor discusses the didascalic tradition in his "Introduction" to *Didascalicon,* pp. 28–36.

[61] *Didascalicon,* II, i, 61. (All references to *Didascalicon* are to the translation by Jerome Taylor.)

parts. . . . We have said that there are four branches of knowledge only, and that they contain all the rest: they are the theoretical, which strives for the contemplation of truth; the practical, which considers the regulation of morals; the mechanical, which supervises the occupations of this life; and the logical, which provides the knowledge necessary for correct speaking and clear argumentation." [62]

When Hugh was listened to, an intense awareness was developed for the natural divisions of human knowledge and for the relationship that existed among these divisions. He changed the thinking of educators, although he may not have reformed the ordinary schoolmasters much, about the aim of their teaching; it was hardly possible, if Hugh was taken seriously, to be content with grammatical, mathematical, or rhetorical competence, for example, because now each of these subjects was related to, and in some ways expected to cover, the whole of human experience. Each had its clear obligations to the realization of wisdom.

The meaning of philosophy and the enumeration of the arts is taken care of in the first two books of the *Didascalicon*. Hugh ends Book II by trying his hand at defining a discipline. In Book II Hugh repeats what he had said before in another way, viz., "Philosophy is divided into theoretical, practical, mechanical, and logical. These four contain all knowledge." [63] And then in chapter thirty, when he is discussing invention and judgment, he wonders whether or not they may be called part of philosophy. He suspects they cannot be fitted into one of his nests, and this leads him to make some distinctions about kinds of knowledge. With this introduction we can let Hugh speak for himself: "It is always true to say that any knowledge which is an art or discipline is a distinct branch of philosophy; but it cannot always be said that all knowledge which is an act of cognition is a distinct branch of philosophy: and yet it is certainly true that all knowledge, whether it be a discipline or any act of cognition whatever, is somehow contained in philosophy—either as an integral part, or as a divisive part or branch." [64] What Hugh is doing now, of course, is not mere quibbling; he is formulating the rules to be followed for segregating knowledge, or philosophy, into its proper parts. He has mentioned four large categories of philosophy, and he does not mean to retreat from this fundamental position. Nor does he mean that further subdivisions are impossible. These further subdivisions are named throughout the *Didascalicon;* here he is content to call them disciplines. What is a discipline? Hugh is ready with an answer: "A discipline, moreover, is a branch of knowledge which has a defined scope within the range of which the objective of some art is perfectly unfolded; but this is not true of the knowledge of invention or of judgment, because neither

62 *Ibid.,* I, xi, 60.
63 *Ibid.,* II, i, 62.
64 *Ibid.,* II, xxx, 82.

of these stands independently in itself, and therefore they cannot be called disciplines but are integral parts of a discipline—namely, of argumentative logic." [65]

Hugh is quite aware of the academic tendency to think of knowledge as being general—the content of the seven arts—and professional; and we shall probably have to admit that this tendency continued to prevail for some time, despite the solid arguments Hugh could bring in favor of revision. If the curriculum of the medieval university is representative of the scholar's idea of what knowledge was available for communication and learning, we are forced to admit that the theory of curriculum set in motion by Hugh was moving below the surface of scholastic practice. We are not, however, forced to deny that it was extant, or even that it was effective. Besides, there is no reason whatever for thinking that Hugh would have willingly diminished the significance of the seven arts; he knew they were important, and in his theory he only wanted to show clearly that neither they, nor professional knowledge, marked the last boundary of knowledge leading to wisdom.

When he speaks of the subdivisions of philosophy and totals their number to twenty-one, he does not mean that the traditional seven arts should not have the first claim on the student's attention. Yet before he speaks in favor of the seven arts, he wants to be sure that his readers know there is something more. We would have liked more precision in Hugh's plan for separating philosophy into its proper parts; and we are sometimes mystified by his ability to find twenty-one parts counting one way, and twenty-eight parts counting another. In any case Hugh is still the best witness, and we should listen to his testimony. After saying that philosophy is comprised of the theoretical, practical, mechanical, and logical, he allows us to see inside these major parts. "The theoretical is divided into theology, physics, and mathematics; mathematics is divided into solitary, private, and public. The mechanical is divided into fabric making, armament, commerce, agriculture, hunting, medicine, and theatrics. Logic is divided into grammar and argument: argument is divided into demonstration, probable argument, and sophistic: probable argument is divided into dialectic and rhetoric." [66] There is knowledge in a nutshell. It all seems very simple. The next problem is for the student to master these parts; and Hugh can give him some practical advice. First, he lists the authors students should read if they want to know the subject matter of these parts. They should not read everything at first, but they are to be selective. And he gives them a bibliography. The justification for selection is that "our effort should first be given to the arts, in which are the foundation stones of all things and in which

[65] *Ibid.*
[66] *Ibid.*, III, i, 83.

pure and simple truth is revealed." [67] In making his selection Hugh can be a true son of tradition; the ancients in their studies selected seven arts to be mastered by educated men, and Hugh does the same.

> It is in the seven liberal arts, however, that the foundation of all learning is to be found. Before all others these ought to be had at hand, because without them the philosophical discipline does not and cannot explain and define anything. These, indeed, so stand together and so depend upon one another in their ideas that if only one of the arts be lacking, all the rest cannot make a man into a philosopher. Therefore, those persons seem to me to be in error who, not appreciating the coherence among the arts, select certain of them for study, and, leaving the rest untouched, think they can become perfect in these alone.[68]

By this time we are fairly certain of the kinds of knowledge Hugh means to emphasize, so we may turn to his method to see how this knowledge is to be converted into an individual possession. But before getting to details of pedagogy we should know something about Hugh's philosophy of man and about the fundamentals he used to build an elementary psychology of learning.[69]

One has a strong temptation to label Hugh a Christian idealist rather than a Christian humanist, despite his interest in the classical heritage, for he seems to have the Platonic conception of body and soul being two disparate natures.[70] His theory of personality is distinctive: soul is the man; the subject of knowledge is not the human composite, but the soul. In Hugh's philosophy man is a microcosm, and he is placed in the center of creation between two contrasting worlds of sense and spirit. The soul is endowed with faculties enabling it to look at both worlds; these faculties of knowing are sense perception, intellectual apprehension of the sensible world through imagination, and intuition, a faculty the soul has for knowing itself. In concert these faculties lead men to a knowledge of the higher world. The hierarchy of being—world, soul, God—marks the route that knowledge should take to fulfill its function of shaping wise men.

Hugh is confident of the reliability of sense knowledge, and in various places he speaks of the subject, act, and object of sensation. He also undertakes to explain the process whereby the form of the external object is impressed on the sense organ and is conveyed to imagination, where it exists as a corporeal image. Sense perception, in Hugh's view, is largely a passive process. Sense and intellect are sharply divided, so sharply, in fact, that one wonders how Hugh was able to move so quickly

---

[67] *Ibid.*, III, iv, 88.

[68] *Ibid.*, III, iv, 89.

[69] See John P. Kleinz, *The Theory of Knowledge of Hugh of St. Victor* (Washington, D.C., The Catholic University of America Press, 1944), pp. 16–28.

[70] *Ibid.*, p. 21.

from the corporeal image to the idea, which is both spiritual and universal. In any case, in Hugh's theory, the idea is the spiritual representation of reality. Knowledge is an assimilation between knower and known; and he accepts the correspondence theory of truth. The traditional distinction between reason, a capacity for knowing temporal phenomena, and intelligence, a capacity for knowing the spiritual and the divine, is accepted by Hugh. Reason and intelligence are not separate faculties; they are two parts of the power of thought, a power which distinguishes men from animals.[71] This broad human power of thought is deeply involved in the educational process, and Hugh wants to use every available resource to develop it. In trying to incorporate a variety of resources into his learning theory, Hugh often becomes eclectic. He borrows from Plato, Aristotle, and St. Augustine—sometimes directly and sometimes through intermediaries—and his borrowing in the end adds up to a Platonic dualism in psychology.

With this quick look at Hugh's philosophy of man, we may now go on to his recommendations concerning pedagogy. He has told us before, in the preface to *Didascalicon,* that he will discuss "how the student should read."

Hugh begins by saying that natural endowment, practice, and discipline are necessary "tools" for those who undertake serious study. By these he means the usual things: natural endowment is the student's ability to grasp knowledge quickly and retain it firmly; practice is the student's constant employment of his natural endowment; and discipline is the combination of moral behavior and knowledge toward the objective of a praiseworthy life.[72] Despite Hugh's admission that endowment, practice, and discipline are necessary equipment, he is at pains to single out endowment for some special attention and, we think, emphasis. "Those who work at learning," he wrote, "must be equipped at the same time with aptitude and with memory, for these two are so closely tied together in every study and discipline that if one of them is lacking, the other alone cannot lead anyone to perfection. . . . Aptitude gathers wisdom, memory preserves it. Aptitude is a certain faculty naturally rooted in the mind and empowered from within. It arises from nature, is improved by use, is blunted by excessive work, and is sharpened by temperate practice."[73] Earlier he spoke of practice and its desirable effect on aptitude, and we want to know more about this. He meant that aptitude is cultivated by reading and meditation. Reading consists of forming our minds upon rules and precepts taken from books, and in Hugh's opinion order and method deserve special attention in reading.

Order of study, or the sequential arrangement of subject matter, is no mere detail in Hugh's approach to pedagogy; yet it is something that

---

[71] *Ibid.,* pp. 29–36.
[72] *Didascalicon,* III, vi, 90.
[73] *Ibid.,* III, vii, 91.

he can discuss quickly and quite philosophically: "One kind of order is observed in the disciplines . . . and another kind on the exposition of a text." [74] He maintained that order in the disciplines is determined by their nature; that is, study which is clearly prerequisite is determined by the nature of knowledge, and any tampering with this natural order is done at the learner's peril. In the exposition of texts—the interpretative lecture on classical or Christian texts—the order followed must be adapted, Hugh says, to inquiry or, we suppose, to the rules of logic and rhetoric.

At this point we come to something new in the school method of exposition. We know that teachers employed two techniques as part of exposition, and we know, too, that medieval teachers were indebted to their ancient predecessors for these methods. The two techniques, to which Hugh added a third, were letter and sense. Exposition according to letter meant construing the grammar of the text; exposition according to sense meant elucidating the precise meaning of literary passages. The technique added by Hugh, which in effect revolutionized the teaching of literature, was exposition according to "inner meaning." He states his position as follows: "The letter is the fit arrangement of words which we also call construction; the sense is a certain ready and obvious meaning which the letter represents on the surface; the inner meaning is the deeper understanding which can be found only through interpretation and commentary." [75] Hugh has provided the method of allegorical interpretation of the texts with a theoretical foundation; the inner meaning of the classical texts may now be explained, not in the obvious terms in the author's intention, but as it fits into the broad plan in the mind of God. A technique for moving from the author's intention to the final cause of the classic, timidly but literally advanced by Conrad of Hirschau, is confirmed in the educational theory of Hugh. There is no doubt whatever that this new technique added to the method of exposition was of immense importance to medieval masters; they used it enthusiastically for all kinds of literature, ranging from the Bible itself to what before had been considered the most dangerous of the classics. But this new technique was not without deficiencies. Unquestionably it broadened the scope of the Christian scholars' intellectual interests and the range of their reading was extended. No longer was there any question about the legitimacy of classical learning, because this learning could be made to conform to a Christian purpose, regardless of its obvious surface meaning. Yet, allegorical interpretation was not allegorical expression. The latter is a way of representing material that is otherwise difficult to handle; the former is a purposeful deformation of literary material which for some reason or other does not meet with the lecturer's approval, or it is an attempt to derive information about some subject in

[74] *Ibid.*, III, viii, 91.
[75] *Ibid.*, III, viii, 92.

which the lecturer is interested from a source that on the surface would be partly or wholly unsuitable. Hugh's contribution to the method of exposition of texts, while it opened the gateways of classical learning even wider than before, had the effect of making the classical heritage wear a different face, or in some respects it masked the face of the authentic classical literary inheritance.

Not only did Hugh's elaboration of method alter the fundamental character of the classics, it also provided us with a key to an emphasis in learning that had been evolving slowly. Most medieval masters up to Hugh's time, and for that matter after, continued to think of education in primarily intellectual terms: the school was a place for the formation and information of the mind; the home and the church were places where moral development could be tended to.[76] But Hugh had held up discipline as one of the necessary outcomes of study, and he meant, as we will recall, that worthy moral behavior must be coupled with knowledge. The moral dimension, then, is firmly nailed to the educational mast, and the teacher, while he is drilling the students in their grammar and lecturing to them on the inner meaning of the classics must also aim at the formation of character. But this is a departure only from the normal medieval ways of pedagogy; it is a return to the classical pattern for education. So Hugh, responsible in one way for allowing some defacing of the classics by exposition, is also responsible for bringing educational purpose closer to the mainstream of classical practices. In doing so he paved the way for the Christian humanists who followed him three centuries later; for Erasmus could use the classics, arguing for their moral qualities much in the same way as Hugh, although using allegory somewhat more shrewdly, and go on to find in discipline, not a content but a method for realizing praiseworthy moral character. Where Hugh seemed to think proper interpretation could lead one closer to good moral behavior, Erasmus argued that the difficulty and the precision of classical learning contributed to the formation of character. One would be on fairly safe ground in asserting that Hugh, first, and then John of Salisbury, had about as much humanism in their educational theory as Erasmus, later, was to have medieval practices in his.

Hugh concludes his treatment of the essential elements in the order and method of study by discussing meditation and memory. Both are important to his total view, so we should not overlook them. Meditation follows the exposition of the text, and, in a way, one could think of it as the "inner meaning" being put to work.

> Meditation takes its start from reading but is bound by none of reading's rules or precepts. For it delights to range along open grounds, where it fixes its free gaze upon the contemplation of truth, drawing together now these, now those causes of things, or now

[76] See W. J. Townsend, *The Great Schoolmen of the Middle Ages* (London, Hodder and Stoughton, 1881).

penetrating into profundities, leaving nothing doubtful, nothing obscure. The start of learning, thus, lies in reading, but its consum-
mation lies in meditation; which, if any man will learn to love it
very intimately and will desire to be engaged very frequently upon
it, renders his life pleasant indeed, and provides the greatest conso-
lation to him in his trials. This especially it is which takes the soul
away from the noise of earthly business and makes it have even in
this life a kind of foretaste of the sweetness of the eternal quiet.[77]

Hugh does not want to be misunderstood: wide reading and sound
knowledge help men meditate; and meditation brings men close to God.
All this is on the level of highest educational purpose, a level where
Hugh is comfortable, but some practical things need to be said too. Man's
knowledge must be retained. No doubt a good memory, a good native
endowment, was of considerable help, but even a good memory could be
overburdened. Hugh has the answer. He tells his readers to reduce what
has been "gathered"—learned—to a brief but compendious outline. The
age of the notebook is just beginning; and Hugh has some general advice
for students who fill their notebooks: "every exposition has some principle upon which the entire truth of the matter and the force of its thought
rests, and to this principle everything else is traced back." [78] The student
must not try to put everything in a notebook, for then he would have a
tool blunted by its own weight. He must find the germ or the principle of
the ideas he has learned, and this is to go into the notebook. When he has
done this, and his notebook is full, it will be possible for him to review
regularly and to keep his learning fresh and up-to-date.

Hugh's parting words to his readers are: "I charge you, then, my
students, not to rejoice a great deal because you may have read many
things, but because you have been able to retain them. Otherwise there is
no profit in having read or understood much." [79] And, finally, "Morals
equip learning . . . let him who would seek learning take care above all
that he not neglect discipline." [80]

IV

JOHN OF SALISBURY

If the *Metalogicon* is the "cardinal treatise on medieval pedagogy," [81] it
deserves careful study; even if it falls somewhat short of the promise
contained in this broad claim, its special place in the history of educa-

[77] *Didascalicon*, III, x, 92–93.
[78] *Ibid.*, III, xi, 93.
[79] *Ibid.*, III, xi, 94.
[80] *Ibid.*, III, xii, 94.
[81] C. S. Baldwin, *Medieval Rhetoric and Poetic* (New York, The Macmillan Company, 1928), p. 155.

tional theory cannot be seriously disputed. It was written by a man who had received the best education medieval institutions could offer; John studied under the best teachers and scholars—Abelard, Theodore of Chartres, and William of Conches, to name only three—the age could boast; and he appeared at a time in history when a synthesis of educational theory was possible, because the ground of theory had been cultivated.[82] Some of the old ground had been cleared away by Alcuin, and the field was opened for an accurate fundamental schooling which could be built on; schools became more popular, and learning began to capitalize on its intrinsic utility; curricula multiplied; syllabi became fuller; the question of knowledge and man's relationship to it was discussed in a philosophic manner by Hugh of St. Victor. In fine, there were now educational alternatives and men needed a theory to guide them along the best routes. They were, moreover, conscious of theory and were quite willing to make it, on the one hand, and to contemplate it, on the other.

John had time, despite his protestations to the contrary, to argue with dead men; yet, he could make his Cornificius seem real because there was just enough neglect of grammar, logic, and rhetoric—what John called "logical studies"—and impatience with the time and effort they demanded of students to infuse his spirited defense with credibility. Cornificius' reasoned rusticity reminds us more of Gregory the Great and St. Benedict—and that whole body of distrustful churchmen who feared or despised the instruments of liberal learning—than it does of a medieval man. John does not identify his antagonist nor does the literature reveal any such person holding such archaic views. Perhaps there were rustics still, well known to John, who had not progressed even as far as Alcuin's moderate position, and possibly there were scholars who did not doubt that one could go directly to philosophy without first overcoming the literary obstacles contained in the "tools of eloquence."

If Cornificius was not real, neither was he unreal; the temerity John charges him with in ignoring logical studies was part of the Christian intellectual (or anti-intellectual) tradition. Once and for all John wanted to rewrite out of that tradition all vague hesitations and miscalculations; he wanted to still the voices that timidly counseled compromise. Alcuin found the arts in divine knowledge in the Scriptures; John wanted to prove that they really belonged to the equipment of a reasonably well educated Christian gentleman.[83]

[82] See C. M. Schaarschmidt, *Johannis Saresberiensis, Nach Leben und Studien; Schriften u. Philosophie* (Leipzig, B. G. Teubner Verlagsgesellschaft, mbH, 1882), pp. 311 ff. John himself alludes to his teachers. See *Metalogicon* (translated by McGarry), I, v, 21–24; II, x, 95–100. References to this translation of *Metalogicon* are referred to hereafter as *Met.*

[83] John of Salisbury, *Policraticus*, C. C. J. Webb, ed. (Oxford, Clarendon Press, 1909), VII, ix, 126.

Should John's reasoned defense of logical studies seem at times to be labored—especially if we take for granted what he had to prove—it must have been because his age, less literate than our own, was preoccupied with the possibilities of literary learning and linguistic excellence. John wanted to mark out a safe route to satisfy these preoccupations. Where we might well become enamoured with science and technology, John's medieval companions could fall in love with eloquence. But in doing this, it should be remarked, they were not rewriting history or even putting it on a new page but only reliving some of the literary predispositions of the ancients. Quintilian's testimony in favor of eloquent speech, while meaningful for a political-social genre that he himself could only faintly recollect, sounds strangely out of place among men who had never seen the Forum and for whom eloquence could be no handmaiden to the determination of political or ecclesiastical destinies. On the broad level of social and political meaning, eloquence was long out-of-date. On a more limited basis, however, it had utility for the individual, and John is quite willing to admit this. It goes beyond the implications of admission: he forthrightly and unabashedly announces that one of its principal uses is to advance the person who is eloquent in the courts, in business and money making, or in the Church.[84] Even Quintilian, who in his best moments was a practical man, would have shuddered at the disembodiment of liberal learning.

But before we disagree with John—if, indeed, we do—we should try to understand how he pieced together a theory of education that stood the tests imposed on it by a medieval world, and one that was not completely out of tune with the intellectual quickening of modern times. John (1120–1180), an Englishman, in search of a good education betook himself to the centers of learning which then, early in the twelfth century, were on the Continent. He tells us something of his own schooling. When he was about sixteen years old—in 1136—John went to Paris, where he studied logic under Abelard. At his feet, he says, "I learned the elementary principles of this art, drinking in, with consuming avidity, and to the full extent of my limited talents, every word that fell from his lips." [85] John's admiration for Abelard's knowledge and teaching skill is unconcealed, for nearly a quarter century after his study under Abelard he is still able to admit that Abelard's departure from Paris was "all too soon." John continued his study of logic under other teachers—Alberic and Robert of Melun—for two years and then returned to the study of grammar under William of Conches. We assume he returned to the study of grammar, since it is unlikely that he would have approached logic without having first had elementary studies in grammar in the schools of his homeland. William was his principal teacher, and grammar was his

---

84 *Met.*, I, vii, 26.
85 *Ibid.*, II, x, 95–100.

main occupation for three years; then under Hardewin and Richard he delved into the subjects of the quadrivium. At this point the chronology of his study becomes difficult to follow, but he says he reviewed rhetoric, which he had previously studied under Theodore of Chartres, and attached himself to Peter Helias, a teacher from whom he learned a great deal more rhetoric. After all these years of study his finances were running low, so he became a teacher of grammar and taught this subject, apparently with considerable skill and success, for three years, and then returned to his studies. Now he was ready for more advanced courses in dialectics and for theology; his teachers, in turn, were Gilbert of Poitiers, Robert Pullen, and Simon of Poissy. In all, according to his own testimony, John spent twelve years of fairly advanced study in the subjects of the trivium, and during this period he made a commitment to the importance of these studies that even time, science, or theology itself could not erode. In the entire history of education grammar, rhetoric, and logic had no greater champion than John; he did not think of them as essentially elementary subjects but argued, and with a great conviction, that they were essential instruments for building and maintaining the citadels of higher learning. In an age when no effort was made to offer a distinction between philosophy and theology, John could say that the trivium was not only a gateway to philosophy but a necessary ingredient to it all along the way.[86]

Grammar had matured greatly by the twelfth century; it still remained true to its past, as that past was explained by Alcuin as rules of correct writing and speaking, but it could go on to bigger things, or rather, it could go back beyond Alcuin to Quintilian and try to fulfill the commission that the ancients had given it—it could try to become again the custodian of general knowledge. So when John extols the virtues and the possibilities of grammar, he is thinking of a study much richer and more broadly educative than anything Alcuin would have devised or countenanced. John could go so far, indeed, in part because Alcuin's words of pedagogic advice had been heeded. In the first part of this chapter we indicated the nature of grammatical study under the auspices of Alcuin; for a long time Alcuin's ideas remained intact, but now, somewhat before John, the boundaries were changed. Grammar teaching in the hands of Bernard would have been barely recognizable to Alcuin.

Bernard, of course, was able to make assumptions about the students' preliminary education, which Alcuin, because he was an elementary teacher, could not make. Both Alcuin and Bernard lectured, but the lecture, in the hands of Alcuin usually a dictation to students of the rules and vocabulary of Latin writing, as a tool for Bernard was used to "point out, in reading the authors, what was simple and according to rule. On

---

[86] *Ibid.*, I, xxi, 60–62.

the other hand, he would explain grammatical figures, rhetorical embellishments, and sophistical quibbling, as well as the relation of given passages to other studies. He would do so, however, without trying to teach everything at one time." [87] It seems clear that both Bernard and John knew enough of Quintilian's *Education of an Orator* to heed his advice that the child's mind is like the narrow neck of a bottle; a little liquid must be poured in at a time. Once the point was made by the teacher, students would set about to apply it in their own writing, for John assigns to Bernard the pedagogical principle that "exercise both strengthens and sharpens our mind"; [88] in following this advice students would seek out the best examples. The heart of classical pedagogy, executed first in the teaching of Isocrates, rules and models, is honored again in the teaching of Bernard, and John is enthusiastic in endorsing the method that is able to make such great use of imitation. The good will of students toward learning their lessons is heavily depended on, but when good will was lacking or somewhat diminished, probably by outside interests or simple neglect, Bernard would try exhortation. When this did not work, flogging the student or some other form of punishment, could renew his determination to master his studies. [89]

Everyday students would recite what they had learned the day before; "each succeeding day thus became the discipline of its predecessor." [90] This practice, later called simply "repetition," was known to Bernard and John as the "declination," probably because of the characteristics of the exercise, or possibly because it came as the day was declining.

Another side to the teaching practices of Bernard remains to be touched: reading. When the lecture was finished students were presumed to know the rules of grammar and the authors they should consult; all this was part of the close instructional contact between the teacher and the student. In the reading phase the classics themselves were now the students' teachers; from these literary teachers the live master would demand something daily, "a daily debt, something committed to memory." [91] If the student selected poorly, he would be criticized by the master and admonished not to make the same error in judgment again: "To examine and pore over everything that has been written, regardless of whether it is worth reading, is as pointless as to fritter away one's time with old wives' tales." [92] The point to be made was simple enough; one of the marks of a good grammarian is his ability to recognize what is unimportant and to ignore it. Part of reading was also writing, and then

[87] *Ibid.*, I, xxiv, 67.
[88] *Ibid.*, I, xxiv, 68.
[89] *Ibid.*
[90] *Ibid.*
[91] *Ibid.*, I, xxiv, 69.
[92] *Ibid.*, I, xxiv, 70.

taking what was written and submitting it to the hopefully discriminating eyes of all the students. This exercise was called the "conference," and John maintained that "nothing serves better to foster the acquisition of eloquence and the attainment of knowledge than such conferences, which also have a salutary influence on practical conduct, provided that charity moderates enthusiasm, and that humility is not lost during progress in learning." [93]

The method of Bernard, if it may really be called his method, must have been in common use for some time in the late eleventh and early twelfth centuries, but John observed that during his own lifetime, probably even during his own school studies, teachers began to make departures from the method by taking all kinds of shortcuts that would get students past their preliminary studies more quickly to make a premature but complete invasion of the field of philosophy. In the long run, it may have been the shortcuts that John was declaiming against rather than the total neglect of logical studies with which he charges the Cornificians. The exaggerated claim may simply have been employed as an effective rhetorical device.

But the method and the content of Bernard's teaching, a method in which John had unwavering confidence, should not be left before its totality is known. What remains is related to religious instruction, intended to foster faith and morality: no school or day, John says, should be without religion. Thus the grammar teacher should cull from the classics those things that will add to faith and morality and use them as supplements to prayer, devotion, and recitations from the Fathers of the Church and from the scriptures themselves.[94] This is the syllabus that Bernard followed and it had John's wholehearted endorsement. We may assume that his theory of teaching used this method as its starting point.

Alcuin broke the ground; Hugh added much in the way of curricular and methodological theory; John supplied the reasoned defense for the validity of human knowledge. The eyes of the scholar were to be lifted above the books he used; the world of learning—where reason now was to have an honored place—suddenly began to wear a different face. Abelard could be doubted and, at times, discredited, because he put too much confidence in reason and apparently subjected everything to doubt, but he could not be ignored because reason was still man's most precious human possession, and education's object was to perfect reason. This was the simple message of John of Salisbury, although in carrying it out its simplicity was disguised by unexpected dangers. Disciplined and undisciplined reason could apparently, and under certain circumstances, be enemies of faith. John was not oblivious to the limitations of human knowledge; the best safeguard he could think of, added to those already

93 *Ibid.*
94 *Ibid.*, I, xxiv, 68.

devised, was a sound training in the fundamentals contained in the trivium.

This training was, of course, expected to guide the scholar up the ladder of learning: from opinion, to science (to use John's own word), to wisdom. Knowledge, John said, agreeing with Aristotle, is obtained discursively; the senses are the starting point. Along with the cultivation of the senses, there must be a cultivation of reason, and this is where John comes to grips with the allegations of Cornificius that the arts are superfluous because effective reasoning and expression are innate gifts rather than the products of training.

This argument favoring natural eloquence had to be blunted if education was to be taken seriously; there is no doubt that John was entirely serious about the importance of education, an importance derived from its relationship to man's principal intellectual occupation: the search for truth. John's basic assumption is that finding truth is possible and that without it men will be lost in the entanglements of a complex universe. But truth is gained only after long and careful application of trained reason; here is where we meet education, and we note again that it has a clear instrumental character. Education cultivates reason, not simply for the sake of cultivation, but because cultivated reason is the only dependable way to truth, and the eloquence which John is so anxious to applaud is an externalizing complement to it. Truth, once discovered, must be projected beyond the individual or individuals who make the discovery, if it is to have any social significance; and such a projection is not possible, at least it cannot be done well, without eloquence. Undoubtedly the eloquence that enables men to disseminate truth and make it effective is also an instrument in mining truth from the treasuries—literary or scientific—in which it is locked. The cultivation of reason and the development of eloquence, then, are the objectives John sets for the educational process, and in setting these objectives he follows advice given by Plato and by St. Augustine, Hugh of St. Victor, and other Christian sources. John is as able to "sit atop the shoulders of giants" to see what they saw and to go beyond them in applying it to his own age and time. He uses them as he would have students use education, as an efficacious tool, fashioned by reason in the light of experience—an expeditious shortcut to the achievement of results which would otherwise be too difficult or even unattainable.[95]

John's views on curriculum and technique flow rather naturally, or logically, from his statement of educational purpose, and in one way or another they are both set forth in the *Metalogicon.* The primary purpose of the *Metalogicon,* of course, was to defend the subjects in the trivium, but John had no intention of stopping with these studies as they appeared in an elementary syllabus. He is concerned with the whole of

95 *Ibid.*, I, ix, 31; and I, xi, 33; and IV, xii, 222.

education, and he repeatedly makes clear his stand that the subjects of the trivium are but the foundations on which all later learning must stand or fall. Throughout the work he is concerned with a broad and generous education; especially from Hugh of St. Victor he had learned that all the disciplines are connected, and he maintains that each borrows from the others if it is to achieve fulfillment. The complete curriculum, then, has the subjects of the trivium as a starting point and then goes on to moral and natural philosophy and to the whole expanse of organized learning.

Yet, if one looks beyond John's message on logical studies to the broader limits of his educational theory, he is likely to lose some of the pregnant meaning contained in the *Metalogicon*. The claims of grammar and logic needed to be articulated to an academic world that was often confused by the claims and counterclaims made for one or the other. The logicians were inclined to insist that logic alone could point the correct way among the many propositions that were culled from the writings of the ancients and the Fathers; sometimes they thought they did not need the help of grammar.[96] And some grammarians still took too seriously the definition of grammar given by Alcuin: the science of correct speaking and writing. According to John grammar was a subject with much greater scope than this; as a matter of fact, when John finished his defense of the trivium, it was really no longer necessary to speak of the three subjects that made it up, because John had put them all under the broad umbrella of logic. Still, we should try to see what John meant when he defended grammar; what in it was so important once its rudiments had been mastered?

John did not despise the elementary stages of grammar, the rules of correct writing and speaking, and his students would spend as much time as was needed to master them. From that point on, grammar was almost a complete curriculum in itself: general literature, the classics, composition, literary forms, prose, poetry, history, rhetoric, elocution, writing, spelling, punctuation, definitions, etymologies, and memory-training.[97] John does not find a separate place for the treatment of rhetoric in his *Metalogicon;* considering the broad vistas through which grammar could roam, he did not have to because part of rhetoric was clearly included in grammar, and what was left over fell into the province of logic. With this view of grammatical studies, it was not at all difficult for John to main-

[96] It is easy to overstate the case for the redundancy of grammar studies; yet, if we ignore the point that one should fly by grammar to dialectic, we at once jettison the entire structure of John's argument in *Metalogicon*. Examples of logic's supremacy may be found in B. Smalley, *The Study of the Bible in the Middle Ages* (Oxford, Blackwell, 1941), pp. 29–31; and J. G. Sikes, *Peter Abelard* (Cambridge, The University Press, 1932), pp. 86–88; 98–99. Haskins, *op. cit.*, chap. ix, has an illuminating discussion on how philosophy was supported by logic.

[97] *Met.*, I, xiii, xvii, xviii, xix, xx, xxi, xxii.

tain that they form the cradle of philosophical study and that "One who is ignorant of grammar cannot become learned and wise any easier than one who is blind and deaf from birth can become an eminent philosopher." [98] The sources John used to form his broad view of grammar range all the way from Quintilian to Hugh of St. Victor, and he quotes many of them liberally. We are always sure that an author has read the things he quotes, but we are not always certain that he has read the whole of the treatise from which they come. Thus, while John's reputation for learning remains intact, we must be cautious about believing that he came directly in contact with all of the authorities he quotes. The medieval period was the birthplace of anthologies, and many a learned medieval scholar had read parts of all the notorious works on grammar and philosophy in his anthology but had consulted few of the sources from which these parts were drawn. If John was a victim of the anthology, he suffered from it much less, we think, than some of his contemporaries; moreover, he gives a good deal of evidence of having read with care Quintilian, Cassiodorus, Isidore, Capella, and Priscian in an undiluted form.[99]

Once John has taken care of grammar, telling us what it should include and describing Bernard's way of teaching it, he is ready to confront the main issue in the *Metalogicon:* the science of reasoning. This is logic proper, and its place in the educational process is an important one; its role is to devise a science for arriving at truth, and as such it must be learning's central consideration. Logic, to use John's expression, is the gateway to learning and the foundation of virtue. With these credentials, little wonder that John should pay it such heed in a book on educational theory. And if John's position is valid, logic does not need any further justification for being accorded a dignified place in the school's curriculum. Yet even with its place secure, the question of what logic's content is as a school subject could still be asked. John takes a long time to answer this question, but he answers it, and the answer is, without the details here, that the syllabus of logic should be made up by following Aristotle's *Organon.* John can give all of the subdivisions of the subject their proper due and cap off his discussion with the admonition that the great intellectual leaders of antiquity accepted logic's importance and that anyone "who charges that it is foolish to study this [art], thereby shows himself to be a fool of fools." [100] This, in itself, may not have been the most astute application of the science of logic, but it was effective polemic; and time and time again John demonstrated that he was no "small fry" when it came to using the thunder of rhetoric.

98 *Ibid.,* I, xiii, 37–38.

99 See Hans Liebeschütz, *Medieval Humanism in the Life and Writings of John of Salisbury* (London, The Warburg Institute, 1950) , pp. 63–73.

100 *Met.,* IV, xxv, 241.

Logic and grammar are clearly the staples of good education; they carry the principal burden in cultivating reason and in formulating a science of reasoning; but they do not stand alone in the diet of the educated man. John is not a narrow thinker who is willing to leave his theory open to the charge of inadequacy. He goes on to mention the importance of other subjects, some of them in the traditional quadrivium, that must be taken if the young man who goes through the scholastic process is going to be decently educated.

The curriculum, then, would have to find room for geometry and astronomy especially; music and arithmetic are not emphasized; John himself had undergone some study in mathematics and obviously considered mathematics essential to a complete education. Although he could think of the trivium and the quadrivium as being part of philosophy, a sort of important and essential preliminary branch, neither one contained all the learning that was needed for a good education. The trivium contained the logical branch of philosophy, and the physical and ethical branches needed attention too. By physical philosophy John meant the natural sciences, from which he would try to obtain the secrets of nature; and by ethical philosophy he meant individual and social ethics (moral philosophy), political science, sociology, and theology. Theology, for John and for many medievalists, was a part of philosophy, and in this branch of philosophy, as in all knowledge, faith—a comprehension of divine things, is affirmed to be a prerequisite for real understanding.[101] But even now John has not said all that needs to be said about the subject of education and the content of the school's syllabus: there are arts, falling naturally outside logical, physical, and ethical philosophy, that may be learned and that are probably important to learn. John is not troubled to specify them; he calls them "the arts of doing all things that we are to do," says that they "should be taken up and cultivated," [102] and justifies them by adding that they are drawn from nature and that their good is attested to in the objects of their application. These, we should judge, are the useful arts, and they are to have a place in learning, although we are not quite sure where that place is.

With the answer given to the question of what to teach, John can turn to the methods involved in teaching. At some points in his disquisition on education he goes into considerable detail, as when he recapitulates Bernard's method for us, but we can be content with a more general approach to method and, in fact, summarize John's attitude toward the art of teaching. There is no doubt whatever that John was a firm friend of any technique that centered on student activity. So this is a corollary to whatever else he says about methods. In general, method begins with

101 *Ibid.*, IV, xiii, 222–223.
102 *Ibid.*, I, x, 33.

reading, and in medieval educational language reading meant two things: students' reading of the authors and the teacher's commentary on the authors. The former obviously depended on student activity, and even in the latter, in John's opinion, the student could be brought into the prelectic by making it an intercommunication between the student and the master. In other words, this lecture was to be an explanation by the teacher and a recitation by the students, ample time being set aside for the correction of student errors. The complete method consisted in reading, active participation in lectures, reflection on the reading from the authors and explanations on them, memorization (the daily debt referred to before), exercises in composition following accepted classical models, original compositions, recitation, and review. In all these parts of method, as we have said, the student was supposed to be an active agent. To prove his point, John paraphrases Quintilian with obvious approval: "Iron is sharpened by iron, and one's mind is more cogently and effectively stimulated by the sound of the words of another, particularly if the other person is wise or modest." [103]

The name of John of Salisbury is usually mentioned in connection with a defense for a renewal of classical studies, and if one were asked to select one part of his educational theory that stood out above the rest, it would be this: his emphasis on the importance of the classics in building a foundation for the education of men. John shared an assumption made by many before and after him—namely, that the classics contain all knowledge most worth knowing. But where others, in making this bold assumption, seemed to leave much unsaid about the actual and potential worth of classical literature, John could be clear. He did not mean that scholars should stop with the words of the ancient authors; they should start with them and build on them and thus come to know even more about the world in which they lived. In other words, by continuing to study the words of the ancients and adding modern interpretations to them, scholars "could be lifted up and borne aloft on their gigantic stature." This was no doctrine for an academic reactionary, but it was one that had a healthy respect for traditional classical learning. John speaks for himself: "Accordingly the words of the authors should not be lost or forgotten, especially those which give [their] full opinions, and have wide applicability. Such words preserve scientific knowledge in its entirety, and contain tremendous hidden as well as apparent power." [104] In many instances, of course, students would find the classics too difficult for preliminary study, and then, according to John, they should begin with the simpler supplementary commentaries. In general, John is telling his readers that they should read not only the classics but also works that

[103] *Ibid.*, III, x, 200.
[104] *Ibid.*, III, iv, 168.

interpret the classics; they should read everything they can if they want to be well educated: "Rather, let him [the student] go on [to read], as authors mutually explain one another, and all things in turn help to explain other things. For which reason there is little or nothing that lies concealed from one who is well read." [105]

We know how John objected to shortcuts to learning, especially to philosophy, and in this objection he anticipated some of the criticisms later levelled at the scholastics, who were so intent upon philosophizing that they could not be bothered with the ordinary rules of grammar; moreover, he objected to the pedantry that crept into the method of some scholastics, whose inquiries concealed more truth than they revealed, when they quibbled over words and allowed their ideas to deteriorate to a point where they would spend countless hours trying to decide, for example, "whether the pig being taken to market is being held by the man or the rope." We have seen how he was an ardent enemy of super-ficiality in all study—there is no doubt that he wanted a thorough academic program for logical studies—but where he could counsel broad, almost limitless reading, he could at the same time maintain that selection was a sound principle to follow in laying the solid foundations of education. Despite his friendship for the subjects in the trivium, nowhere concealed, John advocated the employment of moderation and judgment in the study of grammar and logic. Good sense should always preside in the educational process, and more time than is necessary for their mastery should not be spent on logical studies, for, as he said, "It is foolish to delay a long time, with much sweat and worry, over something that could otherwise be easily and quickly expedited." [106]

The day-to-day methodology of teaching endorsed by John was unquestionably a recapitulation of the teaching techniques his own masters had used; it was one whose elementary characteristics had been developed by Alcuin, but succeeding ages of schoolmasters had "stood on the shoulders of their own giants" and had embellished these elements with the technical insights of classical pedagogy. In many respects, John's theory of education emerged in the same way: as an evolution of ancient educational theory shaped to meet the needs of the twelfth century. Although it is hard to maintain that John's theory is original, and it can hardly be claimed to have many novel features, it was a theory that communicated with its own time, and in the end it became the representative educational theory for the twelfth century. Yet, it did not cease to be influential when the twelfth century came to an end; it remained a mature force in the history of medieval education from the twelfth through the fifteenth centuries—the grammar and logic teaching in the

---

[105] *Ibid.*, III, i, 150.
[106] *Ibid.*, I, x, 32–33.

universities of the thirteenth and fourteenth centuries attests to its influence in the schools—and, moreover, it paved a few educational avenues for the pedagogic humanists of the great Renaissance.

John articulated a theory of education that made training of the reasoning faculties the central function of all teaching; this end could be achieved most fully, John argued, by welding together Christian and classical elements and offering a broad syllabus taking into account reason and faith, philosophy and education. The product of such teaching, built upon John's personal example of scholarship, would be a critic and a dialectician, a humanist and a Christian scholar. To John and, we may believe, to many of his contemporaries this represented the fairest type of the learned man.[107]

107 Two additional studies on John of Salisbury bear mentioning here: M. B. Ryan, *John of Salisbury On the Arts of Language in the Trivium* (Washington, D.C., Catholic University of America Press, 1958) ; and Daniel D. McGarry, "Educational Theory in the Metalogicon of John of Salisbury," *Speculum,* 23 (October, 1948) , pp. 659–675.

☙ 7 ☙

Erasmus: Promoter of Christian Humanism

I

LIFE AND SERVICE TO LEARNING

Gutenberg printed a Latin Bible in 1456, a technological advance of enormous importance which enabled scholars to continue their great war on ignorance. Whether or not Gutenberg's Bible was the first product of movable type is a question too burdensome for these pages; [1] in any case, and without assigning any primacy for printers, we can fairly assume that the stage was properly set for an assault on the citadels of learning. The invention of movable type served learning in two ways principally: books could be multiplied a thousandfold; and scholars could cooperate in their efforts to understand the physical, human, and spiritual worlds in which they lived.[2]

Multiplication of texts, a fact of immense significance, requires no further amplification. The point of cooperation may not be clear. With printing, every book of the same edition was identical, and this identity was the key. Manuscripts in libraries, for all their excellence, were the products of scribes, who, even when taking their copying with the utmost seriousness, were liable to error. And when they produced several copies of the same manuscript such seemingly minor items as handwriting style

[1] See E. P. Goldschmidt, *The Printed Book of the Renaissance* (Cambridge, Cambridge University Press, 1950); D. C. McMurtrie, *The Book: The Story of Printing and Bookmaking* (New York, Covici, Friede, Inc., 1938); W. D. Orcutt, *Master Makers of the Book* (New York, Doubleday, Doran & Company, Inc., 1928); and P. Butler, *The Origin of Printing in Europe* (Chicago, The University of Chicago Press, 1940).

[2] See W. Wattenbach, *Das Schriftwesen im Mittelalter* (Leipzig, B. G. Teubner, 1896); J. W. Clark, *The Care of Books* (Cambridge, The University Press, 1909); and G. H. Putnam, *Books and Their Makers During the Middle Ages* (New York, Hillary, 1962).

and page size led to marked differences from one copy to another. Whenever it was necessary for medieval librarians to identify manuscripts in their bins, they did so not by referring to title pages, dates of publication, or authors, but by incipit sections on the second leaf of the manuscript. By the time the reader or librarian reached the second page of a manuscript, it was apparent that uniformity was lacking, and the variations in evidence were due either to scribes' unwillingness or inability to follow originals exactly. Reasons for variations in the texts need not be belabored, for they did not bespeak either a conscious subversion of scholarship or an erratic approach to it. A simple experiment in copying two printed pages will expose the hazards to accuracy.

A scholar preparing his own manuscript could elect to number the pages, but in doing so he had no assurance that copies of his work would retain the original pagination; and when he numbered pages of a finished manuscript in his possession for reference purposes, he could not assume that other scholars using the same manuscript could find the reference on the page he cited. The advantage of the improvement introduced by printing was not at once perceived. To begin with, printers signed their pages by quires of either four or twenty-four pages, depending on their preference, as the scribes had written them. But these signatures were intended to guide the binder, and when he had the directions he needed they were sheared off; subsequently the reader's convenience was noticed and these signatures were put at the foot of the page. The next step was to number the pages, not at the top corner of a page, but in the middle of the right-hand margin. This was done about 1470, perhaps by a printer in Cologne, yet it was an innovation not immediately imitated by other printers. Even chapters or parts of books were not clearly distinguished—the original manuscripts did not distinguish them either—and it was the rare printer who bothered to note the edition of the manuscript used as a basis for the printed text. In time all this was regularized, and when it was the book became a foundation on which scholars could build. They could exchange interpretations of the classics and contemporary works, and the book, with its permanence won in print, preserved an intellectual tradition and guaranteed a long life to scholarship. The standard text became the most important tool in the new world of learning that faced the genius of Erasmus.

According to a tradition, which he himself does not dispute, Erasmus was born ten years after Gutenberg's Latin Bible was printed in Mainz. The place of his birth was Rotterdam. Details of his parentage are clouded by myth, romance, and gossip, a point not missed by his adversaries, who, in later years, found such ammunition useful when they tried to discredit Erasmus.[3] At best, if we take his own testimony at face value,

---

[3] Erasmus' father is said to have been a parish priest of Gouda. See P. S. Allen, *The Age of Erasmus* (London, Oxford University Press, 1914), p. 32; and W. H. Wood-

Erasmus' early years were hard and unhappy. Primary education was pursued in the town school of Gouda, and, after being introduced to the Latin grammar of Donatus, Erasmus was sent to the Deventer School, where he was exposed to the teaching practices of the Brethren of the Common Life.[4] The Brethren were not charged with the management of Deventer, but many of its teachers had been associated with their schools and knew both their theory and practice of pedagogy. He spent eight years at the Deventer School and despite its considerable excellence, regularly attested in the pages of educational histories, had some hard things to say about it when, in later years, he reflected on the quality of his early schooling. His aspersions may only have been dictated by negative nostalgia, or by his abhorrence of the scholastic character impressed on the educational program. We know he had some renowned teachers—Hegius is an example—but we suspect that several grains of truth are lodged in his criticisms of the school. It had a good reputation for careful organization, demanded no doubt by an enrollment of upwards of 2200, yet each of the classes averaged about 275 pupils, and all too frequently the entire class was instructed by one master. There is a story that on some occasions the headmaster tried to teach the entire student body. But this perhaps was better than the ordinary instruction provided through conventional methods, when sometimes as many as nine teachers read their lectures to the boys at the same hour in the same room. All in all it was wearisome business.

We are ill-informed on the books employed in the curriculum of the Deventer School. The story is extant that few other than *Aesop's Fables,* the moral distichs of Cato, and the *Parables of Alan* found their way into the syllabus.[5] Yet this story is contradicted by others leading us to believe that the curriculum was filled with the choicest of modern and ancient authors.[6] Whichever version is correct, the course of study required the boys to be industrious, and they left the school having been exposed to the most advanced teaching afforded at the time.

Erasmus completed his study in the Deventer School about 1483 and after an interlude of approximately two years entered the Augustinian novitiate at Steyn.[7] Commentators often appear certain that Erasmus

---

ward, *Desiderius Erasmus Concerning the Aim and Method of Education* (New York, Bureau of Publications, Teachers College, Columbia University, 1964), p. 1.

[4] See Albert Hyma, *The Brethren of the Common Life* (Grand Rapids, Michigan, Eerdmans, 1950).

[5] J. H. Lupton, *A Life of John Colet,* pp. 271 ff.

[6] See Albert Hyma, *The Youth of Erasmus* (Ann Arbor, University of Michigan Press, 1930), pp. 88–104; J. A. Froude, *Life and Letters of Erasmus* (New York, Charles Scribner's Sons, 1905), pp. 3–4; and F. M. Nichols, *The Epistles of Erasmus* (New York, Russell & Russell, Inc., 1962), I, pp. 7–25.

[7] The chronology at this point is hard to follow: Woodward, *op. cit.,* p. 5, puts Erasmus in the monastery in 1483; Allen, *op. cit.,* pp. 66–67, seems to prefer the date 1485.

had neither the temperament nor the fundamental spirituality of a monk; they take both his trenchant remarks on monastic life and their own psychoanalytic conclusions too seriously, for if it was difficult for Erasmus to fathom his own motivations or the strength of his religious vocation, it is certainly infinitely more hazardous for his biographers and critics to identify them. Whether cut out for monastic life or not, Erasmus made the most of it; doubtless any other state of life should not have given him either the opportunity or leisure for scholarship, and the monastery turned out to be a good place for him to study. By 1492, when he was ordained to the priesthood, Erasmus was certain of his interest in scholarship and was determined to devote his life to it. So, beginning with a solid and sincere Christian persuasion, which did not go unchallenged by his more conservative confreres, Erasmus set his goal on literary excellence in the service of sacred learning, and after entering the official entourage of the Bishop of Cambrai—a tour of duty freeing him from monastic routine—matriculated at the University of Paris in 1495 to prepare for a degree in theology.[8]

The degree he sought was the doctorate, and to obtain it he had first to pursue preliminary studies which often seemed to him to be deprived of substance. Without trying to defend the basic arts course at Paris, it is only fair to say that Erasmus, now a man of twenty-nine and surprisingly well read, was studying subjects normally intended for boys ten or twelve years his junior.[9] He commented to his friends that he sat in class looking puzzled to impress the master with his serious intent, but really all that success required was to forget almost everything he already knew. His opinion of the course was low, yet he persisted long enough to obtain the first degree in theology; this took about three years. He could not remain for the full course. The great outcome of his Parisian study, to say nothing whatever about his fuller knowledge of theological canons, was a better-than-average competence in Greek, produced no doubt largely by independent study.

Now with fair competence in Greek he had the tool he needed to delve deeply into sacred learning, and he made the most of it. When he left the University of Paris he took what first appeared to be a detour in his route toward scholarship by getting into the publishing business.

---

[8] At this time the sixty colleges of the University of Paris may not have been intact (see H. Denifle, *Die Universitäten des Mittelalters bis 1400* (Berlin, Graz, Akademische Druck-u-Verlagsanstalt, 1956), vol. I; and Rashdall, *op. cit.*, I.) The college Erasmus attended was Montaigu. For additional information on Erasmus' early scholastic career, see, Woodward, *op. cit.*, p. 7; Allen, *op. cit.*; R. W. Chambers, *Thomas More* (London, Jonathan Cape, 1953); M. M. Phillips, *Erasmus and the Northern Renaissance* (London, Hodder & Stoughton, 1949); and Preserved Smith, *Erasmus* (New York, Harper & Row, 1923).

[9] A good description of this course is found in L. J. Paetow, *The Arts Course at Medieval Universities* (Urbana, Ill., University of Illinois Press, 1910); and Rashdall, *op. cit.*, vol. I.

Quite fortuitously he came to the notice of the printers, first by correcting proofs and composing dedications and prefaces, and then by writing reviews of new books. The latter were used regularly as advertisements and were given wide circulation. As the quality of his work became obvious, the printers, always anxious to produce salable goods, wanted more of his work and accepted some of his early verses and essays for publication. This was employment that kept open the gates of publication and along with private teaching enabled him to support himself. But this employment was below the level of Erasmus' aspirations, and while it created conditions for subsistence living, it also erected obstacles to scholarly achievement. Erasmus needed, and wanted, a patron who, in the best Renaissance tradition, would support his personal and his scholarly ventures generously and without question. A certain Lady of Veer appeared to fill the bill and Erasmus acceded to her munificence.[10] But in the long run neither the Lady nor Erasmus was happy about the arrangement. She did not have either the vision or the tastes of a Renaissance patroness, and Erasmus was not a man either ready or willing to account for his actions or his expenses. Erasmus' admirers read this page of his biography with chagrin, for when the Lady showed signs of niggardliness Erasmus upbraided her and demanded funds almost as a matter of right. He apparently felt no pangs of conscience over these outbursts and allowed the letters containing the diatribes to be published when only a word from him would have suppressed them.

With his patronage gone, Erasmus sought another course. He went to England in the summer of 1499 and spent some time at Oxford attending the lectures of John Colet. Colet, then engrossed with the Epistles of St. Paul, fascinated and inspired Erasmus by the breadth and depth of his learning. A close scholarly relationship and firm friendship were cemented before Erasmus left England—Colet wanted him to remain to continue his scholarly work in England—and the example of Colet must have had a permanent influence on Erasmus' firmly felt dedication to sacred learning. Still Erasmus did not believe that his tools, especially his Greek, were good enough to tackle the self-assigned job of illuminating sacred learning; his Greek was not flawless, and he knew almost no Hebrew. A cadre of English scholars led by Colet and Thomas More could not convince Erasmus to remain with them, although their scholarly expeditions and purposes were closely correlated with Erasmus' own goals.

He returned to the Continent to study the Greek classics and to continue his writing. In 1500 the first collection of the *Adagia*—a compilation of proverbs, maxims, and witty sayings culled from the classics—appeared in print. Then, to earn money, he edited Cicero's *De*

---

[10] Woodward, *op. cit.*, pp. 8–9.

Officiis and began to lay the foundation for *De Copia Verborum et Rerum* and for an enlarged version of *Adagia*. At about the same time he began, and then interrupted, a commentary on the *Epistle to the Romans*, because he doubted his command of Greek. An offer to asume the chair of Rhetoric at the University of Louvain was declined, possibly in 1502, because Erasmus did not want to be confined either intellectually or geographically and Louvain offered almost no hope for finished scholarship in Greek.[11] Erasmus was still determined to perfect the tool that could put him on entirely intimate terms with the Greek Testament.

In 1505 he returned to England in response to an invitation from Colet and other English scholars, but he stayed in England only briefly. Despite the excellence of English scholarship at this time, England was not the prime center of Greek learning, and Erasmus, now in command of the best Latin style of his time, widely read in Latin, patristic, and classical literature, and an adviser and friend to scholars in the north of Europe and England, wanted to secure his reputation as a scholar by sitting at the feet of Italian scholars and Greek teachers who even yet had not crossed the Alps. With superior credentials, the maturity of a scholar, and a new translation of the New Testament, complete except for Acts and Revelation, to his credit, he seized an opportunity to go to Italy, leaving behind the unfinished writings of his English sojourn.

In 1506 he was en route to Italy and while passing through Turin he took his doctorate in theology at the university, a degree that until then had eluded his academic grasp.[12] Then on to Bologna, Florence, and finally Venice where he was associated with the great printing firm of Aldus Manutius and its community of scholars, who used Greek as a living language. At long last Erasmus was where he needed to be: in the company of men from whom he could learn and with whom he could work. Plato implied that fifty years were needed to make a man; Erasmus met most of Plato's requirements with about ten years to spare. From Venice, where he spent the greater part of two years, he went on to Rome, and not being greatly impressed with the city he returned to England in the spring of 1509. The Italian experience was brief, but it paid huge dividends both in learning and writing; we are almost forced to admit that Erasmus never wasted an hour. Original writing, editing,

11 *Ibid.*, 12–13. See also P. A. Duhamel, "The Oxford Lectures of John Colet: An Essay in Defining the English Renaissance," *Journal of the History of Ideas*, XIV, No. 4 (October, 1953) , pp. 493–510.

12 Erasmus is surprisingly silent about the details of his journey. Perhaps he took no time to breathe in the spirit of the cities through which he passed. So little evidence exists of study or residence at the University of Turin, we are almost compelled to believe the degree was practically a gift from an admiring faculty. Yet this is a hasty conclusion and it may do Erasmus an injustice; a quick degree from a sixteenth-century university was not necessarily a cheap one. See Woodward, *op. cit.*, p. 15.

and translation flowed from his pen; in three years in Italy he published enough to do credit to a lifetime. And when he left Italy he left as a new man: he was now acquainted with princes of the Church; he had watched the complicated ecclesiastical apparatus at work; with his Italian degree his academic pedigree was assured; he was admitted to the inner circle of scholars, editors, and publishers; and most of all he had gotten the one thing he wanted most from Italy—a sound working knowledge of Greek.

From this point on we need not try to follow Erasmus around Europe. He is almost always on the move. His first stop after Italy was England, and while he was in England he turned once more to translating the New Testament, an enterprise completed in 1514, although styling and editing the manuscript delayed its appearance in print until the first months of 1516. His determination to have an entirely accurate version of the Bible never lessened during his illustrious career; it stands as the consuming occupation of his life and is convincing testimony to his dedication to Christian scholarship, but in conjunction with this overriding occupation he found time to translate and edit Jerome, Chrysostom, Augustine, Origen, and other Fathers, along with a long list of classical authors. His place in learning thus guaranteed, he could thereafter answer to the appellation, Prince of the Humanists.

Although Erasmus was never a schoolmaster, he saw clearly the many defects in the educational process. Schools were poorly managed, teachers badly prepared to lead students down the multiple avenues of learning, curricula disorganized and rarely constructed following any principles of selection. Even when scholarship was good, as it was in Erasmus' case, the schools were in no position to profit from it. There was an urgent need to create a living tradition of sound learning and a respectable atmosphere for it to grow in, for unless this was done the accomplishments of the best humanists would be but ephemeral specks on the academic horizon. Erasmus was too much a humanist to allow its accomplishments to go unnoticed, so he tried to translate its scholarship, and its real literary achievements, into a syllabus for the classroom. Bringing scholarship down to the level of the schools without diluting it or making it mere rote was a striking failure of the earlier humanists, beginning with Vergerio, excepting only Guarino and Vittorino; and to say they failed is to give them the benefit of the doubt; they may never have had any vision that such transference was important or imperative.[13] Educational reform, all

13 See Woodward, *Vittorino da Feltre and Other Humanist Educators* (New York, Bureau of Publications, Teachers College, Columbia University, 1963), pp. 22–27; and by the same author, *Studies in Education During the Age of the Renaissance, 1400–1600* (New York, Cambridge University Press, 1924), pp. 93–112. A somewhat less enthusiastic appraisal of Vittorino's accomplishments in education is made by F. Prendilacqua, *Intorno alla vita di Vittorino da Feltre,* translated and edited by G. Brambilla (Como, Guido, 1871). See also, A. Gambara, *Vittorino da Feltre* (Turin, G. B. Paravia, 1946).

the way from school objectives to methods of teaching and learning, was required; and to be in the vanguard of this pedagogic reform was not beneath the dignity nor beyond the ability of Erasmus. It may be argued that Erasmus, despite his enviable credentials as a writer and man of learning, was ill-equipped to advise teachers in the lower schools or professors in the universities. He had never spent a day teaching a class of boys in an ordinary school nor had he ever held a regular appointment to a chair at a university; moreover, his blind spot—a persistent refusal to reclaim the vernaculars as proper vehicles of learning—made him an uneasy champion for revitalized and popularized school learning. Yet, he forged ahead to restate education's best goals and to revive its best methods, based always on a balanced view of a learner's capacity. But there was a limit: Erasmus led an educational reform centering on a teaching of the classics; he was willing to ignore, or leave to others, any updating of vernacular schools or broadening of educational opportunity for the mass of mankind. Despite the acknowledged narrowness of his approach—which makes us say later that it was out-of-date almost the day it was offered—it had a certain universality making it applicable to any school or level of education. The content of the curriculum—Latin and Greek for Erasmus—while never sold at a discount in the tradition reborn with him, turned out to be less important than teaching goals and methods, and in dealing with these items Erasmus displayed pedagogic insight and even genius.

Erasmus "did not invent humanistic education, nor was he by any means its only distinguished advocate; but he was perhaps its most accomplished one"; [14] or "He is the greatest man we come across in the history of education," [15] are two comments not to be taken lightly. While the evidence to support or contradict them, or even evidence to establish a balanced estimate of Erasmus' place in educational history, cannot be offered on these pages, we must be aware of the stature of the man with whom we are dealing. And the best way to consolidate this awareness is to display his educational dicta as best we can. Unquestionably he was always conscious of the pedagogic issue, and he dealt with it in three ways: first, he devoted generous space in several of his autobiographical writings to his own school experiences and added acid criticisms on what he believed were remnants of medieval teaching practices; second, he supplied textbooks for the schools by aiming many of his scholarly works at an academic public; and, third, he produced books on education that recommended procedures for formal teaching and learning. The last genre concerns us now, not that we intend to review them in Erasmian

14 Craig R. Thompson, in forward to Woodward, *Desiderius Erasmus*, p. xx.

15 R. R. Bolgar, *The Classical Heritage and Its Beneficiaries* (Cambridge, Cambridge University Press, 1954), p. 336; for a highly perceptive analysis of humanistic education from Petrarch through Erasmus, see pp. 248–282; 329–340.

style, but merely to name and annotate them in order to set the stage for a subsequent rendering of Erasmus' pedagogic creed.

Between 1511 and 1529 Erasmus wrote three strictly educational books: *Upon the Right Method of Instruction* (1511), *The Education of a Christian Prince* (1515), and *The Liberal Education of Boys* (1529).[16]

His theme in the first book was essentially practical. The educational fraternity, he believed, needed help of the most basic kind: it needed to know what and how to teach. Although Erasmus has been condemned for his preoccupation with the classics in this discourse, he has never been charged with impracticality. His readers could go to him as John Colet did when he started his school in England, for guidance in the management of a school. When they did they learned that he wanted them to emphasize skill, expression and physical and spiritual training, but knowledge of truth and knowledge of words were to be attended to also. Literature and grammar must be mastered; memory must be strengthened through use; games, plays, contests, rewards, revision, and repetition, all find their way into the instructional apparatus and all are important. But they are really aimed at mastery of literature, a mine that must be excavated of all its treasures, and nothing is to be left to chance. The purpose of the whole business is clear: boys begin their study with literature and they end it with literature; but they are not just marking time; they move steadily—but not swiftly—from a knowledge of their authors to a critical and objective attitude toward literature. The goal is clear, and the means, Erasmus thinks, are certain, but he does not give us all the details we would like.

The Education of a Christian Prince [17] articulates the principal thrust of Erasmus' educational philosophy as well as the central theme in his philosophy of life: morality. It is a solid Christian view to which all life's labor is subordinated; even the erudition of the humanist could not submerge or subvert the objective of salvation, which is attained not through intellectual excellence but through moral formation. And, as we shall see, Erasmus' literary education was not a closed system sufficient in itself, for the syllabus of classical learning both generated and supported morality, as Erasmus could prove by historically and philologically based arguments. The prince for whom he wrote was every noble child, not just Charles V, and the education he endorsed was not just for monarchs but for every man who had first to control himself before he could lead others. Such a man needed to be a philosopher, and in this context the

[16] Rather than follow Richard Sherry's sixteenth-century translation of *De Pueris Statim ac Liberaliter Instituendis* (That Children Ought to be Taught and Brought Up Gently in Virtue and Learning—and That Even Forthwith From Their Nativity) I have used the simpler, and I believe more meaningful title: *The Liberal Education of Boys*. See Edward J. Power, *Main Currents in the History of Education* (New York, McGraw-Hill Publishing Company, Inc., 1962), p. 296.

[17] Translated by L. K. Born, New York, 1936.

philosopher was not Plato's student searching for intimations of being but a man whose mind was free from false opinions and predilections. He was to be a good man, skilled, not in speaking, as Quintilian advised, but in wisdom. And what better way was there to exploit the natural impulse for goodness than by exposing students directly to the great ideas and the grandest expressions literature contained? The contrast between Erasmus' and Machiavelli's prince is striking; the latter emphasized political skill—and in a sense followed Quintilian, for whom eloquent oratory was the greatest political skill of all—while the former thought more highly of wisdom, prudence, justice, and integrity.

In what is often described, without much meaning,[18] as his most mature work on education—*The Liberal Education of Boys* [19]—Erasmus restates the importance of education and makes a final attempt to provide a theoretical foundation for translating scholarship to education, for bringing the best in the intellectual tradition within the range of boys in the schoolroom. It is a broad, yet brief, essay on the meaning and purpose of education wherein he treats of the following topics: beginning education early, judicious selection of a boy's first teachers, nurture's superiority over nature, the priority parents must give to the education of their children, the dangers of neglected education, the role of reason in man's life, formation of habit, the role of experience, the character of teachers, the individuality of the child, the effects of education, the age for beginning formal education, expression in the hierarchy of educational goals, ancient literature in the curriculum, private schools, the punishment and discipline of children and students, and varieties of methods of teaching. When the catalogue was complete Erasmus was satisfied with his theory, and he offered it unhesitatingly to the educational world. What is more, for the next 200 years the educational world followed him almost without reservation. Seven years after the publication of *The Liberal Education of Boys* Erasmus died; in four centuries the luster to his scholarship and educational influence has not tarnished, although it is sometimes misunderstood.

II

A PERIOD OF TRANSITION

The genius of Erasmus is found mainly in the synthesis he arranged between the various promises of the new humanism, which by his lifetime

---

[18] What should perhaps be said instead of "his most mature work on education," a statement implying qualitative judgment, is "a work of his more mature years," or "his last book on education."

[19] Printed in Woodward, *Desiderius Erasmus*, pp. 163–180.

had been given general credibility, and the lingering manifestations of medievalism that were validly Christian and pointed men toward otherworldly values. The Renaissance at its height proved that Europe was a cultural unit with a profound reverence for its Christian traditions; the Renaissance way of life was not a reflection of a sharp break with the past but the result of a long, slow development which can be traced through the preceding centuries.[20] In a sense, scholasticism dealt with the same issues that faced humanism—constructing a world view wherein classical material and secular culture should subserve Christianity—and on the intellectual level scholasticism succeeded; yet the scholastics did not take into account the changes that were coming over the world and, in the last analysis, many of the factors responsible for these changes lay beyond the reach of scholastic thought.[21]

Scholasticism had its remarkable personalities; humanism had them too. If we are to sense the role of Erasmus' humanism vis-à-vis pedagogy, we must see how the stage was set for him and how the humanistic movement which had its authentic origin in classical Greece was transformed for European use. Humanism in Europe evolved slowly, and it is hard to know how long this evolution might have taken without acceleration; the person responsible for humanistic acceleration was Petrarch.[22]

Petrarch made his first appearance in the early decades of the fourteenth century as a poet, and he attracted the attention and won the admiration of a vast public. He could have enjoyed the luxury of his position and turned his back on intellectual issues, but he chose not to do so; instead he developed a cult of fame. One of the precepts of this cult was to use human talent to obtain genuine public recognition. In Pe-

[20] See C. H. Haskins, *The Renaissance of the Twelfth Century* (Cambridge, Mass., Harvard University Press, 1927) ; Gilbert Highet, *The Clasical Tradition* (New York, Oxford University Press, 1949) ; J. E. Sandys, *A History of Classical Scholarship,* vol. I (Cambridge, The University Press, 1906–1908) .

[21] "The reach of scholastic thought" used to be an old debate and many Catholic writers gave the impression that the structure of their faith depended on their success in the debate. Thus, the literature is full of a variety of interpretations of scholasticism. If the reader is interested in illumination rather than polemic, he may obtain insight into scholasticism's origins from R. L. Poole, *Illustrations of the History of Medieval Thought and Learning,* 2d ed. (New York, The Macmillan Co., 1940) , pp. 116–222; C. H. Haskins, *op. cit.,* chap. XI; M. Grabmann, *Die Geschichte der scholastischen Methode* (Berlin, Akademie-Verlag, 1956) ; and C. C. J. Webb, *Studies in the History of Natural Theology* (Oxford, The Clarendon Press, 1915) . For examples of rejections in scholasticism, see E. K. Rand, "The Classics in the 13th Century," *Speculum,* IV (1926) , pp. 249–269; L. J. Paetow, *Two Medieval Satires of the University of Paris* (Berkeley, University of California Press, 1927) . See also, Bolgar, *op. cit.,* pp. 239–244.

[22] Although we would find it unacceptable to omit Petrarch as a groundbreaker for Erasmus, it is impossible to give him the attention he deserves in these pages. See J. H. Whitfield, *Petrarch and the Renaissance* (London, Oxford University Press, 1943) ; H. W. Rolfe, *Petrarch: The First Modern Scholar and Man of Letters* (New York, G. P. Putnam's Sons, 1909) ; Hans Baron, *The Crisis of the Early Italian Renaissance* (Princeton, N.J., Princeton University Press, 1955) ; and Denys Hay, *The Italian Renaissance and Its Historical Background* (Cambridge, Cambridge University Press, 1961) .

trarch's case this meant trying to formulate a reasoned justification for the employment of classical learning, for which he was a most zealous champion. The old dilemma that had plagued Christians for fourteen centuries was still alive; [23] yet the dilemma that faced Petrarch was hardly identical to the one with which Jerome, Basil, and Augustine had wrestled.[24] Petrarch's problem, or goal, was simpler and it can be stated quickly: to offer bases upon which a full individual life could be led and at the same time to exploit and perfect man's natural inclinations for social relations. Both dimensions of the goal, he was convinced, could use the means of classical knowledge to good advantage; in fact, classical knowledge may have been judged indispensable.

Petrarch began where his medieval predecessors had also begun: with Latin. An unbroken tradition, not, to be sure, authentically classical, held Latin to be the language of literature; besides, a firmly held conviction among many Christians elevated Latin as a divine language invented by God especially for sacred use, but Petrarch refused to make such a precarious commitment. He never doubted, however, that true learning was impossible without a mastery of Latin, and thus he perpetuated a tradition with which he could have broken had he mustered sufficient cultural self-confidence. When he rejected scholasticism his cultural aspirations demanded that he cling to Latin and Greek, although Greek, it must be admitted, was a kind of cultural afterthought.[25] In addition, there was a personal reason: Petrarch abhorred the products of scholasticism, but he enjoyed Latin authors and found spiritual comfort in reading them. Yet, despite his estimate that everything the ancients had written was good, he could be selective when he consulted the shelves of his library. Only in theory did he embrace the whole of the classical heritage. Logic and metaphysics, law and medicine, were either despised or paid scant heed; and on the other side of the ledger, in space reserved for the budding sciences where classical allegiances did not count for much, Petrarch made no debit entries.[26]

Petrarch's overriding interest was in the good life, and for it Greek and Latin were the only suitable languages. This precept began as a stumbling block, and so it remained, to the development of vernacular language, which in turn was a natural vehicle for the growth of national-

23 The dilemma had perennial qualities. See examples of its application in J. E. Sandys, *op. cit.*, I, 618; A. O. Norton, *Readings in the History of Education* (Cambridge, Mass., Harvard University Press, 1909), pp. 64–66; C. H. Haskins, *op. cit.*, pp. 96–97; M. Manitius, *Geschichte der lateinischen Literatur des Mittelalters* (Munich, Beck, 1959); and Bolgar, *op. cit.*, pp. 246–247.

24 See E. K. Rand, *Founders of the Middle Ages*, (Cambridge, Mass., Harvard University Press, 1928), pp. 1–68.

25 P. De Nohlac, *Pétrarque et l'Humanisme* (Paris, Banelon Thiolier, 1921), p. 16; and Bolgar, *op. cit.*, pp. 249–250.

26 Petrarch, *De ignorantia*, edited by Capelli (Paris, H. Campion, 1906), p. 68.

ism and the spread of education.[27] Petrarch cast his lot with imitation, believing that the most certain way to achieve individual and social excellence was to follow the tone and style of ancient models. He endorsed a procedure whose ultimate implications he could neither have realized nor approved. The imitation Petrarch supported could not be learned in a day, nor was it simply a matter of writing a Latin corresponding exactly to the usage of Cicero. It is important for us to know what Petrarch meant when he advocated the imitation of ancient authors. He wanted potential writers to use the classics as models to find in them, not themes, but styles of expression which would enable writers to develop their subjects naturally; above all, by using the classics in a broad, rather than narrow, sense, he hoped to develop a student's power of expression.[28] Petrarch would have been content with accomplished and refined expression; unfortunately, too many of his successors took this to mean collecting storehouses of classical words and phrases.[29]

It was not until the end of the fourteenth century that humanism began to invade the educational world. Then certain teachers working within the established systems caught the spirit of Petrarch's doctrine of imitation and tried to give their lessons in grammar and rhetoric a wider range. Bruni,[30] Marsuppini,[31] and Poggio [32] were such teachers, as was Giovanni da Ravenna,[33] who, while he was a master at Padua, taught both Guarino [34] and Vittorino da Feltre,[35] and wrote his autobiography,

27 See Daniel D. McGarry, "Renaissance Educational Theory," *Historical Bulletin,* 32 (May, 1954) , pp. 195–209; and Bolgar, *op. cit.,* p. 252.

28 *Ibid.,* p. 266.

29 See H. H. Gray, "Renaissance Humanism: The Pursuit of Eloquence," *Journal of the History of Ideas,* XXIV (1963) , pp. 497–514.

30 Woodward, *Vittorino da Feltre,* pp. 123–133.

31 Carlo Marsuppini carried some of this pedagogic inspiration to Florence, where he was a highly successful teacher. See Bolgar, *op. cit.,* p. 329.

32 The literature on Poggio is not as full as we would like. See William Shepherd, *The Life of Poggio Brocciolini* (Liverpool, J. M'Ceery, 1802) ; and E. Walser, *Poggius Florentinus: Leben und Werke* (Leipzig, B. G. Teubner, 1914) .

33 A brief but good sketch of Giovannia Conversino da Ravenna's teaching and influence is given in Woodward, *Vittorino da Feltre,* pp. 3–4; see also, Bolgar, *op. cit.,* pp. 257–258, 429.

34 Guarino Veronese, accounted to be the finest ornament of Chrysoloras' and Giovanni's teaching, makes the historical record only through his son, Battista Guarino. In *Concerning the Order and the Method to be Observed in Teaching and Reading the Classical Authors* (Woodward, *Vittorino da Feltre,* pp. 161–178) the son writes: "It [this book] is indeed a summary of the theory and practice of several scholars, and especially does it represent the doctrine of my father Guarino Veronese; so much so, that you may suppose him to be writing to you by my pen, and giving you the fruit of his long and ripe experience in teaching" (*ibid.,* p. 161) . See also, G. Bertoni, *Guarino da Verona,* 1429–1460 (Geneva, L. S. Olschki, 1921) .

35 Vittorino's reputation as the greatest modern schoolmaster is based on an oral tradition. He left no written account of his educational views or practices. Woodward's book, *Vittorino da Feltre,* pp. 1–92, along with Gambara's, *op. cit.,* are our best sources on his career as an educator.

in which he expressed Petrarchian ideas on education. But this was not educational literature in any strict sense, and the practical recommendations relative to technique that he made for carrying Petrarch's program forward were easy to overlook. In 1404 the aims of education distilled by Petrarch were given a strict pedagogical formulation by Vergerio in his *On Noble Character and Liberal Studies*.[36]

There is no need here to give Vergerio's treatise a close and thorough examination. It is not worth such care. Yet he must have shocked his contemporaries with the originality of his approach: he clearly makes the formation of character, not the acquisition of knowledge, the principal emphasis in teaching.[37] And he took time to assert the importance of manners—which must have endeared him to a shop-keeping public—in a way that makes us think he was writing a constitution for a business college.[38] Literature is important, he says, because it occupies leisure hours, but it also teaches a power of expression which is of great help to the businessman or administrator. But these are justifications which can be noticed and then left; the real value to literature is that it is a moral guide and as such is basic instruction for everyone. Here was the key for integrating the individual and social goals that Petrarch had erected. The schools henceforth must accept the classical commission and train their students for character. In Vergerio's work, Petrarch's educational hopes are brought nearer realization.[39]

Vergerio's auspicious beginning in *On Noble Character and Liberal Studies* is spoiled by his refusal to make detailed suggestions on educational practice. He does not bother to tell us what the boys are to study or how long their course should last. When he does treat of one subject, logic, in some detail—perhaps he felt competent here because he had been a professor of logic—he tells us it must be practical,[40] and thus, ignoring four centuries of scholarship in connection with logic and its many contributions to a science of exact thinking, he creates a gap between the humanist and medieval educational outlook.[41] Even when we are not impressed with Vergerio's theories in a book largely barren of educational suggestions, we should know that both they and the practices represented mark the high point of educational achievement in fourteenth-century humanism. Vergerio could write on education without any real sense of involvement, and schoolmasters could read him without being motivated to alter their school practices. If we think humanism transformed the schools of the fourteenth century, we are

---

[36] For a brief sketch of Vergerio's life and a translation of his educational tract, see Woodward, *Vittorino da Feltre*, pp. 93–122.

[37] *Ibid.*, p. 102; and Bolgar, *op. cit.*, p. 258.

[38] *Ibid.*, p. 259; and Woodward, *Vittorino da Feltre*, p. 99.

[39] *Ibid.*, p. 104.

[40] *Ibid.*, p. 107.

[41] See Bolgar, *op. cit.*, p. 259.

mistaken, for they followed the dead hand of habit and turned to the collecting and copying of classical manuscripts, an occupation that in the long run brought them an enormous amount of fame but did nothing to alter the educational course little boys had to run. It was an occupation, too, eventually making Petrarch's theory and Vergerio's ringing endorsement impossible to follow without some important alterations or additions.

Petrarch had started a movement to recover the literatures of the past, and his followers were remarkably successful not only in collecting poetry but in gathering together for criticism and examination manuscripts devoted to law, medicine, and philosophy. Coupled with this achievement was a further cultural enrichment made by a revived interest in Greek studies. Petrarch set the compass, but he left it to others to follow the course. Collectors and students were uncomfortable handling and storing Greek literary treasures whose meaning was inaccessible to them, and there were still remnants of cultural inferiority in the Latin tradition left over from the finest period of Roman eloquence. Humanistic cultural aspirations were high enough to motivate scholars to return to the study of Greek, a language long wilted by obscurity, and place it on a level of scholarship alongside Latin. Besides, printing presses were churning out books of all kinds, and the breadth of classical literature— both Latin and Greek—was so great that basic conditions of education and research needed altering.

Petrarch could easily talk about the worth of imitation and expect students to follow his advice when there were so few classics to choose from. A student would read and reread the manuscripts available to him, and from his constant study he could expect to capture not only the style of the classical authors but also all the knowledge the classics contained. It was not too much to expect that a scholar would know most of his classical literature by heart. But with almost the whole of the classical legacy in their possession the humanists could no longer rely on the unorganized workings of sheer memory; if the classics were to have any effect on education, schoolmasters would have to devise some new techniques. Vergerio was by now hopelessly out-of-date, although the educational goal he acknowledged was still regarded as fundamental; the task of translating scholarship into education required more than pious advice. Rules and procedures were necessary if imitation of classical language and style were to be handled successfully to the extent that ancient ways of thought could be mastered.

We have already said what Petrarch meant by imitation, and his creed might have worked when the classical corpus was less complex, yet even then it did not prove to be an entirely adequate tool for directing an assimilation of classical thinking. It made effective writing possible, but it was too unsystematic for general use and for the larger role now expected of it. Petrarch had recommended nothing more than ordinary reading, but now ordinary reading could not serve the object of recovering the culture of the past. Even Petrarch, when he followed his own advice, was remarkably little affected by his excursions into the classics: the classics did not remake him, they simply provided him with greater facility in expressing ideologies having prior existence in his mind.

So when Petrarch's advice was found wanting another guide was sought. The humanists found that guide in Chrysoloras (1350–1413),[42] who opened the door to Greek studies. He became the leading man of his age and exerted a formidable influence on the men who were to invent and popularize a new pedagogic technique. From Chrysoloras the humanists not only learned greater facility in Greek, but they learned also that the gateway to classical culture was opened by finding categories in classical writing and by placing inordinate confidence in minutiae. Now they could not be content with the sound or the sense of the classics; they had to embrace a comprehensive approach that would enable them to dissect every classic, analyzing and noticing everything they contained. Of course they would pay particular attention to words, syllables, figures of speech, and all ornaments of style, for these, they thought, were the ultimate building blocks of good writing. The new method was not explained in great detail by any humanist educator, although Leonardo Bruni came closest to doing so when he wrote a handbook on the education of women.[43] Yet women were never expected to undergo the same grammatical and rhetorical regimen as men.[44]

What we notice especially in Bruni, and in the other educational theorists of this time, is a recommendation that good pedagogy is grounded in attention to detail.[45] Even when they do not follow their own advice and go into detail, they tell us that successful imitation— whose value they never doubted—stands in the last analysis on grammatical and rhetorical exactitude. From this time to the time of the more balanced and fuller statements of Erasmus, we are caught in an educational program that loved and honored the doctrine of detail.

How was detail to be handled in the school? We know that the enriched classical heritage available now in print could hardly be

---

[42] See John A. Symonds, *The Renaissance in Italy* (New York, Modern Library, Inc., 1935), I, pp. 93–122.

[43] For Bruni's treatise, see Woodward, *Vittorino da Feltre*, pp. 123–133; for an evaluation, see Bolgar, *op. cit.*, p. 269.

[44] See R. Kelso, *Doctrine for the Lady of the Renaissance* (Urbana, Ill., University of Illinois Press, 1956).

[45] "To this end we must be supremely careful in our choice of authors, lest an inartistic and debased style infect our own writing and degrade our taste; which danger is best avoided by bringing a keen, critical sense to bear upon select works, observing the sense of each passage, the structure of the sentence, the force of every word down to the least important particle. In this way our reading reacts directly upon our style" Woodward, *Vittorino da Feltre*, p. 124).

mastered and remembered without some pedagogic device, and the humanists knew it too. Most of them, however, were unwilling or unable to say what form the device should take. Here is where Bruni comes again to our aid, although we are fairly certain his ideas lack originality, for they reflect mainly the techniques worked out earlier by Guarino, but until now Guarino's methods had gone unnoticed.[46] In any case, questions of origin aside, we are told that reading on every educational level must be analytical and that every student must read with a notebook on the desk ready to receive under proper headings everything coming to the reader's attention. Now schoolmasters had a technique which could complete the cycle between the corpus of classical writing and day-to-day pedagogy.

With notebook at the ready boys could now make a brave beginning into their classical study with the hope of mastering not only content but style as well. Eloquence was no longer the supreme intellectual accomplishment, yet no humanist was ready to sell good writing or powerful speaking at a discount. When a student's reading was finished and his notebook was full, composition could begin. As the notebook age progressed scholars were at pains to refine the categories or the notebook headings in order to make the contents of the notebooks readily accessible to intending writers, and as they succeeded their systems gave birth to a short-circuited pedagogy. The best notebooks—ones filled not by mere schoolboys but by finished scholars—were published, and pupils could use them as guides to reading and as almost inexhaustible sources for their own writing. Perhaps in theory there was no substitute for taking one's own notes, but in practice these ready-made notebooks made a schoolboy's life less complicated. The more capable schoolmasters and the students who showed a disinterested determination to achieve excellence must have demurred from these violations of the spirit of the notebook technique, but if they did, or when they did, they left no permanent record of their objections.

The cycle, it is true, was then complete, but much remained to be done. The best humanist writers turned their not inconsiderable talents to developing a science of notetaking. And it should be mentioned that in doing so they were largely converting to their own use a system of classifying knowledge that was commonly used in medieval education.[47] The humanist break with the recent past could achieve only a superficial reality; the most astute humanist educational writers knew of the medieval categories, most obviously displayed in medieval sermon books, but they nevertheless maintained their aloofness to everything medieval

---

[46] I mean only that they had to await publication by his son. See Bolgar, *op. cit.*, pp. 269–270.

[47] For some examples, see G. R. Owst, *Preaching in Medieval England* (Cambridge, The University Press, 1926) , pp. 279–308.

by simply acting as if their relationships to the medieval world of life and letters did not exist. We should not, of course, insist that humanistic educational practice or theory was simply medieval educational theory and practice all over again, for this was never true; neither should we allow the humanists to pretend that their approach to learning was entirely fresh without any indebtedness whatever to their medieval forebears.[48]

The notebook technique brings us to Erasmus again, for the most detailed account of the whole business of notetaking and the theory supporting it is given in his *De Copia*.[49] Here Erasmus, perhaps building on the false starts of Bembo [50] and Vivès [51] and others, distinguishes two approaches or two applications of the technique. And he is not inventing; he is simply being systematic in recording a tradition begun by Guarino. In the *Copia Verborum* he concerns himself with vocabulary and recommends various ways of arranging material; in the *Copia Rerum* he enumerates the ways illustrative materials can be presented and he gives us ample examples to follow. In other words, he not only tells his readers how the job of writing should be done, but he also offers models for them to follow.[52]

The last part of *De Copia* is devoted to the method of notetaking. Erasmus wants to be sure that students know how to collect their examples of classical treasures and how to record them for future use. In an age that placed such great value on what literature contained and the style of its presentation, this was no insignificant undertaking. He shows the student how to divide his notebook into various sections, and he recommends headings that will be most useful. He shows him the proper divisions, subdivisions, headings, and subheadings. But this is not all. Despite great care and judicious selection in notetaking, a student would soon have a mass of information neatly filed on the shelves of his bookcase. One might wonder if the germs of knowledge and style were any more accessible so stored than in their original form. It is apodictically clear that these notebooks were next to valueless unless their contents were in useable form, and while classification could help, it could not do everything. Even the clearest and best notebooks could not be packed

---

[48] See again, D. D. McGarry, "Renaissance Educational Theory," *Historical Bulletin*, 32 (May, 1954), pp. 195–209.

[49] It is easy to miss *De Copia* as an educational work—a textbook and a guide—designed for wide circulation. It appeared in more than fifty editions, before 1555. See D. B. King and H. D. Rix, *On Copia of Words and Ideas* (Milwaukee, Wis., Marquette University Press, 1963).

[50] Cardinal Bembo (1470–1547), *De Imitatione* (Basil, 1556).

[51] See Foster Watson, *Vivès on Education* (New York, G. P. Putnam's Sons, 1913); and *Vivès and the Renaissance Education of Women* (New York, Longmans, Green & Co., 1912). Both Vivès' impact on the notebook technique and the education of women have been exaggerated.

[52] See King and Rix, *op. cit.*, and Bolgar, *op. cit.*, p. 273.

around by the scholar; he could not carry them everywhere he went. Notetaking and notekeeping must therefore be regarded as a technique, a step toward something greater and even more useful: it was a way of setting the stage for the titanic task of remembering everything excavated from classical mines.

Erasmus was only recommending a way of studying the classics that he himself had found eminently useful. The techniques of *De Copia,* supported by ardent memorizing, contain the clue to the proper employment of imitation and composition; moreover, the clue is there too for mastering the entire field of classical learning. Portions of the classical legacy had for too long been neglected—sometimes for compelling reasons; now the means were at hand for absorbing all classical learning into the European intellectual tradition. The scholar most responsible for making this assimilation possible was Erasmus, and it is left for us now to see how he transformed this clue into a code of teaching and learning, into a new method of study giving humanistic schools life and meaning.

The humanistic educational inspiration and method were intended to have a broad application; not only were literary studies the objects of humanistic interest, and with them humanists felt most at home, the specialties were to be beneficiaries of humanist genius too.[53] Yet the great professional specialties of philosophy, law, and medicine had already developed their own elaborate methods, and the humanists could do little to alter or invade them. Still with all of life the humanists' proper arena of action, nothing was to be allowed to assert its independence from their sphere of influence. They tried to reform or humanize philosophy by going first to Aristotle and then to Plato. But humanists who were not really philosophers could hardly be expected to illuminate the thought of either, or to apply that thought to the vital questions of the day. They produced new translations of Aristotle and Plato, and to this extent should be commended, but with respect to their larger goal of adopting Aristotle and Plato and making the philosophical enterprise up-to-date and meaningful, they were failures. To begin with, Aristotle's style did not appeal to them, and given their ineptness in scientific philosophy they had difficulty in understanding him; but he was Greek and they would not leave him alone. In the end, they looked at his works, not for philosophical insights, but as philologists trying to understand his use of language. Plato had better literary credentials than Aristotle and was therefore more eagerly welcomed into humanist circles; but if Aristotle had been too tough for them to master, what could they really expect to learn from Plato? Apparently they learned nothing of consequence philosophically, for the Plato they pretended to know was not really Plato at all, and they regularly misinterpreted and misunderstood him. What they did, however, which had no meaning as philosophy, was

[53] See Bolgar, *op. cit.,* pp. 282–295.

to construct a philosophical fabric that would bolster their preconceived notions and support their private view of life. Somewhat negatively they served philosophy by bringing it to such low repute that modern men rejected traditional philosophy and turned instead to new systems of philosophical thought holding greater promise for solving, or at least illuminating, some of the burning questions of the day.

In medicine the humanists were only slightly more successful, and here the worth of their work is not demonstrated in additions to medical science, but, rather, in making available to medical men the little-known works of ancient medical writers besides Galen and Hippocrates.[54] Galen, of course, was the medical authority to whom all doctors turned, and for years he had been the principal textbook in the university schools of medicine. But the humanists were quick to see Galen as primarily a medical philosopher and were prone to label as quacks the doctors whose medical prescriptions were based solely on his works. If medical authorities were not dependable, where could doctors go? At this point the humanist, acidly critical of Galen, could not give the medical profession any guidance; he could not foresee the development of medicine with its allied sciences as an empirically based discipline. When he told doctors to return to the literature, he ignored the possibilities of a new medicine with scientific knowledge then lingering on the fringe of medical respectability. There were medical innovators, yet unsupported by their colleagues or by the humanists. The humanistic admonition to the doctors to return to the literature may have been better advice than we would at first think, for with the list of authorities lengthened medical practitioners were no longer confident of their mastery of medical knowledge. This doubt led in time to innovation and to a more empirical approach to medicine and the sciences supporting it.

In law the humanist effort bore better fruit; jurists finally adopted the humanist apparatus for reinterpreting legal authorities and undertook to formulate a legal code in which Roman law, with its authorities and precedents, was adapted to a capitalistic society no longer content with legal formulas devised for a society whose basic structure was feudalistic. Time was running out for the old law; men were ready for legal systems meeting the needs of their age; but in revising and updating law, the lawyers retained almost as much as they discarded from the past. Here the literary skills of the humanist were put to work in sifting the true from the false and the just from the unjust; language had a legitimate role in legal studies, especially because medieval jurists had made grave errors in interpreting the *Digest*. They were not faultless Latinists; the humanists were.

To our modern minds law, philosophy, and medicine do not account for all human knowledge, but to the humanist anything not

[54] *Ibid.*, pp. 290–295.

clearly part of one of the specialties was packed together in an amorphous mass of material labeled literature. For this reason the humanistic techniques applied to education became all the more important; imitation, analysis, and memorizing were brought face to face with a vast sector of human knowledge. In the absence of other disciplines commissioned to organize all knowledge outside the specialties, the power of literature to shape the intellectual future of men was almost absolute.

It is against this background that we must look at the new method Erasmus proposes; his recommendations form a handbook for making the wisdom of the ancients accessible and useable, and it was a handbook used not only by schoolmasters of his own generation but for the next 400 years as well.

III

THE NEW METHOD OF STUDY

Medieval education had maintained a liaison with classical antiquity for reasons understood by everyone who has studied the curriculum of medieval higher schools.[55] Yet medieval teachers and students were disadvantaged if we compare them with their humanist successors: first, they were dominated by a basic educational theory which, despite its inner logic, centered on otherworldly objectives. Understandably they approached the classics with a reserve nurtured not only by this theory but also by their fundamental view of life. They were convinced that many of the authors of antiquity were dangerous and they eschewed their artistry while at the same time recognizing it. When they exercised an age-old pedagogical device of "selection" and turned aside from the authors they distrusted, little was left for them to use. This brings us to their second disadvantage: too few of the classics were readily available for schoolmasters to pick and choose those which could be used with impunity. In a word, then, the humanist stood on firmer pedagogical terrain. He was working within a theoretical framework which, rather than looking past this world of time and space to an eternal one, accepted the world of man and sought to exploit all of the means available to elevate man as a temporal being. Besides, human goals were now seen in a new light; they were judged good in themselves and needed little tempering in the forge of supernaturalism. It was not that Humanists rejected the supernatural; they were not anti-Christian in any fundamental sense; they did not deny Christ, but they did emphasize the human dimension so long minimized by the ascetic and monastic spirit of the Medieval Age.[56]

[55] See Hastings Rashdall, *op. cit.*, vol. I.
[56] Again, see McGarry, *op. cit.*, pp. 195–209.

This new spirit would have counted for little had not the scholarly expeditions into the ruins and libraries of the past broadened the scope of classical literature. The humanist lived in a richer literary world than his medieval predecessor: he could still honor the principle of selection and avoid many of the dangers and temptations detected in classical literature, but in doing so he was not emptying the larder. There was so much more to choose from.

The spirit of cultural enrichment with which the humanist age began was strengthened further by taking many long-lost Greek classics and placing them alongside Latin studies. The humanists were not returning to an authentic Greek classical model when they did this but were resuscitating a Latin classical model which had come of age in Rome with the adoption of a bilingual educational program.[57] Moreover, irrespective of the models to which they might turn, or of the fervor or accuracy with which they might follow them, the humanists became the happy beneficiary of invention—printing made the cultural world wear a different face.

If we were to stop at this point we would in effect be asserting that the humanist movement in its educational dimension generated a lasting and basic educational reform and that pedagogy as well as the broader world of cultural opportunity suddenly became new and up-to-date. We would begin almost at once to look for curricula, objectives, and methods marking an end of one era and the beginning of another. This did not happen, for as humanism made its way slowly through the centuries it found itself immersed in a thicket of school practices that did not respond to newly-stated cultural ideals or educational theories.

We need only read the educational articles of humanists to see how far theory really reflected the cultural renewal taking place.[58] In the last analysis most school practices of the fifteenth century differed little from those of the thirteenth, and the great curricular opportunities offered by Greek studies, on the one hand, and a vastly expanded literary syllabus, on the other, were blithely ignored.[59] If the schools were to wear a different face, as they in time did, it was a face that reminds us how often human endeavor misses the mark in achieving the ideals it grasps only fleetingly and intuitively.

The chronicle of humanist education begins with Petrarch, is shaped by Chrysoloras, is tested by Vittorino and Guarino, and is finally synthe-

---

[57] I know of no better exposition of the bilingual tradition than the one made by H. I. Marrou, *A History of Education in Antiquity* (New York, Sheed & Ward, Inc., 1956), pp. 255–264.

[58] The best one-volume source is Woodward, *Vittorino da Feltre and Other Humanist Educators.*

[59] See A. F. Leach, *English Schools at the Reformation* (Westminster, England, Constable & Co., Ltd., 1896); and C. P. McMahon, *Education in Fifteenth Century England* (Baltimore, The Johns Hopkins Press, 1947).

sized, and perhaps finalized, by Erasmus. Whether or not Erasmus should be allotted pride of place among the world's great educators, as some scholars assert,[60] is an inquiry falling outside the ambit of this work. But while we readily admit our inability to place him in a definitive position in the hierarchy of educational statesmen, we have no difficulty in seeing him as an educational theorist worth our careful attention.

To begin with, Erasmus' own work, either as it detailed methods of study or set goals for Christian education, could be justified, and we could honor him with an exegetic treatment, but still we would be missing the real genius of his work. To see Erasmus' pedagogy in full light, we must first see how the stage was set for him and for the scenery it contained.

One looks in vain for a criterion more characteristic of humanist (and modern) pedagogy than imitation, a criterion formulated by Petrarch and one regularly accepted by all humanists who followed him. Yet, what was Petrarch recommending when he asked his followers to imitate the ancient authors? Too often his followers misunderstood him and built up dry-as-dust curricula and methods aiming at linguistic accuracy—literary achievements conforming in letter to the compositions of ancient authors. But, in spite of what he got in return for his advice, what did he want? Petrarch's main guide was Cicero, who does not recommend linguistic accuracy but looks to imitation as a means for building up an orator's power of expression, and it would surprise us greatly if he wanted a mere literary exactitude, for then we would be in a position to claim that Petrarch's ideals were so low, and his use of imitation so adroit, as to be achieved rather quickly and without any great expenditure of effort by a reasonably clever schoolboy. It is reasonable to suppose, as we have said, that when Petrarch encouraged students to use the classical writers as models, he wanted them to take the whole of a classic, digest it, and be guided by it toward a more refined and eloquent expression. Thus, the method of imitation, as Petrarch developed and used it, was to make effective writing possible. He was not greatly concerned (he may not have seen any need to be) about men grasping ways of classical thought. In any case, the method he advocated and the way it was employed, was ill suited to an assimilation of classical culture. One could read through the classics, or a wide selection of them, and, depending solely on the unorganized workings of his memory, would come to the end of the readings remembering only a few of the novelties they contained. In time an effort was made to do something about this, but Petrarch seemed undisturbed at the prospect of the student forgetting most of the wisdom spread out for him by the giants of ancient literature.

At this point another actor appeared on the scene. At first he was not

---

[60] Bolgar, *op. cit.*, p. 336, says of Erasmus: "He is the greatest man we come across in the history of education." See also, pp. 266–267.

a teacher at all, for he came to Florence as an emissary on a diplomatic mission. But he was Greek and the demand for teachers of Greek studies, resulting from the cultural evolution we have already noticed, prompted him to remain as a teacher. This was the famous Manuel Chrysoloras (1350–1413). His followers were anxious to testify to his greatness as a teacher, and from him they learned two things which they were to apply with devotion and zeal to all their humanistic study—everything in the classics must be analyzed and everything must be noticed.

How analysis and notice were to be handled became the subject for a number of short books on education. The first such book was by Leonardo Bruni, who wrote on the education of women, but it was by no means the last.[61] And however many there were or who wrote them is not especially important here. What needs our attention is the testing of this advice. The testing was done best by Guarino and Vittorino. Both have been given their due as effective humanist schoolmen; their schools were models of humanist pedagogic effectiveness. Yet, it should be remembered that they were but two men and they conducted only two schools; perhaps none of their contemporaries and only a few teachers in later years who tried to follow in the main stream of their practice ever matched their success. We must look elsewhere if we are to find the definitive codification of humanistic educational theory and practice. When we do we come face to face with the unassailable educational stature of Erasmus.

Erasmus was a many-sided man and it was easy for him to do the two things for education that most needed doing. The message of Petrarch was dimmed by time and only a faint echo of Chrysoloras' formulations could be heard past the din of the faint-hearted and too often confused humanist theorists who followed him. Erasmus was able to measure the techniques associated with imitation, set them all in precise correspondence, and then construct a theory to hold them together. Let us begin on the level of method.

Method was needed for what? It was to be an instrument for achieving eloquence. Why eloquence was set as a goal is a point we must defer until later. Now we may simply assume it was taken as an objective worthy of man's best efforts. Method, of course, could have no meaning separated from the object of writing like the ancients had written; but even this goal was but a step along the way—the final goal was writing well. Erasmus is probably more fully aware of this than any of his predecessors, although in fairness to them it should be noted that they too had a vision of this goal. Visions, however, are perceived with varying degrees of clarity. Yet, unquestionably this tradition Erasmus was heir to had originated with Guarino.

[61] See M. A. Cannon, *The Education of Women During the Renaissance* (Washington, D.C., Catholic University of America Press, 1916).

Operating within the friendly confines of this humanistic tradition, Erasmus delineated his approach to method. Perhaps what he did was not novel, but it was systematic, and as surely as ever before sights were set on effective writing. First, there were words that had to be known, for who could write or speak well without a rich vocabulary? This was part of the matter of eloquence and, important as it was in itself, it needed to be completed by form. Form could no doubt be placed under the heading of rhetorical techniques and devices, all of which could be learned on the level of rules, but rules would stand as sterile vehicles until fertilized by application and exercise. Erasmus did not invent the dictum—practice makes perfect—but he certainly understood it. Next came classification of subjects and data. Who could write without topics, and how barren would the topics be without information?

Again, with classifying there is a return to tested practices from the past. The medieval sermon books had arranged and classified and so had Agricola. Vivès recommended putting things into their proper nests, and Erasmus does the same.[62] Finally we come to the climax of the whole system and perhaps to the hardest part; remembering everything that had been classified.

The notebook age was well begun by Erasmus' time. There was no other way to keep ready and waiting vast stores of classical knowledge. He could recommend that his own practice be followed: let every serious student read through the classics at least once with notebook in hand. In this way everything could be noticed and everything could be analyzed.[63]

In a number of books Erasmus delved into the problems of formal education, but in one—*Upon the Right Method of Instruction*—he is most articulate and detailed concerning the day-to-day practices teachers should use. If for no other reason than the attention he pays to learning on the pedagogic level, we would be interested in him, for the age of humanism was one which had no trouble ignoring the practical issues involved in teaching and learning.

Let us see what a great humanist saw in teaching and what methods he recommended for most efficient learning. Rather simply and quickly he sets the goals of formal education as being thought and expression: the effort of learning is directed at "knowledge of truths" and "knowledge of words." It would be well if the student could move directly to the former, but he cannot. He must seek truth through the instruments of words. Seeking truth is first in importance, but expression is first in time.[64] Yet Erasmus does not choose to make expression a simple

[62] Foster Watson, *Vivès on Education*, p. XXXIX; and Woodward, *Desiderius Erasmus (De Ratione Studii)*, pp. 173–176.

[63] Bolgar, *op. cit.*, pp. 274–275.

[64] Erasmus *(De Ratione Studii)*, p. 162.

handmaiden to knowledge. He respects expression too much for that and shares the humanistic reverence for the charm of eloquent speech. So he is able to establish true education as one which includes both kinds of knowledge—theoretical and practical—presented, he says, under the best guidance.[65]

But it is easy to overlook Erasmus' limitations by neglecting his adherence to tradition. There may have been a time in his life when he did not condemn the vernacular tongues—perhaps it was unavoidable that he use them—but in his mature years, it is said, he simply refused to respond to any address in the vernacular. He saw little need to fortify any level of education with nonclassical language; he was always certain of the preeminence of Latin and Greek in the curriculum because their literatures contained everything that was most worth knowing, and studied together there was positive transfer between them.[66]

The handbook had kept many a teacher in his position of some esteem; without it he would have been lost. And hammering in rules had been his favorite and unchallenged technique. Erasmus has no time for either. He notes the good grammar texts among those available and approves those most carefully planned and written. Clearly he interdicts the dry-as-dust technique of memorizing rules of grammar: "I have no patience with the stupidity of the average teacher of grammar who wastes precious years in hammering rules into children's heads. For it is not by learning rules that we acquire the power of speaking a language, but by daily intercourse with those accustomed to express themselves with exactness and refinement, and by copious reading of the best authors." [67]

Before Erasmus goes too far into questions relating content and method and on to a kind of curricular theory, he pauses to say a word about the instruction of beginners. If we think we are to catch him in a pose where he is treating elementary learning, we are mistaken, for he does not operate on such a level: children for whom his education would apply would already have had their rudimentary instruction. Erasmus is thinking of teaching Latin and Greek to boys for whom neither language is a native tongue. This was a problem in teaching that had stymied schoolmasters for half a millennium; it was an issue for which the ancients had no ready-made solution. Why should they? They were never faced with the task of teaching Latin or Greek to boys who did not already know something of the language. Alcuin had made a long step forward in constructing a pedagogy to ease this situation, so by the time we meet Erasmus there is nothing particularly acute about the issue. Schoolmen between Alcuin and Erasmus had rewritten the old grammars and had

---

[65] *Ibid.*

[66] "For I affirm that with slight qualification the whole of attainable knowledge lies enclosed within the literary monuments of ancient Greece" (*ibid.*, p. 164).

[67] *Ibid.*, pp. 163–164.

inserted the vocabulary lists: the stage for Latin learning was properly set.

The first learning is to begin from a reading of the authors. Erasmus is willing to be specific in his recommendations: Lucian, Demosthenes, and Herodotus are the Greek prose writers he thinks best; Aristophanes, Homer, Euripides are his choices among Greek poets, although he would put Menander first if his works were available. The Latin writers who are given Erasmus' approval are Terence, Plautus, Vergil, Horace, Cicero, Caesar, and Sallust.[68] A working knowledge of Latin and Greek is the goal of instruction at this level; these authors are the means. Erasmus does not pretend that these authors are sufficient for a complete education; he admits only that through them the student may make his best start. But he does think that their works are better suited to the purposes of education on this level than is the whole range of classical writing.[69]

As these authors are read the student is to have his notebook in hand ready to record, under proper headings, unusual words, archaisms, innovation, ingenuity in handling material, distinction of style, historical or moral instances, and proverbial expressions. Even the entries in the notebook are worthy of Erasmus' attention: if the student tries to record everything, his notebook will be useless to him; he must capture the pith of his reading and phrase it in such a way that it will enable him to recall what he has read.[70]

The beginner may move from author to notebook and then to logic. When in logic he will travel the path marked out by Aristotle and will not wander from it. Even with this admission Erasmus is making a concession to logic, for he is not certain that it contains any secret paths to an elegant style of writing. If logic can enter under the protection of grammar, dialectic is securely barred from the syllabus. Erasmus was unsure of dialectic, referred to it as verbiage, and cautioned his reader with the advice that "Dialectic is an elusive maiden, a Siren, indeed, in quest of whom a man may easily suffer intellectual shipwreck." [71]

With the good start the student has in his reading and notetaking he should shortly be ready to write. And here, according to Erasmus, is the real key to success: "write, write, and again write." [72] Along with writing goes learning by heart, for which the following conditions should be noted: understand the subject before undertaking memorization, arrange the material logically, and repeat frequently that which has been committed to memory. He notes the success some persons have had with memory crutches but seems neither to recommend nor dismiss them. Finally he recommends as the surest method of acquisition, the practice

68 *Ibid.*, p. 164.
69 *Ibid.*
70 *Ibid.*, pp. 165, 167, 177–178.
71 *Ibid.*, p. 165.
72 *Ibid.*

of teaching what one knows. "In no other way," Erasmus writes, "can we so certainly learn the difference between what we *know,* and what we *think we know.*" [73]

The arsenal of rules for composition is still large and imposing. No one could ignore these rules with impunity, although a man of Erasmus' stature could advise teachers to be most careful of those rules which are decidedly essential, and, further, he could insist that rules alone are almost useless—they must be applied through practice.[74]

Practice evidently takes us out of the realm of beginning instruction, for now we have both our matter and form and should be prepared to write under the discerning eye of a good master. Both the student and the master must keep before them the code of good writing. This code may be reduced to three points: selection, treatment, and imitation.[75] The student must select a subject and material for its development; he must treat his material in concert with the accepted grammatical and rhetorical canons; and he must ensure the greater acceptability of his composition—sort of guarantee that it is good writing—by seeing that it follows in tone and style some classical masterpiece.

It is hardly to be hoped that all of these canons can be kept intact by the novice writer. The teacher, with the code before him, can test the suitability of the composition, he can point to its weak spots, and he can recommend items for care in rewriting. The certain path to good writing is to keep the canons in mind and to apply them in writing and rewriting.

When writing begins, reading must not stop, for the world of literature is an almost inexhaustible source of knowledge that counts. But as writing can become more precise and generally more sophisticated, so also can reading. Reading in class becomes now a demonstration of what an author contains; like a mine the book is subjected to techniques of excavating its treasures. This was an old technique dating no doubt from the Hellenistic grammarians and rhetors. Erasmus made no claim to invention. He simply asked that masters keep their commentary relevant and that they not take this occasion to display their erudition.[76] Most of all he wanted to be certain that the author's meaning was understood and respected. A systematic presentation of the book's meaning and principal arguments—nothing more and nothing less—was recommended. And in this reading authors should be selected according to the capacities and interests of the readers. Erasmus did not use the word, but he was simply asking for a grading of instructional materials.

Neither in *Upon the Right Method of Instruction, De Copia, The*

---

[73] *Ibid.,* p. 166.
[74] *Ibid.,* p. 169.
[75] *Ibid.,* pp. 172–173.
[76] *Ibid.,* p. 173.

Liberal Education of Boys, nor in *The Education of a Christian Prince* does Erasmus present us with something strikingly new. It is hard to see him as an innovator save on the level of organization, on the one hand, and in sympathy for the learner, on the other. In *The Liberal Education of Boys* he is aiming at virtue, but he does not allow us to forget that one of the roads to virtue is kept open by attachment to study. *The Liberal Education of Boys,* moreover, provides a base for *Upon the Right Method of Instruction* by touching on a variety of preliminaries to secondary schooling. Erasmus does not want to forget the educative influences of the home and the church, nor does he want to minimize them.[77]

Erasmus could propose a revision and a reawakening of educational methodology without ever touching essentially on the rationale supporting classical teaching. Whenever he invades the province of method he proceeds from the dogmatic assumption that classical education can be given a theoretical justification, or, better, that a theory of education can be constructed which contains the classics as necessary means to valid ends.

Christians had begun by being suspicious of the classics; some Christian leaders had counseled their followers to ignore the classics; others had said the classics could be used with certain safeguards under certain circumstances; still others saw little to fear from the classics or so-called pagan learning.

By Erasmus' time the issues surrounding the use of classical content in Christian education should have been resolved. Doubtless most of them were, but behind the bold confidence of the Christian who was attracted to the classics lurked a seed of doubt. It was this doubt that Erasmus' theory sought to remove. In place of doubt he wanted the clear understanding that one of the goals of education was piety (moral formation) and that another was eloquence (intellectual development). Classical learning could be, he asserted confidently, an instrument for the attainment of both goals.

Fortunately for the theory advanced by Erasmus, his age was both vigorously individualistic and fundamentally moral. Had it been predominantly one or the other, so that either intellectual or moral formation was required to assume a subordinate role, we would remember far less of Erasmus and see his name less frequently cited on the pages of intellectual history. The climate was right, and a theory seeking to integrate ancient wisdom and Christian devotion could be nourished by practice and cultivated to flourish by a willingness to accept almost uncritically its fundamental assumptions.

Had Erasmus stopped with his artful and sound recommendations on how the classics were to be taught—only a few at first and then, when the student was ready, the entire classical corpus—he would have secured

[77] *De Pueris Instituendis,* in *ibid.,* pp. 200–201.

for himself an impregnable position in the history of pedagogy; but because he chose to go further—to inquire deeply into the reason for their being taught, he organized a code of teaching and learning that dominated modern education and made him a giant in intellectual history. The problem facing him may be stated quickly and simply: if in an age which valued Christian moral formation there was also an almost insatiable desire to feast at the banquet table of classical wisdom, how were these historically disjointed objectives to be remade to play complementary roles? Why were the classics, with the complex apparatus devised for teaching them, important in Christian learning?

Erasmus' educational aims have too often been misunderstood: by misreading his objectives and his own solid Christian standards we are left with no problem at all. The tradition that Erasmus was a man without true Christian instincts is no longer conventional wisdom. Where it remains it should be corrected. In other words, Erasmus' theory of education did not proceed from the dogmatic assumption that intellectual refinement, itself a product of classical learning, was sufficient for men. He was not a narrow pedant, for all his eccentricities, and he did not ignore the need to weave more strongly into men's souls the inexhaustible value of a Christian ethic. Why, then, defend the classics as an indispensable content for sound and complete education? In the answer given by Erasmus we find his theory of education, often rendered in the literature as *pietas et eloquentia,* or *pietas litterata.*

The theory was founded on two fundamental propositions: one was drawn from history, the other from the study of language evolution and use—either advanced grammar or philology.[78]

Erasmus was able to show that the Christian culture was an admixture of classical thought and Christian idealism; he could point to the uses that even the Fathers had made of pagan learning and how they had been influenced by it. If the very culture which sixteenth-century men imbibed was partially excavated from classical mines, was it not unreasonable to think that the schools could ignore these treasures with impunity? There was a greater danger in indifference to the classical heritage—for then contemporary culture would lose its vitality—than there was in keeping that culture current, meaningful, and up-to-date. Moreover, if the best of the Fathers had seen fit to borrow—and to be influenced by—pagan learning, why should contemporary Christian thinkers eschew it. Of course, the Fathers could have been wrong. But such an admission, especially if evidence were gathered to support it, would challenge the substructure of all that was distinctively Christian. Such an assumption could not be entertained seriously or for long. Quite clearly the historical justification for the use of classical learning was not new, and in no sense did it originate with Erasmus. Yet, he made this

[78] Bolgar, *op. cit.,* p. 337.

theoretical dimension go a long way, and as it moved forward along the road to more general acceptance it was bolstered by and advocated in the works of other humanists.

The second support for the theory was more distinctive of Erasmus' own thinking and more, too, a product of his own scholarship. He maintained that a thorough study of a culture distilled in the language and literature of the most civilized of man's predecessors would reveal ethical foundations similar to the moral precepts of Christianity. Some humanists, it is true, had concentrated on parts of classical literature for display and had flooded the literary world with excerpts not at all representative of ancient moral convictions. The bawdy, irresponsible epistles were, he argued, either *sui generis* or out of context; the main body of classical literature was responsive and responsible to ethical standards. In addition, there was, Erasmus opined, a discipline of intellect needed to master the thought of the ancients, and this discipline was either a condition for scholarly excellence or a product of it. In any case, careful scholarship was in itself a kind of individual moral exercise.[79]

Thus was laid the theoretical foundation for piety and eloquence through the vehicle of classical learning. But the theory in its implementation needed some insulation: if the classics were to be used following the traditional methods of humanism—analysis of texts, excerption, memorizing, and imitation—some safety devices needed to be added. Besides, even though Erasmus had not thought these devices imperative (which apparently he did), his audience, still feeding on the uncertainties and prejudices of the past, would have been uncomfortable with the classics unless there were pedagogic techniques for rendering the least suspicious student, teacher, prince, or cleric immune from criticisms of moral, albeit theoretical, infidelity. So the safety devices must be looked at as essential parts of the theory, for without them no one, possibly not even Erasmus himself, would have felt able to implement the theory.

Quite independent of the theory the broad methodological recommendations of Erasmus are interesting. He begins where Christian education in its most nascent stages had really begun: with the moral training of the young.[80] This was principally the work of fathers and mothers. The student presenting himself for classical study with the sure grounding of home-instilled piety could feel secure with his literature, and his teachers could be confident that even the worst parts—those which had shocked or infuriated the appointed guardians of morals in the past— would be rendered innocuous. There is something naive in this assumption that the home can supply unassailable and permanent defenses, and we have no incontrovertible evidence that Erasmus was willing to take it at face value. He established this safeguard, but he went on from there to

[79] *Ibid.*
[80] See Woodward, *Desiderius Erasmus,* pp. 154–160.

reclaim a well-worn medieval device—allegorical interpretation of the text.[81] Medieval masters were in a touchy position; they had to use the classics available to them if they were to use any, and so few were available that picking and choosing was almost out of the question. To decontaminate the classics they insisted on formal study of them in addition to allegorical interpretation. In the process of formal study they would separate as fully as possible the content from the form (ignore the story and its details). Yet this was not always possible—for excision often violated form—and when it was obviously impossible to ignore questionable content it was reinterpreted in a wholesome way. Medieval scholars were sometimes hard put to find good and moral lessons in every classic used, but they should be applauded for their valiant if often extravagant efforts. While Erasmus approved reading for form, he also insisted upon a second reading for content, and since many pagan myths seemed offensive he counseled ways to render them harmless.[82] Perhaps he would have stopped short of medieval practices, but the mere fact that he recommended allegorical devices puts him in step with the main stream of conventional medieval teaching.

Too often the medieval teacher, perhaps tiring in his effort to interpret every classic coming into his hands in a favorable moral light or finding it impossible to sterilize the offensive stories told by ancient authors, turned away from his classical texts to introduce contemporary works. Few of the contemporary productions were original; medieval writers were great excerptors and intrepid encyclopedists. On many an occasion, however, in trying to be moral they turned out only to be dull. Their books were unfit models to encourage good composition. Considering Erasmus' objective, we should be surprised indeed if he had followed their lead. Yet they had a good idea despite its being overlaid by faulty execution—it was selection.

Erasmus, too, recognized selection of texts as a useful devise for protecting young minds from literature capable of contaminating them.[83] But where the medieval teacher had to emasculate texts, the humanist, by Erasmus' time, could simply take those texts he approved of from the fuller shelves of the library. It is hard to become ecstatic about Erasmus' recommendation, although value should perhaps be recognized even when it is not clothed with the excitement accompanying originality. The point is simple and may be made quickly: there were many more classics to choose from; unknown or lost works, in any case works unavailable to the medieval scholar, were now ready and waiting for the reader's perusal. With a careful and discreet Christian mentality Erasmus suggested that the best authors be studied, and we have his word for the

[81] *Ibid.,* pp. 48–51.
[82] *Ibid.,* pp. 173–176; and Bolgar, *op. cit.,* p. 339.
[83] *Ibid.;* and Woodward, *Desiderius Erasmus,* pp. 111–115.

authors he judged best.[84] It may be fairly assumed, however, that these choice authors were not to be the only ones: a scholar did not begin and end his study with them. Once maturity in scholarship was achieved, we doubt that Erasmus would have limited what was to be read. When we evaluate the import of Erasmus' literary liberalism we see how far Christian thinking had progressed from the time of St. Basil, who in his more liberal moments had composed *On the Reading of the Profane Authors,* in which he tried to show Christians how they could be educated without the classics or, if they could not avoid them, how they might be rendered harmless. Yet even here, Christian thought, though it had progressed, could not cut its ties with its past. Erasmus did not say avoid the classics, but he did say take those which are edifying and avoid the rest.

The final safeguard shows how Erasmus wanted to be an intellectual man of his time; but if his head was in the present his heart was still in the past. He seemed to want an up-to-date meaningful education but he excised from the curriculum the intellectual exercises that carried the greatest promise. Philosophy or dialectic was thought to be too dangerous and too confusing to be admitted to the school. He cited many of the same reasons for excluding it as had the monks in the early monastic school. Later, when logic was seen as a useful tool the nose of philosophy got under the academic tent, and still later, when the broader reaches of philosophy became indispensable to the theologian and important to the lawyer, its body followed. In this context philosophy was used but not loved, and it stood in relation to the other academic sciences much in the way a computer does today—a kind of scholastic machine that can churn up or out but has no independent status. In this context philosophy had to accept Erasmus' censorship, and perhaps it was earned. But in a more viable context, where philosophy could have tested society's most pressing human problems, philosophy was called a siren, too ready to mislead and destroy.[85] In trying to avoid the sterility of much medieval philosophy, Erasmus missed the point of the real value of the study or the exercise. The education that he endorsed, for all the good in it and for all the influence it had, was out-of-date the very day it was offered. Historians have often deplored the fact of history that Machiavelli's *Prince* had influence when Erasmus' *The Education of the Christian Prince* had virtually none. In the nature of things this was inevitable. Erasmus represented humanism; Machiavelli represented contemporary life. The rift between the two was so great that the developments in contemporary thought escaped Erasmus.[86] One who ignores contemporary thought can hardly expect to influence it.

Yet, despite what would now seem to be weaknesses in his system,

[84] *Ibid.,* p. 164.
[85] *Ibid.,* p. 165.
[86] Bolgar, *op. cit.,* p. 340.

Erasmus did set a pattern for modern education in which the objectives of piety and good writing were given due recognition and where the avenue to both was built of classical literature. The key to method was always imitation; the learner was regularly protected from moral contagion by the devices of allegorical interpretation, selection, suppression of dialectic, and a foundation of piety laid in the home.

8

Comenius: The Champion of Realism

I

INTRODUCTION

Slightly more than a half-century separated Erasmus' death from Comenius' birth. If it can be said that the educational theories of Erasmus were out-of-date when they were completed, because the social climate had bypassed them, it can also be said that Comenius' theories were too progressive for the schoolmasters of his time.[1] Again, both time and interpreters were needed to move theory from the library to the schoolroom. Despite the importance of the scientific quickening that occurred late in Erasmus' and early in Comenius' lifetime, which marks sharp educational differences between them, Comenius in a way continued the Humanism of Erasmus. Although Comenius did not rely so heavily on the classics, or know them so well, his school program was bookish, and he always remembered the social, literary, and religious significance of ancient languages.[2] By teaching vernacular language, moreover, he acted on the recommendation Erasmus allowed to lie fallow.[3]

[1] W. S. Monroe, *Comenius and the Beginning of Educational Reform* (New York, Charles Scribner's Sons, 1900), p. 165, maintained that "the name of the great Moravian reformer was quite if not entirely forgotten, and his writings practically unknown, for more than a century after his death." J. E. Sadler, *J. A. Comenius and the Concept of Universal Education* (New York, Barnes & Noble, Inc., 1966), pp. 26–27, modifies this assertion when he argues that Comenius' textbooks were frequently known and used in Europe in the later years of his life as well as in the century following his death.

[2] Comenius' attachment to the classics is clear in his writings. See *The Analytical Didactic of Comenius,* translated by V. Jelinek (Chicago, University of Chicago Press, 1953), p. 69.

[3] See M. W. Keatinge, *Comenius* (New York, McGraw-Hill Book Company, Inc., 1931), p. 200. This book is a reprint in a slightly shortened form of *The Great Didactic of John Amos Comenius* (London, Adam and Charles Black, 1896).

It is hazardous to dwell on the intellectual and educational compatibility of Comenius and Erasmus, but it is wrong to deprive them of any kinship. Continuity is an indelible feature of educational theory, and Comenius stood on the shoulders of his predecessors as his successors were to stand on his.[4] This coign of vantage, of course, did not always give theorists unobscured educational vision.

We should begin by wanting to know something of Comenius' credentials as an educator. Without going into excessive biographical detail, we can find some of these credentials by reviewing his life's work. And we can begin from the assumption phrased by Nicholas Murray Butler: "His [Comenius'] place in education is one of commanding importance. He introduces and dominates the whole modern movement in the field of elementary and secondary education."[5]

Comenius (the latinized form of the Bohemian Komenský—his full name was Jan Amos Komenský) was born in the village of Nivnitz in Moravia, now Czechoslavakia, 100 years after the discovery of America. The village seems to have been a haven for members of a religious sect known as Unitas Fratrum or the Moravian Brethren, a sect tracing its ecclesiastical origins to the Bohemian reformer and martyr, John Huss. Despite unrelenting persecution the sect persisted in its religious reformation; its members were determined to "abandon the theology, dogma, and form that smothered the spirit of Christ's teachings and return to the Bible."[6] This confidence in free Biblical interpretation and application can be detected in Comenius' ministry, his teaching, the reforms he advocated, and his theories of education. The assertion has been made that "whatever the point to be proved, in all his writings Comenius sooner or later turned to the Bible."[7]

Comenius' lifelong determination was to serve God and by serving God to serve man; he looked to education for means to promote and achieve the salvation of men. Yet even with this high purpose his projects, his life itself, were not absolved from sorrow and reverses. When only twelve years old Comenius was orphaned and committed to the care and training of an aunt, who, it is said, dissipated his inheritance, disrupted his youth, and neglected his education.

In the face of these obstacles he nevertheless pursued educational avenues which led eventually to the university. He spent four years in an

---

[4] "Comenius took over from the Renaissance much of the confusion of thought that hid the complete re-orientation from the Middle Ages [sic.]. He kept the old language but gave it a secular application" (Jelinek, *op. cit.*, pp. 55–56) . Monroe, *op. cit.*, pp. 15–38, examines the educational and intellectual influences on Comenius.

[5] N. M. Butler, *The Place of Comenius in the History of Education* (Syracuse, N.Y., Bardeen, 1892) , p. 4.

[6] J. A. Comenius, *The School of Infancy*, E. M. Eller, ed. (Chapel Hill, N.C., University of North Carolina Press, 1956) , p. 4.

[7] *Ibid.*, p. 8.

elementary school at Strasnic. When he was sixteen he entered a Latin school operated by the Unitas Fratrum at Prerau, and in this school he received enough of a classical education to prepare him for the Lutheran College of Herborn (now in Germany). During his scholastic sojourn at this college he came under the influence of John Henry Alsted, and from Alsted he derived his first formal interest in education.[8] It is not too much to say that from Alsted he learned some of the educational principles later used to form the bases for reforms in school practices; in 1613 Comenius left Herborn for the University of Heidelberg and finished a formal education intended to prepare him for the ministry.

Comenius' student experiences served not only to form him intellectually, they also made him stop to think about the process itself. When he did he was dismayed. The educational process to which he was exposed was so filled with defects that it nurtured much of his didactic enterprise. When he studied educational practice in his more mature years, with the deficiencies of existing instructional practice still fresh in his mind, he was even more determined to find the methodological key to quality education. He spoke with feeling about the schools he had attended: They were, he said, "the terror of boys, and the slaughterhouse of minds —places where a hatred of literature and books is contracted, where ten or more years are spent in learning what might be acquired in one, where what ought to be poured in gently is violently forced in and beaten in, where what ought to be put clearly and perspicuously is presented in a confused and intricate way, as if it were a collection of puzzles, places where minds are fed on words." [9]

It is right to emphasize methodology in the educational plan of Comenius, for whatever use schoolmasters made of the methods Comenius himself devised, and despite their often implicit naïveté, they marked the awkward beginnings of modern school methods. Many of them remain with us in almost constant use today. But we would miss much of the significance of Comenius' program of educational reform if we started with methodology and tried to follow him along the path of natural learning without first looking to see what he wanted education to be. In other words the place to begin is with purpose or goal, for Comenius never confused means with ends; educational methods in his system were always subordinated to learning objectives. And here particularly, on the level of learning objectives, Comenius' philosophy of life and learning, partly formed from the froth and the foam of his own educational career, are relevant. In spite of defects in his own education, to say

[8] See P. R. Cole, *Alsted, A Neglected Educator* (Sydney, Collins, Ltd., 1910); and Sadler, *op. cit.,* p. 303. Alsted was only four years older than Comenius; yet, despite this, his influence on Comenius was great. It should be added, however, that Comenius and Alsted did not always agree. See Keatinge, *op. cit.,* p. 211 (1931 ed.).

[9] Quoted in S. S. Laurie, *John Amos Comenius* (Syracuse, N.Y., Bardeen, 1892), p. 21.

nothing whatever about the unhappy circumstances surrounding his domestic and religious life, Comenius had two qualities that consistently permeated his approach to education: First, in an atmosphere of almost constant personal adversity he developed a gentleness that stands in sharp relief to the dogmatic and domineering character of the period in which he lived; second, he kindled a love for learning that is hard to explain solely on the grounds of personal motivation; his teachers had a spark of genius that even Comenius himself was unable to detect. In some ways, perhaps, his education was better than he wanted to admit, or, at least, his school experiences were not so debilitating that they crushed all curiosity and zest for self-improvement. Evidently his talents did not always go undetected by his mentors. For example, the rector of the Unitas Fratrum school, where Comenius was introduced to the classics, cited Comenius as his star pupil and gave him the name Amos—loving of knowledge—in recognition of his quick mind and tireless efforts to learn. And John Alsted, whom we have mentioned before, communicated to Comenius something more than basic ideas about school reform; Alsted was a broadly educated man, interested in everything, and he may have infected Comenius with the spark of intellectal curiosity.

When Comenius completed his studies at the University of Heidelberg, in 1614, he was too young for ordination to the ministry and the responsibilities of a pastorate, so he used these two years to bring learning to the youth in his community. Now as a teacher for the first time, he saw more clearly the ineffectiveness of the teaching around him and the inadequacy of many of the methods used in instructing the young. Latin teaching interested him most at this time, and he was greatly disappointed in the results normally obtained. "Ten years," he testified, "are given to the study of the Latin tongue, and after all the result is disappointing. . . . Boys are stuffed with vocabularies without associating words with things, or indeed with one another syntactically." [10] Merely noticing the ineffectiveness of Latin teaching was not enough; it had been noticed before. Comenius tried to remedy the defects of Latin instruction by writing a grammar book incorporating his progressive pedagogical ideas. About the same time, and little more than a novice teacher, he wrote a thesaurus entitled *A Theater of All Things.*[11]

In 1616 Comenius, now an ordained minister, and pastor of a Fulneck congregation, was appointed town-school superintendent. Record of his work in this capacity is scant, but time and circumstances were against him: the Thirty Years War was being waged, and society, intent on preservation and political security, ignored educational quality and reform. Disorganization of life and religious turmoil bred persecution

[10] *Ibid.,* p. 22.

[11] I am unaware of any translation of this work. In any case, only fragments of it now exist. See Eller, *op. cit.,* p. 10.

and eventual banishment for members of Comenius' sect.[12] Seeking asylum away from his native land, he was forced to abandon his wife and child, along with his library and manuscripts for books he was writing. After some years of hiding from political and religious enemies, he found a reasonably happy refuge in Lissa, Poland. While there—he stayed for twelve years—Comenius taught in the Gymnasium, wrote books on education, and experimented with teaching techniques, all aimed ultimately at correcting religious misapprehensions and misunderstandings. The schools, he thought, could be principal means in religious reform, if textbooks were good and if instruction followed a simple and lucid method.[13]

The books embracing Comenius' educational plans—all written in Poland during his interlude as a practicing teacher—were *Janua Linguarum Reserata* (The Gate of Tongues Unlocked), *The Great Didactic,* and *The School of Infancy.*

Janua, a book on Latin teaching,[14] met with extraordinary success. Translated into twelve European languages, according to Keatinge: "It is an undoubted fact that in every European country generations of children thumbed the *Janua* and no other book until they were sufficiently advanced to begin Terence or Plautus, and that for years after its publication Comenius' name was familiar in every schoolroom." [15] It was used in some American colonial schools and, apparently, as a Latin textbook in Harvard College. Despite its popularity as a schoolbook, Comenius believed it too difficult and too complicated for beginning students—for example, it introduced 8000 Latin words—so he tried to remedy its deficiencies by writing an introduction, aptly titled, *Vestibulum.*[16]

Other books, all intended to ease a boy's study of Latin, followed *Vestibulum: Atrium* (Entrance Hall), *Sapientiae Palatium* (Palace of Wisdom), *Orbis Sensualium Pictus* (The World of Sense Objects Pictured), and *Schola Ludus* (School Plays).[17] None needs specific attention here, for each reflected a method of teaching more than a philosophy of education. The bases for method belong to Comenius' theory of education, pronounced most comprehensively in *The Great Didactic,*

[12] See J. E. Hutton, *A History of the Moravian Church* (London, Cadell and Davies, 1909).

[13] S. S. Laurie, *John Amos Comenius, Bishop of the Moravians: His Life and Educational Works* (Boston, Willard Small, 1885), p. 25; and F. Kozik, *The Sorrowful and Heroic Life of John Amos Comenius* (Prague, State Educational Publishing House, 1958).

[14] The most recent translation is by A. Turek, 1951.

[15] Keatinge, *op. cit.,* p. 23 (1896 ed.).

[16] *Vestibulum,* (Porch of the Latin Tongue), was translated into English by J. Bookbank in 1647.

[17] So far as I know, only *Orbis Pictus* has been translated to English. This was done first by C. Hoole in 1659. We may note that Comenius' conception of the world was quite unscientific and naive. See Jelinek, *op. cit.,* pp. 60–66.

and it serves as our guide as we follow Comenius along the road of educational doctrine. *The School of Infancy*, where Comenius adds new ideas on educational organization, will be referred to later.

Comenius was not a prophet in his own land or time, for his proposed reforms did not become part of school practice until decades after his death. Yet, neither his books nor his theories were entirely unnoticed by his contemporaries.[18] His services as an educational advisor were enlisted by many European countries. Sweden offered Comenius an educational directorship about 1632, but he declined it because he was engaged in translating *The Great Didactic* into Latin. Moreover, just elected bishop of his sect, he hesitated to assume any role that might interfere with episcopal duties.[19]

Comenius' work caught the interest of other realists committed to educational reform; one was the Englishman, Samuel Hartlib, who, finding Comenius' educational writings worthwhile, translated some of them into English. Hartlib's connection with Comenius was developed further, first through correspondence and then, when Comenius accepted Hartlib's invitation to come to England in 1641, by direct association.[20] Despite Comenius' high hopes when he sailed for England, he could not have known that events would once again stand in the way of practical achievement. Either Hartlib had not cultivated the ground for Comenius, or the English were unready for his pedagogy; in any case, Comenius found the English indifferent to his plans for remaking education or for reforming the schools.[21] This attitude toward Comenius' work is explained partly by the unsteady political and economic situation then prevailing and, moreover, by basic suspicions about his pansophism and internationalism. Besides, the Irish rebellion left little time to think about educational affairs. Sadder and wiser, Comenius left England and returned to Poland. Now Sweden invited him a second time and asked him to reorganize teaching and to supervise the preparation of textbooks for elementary and secondary schools. For the first time Comenius could apply on a broad scale techniques and theories for revitalizing education. We judge that Comenius' hopes for Swedish education were not fully realized, but hopes never are, although while there he wrote five major textbooks, all quickly adopted by Swedish schools.[22]

Comenius' association with English and Swedish education is clear and well documented, but there is something else that whets our curios-

18 See J. W. Adamson, *Pioneers of Modern Education* (Cambridge, Cambridge University Press, 1905) ; and J. Needham, *The Teacher of Nations* (Cambridge, Cambridge University Press, 1942) .

19 See I. L. Kandel, "John A. Comenius, Citizen of the World," *School and Society*, LV (April 11, 1942) , pp. 401–406.

20 See G. H. Turnbull, *Samuel Hartlib: A Sketch of His Life and His Publications on John Amos Comenius* (London, Oxford University Press, 1920) .

21 See R. F. Young, *Comenius in England, 1641–1642* (London, Oxford University Press, 1932) .

22 Keatinge, *op. cit.*, pp. 58–70 (1896 ed.) .

ity. An unconfirmed story is extant that sometime between Comenius' trip to England and his longer visit to Sweden, he was invited to become president of Harvard College.[23] No record of the invitation exists, nor does Comenius mention it, so we hardly know what to make of Cotton Mather's account, which asserts positively that the invitation was extended. But this is the small change of history. Yet, whether or not an invitation was made, the mere fact that Comenius was considered for Harvard confirms the tradition that he enjoyed an international reputation.

Comenius remained in Sweden until the press of ecclesiastical duties persuaded him to return to Poland, but even then, amid the multiple duties of a bishop, he continued to think and write about education and, on occasion, to personally superintend schools to implement a conviction that both students and instructional materials should be graded. Comenius, always devoted to education, tried to remake men in God's image by first reforming their schools.

With this brief summary of Comenius' educational career, along with intimations of his life's mission, we are ready to see more of his educational theory.

II

EDUCATIONAL DOCTRINE

Comenius was an educational pioneer of the first order of importance, but neither his theory nor the practices implied in his pioneering were products of his own experience and thought. A basic eclectic attitude enabled him to draw from the thought of earlier philosophers and educators who were concerned with rebuilding education and allowing students to know and understand their own world, not just the world known and interpreted by classical authors.[24] This attitude did not lead to an outright rejection of the totality of classical humanism—Comenius' long vision enabled him to see great formative value in the treasures of the past, and he never doubted for a moment the worth of the ancient languages—but it did serve to broaden the curriculum of the school and eventually to shape a transition of school learning from bookish classicism to realistic naturalism.[25] Educational predecessors who both

[23] Cotton Mather, *Ecclesiastical History of New England* (London, 1702), I, iv, 128. For a skeptical reaction to this reported invitation, see Monroe, *op. cit.*, pp. 79–80. Eller, *op. cit.*, p. 36, appears to accept Mather's account.

[24] See Adamson, *op. cit.*, pp. 64 ff.

[25] For some confirmation of this, see *The Great Didactic*, XXIV, 12; and *Labyrinth of the World and the Paradise of the Heart* (Chicago, 1942), XI. See also, E. Rice, *The Renaissance Idea of Wisdom* (Cambridge, Mass., Harvard University Press, 1958), pp. 125; 160–161.

inspired and guided him toward making this transition and to whom he regularly gave credit were Vivès, Francis Bacon, Ratke, William Bath, and Campanella.[26] By opening the gate of learning to the physical world and its contemporary issues and by recognizing the young but energetic physical sciences, Comenius embraced a philosophy of realism and, in turn, was instrumental in bringing into being a realistic-scientific philosophy of education.[27] Whether considered as a theorist or as a reforming schoolmaster, Comenius must be placed in the vanguard of the realistic movement and must also be acknowledged as one of the leading characters in the history of education.

In its progress through history, realism has often kept company with scientific naturalism, and in the past century it has encouraged a positivistic association; that is, it has regarded as valid only that knowledge supported by the weight of experimental evidence. Whether or not positivism is unavoidably part of contemporary realism need not concern us now, but we should know that the positivistic tradition was neither implicit nor explicit in Comenius' doctrines. His undoubted starting point was neither naturalistic nor scientific: man is a child of God and must be educated to serve God in this and the next world.[28] So Comenius was able to reject the intellectualism of medieval academicians and replace it with piety. For him, as for the humanists who inspired him, "Our schools, therefore, will then at length be Christian schools when they make us as like to Christ as is possible. How wretched is the teaching that does not lead to virtue and to piety." [29] Neither piety nor virtue are inculcated in a vacuum, so it was futile only to hope for moral formation; moral formation, generated by truth, was Comenius' educational goal. In endorsing knowledge he subordinated it to virtue and endowed it with instrumental character, and steadfastly refused to countenance knowledge for its own sake—liberal education—or for independent application—practical education. The virtue Comenius aimed for was not natural virtue—although he never demeaned it—but supernatural virtue, infused with the spirit of a living God. Thus, it is impossible to take Comenius seriously without adverting to his unalterable commitment to supernatural religion and his determination to make formal education serve religious objectives. But from this point on, Comenius sounds more like an orthodox pedagogue than like a Christian bishop.

These high purposes for education could be achieved, according to

26 Sadler, *op. cit.*, p. 54; Monroe, *op. cit.*, pp. 28–37. William Bath, born in Dublin in 1564, died in Madrid in 1614, wrote a book entitled *Janua Linguarum* around 1611. Thomas Campanella (1568–1639), author of *The City of the Sun*, and noted especially for his antischolasticism, is thought to have influenced Comenius while the latter was a student at Herborn and Heidelberg. Wolfgang Ratke (1571–1635), a German educator, was notorious for his natural methodology.

27 Comenius, *Natural Philosophy* (London, 1651), Preface.

28 Keatinge, *op. cit.*, p. 23 (1931 ed.).

29 Keatinge, *op. cit.*, p. 166 (1896 ed.).

Comenius, if pansophism were adopted as a guiding doctrine. And when we come to the doctrine of pansophism, we find many serious misunderstandings of Comenius' point of view. Perhaps the natural, almost inevitable, reaction is to translate pansophic as "all knowledge," and to interpret the Comenian doctrine as one which assigns to schools the general function of teaching everything. It is not unusual, as a matter of fact, to see Comenius' program referred to as one advocating encyclopedic learning. Yet, this was not what he wanted, nor did he ever advocate the school's trying to teach everything, and had he affirmed such a mission for the school we would have a difficult time trying to defend his realism.

When Comenius called for pansophism, he was supporting an educational program aiming not toward universal knowledge, but universal wisdom.[30]

Comenius wrote: "There is nothing in Heaven or Earth, or in the Waters, nothing in the Abyss under the earth, nothing in the Human body, nothing in the Soul, nothing in Holy Writ, nothing in the Arts, nothing in Economy, nothing in Polity, nothing in the Church of which the little candidates of Wisdom shall be wholly ignorant." [31] And it was entirely possible for him to accept this objective for schools, with all their different levels and different grades, to be completely serious about the objective, and yet not advocate teaching everything to everyone. In a recent book the author writes: "in the 20th century nobody in his right senses would hazard such a suggestion, and even three hundred years ago it was a palpable exaggeration." [32] This comment is justified only if Comenius meant what some critics think, namely, teaching universal knowledge. But nowhere does he suppose that universal knowledge can substitute for universal wisdom. The road to universal wisdom was paved by both the humanists and the scientists; it was long for some students and short for others. Not every product of Comenian-inspired education would see the world and man as Plato or Aristotle had seen them; not every student would eventually become a philosopher, a scientist, or a theologian; but all would have a basic intimation of the meaning of God's universe. For some these intimations would be more complete than for others, but all would somehow be touched by wisdom, all would be partially wise in the ways of men and God.[33] We are aware that univer-

30 Comenius' *Outline of the Pansophic School* may even mislead us on this point. For reviews of the *Outline*, see Monroe, *op. cit.*, pp. 64–69; and Sadler, *op. cit.*, pp. 229–233. His *Outline* may be compared with a similar plan toward pansophism in *The Great Didactic*, XXX.

31 Quoted in Laurie, *John Amos Comenius* (Syracuse, N.Y., Bardeen, 1892), pp. 199–200.

32 F. Eby, *The Development of Modern Education* (Englewood Cliffs, N.J., Prentice-Hall, Inc., 1952), p. 192. Jelinek, *op. cit.*, p. 20, is critical of Comenius' preoccupations with pansophism, but he does not claim that Comenius advocated encyclopedic knowledge. See also, Sadler, *op. cit.*, pp. 120–121.

33 See Jelinek, *op. cit.*, pp. 25–26; and Sadler, *op. cit.*, p. 135.

sity studies do not guarantee a person's orientation in society; advanced learning and wisdom are not synonymous. The product of the elementary school may eventually become a wise man and more fully understand his place in the world than the most erudite scholars. In the phraseology of modern philosophers, Comenius was asking for a basic liberal education for all students, an education that would be meaningful and useful; it would put them in touch with the fundamentals of living, but it would not necessarily make them masters of all the fundamentals. In this light, Comenius' pansophic education is neither so farfetched nor so unreal as his critics say. Comenius knew as well as anyone that memorizing encyclopedias does not ensure either understanding or wisdom, and he knew, moreover, despite the classical compendia that lined even the shelves of his own library, that an educational goal obliging everyone to know everything was impossible.[34]

A necessary concomitant to his doctrine of universal wisdom was his theory of universal opportunity for education.[35] The conventional view of human nature worked to exclude too many children from educational opportunity, either because they lacked ability or because they had no need for formal education. Comenius disbelieved both versions of this judgment of mankind. He was convinced, first of all, that everyone is capable of some learning, that all men, irrespective of intelligence, can approach wisdom; and he was certain that with such basic learning, society would be better and men would lead happier and more regular lives. He rejected the argument that education is unnecessary for common men and asserted instead that it would both unify society and integrate it spiritually. We are never allowed to forget the theological dimensions of his theory, and with these convictions uppermost, he wrote: "The education that I propose includes all that is proper for a man, and is one in which all men who are born into this world should share. All, therefore, as far as is possible, should be educated together, that they may stimulate and urge on one another." [36]

The practical implications of this will be discussed more fully in connection with Comenius' methodology, but even now we see something revolutionary in his doctrine of universal education. Universal education, wisdom's instrument, could mold virtuous men and good citizens. Political leaders were blind to the possibilities of Comenius' proposal,

34 In a sense Comenius was continuing a tradition that had its origin in the Medieval world of learning. His pansophism has much in common with the elaborate organizational scheme of Hugh of St. Victor. See pp. 165–169.

35 Keatinge, *op. cit.*, p. 41 (1931 ed.). "The following reasons will establish that not the children of the rich or the powerful only, but of all alike, boys and girls, both noble and ignoble, rich and poor, in all cities and towns, villages and hamlets, should be sent to school."

36 *Ibid.*, p. 418 (1896 ed.) .

and this explains why universal education was not realized in the seventeenth century. When universal education was tested it was found both politically useful and manageable. If Comenius was a prophet for universal education, he commands our admiration, for there is something fine about a man who sees preeminently human values in universal education, and he could be quite specific about his meaning. He intended boys and girls to have the same educational opportunities. Comenius doubted that many girls would become scholars, nor did he believe that many boys would go so far, but this is beside the point and does not detract from his plan for universalizing opportunity enabling men and women alike to share wisdom.

These high hopes for universal education, a most important avenue of universal wisdom, were meaningless without an educational organization, and Comenius says something about this too. First, all schools should be public.[37] It was too early to think about publicly supported schools, so Comenius may be forgiven for not mentioning them; and when he wrote of the superiority of public over private education, he was talking about the scene of instruction. He entertained decent doubt about the efficacy of tutorial instruction, and that is what private education was. His sincere belief in education's social role, whereby persons could understand themselves and others, led him to argue for a liberal school environment embracing children from all social levels. Considering the social philosophies prevalent in seventeenth-century Europe, it is not surprising that this part of Comenius' educational plan went untested. He realized his heterodoxy but he wanted to record his conviction that public schools were society's best servants. If this is to be up-to-date, we should mention Comenius' dream of having all schools conducted in the language of the people.[38] Instruction in the vernacular, known of course in Comenius' day, was yet uncommon, but Comenius did not invent vernacular teaching; the humanists before him wrote about it with some fervor. Yet talk and luke-warm action did not make vernacular teaching respectable, and the humanists never helped even one school inaugurate such a teaching program.[39] Even Comenius' full allegiance to vernacular teaching may be questioned, for as students advanced in his school plan the demands of Latin learning were unrelenting.[40] Still, his suggestion for universal education has no meaning unaccompanied by a

---

[37] *Ibid.*, pp. 40–41 (1931 ed.).

[38] *Ibid.*, pp. 214–215 (1931 ed.). Comenius commissioned the Vernacular school to teach reading, writing, counting, measuring, and singing. In addition some psalms were to be memorized, the catechism mastered, principles of morality absorbed, and economics, politics, cosmography, and mechanical arts learned.

[39] See H. W. Woodward, *Vittorino da Feltre and Other Humanist Educators* (New York, Bureau of Publications, Teachers College, Columbia University, 1963), pp. 40–41.

[40] See Keatinge, *op. cit.*, pp. 221–231 (1931 ed.).

recommendation that elementary schools employ the language of the people.[41] By refusing to use the vernacular, schools were guilty of perpetuating what for most students was irrelevant learning. But this made no difference, and they continued to teach Latin while ignoring foundations, intentions, and relations of more important subjects. But even Latin was not taught effectively. According to Comenius, they wasted years—from ten to twenty, he said—on grammar rules and dictionaries instead of teaching the vernacular, where competence could be achieved speedily.[42] His plan was simple and straightforward: the vernacular school—the second level in his projected school organization—was, for most children, the beginning and end of formal education. Thus, here we should expect to find every principal element of his theory at work. Instruction, beginning with reading and writing the mother tongue, moved next to simple composition and computation. Singing, religious instruction, the Bible itself and Bible history, ethics, economics, politics, and general world history followed, and finally students studied geography, physics, arts, and handicrafts. This took six years.[43]

In an age when schools were few and good teachers hard to find, Comenius must have puzzled over a way to bring the benefits of this program to the people. Obviously, tutorial programs would not do. In keeping with his hope for universal schooling, Comenius supported and refined the method of class teaching. Rather than having teachers deal with students on an individual basis, they would teach them, hear their lessons, and guide them toward deeper learning simultaneously.

We would surely be wrong in maintaining that Comenius invented simultaneous or class teaching. No record in educational history identifies the originator of this plan; quite possibly no one person could be singled out, for instruction in groups must be a practice almost as old as human society itself. But for centuries group practices in learning were not used and received little notice, except when the Sophists offered the people of Athens the fruits of learning in lecture halls and when medieval masters dictated their texts to their students. Now and then a bright educational figure appeared, for example, Abelard, to test the value of large group methods, but for the most part these educators were not innovators because they conducted their classes within the lecture halls or universities and dealt with students well past the rudimentary and formative stages of learning. Yet, even when these practices fell within the purview of innovation, or near innovation, they seldom qualified, for they were used inartistically. Simply having several students in a class with the teacher telling them what they should know is not artistic, and if there is no

---

[41] "To attempt to teach a foreign language before the mother-tongue has been learned is as irrational as to teach a boy to ride before he can walk" (*ibid.,* p. 213).

[42] See Laurie, *John Amos Comenius* (Syracuse, Bardeen, 1892), p. 22.

[43] Keatinge, *op. cit.,* pp. 214–215 (1931 ed.).

artistry in the pedagogical process there is no real teaching. Comenius' plan lacked refinement but embodied many awkward beginnings of modern classroom techniques. Wherever class methods were used, he recommended a division of the school day—two hours in the morning and two in the afternoon. Some part of each daily period was used for private study—probably supervised study. In the morning period emphasis was placed on memory and thinking; this was the time for mental accomplishment.[44] In the afternoon attention was given to vocal and manual exercises. The class was to have books, written especially for it, containing everything to be learned. The teacher read the lesson, explained it, and reread it to the class. Now the students, each in turn, read the lesson aloud and tried their hand at explaining it. Finally, the lesson was summarized and explained as a written exercise by each student.[45]

Schoolbook lessons were not supposed to be abstract or unreal, but concrete and meaningful. Comenius deplored the separation of words and things in education, and he doubted if quality learning was possible so long as the senses were ignored in the educational process. Out of this doubt was reasserted one of the most far reaching of educational principles: the five senses are the gateways to man's soul; there is nothing in the mind which does not have its origin in the senses. Unquestionably this was a principle that most educators, when pressed, would admit; certainly the Latin rendering of this principle among medieval masters had given it a certain indelible quality. Unfortunately most teachers paid it scant heed.

In a chapter of *The Great Didactic* devoted to the foundations of easy teaching, Comenius tried to show how this principle could be exploited in the interest of good teaching and learning. He began by saying that children will learn if they are taught what they desire to know, assuming that their maturity is sufficient and the methods of instruction proper, and if everything is taught by means of the senses. We have said that Comenius did not originate the doctrine, but he was the first modern educator to lay great stress on it. It is, in fact, the bedrock of his theory of teaching and learning: learning must be directed first to the senses, then to the memory, and finally to understanding. Not only would this order make learning more efficient and efficacious, it would also ensure its pleasantness.[46] For the first time in the history of schooling someone thought of the pleasure children might have in learning what they do not know.

If Comenius had stopped with education of the senses and with his ardent determination to bring about a working relationship between words and things, he would have introduced a great change in education

44 *Ibid.*, pp. 219–220.
45 *Ibid.*, pp. 220–221.
46 *Ibid.*, pp. 74–75.

by making it less literary. But he did not stop here, and we do not obtain anything like a full view of his theory if we take him at his word that we learn, not from books, but from the great Book of Nature, from heaven and earth, from oaks and beeches. He did believe that we learned from books, otherwise he would not have spent so much of his energy in writing some forty-two books on and for education. And he did not mean that learning could stop with the senses, any more than he meant that all learning was undisguised pleasure; it only began with the senses. He was sensitive to man's memory, which he felt could be trained and strengthened, to man's imagination, and to the education of man's emotions and will. And the place of these faculties in education according to the Comenian system should be discussed.

Comenius aimed at the complete education of men, and he was enough of a psychologist to know that training the senses—making them ready and receptive—was only a beginning, though a highly important one. What came to the mind through the senses had to be stored in the memory. This storehouse of knowledge enabled the student to extend the boundaries of his quest for truth, because it gave him guidance concerning what to look for, and he could persevere in his search for a firm base. While Comenius could take for granted the indispensability of bodies of knowledge stored in the memory, he was unwilling to accept the practice of leaving memories uncultivated or their development to mere chance. A good memory was not a natural phenomenon; it was made good through training.[47]

Again the principal technique associated with the memory was understanding. This was not new, surely, or original with Comenius, but it was unquestionably stressed by him. Before a child should try to memorize his lesson, he should understand it.[48] This doctrine is now adequately supported by experimental evidence, and we hardly ever demand more proof of its validity, but Comenius asserted the necessary relationship between understanding and memory without the benefit of the evidence now available. Thus we are almost forced to admire his educational intuition.

He believed, moreover, that memory practice should begin early in youth and that as a faculty it could be strengthened by use. He followed Vivès on this point and quoted him with approval.[49] There is little reason to doubt that Comenius aligned himself alongside the formal disciplinarians, yet he was no advocate of mere cramming; the memory should be employed in connection with important knowledge, and what is important should be fixed or stamped in by a variety of exercises.

[47] *Ibid.*, pp. 109–116.

[48] Comenius emphasized the relationship between memory and understanding in *The Great Didactic (ibid.*, pp. 111–113) , but his advice is elaborated considerably in *The Analytical Didactic.* (See Jelinek, *op. cit.*, pp. 140–151.)

[49] Keatinge, *op. cit.*, p. 304 (1896 ed.) .

Thus, writing, pictures, diagrams, and blackboards found their way naturally into his learning exercises.[50]

It is easy to form a picture of Comenius the schoolmaster and educational thinker coldly examining the curriculum and admitting to the learning process only those things that seem to have special relevance to sense training. No doubt he attached great significance to the training of the senses, for he firmly believed that they were the only gateways to the mind, but there was more to education than absorbing what the outside world had to offer, whether this came through direct contact with nature or through books or other vicarious channels. There were inner senses as well as outer ones; these were lodged in the imagination, another of man's faculties, and they too had to be considered in the learning process. It was not easy to deal directly with the imagination, as it was with the senses, but Comenius felt, nevertheless, that stimulation of the imagination was not only a boon to learning, that is, the day-to-day processes of mastering content, but was a way of opening the minds of men to different ways of looking at the world.[51] In a word, imagination at work almost guaranteed violations of the status quo. While it would be wrong to think of Comenius as an educational dreamer, or even a political or religious visionary, he did want the imagination of students kindled so they might see novelty in their learning and cultivate their experiences for unexpected meaning. The humdrum routine of schooling would have ended a century earlier had Comenius been listened to more carefully; as it was, the parts of his system most often noted had to do with matters of grading students, selecting instructional materials, and organizing the school day. Perhaps this was inevitable, because Comenius did not make the liberal elements in his plan especially visible. Some of the important points he had to make were lost on his contemporaries.

Along with imagination was reason or judgment.[52] This, too, was to be formed in the school, and, in a sense, it was one of the most important outcomes of formal education. Pedagogues of the past had paid scant heed to the outcomes of their educational programs. They were confident these programs would make students erudite and keep them in touch with the thinking of some of the best minds of antiquity. Students of the classical curriculum had minds well stocked with the lessons of Greece's fictional and Rome's historical heros; they knew the parts of speech and were able to write a composition the way Cicero would have wanted it written. But far too often they knew little, if anything, more than this. They did not know, for example, how to apply their knowledge to everyday life, nor were they able to say whether a given action should be taken

---

[50] *Ibid.*, p. 131 (1931 ed.).

[51] Jelinek, *op. cit.*, pp. 98–99.

[52] Comenius, *A Reformation of Schools*, translated by S. Hartlib (1642), p. 57; and *The Great Didactic*, XXVIII (Keatinge, *op. cit.*, p. 205, 1931 ed.).

or avoided.[53] Comenius wanted people educated to make decisions, to exercise their faculty of reason in the important daily affairs of living. This was certainly education for what is real.

While there was nothing new about Comenius' interest in the development of character—this had been the prime aim of education for centuries, and despite the seeming inconsistency, it was the overarching aim of the humanists, who spent so much time with the classics—he stayed in step with the past by asserting its importance and assigning to it the foremost place in human experience; the forming of the will, the development of man's moral nature was the capstone of the educational process. Yet, in Comenius' thinking there is something different: the emotions influence men and affect action; their effects must be heeded in school learning, for the emotions are a motive force and drive or stop curiosity, interest, attention, and sensory activity. We should not expect to find in Comenius anything more than a sympathetic approach to what later became a whole field of child psychology, but what we do find and what seems to be of immense importance was Comenius' sympathy for the emotional needs of children.[54]

Long before Comenius began to write on education, theorists had noted differences among children and had guardedly suggested that wise teachers should make some allowances in their pedagogy for these differences. But this was easier said than done, and it was especially difficult when teachers concentrated on mastery of knowledge. If the content of the grammar book or the form of an essay counted most in education, it was understandably hard for a teacher to know how to provide for these differences. The body of knowledge was there to be learned by all, and if Erasmus' advice was taken seriously, and often it was, everything was to be noticed, analyzed, and learned. This left little room for adjustment from one child to another. So given this emphasis on mastering bodies of knowledge, teachers tended to ignore the advice about individual differences; the message they heard from the best theorists on this subject was not always clear. While Comenius did not advance beyond what had already been said about the importance of treating students as individuals and adapting the educational program to their needs, he offered techniques whereby this might be done with relatively little effort by the schoolmaster. There were many minor ways in which these techniques found their way into the classrooms of modern schools, but the most important advice that Comenius could give dealt with adapting the level of instruction to the maturity and the age of the

---

[53] The old problem of pagan literature is revived by Comenius, even though medieval theorists thought they had resolved the dilemma. In *The Great Didactic (ibid.,* p. 190) Comenius wrote: "If we wish our schools to be truly Christian schools, the crowd of Pagan writers must be removed from them."

[54] This is plain in *The Great Didactic (ibid.,* pp. 86–87;) he sees emotion as an aid to memory too in *The Analytical Didactic.* (Jelinek, *op. cit.,* pp. 144–145.)

student. This was, we judge, his most important contribution to the science of pedagogy. And when he added that the child's interests should be taken into account too, we are almost at the threshold of modern techniques. The accepted practice of trying to teach boys philosophy, or even allowing them in the lecture halls, before they could read or write—a not uncommon practice in the two centuries that preceded Comenius—could find no favor with him. He reacted to these practices in a clear-headed way: "to attempt to cultivate the will before the intellect (or the intellect before the imagination, or the imagination before the faculty of sense perception), is mere waste of time. But this is what those do who teach boys logic, poetry, rhetoric, and ethics before they are thoroughly acquainted with the objects that surround them. It would be equally sensible to teach boys of two years old to dance, though they can scarcely walk." [55]

Comenius lived in an educational world where it was believed that children could learn to write well by reading about good writing or by learning long lists of grammatical rules, that they could learn to make good decisions affecting their own lives by knowing the classical prescriptions or applying the rules of scholastic logic, or, in general, that they could prepare themselves better for life in society by remaining largely ignorant of the real situations in society. In short, that the best preparation for life was a carefully contrived and antiseptic educational program divorcing life from learning. Comenius was perceptive enough to see the drift of educational practice, a drift unchanged almost from the time of Cassiodorus, despite his best efforts to make classical-Christian education practical.[56] Comenius must have known of the bitter failures of the reforming educators who had preceded him.[57] Yet he was not deterred from advancing the theory that the best learning is achieved by making learning real and allowing the learners to learn by doing. This creed, learning by doing, has a pragmatic ring, and many schoolmen of Comenius' own day, as well as our own, hastened to denounce it.[58] But Comenius was no pragmatist, except in the sense that all men must sometime be pragmatic, when he adopted the view that "What has to be done must be learned by practice. Artisans do not detain their appren-

[55] Keatinge, *op. cit.*, p. 409 (1896 ed.) .

[56] See pp. 144–145.

[57] See Matthew Spinka's excellent book, *John Amos Comenius: That Incomparable Moravian* (Chicago, University of Chicago Press, 1943) .

[58] See F. Eby, *Early Protestant Educators* (New York, McGraw-Hill Book Company, 1931) , pp. 32 ff; T. Hughes, *Loyola and the Educational System of the Jesuits* (New York, Charles Scribner's Sons, 1892) , pp. 160 ff; and R. H. Quick, *Essays on Educational Reformers* (New York, Appleton Company, 1891) . Despite our willingness to accept Comenius as a progressive thinker who was on the side of change and quality, we should be ready to listen to discordant notes. Sadler, *op. cit.*, p. 286, calls him "a child of his time. In some respects he was even behind the more advanced thinking of his time and he was not able to emancipate himself altogether from the traditions which he inherited."

tices with theories, but set them to do practical work at an early stage; thus they learn to forge by forging, to carve by carving, to paint by painting, and to dance by dancing. In schools, therefore, let students learn to write by writing, to talk by talking, to sing by singing, and to reason by reasoning." [59] This, perhaps, is the soundest doctrine of all in *The Great Didactic*.

Since this approach to learning would have little or no meaning if the student were isolated from reality, his final recommendation is aimed at the schools' pruning from their curricula all useless things. Useless content stands as an insuperable obstacle to a good education. But when Comenius spoke of useful learning, he did not endorse the doctrine of the narrow utilitarian—he thought of man as more than a machine, so use had far-reaching consequences. This was his admonition to educators: "Nothing should be learned solely for its value at school, but for its use in life. . . . Whatever is taught should be taught as being of practical application in everyday life and of some definite use. That is to say, the pupil should understand that what he learns is not taken out of some Utopia or borrowed from Platonic Ideas, but is one of the facts which surround us, and that a fitting acquaintance with it will be of great service to life." [60] Clearly, a pupil might not be able to see the use of everything he is to learn—and Comenius would make his students learn [61]—so the teacher, in addition to being a communicator of knowledge, would have to indicate the application and the relevance of his teaching. In this way, on the purely pedagogic level, relevance was returned to the schoolroom. And the plea for relevance in learning was undoubtedly the most important plea Comenius made in all of his educational writings. His entire system of schools, and his total educational theory, is built on relevance.

III

EDUCATIONAL PRACTICE

Comenius began with the assumption that contemporary schooling was full of defects. His own education, he noted on many occasions, was uninspiring. While we feel no need to recite these defects here, it was as a reformer that Comenius turned first to theorizing about the schools and

---

59 Keatinge, *op. cit.*, p. 347 (1896 ed.) .

60 *Ibid.*, p. 341.

61 In *The Analytical Didactic* Comenius considers the word "discipline" and notes its various meanings. He intends to use it in the context of teaching and learning: "the word is used most properly, as here, to denote a means of enforcing instruction" (Jelinek, *op. cit.*, p. 117.) See also J. K. Clauser, "Comenius Considers Discipline," *Peabody Journal of Education*, XXXIX (July, 1961) , pp. 50–53.

then tried to create means whereby the goals of his theory could be realized. The ends are stated quickly and simply in the title of *The Great Didactic:* youth of both sexes are to become learned in the sciences, pure in morals, trained in piety, and instructed in all things necessary for the present and future life. It was, he wrote, the main object of *The Great Didactic* to show teachers how these large goals could be realized.[62] Thus, when we turn to Comenius as a methodologist, we are not discounting theory, but are merely completing his theory. Without his articles of school practice the doctrines of Comenius would be sterile, and Comenius himself would have remained largely unnoticed as an educator of consequence.[63] It is not possible to deal with every aspect of Comenian methodology here, but we can concentrate on the methodological advice that played a central role in his plan of teaching.

Comenius' educational attitudes were formed in a century having many intuitions about natural methodology. The famous Ratke preceded Comenius on the educational stage, and despite his effort to maintain secrecy concerning his method, enough leaked out for his contemporaries to know that amid his exaggerated claims there were seeds of truth.[64] Vivès, Andreae (1586–1654), and Alsted, to name only the most well-known proponents of naturalism in teaching methods, taught Comenius something, and Comenius himself was always at pains to acknowledge indebtedness to his predecessors. There is no hint whatever that Comenius ever tried to conceal the fact that he learned from others or that his system of education was not entirely original. So when we review the principal tenets of Comenian methodology, we shall at certain points be inclined to doubt Comenius' importance, because we shall have met the same suggestions before. The point is that Comenius synthesized many methodological items and welded them into a total teaching plan.[65] And he did this without much knowledge of psychology and without support from experimental data, now confirming most of his treasured beliefs.

There is a healthy relationship between theory and method, between goals and practice, in Comenius' educational plan; the only reason he talks about method at all is to show how instruction might best be imparted. He was determined to find a way whereby the school's instructional goals might be attained "surely and thoroughly, certainly and clearly, easily and pleasantly." His intuition enabled him to make a large logical step from the quest for a solution to the solution itself: a natural

---

62 Keatinge, *op. cit.*, p. 17 (1931 ed.).

63 See O. H. Lang, *Comenius: His Life and Principles of Education* (New York, E. L. Kellog and Company, 1891).

64 See K. Seiler, *Das Pädagogische System W. Ratkes* (Erlangen, 1931).

65 See W. W. Brickman, "Three Centuries of Comenius' Contributions to Education," *School and Society*, LXXXVI (April 26, 1958), pp. 192–194; and Max A. H. Möhrke, *Johann Amos Komenius und Johann Valentin Andreae, ihre Pädagogic und ihr Verhältniss zu einander* (Leipzig, 1904).

methodology. It was not Comenius but Rousseau who said that if we follow nature we shall almost always be right, yet Comenius was in sympathy with this idea. Now the problem was to find the natural learning process. This could not have been either clear or easy for Comenius, for it is not today; yet with crude tools he tried to uncover the natural method.

Economy of presentation recommends a simple listing of the principal components of natural method:

1. Comenius, observing that plants, animals, and birds began to grow in the spring, concluded, reasoning by analogy, that education was proper to youth; he came close to saying that teaching cannot begin too early. In any event, carrying into practice the belief that education was right for the springtime of life, he proposed the Mother School.[66] This was a school at home, directed by the mother, dealing with the first six years of life, when the most basic virtues and attitudes are formed. No time must be lost before teaching in the Mother School begins. Although some authors claim that Comenius, in proposing infant education at home, was really founding the kindergarten, his infant education and Froebel's kindergarten were supported by quite different theories. Yet, the relationship between Comenius and Froebel as supporters of preprimary education may be a moot point.[67]

2. Again looking at the world around him, Comenius observed that nature prepares materials before she develops them. Transferring this to learning, it meant, according to Comenius, that children must be ready to learn. This involved maturity, interest, attention, and physiological development of the senses, but it meant, too, that the form or the structure of a lesson should first be made clear to students. It is noteworthy that this principle is now recognized and applauded in contemporary education.

3. Comenius, a devoted believer in internal development, did not believe a gardener could make plants grow, although he could aid their natural operations. A teacher, Comenius asserted, neither learns for the student nor makes him learn; [68] he aids most by helping identify relations and clarifying material that students are expected to master. The most obvious and flagrant violation of this principle, according to Comenius, occurred in language teaching. Instruction began with grammar rules that had to be memorized before anything else was done. This was the classical method almost exactly, except on one important point: the

66 Keatinge, *op. cit.*, pp. 203–211 (1931 ed.) .

67 See Eller, *op. cit.*, pp. 3–53.

68 Comenius' view of enforcing instruction was not the same as compelling a child to learn. See Jelinek, *op. cit*, pp. 117–119; and J. C. Halliday, *The Pampaedia* (St. Andrews University, Edinburgh, 1963) , IX. In *The Great Didactic* Comenius quotes Quintilian with approval: "The acquisition of knowledge depends on the will to learn, and this cannot be forced" (Keatinge, *op. cit.*, p. 78, 1931 ed.) .

grammar teacher of the classical age could begin with rules because his students already knew the language—Greek or Latin—and used it in daily communication.

4. According to Comenius, nature begins with universals and ends with particulars.[69] Whether or not Comenius was right may be debated, but following what he saw in nature, and stretching the point, he maintained that in education, if it follows natural processes, teaching must begin with broad principles and go next to details.[70] This reinforced his earlier principle that teachers should begin by demonstrating the structure of a lesson.

5. In Comenius' day pedagogues thought that children moved from one stage of development to another and that there were discrete periods where certain types of teaching were appropriate. Without contradicting the old-fashioned theory, Comenius modified it by affirming that development exists, with its stages for appropriate teaching, but he discarded the notion that steps in development are discrete. He did not find any leaps or sharp breaks in nature, and he did not want any in teaching and learning.[71]

6. Comenius argued warmly for graded instruction, and not according to age alone, although age was a factor, but according to student need. Nature does not compel her operations, and if school methods are natural they will not compel students to learn subjects unsuited to their degree of maturity.[72] Comenius wanted to teach children only what they needed, and teachers could learn what this was by studying children themselves. Now Comenius is hard to believe, and there are signs that his own teaching controverted his advice. Children were regularly exposed to subjects they neither wanted nor needed; and Comenius' justification for this is no different from today's.

7. Nature, Comenius held, was never overburdened: one thing was done at a time. The correctness of this dogmatic assumption cannot be tested here, but Comenius interpreted it to mean that teachers must present only small segments of knowledge. Too much should not be expected of students, nor should they be asked to study several subjects in any school period.[73]

8. Still true to the lessons taught by nature, and believing that natural growth processes occur slowly, he argued that school sessions should be short and that there should be time for study and recreation and short periods for recitation and instruction.[74]

The foregoing principles, drawn, Comenius maintained, from in-

[69] Comenius, *A Reformation of Schools*, 27.74, 57.
[70] Keatinge, *op. cit.*, p. 67 (1931 ed.).
[71] *Ibid.*, pp. 69–70.
[72] *Ibid.*, pp. 88–89.
[73] *Ibid.*, p. 86.
[74] *Ibid.*, pp. 87–88; and Jelinek, *op. cit.*, p. 81.

sights into nature's processes, were supported by additional precepts. One of these was addressed to school discipline. Comenius never doubted the importance of good order in the schoolroom, or that inattentive, obstructive, or recalcitrant students would be obstacles to superior instruction. Wherever moral offenses were the foundation for bad discipline, corrective measures by the teacher included corporal punishment. Beyond this, corporal punishment was interdicted: a slow-learning child should not be beaten, nor should any child be punished for inability to learn. The edict went further: "No blows should be given for lack of readiness to learn; for if the pupil does not learn readily, this is the fault of no one but the teacher, who either does not know how to make his pupil receptive of knowledge, or does not take the trouble to do so." [75] This was an exaggerated indictment of teachers, although Comenius does not think so, for it failed to account for the few children who, for whatever reason, refuse to learn. To make teachers responsible for all learning failure—to lay all the blame at their doorstep—is a defect in Comenius' theory.

Yet we should not dwell on slight imperfections. The praise Comenius gets for promoting the idea that the school is a happy place, that learning can be pleasant with a little help from the teacher, and that students pushed beyond their ability into studies too difficult are intellectually and morally mistreated, is entirely deserved. By concentrating on the natural attractions of learning and the willingness of youth to exploit its own natural talents, Comenius generated a methodological awakening.[76]

Never losing sight of artistry in teaching, Comenius was perceptive enough to know that teachers need the right textbooks and other teaching aids to direct superior learning. He spent precious years writing textbooks, and he never complained about his investment in this kind of scholarship. In all the books he endeavored to apply the principles drawn from observations of nature, and his textbooks represent a natural methodology at work. They were as important to education as his theories about the quality and goals of teaching.

He thought the old lecture—a student taking the teacher's dictation —a sheer waste of time. Fortunately, Comenius could give students textbooks prepared especially for them, for he lived after the invention of movable type and took every advantage of it. The textbook was common to a class and it contained everything a class was expected to learn.[77] Materials, presented with all the artistry Comenius possessed, were directed at the senses to reinforce a relationship between words and things. Foremost among the innovations employed in Comenius' books

---

[75] Keatinge, *op. cit.,* p. 91 (1931 ed.) .

[76] See P. H. Hanus, "The Permanent Influence of Comenius," *Educational Review,* (March, 1892) , pp. 226–236.

[77] Keatinge, *op. cit.,* pp. 56–59 (1931 ed.) .

was illustration, and even in Latin grammar texts he was successful in employing it.

To give unity and meaning to his educational plans, Comenius designed a system of schools wherein universal opportunity for learning held a central place. The Mother School, described in *The School of Infancy* [78]—a book intended to guide mothers in teaching children from birth to age six—was the first rung of the educational ladder. Next the Vernacular School, for six- to twelve-year-old children, was directed to open its doors to all and to teach them in their mother tongue. Although most children were expected to terminate their formal learning in the Vernacular School, the Latin School was available to students who wanted, or needed, a conventional classical education, modified only by the new methods of Comenius. At the end of the educational line we find the University, geared for communicating the literary and scientific inheritance and research. Although Comenius obviously placed considerable value on university studies, he was never very detailed or precise about them.

IV

GENERAL ASSESSMENT

Comenius' influence, although clearly impressive, is hard to measure exactly. In the past century or so, with more notice being accorded his pedagogical posture, he has often been called the father of modern education; [79] a more recent assessment contains more explicit and perhaps even higher praise: "He was not merely a reformer of method but also a pioneer in the attempt to educate a whole nation and later the whole world." [80]

No doubt Comenius always entertained great hope for education as a social instrument, and this hope contained some prophetic anticipations; there is a relationship between Comenius' stated aim for education —the development of souls, bodies, and minds—and the modern goal of educating the whole man. His determination to popularize the idea of universal learning foreshadowed both national school systems and democratic ideals for education. Perhaps without realizing it, he was a democrat, because "the most democratic proposals of all were stated by the Moravian leader, Comenius, who urged the establishment of a complete 'ladder' system of schools reaching from the lowest levels to the univer-

---

78 Eller, *op. cit.*, pp. 59–123.

79 See W. S. Monroe, "Comenius, the Evangelist of Modern Pedagogy," *Education,* XIII (1892–1893) , pp. 212–219.

80 Jelinek, *op. cit.*, p. 6.

sity." [81] Further emphasizing his democratic commitment, he rejected dualism in educational organization—one system of schools for upper-class children and another system for those who remain—and he insisted on equal educational treatment of the sexes: "Why should [the female sex] be altogether excluded from the pursuit of knowledge (whether in Latin or in their mother tongue). They also are formed in the image of God, and share in His grace and in the kingdom of the world to come. They are endowed with equal sharpness of mind and capacity for knowledge (often with more than the opposite sex) . . . why should we admit them to the alphabet, and afterwards drive them away from books?" [82]

Since most of Comenius' books were written in Czech, it was not until they were translated into Latin that his influence in education began to be felt. *The Great Didactic* is a treasury of his keen educational insights: "In tracing contemporary movements and ideas back to their sources, a surprisingly large number of them were absorbed from the progressive tendencies of the time and formulated for the school by Comenius." [83]

John Dewey is sometimes called the "founder of progressive education." However, Comenius had earlier advocated a return to the ancient practice of learning by doing. Long before the science of psychology testified to the importance of child growth and development, theories of learning, role of motivation, and individual differences and needs, Comenius had considered them. "There are few problems in education that are not discussed by Comenius, and teachers cannot fail to derive stimulus from a perusal of the answers that this great schoolmaster . . . gave to the questions that are still being asked at the present day." [84] Comenius looked at education from the child's perspective; his school plan had four levels of education; he based his idea regarding growth and development of children on nature, much the same as we do today.

"In method, Comenius laid the foundation for our division of periods of education and type of instruction in each, graded textbooks, pictures, and other training aids, the laboratory of things to teach ideas." [85] He wanted to make learning pleasant and meaningful by using all the senses and by going from the known to the unknown. Subject matter and method were inseparable parts of teaching, and all basic studies were to be in the mother tongue. The curriculum became broader when Comenius added history, geography, drawing, and manual training.

The list of Comenius' innovations presently found in education is almost endless. The influence of Comenius on later ages is one of com-

81 R. F. Butts, *A Cultural History of Education* (New York, McGraw-Hill Book Company, 1947), p. 257.

82 Keatinge, *op. cit.*, p. 43 (1931 ed.).

83 Butler, *op. cit.*, p. 15.

84 Keatinge, *op. cit.*, p. 15 (1931 ed.).

85 Eller, *op. cit.*, p. 30.

manding importance as we compare his theories to today's educational practices. "His voice was heard, but not until many years later, for it was the nineteenth rather than the seventeenth century that benefited most from the educational views of Comenius." [86] This tardy appreciation of Comenius' theories may be attributed to cumulative disadvantages, which if taken separately should not have been major obstacles in the path of his advanced ideas: he was the religious leader of a persecuted sect; his *Great Didactic* was not translated into English until 1896, and his complementary *Analytical Didactic* not until 1953; his democratic ideas in education ran counter to seventeenth- and eighteenth-century social and political preconceptions, and Comenius lacked the literary facility to make them appealing; and, finally, the inevitable lag of educational practice behind theory put his human and progressive educational plans at a disadvantage. Educational reform, like other reforms, comes slowly, but "In spite of the neglect into which the reforms of Comenius fell, his influence has been lasting because his work was constructive and his reforms were far reaching." [87]

[86] Power, *op. cit.*, p. 346.
[87] Monroe, *op. cit.*, pp. 167–168.

⇝ 9 ⇜

John Locke: The Utility of Learning

I

INTRODUCTION

Comenius alerted teachers to the importance of sense training and real-ism in school instruction. For this students and teachers the world over owe him some measure of gratitude. Where Comenius set the wheel of progress in motion, Locke gave it additional momentum. Along with accepting the principal Comenian theses—although any direct indebted-ness to Comenius is impossible to prove [1]—he added emphases of his own. These emphases allow us to call Locke's educational and philosoph-ical outlook empirical; but it is a qualified empiricism, for Locke was not a narrow sensationalist who eliminated the possibility of internal experience.[2] The point he stressed, and some of his followers overstressed, was that the only avenue for knowledge of the physical world is through the senses; ultimately all our ideas are grounded in what enters our minds through the senses. While this may not strike us as particularly hard doctrine, in Locke's time it was subjected to acid criticism; several leading philosophers insisted that fundamental ideas were innate.

Comenius before Locke stimulated scientific thinking while being himself highly intuitive; he was neither enough a philosopher nor enough a psychologist to go much beyond analogical reasoning or deduc-

---

[1] I am unaware of any declaration of indebtedness on Locke's part, and, so far as I can discover, Locke never quotes Comenius. An analysis of his library does not help us much on this point. See John Harrison and Peter Laslett, *The Library of John Locke* (London, Oxford University Press, 1965).

[2] See James Gibson, *Locke's Theory of Knowledge and Its Historical Relations* (Cambridge, Cambridge University Press, 1960), pp. 52–55.

tive processes in thinking. Locke, however, doubted the efficacy of intuitive solutions for philosophical issues; moreover, he accepted what is now called the Baconian thesis: important knowledge is produced by induction. He was a sophisticated thinker able to create philosophical and psychological principles out of pious moralisms and copybook maxims.[3]

Despite Locke's unquestioned influence on educational practice for more than two centuries after his death, it is probably unfair to study him in comparison with Comenius, or any earlier educator, or, for that matter, to think of him as a complete educator at all. The completeness and consistency of his educational theory are hard to prove; more accurately, he had attitudes about education—about teaching and learning processes, what should be taught, and where and how teaching should be organized.[4]

Yet, despite what may appear to be poor credentials as a schoolmaster, Locke's comprehensive social and political attitudes, along with profound philosophical and psychological convictions, led him to consider basic theoretical and practical educational issues most carefully. While, it must be admitted, every educational question did not come within the purview of his thought, he seldom missed the important ones, and his answers, tempered by a fundamental allegiance to utilitarianism, were ardently scientific and empirical. Locke's principal educational position flowed from his conception of psychology, and its implications paved avenues for teachers and enabled them to retool much of educational practice; in addition, he broke ground for Rousseau and Pestalozzi —not to mention lesser naturalistic educators—and this alone should be enough to canalize our interests toward him.

Locke's educational thought is two dimensional: his psychological doctrines relative to the origin of ideas and the stature of knowledge; and his attitudes on schooling. The first are found mainly in *An Essay Concerning Human Understanding*,[5] and the second in his book *Some Thoughts Concerning Education*.[6]

---

[3] A. Meiklejohn, *Education Between Two Worlds* (New York, Harper and Brothers, 1942) , pp. 26–35, makes some interesting comparisons between Comenius and Locke.

[4] This, I think, is the central point missed by M. L. Cuff, *The Limitations of the Educational Theory of John Locke Especially for the Christian Teacher* (Washington, D.C., The Catholic Education Press, 1920) , pp. 131–145.

[5] John Locke, *An Essay Concerning Human Understanding*, 28th ed. (London, T. Tegg and Son, 1838) .

[6] *John Locke on Education*, Peter Gay, ed. (New York, Bureau of Publications, Teachers College, Columbia University, 1964) , contains *Some Thoughts Concerning Education. John Locke's Of the Conduct of the Understanding*, F. W. Garforth, ed. (New York, Teachers College Press, Teachers College, Columbia University, 1966) , is related to the *Essay* and *Some Thoughts,* although my own view is that it supplements the *Essay* more than it complements *Some Thoughts.* See *ibid.,* p. 5.

II

LIFE AND WORK

John Locke was born in 1632 into a middle-class English family; his father, a country attorney, sometimes dabbled in politics.[7] His father's attitude on education reflected the traditional conception that the best training for young gentlemen is careful parental nurture, and the elder Locke managed his sons' education until they were ready for grammar school. When John was fourteen he enrolled in the Westminster School, a grammar school of considerable fame following the humanistic tradition in education.[8] This was a classical school essaying to prepare students for life by immunizing them from it. No doubt Locke had his Westminster experiences in mind when he wrote, in *Some Thoughts Concerning Education,* that the time wasted in learning languages could have been better utilized by teaching boys subjects of use to them.[9] In addition to a thorough classical education, the school offered young Locke, and, we suppose, all its students, a regimen aimed at disciplining young minds. Whatever merit this schooling had—and it must have had some—Locke refused to offer any compliments, and instead he recited the negative effects of school experience, hoping young men would thus be motivated to take full advantage of their tutorial opportunities.[10]

Even though Locke could write disparagingly of his life in one of England's finest secondary schools, he profited from it and matriculated at Oxford University in 1652 with an excellent recommendation for scholarship. Later, as a King's scholar, he received an annual allowance, and in 1660 he was elected a tutor in Christ Church College; this was a renewable position and Locke held it for several years.[11]

Prolonged periods of schooling enabled Locke to test, or, at least, to think about various professional goals. He considered holy orders, a diplomatic career, then medicine, and finally settled for being a professional philosopher. The latter, if a profession, is hard to identify apart from writing or teaching, so if Locke belonged to any profession it was the teaching profession. Yet his connection with teaching, always tangential, was more as a tutor or censor than as a lecturer; but his closest professional association was an academic one.

---

[7] See M. Cranston, *John Locke* (London, Longmans, Green & Co., 1957), pp. 1–10.

[8] *Ibid.,* pp. 18 ff.

[9] Gay, *op. cit.,* 147.

[10] *Ibid.,* 70.

[11] H. R. Fox Bourne, *The Life of John Locke* (New York, Harper and Brothers, 1876), 2 vols., I, 53 ff.

In true Socratic-like fashion Locke refused the label of teacher to say, in *An Essay Concerning Human Understanding*, that he is not elaborating ideas, knowledge, or philosophy, but is merely inquiring into the nature of things.[12] He is at pains to emphasize his inability to answer man's most searching questions; at the same time, however, he is careful to assert that ready-made answers, to which allegiance was regularly paid, were invalid. Locke knows with certainty what is false; he is less definite about the truth. Still, Locke cannot always be taken at his word: he teaches what the evidence tells him is true.

Because Locke writes without citing authorities, a fact that in itself does not bespeak a paucity of literary knowledge, it is hard to ascertain his literary and philosophical indebtedness. Locke tells us almost nothing about his bibliography, yet we know he was nurtured by scholastic philosophy, and we detect scholastic terms and ways of thinking in his books; but we know, too, that he abandoned scholasticism because he became convinced of its decadence.[13] His principal criticism of scholasticism, and a devastating one at that, was its handling of meaningless questions in abstract and unreal ways. Despite Locke's aversion to scholastic philosophy, he was never able to eliminate all its methods and terms from his own philosophy.

His rupture with scholastic systems was precipitated by Descartes, who, it is said, was Locke's liberator: Descartes' philosophy demonstrated at once the aridity of verbalized rationalism and the exciting possibilities of mathematical exactitude. Locke always credited Descartes with asking the right questions in philosophy—and for a time he accepted Descartes' "I think, therefore, I am"—but he was not at all certain the Cartesians were right in their answers to these questions. The principal point of disagreement between Locke and the Cartesians involved the validity of intuitive knowledge and the existence of innate ideas: Locke denied, and the Cartesians accepted, both.[14]

Sir Robert Boyle and Isaac Newton impressed Locke with the possibilities of scientific philosophy, and from both he took something for his empiricism, but neither was his philosophical mentor.[15] In common with Descartes, Boyle, and Newton, Locke began by agreeing to the importance of reason in philosophy, but later he went beyond this to assert that all man's beliefs, even those involving revelation, must be subjected to

12 *An Essay Concerning Human Understanding*, I, i, 2. (Hereafter cited as *Essay*).

13 See R. I. Aaron, *John Locke* (London, Oxford University Press, 1937), pp. 8–9; 26–38. Locke's philosophy was built on the traditional foundations he inherited from the schools of philosophic thought. Although he was not in any formal sense a disciple of Descartes, he was nevertheless greatly indebted to him. For Locke's relationship to scholasticism, see A. Tellkamp, *Das Verhältnis John Locke's zur Scholastik* (Münster i. W., 1927); and Gibson, *op. cit.*, pp. 182–204.

14 See Aaron, *op. cit.*, pp. 75–82.

15 See Gerd Buchdahl, *The Image of Newton and Locke in the Age of Reason* (New York, Sheed & Ward, Inc., 1961).

reason's test.[16] Now Locke's thought was anathema to Christians. But Locke was not merely concerned to dislodge men's awkward superstitions, he wanted to subject vital social and political issues to coldly objective reason. Still Locke would not qualify as an authentic rationalist, although he trusted reason, because he found the substance of reason in empirical data. All social relations, he said, should be dominated by reason, for in the absence of reason only whim is left. And reason's test would be used in religion too.[17] This attitude proved intolerable to English and Roman Catholics, who, while extolling reason, too often carefully proscribed its use; so Locke's best books were formally condemned—a blessing in disguise, for now on the *Index of Forbidden Books* they attracted even more attention.

Descartes, Boyle, and Newton helped Locke form his disturbing thesis; at least, they were in the vanguard of modern philosophical thought. Sometimes Thomas Hobbes' name is put on this list, for Hobbes is said to have affected Locke with his philosophical nominalism and his association-of-ideas doctrine. Aaron, however, the principal interpreter of Locke's philosophy, rejects this, and asserts instead that Hobbes' influence on Locke was entirely negative.[18]

Inconsistencies appear in Locke's books, and it is usually futile to try reconciling them. A litany of apparent contradictions here would be superfluous, but a few of the outstanding ones may be mentioned. Locke was both liberal and conservative. His social and political ideas, at least the best ones, were liberal, but it was liberalism in a narrow context. When he wrote about liberty and the rights of citizens in political society, his mind was on gentlemen not on hoi polloi.[19] When he wrote about education and tried to broaden it, he meant only the education of upper-class children.[20] And when he was enthusiastic about reason as a social guide, he, in company with the intellectuals of the time, decried enthusiasm.[21]

Locke's thought is always mature, due, no doubt, to the fact that his most important books were published when he was nearly sixty. He never rushed into print and apparently revised his manuscripts several times. When they appeared in printed form, they were usually anonymous.

The *Letter Concerning Toleration,* a plea for more tolerance from the English government; *Two Treatises of Government,* both a diatribe defending King William and a political discourse; and, Locke's greatest book, *An Essay Concerning Human Understanding,* all appeared in

16 *Essay,* IV, xviii; xix, 4.

17 *Ibid.,* IV, xviii, 6. See Herbert McLachlan, *The Religious Opinions of Milton, Locke, and Newton* (Manchester, England, Manchester University Press, 1941) .

18 Aaron, *op. cit.,* p. 33; and Gibson, *op. cit.,* pp. 233–236.

19 John Locke, *Two Treatises of Government,* 2d ed. (1694) , VIII, 95.

20 Gay, *op. cit.,* Introduction, p. 13.

21 *Essay,* IV, xix, 3.

quick succession around 1690. What must be regarded as his principal contribution to educational theory, *Some Thoughts Concerning Education,* appeared in 1693.[22] In addition, Locke was the author of more than two dozen books and essays, attesting his interest in scholarship and his hope that by writing he could generate intellectual reform. Coupled with this dedication to philosophical quickening was trust in reason—unless reason could be trusted an intellectual crusade was out of the question. So Locke's emphasis on sense knowledge and empirical data is toned down; what really counts is the use men make of the knowledge they have.

Something should be added relative to Locke's purposes in writing what authorities agree was his greatest book, *An Essay Concerning Human Understanding.* Here inferences and suppositions are unnecessary; Locke states his motive: "It is ambition enough to be employed as an underlabourer in clearing the ground a little, and removing some of the rubbish that lies in the way of knowledge; which certainly had been very much more advanced in the world, if the endeavors of ingenious and industrious men had not been much cumbered with the learned, but frivolous, use of uncouth, affected, or unintelligible terms, introduced into the sciences and there made an art of to that degree, that philosophy, which is nothing more but the true knowledge of things, was thought unfit, or incapable, to be brought into wellbred company and polite conversation." [23]

Locke, then, does not assert or advance his credentials as a philosopher as such, although he essays to define the purpose of philosophy in simple and straightforward terms—the true knowledge of things. His role is, as he defines it, on a lower level: to do work preliminary to building a philosophy in which the truth of things is made clear. As the carpenter may spend a great deal of time setting the foundation to a house before he begins to build, Locke was interested in clearing the ground and setting the foundation for philosophy. He appears content to leave it to others to provide the superstructure, and he may actually have doubted his credentials for doing the philosophical building, for he suggests that everyone cannot be a Boyle, a Sydenham, or a Newton.

We may think Locke was engaged in an enterprise to discredit philosophy and to advance science, for these men, as we read them, or read of them in histories of intellectual progress, seem to be scientists and not philosophers. Was Locke surrendering the search into the true nature of things to the scientist? Although this question would seem to have some meaning today, when the division between science and philosophy is generally sharp, it had little or no meaning when Locke wrote. He con-

22 If one chooses to include *Of the Conduct of the Understanding* as an educational tract, the date of its first posthumous publication was 1706.

23 *Essay,* "Epistle to the Reader," pp. ix–x.

sidered these men, perhaps the most illustrious of his time, to be true philosophers, and with only slight reflection we realize that in the seventeenth century the science-philosophy dichotomies had not been so securely erected. The content of the *Essay* confirms Locke's purpose; clearly it involves an analysis of human understanding—a concern preliminary to fundamental philosophizing—although it engages discovery, synthesis, and method, all common to philosophy. What bothered Locke most, as he approached the problem of clearing away the underbrush around true knowledge, was the philosopher's tendency to put unlimited confidence in the syllogism, a confidence based on the assumption that certain fundamental principles had a priori validity.[24] While Locke did not discard deductive methods, he deplored the willingness of philosophers to depend solely on deduction and ignore or actively oppose any other way of arriving at knowledge. Such narrowness was capable of producing only limited, inadequate, or erroneous knowledge.

The reform was not to reconstruct traditional opinion but to introduce new ideas; it was constructive not destructive. There could be no satisfaction with partial, incomplete, inadequate knowledge; but how could knowledge be comprehensive and valid unless all means available to philosophy were used to test it? Still, releasing men from traditional opinion was dangerous in two ways: first, when freed from tradition, men would rush to obtain knowledge, employing untrained or misguided reason and being unaware of its limitations; second, released from old stable systems promising certitude, men entered a world where certitude was not guaranteed, and they might decide that dependable knowledge was unattainable. They would, then, simply abandon the search for truth resigned to the awful conclusion that nothing could be known.[25] Locke was neither traditional nor skeptical; his philosophy immunized thinking men from both. Finally, and perhaps still a safeguard for philosophers, he hoped to put limits on human knowledge.[26] He wanted these boundaries established in advance and believed he could determine how far man's mind might range in probing the multiple uncertainties of the universe.

Finally, it must be said, Locke never doubted the possibility of human knowledge. He was not tempted to say that all knowledge was above the level of right opinion, but some could be; so he neither begins nor ends as a skeptic. Knowledge, within the boundaries Locke thought could be set, is possible, and learning, although never having first place among his educational objectives,[27] was an effort worth making.

---

24 *Ibid.*, IV, xvii, 4. With thinly veiled sarcasm, he wrote: "But God has not been so sparing to men to make them barely two-legged creatures, and left it to Aristotle to make them rational, i.e. those few of them that he could get so to examine the grounds of syllogisms . . . God has been more bountiful than so; he has given them a mind that can reason without being instructed in methods of syllogizing. . . ."

25 *Ibid.*, I, i, 7.

26 *Ibid.*, IV, iii, 1–6.

27 *Some Thoughts Concerning Education*, 134. (Hereafter cited as *Some Thoughts*.)

III

LOCKE ON IDEAS AND KNOWLEDGE

Hardly any proposition in Locke's famous *Essay* is better known than the doctrine of innate ideas. When Locke attacks and apparently demolishes the doctrine, he insists that human beings are born neither with knowledge of things nor of first principles. *Tabula rasa* is not mentioned in Book I, Chapter Two of the *Essay,* but it is clearly and definitely assumed. Locke's argument is: all men are born without knowledge, and knowledge is obtained only through the senses. At birth the mind is blank, and if nothing is inscribed by experience, it will always be blank. A quick reaction to Locke's thesis might be: has anyone ever thought otherwise? Granted, today few philosophers talk about intuitive knowledge, innate ideas, or native principles, yet the long Platonic tradition asserting the primacy of intuitive knowledge is persistent. And we remember how the Socratic method of "teaching" rested on the assumption that discursive processes in learning are unnecessary. By the time Locke wrote the *Essay* this tradition was almost totally dissipated, although there were Platonists in the English universities, especially at Cambridge, who had sympathy for innate ideas, but they were neither vocal nor prominent. Descartes and his confreres were understood to mean that certain ideas, especially ones about God, are innate; but, according to Descartes himself, this was an incorrect interpretation of his views,[28] and he made several outright denials about the doctrines of innate or intuitive knowledge ascribed to him. Why, then, we ask, did Locke go to such lengths to deny doctrines which, apparently, no one accepted?

If Descartes was not Locke's target, although Aaron thinks he may have been,[29] for he is unconvinced about the full value of Descartes' disclaimers, against whom was Locke writing? Could he have erected a straw man as a pretext for displaying his genius in philosophical and logical reasoning? Can we find anyone of stature, or anything in the philosophical tradition, that Locke felt compelled to controvert? We have noted Locke's decided antipathies for scholasticism—he thought its record dismal and a discredit to philosophy—but he could not have missed the vivid scholastic doctrine that nothing is in the mind which does not have its origin in the senses. The scholastic's physical world was real enough, and Locke was fully aware of this. On the other hand, neither did Locke miss the overemphasis on deduction in scholasticism

[28] Descartes, *Works,* Haldane and Ross edition, I, 442, wrote: "I never wrote or concluded that the mind required innate ideas which were in some sort different from its faculty of thinking."

[29] Aaron, *op. cit.,* p. 79.

and the apparent acceptance of certain first principles as self-evident propositions. From these self-evident propositions, which for reasons of logical necessity needed no proof, most syllogisms proceeded, and from this starting point, sense knowledge was sold at discount, or admitted only as a minor premise. This, Locke said, put the world out of focus. While it is difficult to be certain against whom Locke was writing when he centered on the doctrine of innate ideas, we may suppose he had many philosophers and several philosophical systems in mind, but among them the most prominent were the Cartesians and the Scholastics, and they bore the brunt of his castigations.

Because that part of the *Essay* dealing with the doctrine of innate ideas is written loosely, and because it emphasizes most the things needing emphasis least, Locke's statements are easily misunderstood. At the outset, because language was so often confused, he promised to write in clear, simple, easily understood prose.[30] Locke, it turned out, was not entirely innocent of wishful thinking. We should try to see, nevertheless, what Locke opposed in the doctrine of innate ideas: he never meant to discredit instinctive behavior; innate capacities are distinct from innate abilities, and he admitted the former; however, Locke spent little time on the lower forms of physical activity, or with what he claimed was subrational behavior. Moreover, in denying innate knowledge, Locke did not become a mere sensationalist, or hold that the mind is incapable of using the raw materials of experience.[31] In Locke's system of thought, the mind needed the senses but was capable also of using sensory information to construct general principles and build knowledge by comparisons of experiences not having their source directly in the senses. Finally, and he spent too much time on this point, he did not deny the possibility of prenatal experience, although he doubted its worth.[32]

Knowledge, Locke held, is always discovery, and first principles or self-evident propositions must come, if at all, from the experiences a person has. The principles of contradiction and identity, moreover, are not part of man's original nature, and he will never have them unless they are learned.[33] The mind has no potential sense waiting to be actualized; knowledge is always by discovery, not sometimes by discovery and sometimes by actualization. Thus, necessary relations between experiences are possible, but they come from the mind's rationalization of experiences. Necessary relations and universality remain intact, although their innateness is denied.

Thus, Locke clearly limits the origin of ideas to sensory experience, and by ideas he means the immediate objects of perception and thought.

[30] *Essay*, "Epistle to the Reader," p. xii. He returns to this subject again in Book III, especially in chapter ten.
[31] *Ibid.*, II, i, 3–4.
[32] *Ibid.*, I, iv, 3–4; II, ix, 5–6.
[33] *Ibid.*, I, ii, 4; I, iv, 4.

His conception of ideas is inadequate, as critics have shown, yet this was Locke's meaning, and if our interest is principally in his thought, we shall not be distracted by critics. His definition of ideas placed him close to representationalism, and critics have noticed this too: are the objects of perception themselves in the mind, or are representations of objects in the mind? Here, it must be admitted, Locke's theory is vague, if not actually defective.

Returning to the origin of ideas, we see that all are acquired. The senses convey perceptions into the mind, and how this is done, physically or psychologically, Locke leaves to others to decide. As they enter the mind, they are either simple or complex, depending on what they were objectively.[34] Yet the mind, according to Locke, does not leave them uncultivated. As a separate process, which involves all the mysteries of internal experience, the mind manipulates experience, and in the end it is different from what it was on a perceptual level. This suggests a compositional theory: the mind composes from raw material and arrives at meaning or ideas not explicitly contained in the original perceptions. This brings us to the question: what precisely was Locke's empiricism? It is implicit in the theory of *tabula rasa* for which Locke is famous: the mind is originally a blank page on which nothing is written. Experience stocks the mind; but experience is not narrow or limited, and it consists both of sensation and reflection. In other words, the mind is capable of great departures from sensory experience, although sensory experiences are always the foundations on which these departures stand. This is the gist of Locke's empiricism: "All those sublime thoughts which tower above the clouds, and reach as high as heaven itself, take their rise and footing here: in all that great extent wherein the mind wanders in those remote speculations it may seem to be elevated with, it stirs not one jot beyond those ideas which sense or reflection have offered for its contemplation." [35]

Now we should inquire into the pedagogical implications of Locke's position. Did his polemic on innate ideas alter the course of education? Nowhere in the *Essay* does Locke stop to point to the educational consequences of his argument, and one must look very hard at the *Essay* if he is to find any bridging of the gap between psychological theory and educational practice. Yet, because Locke was often believed, and precisely because his theory was counted as credible, his doctrine on ideas and their origin could not have avoided affecting teaching and learning.

In the first place, by discrediting any claims for innate knowledge or self-evident principles, Locke put both tradition and authority in jeopardy; at least he put them on the defensive. Reason, replacing both, was the instrument for weighing meaning in experience; rational pro-

---

34 *Ibid.*, II, vii–x.
35 *Ibid.*, II, i, 24.

cesses sifted the valid from the invalid, and reason, not tradition or authority, was the judge of what was true, practical, and useful.[36] When the implications here were taken seriously—and often they were not—a school's curriculum jettisoned reams of its old literature. Locke shed no tears about this, for he remembered vividly, and apparently with some pain, his own educational adventures in the Westminster School. If we remember the curricula of the period's humanistically-oriented grammar schools, we shall have to agree that most of their subjects were justified by a tradition built on ancient educational authorities. Latin, Locke knew, held a privileged position in the curriculum because early Christian humanists had invested it with divine qualities. But this should not, in an enlightened age, be enough to justify its dominance. Locke did not sweep away Latin, although he valued it half-heartedly, and then only when its practical value could be demonstrated.[37]

Locke, we have said, was not a schoolmaster, and he should not be expected to write like one. He was a philosopher, and the problems he dealt with, although having educational consequences, were always kept on a philosophical level. Even in *Some Thoughts Concerning Education,* where his broad educational objectives may be assumed, he remains aloof from, and indifferent to, purely pedagogical issues.

If reason is the only guide to truth, and Locke asserted it was, the principal duty of education was not storing the mind from the treasuries of the past, but training the faculty of reason.

Training reason meant a number of things. First, it meant perfecting understanding; and this was done by having experiences to test and form it. In addition, it meant immunizing understanding from the contagion of emotion. Apart from a basic antiemotional bias, Locke knew that emotions could color experience and destroy its meaning; they could stand as obstacles to the full functioning of reason. Reason could not function at all without information. Here, of course, the senses as avenues for knowledge from the outside world are stressed, but this emphasis alone did not generate a curricular revolution. When the classics were studied, and when their content was accepted as most worth knowing, the senses were employed as much as in a laboratory. So Locke did not enjoin reading, or condemn all traditional knowledge, yet he emphasized the need for scholastic innovation. The books commonly used were out-of-touch with reality, and they perpetuated unexamined, irrelevant assumptions. Locke wanted the mind informed by fresh examinations of the social and physical worlds. Still, he was not so persuasive that schools followed him entirely or at once, but he raised new goals for them and when they were followed empirical rather than rationalistic methods began to make headway.

[36] See *Of the Conduct of the Understanding* (Garforth ed.) , 3.
[37] *Some Thoughts,* 168.3.

Finally, Locke's doctrine on innate ideas and its corollary *tabula rasa* made for a certain theoretical equality among men. At birth no one had any more or better ideas than anyone else. And though Locke may not have intended this (he recognized individual differences in capacity) his theory endowed education and training with additional importance: if men begin with nothing, nurture must take precedence over nature. Thus, though Locke did not cherish the distinction, he must be credited with the extraordinary confidence later generations had in education— sometimes even thinking it a panacea.

While there are psychological implications in Locke's *Essay*, especially in Book II, it is hard to see him as an authentic psychologist. He was more concerned about knowledge itself than about the act of knowing, and thus he was more logician and metaphysician than psychologist. Yet the psychological significance of the *Essay* cannot be gainsaid, for Locke displayed an interest in psychological topics, and attracted a great deal of attention to them.[38]

Locke, as we have said, regarded himself as a philosopher, and the problems of philosophy were his first concern; he was willing to leave to others the task of spelling out psychological and pedagogical implications. Yet, a word here is needed to indicate his main psychological interests, interests he was almost forced to articulate in order to give his *Essay* a quality of philosophical adequacy. Admitting his primary interest to be the *what* of knowledge, he was not thus absolved from considering the act of knowing. And though he does not go very far toward enlightening us on the act of knowing, he did set the stage: to study the act of knowing he recommended, first, introspection, and, second, observation of behavior.[39]

Locke not only recommended but used observation of behavior to arrive at psychological information. He noted what children did at various levels of development, and he watched animals too, and from the employment of this method he was able to deduce some of the external operations of psychology. Even when such information was deemed essential to an understanding of the act of knowing, it was always subordinated, in Locke's method, to reflection or introspection. This was the operation of what Locke chose to call the internal sense. Introspection is a psychological process whereby the mind takes notice of its own operations; that is, it views perception, memory, comparison, and even reflection itself at work. What is learned is pooled, and from this pool of information about internal mental processes something significant can be concluded about human psychology. While Locke undoubtedly knew some information reaped this way would not be entirely accurate or dependable, especially in its reporting, he was nevertheless fairly con-

[38] See Aaron, *op. cit.*, p. 119.
[39] *Essay*, II, i, 4–6. Locke uses the term "reflection" rather than "introspection."

fident that introspection was the best source of man's knowledge about himself. He took seriously the Socratic injunction, know thyself, and thus attributed to introspection a far more central role in giving psychological testimony than do most modern psychologists.

For all his confidence in introspection, Locke did not counsel its uncritical employment. The early years of life were the years for seeking information, for opening the senses and allowing experiences to pass through them. Perhaps these were the years for training the senses to ensure authentic knowledge. But these were not the years when reflection would produce much of worth; adulthood was the period of life when the mind was best able to turn in on itself and try to understand its operations.[40] Locke is not entirely silent about child psychology, and he recognizes this stage of human development as an important one, but he gives far more attention to, and expects better results from, adult psychology.

When Locke used the term faculty in connection with man's two mental powers—thinking and willing—it is easy to believe that he is associating himself with the faculty theory. We know how faculty psychology had defended various mental powers—memory, perception, judgment, understanding, and so on—as distinct agents of the mind, and argued that they, much like muscles, could be developed through proper exercise. This theory, we know too, had made a deep impression on formal education and often came perilously close to dominating curricular theory.[41] It is not easy to determine how Locke, while not an exponent of the theory, reinforced it and prolonged its life.[42] Yet, when faculty psychologists were searching for support, they enlisted Locke among their ranks and did not bother to read his disclaimer of a faculty theory:

> These powers of the mind, viz. of perceiving, and of preferring, are usually called by another name; and the ordinary way of speaking is, that the understanding and will are two faculties of the mind: a word proper enough, if it be used as all words should be, so as not to breed any confusion in men's thoughts by being supposed (as I suspect it has been) to stand for some real being in the soul, that performed those actions of understanding and volition. For when we say, the will is the commanding and superior faculty of the soul, that it is, or is not, free; that it determines the inferior faculties; that it follows the dictates of the understanding, etc.; though these and the like expressions, by those that carefully attend to their own ideas, and conduct their thoughts more by the evidence of things than the sound of words, may be understood in a clear and distinct sense; yet

40 *Ibid.*, II, i, 8.

41 See Walter B. Kolesnik, *Mental Discipline in Modern Education* (Madison, University of Wisconsin Press, 1958).

42 See V. T. Thayer, *The Misinterpretation of Locke as a Formalist in Educational Philosophy* (Madison, University of Wisconsin Press, 1921).

I suspect, I say, that this way of speaking of faculties has misled many into a confused notion of so many distinct agents in us, which had their several provinces and authorities, and did command, obey, and perform several actions, and so many distinct beings, which has been no small occasion of wrangling, obscurity, and uncertainty in questions relating to them.[43]

Locke's statement leaves little room for doubt: he was not advocating a theory of faculty psychology, although he uses the term "faculty" and often with too little precision.

The tradition has not been put to rest that Locke's theory of psychology made the mind a passive agent, capable of reacting but incapable of action. Yet, a more careful study reveals his assignment to the mind of capacities by no means wholly passive. The senses reach out for data, but the mind is involved directing the scope of their quest. Far more important in Locke's psychology than this subordinate issue surrounding mental activity or passivity is the theory of man's nature: Is man material, immaterial, or partly material and partly immaterial? We are now at an important and perennial question in psychology—mind-body relationship.

Locke wanted to be dualistic, and his writings contain clear indications of his preference,[44] but he was not a traditional dualist, and this departure from Christian psychology embroiled him with philosophers in the Christian Church and was the main source of his alleged unorthodoxy. When Locke accepted dualism, it was not to affirm the essential composite of matter and spirit—that man's body is material, his soul spiritual. He could not embrace either spiritual or material monism, because his observations did not allow him to, and evidence was lacking for making the mind an essentially immaterial part of man. He wondered if God could not have added the quality of mind to an essentially material body. He was fairly certain of matter's inability to think, and he knew men thought, but he could not see why God could not have made a kind of human-thinking matter.[45]

While he preferred to believe in a traditional dualism, evidence to support it, he asserted, was unattainable. In fact, he thought, there was better evidence for believing that men are material with the power of thought added.[46]

This doctrine was most dangerous to religion and morality: it called into question the full message of Christian theology by challenging the doctrine of immortality. If man is only a thinking body, nothing whatever can be said about an after life, for man's body ends with death. Why

---

[43] *Essay,* II, xxi, 6.
[44] *Ibid.,* II, xxiii, 15.
[45] *Ibid.,* IV, iii, 6.
[46] *Ibid.*

should moral laws be observed if eternal rewards are myths? In the end, however, Locke demurs from elaborating a definitive mind-body theory; he raised doubts, pointed to good evidence, and concluded that the inner natures of mind and body are forever hidden.[47] Even this agnosticism is unorthodox, for it still questions the traditional psychological assumptions of Christianity, and it kept Locke always in the role of a philosopher to be controverted and avoided.

A word should be added on Locke's moral philosophy, and this is done for two reasons: first, coming after his doubts about immortality, it serves to establish Locke as a firm, even devout, believer in a binding moral law, and, second, because Locke made morality education's principal objective,[48] we should know something about his conception of objective morality.

Locke could be pragmatic without being an ethical pragmatist. On the subject of morality he is obviously practical: morality must be given first place in education because in all human life nothing is more important; social, political, and economic life would become chaotic and unmanageable without a moral code. Ordinary moral knowledge, obtained from conventional sources, is endorsed by Locke, but because it is often unsure and sometimes inexact, more than ordinary knowledge is needed. Locke talks about an eternally true system of morals, a system having a scientific foundation, and he affirms the possibility of a science of morals.[49] He stops there, however, without producing the science. Yet he clearly makes the foundation of moral science rest on the being of God.[50] God is the ultimate source of moral law, but there is a natural moral law that men must observe too.[51] The instrument for codifying and interpeting both divine and natural law is reason.[52] So Locke has made a full circle and is back where he started, with man's reason. The purpose of education, its supreme objective, is to perfect human reason. And now we should try to see Locke prescribing an educational program to ensure an attainment of this objective.

IV

EDUCATIONAL ATTITUDES

While there are intimate connections between *An Essay Concerning Human Understanding* and *Some Thoughts Concerning Education*, it is

47 *Ibid.*
48 *Some Thoughts*, 136.
49 *Essay*, IV, iii, 18.
50 *Ibid.*, I, iii, 12.
51 *Ibid.*, I, iii, 13.
52 *Ibid.*, II, xxi, 49.

by no means clear that Locke's educational views were systematically formed as logical outcomes from the *Essay*. In a broad sense, we may think of *Some Thoughts* as supplementary to the *Essay*, for it is probably true that all Locke's writings are supplemental to it, yet *Some Thoughts* has an anecdotal quality which is somehow inconsistent with objective scientific thought.

The origin of *Some Thoughts* explains its discursiveness: Locke's friends importuned him to write about formal education and give them a guide for the education and upbringing of their children. Locke responded to this appeal by writing several letters in which he gave directions on education, but they always kept him at arm's length from actual pedagogical involvement. He wrote, not as a schoolmaster, but as a generous philosopher willing to share some of his thoughts on education. The title of the compiled letters is entirely accurate: taken together they reveal Locke's attitudes about many educational questions, but they ignore, or only touch, other issues which, if treated, would qualify *Some Thoughts* as a systematic expression of educational philosophy. To achieve adequacy a philosophy of education must apply both to formal and informal education, to ends and means, to all levels of education, and to everyone engaged in the educational process. Locke did not go so far. He avoided practical classroom issues, was preoccupied with informal education, and, in *Some Thoughts,* neglected to say anything about the education of common men.

Despite these lacunae, Locke had many interesting and influential insights to share with his friends. We should be concerned, then, not with pointing to the items he left untouched but with following him on the topics he discussed.

At the outset Locke introduces us to his basic conviction: education makes men. "I think I may say, that of all the men we meet with, nine parts of ten are what they are, good or evil, useful or not, by their education." [53] We should add, however, that Locke is not thinking of the schoolroom or what schoolmasters do, whether they are capable or inept, but of the broader formation of men in their homes and in society generally. His own educational program, encompassing home training, grammar school and universities, gave pride of place to home training; this interlude, supervised by a father, and shorter in duration than formal schooling, was always endowed with superior qualities. Locke, therefore, cannot be absolved from a charge of nostalgia when he writes directions to his friends: he reminds us of an adult who, with feelings of self-satisfaction about his own success, opines that the education which proved valuable for him is certainly good for everyone.

[53] John Locke, *Some Thoughts Concerning Education,* R. H. Quick, ed. (Cambridge, The University Press, 1880) I. Subsequent quotations from *Some Thoughts* are from this edition.

Although these caveats are not easily purged from one's thoughts in reading *Some Thoughts,* they are somewhat beside the point. In the human enterprise of education, experience is the most valid test. An educational program producing the best man is the educational program to be supported and extended. And Locke confidently assumed the test of experience was on his side: he found parts of his own educational experience worth endorsing, but he recognized other parts meriting his most acerbic condemnation.

If we look at the *Essay,* we are reminded of Locke's preoccupation with reason, and we assume that in *Some Thoughts* we shall be told how to train reason. In a way this is done, but always indirectly. Locke is not anti-intellectual, nor is he preoccupied with intellectual training; he begins by remarking on the importance of physical development and good health, and then he treats of moral education. Precedence goes not to intellectual development, or, for that matter, to physical formation, which are mentioned first, but to morality.

The following statements are unequivocal; reading them we know where Locke stands on the question of educational purpose:

> That which every Gentleman (that takes any care of his education) desires for his Son, besides the estate he leaves him, is contain'd (I suppose) in these four things, *Virtue, Wisdom, Breeding,* and *Learning.* I will not trouble myself whether these Names do not some of them stand for the same Thing, or really include one another. It serves my Turn here to follow the popular Use of these Words, which, I presume, is clear enough to make me understood, and I hope there will be no Difficulty to comprehend my Meaning.[54]

> I place *Virtue* as the first and most necessary of these Endowments that belong to a Man or a Gentleman, as absolutely requisite to make him valued and beloved by others, acceptable or tolerable to himself. Without that, I think, he will be happy neither in this, nor in the other World.[55]

Locke supposed that all kinds of natural virtue accompanied maturation, though details about process are lacking, but he stresses neither natural virtue nor reason as the true foundation of virtue. The foundation of virtue, the place where education in virtue must begin, is with a "true notion of God." The child should be taught, or told, in clear and simple language, that God is the "independent Supreme Being, Author and Maker of all Things, from who we receive all our Good, who loves us, and gives us all things: and, consequent to this, instil into him a Love and Reverence of this Supreme Being." [56] This uncomplicated theology was intended to save the child from confusion; it avoided ques-

54 *Ibid.,* 134.
55 *Ibid.,* 135.
56 *Ibid.,* 136.

tions relating to God's nature, content to impress on his mind the fact that God governs everything, He hears and sees everything, and does good things for those who love and obey Him. This was enough to start; possibly, larger theological impressions were never needed, for Locke is concerned to put into place a foundation for virtue, not to indoctrinate the child in a religious creed. However, to reinforce these foundational beliefs, or only to maintain them, Locke told his readers to teach the child to pray. Besides faith in God and prayer, the child should be taught how to be truthful, good-natured, and modest.[57]

Wisdom, the next objective, is, Locke admits, beyond the reach of children, although, as with virtue, they may be prepared for it by their parents and tutors.[58] Locke does not give us many details of his meaning of wisdom or on how to ensure its inculcation. First, he suggests, wisdom is man's ability to manage his business ably, but Locke is not really concerned with businessmen, and, even if he were, such competence would have little meaning for youth who lacked both experience for such affairs and opportunities for practice. By mentioning business actions Locke is able to speak against cunning, which he understands to be the same as deceit, but he really meant to say that children should, from the beginning, be accustomed to the "true Notion of things"; their minds should be raised to great and worthy thoughts and they should be kept "at a distance from falsehood and cunning." This, he says, "is the Fittest preparation of a Child for Wisdom . . . to accustom them to Truth and Sincerity; to a submission to Reason; and, as much as may be, to Reflection on their own Actions." [59]

Once Locke has made virtue and wisdom the principal educational goals, he treats of good breeding. Neither Locke nor his readers needed convincing of its worth, and he is thus freed from proving its right to be listed among the characteristics most important to an educated gentleman. Good breeding means what we expect it to mean; as Locke expressed it, good breeding is a happy combination of humility and assurance. He wants a gentleman to carry himself well—and this, in part, is an outcome of physical culture—and he wants him to meet people easily and good naturedly, to be comfortable in any company, great or small. The dangers to good breeding, or civility, are many, but Locke selects four which, to his mind, are most ominous: roughness, contempt for others, censoriousness, and captiousness. We need not dwell on good breeding; Locke's notice of it may be concluded with this statement: "*Civility* therefore is what, in the first place, should with great care be made habitual to Children and young People." [60]

---

57 *Ibid.*, 139.
58 *Ibid.*, 140.
59 *Ibid.*
60 *Ibid.*, 143.4.

Learning, last among education's purposes in Locke's enumeration, has this place because Locke sincerely thinks it belongs last. He is quite clear when he says that learning can be of great help to virtue, wisdom, and civility, but he goes on to say: "I imagine you would think him a very foolish Fellow, that should not value a virtuous, or a wise Man, infinitely before a great Scholar." [61] Nowhere in *Some Thoughts* does Locke consider learning unnecessary, and he is specific about the intellectual accomplishments most befitting a gentleman, but he wants to be sure that first things are attended to first. In the hierarchy of educational objectives learning is subordinate to virtue, wisdom, and civility.

With the course set for education, we are now in a position to look at some of the topics Locke stressed as young men climbed the educational ladder. At this point, we should see the parts of the curriculum most intimately related to the goal of learning.

Locke never tires of deploring the then contemporary emphasis on humanistic education, which then meant language study. Time and again he returns to a familiar theme: too much time is wasted in trying to teach boys Latin and Greek. But, of course, Locke entertained no special contempt for these languages, and in another time he would have declaimed against other overemphases; what he stressed was a principle of scholastic relevance. He did not see, nor did experience prove, curricular pride of place for either language.

Yet, Locke did not completely proscribe Latin and Greek. He allowed their study when students were ready, but on the condition that they were necessary for a life-time vocation. Usually, only Latin of the classical languages could meet this condition, but even then schooling should not begin with Latin study.[62]

Reading, writing, and learning, Locke wrote, are necessary but they are not the chief business of education,[63] so in the latter part of the discourse he proceeds to the content of schooling.

A long tradition in education, with obscure origins, prescribed age seven as the right age for beginning formal schooling. The Greeks followed this tradition unquestioningly, and the Romans, never doubting Greek wisdom, followed suit. With the weight of tradition to sustain them neither medieval nor humanistic schoolmen stopped to inquire about the validity of this tradition. Locke, however, is ready to jettison all age-readiness assumptions; begin formal learning with reading, he says, and the child is usually ready to read when he can talk.[64]

Play in learning, neither untested nor unknown before Locke, but not generally countenanced in the best educational circles, was revived

61 *Ibid.*, 147.
62 *Ibid.*, 164.
63 *Ibid.*, 147.
64 *Ibid.*, 148.

and made a credible technique in *Some Thoughts*.[65] His point is: the child at the tender age when reading begins is unable to understand the utility of reading, and thus natural motivation is lacking. For good results, motivation must be generated, and the common practice was to drive students to their work and keep them at it with fear; the schoolmaster's rod was the principal instrument of education.[66] Locke refused to accept any of this; and he must have been a heretic to many of his contemporaries when he preferred to allow achievement in studies to lag than to create aversion to learning by resorting to compulsion. In an ideal situation superintended by a skillful tutor, neither delay nor compulsion need intrude on the learning process. Learning to read should not be work, for if it is introduced to the child not as a task, but as a privilege, it should be fun. Here is a hint of soft pedagogy, but Locke did not mean it to be. The natures of children are not adapted to work, and forcing work on them will only injure and distort their natures.[67] He wanted progress in learning, but he was unwilling to destroy the child to get it. And he was convinced, moreover, that the best learning could be obtained by depending on play motivation. All this is good, but it obviously demands a teacher of unusual skill and extraordinary knowledge of children. Unfortunately, Locke says nothing about the preparation of talented teachers. His university career allowed him to know that teachers with these credentials were not produced in English universities, so leaving this matter entirely to chance is, indeed, a curious and notable omission.

The syllabus for beginning reading is given with details in *Some Thoughts*,[68] but here it is enough to say that Locke recommended an easy and pleasant exposure to reading. *Aesop's Fables* were the best, he thought, and although substitutes are possible they are not mentioned in the text. After instruction in reading begins, the Lord's Prayer, the Creed, and the Ten Commandments are introduced and, in the end, are committed to memory. The recommended process for learning by heart is not silent reading and rereading, but one where the teacher repeats aloud the material to be memorized.[69] Selected parts of the Bible need attention too, but the Bible as a whole, Locke was afraid, would overwhelm young students and introduce ideas too advanced for them.[70]

Writing follows reading, and Locke spares few details on the mechanics of good writing, even giving advice on how to hold a pen, but he is indifferent to the content of a child's writing.[71] He thinks this is too

65 *Ibid.*, 148 and 150.
66 *Ibid.*, 147.
67 *Ibid.*, 149.
68 *Ibid.*, 148–159.
69 *Ibid.*, 157.
70 *Ibid.*, 158.
71 *Ibid.*, 160.

early to care about composition, and when the child is able to write clearly and legibly, drawing is added to the syllabus.

Reading, writing, and drawing are all preliminary to foreign-language study; and, of course, Locke assumes the child's general competence in English before any foreign language is introduced.[72] French seemed to Locke the best beginning, possibly because of its general currency among English gentlemen or possibly because its practical value and meaning were clear. The point stressed in connection with the study of French is to learn it according to the conversational method. English boys should learn to speak French the same way French boys learned to speak it. There was no talk about grammar and there was no need to go into the intricacies of the language, important undoubtedly for its written use.[73]

After a year or two of French—Locke is this imprecise, for he no doubt assumes variations in time from child to child—Latin should be undertaken.[74] Again, the method followed in French study is prescribed. Latin, Locke allows, is absolutely necessary to a gentleman, but he is quick to add that it is practically useless to others.[75] At this point concentration in instruction is on speaking the language; the rules of grammar, foolish for this level of teaching, Locke maintains, are to be ignored.

With fundamentals accounted for, and the study of Latin well begun, the student is ready for arithmetic, geography, astronomy, chronology, anatomy, some parts of history, and a general knowledge important for filling in the gaps of experience. Locke treats each of these subjects at some length and his ideas on them may easily be gathered by consulting *Some Thoughts*.[76] His recommendations relative to their organization, or the methods employed for their teaching, are not especially novel. As a matter of fact, there is no very good evidence for believing anything more than a logical approach was recommended, and this is strange because on the earlier levels we are introduced to a carefully formulated plan for a psychological approach to teaching. Either Locke has tired of stressing the role of the teacher, and simply assumes his significance, or he has relegated the teacher to a subordinate position. The evidence for the latter is too strong to ignore: if a good tutor is not available, use good books, Locke says.[77] If this recommendation were taken seriously—and it may have been—Locke would have set back teaching by a half-century. We may be permitted to wonder, too, where these good books, all substitutes for a good tutor, were to be found, and

72 *Ibid.*, 162.
73 *Ibid.*
74 *Ibid.*, 163.
75 *Ibid.*, 165.
76 *Ibid.*, 179–194.
77 *Ibid.*, 167.

what parent was able to make the proper selection. Locke may not have been a disciple of Comenius—he may never have read his works—yet, here he shows some of the same naive confidence in books that Comenius had previously shown.

Locke, we may suppose, has taken us quickly through the syllabus of elementary and secondary education. But he has some afterthoughts, and he wants to share them with his readers. First, he wants us to know, the central problem in all instruction is keeping the learner's attention. He admits that keeping and directing attention is the main talent of skillful teachers, although when the parent must depend more on himself than on a teacher, he can maintain attention by stressing the use the learner can make of the subject he is studying and, further, by showing interest in, and love for, the child.[78]

Earlier in the discourse Locke dismissed grammar, so he wants to return to the subject to clarify his meaning and to retrieve part of the subject he had appeared to jettison.[79] He never intended, he admits, to expurgate grammar entirely from school studies, but he does want to be perfectly clear about its clientele: grammar should be studied only by grown men, and then usually only by scholars. Scholars, of course, have the greatest need for it, but there are others for whom speaking and writing with precision is important, and they may pursue the study of grammar with profit. For ordinary discourse, the kind in which most English gentlemen engage, grammar study is unnecessary. Locke placed no value on grand and elegant discourse, and in his own writing he shows us how far one can go by ignoring both.

If grammar is to be studied, Locke has more to say about it. In general, he has two rules: one, grammar should not be studied until the student is able to speak the language; two, it should come as an introduction to rhetoric, and Locke is plainly critical of rhetoric's prominence in the schools.[80]

Locke concludes *Some Thoughts* by giving us advice on a variety of pedagogical questions, although his advice is largely theoretical. These topics may be handled quickly and directly, for they have no central theme.

Translation exercises which filled the schools were accepted only when they could be transformed into real learning experiences. Locke had no time for translations that stopped with a mere knowledge of words. Compositions were to be written only when students had something to say, and, assuming this would be seldom, themes appeared in school programs infrequently. When these compositions were written, however, English should be used. Here Locke contradicted accepted

[78] *Ibid.*
[79] *Ibid.,* 168.1–3.
[80] *Ibid.,* 168.3.

school practices, for no tutor or teacher would think of excusing any boy from Latin prose writing. If prose composition was infrequently and reluctantly allowed, verse making was always rigorously proscribed. Poetry, Locke stated, is a sheer waste of time. Law, however, is something every gentleman needs to know, and some time should be reserved for it.[81]

Dancing, music, fencing, and riding, additional accomplishments worthy of gentlemen, should be learned. And now, neither we nor Locke's contemporaries expected this recommendation, young men should learn a trade.[82] Locke did not foresee gentlemen working to make a living, but it was good for everyone, he thought, to do something practical. Painting caught his fancy, but, he admitted, others might prefer something else; a country gentleman, for example, is advised to learn something about husbandry.[83]

Finally, travel is mentioned for its educational values.[84] Locke supposed that the young men whose education interested him would travel on the Continent, and such travel had his full approval if trips were taken after the tender schoolboy years.

The part of *Some Thoughts* dealing with learning as a goal of education is terminated by an appeal to see education in broad terms: a teacher "should remember, that his Business is not so much to teach . . . all that is knowable, as to raise in [the student] a Love and Esteem of Knowledge; and to put him in the right Way of knowing and improving himself, when he has a Mind to it." [85]

If Locke had too little to say about teaching and learning processes to satisfy schoolmasters searching for a pedagogical handbook, his attitudes did nevertheless generate a rethinking of educational goals and means by theorists. But because Locke's work, either in the *Essay* or in *Some Thoughts,* never had a handbook character, time again was needed to allow for a transmogrification of educational issues from the library to the schoolroom, from the theoretician to the practitioner. Locke was listened to, but not at once.

As the translations of Locke's attitudes were made and then applied to educational programs some confusion was bound to intrude because Locke's thought often ran counter to accepted conventions, and some of his would-be followers tried to make him entirely orthodox; in other words, attempts were made to interpret his views to support existing school practices. Educators who recognized Locke as a revolutionary thinker and tried to implement his doctrines, sometimes drifted away

81 *Ibid.,* 187.
82 *Ibid.,* 201.
83 *Ibid.,* 204.
84 *Ibid.,* 212.
85 *Ibid.,* 195.

from the fundamentals of his thought. This was fairly easy because Locke is often imprecise and sometimes contradicts himself.[86]

No doubt most confusion was bred around the theory of formal discipline. This theory with tradition's support—great educators from Quintilian to Erasmus had advocated it—stood as the bedrock of educational practice. How could Locke be taken seriously if he doubted or questioned an unassailable educational precept? Naturally the disciplinarians wanted Locke on their side, and when they read Locke they looked for selections tending to support them. When they found him talking about faculties in the *Essay,* they were ready to make him their champion, for if there are faculties in the mind—agents for doing certain things—it seemed reasonable that these faculties could be strengthened through proper exercise. But when Locke used the term faculty, he never meant to join forces with the disciplinarians.[87]

The argument about Locke's stand on the issue of formal discipline has lasted too long. It would long since have been laid to rest if educational historians had taken Locke at his word. Too often they did not, and thus they were responsible for perpetuating a myth making Locke an advocate of the doctrine or, at least, allowing him to be ambivalent about it. Some historians even credited him with founding the theory. However, almost all of *Some Thoughts* could be quoted to controvert the distorted picture of Locke as a formal disciplinarian. And he did not stand at a halfway house undecided about the direction to take. Late in *Some Thoughts* he meets the issue squarely, and is satisfied that his meaning is clear. Although extensive quoting would be illuminating, it may not be necessary to make the point; a few excerpts will do:

> I hear it said, That children should be employ'd in getting things by heart, to exercise and improve their Memories. I could wish this were said with as much Authority of Reason, as it is with Forwardness of Assurance; and that this Practice were established upon good Observation, more than old Custom; for it is evident, that Strength of Memory is owing to a happy Constitution, and not to any habitual Improvement got by Exercise. 'Tis true, what the Mind is intent upon, and for fear of letting it slip, often imprints afresh on itself by frequent Reflection, that it is apt to retain, but still according to its own natural Strength of Retention. An Impression made on Beeswax or Lead will not last so long as on Brass or Steel. Indeed, if it be renew'd often, it may last the longer; but every new reflecting on it is a new Impression, and it is from thence one is to reckon, if one would know how long the Mind retains it. But the learning Pages of *Latin* by Heart, no more fits the Memory for Retention of anything else, than the graving of one Sentence in Lead, makes it the more capable of retaining firmly any other Characters.[88]

[86] See Thayer, *op. cit.;* and Walter B. Kolesnik, "John Locke and the Theory of Formal Discipline," *Catholic Educational Review,* 57 (1959), pp. 181–188.

[87] See *Essay,* II, xi, 14; and II, xxi, pp. 17–19.

[88] *Some Thoughts,* 176.

Locke then goes on to admit the importance of good memories and to give examples from history of men with exceptional memories who could not have had them strengthened according to the conventional prescriptions, and he then adds: "I do not mean hereby that there should be no Exercise given to Children's Memories. I think their Memories should be employ'd, but not in learning by rote whole Pages out of Books, which, the Lesson being once said, and that Task over, are delivered up again to Oblivion and neglected forever. This mends neither the Memory nor the Mind." [89] The best aids to memory, Locke asserts, are use and attention, and he comes close to saying that we remember the things important to us. Then he adds a last charge against the accepted practice of improving the memory by centering studies on Latin and the languages and expresses what seems to him to be a proper view of mental discipline.

> But under whose Care soever a Child is put to be taught, during the tender and flexible Years of his Life, this is certain, it should be one who thinks *Latin* and *Language* the least Part of Education; one, who knowing how much Virtue, and a well-temper'd Soul, is to be preferred to any sort of *Learning* or *Language,* makes it his chief Business to form the Mind of his Scholars, and give that a right Disposition: which, if once got, though all the rest should be neglected, would, in due Time, produce all the rest; and which if it be not got, and settled, so as to keep out ill and vicious Habits, *Languages* and *Sciences,* and all the other Accomplishments of Education, will be to no purpose, but to make the worse or more dangerous Man.[90]

If educators became excited over Locke's stand on formal discipline, they were no less excited about his outright affirmation of *tabula rasa:* the doctrine making the mind of the child blank, devoid of impressions or ideas until experience imprints them. Why this doctrine should have excited educators and philosophers is unclear; yet many theorists spent an inordinate amount of time denouncing the Lockian view. To say the least, it was a most unpopular version of man's mind. Whether or not Locke's evidence was as full as it should have been, or whether or not he was led to the right conclusion by it, *tabula rasa* opened the gates of educational thinking in two important areas: first, by maintaining that the mind was at birth a blank tablet, Locke provided the groundwork for developmental psychology; second, by affirming that everyone began with neither preformed sensations nor ideas, Locke shaped an important plank in the philosophy of human equality. So much Locke was willing to concede: men began from the same place. They differed in their capacities to gain experience and profit from it.

While Locke undoubtedly meant what he said about original equality, he nevertheless gave most of his attention to the formation of

89 *Ibid.*
90 *Ibid.,* 177.

gentlemen. His essay on *Working Schools* was without importance either when written or now, and it hardly qualifies for consideration in his educational theory. Locke's narrowness is strangely inconsistent with all his talk about equality; he is quite clearly interested only in the education of the upper classes.[91]

The theoretical lines between educational utilitarianism and disciplinarianism are sharply drawn, but in practice the demarcation is often hidden. It is easy to advocate the teaching of only useful or practical things, on the one hand, or to defend teaching for forming the mind, leading it to good habits, and guaranteeing a wise and judicial disposition, on the other. But in the schoolroom, the curriculum intended to form the mind may also be useful, and subjects presented because of their obvious practicality and applicability in life may also serve to refine and form the mind. Locke saw all this clearly and was unwilling to be drawn into indefensible extremism. He counseled selection: Latin, for example, could be useful for some students but not for others, and it would always carry its weight in forming the mind. But in doing this it performed no unique service to learning. Locke wisely advises educators to build a relevant curriculum; and when they do neither use nor discipline will be missed. It is incorrect, therefore, to interpret Locke's balanced view as narrow utilitarianism, for neither he nor anyone else would want children to learn meaningless things. He does append a thought, however, warning against any misjudgment of the educational importance of vernacular language: all learning must begin with it.[92] At the same time, despite this emphasis, he nowhere proscribes conventional humanistic education for students who can profit from it. All in all, it is hard to see how Locke can stand as an enemy of any meaningful subject or branch of study.

Locke can be both broad and liberal in his educational thought, but he is a man of his own generation, content to perpetuate apparent educational inadequacies. Nowhere is this clearer than in Locke's assertions about the priority of private over public schooling. His context made private schooling tutorial; public schooling was learning in common with several students. This item, we admit, was of ancient vintage and perennial in appearance; even the best theorists had disagreed about it, and we would have thought that at Locke's point in history the shortcomings of tutorial instruction were too clear for Locke to have avoided accepting public schools as a matter of social necessity. Yet he refused, and his principal reason for withholding approval was that virtue, his first goal for education, could not be guaranteed in them.[93]

[91] See W. Kendall, *John Locke and the Doctrine of Majority Rule* (Urbana, University of Illinois Press, 1941).

[92] *Some Thoughts*, 160 and 162.

[93] *Ibid.*, 94.

Finally, in this account of Locke's educational attitudes, we should mention his willingness to include religion in the educational program. Locke, to be sure not always an orthodox Christian thinker, was never an enemy of religion. We have noted how the child began learning with faith in God and how throughout life divine ordinances served as the foundation for virtue. Locke would be a poor witness for litigants wanting education to reject religion.

We are reluctant to end this chapter on Locke's educational views without appending remarks concerning his indebtedness to educators who preceded him. According to conventional opinion, Locke was a highly independent thinker and depended on his own background and good common sense for the positions he took. This view contains some truth, and Locke contributes to it, for he never notifies his readers when he is following others or when his thoughts are formed from the froth and foam of theories antedating his. Yet, there are striking parallels between Locke and Quintilian, and they should not go unnoticed. They do not compel us to say that Locke followed Quintilian, but they make us wonder.

A principal difficulty in tracing relationships between them, except where Quintilian is writing as a schoolmaster, is that both expressed plain educational common sense. If this is the case, why should Locke be called upon to account for the origin of his ideas, and why should he have turned to Quintilian or anyone else? This, however, may not be an entirely satisfactory answer; for if they dispensed educational common sense and little else, why were they so often separated from conventional school practices? It is surely a curious assertion to say that these men had a monopoly on common sense. But the point is that if both Quintilian and Locke were engaged in writing commonplaces, attribution of influence is impossible.

Despite what may be believed about common sense in pedagogy, there remain interesting comparisons between Quintilian's and Locke's thought and advice, although we must be prepared to admit there are some important contrasts too. First, both agreed on reading as the starting point for formal study; reading was introduced when the child was able to speak well. Locke, we noted, dismissed the whole business of age-readiness imperatives, and in almost the same language Quintilian had done the same.[94] Both were convinced of the educational primacy of virtue, and both thought its formation should begin at home.[95] Although Quintilian is more detailed than Locke, the latter gives home training more than passing notice. Quite plainly, Locke thinks home training in virtue is essential. Quintilian devotes an entire section in the first book of his famous *Education of an Orator* to the techniques of making learning playlike; he has toys and games in mind as instruments

[94] *Inst. Ora.,* I, i, 15–19.
[95] *Ibid.,* I, i, 4, 7–8; and *Some Thoughts,* 136–139.

for maintaining early learning in a pleasant and enjoyable atmosphere. Locke follows suit, and, while he may ignore some of Quintilian's love of detail, he follows the principle almost exactly.[96]

Mild discipline, proscribing corporal punishment, and declamations against the tyranny of schoolmasters are common to both writers.[97] Neither believed in the isolation of subjects; therefore both share a common view when they recommend their concurrent study.[98] And, interestingly enough, both obviously wrote their guides for the education of children of the rich.

The greatest contrast between Locke and Quintilian, one might quickly assume, lies in their apparently different assignment of worth to useful knowledge. Locke, we know, never accepted useless liberal study; he aimed at the education of a useful English gentleman. Quintilian's emphasis is really no different; the code he expounds, if followed, will end up producing an accomplished orator, and the orator, in Quintilian's perspective, was the most eminently useful of all educated men.

Neither had much confidence in philosophy as a study for young men, although both would apparently accept a philosophy which showed men how to live if it avoided the pitfalls of confusion and formalism. Probably Locke saw a greater chance for the development of a scientific moral philosophy than Quintilian, but neither accepted at face value the pragmatic assumption equating knowledge and virtue.

To be somewhat more complete in this analysis, we should take time to show the main departures Locke made from Quintilian. He never allowed public schooling to substitute for private tutoring; and his refusal was based on fear: virtue would surely be jeopardized by public teaching. While Quintilian noticed dangers to the inculcation of virtue, he nevertheless approved public schools, although, we think, somewhat half-heartedly.[99]

Quintilian initiated his students in the study of Greek when Latin was the vernacular; Locke opposed this.[100] And there is no way of explaining away their disagreement here. Nor is there any way of finding a compromise between Quintilian's preoccupations with grammar and rhetoric and Locke's dismissal of these branches of learning with steady derision.

Finally, we may note, Quintilian often wrote as a schoolmaster and meant his book as a guide to teachers; Locke wrote as an interested educational observer, indifferent to schoolmasters, directing his message to parents. Both, however, wrote about education in their mature years, after much experience, and both were vitally interested in education because of its central role in making men.

---

[96] *Inst. Ora.*, I, i, 26; and *Some Thoughts,* 150.
[97] *Inst. Ora.*, I, i, 13–17; and *Some Thoughts,* 147.
[98] *Inst. Ora.*, I, x, 1; I, xii, 1–7; and *Some Thoughts,* 178.
[99] *Inst. Ora.*, I, ii, 2.
[100] *Ibid.*, I, i, 12; and *Some Thoughts,* 162.

❧ 10 ❧

Rousseau and Pestalozzi: Natural Pedagogy

I

INTRODUCTION

At the threshold of an educational enlightenment we meet Rousseau (1712–1778) and Pestalozzi (1746–1827) with new pedagogical ideas and with recommendations for school practice, since refined, perfected, praised, and condemned. But whether applauded or debased, and whatever the contemporary student's evaluation of Rousseau and Pestalozzi, both endeavored to instigate a much-needed educational revolution. Rousseau's literary and scholarly stature is superior to Pestalozzi's, for the former was more a social philosopher than the latter, and he plowed the furrows of human imagination and thought more deeply.[1] Schoolmasters, however, found Pestalozzi a surer guide, and they sometimes became excited about the possibilities in his novel pedagogy. Pestalozzi talked directly to schoolmasters and tried to keep his elaborations relevant to their day-to-day duties as teachers; a general title for Pestalozzi's compiled works could be "Talks to Teachers."[2]

Both Rousseau and Pestalozzi began by recommending a jettisoning of conventional practice, and both invited schoolmasters to recant traditional pedagogical creeds. With such unorthodox views, neither was accused of being practical. Still, educational apostasy should not have been difficult in the eighteenth century, considering the abundance of

[1] See Jack H. Broome, *Rousseau: A Study of His Thought* (New York, Barnes & Noble, Inc., 1963).

[2] See R. H. Quick's chapter on Pestalozzi in *Essays on Educational Reformers* (London, 1890), pp. 290–383. Although this is an old book—and should generally be considered out-of-date—it contains some interesting and illuminating interpretations. Contemporary critical literature on Pestalozzi is scant, which may indicate that much of Pestalozzi's methodology is now taken for granted.

haphazard theories and techniques then prevalent; but natural inertia stood ominously in the path of improvement and even in the path of desire for improvement. Sometimes teachers retained old ways for the worst of reasons: they were ignorant of, or indifferent to, education's real meaning.[3]

Rousseau and Pestalozzi were right to argue that schooling missed its mark: Rousseau meant that educational programs for upper-class children aimed at artificial accomplishments; [4] Pestalozzi meant that poor children were either ignored by the schools or, when admitted, were fed an educational diet causing their natural talents to atrophy.[5] It is easy to recite the tragic misdeeds of seventeenth- and eighteenth-century education: teachers were either totally unprepared or poorly prepared to enter classrooms; materials of instruction, despite the widespread use of printing and the ardent hopes and clear illustrations of Comenius, were too often primitive and unrewarding; methods of teaching ignored the vital principle of activity in learning and disregarded the need children had for meaningful learning exercises; the curriculum depended heavily on Latin and the classics; education lived in the past, convinced that knowledge of words was more important than knowledge of things, and it disregarded any legitimate need children had for training the senses. Children of the poor were neglected; children from the upper classes wasted their time in schools that handled the wonders of discovery and the joys of learning in mechanical and inartistic ways. Some schoolmasters, unusual and ahead of their time, breathed life into schools and either as tutors or class teachers broke the comfortable circle of accepted school practice to find students' interests and to exploit their natural motivations. Yet, such teachers were always an insignificant and unheralded minority.[6]

Neither Rousseau nor Pestalozzi began with intuitive knowledge of these educational deficiencies. Rousseau, probably because of his unor-

3 See S. E. Ballinger, "The Natural Man: Rousseau," in P. Nash, *The Educated Man* (New York, John Wiley & Sons, Inc., 1965), pp. 225–227.

4 See Jean Jacques Rousseau, *Emile,* translated by Barbara Foxley (New York, E. P. Dutton & Co., Inc., 1938), pp. 43–45. Subsequent quotations from *Emile* are from this edition.

5 J. H. Pestalozzi, *Leonard and Gertrude,* "Preface to the Second Edition," in Henry Barnard, *Pestalozzi and His Educational System* (Syracuse, N.Y., C. W. Bardeen, 1874), p. 523.

6 Both the schools of the Brothers of the Christian Schools and those of the Society of Jesus were conducted by well-qualified teachers, but for all their quality they touched only a small minority of school-age children in France. In addition, the ferment of opposition to Church teaching communities, most incisively expressed in Louis-René de la Chalotais' *Essay on National Education* and *The Constitutions of the Jesuits,* was beginning to take its toll. See F. de La Fontainerie, *French Liberalism and Education in the Eighteenth Century* (New York, McGraw-Hill Book Company, 1932); and Power, *Main Currents in the History of Education* (New York, McGraw-Hill Book Company, 1962), pp. 264–277.

thodox schooling with his father, prefers to remain unbiographical; he does not remind us of Locke [7] when he alludes to his own schooling. It was spared waste.[8] And Pestalozzi is less critical of school practices dominating the teaching scene than many of his contemporaries.[9] Yet both knew how schools were conducted, and both had profound distrust for the conventional educational wisdom, despite the fact that neither used many pages to describe their abhorrence of it. Rousseau, we think, speaks for himself and Pestalozzi in the preface to *Emile:* "I shall say very little about the value of a good education, nor shall I stop to prove that the customary method of education is bad; this has been done again and again, and I do not wish to fill my book with things which every one knows." [10]

Rousseau and Pestalozzi entered the field of educational theory by different routes; even so, they had much in common. According to Rousseau's own word, he began *Emile* at the request of a good intelligent woman who was concerned about the education of her son.[11] This simple request—and there is no reason to think it fiction—seemed at first to require only a short essay, but as Rousseau became engrossed in his work, it became longer, and he saw more fully the importance of education. The essay became a book filled with passion and conviction, and written in a clear, uncomplicated style, its meaning was apparent. Pestalozzi, however, sensing the frustrations of the poor, adopted education as an instrument of social and economic betterment. His inspirations were totally humanitarian, and following them he hoped to help his fellow man by action rather than by writing and talking. Pestalozzi was experimental and action-minded; Rousseau's record was made largely by the force of his pen. Only after Pestalozzi had experienced several unfortunate reversals in various attempts to secure selective social amelioration did he become an author. And then, in *Leonard and Gertrude*,[12] a work intended to set the tone and provide a credo for social and educational reform, he succeeded only in publishing an interesting romantic novel that, though widely read, was never recognized as a manifesto for anything. Pestalozzi felt bitter disappointment at his book's failure, and for

[7] B. Rand, *The Correspondence of John Locke and Edward Clarke* (London, Oxford University Press, 1927) , p. 336.

[8] "I grow more convinced every day that if ever a child received a sound and reasonable education it was I" (*The Minor Educational Writings of Jean Jacques Rousseau,* selected and translated by William Boyd (New York, Bureau of Publications, Teachers College, Columbia University, 1962) , p. 23.)

[9] See Carl Von Raumer, "The Life and Educational System of Pestalozzi," in Barnard, *op. cit.,* pp. 50–51.

[10] Rousseau, *Emile,* p. 1.

[11] *Ibid.*

[12] Translated in Barnard, *op. cit.,* pp. 513–665; and translated and abridged by E. Channing (Boston, D. C. Heath and Co., 1906) .

the rest of his literary life he continued to clarify the educational doctrine hidden away in *Leonard and Gertrude*.[13]

Books on educational history usually allow a single chapter for Rousseau and Pestalozzi. A combined treatment is justified because both were engaged in creating a naturalistic environment in which pedagogy could thrive. Historical commonplace makes Rousseau the theorist and lets Pestalozzi, following the trail blazed by Rousseau, invent natural methods for teachers who wanted to be true to the doctrines of natural education to follow. Perhaps this does not tell the whole story, and it pays scant heed to Pestalozzi's impact on the theory of education. Although he admired Rousseau and admitted the worth of his startling educational creed, Pestalozzi was not merely implementing someone else's theory, nor was he Rousseau's technical writer, a thesis giving his innovative and often awkward teaching techniques undue importance.

We now return to the main reason for studying Rousseau and Pestalozzi together. Rousseau is often imprecise about school practice and Pestalozzi dwells on it, but both start with the same fundamental assumptions: man is naturally good, depravations come from society; an amelioration of degrading social conditions is essential to progress; and reformation of society must begin with the training of men for social living. Thus Rousseau and Pestalozzi were intellectually compatible; it was not that one was a leader and the other a mere follower. This sharing of fundamental social assumptions supplies the best reason for a common study of their educational prescriptions.

Rousseau and Pestalozzi together asserted the priority of natural education. However, natural education (education according to nature) is susceptible of misinterpretation, and commentators constructed a variety of caricatures all based, they averred, on the pedagogical principles it espoused. Neither was serious about leaving a child to fend for himself in a garden or forest undirected and unattended, although both were enthusiastic about the kind of experience a child might have if allowed to communicate freely with his physical environment. Rousseau's dictum—"do nothing and let nothing be done" [14]—was not meant to be taken literally; for he is writing about the first part of a child's development and wants to spare the child the acquirements of formal education before he can orient them to proper objectives. To doubt Rousseau's vexation with then current educational practice is impossible; his determination to reform pedagogy by beginning with a thorough housecleaning is clear, but he was not an educational anarchist. Pestalozzi's thesis requires little interpretation or defense: he eschewed extreme language

[13] See R. De Guimps, *Pestalozzi: His Life and Work* (New York, D. Appleton and Co., 1894), p. 80.
[14] Rousseau, *Emile*, p. 58.

for describing the defects of schools, and we read him without visions of total rejection—visions obvious in Rousseau—for his bill of particulars avoids charges that can be vindicated only by annihilating formal education.

To say Rousseau gave all the wrong answers to all the right questions,[15] an interesting but untenable evaluation, gives him credit for too much educational insight and takes too literally the easy solutions he offered. We see this if we probe more deeply the meaning he gave to natural education. First, sensing what other educators too readily ignored, he said that everyone has a natural capacity which can be shaped, and often misshaped, but nothing can be added to it nor can it be altered fundamentally. When Rousseau stresses natural education, he tells teachers to use capacity as a map and to follow it; but they must not try to take the child along routes he is unable to travel. Although he seems to say—and has been interpreted to mean—that the only way capacity can be fully exploited is by adopting a laissez-faire educational policy, this is not what he meant. He knew society abhorred the noble savage, and he knew too that education, with all its defects, was essential: "things would be worse without this education . . . Under existing conditions a man left to himself from birth would be more a monster than the rest." [16]

In the second place, society is full of many things capable of destroying man unless he is successful in finding immunity to them. Immunity to prejudice and convention, to all society's perverse influences, is generated when a boy follows his own natural inclinations. So a natural and negative education is really preventive: it protects a child from a society he cannot avoid. Rousseau wants natural education to form habits and build character as permanent safeguards for social life. Finally, Rousseau wants Emile to live according to the "order of nature," an order established by divine will. The world cannot be remade, nor can men have full, satisfying lives by denying or ignoring the rational principles governing it. Rousseau's educational plan will lead Emile to understand the operations of the universe and to adjust to them; it does not create its own artificial and deceptive world and then contort a boy's nature to fit it. Such education leads to disaster. Throughout Rousseau's *Emile* the conflict between individual natural education and society is everywhere apparent.[17] This conflict cannot be avoided entirely, and the best advice

---

[15] R. Ulich, *History of Educational Thought* (New York, American Book Company, 1950), p. 211, does not go so far, although he did write: "It would be difficult to find a man in the history of thought who with so much half-truth has made as deep an impression on mankind as Rousseau."

[16] Rousseau, *Emile*, p. 5.

[17] But especially in Book I; see *ibid.*, p. 7–8.

Rousseau can give—advice often ridiculed because of its basic contradictions—is to prepare for life by avoiding society.[18]

Pestalozzi may have sensed this conflict, but he neither adverts to it nor bases his educational principles on it. His natural education was less comprehensive in its rejections: in the first place Pestalozzi says nothing at all about running away from the world, and the noble savage is unappealing to him. Social institutions were spared condemnation, and schools were welcomed as important social agencies. Rousseau's exaggerated fear of schools was replaced by a good deal of confidence in them. Pestalozzi wanted common men to have more of life's good things, and he believed schools with the right educational programs and the right methods were needed. From Pestalozzi nineteenth-century educators received special moral support for creating common school systems in Germany and the United States.[19]

Yet, with all his hopes for education as a social instrument, he was most concerned, as Rousseau was, with forming good men. The lesson of the Humanists was taught and learned well; no doubt Rousseau, Pestalozzi, Comenius, Locke, and Erasmus all agreed that the fundamental mission of education was to form a man of good character. This goal made instruction less prominent in the whole enterprise and changed the schoolmaster from a lesson-hearing functionary to an educator in the broader sense. It was hardly possible to be satisfied with the teacher or the tutor who only knew his reading, writing, and Latin; now the teacher was himself expected to be a person who could mold character, admittedly a large order and one not often filled. The unanswered question remained, however, of where these teachers were to be found and how they were to be prepared for their duties. It was much easier to procure a hearer of lessons than to find a teacher who could direct students toward the "one science for children to learn—the duties of man." [20]

Pestalozzi asserts the need for education to be free and natural instead of being cramped, confined, and servile. Learning, he is saying, must be set in a context of liberty sufficient to permit every student to realize his individual character. This is clearly in keeping with Rousseau's view of nature: the natural endowment of the child is unique and must be realized on an individual rather than on a social basis. For Pestalozzi, then, natural education meant first of all an understanding of the child and of his own powers and goals and then a knowledge of natural learning processes ensuring a fulfillment of these powers and goals. To be natural, education had to follow a program for fostering a

18 *Ibid.*, p. 9.

19 W. S. Monroe, *History of the Pestalozzian Movement in the United States* (Syracuse, N.Y., C. W. Bardeen, 1907) .

20 Rousseau, *Emile*, p. 19.

harmonious development of the whole man; Pestalozzi firmly believed that all the child's capacities—physical, moral, intellectual—should be cultivated in a relationship causing none to suffer; one capacity properly nourished would stimulate and help perfect all others.

The starting point for natural learning was the child's intuition; thus, natural education was a highly personal affair. It progressed gradually—never moving forward until all previous steps were mastered —and left nothing unfinished. The dictum, "make haste slowly," found favor in Pestalozzi's pedagogical doctrine, and he accepted its corollary, "leave nothing undone." [21] Rousseau's individual-social dilemma was avoided by making education natural when it found the proper combination betwen public good and private good and when it cultivated a "social and domestic spirit." [22] Finally, Pestalozzi asserted, everything in a syllabus, reduced to first elements, should be practical and the means of development should reside in actual circumstances of life.[23]

In a sense, then, Pestalozzi's theory began where Rousseau's stopped. The principal, though not essential, difference is found here: the former dedicated his educational life to finding the educational means to ensure natural education, and he followed more conventional educational pathways than Rousseau. Rousseau, however, did not operate on the level of application and felt no obligation to do so. But by now enough has been said about the commonality of their purpose to allow us to look more closely at Rousseau's theory, lodged in the *Emile,* and Pestalozzi's, found mainly in *How Gertrude Teaches Her Children,* a supplement to *Leonard and Gertrude.*

II

ROUSSEAU'S RECONSTRUCTION

Although educational views are lodged implicitly in Rousseau's broader social theory, the document Rousseau intended readers to consult when they wanted his prescription for education's ills was *Emile.* It is sometimes helpful in interpreting Rousseau's educational doctrine to read the *Social Contract, The New Heloise,* the *Confessions,*[24] or some of his

---

[21] We may infer this from *How Gertrude Teaches Her Children,* Barnard, *op. cit.,* p. 73; and the more complete German edition, *Wie Gertrud Ihre Kinder Lehrt, in J. H. Pestalozzi's Ausgewählte Werke,* by F. Mann, ed. (Langensalza, 1893) , vol. 3. Rousseau's advice to zealous teachers is "never be in a hurry to act" (*Emile,* p. 57.)

[22] "Preface to the Second Edition" of *Leonard and Gertrude,* Barnard, *op. cit.,* 523.

[23] From *How Gertrude Teaches Her Children,* in *ibid.;* p. 675.

[24] These works are in Everyman's Library edition (London, J. M. Dent & Sons, 1938) .

earlier essays, but it is plainly wrong to concentrate on them as if they were of equivalent value to *Emile* when one is studying Rousseau's educational theory.[25]

So much has been written about Rousseau's *Emile* that one may wonder if any further excursus is necessary.[26] Yet, despite the uncontested value of many such interpretations, the meaning Rousseau intended is not always clear, and sometimes because of a particular bias or predisposition which the critic has for or against Rousseau, his intentions are clouded or contorted out of their original shape. Our purpose here, following *Emile,* shall be to state as clearly and simply as possible the educational message Rousseau left for those who would read him.[27]

To find his intentions we should look first to the preface of *Emile* where he noted in a few words what he proposed to do. *Emile* began, as we have said, as a memoir to a mother seeking advice from Rousseau on the education of her son. He thought he could state the principal elements of education in a few short pages, but, as he says, "I was carried away by my subject, and before I knew what I was doing my tract had become a kind of book, too large indeed for the matter contained in it, but too small for the subject of which it treats." [28]

Despite the tone of dogmatism permeating the entire treatise, Rousseau made no pretense of being a final authority on education. Even if his ideas proved to be unsound, they would, he was confident, stimulate good ones among his readers. The point he wants to make is this: more should be known about children. They should be studied and educated as they are, rather than for what they are expected to be as adults. The great error of the age, Rousseau claimed, was to regard children as small adults, never considering what they are capable of learning.[29] Obviously, Rousseau did not think himself an expert in child psychology, and only after much persuasion did he revise the first drafts

25 This does not mean, of course, that his other work should be ignored. Boyd is correct when, in his introduction to *The Minor Writings of Jean Jacques Rousseau,* he says: "Not to know the *Emile* is not to know Rousseau or the New Education of which he was the pioneer (p. 1). [Yet] . . . The Letter on Education in the *New Heloïse* contains some of Rousseau's best work on educational theory, and would have taken a high place in the literature of pedagogy even if the *Emile* had never been written" (p. 5). See also *Considerations on the Government of Poland and on the Reformation of it projected in April, 1772, ibid.,* pp. 94 ff.

26 For example, see the bibliographies in Pierre Burgelin, *La Philosophie de L'Existence de J. J. Rousseau* (Paris, Presses Universitaires de France, 1952), pp. 579–583; and J. R. Spell, *Rousseau in the Spanish World Before 1833* (Austin, University of Texas Press, 1938), pp. 296–309.

27 Highly valuable, although old, studies on Rousseau are: W. Boyd, *The Educational Theory of Jean Jacques Rousseau* (New York, Longmans, Green and Co., 1911); G. Compayré, *Jean Jacques Rousseau and Education from Nature* (New York, T. Y. Crowell and Co., 1907); and T. Davidson, *Rousseau and Education According to Nature* (New York, Charles Scribner's Sons, 1909).

28 Rousseau, *Emile,* p. 1.

29 This point is stressed in *The New Heloïse* also. See Boyd, *Minor Writings,* p. 49.

of *Emile* to include a discussion of infant years.[30] As it was he anticipated future developments in child study and suspected others would
follow the trail he marked out. If Rousseau had done nothing more than
enter a plea for an understanding of children, he would have made a
lasting contribution to the business of education.[31]

The question is asked now, and it was asked of Rousseau: does *Emile*
contain a practical program for education? Rousseau's answer varied, but
not because of any uncertainty about the content of *Emile*. Is *Emile* a
teacher's handbook? The answer is clearly and always that it is not. Does
Emile contain a theory of education capable of implementation? Rousseau said yes. If we read *Emile* looking for techniques of application, we
shall always be disappointed, for Rousseau plainly states that "particular
applications are not essential to my subject." [32] These techniques, he
knew, depended too much on circumstances to be treated in a general
way and, moreover, always have a subordinate place in educational
philosophy. So Rousseau may be pardoned for refusing to discuss the
execution of theory. A better question is: was the theory of *Emile* "suitable to man and adapted to the human heart?" [33] He does not answer
this question in the preface or anywhere else; yet, in another sense, the
whole of *Emile* must be understood as an affirmative answer. What he
proposed was a top-to-bottom reform of education, and his theory, he
admitted, could not be judged practical or capable of successful application unless it were used as a substitute for, not as a supplement to,
existing practices. When it was suggested that his plan would have
greater feasibility if he attached some of his proposed reforms to existing
practices, to "combine something good with the existing evil," his response was unequivocal: "There are matters with regard to which such a
suggestion is far more chimerical than my own, for in such a connection
the good is corrupted and the bad is none the better for it. I would rather
follow exactly the established method than adopt a better method by
halves. There would be fewer contradictions in the man; he cannot aim
at one and the same time at two different objects." [34]

Among the many misconceptions about Rousseau is one seeing him
campaigning for the suppression of all formal education. In the first part
of *Emile*, where Rousseau is most philosophical in tone, he affirms the
necessity of education with a clear statement that without education
"things would be worse [for] mankind cannot be made by halves." [35] It

30 See Rousseau, *Emile*, pp. 10–14.

31 See L. Proal, *La psychologie de J.-J. Rousseau* (Paris, F. Alcan, 1930) ; Albert
Schinz, *Jean-Jacques Rousseau, a Forerunner of Pragmatism* (Chicago, Chicago Uni-
versity Press, 1909) ; and E. H. Wright, *The Meaning of Rousseau* (New York, Russell
& Russell, 1963) .

32 Rousseau, *Emile*, p. 3.

33 *Ibid.*, p. 2.

34 *Ibid.*

35 *Ibid.*, p. 5.

would be impossible for a man without education to cope with social institutions in which he is inevitably immersed. Yet, it is apparent here and elsewhere that Rousseau is not thinking of preparing the student for sharing in the life of society; he is trying instead to immunize him from the dangers of social institutions.[36]

Education, Rousseau began, is necessary, but it is also three-sided: "education comes to us from nature, from man, or from things. The inner growth of our organs and faculties is the education of nature, the use we learn to make of this growth is the education of men, what we gain by our experience of our surroundings is the education of things."[37]

Every man has three teachers—nature, men, and things—who when they work in concert produce a well-educated person. Unfortunately they seldom work in harmony. Two teachers—nature and things—are relatively independent of man's control, the former always and the latter usually. Education coming from men is under their direct control. Rousseau thinks it possible to minimize the effects of contradictions produced by things and men: remove the learner to a remote environment free from complexities, and put him under the care of one master. By eliminating variables in the educational process the impressions of experience will be more consistent, and, although some conflict will continue to persist, because the three teachers are always present, they will be less harmful. Such education was intended for self-realization and it neglected social features because it intended to. Yet, no one is totally independent and, whether Rousseau liked it or not, must sometime be part of society and prepared to live with others. Here Rousseau becomes entangled in the dilemma of educational purpose—teaching for private good versus teaching for public good—and is mystified by it: "drawn this way by nature and that way by man, compelled to yield to both forces, we make a compromise and reach neither goal."[38] When he tries to resolve the dilemma, he fails, and chooses to ignore public good by concentrating all his attention on the education of man as an individual. Manhood is a common vocation; he will aim at nothing less: "Before his parents chose a calling for him nature called him to be a man. Life is the trade I would teach him. When he leaves me, I grant you, he will be neither a magistrate, a soldier, nor a priest; he will be a man."[39]

After the bases of his theory are given in the first part of Book One, Rousseau notices infant training. Although he is convinced of its importance, he is unable to say much, but what he does say is at sharp variance

[36] The purpose is not so apparent in the Letter on Education in *The New Heloïse*, written about the same time as *Emile*, for Rousseau is thinking of more conventional family education. See Boyd, *Minor Writings*, pp. 44–75.

[37] Rousseau, *Emile*, p. 6.

[38] *Ibid.*, p. 9.

[39] *Ibid.*

with conventional eighteenth-century practice.[40] His views are un-heralded today because they are seldom in conflict with generally accepted practices of child care. The general theme of Rousseau's position here is to allow the child to develop naturally by doing as little as possible for him. Understanding and using his own powers, uncurtailed by the directions of parents and teachers, he will be able to take the first sure steps down the long road to becoming a man.

This road is marked out by Rousseau in four books that follow, each concerned with a different period of human development. But before we see the plan Rousseau devised for the various stages of Emile's development, it is important to identify one of Rousseau's basic assumptions about human nature and to recognize it as the chief obstacle to the acceptance of, or even a fair hearing for, the plan he advanced: "God makes all things good; man meddles with them and they become evil." [41] This far-reaching assertion challenged the Christian doctrine of original sin and laid the foundation for Rousseau's reconstruction of education. Conventional educational practices operated according to the theory that teaching was meant primarily to correct the faults bred in an originally deprived or depraved nature; Rousseau's audacious doctrine makes teaching responsible for guarding the child's originally untarnished nature from the perversions of social living. And because no inner faults needed correction, it was possible for Rousseau to advocate heretofore inconceivable degrees of liberty in education.[42]

Mothers, fathers, and, when necessary, tutors have as their first duty, not protecting the child from himself, which would be inconsistent with the assumption that the child is naturally good, but from the intrusions of men's values and the things that men are successful in misshaping. In the child's first years, the mother must perform the broad and basic functions of a teacher; it is, as a matter of fact, hard to know where the line between maternal care and teaching is drawn. In Rousseau's view it is not important to know. When the child gains maturity, it becomes the father's first duty to instruct him. Rousseau is exceptionally clear about the responsibility of parents and avers that "a heavy curse lies upon those

40 See H. Barnard, *German Teachers and Educators* (Hartford, Brown and Gross, 1878), pp. 479–480.

41 Rousseau, *Emile*, p. 5. See also H. Höffding, *Jean Jacques Rousseau and His Philosophy* (New Haven, Yale University Press, 1930).

42 Rousseau says "well regulated liberty" (*Emile*, p. 56). This position on liberty should be compared with what Rousseau wrote in the *Project for the Education of M. de Sainte-Marie*—"But it is essential for the education of Sainte-Marie to put a curb on him he will feel, one capable of holding him in" (Boyd, *Minor Writings*, p. 27); and *The New Heloïse*—"Do you think," she said at once, "that it is a restriction of their liberty to prevent them trespassing on ours?"—(*ibid.*, p. 63.) See also G. R. Havens, "Rousseau's Doctrine of Goodness According to Nature," *Publications of the Modern Language Association of America*, XLIV (December, 1929), pp. 1239–1245; and J. Tresnon, "The Paradox of Rousseau," *Publications of the Modern Language Association of America*, XLIII (December, 1928), pp. 1010–1025.

who neglect their parental duties." [43] Yet, he does allow a father whose occupations make it impossible for him to instruct his son to secure a delegate, the tutor. Much has been made of Rousseau's failure to supervise the education of his own children; the story is that he packed them off to a foundling home as soon as they were born. Somehow critics see in Rousseau's omissions grounds for attacking his principle that parents bear a grave responsibility in education, or they assume that because Rousseau did not follow his own advice the advice given on this point and on other points too must be bad. Yet it must be clear to us now that Rousseau's own strengths, if we are willing to assume he had any, or weaknesses, which he readily admits, could neither add to nor detract from the validity of his total theory about education. [44]

The tutor whom a father engages must be well educated and young. Above all, Rousseau writes, "he should not be employed for money; should be no hireling." [45] Once attached to the child, the tutor should remain as his play fellow, confidant, teacher, and educator until the child is about twenty-five years old. We are entitled to wonder how such a man could be obtained. Apparently the tutor could have but one student throughout his career. This is all a bit fantastic, and Rousseau must have known it. But on the point of compensation, we are obliged to believe that Rousseau's language was open to misunderstanding. He means to say that the tutor's dedication must be to the education of the child, and this high motive cannot be generated by money alone. If money is the tutor's incentive, he will be a hireling, and hirelings are notoriously insensitive to ideals. No doubt Rousseau would have leveled a heavy charge against the modern teacher who sees in the teaching profession a secure and relatively untroubled life. Rousseau's comment is intended as a test of ideals and is not meant to deprive the tutor of a livelihood.

When the tutor is selected, he must choose a nurse—now Rousseau is talking about Emile, who is an orphan—and accompany the child and the nurse to the country. In the country the child is freed from a contaminating social environment, and he will be allowed all the freedom he can manage; he will be allowed to live and learn according to his own inclinations. Rousseau does not want to rush the child into picking up the tools of education. Even in learning to speak the child should not be accelerated unnaturally; the only advice Rousseau gives here is that both the tutor and the nurse should always speak correctly to him: most important of all "the child ought not to speak any further than he can think." [46]

43 Rousseau, *Emile*, p. 17.

44 See E. Cassirer, *The Question of Jean-Jacques Rousseau,* translated and edited by Peter Gay (New York, Columbia University Press, 1954), p. 15; and for Rousseau's admissions of failure and remorse, see *Confessions,* VII.

45 Rousseau, *Emile*, p. 17.

46 *Ibid.,* p. 40.

Infancy is over when the child is able to speak, and the period of childhood then begins. This period is the subject for the second book of *Emile*, which is concerned especially with the education of Emile up to his twelfth year. This is an important period in formation, and Rousseau takes ample notice of it.

Now he is less a philosopher and more a pedagogue, for he deals with topics that every schoolmaster must ponder. But he does not abandon his philosophical tone or approach: the topics themselves are eminently practical, but Rousseau's discussion of them is by no means technical. It is only on the level of theory that he tells teachers what to do. Much, perhaps too much, of what he had to say was clothed in negativism, but this could hardly have been otherwise, for Rousseau had determined from the outset to reject all existing codes and practices and begin anew.

There is no room in Rousseau's doctrine for unnecessary sympathy for the child; he should learn to bear with whatever fortune brings. This is entirely natural, Rousseau believes. Children, moreover, should be protected from unnecessary teaching; that is, from being taught the things they will learn for themselves—the things they cannot help learning. And the present—whatever learning and living there is in it—must not be sacrificed for the future. Allow the child to be a child, and let him learn what he needs to know. The future can take care of itself.[47]

There is a strong appeal in Book II to recognize that discipline in children is formed most satisfactorily by counting on natural dependence rather than on obedience. They must be allowed to do, within reason, what is attainable and what pleases them; they will soon learn what they cannot do and what is unwise for them to try. They are dependent on persons and things, and to some degree, with their limited freedom, they must conform. This natural, almost inexorable conformity, is always superior to obedience to command, which when not given in a full context of necessity may appear arbitrary and unreasonable.

The bulk of Rousseau's admonitions rests on the maxim: "let children be children." In consequence of this conviction he opposes any program of early education that emphasizes or employs reasoning with children. He does not believe that children before they are twelve years of age are able to reason: "If children understood reasoning, they would need no education. . . . We might as well expect children to be five feet high, as to have judgment in their tenth year." [48]

Jesuit teaching practices were condemned by Rousseau—especially singled out for attention in this treatise because of the tremendous impression Jesuit teaching had made on France—because they placed too much emphasis on the teacher and allowed for little or no student free-

---

[47] *Ibid.*, p. 35.
[48] See *ibid.*, p. 54.

dom and, further, because they employed methods that Rousseau believed to be unnatural and dangerous: emulation, rivalry, competition, and fear.[49] "The usual education of children is such as if children leaped, at one bound, from the mother's breast to the age of reason." [50] This defective assumption led to all kinds of pedagogical perversions, so great and so dangerous, Rousseau believed, that he added a much quoted and criticized principle: "Do the opposite of what is usually done and you will almost always be right." [51] This is the creed of negative education, but it would be unfair to Rousseau to think that he meant there should be an educational vacuum. In Rousseau's view, vacuums were impossible: conditions were present which made for good or bad education; there was no middle or vacant ground between the two.

In Book II Rousseau touches on the importance of conducting education in the country, on moral instruction, where Rousseau takes issue with Locke and contends that the only moral instruction having any value at all is good example, on the tyranny of verbal teaching, on history, reading, geography, and drawing and geometry. On these last Rousseau is concerned most with training the senses and cares very little about the actual accomplishments of the student.

This is the period of life when the child's physical development is especially important. The body must be hardened—Rousseau did not find it difficult to praise a Spartan-like regimen—for the senses are basically physical, and through them the intellect is formed: "Our feet, our hands, our eyes, first teach us philosophy." [52]

Throughout this entire period, although the tutor is not visible, he is important. In the rules Rousseau lays down for the tutor, there is some sound advice which Rousseau must have gathered out of the fragments of his own experience. He counsels tutors to govern their charges wisely; students usually have more perceptiveness than they are credited with, and they see through the tutor's motives more often than he fathoms theirs. Thus, tutors must "govern so that the child shall think itself free"; [53] in other words, they must get the child to follow a proper course of formation by making him think they are doing nothing.

After the twelfth year, curiosity will begin to operate on a somewhat different level, so in the education of the child from twelve through fifteen the tutor must bring a new dimension to his instruction. At this point Rousseau is definitely thinking of Emile. So Book Three is concerned with the third step in the development of Emile.

In a period when Emile is no longer a child but not yet a man,

49 *Ibid.*, pp. 55–56. Although Rousseau does not name the Jesuits, it is clear who his target is. He also takes issue with Locke's supreme confidence in reason.
50 *Ibid.*, p. 133.
51 *Ibid.*, p. 57.
52 *Ibid.*, p. 90.
53 *Ibid.*, p. 70.

Rousseau reverses his direction that the boy be educated in a leisurely fashion and recommends instead the dextrous and prudent use of time. "During the first period of life time was plentiful. We only sought to have it occupied in any way at all to prevent it being put to a bad use. Now it is just the opposite, and we have not enough time to get all done that is useful." [54]

What has happened to change the perspective of education and to give it now a highly imperative quality? Basically, it is curiosity and a drive for happiness, both of which need the support of knowledge. There is now, as before, little room for books, for Rousseau always had a special fear of the written word; curiosity should be satisfied by discovery, and sensory impressions must be developed into ideas. The caution remains, however, "we should not pass too suddenly from material to intellectual objects." [55]

Rousseau gives us a brief, but a not too satisfactory, look at his meaning by examples from astronomy and geography. Perhaps the lesson is too simple to be especially helpful or enlightening, yet there is an undeniable element of validity in the method proposed. Let astronomy be learned by watching a beautiful sunrise and by seeing how the sun rises in the east and sets in the west. Geography should begin with the house where the boy lives and proceed from there to the neighborhood and then beyond.[56] This was advice that Comenius had given before, and it was a method Pestalozzi later tried to perfect.

Authority in teaching is proscribed; the boy should learn what he wants, and not what he is told, to learn. "It is of no use to say to the boy that he is ordered for his own good, and that, when he is grown up, he will see it." [57] The only authority Rousseau is willing to recognize is the authority of utility. The boy must learn to ask himself "What is the good of it?" [58] A quick reaction to this principle is to ascribe its origin to Locke, for Locke had made utility in learning bear a heavy responsibility. But Locke's interpretation of utility was broad; Rousseau's is narrow. What the latter chooses to call the sacred question at this stage of education is always answered in relation to its immediate effects. Thus, Rousseau repeats for this stage an admonition given for an earlier one: guard against all premature learning.

The polemic against verbal education is repeated; things, not words, Rousseau says, are the best teachers: "a boy who is lost will find out better how to set himself aright by the sun, than he would by a long demonstration." [59] Yet, Rousseau does acknowledge that verbal instruc-

[54] *Ibid.,* p. 134.
[55] *Ibid.,* p. 128.
[56] See *ibid.,* pp. 130, 134.
[57] *Ibid.,* p. 143.
[58] *Ibid.,* p. 188.
[59] *Ibid.,* p. 151.

tion may sometimes have to substitute for the teaching that comes from things. This is always a last resort, however, for the overriding fear is present: "from books men learn to talk about what they do not understand." [60] There is one exception, and in Rousseau's view, one exceptional book—*Robinson Crusoe*. In it natural education is depicted clearly. It may be a worthy companion for the boy; at any rate, it will be the only book Emile has in his library.[61]

Rousseau introduced the idea of the workshop to education, although it can hardly be said that he made it a wholly respectable instrument for instruction. Emile and his tutor should enter the workshop and the former should learn a trade. This was not the gentlemanly diversion Locke had talked about in his *Some Thoughts' Concerning Education*,[62] but a skill to be put to use with effectiveness and profit. It served two obvious purposes: first, it made the boy independent, because with such a skill he could provide for himself; second, it schooled him in the value of work and eradicated any prejudice he may have had against trades. The trade Rousseau liked best was carpentry, but this was just a personal preference and cannot be interpreted as having any special significance. More broadly, Rousseau was attempting, by blending mental and physical labor, assuming there was much mental labor in the regimen Emile was following, to achieve reciprocity between training the body and the mind.

All along there is the pious hope that Emile will climb the ladder of intellectual, moral, and emotional development; Rousseau wants him to be a complete man. Yet, his language makes us suspect that Emile is no longer the captain of his fate: to make him a complete man, we must make him also a living and feeling being, that is, we must supplement reason with his feelings.[63] What is the real liberty young Emile enjoys, if we make him the kind of human being we want him to be? Is Rousseau's tyranny any better than the tyranny he would displace?

Rousseau does not seem to notice that Emile is no longer his own master, or if he does he prefers to ignore an apparent withdrawal of liberty, for he quickly recites the virtues Emile has absorbed by his fifteenth year. He yields to no authority; he remembers only what has commended itself to his understanding; he has little knowledge, but no half-knowledge; what is useful to him he values most, and he cares nothing for opinion; he is moderate, laborious, patient, persevering, and courageous; he is destitute of social virtue, but he has no errors or vices, except such as are unavoidable. Do you think, Rousseau asks rhetorically, "that the earliest years of a child, who has reached his fifteenth year in

60 *Ibid.*, p. 161.
61 *Ibid.*, pp. 161–163.
62 See *Some Thoughts Concerning Education*, 201–206.
63 See Rousseau, *Emile*, p. 141.

this condition, have been wasted?" [64] Clearly, if the answer to this question is yes, then the whole of Rousseau's educational doctrine must be rejected. If, however, we agree with Rousseau that the accomplishments, or lack of them, of Emile are meritorious, we should enthusiastically support this plan for education. How much Rousseau would allow us to modify his plan, to choose the good elements and reject those that are contradictory or worthless, is an unanswered question in the history of education. One might guess that Rousseau would countenance no revision. [65]

When we were reading Books I through III, Rousseau allowed us to believe we were being introduced to an educational reconstruction of the greatest import; and everything he said was clothed in strong, incisive language. Undoubtedly he meant to be taken seriously, and no doubt he believed the educational phase covering the first fifteen years of life to be important, but he has no hesitancy in telling us, as we begin Book IV, that so far we have been concerned with child's play; what takes place from now on in the formation of Emile will test the best talents of the tutor, for now, he says, education must really begin. Men are born twice; the first time for existence—and we may assume that education so far has been concerned mainly with existence—and the second time for life— and we are told that the program from now on is education for life. [66]

What has happened to the continuity of learning experiences in which Rousseau put so much confidence? His intimations of adolescent changes were sound, but it is hard to see how natural processes could produce so large a gap as to destroy continuity and demand a totally new approach to learning. [67]

Even though Rousseau does not enlighten us—the strange inconsistencies creeping into his theory here and elsewhere give us pause—we may move along with him into a period of life where, he says, a man's relationships with others become all important. Up to now Emile has been concerned with himself; in a sense he is the world, or, at least, it revolves around him. Now he begins to see and feel outside himself. Truly this is a new world, one that he could not have known before if his tutor and his nurse were successful in immunizing him from life in society.

The transition of which Rousseau speaks from the I-centered existence to an other-centered experience is too abrupt to be realistic; it keeps Emile in the world of a myth Rousseau has created, and it leaves the educator following Rousseau in a state of frustration. He must be creative indeed, to make a meaningful program out of Rousseau's doctrine from now on. About the only thing he can be certain of is that

[64] *Ibid.*, p. 171.
[65] See Ulich's perceptive comments, *op. cit.*, pp. 222–224.
[66] Rousseau, *Emile*, p. 172.
[67] See Davidson, *op. cit.*, pp. 156–177.

Rousseau allows for individual differences in the time it will take for this transition in the boy's attitude to occur.

The young man develops an insatiable desire to know his place in relation to others, and he finds a certain satisfaction in being a social animal, although Rousseau has gone a long way earlier in trying to prove that Emile is not naturally a social being. He plies his tutor with questions of origin, and what he does not learn from his tutor he either discovers for himself or finds in his imagination. Perhaps Rousseau gives us sound advice when he counsels honesty and candor in responding to the natural inquiries of the adolescent mind, but it is not altogether possible to be sure what this advice is. In any case, Rousseau distrusts the imagination and argues that to give it freedom—which is done when valid knowledge is not supplied—is to convert passion into vice.[68]

Social education begins with a knowledge of men, and Rousseau would have Emile know men as they are. Concurrence on this point is easy, but we are never quite permitted to know what this knowledge is or how it is to be purveyed. Emile knows, or is taught, that men are naturally good, that they are perverted by their interpersonal relationships, that he should value each single man, but despise men collectively.[69] Where this advice, or this knowledge, would lead Emile is an open question; too often, we suppose, it would lead to disaster.

Now, however, Rousseau has helpmates; neither the tutor nor Emile must depend solely on himself to supply all the ingredients of social education. Who are these outsiders who at long last intrude on the sacred processes of natural education and in whom trust may be put? Surprisingly enough for the person who has read Rousseau carefully and thinks he knows what Rousseau so far has said, they are historians. But they are not conventional modern historians, who might be expected to give Emile some insights into his social world; Rousseau both distrusted and despised such historians. He wanted a broader and, he thought, more philosophical history, one concerned not with facts or political events, but with personalities of the stature of heroes. He could accept Thucydides and Plutarch, and he thought the latter best of all,[70] for he believed they taught inspirationally; what he must have meant was this: their histories were largely anecdotal and they could deal intimately with the traits of their heroes. Ancient history was enough, for he feared, as we have said, the modern intellectual systems that could cloud the clearheadedness of his young Emile.

Moral and religious education came next on the list, for they too are important in training Emile to remain steadfastly independent of the whirlpool of society. But what moral and religious training will Emile

68 Rousseau, *Emile*, p. 183.
69 *Ibid.*, pp. 197–198.
70 *Ibid.*, p. 201.

have? Moral training is natural morality at its worst, for it has no standard other than Emile's own whim. Religious instruction is surely not catechetical; nor is it in any sense instruction in orthodox Christianity. If Rousseau would not have Emile ignorant of God, he surely would not teach him any of the established creeds. In this view Rousseau is quite precise: In what religion shall we educate him? To this there is only the simple answer, in none.[71] Hopefully, Emile will be able to draw his own conclusions about the relationship of man to God, and this is the best religious creed for him. So, in the end, Rousseau was saying that there should be no religious instruction at all. Finally, Rousseau is entirely satisfied that he has found the key to natural education, but his optimism has been doubted, debated, and damned by his critics.[72]

Book V should be read neither as a chapter on educational theory nor as a marriage manual, for, though it touches on both education and marriage, it really deals with neither.[73] Emile is now ready for marriage and must find the right mate. This leads Rousseau to discourse on the proper training for a woman—where he detects important differences between the sexes—but he has little to say of consequence for education. In a word, the woman—Sophie is the name Rousseau uses to identify her—Emile is to marry should be prepared to serve her husband. But this does not take us very far into the theory of women's education, and for the serious student of the subject, *Emile* is better left unread.

Rousseau at last tells his readers that there is merit in travel, so he has Emile take a grand tour. But there is nothing new here either, for Locke and others had said everything the subject warranted before Rousseau, and were considerably more perceptive about the values of travel. Finally, Emile and Sophie marry; eventually they have a child of their own. At this point Emile's tutor disengages himself, and Emile's son is educated under the direction of his father. With others we may wonder what might become of the boy, for we can hardly accept Rousseau's unguarded and unqualified prediction of inevitable success.

Perhaps no sketch of *Emile* is entirely satisfactory, and none should be taken as a substitute for the book itself. Yet when reading *Emile* the student should know that it contains much that is instructive and much that is corruptive; truth is mingled with error, and too much that is dangerous to the formation of men is disguised as beneficial. No other

---

[71] *Ibid.*, pp. 220–221.

[72] See C. W. Hendel, *Jean-Jacques Rousseau: Moralist* (New York, Oxford University Press, 1934) ; and P. Masson, *La Religion de J.-J. Rousseau* (Paris, Hachette 1916) , 3 vol.

[73] See H. Fuseli, *Remarks on the Writing and Conduct of J. J. Rousseau* (Los Angeles, University of California Press, 1960) ; W. Boyd, *The Educational Theory of Jean Jacques Rousseau*, pp. 315 ff.; and Davidson, *op. cit.*, pp. 185–202. The reader should compare Book V of *Emile* with Rousseau's *Memoir on the Education of the Prince of Wirtemberg's Infant Daughter, Sophie*, in Boyd, *Minor Writings*, pp. 76–87.

educational theorist must be approached with so much caution or read with so much care as Rousseau.[74]

III

PESTALOZZI'S PEDAGOGY

A brief view of Pestalozzi's early life, when his basic sympathies and sensitivities were formed, allows us to see somewhat more clearly the direction he could hardly avoid taking when he reached maturity. John Henry Pestalozzi was born in January, 1746, to a good home of upper-middle-class standing. His father, who died when the boy was six, was a physician; his mother was a sensitive, refined woman from a good family. When Pestalozzi's father died, the boy was incubated in a highly protective household.[75] Apparently there was money enough to live well, although not extravagantly; yet, the boy's experience was narrow, and he seems not to have participated in any of the things that boys from reasonably good homes do. His leisure was spent with the family, and the feminine influences in the family were dominant. Later, he himself related how real life was a stranger to him in his youth and how he "did not live in the world in which [he] dwelt." [76]

Pestalozzi's youth was happy enough, although he found retirement from the world round him more comfortable than being in it. Games with other boys were no fun, for Pestalozzi was poorly coordinated and unpracticed in their activities. Too often he was thought to be a fool by his fellows, but this was a hasty and incorrect view because the boy was highly intelligent, imaginative, and sensitive. He felt much about his fellowmen, although he did not really know or understand them. He stepped over the threshold of life quickly and entered the mainstream of living without much preparation.

His school life, he tells us, was uninspiring, but he did what lads were expected to do and excelled in his lessons without really fathoming their import. Later he was convinced that the lessons were not very meaningful and that much, if not most, of his schooling was a waste of time. What a strain of protest ranges through the writers on education of these years. Comenius, Locke, Rousseau, and Pestalozzi all said much the same thing, and it all added up to the conclusion that formal education was mostly a waste of time and a colossal misuse of human talent.

[74] See W. H. Hudson, *Rousseau and Naturalism in Life and Thought* (Edinburgh, T. & T. Clark, 1903) .

[75] See Käte Silber, *Pestalozzi: The Man and His Work* (London, Routledge and Kegan Paul Ltd., 1960) , pp. 1–18.

[76] Barnard, *Pestalozzi and His Educational System*, p. 50.

Pestalozzi was sixteen years old when Rousseau's *Emile* appeared. He must have read it soon after and, according to his own testimony, was much affected by it: "My visionary and highly speculative mind was enthusiastically seized by this visionary and highly speculative book. I compared the education which I enjoyed in the corner of my mother's parlor, and also in the school which I frequented, with what Rousseau demanded for the education of his Emilus [sic]. The home as well as the public education of the whole world, and all ranks of society, appeared to me altogether as a crippled thing, which was to find a universal remedy for its present pitiful condition in Rousseau's lofty ideas." [77]

Pestalozzi acknowledged Rousseau's influence, and he admitted that *Emile* made a deep impression on him. There is no valid reason to dispute the continuity of natural education running between them, and almost inevitably comparisons will be made between their lives, their temperaments, and the educational reforms they counseled. We have already noted that Pestalozzi was less an apostle of rejection than Rousseau and that he was more deeply humanitarian. His educational views, better his entire social outlook, were dominated by love for humanity, especially the poor who obviously were getting far less than their rightful share of the good in life.[78] Rousseau, on the other hand, to read his pronouncements rather than test his motives, was basically at war with mankind. Ultimately his system would replace what his theory began by destroying, but destruction came first. Everything being done in existing educational systems was to be scuttled, and for Rousseau this was no mere handy figure of speech. Beneath Pestalozzi's fumbling practical efforts to reform education is a warm and penetrating wisdom directed by a deep sympathy for mankind. Pestalozzi loved his fellow men even if he did not always understand them. Rousseau apparently neither fully understood men nor loved them. His system is cold and inhuman, devoid of love and feeling; Pestalozzi, often overly sentimental, is nevertheless more human, and at the bedrock of his plan there is a wisdom outdistancing the flagrant radicalism of Rousseau.

In the preface to the first edition of *Leonard and Gertrude*, Pestalozzi states the theme of his endeavor, a theme to which he remained constant: "I take no part in the disputes of men about opinions, but I think all will agree, that whatever makes us pious, good, true, and brotherly, whatever cherishes the love of God and our neighbor, and whatever brings happiness and peace into our houses, should be implanted in the hearts of all, for our common good." [79]

[77] *Ibid.*, p. 52. See also Sibler, *op. cit.*, p. 10. R. de Guimps, *op. cit.*, p. 13, does not stress Rousseau's influence on Pestalozzi, although he is aware of Pestalozzi's knowledge of Rousseau's *Emile* and *Social Contract*.

[78] See E. Spranger, *Pestalozzis Denkformen*, 2d ed. (Heidelberg, Haase, 1959).

[79] Barnard, *op. cit.*, p. 522. See also H. Hoffmann, *Die Religion im Leben und Denken Pestalozzis* (Bern, Huber and Hans, Co., 1944).

The principal means for achieving this high purpose appeared to Pestalozzi to be elementary education.[80] If it began at the right place and proceeded properly, Pestalozzi was confident men would be reformed and put in a condition to use their intelligence and skill to achieve fulfillment and independence. All this, however, was to be done, not outside the social circle, but within it.

Although Pestalozzi could be confident in the power of education, he could hardly endorse the educational practices he himself had experienced. Reform was sorely needed. But how could elementary schools follow the method and spirit of his pedagogy? Teachers able to apply his principles of natural education could not be found, and institutions for preparing teachers along the lines so indicated were wanting. He had grown up in his mother's parlor and much of his early education was obtained there; thus it was not unusual for him to suppose that he could avoid practical obstacles by placing "the education of people in the hands of the mothers; I will transplant it out of the school-room into the parlor." [81]

The model mother-teacher was Gertrude, and when we read *Leonard and Gertrude* [82] we see how effective she was. Of course, she was much more than a schoolmistress, but this was serving Pestalozzi's purpose effectively, because he wanted education to affect the whole man; and Gertrude directed an educational process touching the hand, the head, and the heart. Still, Gertrude was a talented woman who was herself reasonably well educated. Could other mothers, many of whom were disadvantaged intellectually and educationally, be expected to do as well as Gertrude? Pestalozzi knew they could not, and he anticipated this impasse by preparing teaching materials for mothers to use, materials that if strictly followed would equalize their talent and teaching skill.

In the long run neither *Leonard and Gertrude* nor Pestalozzi's plan was successful. The former was read as a novel and nothing more; the lesson it was intended to teach was largely missed. And the instructional materials contained in *The Mother's Book* [83] proved to be incapable either of capturing the support of mothers or inspiring them to become teachers in their homes. The reception accorded *Leonard and Gertrude* proved to Pestalozzi that neither his educational message nor method was

[80] See J. Payne's old book, *Pestalozzi: The Influence of His Principles and Practice on Elementary Education* (London, 1875).

[81] "Preface" to the 1782 edition of *Leonard and Gertrude*. Shortly after the appearance of *Leonard and Gertrude* Pestalozzi prepared a manuscript for a book entitled "The Instruction of Children in the Home." It was never published. See De Guimps, *op. cit.*, p. 80.

[82] In Pestalozzi, *Sämtliche Werke*, vol. 3, Buchenau, Spranger, and Stettbacher, eds. (Berlin and Leipzig, Walter de Gruyter & Co., 1927). Also Pestalozzi's *Leonard and Gertrude*, translated and abridged by Eva Channing, (Boston, D. C. Heath and Co., 1897); and Barnard, *op. cit.*, p. 513 ff.

[83] P. H. Pullen, *The Mother's Book* (London, S.P.G.F.P., 1820).

clear or perfected. He devoted the remainder of his life to correcting these defects. As we have noted, almost everything he wrote turned out to be a supplement to *Leonard and Gertrude;* moreover, he undertook the management of schools, under varying circumstances and with differing commissions, to learn firsthand the methods of instruction that would be most effective in the hands of mother-teachers. These methods, he hoped, could then be applied in public schools.

It is neither possible nor necessary to follow Pestalozzi through his school experiments, or through all his writings, to get at the bases of his program.[84] Fundamentally he established three principal means for the education of men: domestic life, intellectual education, and religious training. His educational efforts were bent on creating conditions and methods whereby these means could be utilized in the superior education of men.

The temptation is ever present to dismiss Pestalozzi as a visionary, and much of his early labor, both written and practical, is evidence that his ideals were outrunning the instruments at his disposal. Again we see how theory naturally tends to be literary and progressive, more fit for the library than the schoolroom. If Pestalozzi had stopped his educational searches when he was fifty years old, as a lesser man might have done, we should be fully justified in classifying him as an impractical and ineffective visionary. But Pestalozzi learned from his mistakes, and as he learned he moved further from the stance Rousseau had so dramatically taken, one which he had begun by accepting as a dogmatic assumption. After starting his reform of education in the home with a mother-teacher, and after having given extraordinary attention to vocational preparation—so much was this so that in many of Pestalozzi's early experiments what he called a school was really a domestic workshop—he turned over a new leaf and at age fifty began the work of a primary schoolmaster. At last his theories, hammered out in hundreds of pages, and his years of failure in various educational ventures began to pay dividends.

He did not foresake all his earlier principles, nor did he reject everything Rousseau had taught in *Emile*. With Rousseau he shared the conviction that genuine reform, in education and society, must begin with the individual. The person has worth and dignity to be cherished, and social institutions must not be allowed to trample either. But unless the person has the power to help himself, no worthwhile or lasting reform can be effected. There must, therefore, be some social engineering creating conditions for optimum individual formation. This engineering process should result in a system of freedom rather than control; then development along natural human lines will be possible. Here, education came to play an important role, and here, too, Pestalozzi took a different

---

[84] See H. Holman, *Pestalozzi: An Account of His Life and Work* (London, Methuen Co., Ltd., 1908).

fork in the road and parted with Rousseau. He would not, as we have seen, leave the child in a neutral educational climate. Schools would be established consciously augmenting the work of nature in the formation of each person toward a happier and more virtuous life.

From now on we read Pestalozzi in a different light; he is speaking to schoolmasters, not mothers; for he is now convinced that despite its worth domestic education is only a beginning. Yet many of the elements exhibited in domestic education, especially love, unremitting care, and unbounded self-sacrifice, are carried over to the school. A school, Pestalozzi assumes, should exemplify domestic life in all its purity. Teachers should regard the pupils as their children; the children should regard the teachers as their parents, and each other as brothers and sisters. This application of domestic education to school practice prepares the child for mental improvement and religious development and habits. Without love and the real humanitarianism it inspires, religion will gain no access to the heart, and intellectual cultivation will be a means only for satisfying the selfish demands of the animal nature.[85]

Of the three principles of natural education which he shared with Rousseau, Pestalozzi turned the last—natural development—toward useful educational ends. He assumed or accepted as axiomatic the notion that the child is an organism which unfolds according to a clear and definite order in nature. And this natural order of development is three-sided, including the mental, physical, and moral.

In other words, Pestalozzi was saying that educational practice must be in harmony with the child's natural processes of development. But he could go beyond this general proposition now and translate it into pedagogical terms.

1. Education ought to be essentially organic and complete, and not mechanical, superficial, and partial; it should penetrate and regulate the entire being. In modern terms, this means that education should first of all be general, that it should aim at giving the student those things needed for living in the world. It must be balanced between the various demands life may be expected to make and thus be neither entirely vocational nor purely liberal. At bottom, all education must be religious and moral, for neither Pestalozzi nor anyone else could be serious about education touching the child's entire being if religious teaching and moral formation were excluded. And these were far too important to be left to chance, as Rousseau had done.

2. Education should be synthetic; everything taught should be reduced to its first elements. Beginning with first elements, education should then strive to bring about the fruition of mental power; it should not be concerned especially with the acquisition of knowledge.

[85] See P. Wernle, *Pestalozzi und die Religion* (Tübingen, Lauppsche Buchhadlung, 1927).

3. Education should be free and natural; the child should have sufficient liberty to manifest decidedly his individual character. The seeds of capacity should, in other words, be cultivated, and the seeds are innate. Here is a reaffirmation of the principle of individual differences in formation.

4. Education should be based on intuition, on a clear and distinct perception of the subjects to be learned. Two points are apparent here: first, learning must begin at the student's level of experience and, second, this experience must be direct. The fundamental meaning of the direct experience is gained by intuition.

5. Education should be gradual and progressive, united in all parts, like a chain, forming a continued series without gaps. This was a plea for the grading of students and materials to be learned. And along with the idea of grading went the demand that each step up the ladder of learning be made only after the preceding step had been mastered.

6. Education should be practical, drawing its means of development from the actual circumstances of life. Natural development could hardly be protected if learning syllabi were composed of meaningless or irrelevant materials. Pestalozzi used the term "practical" in his plan, but "relevant" is really closer to his intended meaning.

7. Education should be religious and moral, for such development, considering man's relationship to God, was entirely natural.

Despite the overarching interest in religious education, Pestalozzi accomplished most, and set the wheels of method in motion best, for intellectual education. We should see something of the theory and the method involved.

In no sense was Pestalozzi a scientific psychologist, although he intuitively grasped certain sound psychological principles and used them as the bedrock of his system. In company with hundreds of pedagogues the world over who preceded him, he accepted sensory experience as the starting point for knowledge and intellectual development. This alone should not, and would not, call him to our attention, nor would it qualify him for a place among the world's influential educators, but Pestalozzi sorted out sensory experiences and concluded that the most productive sensory experiences were those that put the senses in contact with objects. Besides, he showed no preference whatever for an interpretation of the Lockean doctrine that the mind was a passive receptacle; instead it activated the senses and was, in turn, charged and informed by them. The mind of a child reached out for the world, and following the inner urges of its own being, an entirely natural process, tried to impose order on what the senses gathered.

Following Kant's dogma that perception without concepts is blind and concepts without perception are empty, Pestalozzi sought to construct a method putting the child in contact with reality, a method for ensuring meaning in perception and fullness of understanding. On the level of practical methodology this meant a departure from the conventional practice of beginning with words, of trying to find the basis for all teaching and all intellectual development in books. Pestalozzi preferred to begin with things; when the child knew what things were and what they meant—the things were objects in experience—there was time enough to attach verbal labels to them. This, of course, was the beginning of the famous object-lesson method, about which more will be said later, a technique that in retrospect seems hardly earthshaking in its description, although its implications were extensive, and it proved to be an indispensable instrument in the modern methodological revolution.

The simplicity of Pestalozzi's formula of beginning with objects and deferring linguistic training until later concealed as much as it revealed, for Pestalozzi's psychological intuitions told him almost nothing about distinctions between the logical and the psychological orders of learning. And this same intuition, while often sound, was also often distorted, and on this point blurred the two orders so completely that Pestalozzi could suppose he was teaching language effectively by beginning with meaningless vowel and consonant sounds. Even the foremost promoters of meaning and relevance in learning were sometimes caught off guard and entangled themselves in the mechanisms of their own pedagogy; Rousseau's mechanism was built on a policy of neutralism; Pestalozzi's was more apparent and more elaborate, but it frequently proved to negate the very purpose it sought to achieve in intellectual education.

The aim of intellectual education, according to Pestalozzi, was to develop the faculties, on the one hand, and an executive power, on the other. Apparently Pestalozzi meant by mental faculties about what Locke meant by them; in any case, it would be unfair to Pestalozzi to place too much emphasis on the term faculty or to think he was, in fact, accepting or endorsing the orthodox faculty theory. Faculties in Pestalozzi's plan meant unitary mental power, and he would have all faculties developed together. This development could be achieved only by exercising both the active and the passive power of the mind. In his view the faculties were interwoven; the exercise of one faculty necessarily affected all other faculties as well. Executive power is somewhat harder to interpret; from the context of Pestalozzi's writing and practice one would suppose he meant productive efficiency, or knowing what to do with the products of mental development. In other words, the development of mental power for itself was hardly what Pestalozzi had in mind; he was not a disciple of liberal learning, and he could not have endorsed any view promoting knowledge for its own sake. So we see again the doctrine of use being advocated in educational theory and practice; in Pestalozzi's view use was to be guided and guarded by moral order, and it was always to be responsible. At the same time its potentialities were to be sharpened as an integral part of intellectual education. Thus Pestalozzi either ignores or challenges the distinction, or the separation, of the theoretical and the practical.

Independently of instruction, or partially independent of it, the mind produces certain powers which, according to Pestalozzi, are on the most essential level: number, form, and language. The ultimate element of number is unity; of form, a line; of language, ideas, which are interior, and sound which is exterior. Each of these three means may be employed in two different directions: to develop power of discerning truth and facility in seeing beauty.

No special value is attached to acquiring knowledge, yet in this system a certain amount of knowledge will inevitably accompany the exercises of the faculties toward the production of the three means, number, form, and language. If knowledge is merely a by-product for Pestalozzi, it is an exceedingly important one, for he leaves the impression that an enlightened mind (he must have meant an informed one) will succeed better than an unenlightened one in the acquirement of both knowledge and executive power.

The exercises adopted to develop the faculties should succeed one another in a logical order, and the genius of the exercise is found in the fact that it contains the germ of succeeding experiences. Pestalozzi is not talking about continuity in learning experiences, rather he is thinking of something more fluid, the development of mental power; but surely this view of continuity had direct and effective application in the deployment of school syllabi.

If we are mystified about Pestalozzi's psychology, and often we have every right to be, and by his obscure talk about mental faculties and the exercises of number, form, and language, we find him somewhat clearer when he turns to the scope and use of all this. The development of the principal faculties, and the acquiring of a certain amount of information are necessary to qualify every individual for his duties as a man, a citizen, and a Christian. The degree of this development constitutes the province of elementary education and should be the same for all: here we have a statement of policy on uniform and universal elementary education, a thesis which provided one theoretical foundation for the common-school movement of the nineteenth century. Elementary education, the same for all, is a minimum; and in Pestalozzi's view this minimum might regularly be surpassed by children with special ability or by children who were fortunately placed socially. Thus, individual differences, a fact of life for which Pestalozzi has enduring respect, are by no means ignored, and they do not, it must be noted, rest solely on talent.

Possibly the most distinctive item in Pestalozzian pedagogy is his theory of mental productions; along with this theory he proposed a variety of exercises, and some elaboration of them is necessary for a complete view. But as we proceed, we see the plan becomes less and less theoretical and more and more mechanical.

Pestalozzi was by nature a modest man with more than the normal amount of humility; he never tries to conceal from us the almost accidental evolution of his teaching techniques. In the early pages of *How Gertrude Teaches Her Children*,[86] incidentally an inappropriate title for the book, because it is set in the context of the schoolroom rather than in the parlor and was intended for schoolmasters rather than for mothers, he tells us of his educational work as well as of his longings to produce a more effective teaching system. But nowhere does he presume that he has found any magic formula; moreover, we are struck by the thought that Pestalozzi would not be able to recognize such a formula if it were to appear suddenly and unexpectedly. All this is woven into the fabric of the book.

So at fifty years of age and with greying hair Pestalozzi fulfilled part of his yearning to help mankind by becoming a schoolmaster and educating mankind's children. At this stage in life he was capable of considerable introspective analysis; thus, he could review the several decades of earlier educational interest and effort and conclude with remarkable candor: "I grew careless; and, being swallowed up in a vortex of anxiety for outward action, I neglected to work out to a sufficient depth, within my own mind, the foundations of what I intended to bring about." [87]

Pestalozzi's confession is less important in the long run, for it had no direct bearing on what he accomplished, than the course of a broad method it reveals. Pestalozzi began with practice, or with experience, and then with experience firmly on his side set his course toward explaining the meaning of experience. The parallel between his own intellectual progress and the method he proposed for education is too important to miss. Here was an educational theorist who seemed to preach what he practiced.

He recounts for us his desperate feelings when he first accepted responsibility for almost eighty children. No doubt his was not an enviable situation, although he had sought it willingly: "But imagine my position. . . . Alone, destitute of all means of instruction, and of all other assistance, I united in my person the offices of superintendent, paymaster, steward, and sometimes chambermaid, in a half-ruined house. . . . What a task! to educate, to develop these children, what a task!" [88]

Then he tells us something about his procedure, and if he is not very detailed or precise it is because he had not worked out his plan in detail or with precision. Yet, he says, "I ventured upon it. I stood in the midst

[86] *How Gertrude Teaches Her Children*, translated by L. E. Holland and F. C. Turner (London, 1894) ; and excerpts in Barnard, *op. cit.*
[87] *Ibid.*, p. 672.
[88] *Ibid.*, p. 674.

of these children, pronouncing various sounds, and asking them to imitate them; whoever saw it was struck with the effect. It is true it was a meteor which vanishes in the air as soon as it appears. No one understood its nature. I did not understand it myself. It was the result of a simple idea, or rather of a fact of human nature, which was revealed to my feelings, but of which I was far from having a clear consciousness." [89]

Pestalozzi may have believed that his insights into the elements of instruction were truly intuitive, although we are entitled to assume that they came at the end of a long period of pondering the meaning of education. Perhaps Pestalozzi had the experience many have had, of puzzling over a problem for days with no apparent progress and then suddenly having the answer seemingly without effort. He could call this phenomenon intuition; we can call it productive intellectual labor. In any case, "after long consideration of the subject—or, rather uncertain dreams about it—I at last set myself to conceive how an educated man proceeds, and must proceed, when endeavoring to abstract, and gradually make clear, any subject now floating confusedly and dimly before his eyes." [90]

According to Pestalozzi such a man would have to follow the steps in this process: first, how many subjects, or how various, are before him; second, how do they look—what is their form and outline; and third, what are they called—how can he recall each to mind by means of a sound, a word. The ability to take each of these steps presupposes that certain mental powers have been developed. In his factoring of mental processes, Pestalozzi concluded that the following were of the first order of importance:

1. The powers of considering unlike objects in relation to their forms and of recalling to mind their material.

2. The powers of abstracting these objects as to their number and of distinctly conceiving them either as one or as many.

3. The power of repeating by language, and fixing so as not to be forgotten, the conception of an object as to number and form.[91]

These intellectual powers were to be formed by the art of instruction, which itself was guided by an invariable law. And Pestalozzi was sensitive to the teacher's questions concerning the direction of the instructional process. In other words, they would surely ask: what shall be taught? The answer was now available:

> 1. To teach the children to consider any object brought before their consciousness, as a unity; that is, as separate from whatever it seems to be bound up with.

[89] *Ibid.*
[90] *Ibid.*, p. 675.
[91] *Ibid.*

2. To teach them an acquaintance with the form of each such object; its size and relations.

3. To make them as early as possible acquainted with the whole circle of words and names of all the objects known to them.[92]

The burden, then, of elementary instruction, if it followed Pestalozzi's prescription, was to direct all teaching toward developing, establishing, and strengthening a fundamental knowledge of numbering, measuring, and speaking. Yet, even when teaching was centered on number, form, and speech, the schoolmaster should know that the senses at work could come in contact with qualities not belonging to number, form, and speech. The attributes of objects not fitting into Pestalozzi's essential classification were not ignored; rather, every effort was to be made to show the necessary relationship between the attributes outside the category and those within it. It was Pestalozzi's contention that number, form, and speech were universal in application and extension; to pursue these qualities in all their relationships gave men, Pestalozzi said, definite, clear and intelligent knowledge.[93]

The groundwork is laid and Pestalozzi is ready to deliver his methodological manifesto; henceforth it was the creed which all his teaching was expected to follow.

I thus concluded that the art of educating our race must be based upon the first and simplest results of these three fundamental elements—sound, form, and number; and that instruction in any one department could and would never lead to a result beneficial to our nature, considered in its whole compass, unless these three simple results of our fundamental faculties should be recognized as the universal starting-points for all instruction, fixed as such by nature herself; and unless these results were accordingly developed into forms proceeding universally and harmoniously from them, and calculated efficiently and surely to carry instruction forward to its completion, through the steps of a progression unbroken, and dealing alike and equally with all three. This I concluded the only means of proceeding in all three departments, from indistinct intuitions to definite ones, from intuitions to clear perceptions, and from clear perceptions to intelligent ideas.

Thus, moreover, I find art actually the most intimately united with nature, or rather with the ideal by means of which natures make the objects of the creation known to us; and so was solved my problem, viz., to discover a common origin of all the means of the art of instruction, and, at the same time, that form of it in which the development of the race is defined by the constitution itself of our nature:—and the difficulty removed, in the way of applying the mechanical laws, which I recognize as the foundation of human

---

[92] *Ibid.*
[93] *Ibid.*, p. 676.

instruction, to that system of instruction which the experience of thousands of years has given to the human race for its own development; that is, to writing, arithmetic, reading, etc.[94]

Pestalozzi's awkward and often cumbersome approach to perfecting the elemental mental faculties marked a significant forward step in building a scientific methodology. Even when the psychological principles on which his approach was based were not entirely clear or valid, his methods showed that an analysis of learning processes produced insights into proper technique and disclosed the imperfections of methods then in general use. No one in the history of education had made such an undertaking his chief work; Quintilian and a host of followers, including Erasmus, had a theory of instruction—in a broad sense an educational method—but these theories of instruction concentrated on the manipulation and justification of the subjects pressed into the school's syllabus. Quintilian spent thousands of words proving that grammar and rhetoric formed the core of learning, and Erasmus proved that the classics were most of all worth studying, and he provided a method along with safeguards for doing so. The proofs, however, were meaningful only to those who needed nothing proved to them about the worth of the classics. But no line in the works of the classical theorists touches on the psychological factors themselves, to say nothing at all about physiological factors, fundamental to the learning process. The assumption had always been made confidently, except possibly in the case of Comenius, that human beings could learn and that they would learn if the proper subjects were put before them.

Interest in methodology had been brewing before Pestalozzi's drive to find its essential bases began—we must not think of him as an innovator of the first order—for the talk about natural methods and natural education stems from a common source; but it had almost always stood clear of the question of what happens in the child's psychological and physiological mechanisms when learning occurs. Pestalozzi's problem was fairly simple: if we discover how human beings learn, we shall know how to teach. The presumption is lacking that learning cannot take place unless the proper techniques are used; but learning under such conditions is always uneconomical and to some degree dehumanized.

Efficient and humanized learning and teaching was the goal Pestalozzi embraced, and he began by explaining how the first elementary means of instruction is sound. First, the organs of speech must be trained —this is what Pestalozzi called "instruction in tones." This process involved speaking and singing tones. In general terms Pestalozzi was asserting that even in the cradle children must be exposed to the simple vowel and consonant sounds. These sounds should be repeated over them

[94] *Ibid.*, pp. 676–677.

before they are able to speak. When they are capable of uttering sounds children should be led into pronouncing these simple sounds—ba, da, ma, la, etc.—and later these same sounds should be put in the spelling book, a book that should be found in every home. "This book," Pestalozzi averred, "differs from all previous ones in this: that its method is universal; and that the pupil himself proceeds in a visible manner, beginning with the vowels, and constructing syllables by the gradual addition of consonants behind and before, in a manner which is comprehensive, and which perceptively facilitates speech and reading." [95] Interest in sounds is paramount; no time is wasted on assigning meaning to them, but a great deal of time is given over to repetition. A further step introduces the child to spelling, and here Pestalozzi employed visual aids beyond those of the printed word; letters were cut from stiff paper with the vowels colored red—so the child could easily distinguish vowel from consonant sounds. Shortly thereafter Pestalozzi introduced a threefold series of letters—the German printed alphabet, the German written alphabet, and the Latin alphabet—enabling the child "to read in all three alphabets, without any loss of time." [96] The aids Pestalozzi invented lend themselves to a number of exercises, all intended to develop conversance with sound, and Pestalozzi described some of the exercises in the text. From this beginning, instruction moved on to syllables, where sound, not meaning, was still stressed, and then to simple words. At this point the first reading book was put into the child's hands.

The second department in the domain of sound, which is intended to follow instruction in tones, is instruction in names. Here again the book Pestalozzi wrote contains lists of names drawn from nature, history, geography, and human vocations and relations. These columns of names are to be committed to memory, and in a conclusion not entirely innocent of wishful thinking, Pestalozzi asserts that this will take no more time than is required to read them readily. Pestalozzi believes that by memorizing these names the child has more complete knowledge and that the advantage so gained "is immeasurable, in relation to the facilitation of subsequent instruction." [97]

The third step in the instruction relative to sound is with language itself. Staying close to what he believed is man's ultimate object in language, Pestalozzi tried to detail the means "through which nature herself, by the gradual development of the faculty of language, brings us to this end." [98] At this point Pestalozzi's plan seems confused and inexact. Now form and number are brought into the picture as corollaries in the development of language, and the five senses are pressed into service too, but

95 *Ibid.*, p. 678.
96 *Ibid.*, p. 679.
97 *Ibid.*, p. 680.
98 *Ibid.*, p. 681.

about all we learn is that the names of objects must be recognized and their qualities comprehended and that the child must express himself with distinctness in relation to number and form.

Memory plays an exceedingly important role in the system, and Pestalozzi is entirely content with this. But what he is getting at is that an ability to express oneself must begin on the level of the most immediate personal experiences. When the child is able to express himself clearly and distinctly, it is time to introduce grammar. This is done in order to achieve the last purpose of instruction in language, rendering intelligent ideas; but the whole process, despite the brave beginnings toward reconstruction of methodology, is at best dissatisfying, for Pestalozzi has actually done little more than assert that the basic natural principle of learning is repetition. In a sense, he is saying, teaching on the elementary levels should employ repetition selectively, that is, goals should be determined and kept discrete until each part of learning is mastered. Then the goals may be collated and another aspect of learning begun.

Pestalozzi breaks off his disquisition on sounds with this high-sounding appraisal of his findings:

> My method of instruction is distinguished especially in this, that it makes more use of language, as a means of lifting the child from obscure intuitions to intelligent ideas, than has heretofore been the case; and also in this, that it excludes from the first elementary instruction all combinations of words which presuppose an actual knowledge of language. Any one who admits how nature leads to intelligent comprehension of all things by a clear comprehension of a single thing, will admit also that single words must be clearly understood by the child before he can intelligently comprehend them in connection; and any one who admits this, rejects at once all the received elementary books of instruction; for they all presuppose an acquaintance with language in the child before they communicate it to him.[99]

Thus, finally we see what Pestalozzi's purpose was, and while we can applaud his goal we can still doubt the efficacy and the inner logic of his method.

Pestalozzi turns next to instruction in form, but before he gets into the subject he wants to say something about the source of human knowledge. His view is that all knowledge comes from the following sources:

1. through the impressions derived from things around us, when brought into relation with our five senses;

2. through whatever is brought before our senses by the intervention of methodic guidance, so far as this depends upon our parents and teachers;

3. through our own determination to attain to knowledge, and to

[99] *Ibid.,* p. 687.

obtain intuitions by our independent striving, after the various means of them;

4. through the results of effort and labor in our callings, and all activity which has not mere intuition as its object;

5. through a means analogous to our intuitional knowledge; inasmuch as it instructs us in the properties of things not pertaining properly to our intuitions, but in which we perceive a similarity to things which we know by our intuitions.[100]

In the discussion of form, geometry comes first. It is hardly Pestalozzi's intent to take the child very far into such a complex subject, for we find his interest centering on the child recognizing and naming the relations of geometric forms and knowing and using them independently. From geometry on its simplest level, Pestalozzi moves to drawing, and finally to writing skill, but we can be content with the summation Pestalozzi himself makes of this section: "I say of the study of writing, that it should be completed, not merely as an art, but as a business acquirement; and that the child should be carried to such a degree of facility in it, that he shall be able to express himself as distinctly respecting it, and use it as easily and as universally, as speaking." [101]

At last Pestalozzi comes to number. He does not think he has left the best to last, but he obviously thinks that number—he emphasizes arithmetic—provides the most certain avenue to the formation of clear ideas. "Sound and form often, and in various ways, contain within themselves a germ of error and delusion; but number, never: it alone leads to infallible results; and, if geometry makes the same claim, it can be only by means of the application of arithmetic, and in conjunction with it; that is, it is infallible as long as it arithmeticizes." [102] Yet Pestalozzi's high-sounding confidence in arithmetic leads only to rote learning of number combinations and mathematical calculations. Of course, Pestalozzi uses objects to show the child the difference between greater and less, makes tables for him to commit to memory, and concludes that by following his method arithmetic becomes exclusively a training in reasoning. "In no sense," he says, is it "a mere exercise of memory, nor any routine mechanical process. It is the result of the clearest and most definite intuitions; and leads, by an easy path, through correct understanding, to truth." [103] Pestalozzi wants us to believe he has found a method which is at once natural, easy, and certain; one that will uplift mankind and lead him to a better life and to truth.

Throughout Pestalozzi's writings there is much talk about harmony in the development of the child; Pestalozzi never tires of stressing his

100 *Ibid.*, p. 689–690.
101 *Ibid.*, p. 698.
102 *Ibid.*
103 *Ibid.*, p. 702.

doctrine that man is a moral, intellectual, and physical being and that there should be harmonious relationships among these three dimensions. In the final analysis Pestalozzi would have selected the moral (and religious) side as most in need of careful development, although he is enthusiastic for the physical and intellectual, because he always entertained a clearheaded and uncomplicated approach to man's relationship to God and to the fundamental dependence men have on God. This much is clear in his total philosophy of life, so we are surprised to find that his school methods are not very elaborate when they treat of moral and religious education. No doubt Pestalozzi expected much moral training to occur in the home, and large portions of this training were the work of informal and incidental education, but the school played its part too. His school program for religious education is in no way separate from moral formation; thus both are to be formed by the same instruments. The specific ways that education may promote virtue, goodness, and piety are offered quickly and without extensive justification, probably because Pestalozzi saw no need for justification. Such education begins with pious exercises, the principal of which is prayer; and includes, in addition, religious conversations, wherein the distinctions between earthly life and heavenly and everlasting life are presented to the child in a clear and practical manner, the study of sacred history and the Bible, and, finally, religious instruction "properly so called; or the regular explanation of the doctrine of our Savior." [104] Formal religious instruction did not appear early in the educational program—probably not before age fifteen—but, as a whole, education was always religiously oriented, and this basic plank in Pestalozzi's platform should dramatize his independence of Rousseau's agnostic pronouncements.

How did Pestalozzi affect schools and what were the permanent features of his plan; what remains after his writings and experiments are pushed into the background of history? We have said Pestalozzi was not entirely original in theory, so we must look elsewhere: the object-lesson method remained as a permanent contribution to educational technique, and its use in Europe, the United States, and other countries makes Pestalozzi's name an important one to remember.[105]

Object-lesson teaching aimed at training the senses through exercises in observation and showed particular interest in training the eye.[106] In addition, it sought to develop powers of observation and laws of thought, along with the development of language. When properly used object-training essayed to unite sense-training, thinking, teaching, and language exercises, and work them together. What method will achieve these

104 *Ibid.*

105 See Monroe, *op. cit.;* and A. Pinloche, *Pestalozzi and the Foundation of the Modern Elementary School* (London, 1902).

106 See M. R. Walch, *Pestalozzi and the Pestalozzian Theory of Education,* (Washington, D.C., Catholic University of America Press, 1952).

aims? The following would seem to be the chief laws of the method.

1. Instruction is by actual inspection.
2. Proceed from the easy to the difficult.
3. Go from the known to the unknown.
4. Go from the near to the distant.
5. Go from the simple to the complex.
6. Go from the concrete to the abstract.
7. Instruct according to the nature of the material but also according to the nature of the child; thus, give in each hour, if possible, a little whole in content and form.
8. Use poetry in the service of instruction.
9. Use conversation.[107]

At the end of this section on Pestalozzi, a summation should be made of his principal educational doctrines and contributions. If we nail his flag to the educational mast, we must know why. His faith in the power of education was contagious and to him, in large part, were due the great forward steps common-school education took. He tried to look beneath the surface of pedagogy and methodology to the psychological principles that governed learning. Even when he was mistaken or unclear about these principles he performed a useful service to education, because he called attention to the importance of psychology in education. In stressing psychology he also emphasized natural organic development in place of an abstract, and too often artificial, transmission of ideas.

Besides causing object-teaching to flourish, Pestalozzi invented numerous instructional aids, and because he was interested in popular education he undertook to perfect class methods of teaching, without which popular education would only have been a meaningless symbol. Finally, because of the importance he attached to method, he was in part responsible for forming a new image of the schoolmaster, who now was to be a pedagogical technician. This obviously required special training for which a science of pedagogy had to be found. Thus, both for training teachers and making the study of education scientific Pestalozzi proved to be an important instrument.[108]

---

[107] See Barnard, *op. cit.*, pp. 201–203.

[108] See W. H. Kilpatrick's "Introduction" to *Heinrich Pestalozzi: The Education of Man* (New York, Philosophical Library, 1951).

❧ 11 ❧

Herbart: Scientific Pedagogy

I

INTRODUCTION

After Comenius, Rousseau, and Pestalozzi completed their directions to the educational world—directions explicitly including a firm conviction that observation, employment of the senses, and attendance to simple concrete data in every field of knowledge were the pillars of elementary education—they assumed their work was finished. Considering the context of formal education and the state of psychological knowledge, they were probably right. The real world of everyday experience had been stressed; a trust in nature rather than art had been asserted; and the inner feelings, the human nature, of the child in the educational process had been accentuated. What had been accomplished was to a large extent the result of careful and probing analysis, cynicism, and sympathy. Taken together these approaches sounded the clarion call for a new education. But for all the good work, to ignore for a moment the exaggerations and misconceptions, and the grand desires to lead an educational revolution, the means for achieving desirable ends in education were noticeably lacking. Comenius had talked about learning according to a natural method, but he was never able to deploy this method for the day-to-day teacher; and Rousseau and Pestalozzi had established their pedagogical theories and practices without the steadying direction of a sound psychology. In a word, the emphasis on method in the pedagogical process, which is entirely clear in the writings and teaching of Comenius and Pestalozzi, and dimly recommended in the elaborate assertions of Rousseau, could only encourage awkward progress in the revitalization of teaching and learning because the psychology of learning subserving it was inadequate. Only an adequate psychology could provide a theory which in turn could give scientific precision to instruction and moral training.

We have seen Pestalozzi in action—and he may be counted the inheritor of the tradition of scientific realism begun by Comenius—capitalizing on the empiricism distilled from his intuitions. He recommended techniques of teaching following these major principles: learn the simple before the complex; combine in the teaching and learning process those things that naturally belong together; fix in the mind the objects of thought by employing all the senses in learning them; depend on physical nature to advance and unify the content of instruction; and provide the learner with a rich and varied educational environment. Unquestionably the old patterns of education were challenged by Pestalozzi's hopes for a more meaningful program of learning and for a more generous distribution of educational opportunity, but they were not seriously eroded because Pestalozzi provided little other than his own example as a teacher for other teachers to follow.

Herbart could easily accept Pestalozzi's doctrines relative to the importance of sense perception, verification of knowledge, and object-lesson teaching and at the same time ascertain that much was left to be done.[1] His conception of the unfinished business in education may be stated as follows: the development of a psychology of learning centered on problems of teaching; the application of this psychology to teaching; and the creation of an educational methodology capable of channeling all classroom activities toward the objective of character formation. In 1894 Charles DeGarmo wrote: "We should not regard Herbart's contributions as additions, however important, to an educational mosaic already existing. Such a view would be most misleading. His work is fundamental, compelling a new elaboration of the whole theory of education." [2] This was a strong commission for Herbart, if DeGarmo was correct in his assessment. We shall try to see if his theory was totally new and, at the same time, what it was.

Preliminary to following Herbart's elaboration of educational theory, we should pause long enough to see how he was equipped to fulfill the monumental commission DeGarmo acknowledged for him.[3] There need be no doubt about Herbart's opportunity to obtain a magnificent education; thus he could scrutinize the educational process through eyes that had seen the best Germany could offer. Spared the disadvantages of

[1] See Charles DeGarmo, *Herbart and the Herbartians* (New York, Charles Scribner's Sons, 1896) , pp. 3–11.

[2] *Ibid.*, p. 9.

[3] Biographical works on Herbart are relatively scant and old. See C. C. Van Liew, *Life of Herbart and Development of His Pedagogical Doctrines* (London, Swan Sonnenschein & Co., 1893) ; F. Bartholomai, *Herbart's pädagogische Schriften mit Biographie* (Langensalza, H. Beyer & Söhne, 1903–1906) ; and *Paedagogica Historica*, vol. I (1961) .

Comenius, Rousseau, and Pestalozzi, he was the stable product of a good home and respectable schooling. Born in 1776, the only child of a contented, successful lawyer-father and a highly intelligent, ambitious mother, young Herbart was entrusted to the instructional hands of a tutor, from whom he learned the elements of education plus Greek, mathematics, logic, and metaphysics. His mental gifts were extraordinary, and nowhere in his reminiscences on his own education do we find him doubting the quality or the worth of the things he studied. It may be worth noting at the outset that if Herbart was a reconstructionist, his reconstruction was aimed mainly at the methods of teaching, not at the content of instruction. At age thirteen he was in the Oldenburg gymnasium and naturally found his place at the head of the class. In the gymnasium his favorite subjects were physics and philosophy, but he pursued all his studies with unfailing industry and success and finished what would normally have been a nine-year course in only five. At eighteen he was ready for higher studies and was admitted to the University of Jena to study law. His intellectual appetites, however, were not for the law, so he abandoned legal studies in favor of philosophy. Within the short period of three years he finished the philosophy course and, casting about for something to do, because he was still young and undecided about his future, accepted a situation as a private tutor to three sons of the governor of Interlaken.[4] He held this position for two years, took a decided interest in the intellectual welfare of his students, wrote periodic reports on their progress, and during this period generated an indelible interest in the educational process. At about the same time that he resigned his position as a private tutor, he visited Pestalozzi's school at Burgdorf, where he was able to observe the reformer's pedagogy in action. He was not yet committed to leading an educational revolution of his own, being more intent upon carving out for himself an academic career in philosophy, so he spent the next several years in private study and writing and in 1802 presented himself for the doctor's degree in philosophy at the University of Göttingen.[5] Shortly thereafter he obtained the position of *privat-docent* at Göttingen and, because of his success in this capacity, was shortly appointed as an extraordinary—or associate—professor. At this time, in addition to lecturing on philosophy proper, he delivered lectures on psychology and pedagogy. In 1809 Herbart accepted the chair of philosophy at the University of Königsberg, a chair which he held for twenty-four years before returning to Göttingen, where he completed his

---

4 See G. Compayré, *Herbart and Education by Instruction* (New York, T. Y. Crowell & Co., 1907), p. 10.

5 His knowledge of Pestalozzi's educational writings is attested to, for during this period he wrote: *Pestalozzi's Idee cines A B C der Anschauung* (Göttingen, 1802); *Über den Standpunkt der Beurtheilung der Pestalozzi'schen Unterrichtsmethode* (Bremen, 1804); and *Ueber Pestalozzis neueste Schrift "Wie Gertrud"* (1802).

academic career. He died there in 1841.[6] During this academic career—spanning nearly four decades—he contributed impressively to the literature in philosophy and made brave beginnings in the sciences of psychology and pedagogy. Unquestionably, both because of the positions he occupied and because of the intellectual allegiances he had, Herbart was well suited and well equipped to pronounce new theories pertaining to teaching and learning. And because Herbart was so much the teacher, it is not surprising that he concentrated on formulating what may fairly be called a schoolmaster's methodology; that is, a method of teaching that looks first to what the teacher must do in the instructional process, if the ends for education are to be achieved. Herbart did not ignore the student, but he left it to others to emphasize the psychological and pedagogical problems arising on the learner's side of the teacher's desk.

If Herbart could be thought to have a pedagogical preoccupation, it must surely have been contained in the thought expressed in the opening lines of his *Science of Education:* "The aim of all those who educate and demand education is determined by the range of thought they bring to the subject. The majority of those who teach have entirely neglected in the first instance to construct for themselves their own range of thought in view of this work; it opens out gradually as the work progresses, and is formed partly by their own characteristics, partly by the individuality and the environment of the pupil." [7] Herbart does not argue that educational theory is inoperative or nonexistent; he was too good a scholar, too much in touch with the literature in education to have allowed himself this questionable luxury. In various places in his own writings he makes pointed, and often extended, allusions to other educational theorists. Locke, Rousseau, and, of course, Pestalozzi are paid special heed. So the point of his remark is not that theory is ignored. He complains that theory is not brought down to the level of practical teaching issues; that theory too often, in fact almost always, remains on an antiseptic level and affects neither the mind of the teacher nor the practices he employs. This would not do, Herbart believed, because education was not a theoretical but a highly practical question; teachers needed dependable information about goals and processes before they entered the classroom. Too much valuable time and human talent were allowed to waste away while teachers decided, or determined in their on-the-job training, what they should do and how to do it.

[6] The fact that interest in Herbart's work has waned so greatly in the years since his death, with the exception of a ten- or fifteen-year period toward the end of the nineteenth century, is explained somewhat by H. B. Dunkel, "Herbart's Pedagogical Seminar," *History of Education Quarterly,* VII (Spring, 1967), pp. 93–94.

[7] J. F. Herbart, *The Science of Education: Its General Principles Deduced from Its Aim,* translated by H. M. and E. Felkin (London, Swan Sonnenschein & Co., 1892), p. 78. See Dunkel, *op. cit.,* p. 94.

Thus the interlude in Herbart's Königsberg career, where he actively engaged in conducting a teacher's school, takes on additional importance and stands as a principal component in his profession as an educator; and the doctrine that "education cannot merely be taught; it must be demonstrated and practiced" must be interpreted as a central plank in his pedagogical platform. The plan for teacher training began modestly, with Herbart taking a few promising students from his lecture class on the theory of education to the gymnasium, where he conducted demonstration lessons. There he confirmed in practice his contention that "theory and practice should always go together." Once these select students were introduced to Herbart's theories and classroom techniques, they were allowed to teach the classes themselves, with Herbart on hand to supervise their work. Gradually the student-teachers were trained by a combination of pedagogical principle and active experience in the classroom; their methods were perfected by mutual observation and exchange of experience. Herbart's teacher's seminar graduated into a regular teacher's college and flourished, with surprising attention paid to it, in a German university system where technique had counted for little. Teachers trained by Herbart—for he did not relinquish a central role in the school even when it grew larger—were much sought after in Germany and lavishly praised for their abilities. But the teacher's school at Königsberg closed abruptly when Herbart transferred to Göttingen, because, undoubtedly, of the singular role Herbart occupied in it, and for some reason Herbart did not try to organize another such experiment at his new academic post.[8]

We have drawn a quick picture of the man and his academic background, along with his special commitment to the improvement of teaching. What is left for us now is to see something of the educational code he pronounced, which would guide both teachers and teachers educating teachers in fulfilling their demanding and important intellectual and social roles.

II

DEFINING EDUCATIONAL OBJECTIVES

Many followers and admirers of Herbart's educational thought have been impressed by the newness of his view: "The one and the whole work of education may be summed up in the concept—Morality," [9] and any

8 Dunkel advances some reasons why the school was not continued. See *ibid.*, pp. 93–101.

9 J. F. Herbart, *On the Aesthetic Revelation of the World as the Chief Work of Education*, translated by H. M. and E. Felkin (London, Swan Sonnenschein & Co., 1892), p. 57.

disclaimer now entered has a discordant ring. Yet one cannot read many pages of Locke's *Some Thoughts Concerning Education* or Comenius' *Great Didactic* before meeting virtue securely positioned as the ultimate educational objective. Indeed, neither Herbart nor anyone else would have been required to read only Herbart's immediate predecessors to meet this objective: after many false starts Socrates had come to the conclusion that knowledge is, or leads to, virtue; Quintilian in his definition—"the good man skilled in speaking"—had confirmed in precept the varied traditions of Hellenistic education; Erasmus spoke for the Humanists—and all were included—when he restored character formation as the leading objective of formal education. Herbart, then, was the beneficiary, not the originator, of a cultural and pedagogical doctrine making morality, or character formation, the principal business of education.

In accepting a traditional doctrine Herbart was not making his task of formulating broad educational policy any easier: to have settled for intellectual formation, identified mainly by the acquisition of knowledge, an objective with which many medieval educators felt comfortable, would have simplified every phase of his theory and practice. It is admittedly much harder to find an educational structure to bear the weight of character formation than that of informing the mind. But Herbart would not have been satisfied with an education centered on mental cultivation; he is in complete agreement with others who earlier had expressed the view that men who are only well informed may in fact be dangerous men; they must also be formed morally.

In addition to accepting morality as the principal work of education, Herbart accepted the trained intelligence as the most secure safeguard to morality, and only stopped short of maintaining that right knowledge leads to right action. Nowhere in Herbart's writings do we find him slighting instruction; he never paused to consider what a school would be that did not emphasize instruction, and any such suggestion to him would have been treated as a bad joke. Yet he did not envision the instructional dimension, formed on the impartation of knowledge, as an exclusive or all-dominating one; instruction would, in Herbart's system, take a middle ground between the self-activity of the pupil and the molding force coming from mastering curricular materials. He candidly asserts that "Man's worth does not, it is true, lie in his knowing, but in his willing." But then he adds: "there is no such thing as an independent faculty of will. Volition has its roots in thought; not, indeed, in the details one knows, but certainly in the combinations and the total effect of the acquired ideas." [10] The simple point made is intended to impress on us the need for avoiding formulas in educational theory and practice;

---

[10] J. F. Herbart, *Outlines of Educational Doctrine*, translated by A. F. Lange (New York, The Macmillan Company, 1901), § 58.

most especially in educational practice we must recognize that truly educative teaching is directed toward incitement of mental activity, not toward an encyclopedic grasp of everything worth knowing.

Yet Herbart wants us to know in advance the kinds of mental activity we should foster, and we must make some judgment about varieties of generative instruction. This kind of knowledge about education is clearly philosophic, and Herbart admits the need for continuity and consistency in philosophic thought, beginning with the nature of the person to be educated. We must have authentic knowledge about the nature of man, his soul, and the ethical and psychological principles explaining what he is and what he is capable of becoming. Unless we have clear ideas about these basic considerations, we shall surely run aground when we try to sail the educational ship through the various channels of life.[11] In *The Science of Education* he expresses his thought on the ends of education in this way: "can we know beforehand the aims of the future man, a knowledge for which he will one day thank us, instead of having to find and follow them by himself alone?" [12] His conclusion is, obviously, that we can, otherwise he would not have spent precious time trying to tell his readers what education ought to be. Yet he does not think this is a simple matter, and does not pretend that it is always possible to be clear, and, moreover, he is not at all convinced that in the end he will be able to obtain universal agreement on the subject. Children begin with manifold interests, distilled mysteriously out of their contacts with the world, and these interests are multiplied as they continue through life in and outside the school. While he is unquestionably committed to the view that morality is the ultimate educational goal—and accepting his original assumptions, proof on this point is possible—he is ready to admit that there are other goals in education which must be cultivated, for they are unquestionably conditions out of which the moral objective is developed. "I therefore believe that the mode of consideration which places morality at the head is certainly the most important, but not the only and comprehensive, standpoint of education." [13] To prove his point at this time, he says, would require of him the articulation of a complete system of philosophy, which he believes he has done before in the *A B C of Observation*.[14] In any case, if there was reasonable doubt that the system which he had elaborated was inadequate, and he must have known that universal allegiance to any one system of philosophy was too much to hope for, he declared that "education has no time to make holiday now, till philosophical questions are once for all cleared up. Rather it is to be

11 Herbart, *Aesthetic Revelation of the World*, p. 59.

12 Herbart, *The Science of Education*, pp. 106–107.

13 *Ibid.*, p. 108.

14 J. F. Herbart, *A B C of Sense Perception and Minor Pedagogical Works*, translated by W. J. Eckoff (New York, D. Appleton and Co., 1903).

desired that pedagogy shall be kept as free as possible from philosophical doubts." [15]

It would seem that Herbart has painted himself into a corner: if the philosophical issue is a burning one for pedagogy, if its prescriptions are unavoidable considerations for setting goals in education, but if the philosophical questions cannot be resolved, then what is the educator to do? Would it not seem that he must take a holiday; must he not remain silent on educational issues until he has marked out the route for education to follow? Herbart thinks there is another solution. He himself is willing to depend on the philosophical propositions of his earlier speculations, but if unity of purpose cannot be gained this way—and he does not think that it can—then the mainspring for educational activity must come not from philosophy but from psychology. This is an approach which is, at least, partly empirical, and Herbart wanted to make it even more so. Educational objectives and programs must find their documentation in the human aims of the pupil.

Even here there are some problems, formed mainly because human aims are manifold, and, in order to be adequate, teachers and the programs they direct must contain manifold opportunities for human development. Critical as they are, however, these problems are not without resolution. Herbart is prepared to counsel a course of direct action: "It is not however, here contended that the multiplicities of education cannot easily be classified under one or a few main formal conceptions; on the contrary, the kingdom of the pupil's future aims at once divides itself for us into the province of *merely possible aims* which he might perhaps take up at one time or other and pursue in greater or less degree as he wishes—and into the entirely distinct province of the *necessary aims* which he would never pardon himself for having neglected. In one word, the aim of education is sub-divided according to the aims of *choice*—not of the teacher, nor of the boy, but of the future man, and the aims of *morality*. These two main headings are at once clear to every one who bears in mind the most generally recognized of the fundamental principles of ethics." [16]

Herbart has put before us the broad aim of morality with the candid admission that there are many different systems of moral philosophy, each with its own techniques, maxims, and assumptions. But he does not want teachers to confuse children with varieties of moral arguments and counterarguments. Despite the multitude of theoretical bases to ethics, there are, Herbart thinks, practical bases to which most men will quite readily agree. This should be enough for his purposes. Besides, the business of education is not so much to examine the precepts of a moral philosophy, or even to engage in building one, but to discover how

[15] Herbart, *The Science of Education,* p. 108.
[16] *Ibid.,* p. 109.

ethical ideas are formed and followed in conduct. Once this is done, it should be possible for the teacher to take a set of major ethical ideals, which Herbart supplies, and put it before the students for their ingestion. Herbart knows, of course, that the school is not the only place where moral ideas are communicated or caught: the home environment and the general environment of life are moral teachers, and they are almost constantly at work.[17] But Herbart is certain that the school's moral objectives must neither blindly follow the inchoate teaching of informal educational agencies nor surrender the job of moral education to them. What if the moral education of the child was plainly defective when he entered school? What if the impress of social forces on moral formation were detrimental? The school might not be merely in the position of an agency trying to communicate a good moral foundation; it might, as a matter of fact, have to try in its teaching to counteract the insidious effects of bad moral teaching. All this Herbart could assume, but this assumption did nothing more than underline the extremely significant role the school played in the making of men, and it surrounded the school with an importance that it had hardly ever enjoyed before.

Still, asserting or assessing the school's moral role was not exactly what Herbart had in mind; his principal objective was to trace the pedagogy of moral teaching and learning by discovering the embodiment of moral principles in conduct. So as a beginning he resolved to make two important rejections: the first was a jettisoning of the categorical imperative that reason commands the will.[18] To accept this categorical imperative would mean that morality could not be established as an educational objective; moral education as such would be a mere verbalism. What counted would be intellectual refinement, for in the end the will could only follow the directives of the intellect. On the other hand, Herbart wanted to dispose of the fatalistic conception that human beings are powerless to alter the direction of action prescribed for them by some outside force.[19] If men, or wills, were determined, then, it seemed to Herbart, as it must seem to us, that moral education would be nothing but a meaningless luxury.

Herbart was too positive a thinker to stay long with the ideas or the philosophical presuppositions that needed discarding. His was not a doctrine of rejection. He was more concerned with what educators should do, should be, and should know than with the converse. He was, moreover, somewhat disturbed by the thought that man should be subdivided into various functions and faculties. He had, we know, no time for faculty psychology, and thus it is quite natural for us to find him speaking not of the moral formation of the will but of the moral formation of

17 *Ibid.,* p. 95.
18 *Ibid.,* p. 107; and Herbart, *Outlines of Educational Doctrine,* § 313.
19 *Ibid.,* 3.

men.[20] It is always the man who acts morally or immorally, wisely or unwisely. Thus, for him, there is no need to separate functions of mind or to specifically define functions of institutions which on the one side would be intellectual and on the other moral. His approach is integral; schools should group their forces, take all the resources at their disposal, and work toward the goal of educating a good man. Herbart quite willingly abandoned the last part of Quintilian's famous definition of the orator, although he insisted that the teacher, like Quintilian's orator, be skilled, and he chose instead to dwell on the very dimension, the good man, that Quintilian had abandoned to chance.

If Herbart could not depend upon a code of moral philosophy for his starting point, he had the alternative of concentrating on the pupil, and this is the alternative he selected. He tried to find from his psychological understanding of children the core around which moral formation might be initiated. He was not, we should repeat, trying to state an ethical code; rather, he was trying to find the major ideas or values which constitute moral life and then to make it the business of education to integrate these ideas with every phase of instruction to make them guides to life. Ethical conceptions, Herbart concluded, begin with basic feelings of harmony and pleasure, discord and displeasure. Obviously these basic feelings are unrefined in their original state and thus they would remain unless education does something with them. In other words, they need a shaping and a direction, or an elaboration, which would allow the schoolmaster to establish them as ends toward which his instruction might aspire. The five major ideas of moral life are elaborated as follows:

1. Idea of Inner Freedom. "Inner freedom is a relation between insight and volition," and once this relationship is recognized it forms a double task for the teacher: one of making "actual each of these factors [insight and volition] separately, in order that later a permanent relationship may result." [21] Herbart's point is that inner freedom is the outcome of man's moral insights, on the one hand, and conviction of freedom from external influence in making a choice, on the other. If he does not have moral insights, he will be unaware of a difference between alternatives—one moral issue will appear no different from another—and if he has not experienced freedom from external influence in making choices he will be unable or unwilling to act in concert with his convictions. Early in his classification of moral ideas, ideas expected to affect learning, Herbart applies the principle that "education cannot merely be taught; it must be demonstrated and practiced." [22]

2. Idea of Perfection or Efficiency. Herbart's *Aesthetic Revelation of*

---

20 *Ibid.*, 20.

21 *Ibid.*, 8.

22 K. Kehrbach and O. Flügel, *Johann Friedrich Herbart, Sämtliche Werke,* (Langensalza, 1887) , XIV, 19.

the World clarifies this "idea" and makes us think that he is really talking about a strong will.[23] The will's strength, according to Herbart, is constituted of intensity, concentration, and extension. The two former are products of man's natural endowment and are relatively unaffected by education; the last, however, belongs to the province of schooling. Strength, resoluteness, and determination are generated in a moral and intellectual culture sufficiently broad and appealing to satisfy a many-sidedness of interest. Meritorious action—about which different judgments must be made—is different from strength of will—perfection or efficiency, as Herbart calls it [24]—for one may decide to do something wrong and do it, or select praiseworthy goals and follow them. So the strong and efficient will can make unethical choices. Herbart senses the possibility of a "bad" will and wants to guard against it; but at this point in his discussion of major moral ideas, he is concerned only with the issue of the will's strength.

3. Idea of Benevolence. In the moral formation of men, teaching must lead to an understanding of different kinds of good: my good and the good of others. The end of this teaching is habitual action in selecting the good that, while serving the interests of one person, does not harm others. This is not quite the same as self-abnegation, yet it is entirely compatible with a Christian conception of ethics. Dedication to the common good, however, is not merely a matter of habit: obvious elements of perception are essential. The person about to act must have "good" will toward his fellow men and, additionally, insights into the motives and objectives of his neighbors. Herbart is not preaching that teachers must recite the golden rule, because direct, perceptual approaches to moral teaching are unsatisfactory; yet he wants the idealism reflected by the golden rule firmly imbedded in value systems.

4. Idea of Justice. Herbart refused to endow the virtue of justice with unalterable meaning or to define it in a context insulated from the forces of social evolution. What is justice is a large philosophical question, and for any age new interpretations are needed for justice's efficacious application; and these interpretations are necessary, especially when the bases of virtue are absolute. Pedagogic theory does not demand a definition of justice or a reinterpretation of its meaning, but it must promote the general idea of justice and the social necessity of recognizing the rights of others and acting to ensure their protection and preservation.

5. Idea of Equity. This idea appears at first to be an elaboration of the idea of justice. In any case, its emphasis is one of the consequences of action, of what happens to a person after right or wrong conduct. Herbart wants to underline his conviction that equity means reward for

23 Herbart, *Aesthetic Revelation of the World*, pp. 67–68.
24 Herbart, *The Science of Education*, pp. 110–111.

virtue and punishment for vice; thus virtue becomes eminently practical and, in the end, should make equity pay. In addition, Herbart forthrightly acknowledges human responsibility: men harvest the benefits of right action and intellectually honest decision and suffer the consequences of unethical word and deed.

These fundamental ideas about moral life are huge parts of the business of education, and it must make them corollaries to instruction and ultimately guides for life. Herbart, we think, is telling us something about the foundation of education in values.[25]

III

SETTING THE MEANS FOR EDUCATION

In Herbart's own writing more space was given to analyzing processes of instruction than to identifying and justifying the aims of education. Yet he was always fully aware of goals. He talked about the urgent need for recognizing education as "a harmonious cultivation of all the powers" and interpreted this expression, a common one in his own day, to mean "a proportionate many-sidedness of interest." [26] There is no way for the teacher to decide precisely what the student should know for his future life, although he can be certain of the general structure of life in any historical era. Herbart counsels teachers to take children as they are and capitalize on the interests they have; in turn these interests can be built upon in a way that reminds us of mathematical progression. In the end the manifold interests of the student will be served, and in the end, too, his capacity for insight will be refined. Herbart, then, begins with a commitment to exploit, in the best instructional sense, the multiplicity of interests children have, and he ends with insight, the basis for moral action. "Since morality has its place singly and only in the individual's will, founded on right insight, it follows of itself, first and foremost, that the work of moral education is not by any means to develop a certain external mode of action, but rather insight together with corresponding volition in the mind of the pupil." [27] And at this point Herbart is not thinking of communicating a set of moral principles to young people, for he believes that by doing so limitations will be placed on their course of thought and thus on the possibility of their forming profound and relevant insights. The constant tug of war between individuality, on the one hand, and character, on the other, is noticed by Herbart, and undoubt-

---

[25] For Herbart's discussion of the major ideas of moral life, see *ibid.*, pp. 259–268; and DeGarmo, *op. cit.*, pp. 49–56.

[26] Herbart, *The Science of Education*, p. 111.

[27] *Ibid.*

edly he anticipated that his major moral ideas should have been of some help in reducing the tension between what the person wanted to do to serve his own objectives and what he should do partly in his own interest and partly in serving the common good. This, too, is a pedagogical issue, although we should be somewhat optimistic if we thought that Herbart had an unequivocal answer to it. Herbart phrased the issue in this way: "The teacher aims at the universal; the pupil, however, is an individual human being." [28] And he wonders a few pages later if "individuality [is] consistent with many-sidedness? Can the former be preserved, while the latter is cultivated." [29] Individuality is viewed as a highly desirable trait, one unalterably part of man's nature. It is inward looking and is grounded on self interest; many-sidedness of interest, however, to use Herbart's own phrase "presses outwards in all directions." To complicate the matter even further this individuality of which Herbart speaks is unconscious, while the many-sidedness, or character, where volition plays a determining role, takes place in consciousness. "Character then, almost inevitably expresses itself in opposition to individuality by conflict. For it is simple and steadfast; individuality, on the contrary, continually sends forth from its depths other and new thoughts and desires. Even if its activity is conquered, it still enfeebles the execution of resolves through its manifold passivity and susceptibility." [30]

Education is faced with the monumental task of bringing individuality and character into harmony. The key to achieving this objective, according to Herbart, is to be found in interest. So attached is Herbart to interest, both to its refinement and to its relationship to character formation, that we find him being credited with having formulated a doctrine of interest.[31] In the articulation of this doctrine, Herbart is often imprecise or visionary; frequently it is hard to follow all the avenues down which his thought seems to lead. Yet, it may be possible, while not being unfair to Herbart or distorting his principles, to give the foundations of this doctrine. He begins by dismissing as pure myth the notion that the will is independent of ideas and thought processes. The will is dependent on ideas, and ideas in turn are generated in an instructional process in which interest has an essential role. Interest, in the Herbartian analysis, is not only an instrument for keeping instruction vital and progressive; it is, in addition, an outcome of instruction. It is what is left after the knowledge learned in formal schooling has faded from the mind.[32] Broad and varied interests in the student testify to efficient and effective teaching; more than this though, they ignite the drive toward good

28 *Ibid.*, p. 113.
29 *Ibid.*, p. 115.
30 *Ibid.*, pp. 117–118.
31 F. Eby, *The Development of Modern Education* (New York, Prentice-Hall, Inc., 1952) , p. 475; Compayré, *op. cit.*, pp. 47–48; and Ulich, *op. cit.*, pp. 275–276.
32 See Herbart, *The Science of Education*, pp. 132–134.

character by a development of ideals, the cultivation of moral dispositions, and the acquisition of moral habits. The moral world, Herbart maintains, is not revealed through precepts but through direct contacts in living. Despite this clear affirmation relative to the place of action in moral formation, Herbart does not want to eschew the worth of interests generated from knowledge, nor does he want to deny that learning is one way of illuminating interests and multiplying them.[33]

Interests that come from learning are, according to Herbart, of three types: empirical, speculative, and aesthetic.[34]

Herbart studiously avoids going into detail about curriculum; yet it is in the curriculum, at least on the early levels of education, that empirical interests are cultivated. Wonder is the starting point. From the pleasure and excitement the learner feels from knowing what he did not know before about things that seem meaningful to him, he gets the motivation to discover and understand the novel and the unknown. The field for empirical interest must be broad and inexhaustible, but Herbart does not say much about it because not much needs to be said. Undoubtedly it is not a period of education through which the student passes only once on his way to virtue; he must be kept in constant contact with empirical knowledge and thus constantly recharge his empirical interests.

Speculative interest drives one toward the reasons behind things; it goes below the surface of mere empirical interest to look for causes and relationships. Aesthetic interest is more elusive and probably even more personal than the others, for it rests on the enjoyment one has from contemplating something regarded as an ideal.

These interests related to knowledge are called individual, for in Herbart's interpretation they are almost purely subjective. But knowledge interests are not alone in the human make-up; interests generated by association are in evidence too, and they are classified by Herbart as sympathetic, social, and religious.[35] These interests of association are of supreme importance for civilized living, and if they are left uncultivated, or if they become one-sided or narrow, they become threats to the stability of society.

In the school's program care must be taken not to allow any one of the six main classes of interest to be slighted. While this would seem to be good advice, it is not easy to know what tactics are best for securing a proper balance. Herbart does not help us much. While he does allude to the problem in his *Outlines of Educational Doctrine*,[36] he hardly goes beyond affirming his belief that dangers reside in allowing one class of interests to be given extra attention at the expense of others. In the end

33 Herbart, *Outlines of Educational Doctrine*, § 135.
34 *Ibid.*, § 83–94.
35 *Ibid.*
36 *Ibid.*, § 85–89.

the balance of interests hoped for may not be the special province of instruction at all, and this surely creates another pedagogical puzzle for teachers. This is the way Herbart expresses himself on the point: "But no instruction is able to prevent the special varieties of one-sidedness that may develop within the limits of each main group. When observation, reflection, the sense of beauty, sympathy, public spirit, and religious aspiration have once been awakened, although perhaps only within a small range of objects, the farther extension over a greater number and variety of objects must be left largely to the individual and to opportunity. To pupils of talent, above all of genius, instruction may give the necessary outlook by enabling them to see what talent and genius achieve elsewhere; but their own distinguishing traits they must themselves answer for and retain." [37]

Despite Herbart's affirmation that instruction can do little to ward off exaggerations or preoccupations with one or another kind of interest, it can do something. He never doubts for a moment that formal education has a part to play and, indeed, a very important part in stimulating interests and keeping them alive. Education, perhaps more than any other social force, marks out the road to good character, and education without instruction is nothing.[38] So Herbart approaches the instructional dimension with enthusiasm, and it is perhaps on this level that he performs his greatest service to pedagogy. It may even be correct to say that scientific pedagogy actually begins with him. The materials of instruction, as we have said before, do not claim much of Herbart's attention. He willingly leaves to others, hopefully to those who understand the objectives of his theory of education, the task of building curricula, but he is fairly certain that the materials of instruction are to be formed out of the literature and science constituting human knowledge.[39] Herbart's curriculum is not narrowly classical; although the classics are surely there, they are supplemented by bodies of knowledge supplied by empirical science. In many respects Herbart is quite traditional; the school's curriculum should embrace all subjects that have found their way into the intellectual arena. What can be called the progressivism of Rousseau is rejected summarily: "To leave man to Nature, or even to wish to lead him to, and train him up in, Nature is mere folly. For what *is* the nature of man? To the Stoics and Epicureans, it was alike the convenient peg on which they hung their systems. Human nature, which appears to be suited for the most diverse conditions, is of so general a character that its special determination and development is entirely left to the race. The ship constructed and arranged with highest art, that it may be able to adapt itself to every change of wind and wave,

37 *Ibid.*, p. 89.
38 Herbart, *The Science of Education*, p. 84.
39 *Ibid.*, pp. 147–152.

only awaits the steersman to direct it to its goal, and guide its voyages according to circumstances.

We know our aim. Nature does much to aid us, and humanity has gathered much on the road she has already traversed; it is our task to join them together." [40]

The world is opened to the learner by three things, and each is important, although only one is really the business of formal education. The first is experience, by which Herbart means what is learned from contacts with the physical world; the second is intercourse, and Herbart means by this learning from social connections; the third is instruction. The two former leave large gaps in our knowledge, and they must be closed by instruction. Instruction therefore is a complement to the informal education offered by the physical and the social worlds. To begin with, while one must recognize the utility and significance of instruction, he must know too what it is incapable of doing. Only then can he be confident of the worth of instruction. The genius of instruction is identified by Herbart: "instruction alone can lay claim to cultivate a balanced all-embracing many-sidedness." [41] With this brief justification of instruction's special role in the formation of men, he is ready to move to practical considerations in instruction. He understands these practical considerations to be methods of instruction and steps in instruction.[42]

Methods of instruction are the broad approaches to teaching, described by Herbart as presentative, analytic, and synthetic, while the steps of instruction pertain to what the teacher does on the level of day-to-day techniques. Neither methods nor techniques follow naturally from the subject being taught, although Herbart is willing to acknowledge a relationship between subject matter and method. Yet, he does not want to depend on this relationship, and he comes close to challenging the whole doctrine of logical methodology. "The teacher," he says, "in charge of a given branch of study only too often lays out his work without taking account of pedagogical considerations. His specialty, he thinks, suffices to suggest a plan; the successive steps in its organized content will, of course, be the proper sequence for instruction to follow. . . . The good pupil, accordingly, is one who fits into and willingly submits to these arrangements. The natural consequence of all this is, that little heed is paid to the condition of attention, namely, the gradual progress of interest." [43]

The claims previously made for natural methodology made a deep impression on Herbart. The work of Comenius, Locke, and Pestalozzi, despite its inability to isolate the steps in natural learning, had generated doubt in the minds of the best educators about the time-honored practice

40 *Ibid.*, pp. 135–136.
41 *Ibid.*, p. 141.
42 *Ibid.*, pp. 142–147; 154–169.
43 Herbart, *Outlines of Educational Doctrine*, § 96.

of allowing the subject matter to dictate teaching procedures. Herbart does not want teachers to ignore the subject; he is convinced that without a clear content instruction is a meaningless exercise; [44] and he is quite certain that a good school must be content-centered. The curriculum must contain solid things for students to learn; and they must learn them. Herbart pays full heed to tradition in his curricular views; but he wants subjects in the traditional curriculum taught not for their own sake but for student development. And he is ready to say how this should be done.

Presentative instruction—Herbart refers to it as merely presentative —has but one law; "to describe in such a way that the pupil believes he sees what is described." [45] The teacher's role in this type of instruction is obvious: he must, either by oral presentation or by ordering curricular experiences for the student, give a picture of experience. Although presentative instruction has a limited use, it is, according to Herbart, so effective that it merits separate consideration. Teachers must be prepared to use it carefully, for skill in presentative instruction is the surest means of securing interest. What the teacher leaves undone, the student, it might be supposed, can fill in for himself by reading; but Herbart has more confidence in the spoken than in the written word, and he admonishes teachers to develop skill in narration and description. "At the most," he wrote, "we may let the pupils that read exceptionally well read aloud to the class. By far the sure means to the end in view is the oral presentation by the teacher. But in order that such presentation may produce its effect undisturbed, it needs to be perfectly free and untrammelled." [46] What skills must the teacher have to accomplish the objective Herbart sets before him? First, he must have developed a cultivated style of speech; he should be easy to listen to, and his presentation must be interesting; second, he must use a vocabulary adapted to the understanding of the children. It does no good to talk to them in phraseologies beyond their grasp; they will neither learn anything from such presentations nor will they be able to sustain interest. Finally, Herbart maintains, the teacher must be in full command of his subject; and this means his presentations are prepared carefully, even committing some of them to memory.[47] All facts should be at his finger tips, and everything he says should be accurate.

In presentative instruction the teacher and the subject matter seem to loom largest, but the student must not be forgotten. The purpose of this kind of instruction is to inform the student and at the same time activate his interests, and neither can be done unless the teacher, by his

44 Herbart, *The Science of Education*, p. 84.
45 *Ibid.*, p. 155.
46 Herbart, *Outlines of Educational Doctrine*, § 107.
47 *Ibid.*, § 108.

example and his scholarship, is able to excite the affection of the students for him and for learning.

Once Herbart moves away from presentative instruction, the student is given a more active role in the learning process. In analytic instruction, particularly, the student's role stands out, for such instruction begins with the student's own thoughts, "and these thoughts, such as they chance to be, are then, with the teacher's help, analyzed, corrected, and supplemented." [48] The other side to teaching is found in synthetic instruction. Herbart never believed that the student could be educated sufficiently toward the end of good character by his own unaided efforts. In other words, analytic instruction was not enough; synthetic instruction, where the teacher determines directly the sequence and the grouping of the parts of the lesson must supplement it. "There is one kind of synthesis which imitates experience; there is another kind which consists in constructing designedly a whole whose component parts have been presented one by one previously." [49]

Much in Herbart's *The Science of Education* is vague because it is so highly theoretical, and in Chapter Five, "The Course of Instruction," he treats of analytic and synthetic instruction in a way that would not have been of much help to the average teacher.[50] Fortunately, he is clearer in the *Outlines of Educational Doctrine,* where he again examines these methods.[51] The burden of analytical instruction is to dissect the particulars of experience and to move from the particulars of experience to generalizations about it.[52] To put it another way, Herbart expects that analytical instruction will make something out of the student's experience; the facts of experience have to be made clearer and more definite, and, moreover, they must be given an appropriate embodiment in language.[53] Before analytical instruction can really begin in earnest, the teacher must examine the child's experience and sort of total up the child's impressions. When he does this, Herbart maintains, he will find that children vary remarkably both in the quality and quantity of their impressions; and he will find also that neither concepts nor abstractions will have been formed as a result of the child's multiple impressions and observations. Herbart cautions teachers to look for exceptions among children, because he admits that no generalization applies fully or equally to all children, and he wants teachers to know that in the child's individuality the one-sidedness of interest and character formation have already begun.

Studying the experiences of the children in class is a preliminary,

48 *Ibid.,* § 106.
49 *Ibid.*
50 Herbart, *The Science of Education,* pp. 154–169.
51 Herbart, *Outlines of Educational Doctrine,* § 105–130.
52 Herbart, *The Science of Education,* p. 156.
53 Herbart, *Outlines of Educational Doctrine,* § 110.

but it is a very important one. When the teacher has completed his study, he is ready to begin with analytical instruction. The first step is to make children more alike in their knowledge, and to achieve this end Herbart advises teachers to "work over" the store of experiences the students have. Yet, even while they are doing this, and while their objective is a certain homogeneity of knowledge, they must be ready to act upon, or react to, what is distinctive about each child's knowledge. It is easy for teachers to forget that they can learn much about each child from the child himself, so they are admonished to talk to children about their experiences. Whatever they learn from children is considered to be a suitable starting point for analytical instruction, for above all else a good teacher will begin with the experiences of the child. He must come down to meet the child on the child's level, for the child cannot come up to his.[54]

The next step is to take an experience, the more common the experience among the students the better, and examine the main facts in it. The teacher should help the students see what the whole of the experience is, or what its meaning is, and then break down this meaning into its component parts. He should even go so far, whenever possible without distorting the meaning of the experience, to interchange the parts or the principal facts and in this way illuminate the experience. What is important in this instructional process is not the experience itself, but what it means, how it is formed, and what can be learned in general from it: what generalization is possible? When the student is able to do this, either with the teacher's help or without it, he has stepped over the threshold of quality learning. When the teacher has completed step two, he is well on his way toward grasping the significance of analytical instruction, but he is not finished with it. The next step is to classify experiences, to compare them, to discriminate among them, and to learn to observe more about experiences and in a better way.[55]

Much of what is to be done under the auspices of analytical instruction will be on the order of direct teaching, and everything possible must be done to sharpen the student's tools of analysis with respect to the formal aspects of the curriculum, but there is always room for incidental learning in Herbart's plan. The point is that the products of incidental learning must not be ignored or pushed to one side when analytical instruction is emphasized. This method of instruction might achieve the best results when applied to things learned, almost as asides, by the exceptional student.[56]

When the presentation is made and when the experiences students have are put into the instructional pool, the most direct parts of analytical instruction are applied. But Herbart wants teachers to know that

54 *Ibid.*, § 128.
55 *Ibid.*, § 114; and Herbart, *The Science of Education*, pp. 156–158.
56 Herbart, *Outlines of Educational Doctrine*, § 71.

analytical instruction does not come to any abrupt end; it reappears in reviews, written exercises, and corrections of all work that students may do.[57] Herbart is convinced that review, which is something more than mere repetition in drill-like fashion, provides additional opportunities for careful analysis. And he is quite anxious for teachers to use review techniques carefully and not to confuse review with examination. Repetition has its place in learning exercises, and examinations seem to be necessary; at least Herbart is not displeased with examination systems, but he does not want teachers to think that either takes the place of the good review under the teacher's careful direction.

Throughout the process of instruction students should be given ample opportunities to express themselves, to try to make analyses of their experiences, and to reconstruct their learning into meaningful wholes. Since oral recitations do not quite fill the bill for what Herbart has in mind, he recommends generous employment of written exercises. The teacher should help the student organize his thoughts for writing, although he should allow students to select topics for their themes. Hopefully, the topics will come from their own experience; in any case, the principal purpose of writing should be to provide opportunities for exercise in analysis.[58]

Herbart has high hopes for analytical instruction: "[it] rises upwards to the general, it facilitates and assists all kinds of judgments. . . . The association of premises likewise, upon which facility in drawing logical conclusions entirely depends—the scientific imagination —gains much by repeated analysis of what is given. For just because experience is no system, it best provides for the varied mixture and fusion of our thoughts, if we do but always accompany our experience with thought." [59] But for all the virtues claimed for analytical instruction, and Herbart claimed many, he could see its limitations: "But all the advantages of analytical instruction are fettered and limited by the limitation of that which experience and intercourse, together with the descriptions connected with them, have been able to supply. Analysis must accept material as it finds it. Further, the repetition of sensuous impressions, by which a preponderance is created on one side, is often stronger than the artificially produced concentrations and considerations by which the teacher strives to counteract it on the other. Moreover the general, which only in certain cases is brought into notice by abstraction, reaches with effort that free position in the mind by which it proves equally efficacious whether as general or in dealing with all special combinations. And, properly speaking, analysis is not able to do more for speculation and aesthetic judgment than lay bare the points with which

[57] *Ibid.*, § 117.
[58] *Ibid.*, § 124.
[59] Herbart, *The Science of Education*, p. 157.

they are concerned. . . . Even analytical examination of accepted speculative and aesthetic modes of presentation, although it could make us feel what is wrong, nevertheless seldom attains to that strength of (the new) impression necessary to erase the earlier one; it never reaches that sufficiency which is a necessity to the awakened mind. Confutation and criticism alone can effect little; the right standard must be set up." [60] The business of setting up the right standards is the business of synthetic instruction.

Herbart's meaning is often obscure, and nowhere is he less precise than in the section of *The Science of Education* dealing with synthetic instruction. It is possible to understand the separate items in his discourse on the subject, but it is hard to synthesize them. For example, we can understand what he means when he argues for the necessity of presentative and analytical support of synthetic instruction, and we can agree with him when he says that without the support of these two sides of instruction the results of synthetic instruction will be problematical, especially as regards the union of learning and life. It is also clear that synthetic instruction will introduce much that is new and strange; it will try to ask more questions than can be answered; it will not aim at perfect mastery; and it will constantly aim at arousing interest, maintaining attention, and avoiding indifference to learning and fatigue from learning exercises. On all these points Herbart is perceptive and his advice is good, but we are nevertheless unable to grasp the genius of synthetic instruction after having studied them.

There is some poetry in Herbart's comment that "synthetic instruction, which builds with its own stones, is alone capable of erecting the entire structure of thought which education requires." [61] Is he saying only that synthetic instruction begins to pay dividends when a solid educational foundation is laid and that the learner is capable of seeing relationships between the elements of knowledge he has previously mastered? Or is he following the Platonic program which aims at freeing the student from the bonds of sensory knowledge, a freedom enabling him to cross the threshold of wisdom and gain intimations of immortality? In other words, is Herbart's synthetic instruction the famous, productive, and possibly dangerous dialectic Plato had championed? It is by no means certain that Herbart's writings contain a definitive answer to these questions.

Synthetic instruction is concerned, Herbart says, with a twofold object: "it must supply the elements and *prepare* their combination. . . . The most general kind of synthesis is combinative. . . . Speculative synthesis proper, entirely different from the logical-combinative, rests

60 *Ibid.,* pp. 157–158.
61 *Ibid.,* p. 158.

on relationships. But the method of the relationships no one knows, and it is not the business of education to exhibit it." [62]

Perhaps the easiest explanation of the meaning implied in synthetic instruction, although not necessarily the most accurate, is that it is an exercise of the human powers of speculation and contemplation. No handbook could adequately illuminate all the steps a teacher must employ in superintending synthetic instruction, and Herbart nowhere essays to write one. He believes in the educational force of the best literature and specifically recommends the classics, beginning with Homer. In addition, he declares that methods of teaching the great masters of literature must be exactly defined,[63] and the great books must themselves be supplemented by auxiliary commentaries illuminating them.

All too soon he tells us that "enough has been said about synthetic instruction. It must begin early, and its end is not to be found." [64]

The educator interested only in methodology may not find Herbart's discourse on presentative, analytical, and synthetic instruction very helpful. Yet, these points provide an important background for the broad goals he sets for teaching. The pedagogue's quest is satisfied more fully when, in *The Science of Education* [65] and the *Outlines of Educational Doctrine*,[66] Herbart offers a theory of teaching which can be translated into classroom practice; the translation was, in fact, done partly by Herbart himself and, then, more fully by his disciples. The result was the five formal steps.

These steps came to be cut-and-dried techniques for teachers to follow, and, although they were related to a psychology of learning, this was more than Herbart had bargained for. He had written about conditions of many-sided interest and had maintained that in order to secure such interest teachers should keep certain cardinal points in mind: clearness, association, system, and method.[67] He did not say that teaching could follow only one method or that its environment was uniform; and he admitted that some teachers preferred explication, others conversation, others a structural approach following leading ideas, and still others wanted their students to be active in exercising their minds in systematic thinking. In other words, Herbart acknowledged and approved variety in teaching method and asked only that teachers, whatever their individual approach might be, impose a general order on teaching. The content of instruction should be clearly arranged and presented; it should be associated with what the student already knows; it should be a content

62 *Ibid.*, pp. 159–161.
63 *Ibid.*, p. 168.
64 *Ibid.*
65 *Ibid.*, pp. 126 ff.
66 Herbart, *Outlines of Educational Doctrine*, § 67–70.
67 *Ibid.*, § 67; and Herbart, *The Science of Education*, pp. 126–128.

capable of belonging to recognized classifications of knowledge; and, finally, it should be put to use or applied in the student's world of life and learning: "in his own independent attempts and their correction." [68]

In *The Science of Education* Herbart explains what he means by clearness, association, system, and method.[69] While extensive quoting tends to be wearisome, it is best to let Herbart speak for himself at this point.

> Quiescent concentration, if it be but clear and pure, sees single things distinctly. For it is only clear when everything is kept at a distance that makes the act of presentment a turbid mixture, or when several varied concentrations disintegrated by the teacher's care are presented one by one.
>
> The presentations are associated by the progress of one Concentration into another. In the midst of the crowd of associations hovers imagination; it tastes every mixture and despises nothing but the tasteless. But the entire mass is tasteless as soon as the elements can commingle with one another, and that is possible only, if the clear antithesis of single things does not prevent it.
>
> Quiescent reflections see the relationship of the many; it sees each particular thing as a member of the relationship in its right place. The perfect order of a copious reflection is called System. But there can be no system, no order, no relationship without clearness in single things. For relationship does not lie in mixture, it exists only amid separated and re-united parts.
>
> The progress of reflection is Method. It runs through system, produces new members of it, and watches over the result in its application. Many use the word who know nothing of the thing. The difficult business of cultivating the mind according to method must be on the whole left to the teacher; if the present book does not show how indispensable it is to order methodically one's personal thoughts on education, it will have availed nothing with the reader.[70]

Educators and psychologists who followed in Herbart's footsteps maintained that his four steps had taken into account the three principal parts of the act of learning: perception, thought, and application. Yet they found Herbart's four steps—clearness, association, system, and method—somewhat too abstract and involved for teachers to follow, so they elaborated these steps into a methodological doctrine which contained five parts, each of which could be followed by the teacher as he instructed his pupils. In elaborating the Herbartian scheme, some departures from strict Herbartian thinking were inevitable, and not the least of these was a shifting of the emphasis in learning from the student to the

---

68 Herbart, *Outlines of Educational Doctrine*, § 69.
69 Herbart, *The Science of Education*, pp. 126–127.
70 *Ibid.*

teacher. It is not unusual, when one follows the so-called Herbartian formula, to put the teacher in the center of the educational stage; and we should not be surprised, then, when we come to Dewey and some of the more progressive educational theorists, to know that they did not accept Herbartian techniques, nor did they, as a matter of fact, accept the psychological doctrine on which those techniques were based.[71] Perhaps they were not rejecting an authentic Herbart when they rejected Herbartian pedagogy, but they were putting the learner back in the central position from which many Herbartians had seemed to push him.

The five steps in method distilled from the four steps in learning are preparation, presentation, association, systemization, and application. Here teachers had directions not difficult to understand or to follow. Preparation meant a cultivation of the receptive powers of the student's mind; to the teacher it meant getting the student ready for the lesson. This step may also be referred to as orientation, or introduction; in humanistic pedagogical practices it meant the old *prelectio*. Preparation did not, of course, imply that the teacher, regardless of the level of teaching, could follow a set formula. He readied the minds of his students, whatever their level of educational accomplishment, for the material he was going to present. Presentation could have taken several forms, and in the hands of the best teachers undoubtedly it did, but in the usual classroom dominated by Herbartian methods, presentation meant a recitation by the teacher of the facts contained in the lesson. Herbart said this was only one way of making a presentation, and he cautioned his readers against becoming narrow or exclusive in their presentative approaches, but for the most part his advice was paid scant heed. With the preliminaries out of the way and the content of instruction now in the students' possession, the teacher could lead his students into the more meaningful and productive aspects of learning. By employing association, or aiming for it, he leads students to see the rational connection between what they have just learned and the bodies of knowledge they have already in their possession. From association he moves to system, which, however involved it might be in attainment, is, nevertheless, simply a matter of appropriate mental classifications of knowledge; its key is generalization. The last step, application, involves a process of converting knowledge from the level of theory to that of practice, from knowing to doing. If the teacher follows these steps, he has at the same time kept pace with the act of learning, and, though it may appear less complicated in precept than in practice, he will have fulfilled his duties as a teacher. Herbart is quick to admit that teachers can do only so much for students, and the methodological steps formulated by his followers seem to confirm Herbart's view. Teaching starts the student on the way, but at its best

71 See John Dewey, *Democracy and Education* (New York, The Macmillan Company, 1930), pp. 83–84.

learning is a process that continues long after the student-teacher relationship is abrogated.

The influence of Herbart's pedagogy, especially in American education, was considerable, and vestiges of it are still much in evidence, but this is another side of the story—one that cannot be told here.[72] In the end, we are almost forced to regard Herbart's contribution as being one of shaping a schoolmaster's approach to education; despite his unwillingness to lose sight of the student in the teaching-learning process, losing sight of the student is almost exactly what happened. It took the pragmatic revolution in education to repair the distortions that were, at least in part, attributable to Herbart and his followers.

[72] See Dunkel, *op. cit.*, pp. 93–101.

❧ 12 ❧

John Dewey: Reform for Relevance

No history of educational theory could be judged adequate unless attention were given to the Sophists of Greece; yet, we should be prepared to admit that the Sophists can hardly be represented fairly because most of our knowledge about them comes from their enemies. With the Sophists we have too little evidence; with Dewey we have too much: Dewey's bibliography is long enough to fill a small book, and commentators on Dewey's viewpoints in education have written more volumes both praising and condemning his educational theory.[1] One must be cautious in elaborating the Sophists' fundamental theories; but with Dewey, too much evidence leaves us in a quandary: what period of Dewey's work should be taken as representative of his best and most authentic thought; and which commentators should one trust for assessing the strengths and weaknesses of this theory?

At the outset we should set some limits for the chapter: it is concerned mainly with Dewey's ideas on the purposes and processes of education; general philosophy is considered, not as a side issue—for it could not be a side issue in Dewey's conception of educational theory—but only as a background against which persistent educational problems may be viewed. And even with this limitation on the chapter's goals there are difficulties, for, obviously, in one relatively short chapter all Dewey's educational ideas cannot be considered. In trying to examine what seem to be Dewey's principal ideas on education, we leave ourselves open to criticism because there is hardly any agreement among scholars on what these principal ideas were.[2]

[1] Although neither claims to be definitive, including every authentic Dewey writing, the most complete guides are: M. H. Thomas, *John Dewey, A Centennial Bibliography* (Chicago, The University of Chicago Press, 1962); and P. A. Schilpp, ed., *The Philosophy of John Dewey*, 2nd ed. (New York, Tudor Publishing Company, 1951).

[2] See R. D. Archambault, ed., *Dewey on Education, Appraisals* (New York, Random House, 1966).

If we cannot avoid the difficulties in writing about Dewey's theory of education, we can, at least, postpone them while we treat quickly of the theoretical developments in education separating Herbart and Dewey.

I

EDUCATIONAL THEORY FROM HERBART TO DEWEY

By the end of Herbart's life the main foundations for a science of education had been laid. The purpose of education, according to Herbart, was to form good men: morality was education's foremost objective.[3] In settling for this objective, it should be noted, Herbart was not original, although there was originality in his approach: he wanted to find a formula for converting the usual appurtenances of the educational process to specifically moral rather than intellectual ends. In Herbart's plan knowledge was not sold at a discount, and he was, moreover, prepared to admit that its communication formed an important part of educational processes; but he wanted more than knowledge from education—he wanted good men. In the end, however, despite the high hopes, his ambitions proved too large for the educational machinery of his system, and he was left with a subject-centered school, dominated by a teacher whose principal pedagogical tools were extracted from a four-step analysis of the nature of learning. Herbart's disciples converted these four steps into the five formal steps of teaching, which we have already noticed.[4] It is probably fair to credit Herbart with the invention of a schoolmaster's pedagogy; for if teachers followed its methodological prescriptions and were sensitive to the development of a pupil's many-sidedness of interest, they could be confident about their role in instruction. Undoubtedly, Herbart's contributions to educational theory and practice were great, and his advice was heeded, for his system had many apparent advantages. His voice, however, was only one among many to chant the refrain of educational reform.

In the wake of Herbart's scientific approach to education, we find Friedrich Froebel (1782–1816): he stood for many of Herbart's educational gains,[5] but in the long run he belonged to a loyal opposition because, by adding new dimensions to the persuasive educational testimony already in the record, Froebel literally revolutionized educational

---

[3] J. F. Herbart, *Aesthetic Revelation of the World*, p. 57.

[4] See Charles A. McMurry, *The Elements of General Method Based on the Principles of Herbart* (New York, The Macmillan Company, 1903).

[5] See P. R. Cole, *Herbart and Froebel: An Attempt at Synthesis* (New York, Columbia University, Teachers College, 1907).

thinking. Admittedly, Froebel's educational theory is complicated; its mixtures of idealism and naturalism often leave students perplexed.[6] But apart from the commitment to the kindergarten, which was a structural addition to schooling, Froebel's most penetrating doctrine highlighted the need for freeing children to pursue their own interests. Self-development, he held, expressed education's most fundamental meaning, and it could be secured only as a result of self-activity, a self-activity unencumbered by prescriptions from either a teacher or a system.[7] Froebel reintroduced the idea of growth to the psychology of learning and argued, somewhat naturalistically, that learning is a natural process, like physical growth and, moreover, that it should be allowed to proceed in the same way as physical growth.[8] Whatever inroads Froebel was successful in making on the accepted doctrines of education, and they may not have been especially impressive, we must remember that his theory counseled student involvement in directing the educational process. If Herbart pronounced a schoolmaster's pedagogy, Froebel surely articulated a creed placing the learner in the center of the educational stage. Possibly Froebel's ideas were too radical for his time, when national education was beginning its ascendency and when superintendents of education regarded formal education as a tool to state objectives rather than a human occupation for the advancement and perfection of personalities. Quite clearly the essentials of the Herbartian system were more compatible with state interests in education than the free-wheeling program of teaching and learning endorsed in the writings of Froebel.

While Froebel was still alive American education passed through a state of ferment leading to an awakening. In the United States basic ideas of freedom were more in keeping with people's tastes than in the class-structured societies of Europe. Froebel's kindergarten was banned in Prussia by a reactionary Ministry of Education, while in the United States the ideal of educational freedom was theoretically acceptable. But freedom in the classroom was still only on the distant horizon of American educational practice. Too much confidence was still vested in a kind of education guaranteeing a reasonably efficient school product who could perform the many necessary social and economic tasks of life. Education was regularly interpreted to be an instrument preparing children for life in society, and its goals could be determined, and should be determined, by wise men who knew what these goals were. The ends of

6 See E. Lawrence, ed., *Friedrich Froebel and English Education* (New York, Philosophical Library, 1953) , pp. 179–233.

7 F. Froebel, *Education By Development,* translated by J. Jarvis (New York, D. Appleton and Company, 1905) , pp. 246–248; see also H. C. Bowen, *Froebel and Education by Self Activity* (New York, Charles Scribner's Sons, 1901) .

8 J. L. Hughes, *Froebel's Educational Laws for All Teachers* (New York, D. Appleton and Company, 1900) , p. 11.

schooling were outside the boundaries of student responsibility, and few educators paused to consider the legitimate dimensions of student interest in their own learning.

Despite the unwillingness of national states to subordinate their political interests to personal education, there were undercurrents of educational thought counteracting the state's drive to make its definition of education prescriptive and universal. The main source of these undercurrents was the liberal-idealistic doctrine of Froebel; he left educational theorists a good many things to think about.[9] First and foremost was his assertion that an educational program must be based on the natural evolution of a child's activities. It is easy to see why national leaders might take a dim view of such a preamble to any educational theory, since it would effectively demolish their claim that education was a tool to perfect citizens for the state to which they owed allegiance. If Froebel's innovations had stopped with the kindergarten, if he had offered it as merely an addition to the existing educational structure, he should have been put up with; his evolutionary hypothesis and his doctrine of self-activity were too directly aimed at state self-interest to allow them much currency. Coupled with his advocacy of evolution as a way of explaining the development of man, Froebel advanced the view that all significant human development comes from within the person and not from an accumulation of knowledge.[10] Besides, by giving play activities a valid, even a central, role in the educational process, Froebel made it easy, even for sincere men, to discount his educational thoughts as being nothing more than frivolous tinkerings with pedagogy.[11] How could a man who thought play was significantly educative be taken seriously? Of course, Froebel did not advocate political anarchy, and he would never have supposed that his theory supported any disintegration of society, although it might have generated social reforms. One of the reforms he espoused, and one which seemed to hardheaded nationalists to be singularly inconsequential, concerned the education of women. He could not understand why society should ignore the education of women, for in his thesis the cultivation of civilized society depended mainly on their further education.[12] Finally, Froebel argued that knowledge should not be accepted as an end in itself. Schools should surely encourage the acquiring of knowledge, but they should try to employ it for the further development of mental and physical power and for the production of skill in putting it to use.[13] Even as early as the kindergarten years, the school's

9 See R. Ulich, *A Sequence of Educational Influences* (Cambridge, Mass., Harvard University Press, 1935), p. 17.

10 F. Froebel, *The Education of Man,* translated by W. N. Hailman (New York, D. Appleton and Company, 1892), p. 17.

11 *Ibid.,* pp. 54–55.

12 See Ulich, *op. cit.,* pp. 26–27; and Hughes, *op. cit.,* pp. 28–30.

13 F. Froebel, *The Education of Man,* pp. 34–35; 94–95; 236–237.

instructional process would be three-sided: absorbing, assimilating, and expressing were interdependent. In Froebel's pedagogy, instruction that terminated with mere absorption of knowledge was unacceptable; moreover, he made no effort whatever to reconcile his views on the breadth of the instructional process with the traditional doctrines of liberal learning. On this point of knowledge's utility Froebel is much nearer Herbert Spencer than he is to either Herbart or Locke.[14]

While educational theory was undergoing mild fermentation in Europe, largely because of the catalytic efforts of Froebel, when good questions were raised concerning educational purposes and means—but almost always with few discernible results—American educators were faced with the problem of educating children to become citizens capable of self-government. Thomas Jefferson laid the theoretical foundation for a system of education to produce men capable of performing the essential processes of citizenship; he concluded that universal opportunity for elementary education was essential to the success of the American experiment.[15] During Jefferson's lifetime his educational proposals were considered avant-garde and the possibilities of their acceptance were unusually dim in a political and economic climate that paid homage to aristocratic ideals. But even when aristocratic notions were discounted, sympathetic observers believed the financial demands of such a broad system of education to be prohibitive.

Yet within a half century after Jefferson advanced his plan to universalize educational opportunity, the common school was a reality. If it is too much to say that universal opportunity for some education was achieved with the creation of the common school, then, at least, it was an important forward step that eventually led to the realization of the ideal. Horace Mann, James Carter, and Henry Barnard were acknowledged leaders of a crusade for expanding educational opportunity, and the schools they fought to establish had one principal objective: the preparation of good citizens.[16] Despite their high aspirations, however, the kind of education offered in these schools was patently elementary. The door to good citizenship was opened with literary skills; so common schools stressed, and frequently never went beyond, the three R's. Even if the tools for citizenship had been defined differently, it is probably unreasonable to expect that the school could have done much more. In common schools no one talked about the inner development of persons or the

---

14 See Herbert Spencer, *Education: Intellectual, Moral and Physical* (New York, D. Appleton and Company, 1927).

15 See C. F. Arrowood, ed., *Thomas Jefferson and Education in a Republic* (New York, McGraw-Hill Book Company, 1930); and R. J. Honeywell, *The Educational Work of Thomas Jefferson* (Cambridge, Mass., Harvard University Press, 1931).

16 See A. E. Meyer, *An Educational History of the American People* (New York, McGraw-Hill Book Company, 1957), pp. 150–166; and N. G. McCluskey, *Public Schools and Moral Education* (New York, Columbia University Press, 1958).

goals children might attain if they were free to follow their own interests; the curriculum was formed on skills and abilities believed necessary for living in American society. Departures from such curricular formulas were rarely countenanced.

Once the common-school system was securely established,[17] and its objectives of forming the foundation for good and effective citizenship taken for granted, some time could be spent speculating about improvement of methodology, about taking into account some of the child's interests, and about allowing for greater spontaneity in development. In its preliminary stages, this was work undertaken by Francis Parker (1837–1902), an early promoter of progressive education and groundbreaker for John Dewey.[18] Yet, while Parker was initiating educational reform—first, in Quincy, Massachusetts, and then in Chicago—other forces began generating energies for affecting education profoundly. Darwin's theory of evolution created intellectual upheavals both in Europe and America: although it is hard to demonstrate how education was directly affected by Darwin's daring hypotheses, inevitably men who took Darwin seriously had second thoughts about the quality and purpose of the educational process. If men were evolving in a constantly evolving world, was there not some good reason to call a halt to obviously archaic school programs? The implications of evolutionary hypotheses reached education by many different routes.[19]

When evolutionary hypotheses did not contain enough ammunition to upset traditional theories of education, men like Herbert Spencer and Thomas Huxley could add more.[20] Both effectively challenged educational conventions and asked deeply disturbing questions. Finally, especially in America, the implications of evolution and scientific theses for education could be made even more explicit with the rise to some prominence of the genetic psychology of G. Stanley Hall.[21] The educational stage was set for reform and awaited the appearance of a theorist capable of synthesizing various reforming elements. The ground for educational reform was cultivated for John Dewey.

17 See L. A. Cremin's excellent book, *The American Common School* (New York, Teachers College, Columbia University, 1951).

18 See R. E. Tostberg, "Colonel Parker's Quest for 'A School in Which All Good Things Come Together;'" *History of Education Quarterly*, VI (Summer, 1966), pp. 22–42.

19 See Charles F. Donovan, *Education in American Social Thought, 1865–1900* (Yale University, doctoral dissertation, 1948); and Harvey Wish, *Society and Thought in Modern America* (New York, Longmans, Green and Company, Inc., 1952).

20 See Cyril Bibby, *T. H. Huxley: Scientist, Humanist and Educator* (London, The Macmillan Company, 1959); G. Compayré, *Herbert Spencer and Scientific Education* (New York, D. Appleton and Company, 1907); and K. D. Benne, "The Educational Outlook of Herbert Spencer," *Harvard Educational Review*, 10 (October, 1940), pp. 436–453.

21 See G. E. Partridge, *Genetic Philosophy of Education* (New York, Sturgis & Walton Co., 1912). This is an anthology of Hall's most important educational writings.

II

DEWEY'S PLACE IN EDUCATION

Despite the bitterness evidenced in the writings of many of Dewey's critics, his right to a prominent place among the world's great educational theorists needs no defense. It may be extravagant to maintain, along with his most ardent admirers, that he is a peerless educator and philosopher; yet, undoubtedly he asked most of the right questions about education at the right time. Whenever they were asked, and some had been asked before, they were valid; but Dewey's inquiries were made before an audience willing to listen for answers. Should one argue that Dewey's answers were wrong, even dangerous, he is not absolved from acknowledging the validity of the questions themselves. Dewey's mark on twentieth-century education could not have been made at all, if he were as steeped in error as some of his critics charge; even the high praise of his disciples could not have saved him if his adherence to error were as consistent as his opponents aver.

History, we have said, was probably on Dewey's side—again, the right man at the right time—and he became a spokesman for educational reform when reform was a reasonable possibility. His counsel was heeded almost at once; he was, in fact, a "prophet in his own country."

Dewey's overarching purpose was not original; even its phrasing was not entirely new: he wanted a kind of education that theorists since the time of Comenius had demanded, an education both meaningful and relevant.

All educators, regardless of their pedagogic creeds, agree that learning should be relevant, although there may be sharp differences among them about the meaning of relevance, and judgments on what learning experiences are relevant, or most relevant, differ markedly. For some, literary education was assumed to be most relevant; for others, preparation for a job by mastering the skills necessary to it meant relevancy. Dewey, however, did not find relevancy in either extreme. Life alone, as the learner lived it, was for that learner the source of the most relevant kind of education; and the kind of education that enabled him to live a full and productive life was the kind of education he should have.

PHILOSOPHICAL INFLUENCES ON DEWEY. Dewey was a product of the public schools (except for his graduate study at the Johns Hopkins University), and it seems somewhat unlikely that academic-historic philosophy made any impression on him until, during his undergraduate study at the

University of Vermont, he was exposed to realism.[22] Whether or not he became a convert to realism is a moot question, yet this exposure generated an interest in philosophical issues: after three-years' teaching experience on the high-school level, he returned to the University of Vermont for a year's private study in philosophy. The following year he enrolled as a graduate student at the Johns Hopkins University, and in 1884 he finished his work for the Ph.D. degree in philosophy. As a doctoral student he quite obviously made a commitment to philosophy as a field of study, but we are not certain of the philosophical school to which he paid allegiance. Although realism was not represented at Johns Hopkins, Dewey's knowledge of this brand of philosophy was far from being superficial; idealism was the philosophic preference of his principal mentor, George Sylvester Morris; and the experimentalism of G. Stanley Hall and the pragmatism of Charles Sanders Peirce were philosophical positions not escaping his notice.[23]

Despite these mixtures of philosophic influence, Dewey left Johns Hopkins with decided preferences for idealism. Although he could be apparently unsure about the metaphysical assumptions of idealism, he could and did adopt both the idealist preoccupation with ethics and its attachment to the individual and the highly personal aspirations idealism had for each personality. This interest in the individual and the unfolding of his personality as the principal business of life, and thus of education, never left Dewey; it did, in fact, become a principal plank in his pragmatic philosophy of education. And the early ethical preoccupations were later converted into a theory of education that on the broadest level recognized moral objectives as the principal concern of education. Some of the frames of reference needed adjustment and the constructs differed from those of orthodox moralists, yet if Dewey's theory of education had a message, it was that men should have the means and opportunities to live the good life.

Dewey's conversion to pragmatic ways of thinking must have been a hard intellectual experience. We do not know how much he learned from Peirce while both were at Johns Hopkins, nor do we know how aware Dewey was of Peirce as he began his career in philosophy, but Dewey came to see value in the pragmatic criterion pronounced by Peirce. Meaning in idealism was an elusive and highly abstract phenomenon; according to the Peircean code, meaning came after experience; only after an idea was put into practice could its meaning be assessed. An element of common sense permeates this point of view, but, of course, in the hands of pragmatists implications were extracted going beyond the

22 See George Dykhuizen, "John Dewey, The Vermont Years," *Journal of the History of Ideas*, XX (October-December, 1959), pp. 515–544.

23 See M. G. White, *The Origin of Dewey's Instrumentalism* (New York, Columbia University Press, 1943); and James Fiebleman, *An Introduction of Peirce's Philosophy of Education* (New York, Harper and Brothers, 1946).

boundaries of mere common sense. Still Dewey took the criterion proposed by Peirce to refine and install it as a principal thesis in his philosophy. It proved to be a foundation for Dewey's theory of knowledge, and its effects on education were similarly enormous.

The entire history of pragmatism, beginning with Heraclitus and the Sophists, could be recited as having influenced Dewey, although one would hesitate to name the most critical elements in it. No one, and surely no philosopher, is immune to his philosophical past or the intellectual heritage of the race; on the other hand, it is unreasonable to suppose that every philosopher must in some way perpetuate in his own thinking the doctrines of the past. It was possible for Dewey to be keenly aware of the pragmatic tradition, diffused as it was, and not to follow it slavishly. He could have been inspired by the promise of pragmatism in its popularization by William James and yet not have been in any strict sense a disciple of James. Surely Dewey stood on the theoretical foundations of pragmatism, and he accepted most of its assumptions about change, but he blazed new trails for these foundations and assumptions to follow. In the end he built a system whose most obvious characteristic was relativism and whose clearest indebtedness was to the doctrine of evolution. Dewey willingly took evolution seriously, and it became a dogmatic assumption in his theory. But these speculations took time; a philosophical system is not built in a day, and Dewey's thought progressed and evolved. We should not be surprised to learn of changes and shifts in his philosophic stance; indeed, had his later work not differed from his earlier, we would think it strange and Dewey a poor pragmatist. This fact goes a long way toward explaining why Dewey's commentators have found him so difficult to follow. He would surely have been charged with doctrinal inconsistency if he had not allowed for modifications in his theories; however, in adhering to the principal thesis of pragmatism—change—he was often castigated for having departed from previously assumed theoretical positions.

PEDAGOGICAL INFLUENCES ON DEWEY. Any list of leading theorists in educational history is remarkably free from names of schoolmasters; although some important educational thinkers—Plato and Erasmus would be good examples—engaged in the teacher's art, they regarded teaching as ancillary to their principal interests. We like to think of these educational theorists, not as pedagogues, but as scholars. The day-to-day activities of the teacher may generate initial inspiration for probing the theoretical complexities of pedagogy, but the schoolroom has never been an environment conducive to the production of educational theory. The historical record, with the apparent exception being Pestalozzi—who theorized first and practiced later—offers little evidence for believing that teachers have the time or even the inclination to be educational thinkers. Considered in the light of this consistent tradition, Dewey's entrance into the arena of educational theory was not unique: he took the same route his most illustrious predecessors had taken. Thus, after a brief encounter with teaching on the secondary-school level, he turned to deeper issues in education and pondered them in the setting of higher learning.

In following a university career—first as a graduate student and then as a professor—Dewey was an accredited member of the teaching profession, but it is easy to make too much of this, for he himself would have pointed to sharp differences between the purposes of higher education, on the one hand, and of elementary and secondary education, on the other. Yet, even as a university man, he maintained some contact with the lower schools and organized the Laboratory School—as much a laboratory for him as a school for students—to test the meaning of his educational ideas on the crucible of day-to-day teaching and learning.[24]

Despite his relative immunity from the problems of pedagogical practice, he was by no means an antiseptic theorist: his expressions on education were intended to make a difference in the schools. He was aware not only of what had been done in education and psychology; he was aware also of the contemporary situation in education; he kept abreast of contemporary practices, philosophies, and psychologies of education. The educational movement which must have interested him most, because of its affinity to his pedagogical beliefs, was the progressive education advocated by Francis Parker in the schools of Quincy, Massachusetts, and later, and more systematically, in the Cook County Normal School in Chicago.[25]

Parker began his educational career as a country schoolmaster in 1853, interrupted it for military service during the Civil War and for travel in Europe after the war, and then, in 1873, assumed the position of superintendent of the Quincy, Massachusetts, schools. An inspection of the schools in Quincy shortly before Parker came revealed a startling lack of correlation between classroom learning and its application to the practical needs of life. Children who knew their rules of grammar perfectly, the inspection revealed, could not apply the rules in ordinary written correspondence; and students who read with facility in the schoolbooks were unable to read anything else with comprehension. Parker was appointed to correct these deficiencies.

It is not necessary either to follow Parker through his educational career from Quincy to Chicago or to relate the particular reforms installed in the Quincy schools while he was there to discover the principal

24 See K. C. Mayhew and A. C. Edwards, *The Dewey School* (New York, D. Appleton-Century Company, 1936).

25 Work on Parker is neither so good nor so complete as we might like, but for the main facts of his career, see I. C. Heffron, *Francis Wayland Parker: An Interpretive Biography* (Los Angeles, Ivan Deach, Jr., 1934); and C. F. Adams, Jr., *The New Departure in the Common Schools of Quincy* (Boston, Estes and Lauriat, 1879).

tenets of progressive education, most of which were implicit in Parker's thought and many of which came to be adopted by Dewey and his followers. Progressive education in the hands of Parker was largely a practice without a theory; eventually Dewey proposed a philosophy of education which was attractive to progressives, and they embraced it. But it is plainly incorrect to think of Dewey as the founder of progressive education—for it antedated his entrance on the educational scene by more than a decade—or as a philosopher who was commissioned to construct a theoretical foundation on which progressive education could stand. Even though Dewey was not part of the progressive-education movement, he was sympathetic to its goals for reforming education, and his philosophy of education, it must be admitted, contained many pronouncements giving a great deal of aid and comfort to progressive educators.

Building on the work of Parker and others who were deeply committed to educational reform, progressive educators came to adopt a creed which may be outlined as follows:

1. Education should be an active process built on activities arising out of the child's life. Progressives, moreover, never tired of calling attention to the whole child, who, they said, should be the educator's principal concern. It was never sufficient, they argued, to think only of the child's mind, because they had no direct contact with minds; even if some exclusive kind of mental education were actually possible, it would be inadequate, because in modern society the child may make legitimate demands on the school for instruction and formation falling outside the ambit of pure intellectual training. What previous ages had supplied through home and simple social processes were now the school's responsibility. Progressives regularly interpreted the school's role as an all-embracing one; special functions were added to formal education because other institutions in society were remiss in fulfilling them. Building the school's program around the activities and interests of children obviously emphasized the child's place, and thus we have what is correctly called the child-centered school. When this type of school was evaluated unemotionally, and when old biases were discarded, it was not such a sharp break with educational traditions: if schools were not interested mainly in the education and formation of children, what were their interests? Yet, progressive education was seldom discussed without introducing rigid preconceptions concerning the meaning of child-centeredness: to confirmed enemies of the new education, the child-centered school had surrendered to children and allowed them complete control over their educational destinies. But from a progressive's coign of vantage, instead of surrendering any vital values, they were simply introducing a way for capitalizing on the educational advantages of children discovering educational goals for themselves and then finding the means, sometimes with the teacher's help and sometimes without it, for reaching these goals. Even on this basis the

student was not entirely free, because progressive doctrine commissioned the teacher to shape an educational environment generating creative self-activity, and this activity was set in a context not of anarchy but of purpose. In other words, although child activity was little encumbered, teachers were deeply involved in helping the child see valid goals for his action. Despite their hopes for maintaining such an obviously attractive educational setting—one where teachers were not drillmasters and students were not dictators—idealism was forced to mark time when practical achievements fell short of theoretical promise; although progressive educators were always ready to apply progressive practices within the generous boundaries of theory—and to recognize, too, that the best goals were not always possible—their critics too frequently refused to look beyond the level of practice itself and were satisfied to wage a war of polemic against an educational reform whose theory they did not fully understand.

2. Learning should concentrate on problem solving rather than on instruction. Progressive education regularly regarded knowledge as a means—a tool rather than an end in itself; moreover, the theory reasonably doubted the school's ability to teach a total arsenal of tools necessary to every eventuality of life. If it were possible to predict what skills and knowledge students in school would need a generation hence, it could be fairly doubted that they could be taught by employing conventional instructional processes. Children should learn for their current needs and interests, but more importantly they should be learning how to learn by exposure to the finest problem-solving techniques. Techniques of learning how to learn are the permanent products of formal education. Outright rejections of traditional subject matter did not dominate progressive theory—progressive educators agreed that children should be able to read, write, compute, and so on—but they did abandon nonfunctional techniques in teaching conventional subjects. Learning is quicker, easier, and more permanent if the student needs what he is learning for something important to him. Yet, progressive theorists, taking into account the complexities of social living, admitted that the exclusive use of any technique, even functional problem solving, circumscribed learning, so as students mature their approach to learning must be broadened, and when problem solving is used on more advanced levels it must be geared to grapple with abstract considerations of life.

3. Progressive education jettisoned the doctrine that education is preparation for life; instead, its proponents said, education must become an integral part of the process of living. Children should learn what they need to know for their time and place in life; they are not little scholars who will one day enter life.

4. A teacher's role is not to direct but to advise; in progressive codes teaching was guiding students rather than instructing them and filling

their minds with information. Despite the importance and validity of a distinction between instruction and education, progressives had a difficult time convincing their noninitiated brethren that teachers could be effective guides in the educational process, or that their guidance would have any educational significance. Perhaps convictions from the past were too deeply imbedded for teachers to be relieved from the simple, single responsibility of teaching children the things they do not know.

5. Education should encourage cooperation among students rather than competition. As progressive educators looked at education's long history they were deeply disturbed by the heed traditional practices paid competition; learning was set in the context of a contest and the prize was not self-improvement but winning. Their hope was to change this perspective of the teaching-learning process and to open an entirely new area where students could learn from and with one another. Being part of an educational society would in itself be educative, and this experience would transfer to adult society, where the benefits of cooperation, progressives said, were obvious.

6. Because true human growth is possible only in an environment of freedom, the educational process, progressives averred, should be completely democratic. This principle, of course, was subjected to a number of interpretations, many of which heaped ridicule on the democratization of education. Too often it seemed to mean determination of the school's direction would be relinquished to the very persons the school was intended to form. How, the opponents of progressive education could ask, will students be able to control their educational environment when they themselves do not know what it should be?

With these positions outlined, and sometimes adhered to in practice, progressive educators cultivated the field of educational reform for John Dewey. He was fully aware of the movement initiated by Parker in Quincy, and he became even more aware of it, and its possibilities, when Parker came to Chicago to prepare teachers for applying his prized educational ideas.[26] Almost from his first encounters with progressive education, Dewey recognized the insufficiency of the movement's theoretical foundations, and, while it would hardly be accurate to say he was enlisted to supply progressive education with a philosophy, he was unquestionably intrigued by the possibilities of this new education and believed a doctrine incorporating some of its practices could contribute materially to educational progress. How much or how little Parker's views and methods influenced Dewey's *My Pedagogic Creed* is a question not easily answered. Dewey was aware of Parker's views and approved of them; so much is admitted, yet we need not maintain that Dewey borrowed from Parker. Dewey's philosophical ideals were undergoing considerable revi-

26 Tostberg, *op. cit.*, pp. 33–37; and G. Dykhuizen, "John Dewey: The Chicago Years," *Journal of the History of Philosophy*, II (October, 1964), pp. 227–253.

sion in the late nineteenth century, and it is probably safer to assume that his educational reconstructions, which happened to be similar to progressive education, arose out of these revisions rather than by any transfer from progressive education. Dewey was sympathetic with the hopes of the progressives, but we should not forget his critical attitude toward the rugged individualism of progressive educators, each of whom seemed to be going his own way. In 1928, after the progressive movement had lasted more than four decades, Dewey could make these pertinent inquiries of progressive educators: What is progressive education? What is the meaning of experiment in education and of an experimental school? What can be rightfully expected from the work of these progressive schools toward a more intelligent and stable educational practice; especially, what contribution is being made to educational theory? Is each school going its own way, having for its foundations the desires and preferences of the particular person who happens to be in charge? Is experimentation a process of trying anything at least once, of putting into immediate effect any "happy thought" that comes to mind, or does it rest on principles adopted at least as a working hypothesis? While Dewey had no difficulty in making a general endorsement of progressive education's aspirations, he did warn that the movement was on the verge of dangerous superficiality: "if they do not intellectually organize their own work, while they may do much in making the lives of children committed to them more joyous and more vital, they contribute only incidental scraps to the science of education." [27] In addition to the theoretical assignment Dewey gave progressive education, he asked for a closer examination of its conception of individuality. Progressive teachers were exhorted to attend to and take cues from children's interests, likes, and dislikes, and Dewey thought that some of these emphases were unavoidable. Yet, if progressives believed this was educational attention to individuality they were in error: "A child's individuality cannot be found in what he does or in what he consciously likes at a given moment; it can be found only in the connected course of his actions." [28] Thus, Dewey did not approve of departures from organization of learning experiences in the school; he argued, rather, that only by means of some organization of subject matter through serial activities or planned projects could real individuality be reached. Organization, he averred, is not hostile to the principle of individuality.[29] Isolated or disconnected activities could not, he said, provide for the development of a coherent and integrated self. Only doing, however interesting or active it may be, is not a sufficient basis for educational practice. Teachers in progressive schools are not

27 John Dewey, "Progressive Education and the Science of Education," *Progressive Education*, V (1928), pp. 197–204, reprinted in R. D. Archambault, *John Dewey on Education: Selected Writings* (New York, Random House, 1964), p. 175.

28 *Ibid.*, p. 176.

29 *Ibid.*, p. 177.

dispensed from some old-fashioned teaching, although they should eschew its "pouring in" features; because of their maturity, experience, and insight they must suggest activities for students. But responsibility in teaching does not cease with suggestion: they must try to organize experiences for students, and these experiences should be soundly literary and scientific. Besides, their methods and organization must be pedagogically sound. Teachers' most critical responsibilities lay in creating conditions favorable to learning; conditions where the child's mind is preoccupied neither with subjects nor with learning itself, but with doing things the situation calls for: learning is the result.

In general, Dewey's rapport with progressive education was good— and progressives were confident Dewey was on their side—but he was, nevertheless, impatient with progressive education because he thought it was tardy in producing important additions and insights for the science of education and because it had not capitalized on its great opportunity to create an educational methodology which could deal squarely with the learning objectives of the new education. Although Dewey couched his rebuke in mild language, it is not easy to miss the generality of his meaning: progressive education was lagging on the essentials in the educational process—ends and means.

III

DEWEY'S PHILOSOPHY—MAJOR REJECTIONS

Because it is plainly impossible to present a competent summary of Dewey's philosophy in these few pages, the most satisfactory approach would seem to be one which emphasizes the distinctiveness of Dewey's pragmatism, or the principal rejections he built into his system of thought. At the same time, because we are primarily interested in Dewey as an educational theorist, we can select those elements in his philosophy having most relevance for a theory of education. Thus, we do not pretend either to be complete or to evaluate Dewey's philosophic doctrines; we hope instead to present those parts of his philosophy that helped him formulate a new approach to education.[30]

When we examine the field of philosophy and separate it into its various emphases, we notice almost at once those parts that should be most meaningful for educational theory. Every philosophy of education begins with a view of man, so we should want to know where Dewey stood on this point. We should also want to know his interpretations of

[30] See C. W. Hendel, *John Dewey and the Experimental Spirit in Philosophy* (New York, Liberal Arts Press, 1959) ; and Oscar Handlin, *John Dewey's Challenge to Education* (New York, Harper and Row, 1959) .

reality, his conception of knowledge, and his ethical theory. Each of these parts of philosophy illuminate the world in which the educational theorist must work, and, since Dewey confided to us his belief that philosophy's most important objective was a theory of education, they should have a special meaning for education.

Possibly as significant as any of Dewey's rejections was his refusal to accept philosophy as the custodian and unifier of all knowledge.[31] Plato had assigned philosophy a preeminent role in the affairs of intellect, and from Plato's time forward philosophers had liked to think their discipline had an unequivocal mission: the duty of finding in the world ultimate and essential meanings. In some genres even theology was subordinated to philosophy, and even when their positions were reversed, with theology gaining ascendancy, the philosopher could hold his own because he could make the distinction between reason and revelation and claim for philosophy everything that belonged to the science of reason. Dewey had little patience either with these distinctions or with the inordinate confidence of philosophers in finding eternally valid meanings for reality. He regarded the philosopher as a social scientist, and assigned philosophy the task of reporting on social life. Philosophy was not, in his view, a matter of discovering the inner meaning of the universe and drawing unassailable conclusions about man's relationship to the universe; rather, it was a discipline for observing data of human experience and extracting meaning from them. Philosophy was not a traffic officer directing mankind toward a predetermined destination along roads incapable of being rerouted; it was a planning committee trying to find where travellers wanted to go and then helping them prepare routes. A philosopher's most important knowledge was not about metaphysical reality, about some kind of true being, but about the capacities and interests of men—not men in the abstract, but the men of the philosopher's own generation.

On another philosophical level, Dewey rejected the absolutisms he believed to be intimately related to the philosophic traditions begun by Plato and Aristotle.[32] Plato, we know, distrusted sensory knowledge. Everything in the educational program he proposed for his utopia would have reduced the importance of the senses; in the last analysis the best students were almost entirely free from sensory knowledge; only then would they be able to meet truth face-to-face. At the end of the long road to dependable knowledge, Plato's students would have been ready to govern the state: they would by now have seen the place for everything, and their principal duty would have been to keep everything in its place. Plato had elevated the idea to a point where unquestioned allegiance was paid to intuition, with the clear implication that ideas were not subject

31 See John Dewey, *Democracy and Education* (New York, The Macmillan Company, 1916) , pp. 378–387.
32 *Ibid.*

to metamorphoses; if anything was stable in the Platonic system, it was the idea. The steps between Plato's idealism and rationalism are easy to make; they had often been made in the history of philosophy, and their effects on men and society had been quite real. Dewey deplored the absolutism of the idea because it led to rationalism. At the same time, he seriously doubted the Aristotelian doctrine of essence which had grown up around the theory of matter and form. In either case, whether in the idealism of Plato or in the essentialism of Aristotle, reason was regarded as the only reliable approach to knowledge; sensory knowledge and experience were paid scant heed. As Dewey interpreted this philosophic tradition, it had given rise to two convictions which had considerable significance for education. In the first place, by placing a heavy emphasis on the idea or on the essence of a thing or an event, and by discrediting experience, a dichotomy had been erected between theory on the one hand and practice on the other. In the traditional conceptions, theory was by far superior to practice; thinking was always better than doing. If practice were considered at all, it was always clearly subordinate to theory; in science, pure science was superior to applied; in morals, knowledge of the right principle was somehow more important than right action. And naturally, in schools, the curriculum dealing with theory and things of the mind was always superior to a course of studies preparing students for practical accomplishments. The whole history of education, from Plato and Isocrates to Dewey, had been the scene of a battle between the contending emphases in education: theoretical and practical. In the second place, the philosophic tradition, while reluctantly admitting change as a reality, restricted the arenas in which change could occur. Change was almost always a surface phenomenon, an accident, taking place without altering the essential nature of reality. To take this doctrine seriously—that permanence is the overriding principle—meant, Dewey maintained, closed systems of philosophy and education, and he rejected it because it ran counter to the evolutionary hypothesis he embraced. In such a closed system of education, growth—"cumulative movement of action toward a later result" [33]—is attenuated or arrested. His net conclusion was that life is development, and that "developing, growing, is life. Translated into its educational equivalents, this means (i) that the educational process has no end beyond itself; it is its own end; and that (ii) the educational process is one of continual reorganizing, reconstructing, transforming." [34]

While philosophers before Dewey argued their differences, their conclusions usually stayed with them in the ivory tower; like Kant they were content to leave their philosophies in their offices when the time came to live in the real world. But Dewey was not disposed to propose a philos-

[33] *Ibid.,* p. 49.
[34] *Ibid.,* p. 59.

ophy and allow it to remain on the relatively antiseptic level of theory. Man was the central issue in education, not knowledge, and Dewey felt compelled to reinterpret man's nature and thus alter the tragic course he believed most educational programs were following. If we look again to the principal rejections of traditional positions, we shall see Dewey denying a Christian interpretation of man's creation—or if he did not deny it, he disputed its scientific meaning—and supplanting it with a purely natural one in which man is a product of the evolutionary process. At some point in the process, the biological organism, later to be man, gained an advantage over other organisms in nature and accelerated its biological evolution. Concurrently, psychological and sociological evolutionary processes were functioning, and of the two the latter was the more important.[35] Thus, we have men capable of doing things that other organisms are, as yet, incapable of doing. Coupled with this rejection is the rejection of the doctrine of mind-body dualism; spirit and matter are not accorded separate places in Dewey's philosophy. The mind, Dewey wrote, "appears in experience as ability to respond to present stimuli on the basis of anticipation of future possible consequences, and with a view to controlling the kind of consequences that are to take place." [36] But the mind—or the soul—is not the seat of intellectual power; it is not a spiritual force ordained to control and direct man's bodily activities. It is part of material reality, and its powers are shaped by the experiences it has. There is no need, when following Dewey, to speak in conventional terms about intellectual education, or the education of the mind. Nothing is exclusively mental. In concert with this rejection of mind-body dualism was Dewey's rejection of the doctrine of formal discipline, a doctrine enjoying considerable privileges in educational circles.[37] If there were no mind with spiritual faculties awaiting formation, there could be no authentic educational program devised for it. And when formal discipline was swept away, much of the theoretical support for formal subject matter was jettisoned with it. Dewey did not like Locke's empiricism, nor did he accept the sensory passivity and lack of selectivity which Locke seemed to impose on man's learning activities. There was a dualism in Locke's psychology that ran counter to Dewey's conception of mind. Yet while Dewey could have differed with Locke on *tabula rasa*— perhaps it was unavoidable that he should have rejected most of Lockian psychology—he must have misread Locke's views on faculty formation or formal discipline of the mind. In *Democracy and Education* Dewey maintains that the classic form of this theory was expressed by Locke,[38]

---

35 See P. P. Wiener, *Evolution and the Founders of Pragmatism* (Cambridge, Mass., Harvard University Press, 1949).

36 Dewey, *Democracy and Education*, p. 153.

37 See pp. 256–257; 267–268; also H. B. English, *Historical Roots of Learning Theory* (Garden City, N.Y., Doubleday & Company, Inc., 1954).

38 Dewey, *Democracy and Education*, p. 71.

but Locke, although he used the term faculty—mainly, he says, because he could find no other—was careful to explain his doubts about the mind being formed out of discrete faculties capable of perfection by specific training.[39] Perhaps Locke's connection with the doctrine of formal discipline was stabilized by Dewey's criticism, although Locke himself did not entertain the position Dewey attributed to him. But Locke's theory vis-à-vis Dewey's is not the issue here. Regardless of what Locke held, the point is this: Dewey underscored intelligence and insight, not as products of man's soul, but as outcomes of man's transactions in life. Both man himself and his experiences are continuous with the world of nature; in a word, there are no transempirical realities.

Finally, in connection with any analysis of man's nature, a word should be added on will. Is or is not a man free; is he or is he not an active cause in the world? Here were two traditions available for rejection, and Dewey rejected both the tradition of freedom and the tradition of hereditary and environmental determinism. In place of both traditions Dewey substituted this interpretation of will: "will means an attitude towards the future, towards the production of possible consequences, an attitude involving effort to foresee clearly and comprehensively the probable results of ways of acting, and an active identification with some anticipated consequences." [40] In other words, man does not stand above the course of events; he is part of it. The influence he exerts may vary from time to time and it may not always, it may never, be determining. He neither controls the direction of social or material events nor is he helplessly subject to them.

Obviously Dewey's philosophy of education is unmanageable unless his interpretation of man's nature is understood; at this point most of the opposition to Dewey's theory was aimed.[41] If Dewey's conception of man is invalid, then much of his theory of education has a highly problematical meaning. But if Dewey's assumptions about the philosophy of man are accepted, his plan for education is both reasonable and praiseworthy. He followed the revolutionary plan pronounced by Rousseau, but avoided the pitfalls of negativism and ardent anti-intellectualism that made Rousseau's specific recommendations archaic the day they were written.

Dewey's elaboration of his philosophy of man was both clear and concise.[42] It is not quite so easy to grasp his metaphysical position, for he seemed to doubt the importance of a general theory of reality either for

39 John Locke, *An Essay Concerning Human Understanding*, II, xxi, 17–18.

40 Dewey, *Democracy and Education*, p. 157.

41 For some examples, see John Blewett, ed., *John Dewey: His Thought and Influence* (New York, Fordham University Press, 1960).

42 Although he deals with this issue in a number of his works, his most formal treatment was in *Human Nature and Conduct* (New York, Henry Holt and Company, 1922).

education or anything else, and he came dangerously close, at times, to saying that one could not be built. In his philosophy of man he eschewed metaphysical complexities and chose to deal with men as they conducted themselves in the day-to-day world rather than to become involved in erudite speculations about their origin and destiny. He was content to take men as he found them, and he was comfortable with the reality he knew. Knowledge of reality was confined by experience; once a theorist went beyond his experiences he became involved in what might be interesting, but meaningless, speculations. For this reason Dewey could affirm, in *Creative Intelligence,* that "the chief characteristic of the pragmatic notion of reality is precisely that no theory of Reality in general . . . is possible or needed." [43]

While this should have settled the question—and Dewey might have been taken at his word—some of Dewey's followers, not entirely content to leave reality theory uncultivated, undertook to make their metaphysical views, or reservations, more explicit.[44] Although one cannot contend that their metaphysical propositions were embraced by Dewey, or made part of his philosophic outlook, he seems not to have raised serious objections to them. Still, we must be cautious, for silence should not be interpreted as consent. In the absence of a unified metaphysic, these positions would, in general, express the pragmatist's principal responses to questions about a general theory of reality: [45]

1. Whatever is used to construct a theory of reality must come from experience itself and this, almost inevitably, leads to the conclusion that there is no all-embracing reality against which human experience may be observed, interpreted, or judged.

2. While it is essential to avoid broad commitments to what is or is not real, especially since so much of what men like to call reality is outside the boundaries of their experience, change is a reality confirmed time and time again in experience. Thus, pragmatic theory of reality would seem to be in the position of accepting half the traditional doctrine erecting principles of permanence and change. The pragmatist does not merely neglect the principle of permanence; he denies it. And considering his commitments to evolution—which is in itself a doctrine of flux—he must deny the principle of permanence if he is to be consistent.

3. Reality is unfinished; it is in a process of becoming. Unquestion-

[43] John Dewey, *Creative Intelligence* (New York, Henry Holt and Company, 1917), p. 55.

[44] For example, see Sidney Hook, *The Metaphysics of Pragmatism* (Chicago, The Open Court Publishing Company, 1927); and John L. Childs, *Education and the Philosophy of Experimentalism* (New York, Century Company, 1931).

[45] These may be compared with the summary in J. Donald Butler, *Four Philosophies and Their Practice in Education and Religion,* revised ed., (New York, Harper & Brothers Publishers, 1957), pp. 453–459.

ably pragmatic theorists admitted the reality of matter in the physical world, but it was an incomplete and indeterminate reality. Its meaning could be revealed episodically, or as individual knowers came in contact with it and made something out of it. What it is in general, or what it is when separated from the transaction of knower and known is scientifically meaningless.

4. Order in the world is achieved as a result of creative experience; it is not something concealed in nature to be discovered and submitted to. The processes of nature are not fitted into a prescribed system with a foreordained end; there are as many ends in the world as there are persons coming in contact with reality.

In a sense, of course, these fundamental positions do add up to a theory of reality. Undoubtedly they do affect man's attitudes toward what education should be—and they affected Dewey—yet Dewey remained aloof to any opportunities to amplify them. Perhaps he was right: what else was there to say?

The key to pragmatism, it is said, is its theory of knowledge; possibly an explanation of pragmatism should begin with a theory of knowledge. However, our interests are not especially with pragmatism as a philosophy, except as it provided a starting point for Dewey's theory of education, and we do not feel compelled to elaborate its principles. Yet on the level of knowledge Dewey began by rejecting both rationalism and empiricism as adequate accounts of the phenomenon of knowledge; in their place he put instrumentalism.[46] When all the implications of instrumentalism are seen, the educational plan proposed by Dewey follows inevitably. Knowledge, for Dewey, was not made up of facts, and though he recommended the experimental method as a way of having experience,[47] he was by no means certain of this method's ability to produce dependable and permanent data. The process of knowing, moreover, could not be carried on outside an operational, experimental context: thus, he rejected the familiar and time-honored deductive process. At best, knowledge was an instrument gained in a learning process—part of what might be called knowledge was supplied by the learner, himself an essential unit in the process, and part came from the events to which the learner was exposed. And what he learned depended mainly on the situation. The point is, there was no mine from which knowledge could be hauled by the industrious student; knowledge was not just waiting to be known. It arose only out of a transaction between the knower and that part of reality in which he lived.

This was the relativism for which Dewey was praised and blamed. It

[46] See M. C. Baker, *Foundations of John Dewey's Educational Theory* (New York, King's Crown Press, 1955).

[47] See John Dewey, *Experience and Education* (New York, The Macmillan Company, 1938).

rested on the assumptions that: (1) there was no dualism of subject and object; (2) there were no absolutes in knowledge or elsewhere; (3) there was no rational test of truth—truth was not a question of right or wrong, but of what had meaning and what had none; (4) there was no meaning to experience prior to the act of experiencing; and (5) the closest thing to knowledge was the tested hypothesis extracted from a careful application of the experimental method. With these convictions about the knowing process and knowledge itself, it is easy to see why Dewey campaigned for curricular reform and why he consistently rejected formal textbook teaching.

He could, moreover, reject the narrow approach to knowledge codified time and again in the curriculum of the school, for he entertained serious doubts about the worth of knowledge revealed by following either the prescriptions of classical humanism, which made the Latin and Greek classics the reservoirs of universal wisdom, or those of scientific positivism, which promised utility in learning if scientifically-oriented syllabi were followed. But this was only part of the issue, for Dewey was not preoccupied with knowledge; he did not identify instruction and education; and he found the old formulas stressing intellectual goals for education seriously deficient. The school should surely encourage students toward learning how to learn, but this goal was subordinated, in Dewey's thought, to learning how to live. The process of education could not avoid taking into account man's most pressing need—living productively and intelligently in society. None of the traditional syllabi met this issue squarely; some of them, as a matter of fact, hardly acknowledged its reality.[48]

Living, in Dewey's view, is primarily a moral experience. Intelligence is involved obviously, and Dewey wanted men's intelligence trained as fully as possible. But mental training was only one step toward building a system of values, a valid ethical code, for social living. What is needed most from mental and emotional training is judgment or "what is ordinarily called good sense."

> The difference between mere knowledge, or information, and judgment is that the former is simply held, not used; judgment is ideas directed with reference to the accomplishment of ends. Good judgment is a sense of respective or proportionate values. The one who has judgment is the one who has ability to size up a situation. He is the one who can grasp the scene or situation before him, ignoring what is irrelevant, or what for the time being is unimportant, and can seize upon the factors which demand attention, and grade them according to their respective claims. Mere knowledge of what the right is in the abstract, mere intentions of following the right in general, however praiseworthy in themselves, are never a substitute

[48] Dewey, *Democracy and Education*, pp. 286–291; and John Dewey, *The Child and His Curriculum* (Chicago, University of Chicago Press, 1912) .

for this power of trained judgment. Action is always in the concrete. It is definite and individualized. Except, therefore, as it is backed and controlled by knowledge of the actual concrete factors in the situation demanding action, it must be relatively futile and waste.[49]

Pragmatists are often charged with indifference to moral values. Moral nihilism, it is said, must inevitably result from a pragmatic value theory, for this theory does not stand on the foundation of intrinsic values defined either by God, and interpreted by men, or on the law of nature, the natural law.[50] Yet, it was not Dewey's intention, nor the intention of his followers, to lead men into the abyss of moral anarchy; society's ethical conventions were affirmed, although with some misgivings about the universality and inflexibility claimed for them. By no means was Dewey in the business of doubting virtue or destroying conventional morality; yet he could, and did, express major rejections concerning traditional theories of morals.[51]

We know Dewey did not countenance any doctrine allowing ends to justify means. In a charming and amusing chapter in his *Theory of Valuation,* he reminded his readers of Charles Lamb's essay on the origin of roast pork. Lamb had written about man's first aquaintance with roast pork through the accidental burning of a pig barn. While trying to remove the debris, laborers touched the burned pigs and scorched their fingers. They soothed their fingers by putting them in their mouths and discovered with delight the taste of cooked pig flesh. Thereafter, according to the essay, in order to satisfy their appetite for cooked pig they put pigs in houses and then burned the houses to the ground. The end was good—at least, it gave enjoyment to hungry men—but the means were ridiculously inappropriate, and Dewey extracts from the incident this meaning: "Now, if ends-in-view are what they are entirely apart from means, and have their value independently of valuation of means, there is nothing absurd, nothing ridiculous, in this procedure, for the end attained, the *de facto* termination, was eating and enjoying roast pork, and that was just the end desired." [52]

This incident may be used to illustrate Dewey's rejection of traditional solutions to two questions: (1) where do values originate; and (2) how are men able to determine the appropriateness of any particular value in a specific social situation? Put quickly, in the traditional answer, values came either from God or from the laws of nature. And these intrinsic values do not have to be weighed for one situation or another;

[49] John Dewey, "Ethical Principles Underlying Education," *Third Yearbook,* National Herbartian Society (1897) , and reprinted in Archambault, *op. cit.,* p. 134.

[50] See P. K. Crosser, *The Nihilism of John Dewey* (New York, Philosophical Library, 1955) .

[51] See Dewey, *Democracy and Education,* pp. 402–417.

[52] John Dewey, *Theory of Valuation* (Chicago, University of Chicago Press, 1939) , and excerpted in Archambault, *op. cit.,* p. 97.

they have eternal worth and general application—what is good is always good and what is bad is always evil. Reminded of Lamb's essay, it was obvious to Dewey that the value of enjoyment in eating roast pork occurred not from intent, not as an end-value, but as an outcome of experience. The appropriateness of the end-value could not be determined by enjoyment alone, but only by taking into consideration the material and social costs involved. Regardless of the delight of eating roast pork, it is not worth the waste of burning down one's own home, and it is too great a luxury if having it requires burning a neighbor's home. Yet, no one could argue, and Dewey does not, that eating roast pork must be prohibited. Thus, in rejecting the maxim that the end justifies the means, Dewey also rejected, as being cut from the same cloth, the traditional moral conception of ends-in-themselves. "The conception," he wrote, "that certain things are ends-in-themselves can warrant the belief that the relation of ends-means is unilateral, proceeding exclusively from end to means." [53] By assuming these positions, Dewey continued, moralists ended up holding one of two views, neither of which could be validated empirically:

> One of the views is that only the specially selected 'end' held in view will actually be brought into existence by the means used, something miraculously intervening to prevent the means employed from having their other usual effects; the other (and more probable) view is that, as compared with the importance of the selected and uniquely prized end, other consequences may be completely ignored and brushed aside no matter how intrinsically obvious they are. This arbitrary selection of some one part of the attained consequences as the end and hence as the warrant of means used (no matter how objectionable are their other consequences) is the fruit of holding that *it*, as *the* end, is an end-in-itself, and hence possessed of 'value' irrespective of all its existential relations. And this notion is inherent in *every* view that assumes that 'ends' can be valued apart from appraisal of the things used as means in attaining them.[54]

Dewey found a dangerous fallacy in the creed that ends have value independent of any appraisal of means used to attain them, or that in attaining the end desired the process is terminated: ends must always be appraised as causes or means to further ends. Society, Dewey knew, accepted certain standardized ends uncritically and was concerned only with means used to attain them. But this human experience, he argued, did not illuminate value theory because these ends were either nominal or habitual. What interested him most was the possibility of freeing the human resource by discarding the notion that some objects are ends-in-themselves, and this abandonment should be "not merely in words but in

[53] *Ibid.*, p. 99.
[54] *Ibid.*

all practical implications, [then] human beings would for the first time in history be in a position to frame ends-in-view and form desires on the basis of empirically grounded propositions of the temporal relations of events to one another." [55]

Dewey regarded formal education as an important instrument for building a moral order, but it had to begin with the individual. We know how he wanted the curriculum to be relevant, and on the same level of significance and urgency he wanted the moral formation of students in school to be relevant. The condition for moral relevancy was that the school be part of social life, for "apart from the thought of participation in social life the school has no end or aim. As long as we confine ourselves to the school as an isolated institution we have no final directing ethical principles, because we have no object or ideal." [56]

The lamentable separation of intellectual and moral training in formal education was, Dewey said, only one indication of the school's failure to be a society with its own life and values. Unless the school became an embryo of typical community life, this separation was bound to continue, and moral training would always be partly pathological. Of course, not all the school's equipment for moral training would have to be channeled into socialized living; moral training in school had a formal side. Such moral habits as promptness, regularity, and industry need attention, for they are morally necessary simply because the schools are what they are; but the duties they dictate, it must be clear, are distinctly school, not life, duties.[57]

The school's special function as a moral agency must be fulfilled, Dewey said, by making the pupil conscious "of this social environment, and [confer] upon him the ability to interpret his own powers from the standpoint of their possibilities in social use." This, Dewey wrote, is the "ultimate and unified standard." [58] There could not be two ethical theories, one for the school and one for life. "As conduct is one, the principles of conduct are one also." [59] Moreover, if the school is to perform its function as a moral agency, it must exploit the legitimate relationships between morals and knowledge. In *Democracy and Education* Dewey employs trenchant language to state his position:

> Moral education in school is practically hopeless when we set up the development of character as a supreme end, and at the same time treat the acquiring of knowledge and the development of understanding, which of necessity occupy the chief part of school time, as having nothing to do with character. On such a basis, moral educa-

55 *Ibid.*, p. 100.
56 John Dewey, "Ethical Principles Underlying Education," in *ibid.*, p. 114.
57 *Ibid.*, p. 117.
58 *Ibid.*, p. 121.
59 *Ibid.*, p. 108.

tion is inevitably reduced to some kind of catechetical instruction, or lessons about morals. Lessons 'about morals' signify as matter of course lessons in what other people think about virtues and duties. It amounts to something only in the degree in which pupils happen to be already animated by a sympathetic and dignified regard for the sentiments of others. Without such a regard, it has no more influence on character than information about the mountains of Asia; with a servile regard, it increases dependence upon others and throws upon those in authority the responsibility for conduct. As a matter of fact, direct instruction in morals has been effective only in social groups where it was a part of the authoritative control of the many by the few. Not the teaching as such but the reenforcement of it by the whole regime of which it was an incident made it effective. To attempt to get similar results from lessons about morals in a democratic society is to rely upon sentimental magic.[60]

IV

EDUCATIONAL THEORY

With some insights into Dewey's general philosophy, especially into his views of man, reality, knowledge, and ethics, we are ready to look more closely at his educational theory. It is not easy to separate sharply Dewey's philosophical and educational thought, even for purposes of analysis, because Dewey did not separate them in his own thinking. "If a theory makes no difference in educational endeavor, it must be artificial. The educational point of view enables one to envisage the philosophic problems where they arise and thrive, where they are at home, and where acceptance or rejection makes a difference in practice. . . . If we are willing to conceive education as the process of forming fundamental dispositions, intellectual and emotional, toward nature and fellow men, philosophy may even be defined as the *general theory of education*." [61] This attitude toward philosophy vis-à-vis education did nothing to diminish the importance of education; in it consideration of special educational problems became imperative and urgent; and it did not make it impossible for us to know Dewey's conception of the purposes of education and the means used to achieve them.

Most of Dewey's writings could be quoted to illuminate his educational thought, but such a broad approach is obviously impossible here, for we cannot hope to introduce the totality of his thought on either education or philosophy. The parts of his theory which seem to be fundamental may be found in two highly important books: *My Pedagogic Creed,* written in 1897, and *Democracy and Education,* published in

[60] Dewey, *Democracy and Education,* p. 411.
[61] *Ibid.,* p. 383.

1916. In addition to the remarkably penetrating ideas advanced in these two books—the former only of essay length and the latter of full book length—we are impressed by the consistency of his theories over a period of two decades. Despite his strong attachment to the pragmatic doctrine of change, Dewey's basic attitudes toward the educational process have a quality of permanence, and *Democracy and Education* may be interpreted as an elaboration of principles contained originally in *My Pedagogic Creed.*

The distinction between formal and informal education was no mystery to Dewey,[62] and the charge that he sought to preside over the dissolution of formal education until it became totally informal and incidental is plainly wrong. Dewey was not intent on destroying schools or even on making them miniature societies, but he did want to underscore the dangerous tendency of formal education to ignore social necessity and be preoccupied solely with imparting instruction. Thus, Dewey's theory of education was concerned both with formal and informal education, but because of the place formal education had achieved in society and because of society's obvious need for it, formal education got the bulk of his attention.

When Dewey elaborated his view on "what education is" in *My Pedagogic Creed* or the "aims of education" in *Democracy and Education,* he was not restricting his theory, although it was clear to him that informal education, by its very nature, followed a more realistic and relevant course and was less in need of theoretical direction. He was willing to emphasize such things as how schools are organized, how curricula are built, how students are motivated to learn and how they apply what they learn, and what teachers do. What is the reason behind all these activities?

In *My Pedagogic Creed* Dewey expressed himself on the meaning of education in this way: [63]

1. Education is a social process which puts the individual in relationship with the social consciousness of the race. As a process, education begins unconsciously—the learner shares freely in the intellectual and moral resources of humanity long before he is aware of doing so—and it moves gradually toward a conscious relationship with the inheritance of mankind.[64]

2. Education with worth begins with the stimulation of social relations; the learner is involved; he acts and reacts, and as he does he begins to see what his actions mean socially.[65]

---

62 *Ibid.,* pp. 7–11.
63 See John Dewey, *My Pedagogic Creed* (New York, E. L. Kellogg and Co., 1897), and reprinted in Archambault, *op. cit.,* pp. 427–439.
64 *Ibid.,* p. 427.
65 *Ibid.,* pp. 427–428.

3. One side of the educational process is psychological. Educators must have psychological insights, and education must be adjusted to the individual's psychological structure or it will be haphazard and arbitrary.[66]

4. The other side of the educational process is sociological. Educators must properly interpret the child's powers, instincts, and tendencies and translate them into social equivalents. The child must be seen as the inheritor of the social past and as an agent in society's future.[67]

5. The relationship between the psychological and sociological dimensions of education are organically related: mental power cannot be developed without regard for its use, and the good of society cannot be stressed at the expense of individual freedom.[68]

6. The conception of education as a preparation for life is almost meaningless. We cannot know in precise terms what future life means, but we can think of education as being a way of giving the person command over himself.[69]

In *Democracy and Education* Dewey is somewhat more direct and explicit, but he has not altered his earlier position. We can summarize his views on educational aims as follows:

1. In seeking aims for education, Dewey did not try to find an end outside the process itself to which education is subordinate. He did not ignore the existence of such ends, but where they were honored, he maintained they did not "arise from the free growth of [student] experience, and their nominal aims will be means to more interior ends of others rather than truly their own."[70] Here and elsewhere Dewey's assumption is crystal clear: he is concerned with education in a democratic society.

2. Acting with an aim is equivalent to intelligent living: no case is made for aimless education. Aims, however, are neither imposed nor prescribed but appear as a function of student experiences: "to have an aim is to act with meaning, not like an automatic machine; it is to *mean* to do something and to perceive the meaning of things in the light of that intent."[71] The aim, then, must be an outgrowth of existing conditions.

3. Good aims survey current student experience and lead to tentative plans of action which are modified as conditions warrant. "The aim, in short, is experimental, and hence constantly growing as it is tested in action."[72]

4. Education, as such, Dewey maintained, has no aims. "Only persons, parents, and teachers, etc., have aims, not an abstract idea like

66 *Ibid.*, p. 428.
67 *Ibid.*
68 *Ibid.*, p. 429.
69 *Ibid.*
70 Dewey, *Democracy and Education*, p. 117.
71 *Ibid.*, p. 121.
72 *Ibid.*, p. 123.

education." Because persons have aims, they are definitely varied, and in school they differ with different children, "changing as children grow and with the growth experience of the one who teaches." [73]

5. An educational aim must be founded upon the intrinsic activities and needs of the person being educated. "The tendency of such an aim as preparation is, as we have seen, to omit existing powers, and find the aim in some remote accomplishment or responsibility." [74]

In *My Pedagogic Creed* Dewey concluded the section on "what education is" by saying that education must give the person command over himself. In *Democracy and Education* he spoke of aims as ways of acting intelligently. In both places he opposed imposed, rigid aims, but nowhere does he endorse chaos or aimlessness as the guiding principles in education.

If the aims of education are distilled out of the process of living, and according to Dewey they are, then the school's importance is enhanced, because to a large extent it is responsible for the environment where learning and living occur. Without a doubt, in Dewey's conception of education, the school wore a new face. What is the school? In the first place, it is simply a form of community life; its chief role is to maintain an environment for high quality living by representing present life at its best. Contemporary community life is so complex that its full representation in the school's environment is out of the question. Hence, there is need to simplify and consolidate the finest living experiences. Even these condensed versions of life when organized in the school's program must be graded and accommodated to the maturity of students. Educational programs should be grounded on the earlier experiences of home life, but they must also maintain a constant contact with home life in order to assure a continuity of student growth, on the one hand, and to illuminate the values of home life, on the other. When the school is understood to be a kind of community life, it becomes a better agent for moral formation, because it maintains the unity of living and moral training. Dewey was always confident that moral formation had better prospects in a school where moral training was sought through the channels of proper social relations.

Dewey did not mean to disenfranchise teachers or relegate them to unimportant places in the school's environment. Yet, he would not commission a teacher to be the creator of the student's educational environment. Stimuli for learning and control over the conditions of learning should not come from the teacher but from the total social environment of the school, and the teacher's function is to select experiences to affect the child and to assist him in responding to these experiences.

The conventional machinery of conducting schools—grading, promotion, and the like—should not cast such a long shadow over education.

[73] *Ibid.,* p. 125.
[74] *Ibid.,* p. 126.

Each might have its place, but only insofar as each could reveal the student's fitness for social life. In this way Dewey's creed was applied to the school itself.

Dewey's instinct for educational reform evidenced in *My Pedagogic Creed* was eroded neither by time nor by further study of education's problems. *Democracy and Education* is inspired by the same instinct; almost the entire text could be quoted as an elaboration of the principles Dewey articulated in *My Pedagogic Creed*. Extensive quoting might prove to be wearisome, so we shall try to show by selective quoting how Dewey used *Democracy and Education* to illuminate his original ideas.

The first office of the school, he wrote, is to provide children with a simplified environment.[75] The school should begin with fundamental features of society and put them in a context appropriate to the student's experience and understanding. "Then it establishes a progressive order, using the factors first acquired as means of gaining insight into what is more complicated." [76] Once this beginning is made, the school must eliminate "so far as possible, the unworthy features of the existing environment from influence of mental habitudes." Not only does the school need to eliminate undesirable parts of the social environment, it must also work to counteract perverse influences in the social environment. "As a society becomes more enlightened, it realizes that it is responsible *not* to transmit and conserve the whole of its existing achievements, but only such as make for a better future society." [77] Finally, the school has a clear responsibility to educate students away from their past: schools should open new worlds to young minds. But even as it closes the book on much of the past, it must be a steadying and integrating social agency as it throws open the doors to the future.

When Dewey turned to the teacher in *Democracy and Education,* he continued to press views expressed earlier in *My Pedagogic Creed*. He did not doubt the importance of the teacher's role,[78] but he stressed communication rather than transmission as its most central feature. Moreover, he questioned the effectiveness of what he called deliberate teaching.[79] Yet he did not mean for the teacher to "stand off and look on; the alternative to furnishing ready-made subject matter and listening to the accuracy with which it is reproduced is not quiescence, but participation, sharing, in an activity. In such shared activity, the teacher is a learner, and the learner is, without knowing it, a teacher—and upon the whole, the less consciousness there is, on either side, of either giving or receiving instruction, the better." [80]

[75] *Ibid.*, p. 24.
[76] *Ibid.*
[77] *Ibid.*
[78] *Ibid.*, pp. 4–5.
[79] *Ibid.*, p. 20.
[80] *Ibid.*, p. 188.

Many twentieth-century educators who were sympathetic to Dewey's assault on the teacher-subject-centered school, and who were sincerely interested in building bridges between life and learning, were troubled by the apparent jettisoning of content from progressive schools. They could not see how the educational program built on student interest alone could lay the kinds of intellectual and moral foundations necessary for living in a complex, modern society. If subject matter were removed from the school, what would take its place? And would the substitute be truly educative?

When Dewey's *My Pedagogic Creed* was consulted for illumination on this point, although it must be said that Dewey himself was not one of the progressive educators,[81] a rather general endorsement of popular progressive practices was found. Dewey maintained that social life was the basis for training and growth, and the school's curriculum should generate a gradual development of social life. School studies do not, Dewey argued, have an independent value; their relevance and value are confirmed by the social experiences of the learner. The true center for school subjects, Dewey wrote, is social living and activity. From this center flows the justification for studying science, history, and literature; without a social motive these studies have practically no meaning to the child. Literature is a fitting summary of social experience; history is a record of man's social life; science, stressed as a tool rather than a storehouse of knowledge, is important for what it reveals about social living. Cooking, sewing, manual training, etc., have a legitimate place in the school's curriculum, and they are not included as a relief for the students from other important studies but because they have an intrinsic social value.[82]

Thus, the belief that Dewey would have abandoned all subject matter is not entirely innocent of mythical thinking. He did not prescribe subjects for study, nor did he determine their educational order; yet it is entirely clear that the content of any traditional subjects, separated from their conventional and prescribed curricular format, would be part of the student's school experience. The road taken to history, literature, and science, for example, would be paved by the student's attitudes and interests and not by the formalisms or dicta of the school or the conceptions or judgments of the teacher. And once these subjects were met in the daily life of the school they would not be cast into the old mold—in other words, the new education was not merely different on the level of

81 Dewey's relationship to progressive education is complex. See R. H. Beck, "American Progressive Education, 1875–1930," *Curriculum Journal*, 14 (March, 1943), pp. 115–118; L. A. Cremin, "The Progressive Movement in American Education: A Perspective," *Harvard Educational Review*, 27 (Fall, 1957), pp. 251–270; and L. A. Cremin, *The Transformation of the School* (New York, Alfred A. Knopf, Inc., 1961), pp. 234–239.

82 Dewey, *My Pedagogic Creed*, in Archambault, *op. cit.*, pp. 433–434.

approach; subjects would be studied and sustained in the curriculum so long as they fulfilled criteria of meaning and relevance.

In *Democracy and Education* Dewey is more philosophical, and thus his views on the content of education can be taken with the utmost generality, as he intended. When we finish with the section on subject matter in *My Pedagogic Creed,* we are left with the impression that Dewey is counseling a new technique—and an indirect one at that—to teaching traditional subjects. Although such an impression may be invalid in the long run, it is easily obtained. But in elaborating his position later, he is quite clear in not accepting "subject matter . . . as something complete in itself; [or as] something to be learned or known, either by the voluntary application of mind to it or through the impressions it makes on mind." [83] The subject matter of education should "consist of whatever is recognized as having a bearing upon the anticipated course of events, whether assisting or retarding it." [84] Thus, following his pragmatic theory of knowledge, Dewey rejects the traditional dualism of mind and matter, of knower and thing known, and establishes mind as but one factor among many involved in the production of consequences. From this rejection he can move to the problem of instruction and explain it as one "of finding material that will engage a person in specific activities having an aim or purpose of moment or interest to him, and dealing with things not as gymnastic applicances but as conditions for the attainment of ends." [85]

Dewey does not pretend that the task of building and organizing curricula is easy, and he admits to its becoming more difficult when the subject matter employed is intended to foster continuity in social life. Even with a carefully selected curricular content teachers are tempted to endow subject matter with independent value. Despite the worth Dewey readily acknowledges for various kinds of curricular content, its value is never independent of its ability to promote the realization of meanings implied in the present experiences of the child.[86]

Introducing content to education without at the same time considering method, or deploying methods without seeing them in the full context of content, was, according to Dewey, to reconstruct the old dualism of knower and things known, which in this connection became a dualism of what and how: what is to be taught or learned and how it is to be approached either by the student or the teacher are not, Dewey said, separate questions. While educators can distinguish *what* from *how* in analyzing the act of learning, they were warned against separating the process of learning into categories of content and method. The two are

[83] Dewey, *Democracy and Education*, p. 153.
[84] *Ibid.,* pp. 153–154.
[85] *Ibid.,* p. 155.
[86] *Ibid.,* pp. 212–227.

irrevocably related. When teachers separate them they make learning artificial and largely irrelevant. Method has two foundations: the child and the content of instruction. But unless one takes full account of the learner's interests and abilities and begins with them, he shall have no need to consider the implications content has for method. In *My Pedagogic Creed* Dewey lays down some general beliefs about method but he does not support them with theory; [87] theoretical support is supplied in *Democracy and Education*.[88] The general beliefs may be summarized as follows:

1. Method is based on the development of the child's powers and interests. Thus method may not be taken as a static thing; the foundations for it are subject to change.

2. In the experience of the child the active precedes the passive; conscious states project themselves in action. Meaningful instruction, then, must be rooted in the experiences of the child. Instruction that assumes or condones passivity is largely a waste of time.

3. Ideas—the sought-after products of education—are generated in the action the learner experiences in meeting his environment.

4. The instructional benefits to the child are controlled by the image he himself forms about the content of instruction. Rather than making children learn certain things, teachers should try to help them form proper images.

5. Good teachers enter the child's life and try to see learning problems through his eyes. When this is done successfully, the reality of child learning is stressed and his interests are accepted as valid, to be neither humored nor repressed.

6. In learning situations emotions must be recognized and related to activity; emotions do not stand as obstacles to learning when proper habits of action and thought are maintained.

7. Content and method should not be separated; nor should feeling and action be segregated.

These general statements are endorsed and elaborated in *Democracy and Education*. They are also applied more directly to school learning processes. Dewey begins by affirming the general principle he had expressed before: "Method means that arrangement of subject matter which makes it most effective in use. Never is method something outside of the material." [89] And what is sometimes taken to be method—that is, random or ill-considered action unrelated to desired results—is not method at all. In the end, method is only an effective way of "employing some material for some end." [90] Again, Dewey warns us to beware of

87 Dewey, *My Pedagogic Creed,* in Archambault, *op. cit.,* pp. 435–437.
88 Dewey, *Democracy and Education,* pp. 193–211.
89 *Ibid.,* p. 194.
90 *Ibid.,* p. 195.

separating content and method: "Apart from effort to control the course which the process takes, there is no distinction of subject matter and method." [91] Yet, we can and must study the process of understanding the elements which will enable us to control it more effectively. "Getting an idea of *how* the experience proceeds indicates to us what factors must be secured or modified in order that it may go on more successfully." [92]

The isolation of method from content produced, Dewey said, some educational evils. He identified them for us, and we may summarize them as follows:

1. A mechanical approach to method and consequent neglect of the concrete situations of experience is bad. The experiences of teaching and learning are gained under conditions of restraint and they "throw little or no light upon the normal course of an experience to its fruition." [93]

2. Discipline and interest are misunderstood because method and content are isolated. Discipline becomes a matter of forcing interests upon the child and he accepts these interests because he is afraid of unpleasant results if he does not accept them.

3. Learning is made an end in itself when it should be a "product and reward of occupation with subject matter." [94]

4. The unwarranted assumption is made that there is one method, a kind of recipe, that may be handed to teachers, and if they follow it proper mental habits will appear.[95]

Dewey did not discredit the notion that education "has its general methods," for, he wrote, a very important part of learning "consists in *becoming* master of the methods which the experience of others has shown to be most efficient in like cases of getting knowledge. These general methods are in no way opposed to individual initiative and originality—to personal ways of doing things. On the contrary they are reinforcements of them. For there is radical difference between even the most general method and a prescribed rule. The latter is a *direct* guide to action, the former operates indirectly through the enlightenment it supplies as to ends and means. It operates, that is to say, through intelligence, and not through conformity to orders externally imposed." [96] Yet, even with the general method garnered from experience others have had in similar situations, each learner must make his own reaction. The general method may help, or harm, the learner according to the impress it has on his personal reaction and on the exercise of his judgment. The distinctive quality to learning, much neglected in conventional educational practice, Dewey said, must be restored. It is not sound pedagogy to

91 *Ibid.*
92 *Ibid.,* p. 197.
93 *Ibid.,* p. 198.
94 *Ibid.*
95 *Ibid.,* p. 199.
96 *Ibid.,* p. 201.

think of ordinary persons and exceptional persons: in teaching and learning situations every learner is exceptional. He should have the chance to employ his own powers in activities having meaning. Unless method allows for this it is faulty. "Methods remain the personal concern, approach, and attack of an individual, and no catalogue can ever exhaust their diversity of form and tint." [97]

THE SCHOOL AND SOCIAL PROGRESS. Dewey wanted an intellectual revolution, and he wanted the school to lead it. He argued against mere learning and said there is no clear social gain in absorbing facts and truths as an exclusively individual affair.[98] The position he took in *My Pedagogic Creed*—that education is the fundamental method of social progress and reform; that reforms resting on law alone are largely futile; that education is the regulation of the process of coming to share in the social consciousness, and that the adjustment of individual activity on the basis of social consciousness is the only sure method of social reconstruction; that the community's duty to education is a paramount moral duty because through education society can organize its means and resources and thus shape its goals—are clearly reflected in his later works, principally in *School and Society* and *Democracy and Education*. In the latter we have Dewey's word for what he meant by progress, and we can see how education was to be an instrument for it: "Progress is sometimes thought of as consisting in getting nearer to ends already sought. But this is a minor form of progress, for it requires only improvement of the means for action or technical advance. More important modes of progress consist in enriching prior purposes and in forming new ones." [99]

In the end, the aim of education is social progress and Dewey hoped to reform the school, the curriculum and the method of education to ensure the achievement of this aim. Obviously, we have not touched on all the multiple educational issues forming Dewey's educational theory— we did not begin with the intention of doing so—but we have discussed some of the central positions in his educational thought that brought educational theory to a stage of maturity, and have tried to show how much broader he intended education's role to be. Although he should not generally be thought of as an educational humanist, there is hardly any doubt that his principal hope was to reconstruct education and humanize it, that is, make it more meaningful to those who would of necessity be exposed to it.

[97] *Ibid.,* p. 204.

[98] John Dewey, *School and Society,* revised ed., (Chicago, University of Chicago Press, 1915), pp. 12–13.

[99] Dewey, *Democracy and Education,* p. 261.

≫ 13 ≪

Educational Theory in Retrospect

I

THE BACKGROUND

The conservative and conventional attitude long dominating educational thought rested on the assumption that an explicit educational theory was not only essential to but necessarily preceded educational practice. This assumption is weakened or destroyed by a closer examination of the facts of history; hardly any evidence supports a belief that the doctrines of Plato or Isocrates were countenanced in practice in ancient Greece; it is hard to see how the elaborate constructions of Quintilian were adhered to during his own lifetime or even in the two or three centuries following his death. Cassiodorus, unquestionably a revisionist, could make only slight impressions on the schoolmasters of his own genre, although his innovations were remarkably effective in the schools connected with the monasteries he established.

So long as Alcuin remained on the level of pedagogic technique and tried to teach an accurate Latin along lines most useful to the governments of Church and state, his work had a strong ring of relevance; but when he strayed into the arena of theory—which was not often—he displayed a singular ineptitude either for knowing the purposes of theory or for organizing and presenting its ingredients. Yet for all this, Alcuin was a pioneer, without whose work medieval education would have been much retarded; and the point may be that the labor of Alcuin concealed an incipient theory, formulated in tradition, perpetuated by custom, and applied intuitively. But this unconscious conformity to a highly theological view of man and his temporal purposes could hardly count as an educational theory, for both in content and elaboration it missed the mark of being adequate. Hugh of St. Victor and John of Salisbury, compared with Alcuin, were more broadly educated men, and their sensitivity to, and understanding of, theory was somewhat keener than Alcuin's; yet they dealt with theory only when it suited their purpose of opening the mines of classical literature for Christian exploitation. They were committed to using the past for educational purposes, and their methods and theory were both centered on decontaminating texts or proving that decontamination was unnecessary. Textual exposition, illuminated by Hugh and John, was a monumental achievement, and huge benefits accrued to education from its use; but for all their good work here, one can hardly avoid admitting that by staying so close to reading as the one and only means of education they were severely limiting the educational process for their own day and setting almost insurmountable strictures on its evolution. Their use of theory—convictions about education bequeathed by the ancient and early Christian pedagogical writers—was hardly praiseworthy, for their rejections were, in the long run, more significant than the points embraced. Part of the fault was perhaps not theirs, for the full corpus of pedagogical thought was not yet available; on the other hand, much classical educational writing was in the libraries, and we find it hard to believe that their rejections were due to ignorance: they refused to use what they did not want. Despite their determination to preserve their grasp of the Christian educational tradition, and for all the good work they accomplished along lines of allegorical exposition, the schools were little affected by their labor. The road between theory and practice was long and full of obstacles, and not many teachers thought the journey was worth making.

Erasmus was in a better position to speak with authority on the educational views of the ancient authors and on the promises of a good, profound, and complete classical education. An accomplished scholar, Erasmus found ways to achieve distinction in scholarship largely through his own efforts. Enrolling in the cult of fame, he was prepared to admit the reality of success formulas and thought an analysis and emulation of successful careers provided the key to greatness. Erasmus never seriously doubted that almost everything worth knowing was found in the classics; and in analyzing the classics, making heroic efforts to remember everything, he concluded that superior education results from a cultivation of two human abilities, thought and expression. Henceforth, in all his educational writings, he advocated a program of teaching and learning to develop these two human abilities. His *pietas litterata* is remarkably thorough—it considers the nature of man, his purposes in this world, the content of education to form him, the methods to be employed in teaching, and the safeguards imposed—but it does not tell the whole story, because Erasmus never left the classics nor understood why anyone should want to. Yet, despite the onesidedness of his educational plan and its tendency to perpetuate medieval pedagogical edicts, Erasmus' theory was attractive; when translated into practice by Erasmus' own generation it gained almost immediate favor and remained as a directive educational doctrine for centuries. Hardly any other theorist has had as great an impact on educational practice as Erasmus; perhaps this may justify the conclusion that in a list of the world's great educators, Erasmus' name must come first. However, the lag between theory and practice, even when Erasmus himself was the transmogrifier, was perceptible, and we are entitled to doubt either the seriousness or the validity with which practicing schoolmasters endow educational theory.

Comenius stood at the threshold of a new educational era, and part of his greatness was his accommodation to a world in ferment; he, like John Dewey, arrived on the educational scene when education was blazing a new trail, and the reforming theorist was enviably positioned to follow it along the way. But Comenius, when he embarked on the seas of novelty and educational innovation to parade his views on natural pedagogy, was ignored or rejected, either because his message was obscure or because it contained pedagogical language either unwanted or misunderstood by his generation. Comenius upgraded methodology because his instincts were good and he was a highly human person, but the psychological foundations underlying his method were dim and imprecise; and in the final analysis his best advice to schoolmasters was to use good books. In using Comenius' school texts, they were usually on safe ground, but inevitably these texts were dated, and Comenius was all but forgotten.

It would be easy to charge John Locke with indifference and to defend the indictment. He challenged the doctrines of the past to make vague generalizations relative to educating the sons of gentlemen; but he ignored the schools so long as he was confident the gentry would follow his advice and retain the services of good tutors. Yet, behind this veil of indifference was the suggestion that psychology—questions about the nature of learning and the learning process—contained the real key to the educational puzzle box. Locke willingly left to others the task of finding the proper dies for making this key.

Undoubtedly Rousseau was familiar with Locke's recommendations; and he followed Locke, not to articulate psychological precepts—for which he had neither the background nor the scientific equipment—but to counsel indifference to the large-scale educational issues that plagued his century. Even if any schoolmaster wanted to, he could not take any of Rousseau's works—*Emile* especially—and put them into practice on the day-to-day platform of teaching and learning. And Rousseau knew this as well as anyone. Still, it is argued, Rousseau had a message (and so much may be acknowledged) understood only by Pestalozzi, who in turn translated it into pedagogical practice. This overstates the case for Rousseau and understates it for Pestalozzi. Both were engaged on the same effort;

both wanted to reform education; but where Rousseau sought to lead a reform by discarding almost everything forming the structure of education, Pestalozzi tried to reform pedagogy within the broad boundaries of conventional school systems. He tried precisely what Rousseau said should not be done. The affinity between Rousseau and Pestalozzi is hardly one of master to disciple; rather, it is an affinity of inspiration. Pestalozzi, inspired by Rousseau's doctrine of natural education, and from his own long experience with teaching children under the most unfavorable social conditions, tried to formulate techniques of natural pedagogy. In the long run he was remarkably successful, for a century after his death scholars began to recognize excellent points in his writings and practices; but for the greater part of his own career friend and foe alike agreed on the verdict that Pestalozzi was an eccentric who, being deeply disturbed by the manifold problems of mankind and somewhat imbalanced himself, tried to lead an abortive educational crusade.

After amateurs like Rousseau and Pestalozzi had tinkered with the educational establishment, and came close sometimes to upsetting it, the scholars thought it best to take things into their own hands. This was simply a turning back of the clock, or better, of the calendar; in any case, the time had come for men with academic credentials to look closely at the basic issues in pedagogy, make sense out of them, organize them, and present pedagogy with a new face, as a scientific discipline. To be a science, pedagogy needed its facts organized, although it was apparent that before organization began, the facts would have to be determined. What was the purpose of education? What were its foundations in psychology, philosophy, and sociology? What should teachers teach, and how should they deploy their methods for the most effective instruction of the young? Herbart bravely set out to make education a science; in order to do this it needed both a theory and a content, but it needed a method as well. Yet, apart from his own pedagogic seminar, and the relatively few teachers he produced in it, Herbart remained confidently on the level of theoretical pronouncement; his scholar's study was, he thought, despite his highly-quotable advice that education must not just be talked about but also must be practiced, the best vantage point from which to view and understand the pressing questions of education. And for the most part, except when his followers misinterpreted his views on method and codified the five formal steps of instruction, Herbart's educational theory—his science of education—was a scholar's theory; its implementation was cumbersome and curtailed.

However, if Herbart was not entirely practical in his educational message, he did set in motion the idea that education was something to be concerned about: the generalizations of the past, despite the worth implicit in them, had not changed the schools much. Teaching and learning were important human pursuits, and dependable knowledge was

needed concerning their direction and practice. How was this information to be obtained, and how were the facts gleaned from investigations to
be validated? Now we are approaching the stage settings for a science of
education, and we come closer to John Dewey, for it was Dewey more than
any earlier educational theorist who, despite the claim that he ignored
the proper realms of theory and practice, taught that theory's work is to
report on the successes and failures of practice. Thus, theory—what education should do, what teaching and learning should accomplish—cannot
be jettisoned, on the one hand, or be allowed to remain impervious to
the validation of day-to-day practice in real schools with real children, on
the other. With John Dewey educational theory came of age; from his
time on it wore an entirely new face; and for almost the first time in
history, educational theory began to make a difference.

II

THE MISSION OF EDUCATIONAL THEORY

Educational theory, whether as an independent discipline or as part of
politics or philosophy, has never been regarded by its advocates as a
meaningless exercise. Even when school practices ignored the theories,
not one of the theorists studied in this book lost confidence in what he
had said about education. In the course of its evolution, theorists have
wrestled with some of these questions: What is the role of educational
theory? Why is educational theory necessary? What part should theory
have in the preparation of teachers?

THE ROLE OF EDUCATIONAL THEORY. This might seem to be a strange place
to raise questions concerning the purposes of educational theory, how it
should react, and when, to the educational enterprise. But in a book
which essays to examine the evolution of educational thought, this could
be the best place to catch the meaning that the theorists we have studied
thought educational theory should have for teachers and students, with
anyone, as a matter of fact, who is interested in the proper formation of
men.

Without trying to relate the general mission of educational theory to
any particular theorist now, we can begin by seeing the general directions
theory may take. First, we can say, educational theory may be assigned
the function of determining the broad purposes of education and then
trying to evaluate the processes of pedagogy. In this view educational
theory assumes a leadership role. Contained in the theory are answers to
the most pressing of education's questions: Who is being taught? Why is
teaching undertaken at all? What content is employed? How are the

means of education deployed? If the theory is complete, it will contain positive answers to all these questions. Little is left for the teacher: he has his educational prescription and is expected to follow it. Put in these terms, educational theory is a directive doctrine, which asks nothing from educational practice but that it be true to the theory as elaborated, and that it follow its precepts in day-to-day practice. As we look at a list of educators who have labored over theory for the past twenty centuries— both those dealt with in this book and others—we must be impressed by the number who accepted educational theory as a directive doctrine.

There are other faces, and when we look at them in the context of educational theory's role, we find some alternatives. Theory need not necessarily lead practice; it is not absolutely essential for a theory to be ready and waiting for practitioners to accept or reject it. Theory may be a response to educational practice; that is, educational practice takes certain routes because of social, political, and human pressures. It is not drifting in a sense of aimlessness, but it is drifting along with the course of human affairs. Education is fitting people for the tasks of life, and since these tasks are manifold and often unpredictable, the business of education is to deal with them flexibly and imaginatively. Education, as Herbart said, may not make holiday to deal with philosophical questions; it must do what needs to be done. When what needs doing has been done, it is time for theory to interpret, justify, and rationalize the practices employed. Questions about man and his nature are answered by the educational theorist only after he has seen children in the schools. Why are children being educated; what are education's aims? These are important questions, but they are not answered outside the context of a child learning in a particular educational and social environment. What should be taught—the curriculum—is a question whose relevance cannot be gainsaid, but if the answer is given beforehand, without reference to the needs and interests of students exposed to the curriculum, it may be an irrelevant answer. How are educational materials used to arrive at educational ends? This question may be asked anytime, but it can only be answered, say those who reject educational theory as a directive doctrine and make it a liberal discipline, after the educational process begins, only after the children are in the schoolroom, with their interests and needs, and with curricular materials assembled.

A third position is possible, and in it educational theory is neither directive nor liberal: educational theory is delegated to report on educational practice. Teachers faced with instructional problems may repair to theory to note what has been done, and they can get information about the success of a variety of teaching procedures.

When educational theory is either directive or liberal, answers will eventually be found to philosophical questions. As a directive doctrine, they will come quickly; as a liberal discipline, answers must await considerable rationalization and justification. Yet, either way, when answers come they will be infused with authority, and teachers ignoring them do so at their peril. With theory as a reporter, pointing but not leading, infallibility is forgotten and teachers are free to improvise, reject, or improve on the counsels printed in the books.

Can these roles for theory be found in history, and is it possible to follow their evolution in the doctrines of leading theorists?

It is hard to know whether educational theory began as a response to educational problems or whether its initial inspiration lay in the fact that someone thought he had discovered an educational plan of real promise. When we first meet educational theory—wedded to politics and philosophy, as we have said—it is in the hands of Plato and Isocrates, and both are reacting to educational practices pursued by the Sophists. When Plato reacts he does so in a highly speculative way, and in the end he has a set of directives for the state to follow in setting up machinery for education. For the most part, Plato prefers the high ground of education-politics-ethics, and leaves for others the problems of pedagogy that must belong to the lower ground. Yet, there are many occasions in the *Republic,* in the *Laws,* and especially in the dialogues selected for special attention in this book—*Protagoras, Gorgias, Phaedrus*—where Plato does move inside the walls of the schoolhouse. Plato himself gives us no hint that he is willing to wait for educational practice to make the record before he canalizes education's purposes; he does not hesitate to embark on theoretical speculations concerning utopian politics or education, and he never thought it necessary to have day-to-day experience with either before making his pronouncements. Education, along with many other things, was a matter for reason not reaction. Yet, Plato was no conservative, except for his willingness to accept most of conventional elementary Greek education, and he set high, almost unattainable goals for his educational followers. It is only when Plato gives us a good picture of Socrates that we are sometimes inclined to believe in the theory-by-justification hypothesis. Socrates does not come to the discussion with his doctrines intact; at least, this is the impression Plato wants us to have, and it is not merely that he wants us to see Socrates thinking on his feet. Socrates hammers out his doctrines on the anvil of discussion and debate, and without temerity he comes to tentative conclusions about what should be done; yet avenues are always open for improvisation or retraction. And Socrates, we know, was capable of changing his mind: he could take one side of a question and defend it at the beginning of a dialogue and be on the other side of the question at the end. Yet, however much Plato should like to make Socrates his spokesman, in the long run he does not succeed; he must speak for himself. And in all Plato's writings, if one captures their broad thrust, he is elaborating a doctrine, and he does not think for a moment that it needs the blessings of the schoolmasters.

Quintilian, Hugh of St. Victor, John of Salisbury, Locke, Rousseau, and Herbart are all allies of Plato, not so much for the content of an educational creed but because they share his confidence in the prescriptiveness of a sound educational theory. If one catches nothing more than the tone of their writings, it becomes immediately clear that they have a message to propose and that they have made dogmatic assumptions about its validity. Plato is more complete, yet more idealistic, and somewhat less satisfying for the schoolmaster who must face a class next morning, than his allies here, but this is a point of little interest to us now. With him they formed a block of theorists supposing unquestioningly that everything they said about education was good and should be followed by the efficient and conscientious teacher. They left no blank pages in their manuscripts on which teachers might write amendments to their dicta, if perchance the tests of experience should suggest some.

The educational context in which Isocrates, Cassiodorus, Alcuin, Erasmus, and Comenius worked almost inevitably gave their educational writings a strong tone of justification. At times we are led to believe they were educational polemicists rather than theorists. Isocrates wrote his longest and most complete book on education—*Antidosis*—as a personal defense and justification for his half century of teaching. He has forgotten his start as a reforming schoolmaster with tentative attitudes— expressed in *Against the Sophists*—and his implied promise to rebuild them as experience directed. A close look at Isocrates' final ideas about education makes us believe he put unusual value on his original theories; all in all he proves how little a man can change in fifty years of teaching. Centuries later Alcuin, faced with a problem quite different from Isocrates' (elementary education needed quick and drastic upgrading), took the broad and vague implications of Christian literature together with the traditional mission of the Church—neither qualifying as educational theory—and tried to accommodate educational practice to them. When he said anything about theory it was in connection with methods for teaching an accurate Latin, an objective validated nowhere in Alcuin's theory, but by the demands of practical ecclesiastical necessity. He was actually repeating what Cassiodorus had tried before and had documented in *An Introduction to Divine and Human Readings.* Neither Cassiodorus nor Alcuin set educational goals; both accepted ecclesiastical prescriptions and tried to justify an educational practice enabling men to attain them. What they accomplished—and we suspect it was much—is not at issue here; and we are not arguing that their doctrines should have been directive, but they were shaped by attitudes of justification.

Comenius began with an assumption that the senses should form the basis for learning and that the physical world could be a complete textbook. From there he turned to practice, both the practice of others and his own, and wrote a plan for education intended to justify the assumption he had made, but could not prove, and the educational techniques he endorsed. Almost the whole of *The Great Didactic* is a document justifying what Comenius conceived to be sharp breaks with the teaching tradition. But where Comenius could turn toward the world of sense and try to find educational panaceas therein, Erasmus had nailed his educational flag to the mast of the classics. He did not formulate the classical pedagogy, this was the work of Petrarch and earlier Humanists, but Erasmus spent the greater part of his lifetime justifying classical teaching. Undoubtedly, he thought, almost everything worth knowing was contained in classical literature, and this knowledge could help form a man of good character. This was a dogmatic assumption. From this point on, he spares no pains to justify his theory of *pietas litterata,* to surround it with mnemonic techniques, plans for analysis, and safeguards. In the end his doctrine is as directive and unassailable as Plato's, but it began as an exercise in upgrading and justifying the conventional wisdom of classical pedagogy.

Pestalozzi began with plausible doubt about educational purpose, on the one hand, and the effectiveness of pedagogic technique, on the other. His vision was attracted to the plight of the common man, who everyday was finding it more difficult to live a full and satisfying life. Even the essential skills for making a living were ignored in the schools; and when schools themselves were ignored in favor of undiluted apprenticeship training, the common man was dehumanized, because so much of the inheritance of mankind was thus unavailable to him. Even for the child who was lucky enough to have an exposure to schooling, there remained serious shortcomings, and in language that could only partly veil his feelings of despair Pestalozzi pointed to crude and ineffective teaching methods used to teach children things they could neither want nor use. While Pestalozzi could verbalize the shortcomings of the educational process, he eschewed optimism about his ability to supply universally valid solutions to education's most pressing issues. He could praise the work of his predecessors, some of whom he quotes with approval, without being convinced that their directive doctrines contained panaceas. And when he rejected the authority of old doctrines, he included not only the products of rationalism but of the justification process as well. Complexities attending theory's creation bothered him less than inflexible outcomes: children were too much individuals to be shaped in an educational mold built for other generations; and the ferment characterizing any generation was too intense to allow anyone to believe that one generation was simply a carbon copy of another. Although permanent features are attached to human nature, there are, Pestalozzi averred, ephemeral features as well; and when educational goals are at issue these latter features are the more significant. What, then, is theory's role? Pestalozzi's thinking was neither so profound nor so refined as Dewey's, and thus its articulation lacked precision. Yet, in effect, and in often confused and tendentious language, he said what Dewey later could express in clear and trenchant prose: the business of the educational theorist is to keep educational practice constantly in view and to report on meaningful school curricula and practices, on learning goals and children's interests, and thus spark attitudes of urgency about the process of education in teachers' minds while keeping them up-to-date on the almost constant metamorphoses in the lives of children and in the management of schools. Dewey commissioned philosophy and educational theory as social sciences; and to social science he assigned the role of reporting on human affairs.

Beginning almost with the decision of Quintilian to respond favorably to his friends' request for a pedagogical handbook, the building of an educational theory was undertaken with a strong sense of urgency, and often, we must suppose, writers of such theory were not entirely immune to hesitations, compromises, and urgent anxieties about the direction of education as they knew it, or the direction they hoped it would take. They were not, moreover, always able to satisfy themselves with respect to the conflicting opinions their researches uncovered. And with few exceptions they wrote in haste; even the great Quintilian who time and again endorsed the teaching dogma to "make haste slowly," could not follow his own advice about letting manuscripts ripen with age. He rushed into print, and the educators who followed in his footsteps accepted his example with none of the usual hesitations of scholars who spend three-quarters of a lifetime perfecting and polishing a historical or philosophical magnum opus. Perhaps, however, they are due more praise than blame, for the clock could not be made to stand still; education was recognized as an indispensable enterprise for the civilization of men in society, and marking time while literary tastes were being fully satisfied could hardly be countenanced if the good of men stood in jeopardy or if the stability of civilization was being tested. These clear tendencies toward temerity, haste, and sometimes censoriousness may in the long run be pardoned, for the dedicated educational theorist was not at all certain that time was his to spend as he might. Even so, we must recognize that these accounts were prepared while the educational battle was fully joined; despite the willingness of most theorists to retire to the friendly confines of their studies to produce their solutions, the order of battle could not be erased from their minds, and the sounds of educational fury could not be silenced.

Thus educational theory is almost inevitably dated; moreover, it must be examined, criticized, and accepted or discarded within the social contexts of its time. And the modern theorist who accepts the principal tenets of an ancient theory is forced to update them or be rejected as an interesting but irrelevant antiquarian.

The schoolroom, we have said before, has not been a highly fertile field for producing educational theory, for the occupations, the distractions, the currencies of the school day leave too little time for careful thought about the process itself. This should not generate surprise; and as we look again at our list, from Isocrates to Dewey, we are convinced that greatness in theory demands as a condition some immunity from the daily demands of schoolmasters' lives. But it has never required a narrow ivory-tower approach, and we are not led to believe that an educational theory of any worth has ever been offered by a man who is not familiar with the schools. Although our list of educational theorists contains only two teachers—Alcuin and Pestalozzi—who devoted more of their time to pedagogy than to scholarship, we are prepared to admit that the former was more a contributor to technique than a formulator of theory, and the latter was an extremely unusual teacher. But the line, if drawn, between the scholar and the teacher may be drawn too sharply, and our intention here is only to emphasize the record of history, which shows quite clearly that educational theory has been forged by the thinkers rather than by the doers. Yet, Pestalozzi, first of all a man of action, was fifty years old before he began to think seriously about the deeper meanings of education and tried to organize them into a constructive theory; and he, more than anyone else, gave us an object lesson in building a theory of education by going directly to the schools, understanding children and their educational needs, probing the mysteries of learning, and adapting all this to the goals, curricula, and methods of teaching. To some slight degree other theorists—Erasmus and Herbart would be good examples— had done or would do the same thing; that is, they had some experience with the schools before they began to write, but none could boast the intense interest in practical pedagogy of Pestalozzi and none could show a record of devotion to the methods of teaching, before he began to theorize, matching Pestalozzi's. If Pestalozzi had done nothing more for educational theory, his demonstration of it as a practical rather than a theoretical discipline would be impressive and we would be thus compelled to stand somewhat in his debt.

So far we have been preoccupied with the role of educational theory and its service to learning, and this preoccupation may cause us to lose sight of the dependence educational theory has on other disciplines in the scholar's syllabus. Theory began, as we have said, by being tied to the apron strings of politics and philosophy; then it received the benevolent attention of the Hellenistic thinkers and was established as an independent study worth talking and writing about on its own merits. Yet it would be entirely naive to think that educational theory could stand alone and speak to educators in a meaningful way without the fortifications of other disciplines, any more than educational practice could be a technique only without a content. So we understand at the outset that educational theory lacks an objective construction; but where we now make this understanding explicit, it was often little more than a dim assumption among many of the leading theorists. Quintilian was so enamored of the oratorical ideal, an outdated ideal in his own day, by the way, that he subsumed educational theory to rhetoric, which may be analogous to allowing criminals to write the laws. Alcuin, Hugh, John, and Cassiodorus subverted the purposes of educational theory by seeing the objectives of life through the eyes of the institutionalized Church. Erasmus took Humanist enthusiasts at their word and made educational theory a servant of the classics. Pestalozzi wanted to use the disciplines of psychology, sociology, and the social sciences generally to form his educational view; but he was highly disadvantaged, first, because of his own intellectual shortcomings, and, second, because despite the desperate need for social and scientific knowledge about education there was very little then codified. Locke had made brave talk about the relationships between education, philosophy, and psychology, but he refused to meet the issue squarely. He stopped where he should have started. Rousseau only confused the issue, for if one read him uncritically he would end up by discarding the assistance proffered by the adolescent social sciences. Herbart, for a number of reasons, was best situated to dramatize and explain the relationship educational theory must have to psychology and ethics. And from Herbart's time forward, education scholars have tried to follow his advice and strengthen the contacts between educational theory and the various sciences that can illuminate it. There is never any doubt in Dewey's mind, nor any hesitancy either, about going outside educational theory to find dependable data with which a theory of education may be elaborated.

Finally, something should be said about the adequacy of educational theory as it was pronounced by the men we have studied. But first we should be sure of our ground: we should want to know some of the major items necessary to an adequate theory. Among the many that may be mentioned, we should think adequacy rests primarily on the willingness of a theory to take into account all levels of education—elementary, secondary, and higher; formal and informal education—education outside the school as well as within its walls, or aided and unaided discovery; and a commitment to the education of all human beings, by which we mean mainly the education of both sexes. Using these criteria, it is hard to give any of the men on our list of theorists a perfect score, although Comenius and Dewey score highest because they were entirely convinced that educational theory should touch all levels—yet in practice Dewey ignored most of higher education, save for the education of teachers—and be involved with formal and informal education as well as with the complete education of both sexes. If we read Isocrates correctly, we find him engrossed with the purposes of secondary teaching, inattentive to the pressing issues of informal education, and impervious to suggestions that women needed the good offices either of his theory or his school. Plato, second only to Comenius and Dewey on the test of adequacy, simply accepted and assumed the validity of most practices of lower schools and concentrated on making highly erudite scholars for leadership in his ideal state. But he could and did concede to women an opportunity for some education; but, as we have said, we must remain unsure whether he was talking about coeducation or parallel education of the sexes. Quintilian immerses us in details of secondary teaching, concerns himself with formal and informal education, but leaves the whole field of women's education entirely uncultivated. Cassiodorus tried his best to be a good disciple of Quintilian and departs from his creed only when he forgets about informal education. Alcuin, of course, showed interest only in elementary teaching, in school, for boys. Hugh and John altered this pattern only to emphasize secondary teaching to the neglect of both lower and higher levels. Erasmus, who must also be given a high mark, neglects elementary and higher education in his theory and concerns himself with the education of women in a half-hearted way, and then what he has to say is put in an appendix to a work on *Christian Marriage.* Locke was an unalterable advocate of the superiority of informal education, and he fitted his ideas about elementary and secondary education into this bias; but he could find little or nothing to say about the education of women. Rousseau met few of the criteria head on: both men and women should receive the benefits of education—not schooling—but he could think of nothing worth saying about the different levels of schooling. Despite his close association with the German university, Herbart had little to say about the theory of higher schooling; he is unconvincing when he approaches informal education, and he is uncomfortable and brief in talking about the education of women. What he has to say is meant for the education of men. Pestalozzi, finally, with all his sympathy for humanity, rested his whole case and gave all his attention to elementary education, both formal and informal, for boys and girls. Thus, in the history of educational thought, even the best theorists have had to struggle with the test of adequacy.

IN DEFENSE OF A THEORY OF EDUCATION. Despite obvious differences in educational theory among many contemporary educators, one sometimes senses a guarded feeling that there is too much talk about theory; that what counts in education is practice in the classroom; sound and fury aside, theories of education end up at the same place (which may not be a surprising assertion) and they all add up to a confirmation of one universal practice (which is surprising and questionable). It has been argued, as a point against preoccupations with theory, that all teachers do the same things in the classroom irrespective of the theories of education they may entertain. If this is indeed true, what need is there for theory? May one regard educational theory as a kind of codified common sense; and may one conclude that all theories meet on common ground and unanimity of purpose on the teacher's desk?

Surely every educational theory contains what its builders believe is a pattern for obtaining superior education. Among various theories, on this point there is ubiquity and harmony. Yet not all theories agree—nor do all theorists—on the nature of the person to be educated or the content and the method of the process commissioned to educate him.

Let us look again at the theorists on our list and see if we can detect their reaction to a hypothetical question asked of them with respect to the need for a theory of education, a reasoned defense for it, and the doubt that a theory of education makes any difference, because all theories, in the last analysis, affirm identical school practices.

Isocrates was much less enamored of theory than, say, Plato or even Quintilian; yet, Isocrates, despite his reasoned doubt about the theories of the "vulgar" Sophists, on the one hand, and the "philosopher" Sophists —Plato and his disciples—on the other, did entertain the firm conviction that education was important to the state. Citizens needed a kind of education enabling them to understand state purposes and serve them. For the better citizens—those with good native endowments—a special educational program was desirable, one to form them as responsible orators. Scant heed was paid all who failed to make the grade of the category of the elite, for Isocrates was no democrat and found little in the popularizations of government decision worthy of praise. Isocrates did not merely neglect the broad mass of mankind in his educational code, he refused to recognize either in his theory or practice any legitimate educational needs in it. He was intent on educating political leaders, effective statesmen who could bear the burden of civic responsibility; so he kept his school small and selected his students carefully.

Once he had students with native intelligence and a natural facility for oratory, Isocrates was able to affirm the incontestable value of rhetoric as a means for bringing them up to his standards of political acumen and oratorical skill. The best of Isocrates' students were well schooled in political science, thoroughly practiced in the art of debate, and highly sensitized to the responsibilities involved in political issues. From here Isocrates drifts into pedagogy, and what we find must be put down as a theory of rhetoric, supported by a small but sturdy arsenal of rules, aimed at the refinement of speech. Despite the temperamental rejection of too much theory, or better, his refusal to remain always on the level of theory and run the danger of being swamped by it, we have no reason to doubt Isocrates' conviction that behind his practice—behind all practices, indeed—basic answers were needed relative to the abilities of man and the political and intellectual virtues of most worth in society. Finally, if

Isocrates did not see the need for theory, or entertain fond hopes for it as a guide to the correct education, he would never have written the *Antidosis,* which is first a defense of his own theory of pedagogy and then a general defense of educational theory. Isocrates, moreover, was convinced by the evidence mustered in the schools around his own city that neither he, nor Plato, nor the Sophists were conducting their schools along identical methodological lines. Although there is much in common between his view of political society, and those of his contemporaries and pedagogical competitors, there were important differences. Here, differences are more significant than similarities and, in the long run, they must be attributed to differences in theory. The kind of education Isocrates offered in his school stood on the bedrock of his theory; even when he demurred from elevating theory to a Platonic level, he never seriously doubted its relevance any more than he believed that all educational practice, regardless of the theory supporting it, followed a common channel.

Plato nowhere discusses the importance of a theory of education, and we know that he never showed any interest in developing one capable of standing unsupported by political philosophy, yet Plato repeatedly demonstrates the worth of theory in all his dialogues. *Protagoras, Gorgias,* and *Phaedrus* illustrate Socrates, the thinker, applying his wisdom to problems which are surely educational, and Plato never allows us to suppose that Socrates is engaging in frivolous pastimes. Theory is necessary; it must precede practice, for otherwise the teacher should not know how to proceed; and it does not lead to one common pedagogical process. There is hardly any need for Plato to talk about this last point, because he has dramatized how different educational practice becomes when it is directed by the incomplete, vicious, or misconceived theories of the Sophists. The function of Plato's educational theory is entirely clear: it is responsible for forming a pattern of education for men who will thus be raised above the level of mere opinion to the level of truth, and with the benefits of such an education they will be able to lead society by the sheer force of their refined intelligences.

We have seen how Hellenistic masters handled theory, and we know they regarded it more as a custodian of ancient classical culture than as a tool for broadening educational horizons. Even this limiting custodial function amounted to something, however, for in the hands of educators convinced that the civilization of men depended on their ability to perpetuate classical culture, educational theory gained an independent status. Its purpose was to set objectives which could bear the weight of classical cultural traditions in an undiluted form and organize pedagogical practices to ensure proper and complete communication and inculcation of the culture of the classical past. Hellenistic theorists endowed the school with a clear and uncomplicated commission, and they used theory to protect this endowment; following their prescriptions schools assumed the role of instruments for cultural transmission and employed the uncertain and often unsatisfactory means of book learning to fulfill it.

So convinced were these Hellenists of their correct purpose that they spent little or no time either defending educational theory or conjecturing about the route educational practice might take if it were dominated by some other cultural assumptions or educational codes. Despite their single-mindedness, they knew other purposes were possible for education, and they knew technical, as opposed to cultural, curricula could penetrate the schools, but they knew, too, that their theory would never lead to a technically oriented school.

Quintilian saw how educational practice can become bogged down in the swamp of mediocrity, and he noticed the frequent departures from what he understood as Ciceronian oratorical excellence. Cultural transmission of an honored past was certainly part of his educational purpose, and it was somewhat more complicated for him than for his Hellenistic predecessors: where they were concerned only with communicating the cultural excellences of classical Greece, Quintilian had to find means to communicate both the Greek and the Roman classical past. But the content of these cultures was, in the hands of Quintilian, means rather than an end in itself; it was complementary rather than complete, and it added the final touches of ornamentation to a prospective orator's education. So Quintilian must give us something more than his predecessors if he is to satisfy us, and, indeed, he does satisfy us by promulgating a theory of education and then demonstrating his theory's application in practice. Throughout the *Education of an Orator* he pleads a case for educational theory, and much of the skill he developed in the law courts of Rome is used to convince us that education with the object of shaping a good man skilled in speaking, the accomplished orator, is too important to be left to chance; it must have competent direction, or a valid theory to support it. Quintilian is keenly aware of theories of education and pedagogical practices other than those he himself endorses or uses, for his magnum opus is liberally sprinkled with quotations from authors whom he either accepts or rejects. Theory is the heart of the educational undertaking, according to Quintilian, and he would not have it otherwise; he is convinced, moreover, that variety in educational practice is the direct outcome of distinctiveness in educational theory.

Cassiodorus does not have much time to spend on theory. The urgent need for education with a new or different orientation does not allow him to make the long road through theory, so he makes a superficial pledge to the validity of everything Quintilian has said and then tries to convert classical educational appurtenances to Christian use. Although this was done thoroughly and with relative ease by Erasmus, it was a far from easy job for Cassiodorus; yet his purpose can be stated in an uncomplicated way: to use the literary skills evident in the best classical education, while avoiding the content of the classics which may have been dangerous, and ending up with a practical literary training useful to Christians in their everyday business pursuits. Cassiodorus defends his theory of teaching mainly on theological grounds, but he defends it. He is certain, moreover, that such defenses are necessary if educational syllabi and practices are to remain uncontaminated by the values of pagan culture. Educational theory is a guide for Cassiodorus, but it is also a guard, and he could never have taken seriously any claim that all educational practice is identical regardless of the theory supporting it.

Alcuin's allegiance to theory is minimal, and, no doubt, one could argue, taking Alcuin's side, that he was too busy to indulge in theorizing about education when so much basic teaching and learning were needed. Yet, even this should not blind us to the seminality of his theory: an accurate Latin is essential to every decently educated person, and the principal means for teaching an accurate Latin is found in the course marked out by the seven liberal arts. Much of the acridity evident in the earlier debates over the content of the arts is absent in Alcuin's writings; he had come to recognize the arts, not as foreign to Christian literature, as invaders from a pagan world, but as natural components of Christian learning. Had not the Fathers used grammar, rhetoric, and dialectic? And were there any Christians who could boldly gainsay the worth of arithmetic, astronomy, music, and geometry? Alcuin almost certainly placed too much confidence in the literary skill and assumptions of his Christian forebears, for if he had known them better he would have been aware of their hesitations and misgivings about the content of classical education, and he may even have followed the advice given by some about proscribing the use of the classics. As it was, however, Alcuin was not an accomplished scholar; much that the Fathers had said remained a mystery to him; he was, moreover, relatively untouched by classical learning itself and was only dimly aware of its potential dangers. Thus, Alcuin's liberal attitude must not be accounted for as a reasoned leniency: had he known the classics better he would unquestionably have feared them more. But knowing the classics better, as either a personal or a professional goal, seemed unimportant to him; he realized that students with whom teachers of his genre had to deal must learn to creep before they could be taught to walk and run. There was no reason whatsoever for opening the world of literature to them and getting involved in what we would call secondary or higher education, because elementary teaching was what they needed. In earlier Christian periods educational leaders could have told their audiences, as St. Augustine did, that classical literature might be used prudently, by which he meant selectively—choose what was inoffensive and use it, but discard the rest—and this course was open to Alcuin. Had he any need for using the technique of selection, he should have pressed it into service. On the most elemental level of Latin teaching, however, there was seldom much need to employ such a useful device.

The threat to education during Alcuin's lifetime was not another kind of education supported by a theory different from his own; the choice, if conditions permitted a choice, was between some education, chaotic and erratic as it was, and unsteadily directed by theory, or no education. So Alcuin is absolved by his own times from debating the relative merits of educational practice; he spent all his energy in finding pedagogical techniques for teaching an accurate Latin; and neither he nor his contemporaries tested the untroubled waters of educational assumption. Besides their willingness to follow the faint marks of tradition, and to spend their energy only in upgrading technique, they were, depending on one's point of view, either the victims or the beneficiaries of cultural and pedagogical isolation. They had perhaps a fragmentary knowledge of ancient positions on education and were somewhat aware of handbooks for teachers and textbooks for students produced by earlier periods; yet upon examination they found them almost useless, for their assumptions and prerequisites were made for an educational practice rooted in a classical culture, not for one requiring viability and usefulness in Ireland, Britain, or Gaul. If Alcuin's insights led him to understand the threats or the promises of educational codes different from his own, he never shares his thoughts with us.

Hugh of St. Victor and John of Salisbury endorsed the then current medieval doctrine that much of classical literature was useful, even essential, for the properly educated Christian. Despite their preoccupation with educating clergymen and their endorsement of the Church's monopoly over the structure of teaching, they deplored indifference to the style and content of classical literature as a plainly indefensible educational position. Christians must employ the whole of classical culture if they are to understand their own traditions and strengthen the intellectual appurtenances to their faith, but to proceed in this way is dangerous unless there is a clearly defined theory guiding masters and students. The key to good education, Hugh says, is reading. But reading must be from the best authors, both the Fathers and the pagans are included in his bibliography, and it must be done according to a definite plan. A student must learn to read in order to draw from the authors a correct interpretation; he must fathom their inner meaning and cannot be content with either a literal or a sense exposition or interpretation of what he has read. The much-sought-after device is allegorical interpretation, and all the skills of grammar, rhetoric, and logic are required for its proper employment. Now, with allegorical interpretation used effectively, no classic lacked utility for the Christian student and nothing in pagan literature was offensive to his faith or standards of morality.

John accepts all that Hugh has said and, in addition, supplies a reasoned defense of Hugh's theory which he eventually adopts as his own. *Metalogicon*—a defense of logical studies—is John's defense of medieval educational theory, and John, a better classical scholar than either Alcuin or Hugh, is keenly aware of educational theories capable of leading educational practice in other directions. He is at pains to show how the theory of education endorsed in *Metalogicon* is the only one worthy of a Christian's consideration.

Where three medieval educators had been interested mainly in erecting an educational structure with intellectual objectives given pride of place, Erasmus, influenced by the tone and temper of the Renaissance and his own grave doubts about the educational values of medieval pedagogy, turned the educational ship a full 180 degrees: moral or character education concerned him most, and he tried to formulate an educational doctrine to serve the ideal of the good man. Changing the objective of education required a great deal of justification, and Erasmus is prepared to argue his case. In addition, he selected as principal means for attaining this educational goal the literary syllabus of classical education, by now much fuller than it had been even to classical men themselves. Thus, Erasmus is faced with a monumental task; it is plainly one of organizing the content of the classics into a curriculum and teaching this curriculum according to methods that will guarantee a man of character. All this is Erasmus' project, and to a large extent he is successful: in the end he offers us a theory of education: *pietas litterata*. Erasmus knows that a theory of education is essential to the proper direction of the teaching process; he senses, moreover, the need for defending this theory and for supplying it with all kinds of justifications. Finally, we need read only parts of his educational works to know how aware he was of contending positions in education: old theories, largely medieval in orientation, were vying for places of prominence, and Erasmus wanted to reject them; new theories, challenging the doctrine dogmatically assumed by Erasmus— that everything most worth knowing was contained in the classics— needed to be demolished.

Comenius began by taking issue with Erasmus' dogmatic assumption and broke ground for educational practice that would depend less on the content of the classics and more on the real world in which the learner lived. This bold departure from the conventional educational wisdom required considerable elaboration, so the theory for realistic education was supplied by Comenius in his *Great Didactic*. He knew that theory is important and essential; he knew moreover, that he must defend it; and he was fully aware of the kind of educational practice—and where it will lead—defended by theories of education other than his own. On the level of theory, Comenius was brave and uncompromising, but on the level of practice he refused to follow his own advice. In the end he counted heavily on classroom practices that remind us of Erasmus, although where Erasmus would have students read the best of the classical authors, Comenius was content to have his students depend mostly on the textbooks he himself had prepared for them. Comenius, therefore, made a long theoretical journey to prove that book learning was not the genius of education and then, with his journey complete, he settled finally for book learning. Despite what we should regard as an imperfection in Comenius' creed, or the relationship between his theory and his teaching practice, it should be said, to the credit of Comenius, that he laid bare the elements of an education beginning with the senses and concentrating on the real world, rather than a literary world, in which the person would have to live out his life.

Neither Locke, Rousseau, nor Pestalozzi was especially responsive to education's need for a theoretical foundation; yet, even with what may be counted an attitude of indifference to theory, each formulated a partial and sometimes inconclusive code for educational practice to follow. Locke's blind spots—public schooling, opportunity for the common man, and the preparation of teachers—did not prevent him from dealing with psychological issues of tremendous importance to succeeding decades. He could point to routes that might be taken to the construction of a sound psychology, but he could not follow them himself. Although he saw clearly enough the tug-of-war going on among various educational creeds and knew that these creeds made a difference on the twin platforms of teaching and learning, he was not disposed either to affirm a theory of education or to defend the inchoate educational attitudes he had expressed.

Rousseau puts us in a dilemma: either he has no theory of education at all, as some critics aver, or his theory is full and complete, although confidently negative. On the one hand, *Emile* began as a set of instructions to a mother concerning the education of her son, but it soon overran these early limits to encompass a severe castigation of current educational practice and then turned to a broad and optimistic, although often oversimplified, explanation of the promises contained in naturalistic pedagogy. Rousseau was concerned with education in almost all its parts, and he was anxious to defend his conclusions. On the other hand, to take seriously Rousseau's admonition—and he gives every evidence that he wanted us to take him at his word—to do nothing and allow nothing to be done would reform formal education into complete oblivion.

We may, however, avoid this difficulty and get off the horns of the dilemma by admitting, to begin with, that Rousseau may not be judged by ordinary norms. He was an educational theorist, but he was unorthodox: to follow him at all we must accept his terms. His best moments in *Emile* are not when he rejects everything but when he tells his readers to understand children's interests and needs and to follow what is natural to learning processes. Even before we come to Rousseau we have read these admonitions on the pages of older books, but Rousseau's language is more forceful than any we have heard before, and his message goes beyond its literal interpretation. In the last analysis Rousseau's extreme rejections served to drive educators to look again at their own assumptions and sometimes to replace them or reform them along lines recommended by the broad themes recorded in the *Emile*.

Pestalozzi, although a follower of Rousseau, was more than a meek disciple. But where one can talk about the place of theory in Rousseau—because the document itself prohibits any prolonged debate about practice—and look closely at the basic assumptions attached to natural pedagogy, Pestalozzi's attitude distracts us from theory. He begins with the hope that teachers can humanize their educational labor and from this hope is bred a willingness to lose himself in practice. Once the experimentation with educational tools is over, Pestalozzi is willing to turn to theory, but his theory is largely a matter of explaining, justifying, and elaborating the techniques he has found successful. If one were to follow in Pestalozzi's footsteps, he would not linger too long with theory before he begins seriously to teach.

Herbart, however, has seen that educational practice, even when guided by the best of intentions, becomes erratic and unsure of itself. Experimentation, or worse, trial and error, is a great misuse of human time and talent. It is entirely possible, he assumed, for knowledge about education to be clarified, validated, and coded: he spoke for a science of education—a theory—and counted it as an indispensable preamble to pedagogical technique. No teacher could be effective without the support of theory, and throughout his pedagogical works he defends his theory, all the while conscious of what practice may become if theory is not followed.

With only minor exceptions, the best minds—at least the best-known educational thinkers—have argued in defense of theory; their actions indicate their belief that it merits a determined defense; and they appear to be agreed on the proposition that educational theory does make a difference in the day-to-day practices of schooling. John Dewey, perhaps more than any of his predecessors, believed in the importance of theory and countenanced no erosion of its stature.

THEORY FOR TEACHERS. For all their interest in theory and willingness to affirm its worth, our theorists, with the exception of Herbart and Dewey, show remarkably little interest in moving theory from the library to the classroom and allowing it to become a permanent possession of teachers. Details need not be reviewed here—we looked at them earlier—but save for Herbart's seminar and Dewey's long career as a teacher of teachers, the theorists studied in this book remained indifferent to the education of teachers. Perhaps they hoped teachers, becoming aware of theory, would embrace it, for we no longer doubt their confidence in theory's essential functions; or possibly they assumed it would inevitably infect an educated person and thus alter his approach to pedagogy. But for whatever reasons, good or bad—and ferreting them out would not be easy— they appeared content to make their pronouncements about education and then leave entirely to chance, or to others, the matter of communicating them to schoolmasters. Teaching a science of education to prospective teachers is a plank in Herbart's platform—and he is serious about it—but his plan is realized unevenly; in the hands of John Dewey, however, teacher education attains maturity, and educational theory becomes a staple in the future teachers' educational syllabus.

III

CONTRIBUTIONS OF EDUCATIONAL THEORY TO PRACTICE

Although one may be sensitive to positive relationships between theory and practice, the possibility remains that theory can sometimes be an important obstacle to practice, particularly to practices needing revision because they have not met the pragmatic test. In addition, with a great variety of theories and their internal diversities, it should be interesting to speculate briefly about the possibility of consensus. These admittedly huge issues cannot be examined in depth here, yet we shall try to treat them within the context of the theorists and theories studied in this book.

ACCOMPLISHMENTS OF THEORY. In the first place, educational theory gave educators a set of directions to follow in teaching and learning, but because of difficulties encountered in getting these directions to the marketplace, one of theory's accomplishments was simply to command an audience. For this educational theory needed independence and status: both were provided by the Hellenistic theorists discussed in Chapter 1. Yet their contribution was mainly in the direction of codification; none was a highly original thinker; few were visionary. They looked back to the classical age and tried to mine from the writings of Isocrates, Plato, the Sophists, and some lesser schoolmen an educational wisdom useful to them. Their accomplishments as compilers are not discounted, but without their classical predecessors they could hardly have written the first paragraphs of their books.

    Taking for granted educational theory's ability to make itself heard, we can proceed to a quick recitation of *exempla,* by returning to the theorists discussed in preceding chapters. Plato's theory elevated higher learning to an important position in education, for prior to Plato, even in the doctrines of Isocrates and the Sophists, it was largely ignored, but Plato opened its doors by stressing the need for a level of certainty beyond mere opinion. Possibly only the best minds could grasp truth, yet even slow and arduous progress promised rewards worth the effort, Plato said, and he organized a kind of education aimed at truth open to anyone with ability. Plato's syllabus was intended to make leaders, and from him comes the tradition, now an unassailable social conviction, that higher education is essential in any society wanting leaders in all walks of life.

We see how Plato always stayed on a high plane and are dismayed when he does not speak to teachers, but neither his theoretical contemporaries nor his successors always remained aloof to practical dimensions of school life. Isocrates, the ancient world's most illustrious teacher, made his reputation largely by teaching students how to use words. Where Plato centered his teaching on science aimed at truth, Isocrates was untroubled by routes to truth and chose instead to give literary and oratorical refinement to human talent. No greater pedagogical doctrine has ever been devised, or had greater longevity, than the Isocratic theory of imitation. In a word, Isocrates discovered that students become accomplished by being exposed to the finest models of speech and writing; and Isocrates' theory achieved permanent status in educational practice.

Quintilian accepted at face value the theory started by Isocrates, although he modified it somewhat to fit the needs of his day. He essayed to prepare a public man and was entirely willing to share his pedagogical discoveries with his fellow teachers; but even his contemporaries were uncomfortable with the ideal orator and were uncertain about the universality of Quintilian's prescription. Thus, unavoidably, they selected some parts of Quintilian's magnum opus and paid pedagogical allegiance to them while discarding others. The element in his theory impressing his contemporaries most, and best standing the test of time, was his justification of a two-language system of education, later elevated to a dogmatic assumption, wherein the superior way of perpetuating the literary inheritance was to teach the classics in a language other than the student's vernacular. This position was attractive to Cassiodorus, who could easily dispense with oratory set in a classic mold and instead direct teaching within the boundaries of Christian utility. And what had greater utility than taking the apparatus of classical education and converting it to teaching an accurate and practical Latin submissive to the monumental objectives of Christian and ecclesiastical life? Despite Cassiodorus' willingness to heed voices from the past commanding that Latin was a divine language invented by God for Christian use, he looked beyond the classics' content, wherein much of their genius surely lay, to concentrate on form or style. Concessions to aesthetics were made in the Cassiodoran admonition that students of Latin should aim both for accuracy and for beauty of expression. In theory what counted most was Cassiodorus' assumption, undisguised on the pages of *An Introduction to Divine and Human Readings,* that the arts are necessary instruments to divine learning—a position guaranteeing complete security in a Christian school syllabus—and, while unworthy of love, may be used and exploited.

Yet, when Cassiodorus wrote he did not fully realize the appeal to men's minds of classical literature's indelible qualities, nor did he foresee the future tendency to endow the classics with an extraordinary amount of wisdom. The content of classical literature is dangerous, but he wants the style clothing it; for content, for explanations of the world and God's relationship to it, the Scriptures and the writings of the Church Fathers satisfy him. This attitude changes slowly. When we meet Alcuin, the Cassiodoran position is still acceptable; and Alcuin neglects theory—explaining why the arts should be studied by Christians as essential prerequisites to all other study—to concentrate on practice: he must find a way to teach Latin to boys living in a culture almost entirely barren of classical contacts or traditions. Had progress stopped here, Christian learning should have had only a nodding acquaintance with the classics, but progress did not stop. From Alcuin to the beginning of the twelfth century, Christians were unavoidably exposed to the classics, and, becoming more competent in classical languages, they became more confident that the classics contained ideas not incompatible with Christian thought and an ethic sometimes indistinguishable from Christian doctrine. Now cautiously expressed opinions say Christian wisdom is hidden away in the classics, and a Christian scholar may mine these treasures. Used properly the classics support faith. But how are these treasures obtained? A theory defending the classics' worth is implicit in *Didascalicon* and *Metalogicon,* and this theory's implementation made Hugh of St. Victor and John of Salisbury shine as the best pedagogical ornaments of the twelfth century. Education, they said, is fundamentally a matter of reading correctly; and to read the classics correctly Christians must first notice the style, then they must notice the content, and finally they must make the proper interpretations of content. The last part of reading, called textual exposition, was the special contribution—the invention—of these twelfth-century educational theorists. Using it, any classical text could be made not only compatible with Christian belief but a justification and elaboration of Christian dogma as well. Neither before nor after the medieval age has allegorical interpretation of texts—for which all the devices of grammar, logic, and rhetoric are essential—been used so widely (and indiscriminately) or shone so brightly.

Erasmus used allegory, but less generously than medievalists, and gave it the status of a safeguard, for he disbelieved the platitude that everything in the classics had Christian meaning. He could take this position, one more sophisticated than his medieval predecessors', because he knew the classics so much better. While not affirming their unimpeachable significance for Christian doctrine, he nevertheless saw extraordinary value in them and never tired of complimenting the classics as the source of "all things most worth knowing." But Erasmus, despite an affirmation of the classics' worth, made theory most effective by redefining the objectives of education: he spoke of the moral values to be obtained from a good, sound classical education and aimed at building a man of character with an almost entirely literary curriculum, while his medieval forebears were preoccupied with intellectual outcomes from the school's syllabus. Despite the visibility of literature in Erasmus' curriculum, he commissioned schools to build character, and for at least three centuries thereafter they tried with might and main to fulfill it.

Comenius, Locke, Rousseau, and Pestalozzi all tried to apply the test of relevance to schooling: Locke discredited classical language and eventually his words were heeded by schoolmasters; before him, Comenius underscored the psychological bases of learning by insisting on using the senses to contact the real world where students lived; Rousseau spoke for individualism and for natural educational evolution; Pestalozzi championed technique and endeavored to make natural learning processes live in the classroom. Each in his own way expressed an educational point of view that came to rest finally in accepted practice.

Herbart's psychological involvements led him to pronounce an educational doctrine accentuating methods of teaching, and, though his intentions are sometimes misread, he placed the teacher in the center of the educational stage. School learning codified by teachers was anathema to John Dewey: he did not believe one's character could be formed by his hearing precepts, and he did not understand how an educational system could produce useful citizens by ignoring the interests and vital needs of students. Dewey made *relevance* a pedagogical watchword, and his impact on twentieth-century teaching and learning is too great to measure.

THEORY AS AN IMPEDIMENT. Even when we want to be a friend of educational theory and affirm its worth in debate, we should be aware that theory sometimes stands as an impediment to pedagogical progress. No theorist ever anticipated this for his theory, for believing he had discovered the right road, he hoped others would follow. Yet, whenever theory is regarded as a directive doctrine—a set of directions for teachers—certain obvious limits are imposed on educational action. Even when a theory as a whole is not an impediment, subordinate directives within it may retard free practice and thus make innovation and experimentation difficult or impossible. When theory is a liberal discipline, its blocking or short-circuiting of innovation is less likely, although a lack of prescriptiveness may in itself be an obstacle to well-conceived educational practice. In any case, despite educational theory's present popularity as a liberal discipline, no great educator, not even John Dewey, made his theory of education a clearinghouse for discussions of what was educationally trustworthy.

Only a few examples are needed to show how educational theory dominated and sometimes misshaped educational goals and practices. Plato's idealism attached itself permanently to the language of education to emphasize the power of mind over things, to intimations of truth over sensory data gathered in the day-to-day processes of living, of nature over nurture, and of spirit over matter. And we need not go on to discuss how idealism perverted educational practice and made schools uninspiring places. Preoccupation with words, of being able to speak and write convincingly on any subject, and to sell truth at discount, all distilled from Isocrates, have long plagued educational practice. Isocrates' belief—the right word is a sure sign of good thinking—led him to adopt and make imitation an unassailable educational code. When we see how often imitation was misused, for all its good in appropriate contexts, and how it kept generations of teachers mired in the past, thinking a reservoir of all knowledge was in classical models, we cannot blind ourselves to theory's potentially detrimental effects on educational practice. Quintilian's oratorical objectives dominated education for centuries, although political realities once justifying oratory as a principal goal of schooling were no longer in evidence. Many humanist teachers followed everything Quintilian recommended and avoided practices he refused to mention; some of their devoted modern successors imitated them to the letter.

As a principal plank in his theory, Cassiodorus recommended indifference to content; on the level of profane study style alone counted. Artificial and empty formalism eventually overran education, an aftermath of humanist pedagogy we usually say, but Cassiodorus himself must accept part of the blame. Medieval theorists, trying to find ways to decontaminate the classics permanently, added an important dimension to the science of textual exposition, but, implementing their theory, they often ended up by distorting the classic on which allegory was used. Yet, for two centuries or more allegorical interpretation was a principal device for improving and illuminating reading. Erasmus wanted his students to notice and remember everything in classical literature, and with this prescription for learning, mnemonic technique was born and became a serious impediment to competent educational practice.

Comenius sensed the need for fewer words and more objects in schooling, but he spent most of his time writing about the curriculum, and his pansophic theory was used to justify broad, superficial, and largely literary teaching. By concentrating attention on the education of English gentlemen, Locke retarded public education: his theory defended the education of an elite and denied worthwhile opportunity to the masses. Rousseau's inordinate emphasis on natural pedagogy put schools and schoolmasters on the defensive and too often led to erosions of syllabi with the necessary tools of learning. Pestalozzi's devices concealed the real significance of methodology based on a sound physiology of learning; and his assumptions often needed correcting before learning and physiology became compatible. Herbart's formalism, despite his great interest in psychology and its possibilities of becoming the bedrock of pedagogic technique, led to a teacher-centered school and made teaching a mechanical and, sometimes, lifeless process. Dewey's doctrine of educational relevance too often stood in the path of perpetuating the necessary literary inheritance and made the present the be all and end all of educational practice while ignoring the past and remaining indifferent to the future.

No theorist, we repeat, intended or expected his theory, in whole or in part, to impede the progress of decent education, but from our vantage point we can see how theory sometimes weakened or undermined the very things it wanted to attain.

DIVERSITY AND CONSENSUS. In the long history of educational theory we have seen multiple disagreements over the nature of the person, the goals for education, and the content of the curriculum. In the twentieth century, it may be said, less diversity is evidenced by theories on such points as class education, education for state service, commitment to the classics as the sole road to quality learning, and natural processes in learning than in previous centuries; yet diversity remains to center on perennial issues in educational theory: the nature of man, the basic reason for educating him, and the means used for achieving fundamental purposes. What chance has consensus? Imminent agreement on these perennial issues is unlikely among contemporary educational theorists, although, clearly, consensus has been reached at one important point: whatever the nature of the person or the goals of education, opportunities in education should be both generous and superior.

IV

THE ROAD AHEAD

Despite the attention given educational theory for all these 2000 and more years, the last word has not been spoken. New theories, often distilled from older ones, or reviviscences of older ones, regularly appear in educational literature. The dangers that lie ahead are not likely to be found in a dearth of theorizing about education; rather, the danger is that educational theory will not be taken seriously. The current preoccupation is not with probing the fundamentals of the educational act before beginning seriously to teach but with making practice and a correlation of practices an adequate substitute for theory. John Dewey made educational theory a respectable and necessary study for prospective teachers, but his achievements along those lines are in jeopardy. It behooves contemporary educational philosophers to emphasize the significance of their discipline by making it communicate to present and prospective teachers the urgent need for knowing the fundamental goals of their profession. Educational theory will not remain popular, and, what is more important, relevant, unless it rejects an observable tendency to follow the trail blazed by rhetoric and philosophy: to construct and apply a technical language in a pedantic and artificial way to unreal or meaningless issues. When educational theory becomes an arsenal of rules and codes concealed in terms not understood by decently educated men, it will have lost its reason for being and have foreclosed on an opportunity to elicit allegiance from a community of intelligent men.

⊱ Index ⊰